"THE ADVENTURES OF A SOLDIERS WIFE."

Derek & Mary
Happy Reading
Joe Plant
4th July 2016

Pte. S. K. Cunningham.
Q.M.A.A.C.

Sgt. J. J. Plant.
ROYAL FEILD ARTILLERY.

D1350105

Story based on the memoires of

Entrusted to and written by Joe. P. Plant

DEDICATION

This book is dedicated to the memory of Mum and Dad.
Who gave us all a life to live a happy adventurous and fruitful existence.

List of Chapters.

BOOK I. IRELAND / ENGLAND 1915 - 1928

BOOK II. THE MEMSAHIB'S INDIAN EXPERIENCE 1929-1932

BOOK III. CLIMATIC CHANGES BLIGHTY 1932 -1974

PROLOGUE
LONDON - NOVEMBER - 1955

Propped up by pillows, I watched as the fading daylight seeped through the net curtains dimming the interior of the bedroom. Outside it appeared to be a typical miserable dull, damp November day. Amidst the constant drone of the passing traffic, the only sound that filled the room was the loud tick tock of Jack's alarm clock. Glancing at the clock, checked the time as a reminder to take my medicine, prescribed by Doctor Smyth for a condition she had diagnosed as. "Nervous Exhaustion." Confined to rest in bed, with a course of phenobarbital tablets and a bottle of bitter tasting blood red iron tonic that I loathed. I did not feel ill, still with an hour to go stared up at the ceiling. On the rare occasion when I had actually been ill, Jack's usual comment was. 'On your feet soldier.' Then under my present circumstance that was forgotten, exasperated my thoughts overcame me so much that I spoke out loud.

'Whatever am I doing here in bed, when I should be up tending to my family's needs?'

Switching on the bedside lamp, looked at the page of the letter I had been writing to my youngest son Joe serving in Malaya, according to his letters, he was having a wonderful time playing football. To me in a constant state of anxiety about him, that was not wonderful. However his father, a serving soldier for twenty–eight years was unconcerned just commented.

'Sarah. Don't you worry about him. He's a young man in the army. It will make a man out of him and he will have a great time.' Well maybe? But I was born to be a worrier?

My mind totally blank sought for words to write. Picking up his letter, quickly scanned his words, what was evident, his concern for my health. Insisting that I start to write the story of my married life during his father's army career. He like the rest of the family and friends, all enjoyed the stories I used to tell. He was not the only one who had urged me to write my story. For many years my mother had been encouraging me to write a book about my life. Once her family had grown up she took to reading, and according to her. I had a better story to tell than anything she had read. Now nineteen years later, confined to bed, very conscious of the fact that I had so much spare time to reminisce about the old times and reflect on the events of my life, which had not been an easy one. However, it has had its compensations and God had blessed me with a lovely family of seven, all grown up and away from my apron strings. So with Mother's prediction foremost in my mind, what I could do. Was write it all down that would certainly occupy my mind and help me on the long road to recovery? I tasked myself to put pen to paper and write down as many tales and events, either good or bad that I could remember? Diverting my attention back to Joe's letter, where before my mind had been blank, words seem to flow with ease, quickly finished it off, noticed there were only a few sheets left in the writing pad. Addressing and sealing the envelope placed it on the bedside table ready for posting, speaking out loud.

'Nothing like the present Sarah. Once a soldier's wife always a soldier's wife. Your new duty is to write a book!'

With pen poised to write, much to my dismay I did not know where to start. I lay there trying to recapture my thoughts of less than five minutes before. In the quietness of the room; I heard the tuneless whistling of Jack coming up the stairs. It abruptly stopped as he entered the bedroom.

'Any mail for posting Sarah?'

'Yes. One for Joe.'- Picking up the letter handed it to him. He being a postman took the letter checked the address, which I suppose was a normal Postie's habit continued,.. 'Oh, and while you're at the post office. Can you buy me some more writing pads please?' Peering at me over the top of his glasses enquired.

'Who are you writing to now?'

'Nobody. I'm going to write a book.' A huge grin spread across his face, exclaimed.

'You sure you're okay Sarah? The medicine is not affecting you? Who's given you this idea then?' He always treated everything as a joke, quickly I retorted.

'No, don't be so daft. Mother said I should.' At this remark he just burst out laughing and jokingly replied.

'I didn't see her come in today. She's been dead for the past eight years. God rest her soul.'

'Yes we all know that! But it was something she said way back in thirty-six that I should write my story. I think she was right, but as I'm not a writer. I do not know where to start.'

'Writer no! But you can tell a good tale or two. It depends how much you want to put into your memoirs. The point is. How far do you want to go back? A lot has happened over the past years, and you never kept any diaries or, anything like that. But I will say you do have a good memory to work with.'

'I suppose you're right there. Do you remember the time when Bobby.' - He cut me short.

'There you see. You're off again. It doesn't take much for you to start on your tales. It seems a good idea, maybe at this present time it will occupy your mind. I'd better get you a couple of pads to start you off'...about to leave the room another grin creased his face he added...'Before I go I'll get you a cup of tea?' Whistling he left. .

Laying there my mind began to work overtime, as memories of events spanning two world wars began to flood back: *My own enlistment in the Army, our married quarters at so many different postings, our time in India and my dear friend Kitty.* The sound of Jack's tuneless whistle coming back up the stairs interrupted my thoughts. It stopped as Jack came into the bedroom carrying not one but two cups of tea. Obviously one for himself, handing me one he joked.

'Finished your book then Sarah?'

'No! Don't be so silly. It's so difficult to know where to start.' Sitting himself down at the end of the bed he began to drink his tea and asked,

'Well. How far do you intend going back?'

'I don't really know? I have just been thinking about our life together, back in nineteen nineteen?' Surprised, he questioned.

'You intend going back that far? 'Indignantly I replied.

'Yes, and you with your memory. Seem to forget that you were not the only one in the Army in the fourteen eighteen war. I too was in the Army, and a lot happened even before I ever met you.' Having finished his tea, he stood up said.

'Uhm! More to the point. Can you remember back that far? I'll be off now to catch the last post, maybe by the time I get back you might have sorted something out.' He left.

A short while later I heard the front door bang shut. Apart from the monotonous drone of traffic and the ticking of the clock the house fell silent. I cast my thoughts back to my life in the Army to our very first meeting. A picture formed in my mind of a young soldier in uniform stood in front of me, with a shock of grey hair, looking down at me with lovely steel blue eyes, a warm face creased with a broad grin that appeared to spread from ear to ear. This image provided me with an idea for a good opening to the sequence of events that finally led me to meet, fall in love and marry my gallant Sergent Jack. I lay there, my pen poised ready.

[Authors Note] *After Sarah's demise, in 1974 whilst going through family papers, Mum's sketchy story was discovered. It was a surprise to all of us, as she never kept any diaries, but she was a good story teller. Nevertheless it was a collective family effort to remember all the names, dates and places [India specifically Kaye & Jackie] of incidents that Mum throughout her life had constantly reminded and related to us, these events and incidents over a long period of social history, have been researched and compiled into the following manuscript.*

CHAPTER ONE
IRELAND –KILDARE 1915

In disbelief I again read the note my younger sister Margaret had brought to me, exclaimed! 'Is this true?' She began crying and through her tears mumbled.

'Yes. Mother told me to bring this to you. She wants you back home immediately. Michael Whelan is waiting outside in the trap.'

I was near to tears myself. How did it happen? What is going on back there? Who's in charge? These questions rushed through my head. I could not believe what I had just read, this could not be possible. Margaret took my hand and urged me to go with her.

'Wait. I must speak with Mrs. Kilbride and tell her of the tragedy.'

Mrs. Kilbride did not hesitate, urging me to go home at once. But I had to get word to my other two sisters, Bridget and Mary who were working in Kildare. I stopped and quickly wrote down Bridget's address on the back of mothers note, and gave it to Margaret.

'Here take this to Bridget. She is at that address four streets away, she will get Mary and you all come home in a trap. Now go quickly. I will go home with Michael in his trap.'

Having given instructions to Margaret, I pushed her out through the front door and directed her to the right. Fighting back my tears climbed up into the trap, and much against Michaels wishes took hold of the reins and urged the mare into a gallop. I could not grasp the situation, our little Rosaline only two years old the only survivor of twin girls. Her sister Josephine had died two months after her birth. As we galloped along. My mind was racing with questions: *What is going on back there? Who is in charge? How did it happen? I would only find out those questions when I got home.* Our ride back was swift and I was standing on my feet, pulling hard on the reins to bring us to a halt, without any hesitation I threw the reins to Michael and jumped down ran inside the house. Inside it was silent, gone was the normal chattering and playing of the children. Mother was crying. Father was stood talking with a Policeman. Kathleen was sat on the floor in the corner of the room. I could see she was extremely upset. I immediately went to mother putting my arms around her, questioned.

''Mother. What's happened?' Through her tears she mumbled.

'Thank God your here Allahnah. Rosaline had gone out of the house and wandered off on her own. The next thing we knew, someone came running into the house and said. One of the Cunningham girls has drowned in the canal. It was my Rosaline Allahnah.'

This indeed was a tragedy to our family, and with mother expecting yet another baby. I just knew I would be back in charge of the household. Of course there was an inquest into the tragedy and witnesses were called. However, we knew Rosaline had died from fear, but the coroners verdict was announced as by drowning.

Publication: Kildare Observer 1880-1935; Date: Jun 26, 1915; Section: None; Page: 6

Dr. M. F. Kenna held an inquest at Monasterevan on Tuesday touching the death of a child named Rose Cunningham, aged 2 years, who was found drowned in the canal at Monasterevan. A verdict of found drowned was returned, with the following rider added:—"That we call upon the directors of the Grand Canal to take immediate steps to have some barrier or protection erected for the safety of human life in Monasterevan. This unprotected waterway has been the grave of many victims."

Nevertheless. The story of my journey of life, through its trials and tribulations begins in the little village of Hacketstown County Carlow, Where I was born in 1896. Within a few months we moved to Ballybrittas, where my father became the village Postmaster. Over the period of the next ten years, eight more siblings were born, unfortunately two of the boys died. In 1906 mother and father had saved enough money, to venture into buying a general store and greengrocer's shop in Whelan's Row Monastereven. The shop included living accommodation with three bedrooms upstairs, downstairs at the rear of the shop was the kitchen, a small parlour, a tiny washhouse, and outside was the haggard (paddock) with stables, including horses and space for storing root vegetables under straw. Opposite the shop was a row of houses with small gardens at the back, which led down to the banks of the Grand Canal.

In contrast to Ballybrittas. Monastereven was a lively and busy town where there was plenty of work for everyone, at Cassidy's whiskey distillery, the Brewery or the Grand Canal dockside, where the Dublin boats docked to unload their cargo of coal and all manner of heavy goods. A few miles up the road was the town of Kildare and the Curragh Army Camp. One of the largest in Ireland that was built in 1855 to billet thousands of troops. Its very existence provided a very good source of income, to practically all the local trades and professions in the surrounding towns.

Mother was a knowledgeable businesswoman and the brains of the family business. Shortly after my parents opened their business. Father was fortunate enough to secure a large contract to supply provisions to the Officers, Sergeants Messes and the married quarters located within the Camp. Throughout the year my parents normal day's work began at four o'clock in the morning, loading up the daily provisions and supplies to be delivered to the camp, whilst on their return journey they would visit farms to select and buy whole fields of vegetables and orchards full of fruit and I, being the eldest was put in sole charge of the household running the shop, getting the children organised to help during the harvesting of the vegetables and fruit. My parents worked very hard to ensure the business flourished providing a good income for the family, she employed a washerwoman called Annie Whelan and a casual called Maggie Murphy. So, for a few years my parents did very well until unfortunately father became mixed up with a crowd who did little else except drink and back horses. Mother said. 'It was the worst day's work he ever did when he gave up his postman's job back in Ballybrittas.'

With Father spending more time drinking and betting he frittered away the household savings therefore, I had to take over my father's role and to accompany Mother on her trips to the Curragh Camp delivering provisions. It was during my trips to the camp. I first saw something in the married quarters that I greatly admired. The brass souvenirs that different families had brought back from their postings to India. Nevertheless, with father spending the money to cover his betting, more was going out faster than it was coming in, and yet another additional problem came into the equation. The on-going progress of the Home Rule for Ireland that was opposed by the Ulster Unionist, who had organised a large force of volunteers in opposition to the English Governments proposal. So much so that in early 1914 the effects were openly incited by many Army officers in the Curragh Camp, there was a Mutiny of Officers. That had a direct effect on Mothers business interest and temporarily restricted her, therefore Mother had no option but to let her two helpers go. I was not interested in whatever was going on and was only concerned with organising the household, so the elder girls took over their workload. It was a constant ongoing battle as mother struggled to maintain the business. Gradually it deteriorated with me helping mother on her fewer trips. Nevertheless still in full charge of the household, washing clothes and minding babies, I was fed up to the teeth with my life of drudgery. However, one day an old lady by the name of Mrs. Storey called, enquiring if one of the young girls could help light her fire and do her shopping. Although it was not a full time job, realising it gave me a chance to escape for a few hours, immediately volunteered to do the necessaries. Mother knew Mrs Storey very well as she had been employed by her in the Hotel that she owned. Mrs. Storey was very kind to me and paid me well. However, unknown to everyone, looming on the horizon was even a greater threat to our livelihood.

It was on a very hot summer's day in August 1914. We had finished selling all our produce. I was at the reins as we made our way along the main road towards the gate out of the camp. It was very evident that something was up. It was a hive of activity, orders were being barked out and soldiers were dashing everywhere. Nudging me in the ribs Mother muttered.

'Sarah Allahnah! Something is going on around us that I don't like. There's trouble afoot.'

6

I clicked the horse into a gentle trot towards the main gate. Standing in the centre of the road was the figure of the duty Sergeant. He put up his hand to stop us. Pulling on the reins slowed the horse down and came to a halt. Mother was well known and acquainted with nearly everyone in all of the Messes, whereas before we had freedom to pass in and out without any problems, this time he challenged her.

'Whoa Ma. New orders. From now on you and your little girl Sarah shall need a pass to get in and out of the camp.' She questioned.

'Whatever is up now sergeant Phillips?' curtly he responded.

'Orders. Ma just orders. Nothing for you to worry about. Just wait there a moment.'

Striding into the Guardhouse, we waited in silence until he came out and handed over some papers with the curt instruction.

'Here you are Ma. Passes for yourself and your little girl Sarah there. You keep them safe and present them every time you come in and out of camp.'

'Thank you Sergeant Phillips. We'll do that and now we'll be on our way.' Thinking about his remark: *Little girl and me eighteen years of age was rude to say the least.* I clicked the horse into motion that made him step back smartly. As we moved out through the gates and away on the trip home. I asked.

'What's all that about Mother?'

'Allahnah! I don't know. But something big is going on that's for sure.'

Three days later we found out. On August 4th. 1914, war was declared. The activity and passes given was the Army preparing to leave Ireland and join other forces on the Western Front in France. Amongst the first to go were five of my parent's brothers, cousins and friends including, Mother's three younger brothers, Jim in the Leinster's, Tom in the Dublin Fusiliers and Andy in the 2nd. Connaught Rangers. Within weeks of the Army's departure the Curragh Camp almost became deserted and with it our trade virtually became non-existent. So, with a diminished trade Mother sold three of the four horses she kept. My two younger sisters Bridget and Mary left home to work in Kildare and much to my surprise even Father got a job. Carrying parcels from the station to various shops in the town.

As predicted the war did not end by Christmas, instead it gathered momentum, ensuring it needed more men to join in the fight. Men volunteered in their hundreds but had to be trained before being sent out to the battlefront. Bridget on one of her weekends off, informed Mother that the Curragh Camp had been re-opened as a basic training camp, and plenty of recruits were walking about in Kildare. Mother having still kept the business alive was already aware of this and of the different new regiments that arrived at the Curragh Camp. One such regiment was the newly formed. 'Royal Flying Corps' and she took no time in warning us girls.

'No fraternising with those demented men, flying around in those new-fangled aeroplanes.' God help any one of the girls in our family who even dared to look at one, and for me stuck at home there was little chance of me even seeing one never mind going out with one.

One weekend Bridget returned home from Kildare and asked if I was interested in a 'Live-in' job in Kildare, with Mrs. Kilbride a woman she knew. Doing her housework and caring for her six-month-old boy named Antony. Wild horses could not have stopped me. On the premise of getting the job I packed a few clothes and toiletries, together with Bridget got a lift in a trap with Michael Whelan to Kildare. There I met Mrs Kilbride who gave me the job with pay including a tiny room that was adequate for my needs. But what a delight to be able to sleep on my own and even better, it was to be my first venture away from home. I spent the first week doing the housework whilst caring for her baby boy who appeared to idolise me, yet every time he was picked up by someone else he cried so, instead of helping Mrs. Kilbride with all the housework I spent most of my time looking after Anthony. One Saturday morning the 8th. of May 1915, Mrs Kilbride showed me a newspaper with the headlines.

'THE SS LUSITANIA SUNK.'

1,198 Passengers feared drowned. Yesterday afternoon a German U-boat torpedoed the ship eight miles off the West coast of Ireland. Photos of the survivors being brought ashore in Cork displayed their plight.

The significance of this incident proved that the war did not only rage on the land but also the seas, something we had not dreamed of, yet a couple of weeks later in June tragedy struck our family back home and the details of the family tragedy unfolded. Mother had returned from a trip to Dublin and as she always did, she brought back a small present for in turn only one of her tribe. On that occasion it was for Francis. Apparently this upset Rosaline and she wandered off on her own. At the inquest that was held after the incident. Other witnesses revealed that Rosaline had slipped down the bank of the canal, landing feet first in the mud. Although totally dry from the waist upward, owing to her fear of water she died of fright but, at the inquest she was pronounced drowned. Believable or not, even from birth Rosaline screamed at the mere touch of water, we had to lay her on an oilskin cloth in front of the peat fire and dry wash her with damp cloths. My parents decided to bury her back in the old village cemetery at Ballybrittas. After the funeral I returned to Mrs. Kilbride's nevertheless, that was not the end of it. In the July Mother heavy with pregnancy could no longer stand living in Monastereven, found a suitable family house on Church Hill Kildare, and for a pittance sold the business to another trader and moved.

I was nineteen years old and unaware of the process of making babies! All through my growing up there had been no time for me to understand where they came from, as every year my mother saw to it that there was another child and throughout the years of her confinements, Mother gave birth to thirteen girls and seven boys. Jack the youngest boy was the only boy to survive. In those days large families were not uncommon, the boys would tend the land, whilst the girls ran the household reared children and cared for horses and any other animals owned by the household. As each child grew older, specific tasks were allocated to share the workload. I being the eldest was trained to run the household nevertheless, on this particular occasion, Mother close to confinement decided she wanted me back home to resume my duties as 'head cook and bottle-washer'. With great reluctance I had to leave Mrs Kilbride's.

Back in the confines of our home I soon had all the younger girls organised with chores and the house back in order. However, my difficulty was trying to maintain a balance betwixt the family and my desire to lead my own life. I shall never forget the events of the day my new baby sister was born. Early in the morning Mother summoned me to call Dadie (Ellen Kelly) the midwife whom had attended all of mother's confinements. I scribbled down a note and gave it to Kathleen to take to her. Whilst she was gone the postman arrived with a letter for my father. Immediately he opened it, reading through it, he became silent still holding the letter let his arms go limp by his side, I asked him.

'Who is that from?' Sullenly he replied.

'Your aunt Helen. Your uncle Andy has been killed in France.' He then moved into mother's room to tell her the bad news, he should have known better. He came out from the room like a scalded cat.

When Kathleen arrived back with the midwife. Father was still moping around with half the tribe of children fighting. Baby Francis waiting to be fed was screaming her head off, whilst the other half were waiting for me to give them breakfast. Being so fed up with father's attitude, I was running around shouting orders, at the same time trying to assist the midwife preparing for the birth. It was chaotic, a house of bedlam, with me near to screaming myself. After mother had given birth to yet another baby girl named Julia. I managed to quell the noise and get the household back to functioning normally. Later that evening mother, having recovered was being attended to by Dadie and I being party to their conversation, listened in about Mrs Clements the Army Warden's wife. Herself in confinement in their family quarters in the Kildare Barracks. Was seeking the assistance of a young girl to help look after her other children. I quickly offered to go, very reluctantly Mother agreed. Only too pleased to get out of the house and knowing exactly where to go, I practically ran all the way to the Warden's quarter's, knocking on the door that was opened by a young girl, I questioned.

'Can I speak with your mother please?'

She nodding beckoned me to follow her indoors into a bedroom where the woman was in bed. I introduced myself Mrs Clements informed me of what the job entailed. General housework, all the washing, ironing and there were five children to be cared for. I was offered two shillings and sixpence for my time. I certainly was no better off than at home, but at least I was being paid for the trouble. I quickly made up my mind to accept the woman's offer. That little diversion did not last very long and very soon I was back in charge of our own household. But I was desperate to seek the freedom I had at Mrs Kilbride's and found a job at Grahams Bakery looking after two ladies and a gentleman, which included their washing and ironing at five shillings a week. I quickly accepted. It was a total change for me and I revelled in my new position. Nevertheless, that was to last just a few months until my next escapade reshaped my future life.

Wednesday at the bakery was half day. Having finished my chores, I was on my way up the town to meet my two sisters Bridget and Mary. Happily walking along the main street I came across a group of girls gathered outside a shop, their attention drawn to a notice stuck to the glass shop window. I being nosey asked one of the girls at the rear.

'What's the notice about?' Shrugging her shoulders was about to reply, when a buxom red haired girl with a broad Dublin accent retorted.

'Be Japers! Now dare's a ting. Dare looking for us girls to join dare army? Waata a cheek, day won't be getting the loikes of me dat I'om saying. Let dem foight dare own wars. I'om at war wit mi husband every weekend when he feels loikes coming home.'

Looking to hit whoever tried to challenge her, she pushed and shoved her way through the gathering, muttering to herself stormed away up the road. I thought: *There's a Dubliner always fighting amongst them.* Curiosity got the better of me and I edged my way into the group, towards the shop window to read what this notice had to offer. Printed in big black letters were the words:

WANTED
YOUNG WOMEN VOLUNTEERS
TO JOIN
THE WOMEN'S LEGION

It was an official notice issued by the War Office in London, seeking to enlist women to assist in the war effort. The notice stated that the reason for enlisting Women Volunteers was that it would release the men to join the forces fighting in France and Belgium on the Western Front. I read on understanding that Women Volunteers would not go out and fight alongside the men, Instead their services would be required to help in the army camps. This was followed by a list of various jobs that anyone could apply for. The conditions to join were: - A minimum age of seventeen with three references. One from your current or last employer. One from the Clergy and One from the Police. Any fit young women who wished to volunteer should apply to:

THE RECRUITMENT OFFICER
CAPTAIN LADY HOUNDSWORTH
O/C. WOMEN'S LEGION
KILDARE BARRACKS

This presented me with a great opportunity to rid myself from my present household drudgery that I was totally fed up with. Its prospects provided me with a new source of income, a steady job, and the freedom I so sought. Once again reading the list of their requirements thought: *That's the job for me.* Immediately made up my mind and decided to volunteer. Easing my way back out through the gaggle of girls, I left them discussing the whys and wherefores of enlisting. With all the information buzzing around in my head met my two younger sisters Bridget and Mary. Immediately told them about this new opportunity and my intention to volunteer. They in the same type of work as I was were interested and decided to join up with me. Excited at our future prospects. As we walked home, we realised that there was one stumbling block: Mother's approval!

That Wednesday afternoon I told mother all about the War Office notice I had read, and of our intention to volunteer. Patiently she listened to what I had to say and the reasons why all three of us wanted to volunteer. Much to our surprise Mother approved. Unbeknown to us from her own sources in the camp she had found out all about 'The Women's Legion'. Kathleen our younger sister, having listened to all the chatting, although only thirteen, decided she wanted to volunteer too. The four of us set about obtaining the required references. Unfortunately for Kathleen, having never been employed lacked one, although under age still insisted upon volunteering.

The four of us dressed in our Sunday clothes set off for Kildare Barracks to volunteer. Upon arriving at the barrack gates the guards stopped us, requesting what we wanted? We all cheerfully chorused.

'Volunteers for the Women's Legion.'

Letting us through, they informed us where to go. After a short walk we met a large group of girls gathered in front of a hut. Stood on the top step in front of the doorway was a rather officious looking woman dressed in a khaki uniform. Spotting us, she called out.

'Are you four volunteers for the Women's Legion?'

'Yes.' We chorused.

'Right, I require your names and I need to know what references you have?'

Each in turn gave our names showed her the reference's, she added our names to her list. When it was Kathleen's turn looked very quizzically at her, briefly looked at her one reference shaking her head but noted her name.

'Now you four girls, inside that hut behind me. You will all be interviewed by an Officer one by one. Immediately after you will be informed if you have been accepted. Now would you kindly wait over there along with the other girls until your name is called out?'

We joined the group of girls. Gradually others arrived to swell our numbers until it was apparent that there were no more volunteers. The uniformed woman began calling out names in pairs, the first two entered while the rest of us waited outside. It was not long before my name, along with that of another girl was called out. With shouts of encouragement the pair of us cautiously entered.

The hut was sparsely furnished, with two tables in the middle of the room where two women dressed in smartly pressed khaki uniforms were seated. Neatly stacked in front of them were some forms. In front of the tables were two vacant chairs. At the far end there was another door leading outside, or maybe to another room. A stern faced woman in a similar uniform approached

10

us, ushered us to the chairs indicating to be seated. I sat in front of one of the senior women who introduced herself as Captain Lady Houndsworthy she asked.

'Full name please?'

'Sarah Kathleen Cunningham.'

'Do you have the appropriate references?'

'Yes ma'am.' I handed my references over to her she took them placing them down on the table next to the pile of forms, removing one of them she began asking questions.

'Your age, address, married or single, occupation?' I answered each question as she made notes on the form. She asked why I wanted to join? I replied.

'I wish to join the war effort and be usefully employed.' That appeared to be the right one. She asked other questions, about my home life my previous employment and what type of duties I was capable of undertaking. Constantly she making notes on the form asked.

'What type of work are you seeking in the Women's Legion?' Quickly thinking of what I was proficient in answered.

'Domestic and kitchens ma'am.'

Picking up the references she began to study each one with great care, whilst I waited with bated breath she jotted down some more notes, looking up smiled and said.

'Well. Miss Cunningham. Congratulations you have been accepted. However there are conditions that you must accept before you sign the attestation forms. These are. Number one. Upon signing up you will be unable to leave the Army until the authorities officially release you, maybe in a year or possibly more, hopefully less when we win this war. Number two you could be sent to another part of Ireland'...pausing she waited for me to answer. I was taken aback by the prospect of moving away from home but quickly thought: *That was the reason why I had volunteered.* Positively answered

'Yes ma'am. I do understand.'

'Thank you I am pleased about your decision. Now we need to give you a medical examination. Please take this form with you and go through the door at the rear. Hand it to the lady Doctor who will examine you.'

She smiled and pointed in the direction of the door. Much relieved taking hold of the form, stood up, thanked her turned and followed the other girl walking towards the door. Inside the room the lady Doctor told me to stand to the side while she examined the other girl. Then it was my turn - It was very quick she asked some personal questions? Examined me. So long as you could breathe, hear and see you were passed fit. Once she had completed the medical the Doctor wrote something on the form whilst doing so said.

'Now ladies you are both fit for duty. Next Monday you must report to Stewart Barracks on the Curragh Camp. They will be expecting you.'

We were both ushered out to make our way back to the front of the hut, to re-join Mary and Kathleen. Elated with my success I burst out that I had been accepted and before the pair of them could ask any questions, their names were called out. Helped on by another round of cheers they both entered the hut for their interviews. Meanwhile Bridget appeared from around the back of the hut along with another girl. I could tell by her grin she had been accepted. Comparing our interviews we discovered that both had to report to the same place at the same time. Soon Mary and Kathleen emerged through the front door, the expressions on their faces told a different story. Not a happy pair! Mary had a look of despair, Kathleen was near to tears. Re-joining us they informed us they were rejected, too young and Kathleen with only one reference. We returned home to tell Mother our good news. She was pleased for Bridget and me, and advised Mary and Kathleen that their chance would come later. 'This war will not be over for a long time yet.' she prophesied. They made up their minds that later they must go to England.

11

CHAPTER TWO
ENLISTMENT

Monday the following week Bridget and I, dressed in our Sunday best climbed up into the trap owned by Thomas, a friend of mothers who was to take us as far as the gates of the Curragh Camp. As the horse and trap set off into a brisk trot, the whole tribe stood waving and cheering us on our way. Following the same route that mother and I used to take out through Kildare, Thomas wheeled off onto the Newbridge road that ran right across the Curragh plains covered in lush deep green grass. Here and there flocks of sheep were grazing and in the distance we spotted some troops marching in formation. Farther away Cavalry troops on horseback were riding in line at the gallop. Halfway across we took the right fork road along past the hollow called Gibbets Rath, leading up the long incline towards the top of Long Hill, where clearly visible for miles around was the camps square clock tower. We rode past a stream of girls walking up to the camp, when we finally arrived at the main gate we were not the first to arrive. There were dozens of girls queuing up. Stopping at the end of the queue we got down, thanked Thomas for the lift, he in turn bade us farewell and Good Luck. Joining the end of the queue, which gradually approached the entrance where about twenty soldiers were asking each girl.

'Which barracks are you assigned to?'... We chorused.....'Stewart.'

'Okay you're in luck! There are nine different Barrack's along North Road. Ponsonby is the first, Stewart is the second, go past the first Barracks, in between the two blocks is the entrance to Stewarts guard room, that's the one you want. Just follow those two in front.'

Glancing at Bridget I noticed a look of anxiety on her face, something even I was feeling, so as we proceeded on our way, to ease our anxiety with my knowledge of the camp I began pointing out the different places Mother and I had delivered provisions to.

'Bridget that first house is the Quarter Master's; the next one is the Commanding Officers. This road on our right leads down towards the married quarters located at the rear of the Camp'... Passing the first block noticed there were several girls waiting on the other side of that gate...'Look. On the opposite side of the road, directly opposite each Barracks, are all the Officers Messes.... By this time the two girls in front had turned into the entrance of Stewart Barracks. When we got there the Guards stopped us and questioned.

'You two for Stewart?' I answered

'Yes we are reporting in.'

'Right, just around the corner you will find other girls waiting. Join them.'

I felt Bridget's hand grasp mine as we went past them, at that moment a feeling of the unknown overcame me as I'm sure it was with Bridget. Turning the corner there stood the officious uniformed woman we had encountered at the interview. On the right arm of her tunic was a crest indicating a rank NCO (None Commissioned Office) of some sort. In her hand she held a small board she shouted.

'YOU TWO. FALL IN WITH THE OTHER GIRLS.'

The group was stood on the verge of a large square surrounded by ten barrack buildings, five on either side. I recognised one of the girls as the tall girl who had been interviewed alongside me. Very soon our number had swelled to about forty. our chattering came to an abrupt halt when the officious woman ordered.

'As your name is called out, fall up in single file behind me.' When all names had been called out she counted us, checked her list then ordered.... 'Assemble yourselves in three ranks.'...In no specific order of size we formed up in three ranks then she called out...'As a group we are going to march down to the recreation building so keep in that order.'

We set off walking around one side of the parade ground towards the bottom, went through the passage way between the two end barracks, crossed over a road carried on towards a building that became obvious as the Recreation Building. Halting us outside the NCO striding past us went and opened the door called out.

'Right ladies. Proceed inside, find a place to sit down at one of the tables. Do not talk and keep quiet.'

Inside the strong smell of tobacco enveloped us, making some of the girls cough. Noisily we moved into the room and settled down at a table to wait in silence. Bridget and I sat down at one and had a chance to look around. Each table was covered with a green baize cloth, arranged in two rows down the room. Some had a vase of flowers placed on the top, and each had four chairs. In the far corner on a table top lay a neat pile of reading books along with some board games, a few gas mantels were suspended from lines of gas pipes across the ceiling. At the far end there was another door and to one side was a large table behind which sat another NCO. In front of her was a neat pile of papers. It wasn't long before the door behind us was opened and two lady Officers entered wearing peak style officer's caps. Walking purposefully through our midst came to a halt by the big table, smartly turning around faced us. Both were about five feet ten in height dressed in a khaki tunic and skirt uniforms, the hemline of their skirts finished just above the ankles showing a glimpse of stockings and polished shoes. One of the officers addressed us.

'Good morning ladies.'...there were some responses...'My name is Captain French. Thank you one and all for volunteering to enlist in the Women's Legion, whose founder is the Marchioness of Londonderry. It is an honour that you have all been chosen to join the Women's Legion, and you all can be proud of becoming an essential part of the war effort. All of you may be wondering why and what you have volunteered for? Well! Over the past months the war in France has increased in its intensity. Even as I speak more soldiers are being killed whilst more men are required to replace those unfortunate ones. The war office in London has finally approved the enlistment of women into army garrison camps throughout Ireland. Such as those in Dublin, Kildare, Cork and Belfast. The main purpose of your employment is to take over all the domestic duties normally carried out by enlisted soldiers, thereby releasing those men for front line battle, and you young lady volunteers will take over their normal jobs as cooks, waiters, administration clerks and ambulance drivers. You will be issued with army uniforms similar to our dress uniforms that will be worn at all times including walking out. The unit you have been assigned to what is known as the Second Cavalry Officers Cadet Squadron, at Stewart Barracks.

Now our official cap badge is a figure of victory, holding a wreath in her up-stretched hand, which signifies the domestic duties you all shall undertake. However, to some members within the army hierarchy. This badge appears to represent a woman holding a frying pan and has earned us the nickname of. "The Ladies with the Frying-pan." (Her last remark brought an outburst of laughter)...'Nevertheless ladies, you all can be assured you will soon find out that is not the case. Now on my right is Captain Tweedy, the senior administrator in charge of your unit and she will inform you of the rights and wrongs that you may encounter.'

Captain Tweedy, the taller of the two ladies, had a strong round young face. Her hair covered by her peak cap was tightly combed back behind her ears, beneath her dark thick eyebrows her brown eyes quickly scanned the girls assembled before her, then she spoke.

'Good morning ladies. As Captain French has already explained your purpose for volunteering. It is now time for each one of you to sign the document of acceptance into the Army. At all times you must observe the rules and regulation as laid down, which you will learn as you progress through your training. You will be trained in discipline and any other respective duties you will be assigned to do, for which you will receive a weekly payment. You will always be

13

correctly dressed and, when speaking to or, being addressed by any army officer or senior rank. You will address them as sir or ma'am. Disciplinary action will be taken against anyone not observing that rule. You will be billeted on the camp and confined to the barracks for a period of six weeks, during which time you will be taught how to march, salute and generally look after yourself, including how to carry out your respective assigned duties. Upon completion of your training period, subject to week-end duties, you may apply for a pass, which permits you to leave camp, and for those local girls who wish to spend your off duty weekends at home. You must apply for a weekend pass. I would warn you that you might receive hostile remarks about women in uniform. Ignore them...however. A strong word of warning to all of you! Men run this Camp and there is to be absolutely no fraternising with any of the troops. Nevertheless, I am sure you ladies can be trusted. If anyone of you has any problems, you can apply through your senior NCO for permission to seek my help or advice. Now, this building is the soldier's recreation establishment and we only have permission to use it, in order to carry out your enlistment procedures and clothing issue. Before you sign the documents of acceptance. Are there any questions?'...No one ventured to ask any...'After that formality you will all be provided with uniforms. Your senior NCO Benton will guide you through the next stages.' The officious NCO Benton called for our attention.

'As your name is called out please stand, I will tell you of your duty and accommodation billet number. Indicating behind her... 'One by one please present yourself to the NCO sat at the table behind me, who will get you to sign the consenting form as acceptance of your enlistment and intended duty. Once the form has been signed, you will stand on that side of the room. Does everybody understand?'

Nods of heads and mutterings of. 'Yes' came from within our midst. Whereupon her voice rose to a shout.

'I DID NOT HEAR MANY ANSWERS OF. YES MA'AM...I WILL REPEAT. DOES EVERYONE UNDERSTAND?' That brought a spontaneous.

'Yes, Ma'am.' She then began calling out surnames, until. 'Cunningham Bridget Mary. Waitress. Officers mess. Hut twelve....'Cunningham Sarah Kathleen. Waitress. Officers mess. Hut twelve.' Moving in behind Bridget waited for my turn, the NCO presented me with a form and a pen, indicating the appropriate dotted line for me to sign. Having signed she tore off the bottom of the page and handed it to me. 'Your Army number is. W4923. Learn it off by heart. Officer Waitress's pay for your assigned duty will be seven shillings and ten pence per week, all found plus uniform.'

After I signed on, I joined the line of other girls until all were enlisted. Captain Tweedy moved across the room to the NCO and had a brief conversation with her, then together they entered the other room. NCO Benton ordered us to follow behind her through the open doorway where inside around three walls, were rows of tables laden with neat piles of garments. Behind the tables stood eight uniformed girls waiting to serve us our uniforms. Capt. Tweedy called for our attention.

'Ladies, you will now be issued with your uniforms. Blouses, skirts, coats, footwear, underwear, hats, and rainwear. One set for walking out, two sets for assigned working dress and one set for general duties when you are cleaning out your billets. As I call out your assigned work duty, please form a line one behind the other.' She moved to a position in front of one of the tables.... 'First line. Officer Waitresses.' Tugging hold of Bridget's sleeve, I walked in front she followed and others fell in behind her. Moving swiftly down our line Capt. Tweedy counted our numbers and then moved to the next table calling out. 'Next line cooks.' The routine was followed by a further two lines. Satisfied that everyone was in place. Capt. Tweedy addressed us.... 'When it is your turn, the orderly will ask you your duty and issue you with your uniform. One set of duty wear is to be used whilst the other is being washed and ironed by each and every one of you. All will be smartly turned out, and you will all be inspected before the start of every duty. No tardiness will be tolerated. You will pay for any losses.' NCO Benton then ordered.

'First one in each line move up to the tables.' Quick as a flash, with an experienced eye, each women storekeeper looked at our shape and size and gave us an article of clothing from one of the stacks. quickly moving from another pile and so on, passed over a garment until our arms were loaded with clothes. One of the storekeepers plonked a hat on our head, the next storekeeper asked.....'Duty?'...'Waitress ma'am'...'Right.' More garments were added to the growing mountain of clothing cradled in our arms. I had difficulty seeing around them as following others made our way out to reassemble outside. In some bedraggled form of three ranks NCO Benson walked us back to our allotted hut. Once inside she allocated each a bed to place our pile of garments on, then informed all that we were to be fed and issued directions to the canteen, where we would be served a meal. Food! Being so busy we had not realised that the morning had flown by. However, I was in my element, as I knew every part of the camp. I suggested that the others follow me. I led the gaggle of girls back along the road towards the Canteen building located next to the Recreation building. Upon entering we formed a queue in front of a long line of tables, stood behind were several soldiers waiting to serve us, no doubt they were the ones some of us would soon be replacing. Our meal, such as it was, was eaten in silence. Bridget nervously turned to me and in a whisper asked.

'Sarah, have we done the right thing in volunteering?'

'Bridget, whether or not we have done the right thing, do remember we did volunteer and realised it is all going to be very strange at first. This is the army's way of getting everyone sorted out as quickly as possible, don't fuss so much' She did not appear convinced.

Having finished the meal we returned back to our hut where we were to sort through our new uniform. Changing into them helped break the ice had everyone talking about the voluminous undergarments they had been given to wear. Some girls began parading around in their extra-long bloomers, providing some strange sights to see. It was quite hilarious and had everyone in fits of laughter. My blouses were too big whilst others had garments too small, some girls swopped one garment for another and it was obvious that some tailoring alterations had to be carried out. The one piece uniform dress that you stepped into had six cloth-covered buttons. The bottom button was located below the waistband with five equally spaced above up to the neckline. The waistband was a wrap-around belt with one button sewn on the right side that overlapped and secured by two buttons sewn onto the dress. The collars of our blouse lay flat outside the neck of our dress and on each shoulder epaulette, a printed tab stated WOMEN'S LEGION. My dress was far too long for me and with my tiny feet my shoes were like boats, they definitely would have to be changed. The Officer Captain Tweedy and NCO Pulvertaft entered. Pulvertaft shouted.

'ALL PUT ON YOUR HATS AND STAND BESIDE YOUR BEDS TO BE INSPECTED BY THE OFFICER.'

Sixteen girls of varying heights stood with hats plonked at different angles, a wide brimmed hat with a blue ribbon band and adorned on the front was the cap badge. 'The Lady with the Frying Pan'. Having already swopped my uniform dress but according to Captain Tweedy it was still too long, she ordered me to exchange it and any other garment that did not fit. I asked if I could exchange my shoes, looking down at my tiny feet swimming around inside a pair of shoes two sizes too big. Captain Tweedy exclaimed.

'My, you have got dainty feet and they go with a tiny person. Yes, you will have to exchange them. Join the others returning to the recreation building for exchanges. NCO Pulvertaft will escort you.'

Outside on the roadway the girls from the three huts assembled, each holding assorted garments. We were marched back to the building for exchanges. I had practically all that I had been provided with changed for smaller sizes, including the right sized shoes. Back inside the huts we dressed into our uniforms, before NCO Pulvertaft escorted us to the Quartermaster's stores to collect bedding. Having made up our beds and sorted out our working uniform ready for the following day. An evening meal was served in the canteen and after a very eventful and busy first day, sleep.

At the crack of dawn NCO Pulvertaft came into the hut and noisily roused us. First ablutions, then breakfast in the canteen, there were no troops present, the authorities had made certain that all meal times were arranged separately. Back at the huts NCO Pulvertaft ordered us outside to assemble with the girls from the other huts, marched us back to the first barrack square. 'Ponsonby' that had been designated solely to the Women's Legion for training. As there were nine separate barracks on the camp, each one had been allocated a separate unit of girl volunteers to each Officers mess. In addition there were another four units designated to each of the four lower rank troop canteens. We were the second to march on and form up to await the arrival of the other units for the morning muster parade, after which our training routine began. We were taught 'The rudiments of army life' mainly how to march as a unit, how to conduct ourselves around the camp and to recognise and salute all the different officers. Once all units had mastered the skills of the parade ground, so began practicing marching (not as good as the men, I might add), Marching in columns down camp roads to the rear of the barracks, past the married quarters, then up the road towards the centre of the camp, where the clock tower and churches were located, along North road passing Beresford and Stewart the barrack blocks of the Royal Engineers, Army Service Corps, until we were finally back at Ponsonby. It was a route march we did quite often under the strict guidance of our drill instructor NCO Benton and her method of training us raw recruits, was excellent as well as being constantly observed and inspected by the watchful eye of Captain Tweedy. Our spare time was occupied making alterations to our uniforms, pressing and ironing in crease's until we looked like a flat iron ourselves. By the end of each day we were so tired that we just fell into bed, asleep before we had time to pull the blanket up around us. I cannot remember anyone complaining about the conditions or discussing whether we had been right or wrong to volunteer. When we had completed our two weeks army drill, the next part of our training was about to begin.

The following Monday morning, all smartly turned out the girls of the three huts were split up into three separate units. All the girls in hut twelve were all waitresses, girls from the other two huts formed up as cooks, kitchen maids and administration clerks. Fortunately our three units did not have too far to march from our accommodation huts, across the main road to the Stewart Barracks Officers Mess. Arriving at the Officers mess it was very quiet and sedate, the three separate units were divided up and shown to their place of work. We entered the dining room to find a number of soldiers still employed doing messing duties, who set about to teach us what our duties entailed. We were shown where the crockery, utensils, cruets, table centres, wines etc. were located and how we should perform our duties, including information about the seating order of the Officers. We were split into two groups of eight, whilst one group sat at the tables acting as officers, the others learnt the procedure of serving then each group would change places. We did not have time to stop and think about anything else, we were on the go all the time. At the end of the day back in our hut, we would practice serving each other. After three days we had finished our training sessions and were paired off, tallest together down to the smallest. Bridget and I, both nearly being about the same height, were allocated a number of tables to wait upon. We were ready for action.

Our first duty in the Officers Mess was serving breakfast. We were all determined not to make any mistakes, very wary and apprehensive of the situation, all smartly turned out in line, each gripping their silver-serving tray. As the officers took their seats, there was an air of frostiness within the mess, when all were settled NCO Benton gave us the nod to proceed with

16

the serving. She quietly moved around the tables carefully watching each and every one of us perform our duties, if she saw something had not been carried out correctly, she would pass a quiet comment to the offending girl. There was no conversation apart from a little on the Senior Officers table. We were polite and provided the service as we had been instructed, and when the meal was finished we returned to stand in line and wait for the departure of all the officers. NCO Benton then ordered us to clear away. Very quickly we had the table crockery back in the kitchens to be cleaned and put away. Our next job was polishing the cutlery and cruet sets so that they gleamed ready for use. After laying-up the place settings NCO Benton inspected all ready for the midday meal. However, there was a change in attitude by the Officers. Gone was the frostiness their conversations was more open as it was at the evening meal, having accepted the change thought no more about our intrusion.

All our working days were long, up before 5.30 a.m., ablutions, clean billets before breakfast, inspections by Captain Tweedy, March to the Officers' Mess to begin duties. Serving three meals a day, within an allotted time to the officers was demanding work, you had to be very quick during mealtimes in order to serve hot meals. After the evening meal our final daily task was laying the tables for breakfast next morning, finishing around about eight or nine o'clock in the evening. Quickly we settled down to the standards set and carried out our duties without any grumbling. As a team Bridget and I worked well together, I being so small eager and quick on my feet, nobody noticed, long before officers on other tables had finished their first helpings, I had served seconds to some of the officers on my tables, however this did not go unnoticed by the officers. As there was not much to spend my weekly wage on I did not smoke or drink, except for my bare necessities, I could have kept it all for myself, but could not think of my mother in want at home, so I was able to save a few pence out of the remaining two shillings and ten pence to give to her. One Saturday I received a surprise a sum of £1.00 handed to me by the senior officer Mr. Green. As a gesture of appreciation for the excellent way in which both of us looked after them, with a promise of a little extra money at the end of each week. We were extremely grateful for their generosity. I was more than satisfied with joining the Army, a period of tremendous change, which provided me with a purpose to my life. However since joining, the time came when being confined to camp was lifted and we could apply to leave camp to visit Mother. Unable to be away at the same time I arranged with Bridget to take it in turns, so that there was always one of us on call, ready to cover any extra duty that may be required in the Officer's Mess.

As the weeks turned into months the Women's Legion became an integral part of the Army camp. There was no fraternising with the troops, not that we had that much connection with them they all fully engaged in training were quickly dispatched to the Front. The girls in our hut were very friendly, we all got on well together and shared the duties on a rota basis. After the long days we spent on duty, our main off duty periods was Friday and Saturday nights, and possibly a full weekend something we all looked forward to. Like my mother I loved dancing and music it was in my blood and I still love it. In those days people made their own amusement, usually at a Ceilidh with the band playing the reels as the couples danced. Back in the early days when we lived in Ballybrittas, whenever there was a Ceilidh on, if I had been good, Mother would allow me go and watch all the people dancing. I would memorise the steps and tunes. Upon returning home I would dance on my own or, with one of my younger sisters.

On Camp, there were dances usually held on a Saturday evening in either the Sergeants or, Corporal's Mess, the music being played by various regimental bands. The girls of the Women's Legion were invited to these dances, which became the sole source of our entertainment. On the day of the dance, NCO Benton would receive an invite from the M/C of the dance, requesting how many of the off duty girls would be available to attend. She being in charge of the roster could provide that information so, they could organise transport by horse trap for the girls. Much to my delight, on my off duties I did attend. However these dances were not

17

the same as the Ceilidhs steps I had learnt as a child, instead the English ballroom style. On my first few visits I only watched, memorising the different steps to the tempo of the music if asked,making an excuse I couldn't dance? I thought: *I am not going to make a fool out of myself not knowing the steps*. It was during our evenings off that, we would practise the dance steps in the hut and soon was able to dance to any of the tunes that were played. Amongst the men there were some good dancers and some bad ones. Due to the fact I would never refuse a dance with anyone even if the men could only stumble around the dance floor, I became very popular, unlike some of the girls who being choosy, would answer an invitation to dance with. 'Sorry. I am engaged.' On one occasion at a Sergeants' Mess dance, a group of us were sitting at the end of the hall waiting for an invitation to dance, when a new young Sergeant, who obviously had a few drinks swaggered over. He asked five of the girls in turn if they would dance with him. Possibly because of his staggering with the drink, each in turn replied 'I am engaged.' The Sergeant took a couple of steps backwards, standing in front of them, placing his hands on his hips swaying he bawled out.

'IF THAT'S THE CASE, IT'S ABOUT TIME YOU WERE ALL MARRIED.' He turned to me and asked.... 'Miss, are you married too?' Truthfully I answered... 'No Sergeant.'... 'Right, Miss. May I have the pleasure of this dance with you please?'...'Yes, I would be delighted,'

That night he turned out to be the best dancer in the hall, subsequently we became good friends, so much so that at later dances I more or less became his dancing partner. We often laughed over that first encounter, but he began to get serious introducing me to his Sergeant Major and wife as 'The nicest girl in the hall'. Of course I was flattered but was too occupied with my Army commitments to become serious about any boyfriends. I did have a few boyfriends, more platonic than anything else, but with the sense of. 'Here to-day - gone tomorrow.' My usual excuse was, I had to go home to my mother and family.

It was about this time that the Women's Legion became integrated with the newly formed Women's Army Auxiliary Corps. (WAAC). Although the style of our uniform or our duties did not change, our hat badge did. 'The Lady with the Frying Pan' disappeared, being replaced by a badge with the letters WAAC surrounded by a wreath. A badge we thought very ordinary and did not take to wearing it very kindly. We were extremely proud of being the original members of the Women's Legion and, as a way of retaining this, we pinned our old cap badge to our tunics (I still have mine as a souvenir). We carried on with our duties, being constantly reminded of the importance of our work by the number of young Cadet Officers arriving for military training, and in what appeared to be a very short space of time, left for the Front. Snippets of conversation overheard in the Mess brought new places to our lips: Mons, Passchendaele, Arras and the Somme. The carnage and horrors of mustard gas causing casualties to be blinded or burnt. Then a new subject cropped up: 'Tanks', a new invention. We did not have a clue as to what they were for or what they did but according to the officers' point of view. 'Along with the Artillery, tanks are bloody good things to have on our side.'

The war seemed to be everlasting, we shuddered to think about how many more young men would die on the field of battle. During conversations in our hut someone would mention, 'Do you remember Lieutenant Goodge? I heard he was killed last week.' This snippet of information would bring our general conversation to a halt, we would all sit there thinking about the reality and senseless waste of human life. Another topic of conversation began with rumours of America joining the war. Having remained neutral was fed up with German U-Boats attacking merchant shipping. It was early April 1917 when they took up arms to fight alongside the British. This was a major development, which brought fresh hopes to our beleaguered forces. However throughout 1917 no quarter was given by either side. Still the fighting raged on, to us it appeared as a stalemate. 'Advance ten yards Retreat ten yards'. Later in the year my two younger sisters, Mary and Kathleen, decided it was time to venture across to England and volunteer for the

WAAC. Both were accepted, even though Kathleen was still too young, she was granted special permission to enlist, based on her determination and the fact that three of her older sisters had also volunteered for service. They were posted to Chatterton Camp in Lancashire. Mary became a cook and Kathleen, became an administrator.

At one of the corporal's dances it was a Fancy Dress do, where I made friends with the M/C a Corporal called Teddy Carr, he was quite a good dancer and had chosen me to become his partner. He had already told me that before he enlisted he had been an M/C at a large dance hall in London, and with that background became the M/C at the Curragh Camp Gymnasium. On one occasion returned back to London for a spot of leave. The day after he returned, I received a message from him asking me to urgently meet him in private at the Gymnasium. I was more than intrigued by this message and after I had finished duties met him and asked.

'Teddy why the secrecy?'

'Sarah, I went back to my old dance halls and they are dancing to three American dances: the Modern Waltz, Fox Trot, and One Step, they are all the rage in England. I've managed to learn them and want to introduce them at the next mess dance. Are you interested?' I jumped at the chance.

'Yes if you want me to.'

So we arranged to meet secretly at the Gymnasium in order to practice the steps. Teddy first showed me how the three different dance steps were formed before we practiced the steps. The steps themselves were not very hard to pick up. Teddy hummed the tune as we danced. Back in the hut I made excuses to the other girls, about doing extra duties but when I didn't turn up, they got suspicious about my disappearing act and started asking questions. One in particular, Nellie O'Callaghan who I had got to know quite well asked.

'Sarah. Who is your new boyfriend?'

'I don't have a boyfriend you know that Nellie'

'Well. Why do you keep disappearing, where do you go?'

I was stumped for an answer and knew how they all liked dancing. I was more than eager to tell them about the new dance steps, but had to keep up the charade. I told Teddy about the girls asking questions. So he simply said.

'Well Sarah. I think we have the solution, we have mastered the steps to the three dances. I've decided it's time to introduce them. When is your next off duty period?'

'This week-end.'...'Right there's a Corporal's Dance this week-end. That's the night we'll demonstrate the steps. Okay.'

We continued practicing throughout the following week, till the night of the dance. Teddy the M/C began the dance, with the normal three introduction dances, after the band stopped playing, the drummer provided a roll on the drums with a clash of cymbals. Then Teddy began his introduction.

'Ladies and Gentlemen. May I have your attention please. Tonight for your very own entertainment. We wish to demonstrate three new dances that are the rage in London. The first dance is called the modern waltz entitled. 'Let Me Call You Sweetheart.' Followed by the fox trot entitled. 'Five Foot Two, Eyes So Blue, Has Anybody seen my Girl.' Finally the one step entitled. 'Rag Street Blues'. To assist me in this demonstration, my dancing partner is Private Sarah Cunningham. A round of applause please.'

This was my cue. I stepped forward and took a bow. My secret was out. Well! The girls just stared then the questions flowed. They all chorused.

'Sarah how could you?' Why didn't you tell us? We could have learnt the steps as well.'

19

However, I was far too concerned about the demonstration I was about to give to take notice of their comments. We took our stance and when the band began to play, we danced the steps for the first time. Whilst the other dancers watched in awe as we performed the slow steps to the Modern Waltz. Clapping and cheering broke out as we finished the dance. The band immediately began the music for the Fox Trot. Silence descended as the spectators became absorbed in the new dance steps, as we glided around the floor to the strains of the accompanying music. We finished that dance amid roars of approval and clapping. A slight pause then the final demonstration- the One Step. The band began to play the music of the quick tempo Rag Street Blues. Once again silence descended, The audience absorbed in watching the lively steps being performed by us before their eyes. We danced the steps well and with a final twirl our demonstration performed without a hitch was over. With a triumphal roll on the drums a crash of cymbals the band stopped playing.

Clapping and more cheering broke out, Teddy twirled me around again, he bowed and I curtsied, before we made our way off the floor. Our demonstration had bowled them over. The band, taking the hint of the ovation, repeated the music of the One Step. Everyone seemed to want to jig about to the music trying to imitate its dance steps we had just performed.-From that night on, the new dances ruled the day. I had to teach all the girls in the hut the new dance steps. At later dances, someone would always ask for the Lancers to be played or one of the other Old Tyme dances. What memories it brings back now when I listen in to the Saturday night radio programme 'Old Time Dancing.' As the saying goes 'You're only young once'.

The war had been raging for four years with no sign of let up. With the constant flow of casualties from the war, being brought into the Curragh Hospital for treatment and recuperation, most suffering from shell shock, gassing, or loss of limbs. A constant reminder of what really was happening on the Western Front. Yet another problem was to take over our lives.

In late spring influenza hit the camp and rumours buzzed around that it was rife in England and America, with many people dying from it. It did not take long before the Camp succumbed to the pandemic. Officers and men alike went down like ninepins, with many Officers very ill. Meal times in the mess became almost deserted. Captain Tweedy organised the waitresses to take hot drinks and soups around to all sick officers in their quarters. However, one by one we too succumbed to the 'flu, until only six of us remained reasonably fit for duty. I was one of the six being run ragged, coping as best we could until the other girls gradually returned to carry on their duties, dragging themselves from sick beds to help out until eventually we caught it. But that was not the end of it. A girl from the Administration unit arrived at the mess and requested me to accompany her. Puzzled by her request, I asked her.

What is the matter?' she replied.

'One of your sister's have arrived at the camp and wished to speak with you.'

Having obtained permission to leave, I accompanied her back to the orderly room where my young sister Eilish sat waiting, a picture of misery, she herself full of the 'flu. In between her spells of coughing she croaked.

'All the family were down with the 'flu and Grandmother has died. Mother has to go to Hacketstown to bury her.'

I was shocked at this news. The only thing I could do was to seek permission to take care of the family at home, which was granted. I informed Bridget of the situation and returned to the hut to collect my bits and pieces. Together with Eilish, was soon on our way home. When I arrived Mother and father having already got over it were waiting to leave. The house was in an awful state, with sick bodies lying around and with me just about fit myself to cope with the sick. Later when Mother returned home, I was only too pleased to get back to camp and carry on with my duties.

20

The symptoms of the flu passed and with all of us fit for duties, the camp continued as normal. As the Officers continued with their conversations, we overheard mention of bombs being dropped by the German aeroplanes on Paris, resulting in many civilian people being killed. With the R.F.C. Squadron located on the Curragh practicing dropping their bombs on the plains, we did have some knowledge of the destruction that bombs did cause but they were not on civilians. Another snippet of information was the name of a giant German gun called Big Bertha, which was being used to shell Paris from sixty-five miles away. We did not like the sound of this and prayed that the war would soon come to an end. It was about this time that we heard that the pilots of the Army Royal Flying Corps were to be amalgamated with the Navy Air Pilots and renamed the Royal Air Force, which still exists to this day.

The month of August saw a dramatic change in the course of the war. According to some of the officers who described events with elation. The tide had turned at last. The final push was a black day for the German Army. As British, Canadian, Australian, French and American troops supported by tanks and aeroplanes, began an attack at Amiens. In September a new wave of flu swept through the camp. The intake of new Officers quickly succumbed to it, which was very evident to see in the Officers' Mess, the empty spaces at the tables. Again I was to receive word from Mother that Theresa one of father's sisters had died from 'flu, even more so close to deaths door was our little brother Jack. As the flu began to wane, Officers and men gradually returned to normal duties. To our families joy, our little brother Jack survived, although he was to suffer from weak lungs for the rest of his life. In addition to the atrocities of the war, with its casualties killed or maimed throughout the war, the Spanish 'flu pandemic claimed the lives of millions of people worldwide.

CHAPTER THREE
ARMISTICE

November 11th a damp chilly Monday morning, we were busy clearing away when suddenly the outer doors burst open. Running through the dining hall came Theresa, a young administration clerk screaming. 'THE WAR'S OVER.' Before disappearing through the kitchens doors. Taken aback by her ravings, in shock we all immediately stopped what we were doing and ran towards the kitchen doors, bursting through them to find all the staff stood motionless inside listening to the ravings of Theresa shouting.

'AN ARMISTICE HAS BEEN DECLARED'. Her outburst was followed by silence, she screamed.... 'DON'T YOU UNDERSTAND? THE WAR IS OVER?' The only person to say anything was the head cook. She yelled back.

'WHAT ARE YOU SCREAMING ABOUT GIRL?'

'A WIRE HAS BEEN RECEIVED AT HQ. WAR WILL END AT ELEVEN O CLOCK THIS MORNING. ALL HOSTILITIES WILL CEASE, THE WAR IS OVER.'

Again there was silence. Until what she had said dawned on us. Pandemonium broke out, cheering, screaming, ladles were being banged against the pots, everyone was hugging each other in groups jumping up and down, some of the girls like me were crying. Bridget grabbed hold of me we just hugged each other, bubbling over with tears of emotion, shaking looking at each other's tear streaked faces, names of uncles and friends, killed in the fighting tumbling from our lip. Instantly we fell to our knees blessed ourselves and said a prayer of thanksgiving. They had not died in vain. God rest their souls. NCO Benson arrived in the kitchens pushing her way into our midst demanding to know.

'WHY IS THERE NOBODY WORKING IN THE DINING ROOM? NON OF THE TABLES HAVE BEEN CLEARED AWAY. ITS IN A MESS.'

Elated with the news, we scurried back to our duties. Just after eleven o'clock the news was confirmed followed by more cheering.

The news of the Armistice had the Officers very buoyant that day. Lunch was served on time, however the midday meal was disrupted and protocol disappeared as they drifted in and out, they taking more time over their drinks. After the meal time their elation spilled out from the mess lounge into their quarters. A group of young Cadet Officers seized another brother Officer and with whoops and shouts carried him spread-eagled above their heads. Someone produced a ladder, all together they manhandled him up onto the rooftop of their quarters, removing the ladder left him stranded. Apparently he was the youngest Cadet Officer on camp. Other pranks went on which we were not witness to. We, elated by the events and goings on, cleared away and began preparing for the evening meal, wondering if that meal would be the same? Our preparations were interrupted by NCO Benson who came in, ordered us.

'Stop what you are doing and fall in outside as you are.' She carried on into the kitchens.

We still dressed in working attire, a motley unit of Waitresses, Cooks and Scullery maids assembled on the roadway outside the Officer's mess. NCO Benson bellowed.

'SECOND OFFICERS CADET SQUADRON. ATTENTION... QUICK MARCH.'

We marched along North Road passing each guardhouse where the duty Guards, gave us a rousing cheer, which was echoed behind us as the other WAAC Unit followed us, passing the Clock Tower and Churches down towards the Camp Gymnasium, where she brought us to a halt and ordered us to fall out and re-form inside.

Upon entering we fell in behind other WAAC units already assembled. Up on the stage in front of the Units, stood alongside a dais, was Captain Lady Houndsworth. After a short wait from behind us the camp Adjutant Major Block, accompanied by the RSM, entered the Gymnasium.

We were ordered to attention whilst they marched towards the front. Capt. Lady Houndsworth saluted the Major, and they had a few words, before Major Block stepped up onto the dais, mentioned something to the RSM, who bristling with importance, stood at attention to one side and with an earth-shattering roar ordered?

'COMPANY STAND AT EASE. STAND EASY.' Then Major Block addressed us.

'This day the eleventh day of the eleventh month in the year of 1918. On the stroke of eleven hundred hours. An armistice was declared! All hostilities with Germany have ceased. Germany has surrendered. Today it is a very important day for the British Army and indeed for the World'....pausing before he continued... 'Ladies of the women's auxiliary army corps. Have all carried out your duties with perseverance and dedication. You should be proud of the fact that you have done a splendid job of work, helping with the war effort, which I might add has not gone unnoticed. However. You Ladies are to be immediately confined to barracks until tomorrow morning. Not I may add. As a punishment. But to enable the men to let their hair down. Moreover as a mark of the Army's appreciation. In three weeks time. I have organised for a ball to be held, In each one of the Officer's Mess. A ball that you shall never forget! And Ladies! Ball Gown's will be the order of dress for the night's festivities. Thank you one and all. Sergeant major. Carry on.'

'YES SAR.' And with another earth shattering roar he ordered. 'COMPANY ATTENTION. COMPANY... TO YOUR DUTIES DISMISS?'

As we were marched back to continue our duties. I thought: *This really was something, after years of wearing only khaki, permission to wear a ball gown to attend a ball in of all places! The Officers Mess. Our one-day confinement to barracks was nothing.* The bar in the Officers mess was busy all afternoon, nevertheless with the lack of officers, the evening meal was a repeat of the midday's. Little activity.

With duties finished, very elated with the day's excitement and preoccupied with the forthcoming event, all being mad keen on dancing, had affectionately named the hut. 'Rag Lane Bungalow.' We all agreed to help each other make our Ball Gowns, but what kind? I remembered on a previous occasion I had worn a light coloured frock to one of the dances. Unfortunately, whilst on my way walked into our Administration Officer who promptly dressed me down, confined me to barracks for five days with no off duty time, in addition, ordered me to pick all the weeds from the front of the huts. A lesson well learnt. Throughout the next three weeks we spent our off duty time busily making ball gowns. On Saturday the day of the Ball, in addition to our normal duties, we prepared all the food and preparations for the evenings ball.

It was dark misty and drizzling with rain, when we set out wearing rainwear covering our ball gowns. Together we all arrived at the Officers Mess, discarded our rainwear, in the vestibule before entering the cleared dining room. There to be greeted with roars of approval and clapping from the Officers. In true military style the M/C lined us up inside, then began calling out each one of us by name, whereas an Officer came forward and took his allotted partner as their escort and beau for the evening's ball. It just so happened that my escort turned out to be. Officer Alan Bradshaw the young Junior Officer who had been stuck on top of his hut. He turned out to be a very pleasant gentleman and if I might say so, he wasn't a bad dancer either. Together we had a wonderful evening. The M/C on behalf of the Officers Mess called for a toast to. 'The Ladies.' With a buffet we had prepared, a raffle with prizes and the band played all night, it was a great success. True to his word Major Block provided us a Ball we would never forget.

Two weeks later, not to be outdone by the Officers, the Sergeants Mess retaliated and laid on a wonderful dinner followed by a Music Hall Style show, the artiste being the Sergeants themselves! Another marvellous evening well remembered.

Christmas and the New Year was a special one and enjoyed by all. In the early spring of 1919, peace had prevailed over the previous months and the War was finally over. It was a time when most of the Officer Cadets began to leave their Training Quarters and Ireland for good. No doubt, they having enjoyed a good time while serving in Ireland and very pleased to be going back home to England in one piece. Subsequently numbers in the various Office's Mess declined rapidly. Rumours abounded as to what would happen to the 2nd Officers Cadet Squadron. Moreover another change to our organisation was announced, the WAAC would be renamed QMAAC. (Queen Mary Women's Auxiliary Army Corps). However, other changes did occur. Bridget and three other girls one being one of the Driscoll twins were ordered to Dublin to serve the Officers at Jury's Hotel. This left the rest of us girls serving the remaining few Officers. I was quite content to stay where I was, nevertheless, wondering where or when we were to be posted. I often say "The Army is built of good men and rumours.' That is all you have, you never get posted to the place you want to go to.

With few officers left there were insufficient duties to keep us girls fully occupied. Very aware of the pending split up, somebody suggested having a group photograph taken. We approached Captain Tweedy who agreed and arranged for a photographer from Kildare to take the photograph.

We assembled outside the Officers Mess dressed in our walking-out uniforms, along with Capt. Tweedy, the NCO 's, not forgetting 'Buster' a little Terrier that we had taken from an Officer when he was sent over to France, unfortunately he never returned.

2nd. CAVALRY OFFICERS CADET SCHOOL, Q.M.A.A.C.
Kildare February 1919.

S. Cunningham. M. Campbell. H. Gibson. K. Murphy . N. O'Callaghan. C. O'Driscoll. M. MacNamarra. B Radford.
H. Fitzgerald. R. Martin. A. Benton NCO. R.M Tweedy (Unit Officer) S.Pulvertaft NCO. A. M'Cormac. NCO. M.Gibson.
A. Hennessy E. M. MacCarthy and "Buster". J. Kenny NCO.

A few weeks later, we received our marching orders. Capt. Tweedy with some other girls was transferred to Cork. A few more were posted to Dublin and some to Belfast, whilst I was to remain at the Officers Mess together with two NCO's and six waitresses. My sister Mary in

24

England sent me a letter to inform me that she and Kathleen had being posted to Press Heath Camp in Shropshire it was a prisoner of war camp.. It wasn't long after her letter that I received one from Bridget advising me that after three months at Jury's Hotel, she was soon to be posted to the Ox and Bucks Officers Mess at Victoria Barracks in Cork. A week later NCO. Pulvertaft told me that the following week I was to be posted to Jury's Hotel to replace Bridget. Something I did not look forward too.

The following week I left for Dublin. I was provided with a lift in an Army GS (General Service) wagon, my very first ride in any automobile. I knew the driver, a girl from the transport hut. On the way our conversation was all about past dances we had attended. In what seemed no time we arrived at Jury's Hotel. I reported to the Duty Officer who provided me with details of my new duties. A very good job that of looking after the Officer in Charge. He took me to where I was to be billeted, a room to myself. However, it was not the same this was a Hotel and what a contrast, the atmosphere there was quiet. I missed the girls and hustle and bustle of the previous Officers Mess. I became lonely and unhappy. I decided to put in a request to be transferred to Victoria Barracks Cork. My reason being that I would like to be alongside my younger sister, also my Mother's concern about me living alone in Dublin. But I knew better, mother and father were very strict. If they had any suspicion and thought I was going down the wrong path, they would have been after me in minutes. Two weeks later I was summoned to the Duty Officer's room and informed my request had been granted. I was to report to the Officers Mess of the 2nd. Battalion Ox & Buck's Regiment, Victoria Barracks Cork. Immediately I sent a letter to Bridget informing her of my impending departure from Dublin and arrival at Cork. The day before I was due to leave I was handed a railway travel warrant from Dublin to Cork on the early morning train. Having packed my kit I booked an early morning call and was provided with a lift to the station.

CHAPTER FOUR
CORK - 1919.

It was dawn when we left Jury's and after a short drive we arrived at a rather desolate station with nobody about to ask questions. Left standing outside with my two rather large bags of kit to fend for myself, the only noise I could hear was the sound of milk churns being moved about. My first thought was: *Sarah just get on with it.* Picking up the bags I moved into the station and quickly spotted a ticket collector near a barrier and headed in his direction. Dumping my bags down at my feet took out my travel warrant from a pocket, handing it to him asked.

'Which is the train to Cork?'

He didn't bother to look at my warrant just directed me to a train at the platform right in front of us, he noticing my stature and the size of my two bags of kit, loudly shouted to a young lad further down the train, busy helping load milk churns onto the train.

'SHEAMUS. CO'ME ON BACK HERE. WILL YEA BE GIVING THIS YOUNG LADY A HAND WIT HER LUGGAGE?'

Sheamus came running back to the barrier, tipping his cap to me, lifted up my luggage and made off down the platform to the far end. Quickly I followed behind him, when he stopped at an open carriage door he threw in the kitbags. I thanked him and I gave him one penny, to which he grunted in appreciation. I climbed in the compartment as Sheamus banged shut the door behind me. Pushing my bags into the centre of the compartment I sat down by the window and thought. *"This is my first train journey."* I sat there very apprehensive about the train journey and my future prospects? From outside the noisy scraping of milk churns being moved and loaded was the only noise that disturbed the silence, until the noisy shouts from some porters as they banged shut carriage doors, then silence. About five minutes later, the blast of a whistle made me jump, frightening the life out of me. Just in case I fell out, I gripped the slats of the wooden seat, I don't know why because I was locked in. With jerking movements the train moved, gradually picking up speed left the station.

Once out of Dublin and into the countryside there was nothing to do, except take in the beauty of the landscape. I sat there in wonderment as we sped along. It stopped at Newbridge on the North side of the Curragh before it jerked and bumped its way out of the station. Stood out like a beacon against a grey sky I noticed the clock tower of the Curragh Camp on the top of Long Hill. It soon disappeared behind, making me wish I was back there. As the train jolted, bucked and squeaked its way across the Curragh plains soon it approached Kildare town. I recognised some parts of the town that made me feel very homesick and near to tears, until once again we were past Kildare back out into the lush green countryside. The rest of the journey was uneventful, all I wished was that the train journey would finish quickly, which did happen just before twelve 'o'clock, when it arrived at Cork. Screeching to a sudden halt I lurched forward to fall onto the floor, my hat fell forward over my eyes, I felt very foolish and burst out laughing as I got up to gather my wits, before dropping the window to open the door. Grabbing hold of my two bags dragged them towards the open door before stepping down onto the platform, with both hands dragged them out dropped them onto the platform, got in between them and with one in each hand, began to walk towards the barrier behind a few other passengers that were ahead of me. At the barrier dropping my kit took out my travel warrant and handed it to the Ticket Collector and was about to ask. *Where and how do I get to Victoria Barracks?* When I heard Bridget's voice. 'Sarah over here.' Peering around the side of the Ticket Collector, I spotted Bridget alongside another tall uniformed girl, someone I did not recognize. Oh how delighted I was to see her! The first time in three months since she had left Stewart Barracks. She came across to me we quickly embraced, then taking hold of one of my bags she said.

'Sarah I found out the time of the train and got time off to meet you. I managed to get a lift back. Come on over and meet Angela, she's one of the QMWAAC drivers at the camp.'

I was formally introduced to this tall girl. We threw my bags on the back of the wagon and both sat in front beside Angela. On our way back, Bridget informed me about the camp and named other girls that had been with us in 'Rag Lane Bungalow' and surprise surprise! Our officer in charge was Captain Margaret Tweedy, and that both of us were to report to her at 1500 hours. This pleased me as she was a good Officer to us girls and had stuck up for us as a unit. I was more than delighted at this news, it was just like coming back home. Bridget also quietly whispered in my ear.

'Sarah. I've met a young soldier and am going out with him, promise you won't tell Mother?' Very surprised at her mentioning that, I quickly looked at her to which she smiled and readily blushed. What could I say, I was sworn to secrecy?

Arriving at the Barracks Guardhouse Angela, stopped the GS wagon to let us get off, go to the rear and hauled off my two bags before she drove off. I reported into the Guardhouse. With that formality over, Bridget took hold of one of my bags and we began walking to our quarters. On the way she pointed out places that I should know about. My first impression of Victoria Camp was not as impressive as the Curragh. There was plenty of evidence of soldiers doing drill or other forms of training. Arriving at our accommodation hut that was much the same as our previous abode, drab and dreary. A couple of the girls, Julia Kenny an NCO and Bridie Radford obviously off duty, were sat talking on their beds. We exchanged greetings and talked a little while before we went to the mess hall to eat. Bridget and I returned to the hut to smartened ourselves up before we reported to Capt. Tweedy. Outside her office we stood waiting until, a senior NCO Birke (unknown to me) came out and marched us in, bringing us to a halt in front of Capt. Tweedy's table. Called out our names.

'Private's. Cunningham. B. and Cunningham. S. Reporting for instructions Ma'am.' We saluted. Looking up Capt. Tweedy said.

'Aah. Sarah Cunningham. I understand you put in a request to be transferred to this Camp?' Quickly I replied.

'Yes Ma'am?'

'Well. I'm pleased that you did and I'm sure you will like it here. This is a good officer's mess, and as you both worked well together in the Stewart's officers mess. I've decided to assign you both to serve the senior officer's tables. Tomorrow your first duty is at o seven hundred hours. Officers breakfast. Bridget, I have already issued instructions about your current duty roster. Now report to NCO Barraclough in the officer's mess. Dismiss.'

The brief interview was over. We saluted and NCO Birke ordered us to about turn and marched us out. Outside the office we were brought to a halt.

'Cunningham B. Take Cunningham S. To the offices mess. Dismiss.'

Elated by our new duties, for all intents and purposes, upgraded we broke rank. With Bridget guiding me and outside of earshot Bridget said.

'Sarah, a word of warning Barraclough was at Jury's with us and transferred here. She's a stickler for smartness and presentation. Whatever you do, do not answer her back, otherwise you will get more than you bargained for? Now then Sarah just wait until you see the Ox and Bucks Battalion silverware. There's a sight for sore eyes.'

Arriving at the Officers Mess, Bridget ushered me through the doors into a vestibule, the bright sunlight shining through a window on a back wall highlighted its dark brown wood polished floors. Bridget taken my arm led me to a room on the left, quietly opened the door allowed me to peek in. All was quiet this was an anti- room, neatly spaced out were round-topped tables with four high backed chairs. Bridget whispered.

'C'mon, the other room is their reading room just take a quick look.' Crossing to the other door I opened it. Oblong tables with comfortable high-backed chairs were evenly placed around a few small settees, a large fireplace with a ornate mantelshelf, in the center was a large clock its steady ticking disturbed the silence, above that was a large portrait of the King in a red uniform. Hung from brass rods on both sides of the windows were velvet curtains reaching down to the floor. A very large oriental carpet covered most of the polished floor, We left the solitude of the room and proceeded towards the Dining room. As she opened the door my eyes were immediately drawn to the centre table, what Bridget had said was true. Laid out on display the silverware of the Ox and Buck's. Trophies, Candelabras, Cup's, Shields, Tankards, Plate Servings, spoons and cruet sets. A truly splendid sight to be admired by all.

Slowly we walked along the table I stopping to read some of the inscriptions on the trophies. The rest of the room was spacious, with individual tables already laid, with rows of seats behind them some with eight place settings others with more. At the far end was the senior officers table the one we had been allocated to, that too had plenty of place settings, like the floor all tables were highly polished like mirrors. The walls were adorned with paintings of various Generals. Bridget guided me towards a double door at the far end, which I found led into the kitchens. Upon entering we came face to face with a line of waitress's being inspected by an NCO. A buxom woman, quite tall, very authoritative and starchy, she turned around and directed her attention to us, she snapped demanding.

'Who are you?' I answered.

'Private Cunningham Sarah W4923. Ma'am'

'Ah yes. Capt. Tweedy informed me about you. You are late. Where have you been? I don't want any slacking in this Dining room. Do you understand?'

'Yes Ma'am.' We chorused. She turned and dismissed the other waitress's, who filed past us into the dining room. Turning her attention at us she began.

'Now. I understand from Capt. Tweedy you are sisters and have been assigned to serve the senior officer's tables. You Bridget will show this new Private where everything is stored. Both of you will attend only as observers at the evening meal and stand to one side of the Officers table, and watch until the meal is finished. After which you will take on your duties to lay up ready for the morning's breakfast. Then you may return to your billet. Private Cunningham S. Your job now is to sort out your uniform and work dress ready for to-morrow morning. I want you both back here in the morning by o six thirty hours, ready for inspection. Is that understood?'

'Yes Ma'am.' We chorused. I thought: *This must be Barraclough.* She ordered.

'Follow me.' She returned back into the Dining hall, striding towards the top table pointing she said. 'These are your tables, now proceed with your duties.'

She left us to it. Out of earshot I turned to Bridget.

'Now I know what you were getting at, Barraclough is a right stickler.'

'Told you so. C'mon I'll show you where everything is.'

I was now more than eager to familiarise myself with the place. In the kitchens, I was introduced to the entire cooking staff. The Head Cook another Angela, was I discovered, a good friend of mothers and the other two cooks, Bessie and Deirdre were from the Curragh camp so, at least we had a few allies amongst the kitchen staff. Deirdre provided me with information on the menu, storerooms, linen, and cutlery cupboard. After that tour we returned to the Dining Hall. I met the two girls we were replacing, Hilary Fitzgerald and Annie Hennessey, who were more than happy to pass over their duties. I renewed old acquaintances, Nellie O' Callaghan was more than pleased to be reunited with me. I was introduced to other new girls, most of who had been at Jury's until they were posted to Cork. I asked the other girls about the Officers, who had been drafted back from the Front.

'Don't be surprised at what you see ' Remarked one of the girls. I asked.

28

'Why?'

'Just you wait you'll see?' Later on we were to meet up with another acquaintance of mothers, Major Kelly also from the Curragh camp, so we had quite a few on our side.

Bridget and I having done what was expected, returned back to the kitchens where we were provided with something to eat and tea. There was nothing else for us to do until the evening meal began. The arrival back of 'Barraclough' put an end to our chatting.

'You two go smarten yourselves up and put your waitress's uniforms on. I want you back here in thirty minutes ready for the evening meal.'

Rather hurriedly we left the kitchens and returned back to the hut. I had not even unpacked my kit, which caused me a problem. Creased uniform. Bridget suggested.

'Borrow some of the other girls, they won't mind and this evening you can iron the rest of your kit.'

With a borrowed uniform the smallest I could find managed to make myself presentable when we lined up for inspection. Arriving in front of me. Barraclough scrutinised my dress snapped.

'Uhm! Not good enough. It will have to do for this meal as you are just an observer. However tomorrow morning I want to see a big improvement. You two stand away from the tables and watch. Waitresses. To your duties dismiss.'

Later the Officers began to drift in from the anti-room, among them walking wounded with walking sticks or crutches, one arm or leg missing black patches covered either the left or right eye, the results of war wounds. At least they had been lucky they were still alive so, that's what the other girl had meant. Watching them take their seats a pang of sympathy rose in my throat. Then they were followed in by senior officers, and once all seated the meal began. Standing to one side we watched Hilary and Annie serve, there was nothing new to learn, the procedure was the same as at the Curragh. I thought: *Here I do not have any problems.* The meal finished and after the last Officers had left we helped the clearing away, then we laid up making certain everything was in its right place for the morning meal before we left for our hut. Me to sort out my kit and prepare for the next morning.

Prompt next morning at 06:30 hrs in the Mess we stood in line waiting for 'Barraclough's Inspection' No comments were passed at me. At 06:45 the Officers began to arrive, all were seated by 07:00hrs. Along with the senior Officers table, occupying another table was a group of young Junior Officers. We decided to nickname their table. "The College Chums." Under the watchful eyes of 'Barraclough' we began our first servings, just as we previously had we worked quickly and efficiently. All meals were issued to the Officers without a hitch, therefore completing the servings of our tables long before the other girls had completed theirs. After the meal had finished and the officers had departed, we cleared away our tables only then did Barraclough come across to us remarking.

'You two work well as a pair.' We must have passed her test. I settled down quite quickly into the new routine. I had been there less than two weeks when one evening, clearing away when NCO Barraclough called me.

'Private Sarah Cunningham. Come here please.'

Wondering what I had done wrong I skirted around the top table, across to where she was standing by the. 'Silver Table. Stood at attention, my silver service tray held correctly in front of me. ...'Cunningham, I've been watching you, I see from your records, along with your other duties, you served wine at the Curragh and Jury's. Is that correct?'

'Yes Ma'am '

'Right, from tomorrow lunchtime you are the Wine Waitress serving the Senior Officers at lunchtime and evening meals. Dismiss.'

'Yes. Ma'am.' Not sure of either to be flattered or annoyed with the extra duty, I had to get on with it. Returning to clearing away, Bridget worked her way towards me and whispered.

'What's that about?'

'She has given me extra duty. I'm a wine waitress as well.'

We carried on. After a week or so serving wine, one of the Officers kindly asked. 'If I would partake in a glass?' As I never drank I politely refused.

Although I never wanted to leave the Curragh Camp, I was more than content with my new posting. Victoria Barracks was also shared by other Regiments and as both the Sergeants and Corporals Mess's of the Ox and Bucks as well as the Lancers, organised various functions including Fancy Dress dances. So if off duty there would always be an alternative function to be invited to, which provided me and the other girls with our weekend entertainment or, take a trip into Cork, which was seldom. I soon got into the dancing routine, once again found good dancing partners at the different functions. Bridget was constantly meeting her soldier man friend, serving in the 'The Royal Irish Fusiliers.' Therefore she spent a lot of her Saturdays at their dances. However, that was not for me, as far as I was concerned all relationships had to be platonic. I had got to know a couple of the Officer's Batmen and as there was always food left over from the officers meals, it was shared out amongst the girls. However, what was left over would be thrown away, which to me was a waste of good food so I would put some aside and pass them over to the Batmen through the pantry window. They returned their gratitude by arranging a trip out for all the girls, by hiring a coach to take us to see the Lakes of Killarney. I discovered that my partner was married and decided not to go, making an excuse that I had been called upon to do an extra duty. In our family we were brought up to keep well away from married men. My chance would come later.

A letter arrived from my sister Mary, informing me that she and Kathleen would be on leave for two weeks, one week in Kildare and the second week   wanted to visit us and stay in Cork.

We had not seen each other for over a year. I discussed this with Bridget and as they were both serving members of the QMWAAC, they might be able to stay on camp. Through the right procedures I requested an interview with Captain Tweedy to ask if they could stay in camp over a weekend with us. After some thought, she gave her permission. I sent a brief wire home to mother explaining the arrangements. I even arranged an invitation, for them to attend the Sergeant's mass dance on the Saturday night. They arrived at the Camp in their uniforms, both looked well and although only sixteen Kathleen had certainly grown up. On the Saturday, dressed in our uniforms we went into Cork for afternoon tea and to have our Photograph taken, as a memento of us serving in the army. At the

4 sisters

Kathleen Bridget Mary Sarah sat evening dance we had a wonderful time dancing the night away. On Sunday we made a   trip to the 'Blarney Castle' to 'Kiss the Blarney Stone'. When we arrived we made our way to the stone and stood watching the antics of others lying on their backs almost upside down, in their attempts to kiss the Blarney Stone. After seeing the way you had to manoeuvre your body into the kissing position, my sisters were too scared to attempt it, but I was game enough. I hadn't come all this way just to look at it. I took off my hat and laid on my back, my sisters held my legs and skirt down, and as the blood coursed to my head, I managed to kiss the Blarney stone. I got up flushed with the exertion and pleasure, at least I had done what the others did not want to attempt. But after a joyful weekend together, they returned back home, then on back to their camp in England, which they informed us had become a German POW Camp.

Bridget was openly courting her man Peter Macdermott. However his Regiment was due to be posted to India, therefore he had asked Bridget for her hand in marriage. Bridget had accepted. Unfortunately she still being in the Army would not be able to go, furthermore she did not want to go. They sought our parent's permission, which was given, she became the first of the girls in our family to get married. They decided to hold their nuptial mass in our Kildare parish church and I was to be her bridesmaid. With the pending departure of Peter time was short. Bridget and I had been unable to get home since we had left the Curragh. With the wedding date set we applied for leave. We spent all our off duty periods busy making her wedding and my bridesmaid dress fortunately, we were helped by one of the girls who had been a seamstress before she volunteered, so with her knowledge the dresses were quickly finished. Together brimming with excitement we left for home. Mary and Kathleen had already arrived ahead of us, it was wonderful to see everyone again. What a lovely wedding it turned out to be. Mother making sure that nothing would spoil the day of her daughter's wedding, it went off without a hitch. Peter had been granted special leave for his wedding and the very next day he re-joined his Battalion en-route to India. Nevertheless, the celebrations continued for a full week and much to our disgust our weeks leave ended far too soon.

Back at camp it was hard to settle into work but soon knuckled down to our normal duties. It was in June that news circulated about two mad airmen (as mother would call them) Alcock and Brown, had crashed landed their aeroplane in an Irish bog at a place called Clifden not far from Galway. They apparently had flown in one of those new-fangled contraptions all the way across the ocean from America. Their heroic flight marked the beginning and future of a new era, travelling by air. Whilst this monumental event was either noted or passed over, the peace process was nearing its climax. The document of peace (the Treaty of Versailles) was signed in a railway carriage at Versailles. On the 28th of June 1919. The Germans officially signed the final document of the conditions, marking Germany's total agreement to the surrender terms. To mark the signing, celebrations had already been planned in Cork City. A day that all the Regiments of the army would take part in the Parade including the QMWAAC.

We had all been rehearsing, marching backwards and forwards until we were as good as the men. On that day the 28th. of June it just happened to be my 23rd. birthday and turned out to be a boiling hot day. As the Army marched in columns of three from the camp to the city centre, to be joined by the rest of the Regiments with all the bands playing, along with the skirl of the pipes and drums of the Irish Regiments. It was a pleasure and honour to be part of it as we marched through the lovely City of Cork with crowds cheering as we passed the dais where the Mayor, along with all the city dignitaries and senior military Officers, took the salute. A delight for everyone watching and by the time we arrived back at camp for dispersal, we were all soaking wet with perspiration. After a wash down and refreshed we prepared for the ball, which the Officers had arranged for the nights celebrations and what a night that was. After four long years of fighting Victory was ours. For me it was a wonderful birthday present. I danced my legs off. Next day we were all back to our duties as normal.

It was much later, on duty one evening, that my close friend Nellie O ' Callaghan another wine waitress, and a good dancer too, were washing up the glasses and above the racket we were making, we could hear in the distance, the strains of a band playing at a dance. It was killing the pair of us to stay on duty, so Nellie suggested.

'Sarah why don't we leave the remaining glasses till the morning and go to the dance?'

Polishing a glass, I was tempted, thinking about her suggestion asked.

'Do you think we will get away with it?'

'Well we'll give it a good try, what do you say?'

I did not hesitate. We disappeared running to the hut to change, then onto the dance. Unfortunately one of the other girls had overheard our conversation, she decided to report us to the OIC. We had not been at the dance for more than a couple of minutes when one of the Officers Batman warned us of the situation. Like scared rabbits we both took off and ran back to the mess, covering our uniforms with our rubber pinafores and began polishing glasses on the tables whilst singing. 'God send him back to me.'

NCO Barraclough arrived on the scene looked quizzically at us, then I spoke up.

'Ma'am we are nearly finished.' She seeing that we had completed all the tables, cast another unbelieving look at us.

'Right well done.' Then left.

We got away with our little escapade scot-free and did go to the dance. Later we heard the other girl received a right dressing down from NCO Barraclough for reporting us without cause. Shortly after that incident, one evening on Company Orders:

"All QMWAAC Personnel to assemble on parade in the Camp
Gymnasium at 1100 hrs next day.
Dress: Walking out Uniforms."

We wondered what this was all about. Next morning, after completing our duty, we returned to the hut to change. NCO Barraclough. Formed us up outside, marched us to the Camp gymnasium to be assembled inside along with other units. It was not long before Captain Tweedy arrived and stood in front of the units, ordered us to stand at ease, then reading from the sheet of paper she held.

'Ladies. Of the QMWAAC. I have received the following directive from The War Office in London. Your Duties to the Crown have now ceased. Serving members on camps where units are operating are deemed 'Surplus to Requirements' and are to be replaced by, nominated men of the Battalion or Regiment present on that Camp.

All serving members of the QMWAAC will all be sent to Dublin for demobilisation. I personally regret the decision, however in an attempt to keep us on the Officer Commanding the Ox and Bucks. Battalion had sent a request through normal channels to the War Office. In return the War Office has refused. Until further notice you will continue with your normal duties, arrangements are underway for soldiers from the Ox and Bucks to take over.

That is all Dismiss.'

The news hit all of us like a thunderbolt. It was demob for all of us. Shuffling of feet and general derision followed this information. With heavy hearts we were marched back to our huts to commiserate amongst ourselves. Following the notice of our pending demob, we had been instructed to train some novice soldiers, who had been selected as. So-called 'Volunteers.' I'm sure that those men declined doing that type of work, but they had been given orders and orders had to be carried out. Within a couple of days of the announcement, we were all clearing away the breakfast tables, when, the crunching of boots disturbed the orderly quietness of our duties. NCO Barraclough entered followed by a file of soldiers. We stopped what we were doing to watch what going on, loudly she ordered.

'LINE UP OVER THERE.' With much shuffling squeals of studs on polished floors, the soldiers lined up at the far end of the dining hall she barked out.

'DO NOT MARK MY POLISHED FLOORS WITH YOUR CLUMSY BOOTS'...waving the sheet of paper in her hand, their shuffling stopped. 'Barraclough' pointed to two of the soldiers...'YOU TWO FOLLOW ME.' 'She advanced towards Bridget and me stood at the top table, she came to an abrupt halt, whilst behind her the two soldiers, bumped into each other, aiming another comment at them. 'I TOLD YOU NOT TO SCUFF MY POLISHED FLOORS.' Looking down at her list, very abruptly presented them to us.

'Cunningham's B. and S. These two Privates. Peak C. and Clements F. Are your replacements? You train them well as I don't want any comebacks after you two have gone. Now get on with it.' She smartly about turned and marched away towards the other soldiers lined up. Her loud voice echoed as she issued orders, sorting out and assigning the other soldiers. She too had a bee in her bonnet about the announcement.

I looked up at these two proud but very embarrassed fair-haired young soldiers towering above me. Stood at attention tucked under their left arm their peaked hat displaying the gleaming, Ox and Bucks cap badge. Their Puttees wrapped neatly and symmetrically around their legs down to their big shiny boots. (The reason for Barraclough's wrath). Both wore Pip, Squeak and Wilfred medal ribbons (so nicknamed, don't ask me why?) on their tunics. Soon the Officers mess became overcrowded with waitresses and their observers. Barraclough herded a group of them past us into the kitchens. I asked the two young privates.

'Have either of you two done anything like this before?'

Still stood at attention The pair of them staring straight ahead, chorused.

'No Ma'am.'... 'What can you do then?'... 'Don't know Ma'am? Only been trained to fight with Rifle and Bayonet Ma'am.' I retorted.

'Uhm that's a good start. Now we know what were up against don't we Bridget?' She replied with a scowl on her face. 'Your right there Sarah.' I asked.

'What are your first names then?'..... 'I'm called Fred.'...Cocking his head in his pal's direction...'He's Cyril.'....'Right Fred and Cyril stand at ease. My names Sarah this is my sister Bridget. We too are just Privates. Just think you are one of us now and we shall get on fine.'

They both relaxed and looked down at us, seeking to be told what to do. I was baffled at where to start teaching them I had an idea.

'Look both of you stand over there.' I pointed away from the top table. Cyril you watch me, Fred you watch Bridget. When we have collected the dishes follow us and just observe what we do. Then we will show you the ropes is that OK?' Cyril answered.

'You are in charge Ma'am.'

We cleared away the dishes, as they watched us like a pair of hawks, then like bloodhounds following on behind us into the kitchen. I had to laugh to myself, I never had seen men doing domestic work before. Hearing the crunch of boots on the floor the kitchen girls looked up, I called out. 'Just call them Fred and Cyril.'

One of the scullery girls attracted by their presence kept gazing at them, she soon got a clip around the ear from the senior cook she shouted.

'GET ON WITH YOUR WORK. STOP GAWPING AT THE POOR LADS.'

We trained as we had been taught, we serving then them serving us. With their own army training, within a few days they had picked up the routine.

On Friday 19th. September 1919. Company Orders stated the arrangements for our departure.

All QMWAAC UNIT Personnel.
Will depart Victoria Barracks.
Friday 26th. September. 09:00hrs.

> Transport has been arranged to take all
> Personnel to Cork station for entrainment
> on the 10:00hrs Dublin train.

The news although expected, came as a shock? Utmost in our thoughts was our pending departure and separation from all the friends we had made. We all walked around with chins on the ground. We continued with teaching the men. We only had one consolation, our last Camp dance to be held at the Sergeants Mess the following day. Although we enjoyed the dance however, the commiserations from the Sergeants did little to raise our spirits. The Sunday meals would be our last day of serving the Officers. They knowing what the situation was we received many thanks and good luck from them.

On the Monday the men took over our duties, the roles reversed, we then became the observers. By Wednesday Cyril and Fred were carrying out their duties satisfactory, although not as efficient or quick as we had been. We had taught them well and were satisfied, as was 'Barraclough' who could only make comments about their clumsy boots?

On the Wednesday night the Officers of the 2nd. Battalion.The Oxfordshire and Buckinghamshire Light Infantry. Laid on our last Ball and presented each of us with a silver brooch of their Regimental Badge. I am sorry to say that later I lost mine at the Curragh racecourse Derby day 1921. I have wonderful memories of their Officers Mess, with a magnificent silver table centre, apparently it was one of the richest Regiments in the British Army? They had two 'Silver Men' just cleaning silver every day. Not forgetting the Thursday nights when their band played in the hall. I can now look back on my Army service days with fondness. They were so happy furthermore, did change my life.

Friday September 26th. Our final day arrived. At the crack of dawn we woke up to the shining sun. Normal routine prevailed then breakfast, for those who cared to take it and finish packing our kit. Bridget and I went across to the Officers mess to say our goodbyes to our protégé's Cyril and Fred. Who thanked us for teaching them the rope's. We handed in our bedding at the stores, returned to our hut looking around for its memories and along with the rest struggling with our kit, went through its door for the last time and made our way towards the road by the deserted Parade Ground, there to join the rest of the Cooks, Waitress's, Scullery Maids, Drivers, Administration Clerks patiently waiting for transportation. Captain Tweedy came along with 'Barraclough' to wish us all goodbye. She went around and spoke to each of us in turn, shook us by the hand and thanked us for our long service and dedication to our duty. Barraclough did the same, as she thanked Bridget and me, she had a smile on her face.

'The Cunningham sisters. You two girls were the best I ever had under my command. Good luck for the future'. She was genuine when she said that to us and we were flattered by her remark. Whilst the goodbyes were being said our transport arrived, several GS Wagons lined up one behind the other. Gradually they began to fill up with their cargo of girls and kit until we were all on board. As the wagon started up and gathered speed, one of the girls started to sing 'Mademoiselle from Marmoutiers.' Some of us joined in half-heartedly, with the 'Par Le Vaux'. As we went past the Guard Room the Officer of the Guard, the Sergeant Guard Commander adorned with Red sash, with twelve men stood at attention. The Officer shouted the Order. 'Present Arms' and with a crash of boots the Guard paid us that final honour - what a splendid gesture. The singing stopped then came the tears. With the camp out of sight someone bravely started to sing again. 'Pack up your troubles in your old kit bag and smile, smile, smile'. It gradually came alive and was sung all the way to the station. It stopped as the wagons drew to a halt. We, a very silent band of girls, got down from the wagons boarded the train and throughout the whole journey, all were very quiet, wondering what the future held for us all?

CHAPTER FIVE
CIVVY STREET

At Dublin, loaded down with our kit, pandemonium and disorder broke out as we fought our way through the barriers, out onto the main road where more GS wagons were parked waiting to take us to the Demob Centre. Once on board the GS Wagons drove off. Arriving at a large building entered through its archway into a spacious quadrangle and formed up in a circle to stop facing a gaunt and dirty building that surrounded the quadrangle, its windows were long and narrow, its main feature the entrance a wide stone staircase leading to two huge black doors. I thought: *Most likely in its past days this building had been a prison?* A Sergeant shouted.

'STAY WHERE YOU ARE AND LISTEN. LEAVE YOUR KIT WHERE IT IS, DON'T FORGET WHICH WAGON YOU LEFT YOUR KIT ON. WHEN YOU GET OFF THE WAGONS FALL IN OVER THERE.' Indicating an open space.

Leaving our kit we got down and moved over to the area he had directed us to. Gone was the discipline of the parade ground as we milled about casually chatting. Through one of the black doors another Sergeant appeared, pausing with hands on hips, surveyed the scene below him and then bawled out.

'SERGEANT BATES! WE ARE ABOUT TO START. CAN YOU MOVE THEM IN PLEASE?' Sergeant Bates responding, Marched in front of us, coming to a halt, turned, holding sheets of paper in his hand, he addressed us.

'Ladies. When I call out your name in alphabetical order. Please make your way up through the front door where Sergeant Lake is now standing.' He began: A's, B's, then the C's Cunningham B., Cunningham S.'

We joined the line of girls entering into a large square vestibule with marbled floor and a marble stairway. The queue snaked through the left door into another very large room, where shafts of sunlight beamed down through the high windows on to a highly polished wooden floor. In-between the windows hung pictures of men in some sort of uniforms staring down with an air of disinterest. Sat behind a long row of tables were soldiers, laid in front of them were piles of papers. Above them, hanging from the ceiling were large notices. A – D. E - H and so on. Upon entering an NCO told us to line up alphabetically. The first table was ours so we joined others in front. Slowly the queue moved forward until it was my turn. The bespectacled Orderly had all these forms ready. I noticed he had Pip Squeak and Wilfred ribbons on his tunic, so he had been out in the front line. However, I did not recognise his regiment. He curtly requested. 'Name and Number?'

'Cunningham. S. W4923.'... Checking his list stopped...'Same as the one before, any relation?'... Busily writing my name on the top of two sheets of paper.

'Yes sisters.'

'That must have been nice for you both at the same camp! Eh?'

'Well we'....turning both sheets of paper around, pushed them towards me, dipping his pen in the inkwell, offered it to me pointing to a dotted line. 'Sign here please. Just there and there'... above it was a lot of writing, I hesitated, he prompted...'It's all right that scribe above just states you have been released from the Army. Just sign!'

With the pen I scratched my signature, first on one sheet then the other so ending my service days in the Army. Placing a sheet of blotting paper over my wet signatures, he took the pen and sheets of paper away, separating them placed one on a small pile on his left, handing over the other said.

'Thank you Miss Cunningham, please take this form to the Orderly on the end table. He will provide you with your pay and if you require it, a rail warrant. Next?'

35

In a split second flash I was out of his mind. Clutching my release papers in my hand I walked away from the table towards the rear of the queues of girls. Turning right spotted the back of Bridget in front, stood in the queue with the sign above. A - D. As I walked towards her the floorboards squeaked with each step I made. Tapping her on her shoulder she half turned and sarcastically said.

'Hello Miss Cunningham'. Far from happy with her remark muttered.

'Don't you dare say another word Bridget?'

In silence we moved forward until it was my turn. In front of me sat a bald headed corporal, bristling beneath his rather bulbous nose was a big walrus moustache, he too displayed medal ribbons. Taking my sheet of paper, scrutinised it questioned.

'Another Cunningham! Any more like you at home?'

'Yes there's....' Interrupting my answer he stated.

'I take it you want a rail warrant Miss?' I curtly replied.

'Yes.'

'Where do I make it out to then?' I abruptly answered.

'Same as my sister. Kildare Station.' He looked at me with distain growled.

'Kildare is it?' Taking a warrant from the pile began to write then signed, blotted it and handed it to me.

'Now then MISS you want paying. Two weeks at seven shillings and ten pence per week equals fifteen shillings and eight pence. In addition to that you will be given two months extra pay. One pound eleven shillings and four pence per month. Altogether three pounds eighteen shillings and four pence'...Opening a drawer under the table he sorted out the required coinage and laid it out on the table in front of me. Three shining sovereigns, four half crown, one florin, two shillings, one sixpence, two three penny bits and four pennies...'There you are Miss Cunningham your final pay and in addition to that you will be allowed to wear your uniform for two months, until that period of time is complete. Now if you would please just sign this form as receipt of your final pay.'...He presented another form to me, dipping his pen into the inkwell handing it to me. Taking hold of it scratched my signature, he blotted the paper took it from me and with a grimace of a smile uttered.

'Take up your money. Thank you very much Miss Cunningham. Now you are a civilian goodbye.' Next Please!

I collected up the coins, left the table clutching the severance pay in one hand and my release papers in the other. The finale and end to four year's service to the Crown. I hurried past the queues of girls out of the building, down the steps and walked back to the GS wagon there to join other girls. For about an hour we stood there, quietly chatting amongst ourselves until the last one in our wagon had completed her signing off procedure. Sometime later Sergeant Bates came out of the building and bawled out.

'MAY I HAVE YOUR ATTENTION PLEASE. RIGHT LADIES SEEING THAT EVERYONE HAS NOW COMPLETED THEIR DEMOBILISATION PROCEDURES. IF YOU WOULD ALL GET BACK INTO THE GS WAGONS YOU WILL DRIVEN BACK TO THE STATION. THERE TO DISEMBARK AND EITHER CATCH YOUR TRAIN OR MAKE YOUR OWN WAY BACK TO YOUR PLACE OF RESIDENCE. GOODBYE AND THANK YOU ALL.' The Army's final word.

We clambered back up into the wagon and waited. Then the face of Sergeant Bates appeared at the tailboard, quickly cast his eyes over the number, smiled at us, with a bang on the wagons side shouted. 'RIGHT OFF YOU LOT GO.'

The driver set the wheels in motion and we were off. Back at the station we disembarked to travel by civilian transport. Having already exchanged addresses back at the hut, we all said our rather tearful farewells before going our different ways. A bunch of us headed for the waiting Cork train and just made it. Clambering aboard banged the door shut behind us. With a shrill whistle the train jerking into motion set off en-route to Cork. It stopped at Nass, Newbridge, finally Kildare, our station. We got off along with Hennessy and the Driscoll sisters. Leaving the others, Martin, the Gibson sisters who would get off at Carlow, with Nellie O'Callaghan plus a few more, all the way back to Cork. It was the end of an era for all of us.

About eight 'o'clock in the evening we finally arrived back home to be welcomed back with open arms. We threw our kit into a corner, discarded like we had been. Whilst mother provided us with food, the first we had eaten all day, we chattering on about the experience of our eventful day before we retired to bed, where for us sleeping together again in mock up sleeping arrangements mother had made. Tomorrow was a new day. So to influence any employers wearing our uniforms began our search for work. We applied to our previous employers and were not surprised upon their refusal; our jobs had been taken over by younger girls. Some employers were considerate but unable to pay us the wages we were asking for even though we thought our charges were low. However, there was little or no work available and was the same, for many men who had become. "Surplus to requirements."

Two weeks later, early in the morning, Mary arrived back from England demobed like us. Our unexpected return became a major problem for Mother. Accommodation had now become very cramped although Bridget was married with Peter away in India, she did not have anywhere to go. Therefore two in a bed became three to share one bed whilst the others slept in another. It was all mother could make available for us. The three of us commiserated with each other as we had expected to remain in the Army for much longer than we had anticipated. However, with so many men returning from the Western Front and other areas of conflict, there was no signing on and the army was certainly no place for women, only if we had volunteered to become Nurse's or Ambulance drivers but that was not to be. Two weeks after Mary had arrived home Mary who had trained as a cook obtained a temporary job for a week, then she was back hunting with us in our search for any type of work. It became fruitless, our future prospects appeared very bleak, we became very despondent. Mary suggested we immigrate to Canada, she wrote a letter asking for forms. When they arrived Bridget declined but we still had to wait for Kathleen still serving in Oswestry England to be demobilisation. So we left them unfilled.

Christmas came and went, January just the same not good. Early February, Kathleen arrived back home finally demobilised, she too was full of woe thoroughly missing her life style in the Army. Whilst playing cards she and Mary commiserated about their life in England and thought of going back, they even roped us into playing a game of Whist. Nevertheless, early one morning our cousin Michael recently demobbed from the Irish Hussars arrived on our doorstep full of greetings.

'Hello. To you four young strapping sisters. Now then, what are you all up to? Still looking for work?

He knowing about our predicament, I was annoyed at his question, so abruptly said.

'Michael. You know damn well we are all looking for work. Anything will do!'

'Sarah listen. You know dat I have a job pulling Flax. Would yus four be interested joining as casual labourers?'

Having laboured in the fields as youngsters, had become accustomed to the hard work required. Looking at the other three's expressions I pondered. Pulling Flax is totally different! But we had nothing to lose. I answered.

'Well we are willing, can you fix it then?'

'I'll speak with der boss and let yus know okay.' He returned later that evening with an answer.

'Yus four can start tomorra, I'll call for you in der morn at six. Be reedy and don't forget, don't wear uniforms, put on yuus oldest set of clothing.'

Daunting, prospects, but at least we had work to go to.

At six the next morning Michael arrived full of the joys of spring, at the top of his voice he called out.

'Now den girls. Ars yus reedy for a hard day's work ahead o'yus?' Bridget retorted.

'Holy Mother of God, not at this blithering hour of the day'...she having become accustomed to having a lie in...'Can't we start later?' Michael spoke.

'Now dere's a ting Bridget, all der tanks o'im gettn, wit me gettn dis foine wonderful job and all yus do's. Is moan about dere toime of day? Tis a foine bright sunny day to be sure. ' Bridget grunted....'Ugh!'

Dressed in our oldest clothes we left a sleeping house and clambered up onto the cart. I got up alongside Michael, who moving over handed the reins to me.

'C'mon Sarah you can take der reins. O'im going to have a smoko while we are on der way.' As I took hold of the reins muttered.

'No smokos now Michael.'

He paying no attention carried on rolling the tobacco into a cigarette. I clicked the horse into action, this appeared to be a prompt for Michael to start talking, Who always had a joke to tell. ...'Did yus evver hear der one about der.'... We took the canal route where I got the horse into a trot, with Michael still cracking jokes the tedious journey soon passed by until we cane to a fork in the road....'Take der roight fork Sarah, not far now.'

Soon we came to the Flax fields....'Along dat track dare Sarah.' Pulling on the horse's reins I guided it into the lane. Half way along we spotted other empty carts, with a large group of labourers all dressed in ragged attire, and with long sacking's covering their arms. Above them wisping into the air clouds of bluey grey smoke rose as they puffed away at cigarettes. Heaving on the reins drew to a halt. We looked at each other, compared to the others, we were well dressed, Michael spoke.

'C'mon yus four down yus get.'

Jumping down stood beside him. In amongst the crowd stood a big burly woman dressed in ragged attire perched on her head was a large flat hat, unfortunately attempted to cover a great mass of red hair tied into a bun at the rear, her red rosy cheeks matched the colour of her hair. Noting something else exclaimed!

'Holy mother of God. Is that a clay pipe sticking out of her mouth?'

Leaving the crowd she approached Michael removing the pipe shouted..

'MOICHAEL. MOICHAEL.' Who interrupted.

'Girls meet Broidie McCann the foreman. Broidie, deese are my cousins.'

He pointing to each of us gave our names. She held out her ham-sized hand in greeting, gripping and engulfing my tiny hand, with a quick strong grasp for each of us, accompanied by a nod. Michael spoke... 'Broidie will show yus der ropes. Doon't be taken in be her, Broidies got a heart of gold. Haven't you Broidie?'

'Enough of dat talk yung Moichael. Yus not be geeven away my secrets now or, I'll be cutting yus down with dat hoss-whip dare.' Cocking her head towards the cart. Michael burst out laughing.

'Now den Broidie no harm meant?'

'Now den yus bucko's. I'll show yus watt to do. Has yus got any arm sackings?'

'No!' We chorused.

'Now den me young bucko's follo me over dere'...She led us over to a pile of sackings picking them up handed a pair to each of us...'Put deese on day will stop yus getting too scratched. Follo ma...Pat follo' ma!'...She hailed another young fellow with a wicker basket slung over his back. He joined us as we followed her into the field right up to the flax...'Dis is wat ye do'...plucking at the flax she nodding her head towards Pat...'Dis young bucko dere will follo yus with the basket, yus jus drop it in. Dat's all dere is te it. Be japers, tis back braaking woirk dat's fer sur!'

With that last remark she left us and began bawling at the other workers to get started. Mary squealed.

'I don't think I'm going to like this.' Impatiently I retorted.

'I don't think anyone of us will. But its work and when the harvest is in and the job done. We will at least have some money to spend. The quicker we get started the sooner we will finish.' Sarah had spoken.

With all the labourers strung out right across the field, we set to work. As we plucked the flax heads, the sackings on our arms did protect us from thorns, but gathering the Flax meant you were bent double, that was back breaking. We worked non-stop except for a break at midday when someone called out the 'Angeles'

We tried to join in but with little enthusiasm, eventually about six o'clock in the evening the booming voice of Bridie could be heard right across the field.

' ALLO DER. YUS CUN ALL STOP. ENUFF FER T'DAY.'

By the end of the day our clothing was torn, snagged, and ragged, we were badly scratched with aching backs. As we dragged ourselves back across the field towards the cart I looked back, only a third had been picked. Michael was leaning against the rear wheel waiting when Bridie sauntered over.

'Yus bucko's had a good day? Yus'll do. Away with yus, sees yus all tomorro' broight un earrly'...Her parting remark made to Michael...'Yus see to that now Moichael.'

Turning around she stomped off. With Michael's help we struggled to get our aching bodies up onto the cart. On the journey home nothing was said, we were far too exhausted and ached all over. Tomorrow, God forbid was another day. I couldn't wait. However it was wage-earning work, although backbreaking it was early to bed, early to rise, which included a full day's work on Saturday, with Sunday a day of rest.

There was no let up during the second week, but on Tuesday evening, relaxing after we had eaten our fill, Mother spoke up.

'Look at the four of you. In the exhausted state you're in'...waving four tickets at us she added...'I don't suppose any of you would be interested in going to a dance on Friday night?'

Her last remark stirred our interest. We all broke out in smiles. When we were demobed the chance of attending mess dances disappeared. I asked.

'Where mother?'

'At one of the Curragh Sergeants Mess. One of my contacts gave me four invitations.' I answered on our behalf.

'Mother. Come hell or high water. We are going to the dance. Thank whomever it is you know and tell him. The Cunningham sisters will be there.'

For the next three days, we worked like Trojans. During that week one field was finished and we all moved into the next field. On Friday evening when Bridie called time. The four of us hitched up our skirts and ran from the field ahead of Michael. Climbing up onto the cart began shouting for him to. 'MOVE HIS LEGS FASTER.'

I taking hold of the reins wheeled the horse around ready for the off. He knowing our urgency delayed our get away by talking to Bridie before leisurely climbing up onto the cart. I clucked the horse into movement before he had sat down. Within a short distance along the cart road, I had the horse stretched at a gallop, Michael, standing up beside me whooping his head off all the way home. Outside reined the horse to a halt, jumped down. Not even giving Michael the time of day, rushed indoors to get washed.

It all became very boisterous, whilst mother prepared something for us to eat, father grumbled about all the fuss that was going on. Changing into our newly pressed uniforms, much to the amusement of all the younger members of the family. Mother lined us up, inspected and handed each of us the invitation and passes into the camp. Talk about Cinderella's. We were ready for an army dance. Nevertheless mother had not finished, she went outside fetched the horse and trap around to the front and took us all the way to the Curragh camp.

Mother was determined to do it right for us. She had her own pass to get in. With that formality over, we carried on passing our old barracks that left Bridget and I rather silent with nostalgia. Continued along North Road passing the clock tower and along down to the Sergeants Mess at the far end of the camp, where she pulled up. Uttering a word of good wishes, turned the trap around and headed back home leaving us there to make our entrance. Bridget said.

'As I'm the only married one amongst us. I think mother wants to get the rest of you three married off.' We laughed at her suggestion, Mary quipped.

'Well I won't be the first one that's for sure.' Kathleen added.

'It's got to be you Sarah you're the eldest. I've got years to catch up with you.'

Laughing and clutching our invitations, we entered the Sergeants Mess into a little hallway, where the cloakroom and toilets were. Stood at the entrance to the mess was a tall smartly dressed Sergeant, above his stripes was a brass badge of a gun. A white lanyard around his right shoulder was attached to a whistle clipped to his tunic breast pocket. He wore Pip, Squeak and Wilfred medal ribbons, horse breeches, with puttees wound from below the knees down to his glistening boots, where straps attached spurs. He politely asked.

'Evening Privates. What can I do for you?'

I took off my hat and politely asked. 'Sergeant is there a dance being held here this evening?' ...'Yes but it's by invitation only.' I presented my invitation.

'We all have invites to the dance, this is mine, and my sisters have theirs.' He took mine and looked at it, now that I was close up to him. I noticed a RHA badge on one shoulder epaulet on his other epaulet was another brass badge, with XXX or something like that.

'Yes that's okay. Let me have the others please'... These were handed to him, looking at them...'Okay, are there just the four of you privates?

In the background, the sound of a band began tuning up, the dance was about to start I responded.

'Yes just the four of us.' He enquired.

'Have you been here before then?' I answered.

'Yes two of us have.'

'In that case, you can show the other two privates where to go. Can't you?'

I was on already on my way towards the door, eager to get into the dance.

'Yes Sergeant. If that's all right.'

'Whoa back privates. What's our hurry? Please leave your hats in the Cloakroom behind you.' jovially adding...'I don't think anyone will run away with them Eh?'

Entering the cloakroom, we placed our hats on a table against the wall, above were several peaked hats hung on hooks. Out of curiosity I took one down to look at the cap badge. It was a gun with a wheel that spun around, above it was the Kings Crown and below was a scroll with some latin letters scrawled on it. I was none the wiser, Bridget asked.

'Who are they?'

'I don't know. But we will find out. C'mon let's get to the dance.' We retreated back outside where the Sergeant uttered.

'Thank you privates, all in order now.'

However we were already through the door and inside, where the band were still playing. Bridget said to me.

'It hasn't changed very much except for the regiment, who do you think they are?'

'I don't know, certainly not infantry. Gunners of some sort?'

40

The band stopped playing, paused, then the conductor waved his baton and the band started to play "Rag Time Blues". I looked at Bridget, she grinned back at me eagerly I said.

'Just like old times Eh. Bridget?' she replied.

'What a lovely sound.'

'I wonder do they dance the same steps then?'

A couple took to the floor, began to dance then were joined by a few more. I stood there watching noting the steps. They were the same. I noticed one of the Sergeants and his partner danced quite well, holding his poise they certainly knew the steps. A few more dances were played before the band struck up and began to play a Modern Waltz. The Sergeant I had spied broke away from his cronies at the bar, walked across the dance floor towards us.

'Excuse me privates. My name is Sergeant Harry Hextall. Can any of you dance?' I was only too eager to get onto the dance floor. I piped up.

'We all can Sergeant.'

'Aah.' Turning to me asked... 'Would you like to dance with me please?'

'Yes thank you, I would be delighted to.'

He was much taller than me, but a smashing dancer, guiding me with ease until the music ended and the band began playing. "Five foot two eyes so blue." Instant memories of Teddy Carr and I dancing the first Fox Trot flashed before me. I began to sing the words as I followed him step by step. After a couple of circuits around the floor, he complemented me on my dancing before asking.

'Forgive me for enquiring. But what are you four doing in uniform? There are no service women on the camp, you all new here?' That tickled me, laughing I said.

'No my three sisters and I live here in Kildare. We are not new to the camp but wished we were. We were demobbed last year.' The music stopped but he still kept hold of me, he wasn't going to let go.

'Oh I see. Where were you stationed then?'

The music began, another fox trot, we continued, he prompting...'I was asking about your last Camp.' I answered.

'Two of us were at Victoria Barracks in Cork. My other two sisters were in England.' .

'Aah, that explains the uniform. You caused quite a stir amongst some of the Sergeants.' I acted surprised.

'Why whatever for?' He replied

'Well! They raised questions about the new intake.' I laughed.

'Oh well. They were wrong then.'

'Is this your first dance here then?'

'No not really. It's the first since we were demobbed. Bridget and I, were originally in this camp serving at Stewarts Barracks. We did receive invitations to the dances the Corporals and Sergeants held. So we know the camp very well.'

'Now that's interesting. By the way what is your name? '

'Sarah! Sarah Cunningham.'

'Well Sarah Cunningham'....politely asking...'May I call you Sarah?'

'Yes, I would like that.'

'Let's see if we can fix you all up with invitations, to our next dance. Would you like that?'

'Yes please we would all appreciate any invitation.'

The music stopped, he thanked me and escorted me back, nodded to the other three, eagerly waiting for my run down. While he returned to the bar and his pals, obviously to spill the beans about the uniformed women. I had broken the ice, with the possibility of more invitations. However the band played a one-step and we were all asked to dance. My partner for the next three dances was a rather short Sergeant. Not a dancer, but we made it round the floor. I

41

danced with two other sergeants whilst Sgt. Hextall danced with Kathleen, Bridget, and then Mary in turn, before he asked me to dance again.

'Sarah, how long were you in the Army for?'

'We all volunteered in nineteen fifteen. Only Bridget and I were accepted, my other two sisters were too young, but two years later they went to England and were accepted.

'Oh that's interesting, I take it you're the eldest?'

'Yes.' Changing the subject he said.

'I know about dancing, as before the war back in Manchester I ran a dancing club, and I can tell you're a very good dancer, much better than your sisters. Mind you Sarah, I don't want to get in their bad books, your all good. The youngest one, what's her name?' 'Kathleen.' I answered...'Yes, she is quite good.' I was flattered by his kind remarks. We danced on until the band stopped for the interval. He offered us some refreshments, which we accepted. Escorting us to a table. bought us tea and cakes, before he returned to the bar.

We chatted about our good fortune. For me, I was back in my element as I idly watched Sgt. Hextall's group stood at the bar. Amongst them I noticed a much younger looking Sergeant, with a big shock of grey hair, who appeared to be the centre of some discussion. All laughing and jibbing with him he appeared to be enjoying the jibbing.

The Band struck up to start the second session. We remained seated waiting impatiently for the forthcoming invitations. We did not have long to wait. Out of the group at the bar, the young Sergeant strode straight towards us. Standing in front of me, a huge grin spread across his face, and in a rather funny accent he asked.

'Scuse me miss yor a nice dancer, I'm sorry, I can't dance, but would you take me round the dance floor?'

Kathleen turning away began to chuckle. I looked up into his lovely blue eyes, I couldn't refuse.

'Yes with pleasure.' I stood up ventured onto the floor. He took hold of me the wrong way, the women's way. I prompted.

'No. This way. You are supposed to be taking me around the floor.'

In the proper manner I took hold of his right hand, placed it on the small of my back, and took hold of his left hand. He blurted out.

'Cor I gotcher.'

Good job he wasn't that tall, being medium height and stockily built. Certainly not lithe enough to be a dancer. We began shuffling about, he kept looking at his boots for inspiration, repeatedly he trod on my foot... 'Scuse me miss.' Looking down at his boots again as if they were the culprits. As I managed to steer him around the floor the best I could, somehow he grasped the basic steps. Every time he looked at me, a big grin would crease his face. I thought: *Thank God it's a Waltz.* The music stopped and he escorted me back to my seat.

'Blimey. Thanks Miss. Didn't do too bad did I?'

'That's alright. Thank you, until the next time?'

Then I realised I had given him an open invitation, he kept coming back for more. Being supportive I did not refuse. Stumbling around as we danced past his fellow Sergeants, they cheering him on.

'Come on Fanny! You know more about football than dancing.' I thought: *Probably he did know more about football, he certainly could not dance.*

Sgt. Hextall had to wait for an. 'Excuse Me' to relieve my agony, clearing his throat apologised.

'I'm sorry Sarah, it was my fault Fanny asked you for those dances.' We joked about his dancing ability, so one of the sergeants dared him to ask you for a dance. Fanny said you wouldn't. I said you would. Just go over and ask the young lady for a dance, tell her you couldn't dance. I bet you, she will take you around. You did. And he had to buy us all a drink. But I sincerely apologise and thank you at the same time.'

'Oh don't worry about it, he's got two left feet maybe someday he will learn.'

Relieved to understand it was only a dare. No more dances with Fanny laughed it off. All with dancing partners, I don't think any of us missed a dance until the last waltz. When with a big wide grin creasing his face. 'Fanny' approached.

'Please Miss. Would you dance the last dance with me.'

I accepted, we stumbled around, the music stopped and we clapped.

'Thank you for the dances Miss. Er. Scuse me Miss. It would be a great pleasure if I could escort you to your home.'

I was not surprised at his invitation, as it was customary to be escorted home from any dances. I thought: *Maybe-another dare*. replied.

'Yes. That would be alright. What should I call you Fanny or?'

'Cor Blimey Miss. Where's me manners? I'm Sergeant Jack Plant. Royal Field Artillery. Just call me Jack. I come from London. I know your name is Sarah and live in Kildare, don't you?' Taken aback.

'That's right.' Obviously he found out from Sgt. Hextall. All of us had escorts from the same group, were taken home in traps, and so began our long friendship.

17/23ᴿᴰ. ROYAL FIELD ARTILLERY R.A.

CURRAGH PLAINS 1919

CHAPTER SIX
COURTSHIP

Early next morning we were back in the flax field. The back breaking work was not pleasant. Nevertheless, we became expert flax pickers with fewer scratches, less aches and pains, but extremely pleased when all the flax had been collected. Bridie cheerful as ever bade us.

'Good Bye, yus furr. C'mon baack nex' yurrr. Dere's a job waating for yus mi bucko's.'

It had been hard work for the pay we received. That was a welcome blessing to tide us over until we found our next job, which each of us picked up just one up here and there, but nothing permanent. Like everyone else, many hours were spent searching for a job at the Labour Exchange, where we being unemployed, received a pitiful amount of money. Of which we gave some to Mother for our bed and board, when not searching we did help Mother with the household chores. With us four grown up young women cooped up at home. Gradually with our miserable existence, our situation became increasingly difficult to come to terms with, whereas we all being used to a life in the Army. If the War Office ever changed their minds we all would be the first to volunteer. Our only association with Army life and salvation was social at the weekly dances at the R.F.A. Sergeants Mess or, to others that we had been invited too. Obviously from the very first invite the word went around the camp of four young ex-Army women that were available for the dances.

From that very first meeting with Fanny. Our relationship had developed into one of platonic friendship. I got to know Sgt. Jack Plant as a rather reserved decent young man, good mannered with a kind heart, always the first to pay for anything yet. he could not dance a step and possibly never would. Furthermore dancing was of no interest to him, his main interest was sports. When I was dancing with someone else he never showed any signs of jealousy, his only dance with me was the last waltz. He would make a beeline for me take my hand, and as we stumbled around the floor he politely asked to escort me home. On other occasions he would arrange for their Battery trap to take us there and back, and knowing Bridget was married, he even insisted she should accompany us to the dances, which she really appreciated as she like me was a good dancer, so much so, the pair of us spent all our off duty time dancing.

At some of the dances they held a Whist Drive before the dance began. Whereas Bridget and I did not care to play cards, Mary and Kathleen enjoyed playing and had become good card players whilst serving in England, they insisted we make up a foursome. Anyway one night after playing a few hands, I not bothering and could not care less ,was urged by Kathleen my partner to check my score card. Much to my delight found I had won first prize. A biscuit barrel the very first item I had ever won, although flushed with that success was only too pleased when the dance began. After the dance had finished, we set off back home with me clutching my prize. When we arrived home Mother was still up and Mary being the best card player amongst us was not happy. She started waving this biscuit barrel in front of Mother, ranting on about my card playing.

'The cheek of that one Mother, un-interested in whist, only in dancing and, she wins the first prize. There's no justice in the world to be sure.'

I took no notice, just a fit of jealousy on her part at me winning, then Kathleen blurted out.

'Another thing Mother, Sarah's got a young Sergeant in love with her.'

Only then did I take notice. Up went my hackles. I glared straight at Kathleen with daggers in my eyes, immediately thought: *The damn cheek of her she's gone one step too far this time.* In those days for a young lady to walk around with a young man was not an easy thing to do. With a twinkle in her eye Mother enquired.

'Is that right Sarah?' Flustered at mothers question had to provide an answer.

'Yes it appears so. Sergeant Jack Plant is a decent fellow with good-natured ways and manners. His intentions are honourable. I know we all can trust ourselves with him when he's in our company.... 'Umm!' She just nodded her head. It appeared that my friendship with Jack had been accepted. That was all that was mentioned about the matter. Now that Mother was aware about my situation, inwardly I felt better. I was allowed to walk out with a young man, but I still had a score to settle with that young madam Kathleen, that I would deal with later.

When we first met. Jack was twenty-one and I was twenty-three. Jack lived for the Army, always smartly turned out charming and good mannered, when Mother was introduced to him, Mother noticed and appreciated his appearance and manners therefore approved of our friendship. For me it was a time of light heartedness, I would take the trap and ride to the camp to meet him. We would walk around the perimeter fence talking about each other's backgrounds and families. What I noticed that he was more aware of my background and circumstances than I of his. He too was from a large family of ten brothers and sisters of varying ages, living in a house in a place called Putney in London. His elder brothers, Harris and Matt, were identical twins. At the outbreak of the War his elder brother Alf had joined the Royal Navy Air Service, the Navy's equivalent of the Royal Flying Corps. (that part of his family I declined to tell mother about). Anyway, apart with the exception of Len his younger brother, all his brothers had joined the army and served in different regiments. Bill was in the Army Service Corps, his twin brothers joined the Duke of Cornwall Light Infantry and later on transferred to the Machine Gun Corp. Jack who was only sixteen and a half, lied about his age and enlisted into the Army, just like thousands of other young men who were far too young but did volunteer. His sisters had been named after flowers: Daisy, Violet, Rose, and May, and with a surname of Plant it tickled my sense of humour, laughing I said.

'That's very curious?'

'Sarah, nothing to do with me, it's all down to Ma and Pop's choice.'

However he avoided any conversation about his experiences on the Western Front. Nevertheless later at the dances, as we had been accepted into the Sergeant's company, I did find out from his pals, he having gained promotion on the field of battle, was the youngest Sergeant in the mess. The battery had come under severe German artillery gunfire, gradually one by one the guns were hit and put out of action. Officers and men were either killed or wounded. Jack took over got the remaining guns to return fire until the barrage was over. For his action he was recommended for a medal, but refused instead took promotion with an increase in pay, far better than a medal. During the battle of the Somme he was gassed, was sent back to Blighty before being sent back again. The only one of very few incidents he mentioned in detail was. He had to escort a young shell shocked Bombardier back to a holding station in Arras. They were travelling in a G.S. wagon along white taped roads potted with shell holes filled with mud and water. As he recalled it was a treacherous ride whilst controlling the horses with a delirious Gunner ready to jump off. Jack had difficulty stopping and was pleased when they eventually got there in one piece. After handing over his charge he decided to go for a drink, asked the orderly where he could get one? He directed him to a Church Army Centre in Arras. Guided by the noise of singing, it wasn't too hard to find. Arriving there tethered, fed his horse before entering into a gloomy room thick with the smell of tobacco smoke and the earthy smell of sweaty soldiers all singing their heads off. Forcing his way up to the makeshift bar he shouted out for a pint of ale, just about to grasp the tankard when a hard slap on his back startled him, as a gruff voice yelled.

'I'll pay for that young Jack.'

Turning around to find another Gunner, an old pal who he had not seen since they had finished their training. Many pints were consumed before he headed back to his unit. Another incident he did mention, was about the time he was in hospital suffering badly from trench fever.

Somehow Matt his elder brother found out where he was, paid him a visit. He had a remedy with him. A bottle of rum that he poured into Jack to sweat it out, he was more than drunk. Nevertheless, the rough treatment probably saved his life. His fever subsided, after which he wrote a letter to his parents telling them about Matt and his medicine cure. Later he was passed A1 fit for duty. Two months later back at his Unit, he was notified that Matt had been killed in action, blown up on the twenty-seventh of May 1918, the very next day after his visit to Jack. However he did take out of his tunic pocket his pay book from which he produced a bit of a photograph, showing it to me he said.

'Look Sarah this is a photo of me and Percy taken on Armistice day in Arras we were celebrating surviving the war. We had been drinking wine and brandy. We did have something to celebrate.

During the summer of 1919 the troubles in Ireland were on the increase. In Dublin the Sinn Fein MPs. tried to set up an illegal Irish Parliament and barricaded themselves inside the Mansion House. The Irish Police and British soldiers surrounded the Mansion House and eventually brought the action under control. That disturbance was something we had first hand experience of when we were stationed at Victoria Barracks, with the unrest around Cork, The troops of the Ox and Bucks were called out many times. Nevertheless the incident at the Mansion House brought about a proposal for two separate Irish Parliaments to govern the provinces of Ulster and Southern Ireland, one in Belfast and one in Dublin. We thought: *That this latest move might solve the problem, which appeared not to be going away.*

Just before Christmas, more trouble flared up in Dublin. One afternoon my father came home to inform mother that there had been an unsuccessful attempt to kill Lord French the Lord-Lieutenant of Ireland? He had previously been the first Commander of the British Expeditionary Force in 1914. I became interested in their conversation. As they discussed the seriousness of this latest incident, they reflecting on the reason why they had moved from Hackettstown where I was born. They moved to Ballybrittas when I was only six months old. By trade my father was a shoemaker and also quite a good musician and played in a band whilst my mother was a smallholder. Those times were very hard and mending shoes was not very lucrative. When he was playing in the band room at Ballybrittas he found out about a Postman's job that was available. Father took the opportunity with both hands got the job and moved to Ballybrittas, a village that spanned the road to the town of Monastereven a few miles away.

It was small, consisting of a group of cottages, three shops, a school the Police Barracks, a small Catholic Church and the Band-room. The prospects of this new job provided a steady income including a two bedroom rented cottage, with a Parlour, scullery and the usual peat fire. Soon after we had moved it was found out my father was a skilled Cobbler and he was offered that job as well. So he became the Village Postmaster and Cobbler which adding money to his postman's income of twelve shillings per week (60n.p.). Together with the income from mother's smallholding, selling Pigs, Chicken's, and having horses stabled in a haggard (Paddock) at the rear of the cottage.

Mother was a good horsewoman and with the help of a horse breaker she would break in any new horse's she had bought. When the horses were fit for sale mother would take them to Monastereven auction them off and buy others. Apart from the rent the cost for necessities in those days was. Halfpenny for a three-quart can of milk, one penny for a loaf of bread, bacon was three pence per pound, whilst other provisions were ready at hand from mother's own smallholding providing sufficient income for the family needs plus savings. Year-by-year the family grew, every year a baby was born, three girls and two boys (both died) and with the limited accommodation and no work in the village, it was becoming increasingly difficult for my parents to maintain their lifestyle. Work had to be sought farther afield. I do remember so well on one occasion when my Uncle Andy arrived home on leave, he was introduced to yet another baby he retorted. 'Mary every-time I come to visit you have another baby.'

Years later mother told me she was very strong, which after her producing such a big family, apparently becoming pregnant did not affect her, she always looked so well. That I can well believe, whereas much later when I was expecting my babies, I always looked half-dead.

We lived in Ballybrittas for about seven years until 1903 when Mother was lucky and found a shop with accommodation in Monastereven, Father gave up his job, as the Postman and Cobbler. I was seven years old and thought: *My heart would break. Missing the village, with those enjoyable Christmas times, when Sir Trench a very charitable man, would provide each and every family with a 'Piece of Beef' for their Christmas dinner table, after we left, it did not matter what parties, Christmas trees or whatever festivities we had, there was none so good as I had experienced there.*

Autumn saw the start of the football season and Jack was picked to play for the Curragh Brigade team. Knowing nothing about football, I went to watch Jack play in the pouring rain, undaunted by the weather they still played. Listening to others spectator's shouts of encouragement, *"Come on Fanny."* Jack responded by running rings around other players, demonstrating his ability as a football player, far better than a ballroom dancer. The Brigade team won and after the game Jack approached me, soaking wet covered from head to foot in mud, he stood in front on me, his hands on his hips with a huge grin asked.

'So what do you think Sarah?' What could I say? But I did ask.

'Who's Fanny?'

'Cor Blimey Sarah. It's my nickname after the Spurs footballer Fanny Walden. I'm not as good as him.' I was none the wiser with his answer.

'Oh I don't know him or, that Spurs thing-a- me what's it'.

Nevertheless, still continued to go to the other football games he played in, what amazed me was to find there was intense rivalry between whatever teams they played against, but afterwards, winners and losers alike drinking in the mess became the best of pals. Both Mary and Kathleen were openly walking out with two of Jacks pals, both Sergeants in the same Battery also teammates in the Brigade football team. Mary with Bert Batten and Kathleen with Frank Lewis.

Just before Christmas 1919. Jack informed me he had received a letter from his mother, requesting his presence at home for Christmas for a family reunion. All his brothers would be home on leave. Jack himself had missed five Christmas's away from home, decided to be there. I thought: *His decision was right and proper, that he should go.* However, after he had left Bridget and I continued to receive invitations to attend various mess "Do's" that we declined, instead chose to be at home amongst our own family. It was during Jack's absence that I realised how much I missed him. Having known him for barely five months, he had become a regular visitor.

The New Year of 1920 did not bring any hope of work for us four, still trying to find something to do. The pattern of our working day had not changed since we had been demobbed, mainly helping Mother out with the workload by which time, Mother had only kept two horses. One a very docile Welsh pony called 'Fan' the other one a Connemara pony called 'Paddy.' He was a real handful and would only allow mother into his stall to tend him, Without warning he would take a bite at anyone who ventured near him furthermore, it was our job to feed him, whoever's turn it was we just threw it over the gate then run for our life. Mother would goad at us.

'Get away with yus, yus a bunch of cowards. Go in with him feed him properly he's harmless.' But there was no way we would venture close to Paddy, let alone go into his stall. On one occasion when Jack was there, it was Kathleen's turn, she suggested.

'Jack there's a good fella would you feed Paddy for me?'

47

'No problem. Where's the feed?' Say's he.

'Next to the paddock in the bin.' She replied.

We, understanding what she was up too, kept quiet as Jack whistling went out, prepared the feed, approaching the paddock opened the gate entered. We watching through the window expected to see him make a very rapid retreat. Instead were all surprised to watch him approach Paddy who without the slightest retaliation, as if they were long lost pals Jack stroked him as he fed Paddy, still whistling to himself he then fed Fan, came out across to the water trough, filled the bucket returned and watered them. Having finished his chores walked back into the house with a big grin across his face quipped. 'All done.'

We were gob smacked, our little practical joke had misfired. Yet unbeknown to us, Mother had been watching the entire proceedings, she came back into the room, looking squarely at us with a knowing nod said.

'Sarah! I'm surprised at you! A quite word won't go amiss follow me.'

Like a naughty schoolgirl about to get a right ticking off, I followed her out. Once out of earshot of the others she said.

'Now listen to me my young girl. I've just seen your young man do something with Paddy that nobody else has ever done before, he must know his way around horses. If I were you I would look no further afield, but towards marriage.'

I too was again gob-smacked and could say nothing. Mother with her understanding of horses and men was indicating to me the direction I should take with her full approval. It was something I had to think about. However it was up to Jack to make the move.

In 1920 Ireland was fast becoming a hostile place. The troubles were on the increase. Day by day neither the political or employment situation was getting any better. Street fighting had broken out in Londonderry and troops from Belfast were sent to reinforce the existing police forces. The Mayor of Cork was assassinated and a magistrate was murdered in Dublin, where roadblocks were erected on the outskirts. To mark the anniversary of the 1916 uprising, many Police stations and civil buildings all over Ireland were torched over the Easter holidays. The diminishing numbers of the Royal Irish Constabulary caused the recruitment of eight hundred ex-army English soldiers who arrived in Ireland (Known as the Black and Tans). Soon after, in protest to the British treatment of Sinn Feign prisoners, workers went on strike resulting in the releases of many prisoners from jail. I thought: *The strike was just plain silly.* As for us, it was still a case of queuing at the Labour Exchange.

At the end of the football season, the Brigade football team won their last game on their way to the final. Their opposing team in the final was against the Lancers, both competing for the Curragh Championship Cup. Celebrating their last win with a Mess Dance, during the evening Jack took me to one side and said.

'Sarah I have some bad news, the RSM had words with me today. He ordered me and the rest of the team to cut out our dancing sprees and spend more time training for the final. According to him it's far more important than dancing and you know what the RSM is like?'

This was a blow to me, having only come to terms with our relationship the previous week. I thought: *Training! I hardly ever see him apart from the dances that I enjoyed so much.* I was very despondent and answered the best I could.

'Well it's not much I can do about it. You're the footballer you'll have to train I suppose.'

I resigned myself to what I had already committed to do, that was not go to dances unless Jack was my escort. Whilst my two sisters going out with Bert and Frank also confined to training, did not share my problem, they still continued to go to the dances. So we saw less of each other that had Mother questioned.

'Why are you staying at home?'

After I had explained the reason she understood and agreed on my decision. On the day of the final, we all went along to shout for our men and the team. As the game kicked off it appeared that it was going to be a hard fought match. Backwards and forwards went the play until, just before halftime, the Lancers scored the first goal. The second half began with more vigorous action from the Brigade team. Bert scored a goal, the Lancers strongly retaliated but could not score. Within the last ten minutes of the game, Jack did some fancy footwork and crossed over the ball, with a mighty leap Bert headed it to score another goal. I jumped up and down with shrieks of approval. With the score in their favour, the Brigade team held their lead to win the Cup and then the celebrations took over.

That night it was my first time back to my very own favourite past time dancing. However unbeknown to us, further celebrations were yet to be announced. Bert Batten was leaving the army to return back to England to play as a professional footballer for Bristol City. During the interval he proposed to Mary, she accepted. With my parent's approval she decided to move across to England, a place she had become to like when serving in the QMWAAC. So it was a double celebrations however, with the football season finished, the athletics season began. Jack had been picked to run for the Brigade Athletic team, in the forthcoming Curragh Camp Athletics Meeting. Therefore he began training again furthermore curtailing our meetings, but I was not aware of how good an athlete Jack was, as he had been entered to run not in one but four individual races including, participation in two relay team races. The event was to be held on a Saturday, followed by a dance in the evening. Of course Jack invited all of us.

'Yes.' Was our spontaneous reply. Nevertheless, on the Wednesday before the meeting, when I met him, he had his head held in a forward position almost on his chest, so asked.

'Whatever is the matter?'

'Boils Sarah'...He showed me the back of his neck that was covered in boils, they looked extremely angry and the rubbing of his tunic collar did not help to ease his discomfort...'I've already reported sick Sarah and all they have given me is ointment. I can't even touch them and I can't compete. I'll report to the RSM tomorrow and request to be excused running.'

I met him on the Friday evening, and he was still in discomfort he said.

'Sarah! I did see the RSM. Do you know what he said?'

'No But I can guess.'

'Plant no excuses. You'll run, with or without boils.'

On the Saturday Jack did compete, his exposed neck above his singlet still extremely red, looking like a bad case of sunburn. That did not stop him, he won all his individual race's, including winning with the team races, in total six events. With his neck swathed in bandages, he escorted me to the dance that evening. His other beaten competitors speaking in good fun passing comments. 'The Medics should have tied up his legs, not his neck.'

His boils did subside. Yet later at another sports meeting, the Royal Horse Artillery's Nery's Open Sports Day and Gymkhana was held at Newbridge. With the athletics meeting in the morning followed by a Gymkhana in the afternoon. What with his football and athletic prowess. Gymkhana was a new name to me I asked Jack.

'What is a Gymkhana? Are you competing in that as well?' To which he laughed.

'Oh no. It's horse jumping events. They make a course out of gates and fences, that the horse and rider jump over without knocking anything down. If they do they lose points. You will see, it's quite exciting. My best pal Sergeant. Percy Larrett is competing in the horse jumping events. He's a Rough Rider and a better horseman than me. I responded.

'Oh I see'...quickly thinking asked.... 'Jack I know by the cap badge that you wear, you're both Gunners but, what is the difference between the Royal Horse Artillery and Royal Field Artillery?'

'Nothing Sarah. The Horse Artillery are referred to as the Cavalry Division of the Royal Artillery, we are referred to as Divisional. There's a long history behind the Royal Artillery going back centuries, and it would take me a month of Sundays to explain it all. But in our brigade which is the thirtieth. There are four Batteries, my Battery the seventeenth. And the others are the ninth, sixteenth Forty-seventh H Batteries. Each Battery has six guns and a limber, each pulled by, six horses and a team of six men. Not all batteries have the same size gun; other Batteries might have different calibre guns, twelve, fourteen, or eighteen pounders or maybe howitzers. But all ours are eighteen pounders. Our job is to support the Cavalry and the Infantry with firepower. Such as Bridget's husband Peter's regiments. So if need be, we provide the firepower down to the last gun. We rely on our horse's, magnificent animals that they are, you've seen them what do you say? Eh? '

'Yes I quite agree, you have some fine horses under your charge. Mother has always made a comment about how well the Army looks after their horses. But you can't say that about Paddy!' We both laughed recalling his meeting with Paddy.

The week prior to the Gymkhana, torrential rain fell until eventually it ceased on the Friday. We thought it might have to be called off. However on Saturday the weather changed and throughout the day the sun shone. Jack, competing in the same events as before, picked us up and took us in the trap. When we arrived the bands were already playing. Jack left us to change into running strip, whilst we joined the crowds milling about the many tents and marquees. A fanfare of trumpets opened the event, so we made our way to the edge of the racing circuit. Jack had told me there would be stiff competition from other regiments and would not be as easy as before. However, he running like the wind, won his first race, his second, third and fourth, leaving his final races in the relays to be run later in the morning, which they won to beat the RHA. His prizes, twenty pounds including cups and medals for each race won.

During the interval. A buffet lunch was being served within a large marquee that was full of senior ranks, wives or sweethearts. As it was warm out in the sunlight, we chose to picnic outside. After lunch in the afternoon, the Gymkhana was to begin. I was intrigued as to what these events were? Jack's pal Percy, proved to be a fine horseman, winning all his Gymkhana events. We returned home to change for the evening dance and Percy was Bridget's escort. It turned out to be a double celebration with both their victories. During the interval Jack asked me.

'Sarah can I buy you a Fox Fur with my prize winnings?'

'NO' was my emphatic response. Taken aback Jack asked.

'Why forever not?' My curt response was.

'In these small towns. If I took a present from a young man. It would not be bought for nothing. I have a good reputation and I intend to keep it.'

'Oh. Don't be so daft Sarah'.

He swung about and returned back to the bar to re-join Percy. The remainder of the evening was carried out with a frosty tinge to it, however they politely escorted Bridget and I home and nothing was said. I certainly was not very happy about their attitudes. They left us at the door, that was the last we saw of them throughout the following week, but we weren't short of friends.

The following Wednesday, Kathleen met four Corporals from the Lancers who invited us all to their mess dance on the Friday night. On our behalf she accepted their invitation. We knew all the Corporals to be good dancers who revelled at dancing. Unlike the Sergeant most were married (and their wives wouldn't let them dance with anyone else, unless it was with themselves) or, too old and would rather do the 'Bar Dance'. Which most of them did?

Friday evening, we were all having a great time dancing away to our hearts content. It was after the interval at about 9: 30 that we noticed the arrival of Jack and Percy, both appeared to be the worse for drink, they took their place at the bar. I was already dancing with one of the

Corporals, as I danced past them Jack waved at me. I turned my head away, I was not going to show him that I was pleased to see him. When the music stopped the four of us joined up again, it was Kathleen who enquired.

'Sarah your Jack's here. What are you going to do?' I retorted.

'Nothing, I'm having a great time dancing. I shall wait and see what he intends to do.'

We were invited to three more dances before the pair of them joined us, sheepishly they chorused.

'Hello. You girls having a good time?' Sarcastically I replied.

'We are having a smashing time. Where have you two been all week?' Jack spluttered out.

'Were both really sorry. We've been out. looking for you girls, at some other Sergeants messes.'…adding…'Have you enjoyed yourselves?' I gave no reply…however Jack continued…'Sarah I'm sorry, but you did not want to accept my present.'….'Well I did explain my reasons but you took it the wrong way.'… 'Oh! Okay will you dance with me please?'…'Well I suppose so.'

We stumbled around the floor, during which time he explained. Both of them had decided to spend Jack's winnings. After that dance Percy danced with me, a far better dancer than Jack and he too told me of their weeks drinking and both of them had stated. "Never again would they go on the drink?" At the end of the dance they politely asked, if they could escort Bridget and I home again? With a sigh of relief I replied.

'Corporal Powell and his pals are our escorts for the evening.'

The pair of them looked at each other. Then walked across to where the Corporals were standing. A few quiet words were exchanged. Jack and Percy escorted us home! I thought: *What a cheek, first they blamed me for their fat heads, which I wasn't happy about, then took over as escorts!* But deep down, I was very pleased, to be back on level terms with my Jack.

By this time, Bert had been informed of his departure date and their wedding arrangements were to take place in Bristol Cathedral. Of course all were invited, but for obvious reasons mainly money, none could attend so, mother arranged a farewell party in their honour. Furthermore, Bert was not the only one? It was only a matter of months before Frank Lewis was due for demobilisation. During the party he proposed to Kathleen. She accepted and with Mother and Father's blessing, they set the wedding day for 8th. February. So, the party turned out to be a double celebration, leaving me the eldest still on the shelf. Within days, Bert and Mary left for England in plenty of time for the beginning of Bert's football career.

It was during August when Jack applied for fourteen days leave to return home to Putney by the river Thames, which I understood to be a lovely part of London. When he left he made a rather curious comment.

'Sarah. We have been seeing each other regularly for nearly a year. When I get home I'm going to tell Ma and Pop's all about you.' Surprised I asked.

'Haven't you said anything to them before in your letters?'

'Er. No it wasn't the right time.' That left me mystified.

After he had left I still kept my word about not going to the dances without him, although Bridget and Kathleen urged me to go. Bridget encouraging me saying.

'Sarah I'm sure Jack won't mind, after all as you well know while my Peter has been away, I have been to all the dances.' That had me thinking before I replied.

'I know but your situation is different. Anyway it's only for a couple of dances over the weekends.'

That did not resolve the point she was making and they attended the dances. Once alone, I had plenty of time to reflect over the previous months I had known Jack, found that I was missing him so much, discovered I was very much in love with my gallant young Artillery Sergeant. I was not happy until he returned. Understandably, this time without any presents.

We resumed our evening meetings. I taking the trap up to the camp to tether the horse and trap close to the Artillery Stables where we used to meet. On one occasion he said.

'Sarah, I am seeking promotion but to gain promotion, I have to sit exams for the Army's First Class Education certificate, which means in the evenings I have to spend time studying. I hope you will understand.' I was not too happy about this latest request but asked.

'What about the dances then?'

'Well there's no problem I can still take you to them. It only means studying during the weekday evenings.' I thought: *At least that is something.*

Together with Percy, Bridget's escort, we did attend. However, it was Kathleen's turn not to attend. She too occupied with her own wedding preparations.

CHAPTER SEVEN
MARRIAGE LINES

The political issues and troubles in Ireland were escalating. Murders were ongoing, whilst imprisoned activists were on hunger strike, some died included two senior politicians, Michael Fitzgerald and Thomas MacSwiney. Their deaths resulted in the outbreaks of further riots. Then in the middle of November, on one Sunday, the IRA shot twelve British officers, later in the day the Black and Tans opened fire on spectators at a Gaelic football match in Croker Park Dublin. Killing twelve people, wounding sixty others. To quell the wave of violence, more British reinforcements arrived. In December, Martial Law was declared in many areas of the South West where savage fighting between the Activists and the Black and Tans took place. In Cork arson attacks occurred. The situation was definitely getting worse.

At home, with our little money dwindling away, hopefully the thought that Christmas might provide some potential work for us did not materialise. With Jack and his pals away on leave in England. It was going to be quite a dreary Christmas without them, so we didn't go to any of the dances. I was lonely without him and spent most of my time helping Kathleen with her wedding gown. On the 29th Jack returned in time for a New Year's Eve dance, although the mood in the Mess was jovial something was not quite right?

Early in the New Year, we resumed our meetings. It was a raw cold January night with thick frost on the ground, that crunched under our feet as we returned to the stables to huddle together, kissing and cuddling. Suddenly Jack stopped, drawing slightly away asked.

'Sarah. Would you marry me?' The very words I had waited for him to ask me. I quietly replied.

'Yes Jack, I would love to, but I can't?' Politely he enquired.

'Why ever not?'

'Because of my religious beliefs. I'm a Catholic and you are not.' He took hold of my hand and quietly said.

'That's not a problem. I have already thought that one through. You know RSM. Swaine and his wife Margaret. He wasn't a Catholic when he asked her to marry him. She refused for the same reason so, he took lessons from the Brother's and became a Catholic. Anything he can do I can do. Would that be acceptable to you?'

Still holding my hands he waited for my answer. I was truly surprised and extremely happy. Here was the man whom I could trust and love that was prepared, not to let an obstacle such as religion stop him marrying the woman he loved and chose to be his wife. I too dearly would love to become his wife. I quietly asked.

'You would do that for me?'

'Yes. I'll make arrangements to take lessons from the Brother's. Now tell me what is your answer?'

'Yes Jack. I will marry you.' I was on cloud nine as he drew me close to him, kissing me said.

'In that case I'll speak with your mother and father this very night. If they agree we will get married very soon. What do you say to that.'

'I'm sure they will approve. I know Mother will and Father will not say no.'

'Right that's it. I'll take you home now.'

I wasn't complaining and could tell by his determined attitude to carry out what he said he would do. He went back to their guardhouse to sign us out. Upon his return helped me up into the trap. Getting up alongside me, taking the reins in one hand, took hold of my hand with his other.

Clicked Paddy into a walk and slowly continued all the way along North road out past the Guards at the far end gate.

Once outside the camp, clicked his tongue to set into a trot, then into a gallop. Helter skelter we careered across the pitch-black plains. Nothing was going to stop him, the horse was still at a gallop as we entered the cobbled streets of Kildare, to endure a bone shaking ride all the way home, where he pulled up with a frightening halt. Not hesitating he jumped down lifting me out of the trap, grabbed hold of my hand and with me trying to keep up with him, pushed me in front of him through the door into the parlour, where mother along with father and a few of my sisters were sitting. Looking up she surprised at Jack's late arrival immediately understood something was up. Father standing up extended is hand.

'Hello there Jack.' Mother too got up and shooed everyone else out.

'Away with yerse. All of yerse.' Nobody hesitated, they all disappeared out through the door, without hesitation Jack answered.

'Evening's Mr Cunningham, Mrs. Cunningham. I have come to ask your permission to marry Sarah. I know there is a religious problem. But I can resolve that!'

I watched in anticipation. Seeing father smile and mothers face beaming with a smile. With a twinkle in her eyes. She enquired.

'And just how will you resolve the problem yourself Jack?'

'I'll take lessons from the Brothers and change my religion.' Taking hold of Jacks hand into both of hers she said.

'You'll do that will you? In that case you have my blessing and Father's.' In response Jack, leaning forward kissed her on the cheek.

'Thank you Mrs. Cunningham'...turning to father he shook his hand...'Thank you Mr Cunningham you've made me a very happy man.' Father asked.

'Now then Jack this is good news, but when is the happy event going to take place?'

'Well we haven't set a date, I have to see the Brothers but I promise you very soon I can say that.' Mother addressing me asked.

'Sarah what took you so long?' My cheeks were still burning and red from the bitterness of the wind whilst on our harrowing ride and spluttered.

'Mother it was up to Jack, he only asked me this evening.'

'Well he didn't waste much time coming forward for our permission. I'm delighted.'...They were both delighted and refreshments were offered. Father suggested.... 'Jack. I will take you back to the camp tonight.'....'Thank you Mr. Cunningham.' Just before getting back into the trap Jack said.

'Sarah, when I was home I told my parents, I intended to ask you to marry me. They did not object, but they would like to meet you. Would you come home with me, Sarah?' He was doing it again!

'No I'm sorry. People in small towns have very small minds.' Jack didn't argue he accepted my reason.

After Jack and father had left, Mother sat me down and told me... 'I met your father at the hotel I was working at in Monastereven. He arrived with a band to play there, he asked to marry him, and I agreed. Me thinking I would have the time of my life going to all the dances. Within two weeks we were married and I only ever went to one dance.' I asked.

'Why only one dance?'

'Well Allahnah. It was at a farewell dance for your father's brother who was immigrating to America, someone asked me to dance. Father became very jealous so, there was no more dancing for me.' Her story intrigued me, as an Irish upbringing did not allow such things and questioned.

'What did Grandmother and Grandfather say about your marrying so quickly?'

'Allahnah they did not object, but Allahnah that is another story, as they themselves had eloped. Your Grandmother was a Nurse at the Rotunda in Dublin and whilst on holiday at her parent's farm in the Wicklow Mountains. Your Grandfather was there buying up an orchard of fruit. They met and it was love at first sight. Your Grandfather asked permission to marry their daughter. He was refused. So, they eloped, married and settled in Hackestown where you were born.' I thought: *That was quite a romantic story however it had taken my Jack much much longer.* The announcement of our engagement brought delight to everyone. Jack was well liked, he never had a swelled head or talked big. True to his word with the help of Mother he went to the Catholic Brother's to be converted. We set the date of marriage as March 30th.'

For the next three months. Jack was very busy, studying for his Army Education Certificate and taking religious instructions, including his football training and playing football twice a week. Fully understanding his commitments, I concentrated on our wedding arrangements, however he did acquire permission for me to enter the camp to discuss the wedding arrangements. Any courting was confined to the stables where it was warm. Jack, a born city boy loved horses, it was unbelievable the way he had with them, not even mother had his gift. Whilst I fed them little treats he groomed and talked to each horse, so much so that I felt jealous as he paid more attention to the horses than he did to me, not that I wanted him to rub my nose or pat and feed me treats. When he had finished his grooming he stated.

'You know Sarah. We slept above the stables. Our routine was drummed into us. Up early at five thirty to muck out, followed by bareback horse riding before breakfast and parade at nine o'clock. Initially I was a driver and forever cleaning, scouring, polishing and burnishing, leather and steel, a tedious job. Whilst the gunners would clean and maintain the guns, which had to completed before stable inspection at eleven o'clock. In the afternoon the horses would be hitched to the gun and limbers for exercise. There was always plenty to do in a gunners day Sarah'...a stallion becoming restless interrupted him...'Whoa there. Steady boy. Sarah feed this one with a treat theirs a good girl.'

I fed a treat to his special horse, in return for my efforts received a neigh and snort. Jack always made sure we left the stable before the Guard picquet arrived. On one such evening when we were leaving Jack noticed my shoes were covered in horse muck, stated.

'Sarah you cannot go through the barrack guardhouse like that. Here give them to me let me clean them up'...grabbing a handful of straw...'Here stand on that. Give me your shoes'...He cleaned them and replaced them on each foot as if he was shoeing a horse saying...'There that's better. Eh Sarah?'

Obviously. I was then fit to be seen in the guardhouse. I was escorted to the gate where he saluted me, shook my hand pressed cheek to cheek and I walked through the gate swinging my arms like a soldier. Climbed up into the stationary trap and went home alone. I'm afraid, my Jack could not dance a step and certainly did not have a romantic bone in his body either. However, I dearly loved my non-dancing unromantic Gallant Young Sergeant.

In January 1921 parts of the South, were placed under Martial Law. British Tanks arrived on the streets of Dublin and certain areas within the city were sealed off. The situation was grim and that added more concern for us at home with the ongoing arrangements for two weddings. Pandemonium broke out, it became a mad house, with Kathleen and Frank's wedding in February followed in March by ours. I was a bridesmaid at Kathleen's and their list of guest included half of the Field Artillery.

The day of their wedding, was a cold misty day, raining in the morning and overcast in the afternoon. With the wedding breakfast in our house, the guest's came and went as they pleased, bringing small gifts and their congratulations. In the afternoon Kathleen and Frank departed bound for Frank's home in Wales. Leaving me with a slight problem to consider, who was going to be my Bridesmaid? Finally I decided on my younger sister Lena and Nellie O'Callaghan, a very close friend from our Army days, who just happened to be the younger sister of the RSM's wife Margaret. After our demob I had only seen Nellie on one occasion, but we had exchanged letters so our ties were not broken. I sent a wire to Nellie asking the question, in return received her acceptance, then sent her a letter to her giving details of the outfit I had chosen. A simple white two-piece suit white stockings white shoes with a similar styled hat like the one we wore in the army. Nellie's return letter was not encouraging, informing me that there was nothing like that to purchase in Cork. However, Bridget came up with a suggestion, she being the same size and height as Nellie, she could try one that certainly would fit Nellie. Easier said than done, the dressmaker did not have anything similar so we went to all the dressmakers in Kildare before we found one that sold a similar style, and more important fitted Bridget. Although the hat was slightly different to mine that would have to do, between us we made a nice suitable dress for Lena, so our arrangements were completed. Whereas Jacks. Was Army uniform with a recently promoted Sgt. Percy Larrett as his best man.

Yet another problem where would we live? According to army regulations Jack had to be twenty–six to qualify for married quarters, he being twenty- three years old was too young. Nevertheless, with his wheeling and dealings he had sorted something out in camp, which I was none the wiser about. But Mother, aware of what went on in married quarters was constantly giving me lectures, drilling me into the Army way of life (which I already knew) on how I should behave after I was married.

'Do not ever wear Jack's stripes(as if I would). Be friendly with everyone. Do not go in and out of other people's quarters. Mind your own business. Keep out of any arguments.' I was fed up with her lectures, nevertheless I did take note of her advice and it was much later I found out why?

Four weeks before our wedding, Jack was confirmed a Catholic. However many unforeseen problems lay ahead. The existing troubles became a serious worry to me, the activists committed several more murders, more British troops being drafted into Ireland, and the Curragh camps security was increased. Only those with validated passes were allowed on camp. All Jack said was. 'Sarah! Do not be surprised if we have to call the wedding off? But do still carry on with the arrangements, and I promise on the Saturday before our wedding we shall go to the jewelers in Kildare to select and buy your wedding ring.'

The banns had been read at the church for a full nuptial mass. The wedding breakfast was to be at our new married quarters, (which I knew nothing about). Everything appeared to be arranged. Then two weeks before our wedding Jack informs me.

'Sarah half of the Brigade, are leaving for gunnery training at Glen Imaal in the Wicklow Mountains. On the Monday after our wedding it's our turn and I will be going with the battery.' I was gob smacked what else could go wrong? Well. I soon found out the following week.

All Military personnel were 'Confined to Camp.' Neither Jack nor Percy could get out and we could not get in, instead we held conversations across the barrier at the main gate. This was a big blow and a major issue! How could Jack and Percy get out? More so, with a wedding list of guest as long as your arm how would they get in for the reception without a pass? The big question was, should we call it off or continue? I consulted with mother and she advised

'Go ahead it will all blow over.' I repeated Mother's advice to Jack and without the slightest bit of concern, he just said.

'Your mother's right. Don't worry everything will be all right. You continue with your preparation. I'll sort the passes out.'

However, he did sort them out. Unfortunately, it was not possible to gain access for everyone on the list. Jack passed over a much shortened guest list with which I had to order the transport for. Saturday arrives and Jack was unable to take me to the jewellers to purchase the wedding ring, instead Margaret Swaine accompanied me to the jewellers. What a job that was, with my tiny hands none fitted. We visited several jewellers in Kildare before at the very last shop, I found a gold ring that fitted.

On the Sunday morning Nellie arrived at Mothers. We fell into each other's arms, we had so much to talk about. She too was fed up with being unemployed, although at least she had a part-time job washing dishes in a Hotel. If it were possible she would gladly volunteer to re-join. Mother invited her to stay for Sunday dinner and if she wanted to stay overnight. She accepted the dinner but declined to stay, she had a pass and was staying at her sister Margaret's on Camp.

On the Monday, Mother, I along with two sisters, having received passes, went to the camp to start preparing the quarters for the festivities. Jack had told me the address so I did know where they were located, having delivered products to them much earlier. On Tuesday we returned to the camp with all the food to lay out the tables ready for the Wedding breakfast the following day. Late in the afternoon Jack and Percy arrived at the quarters. Mother in good voice, told them.

'Everything is Okay. You two do not say anything and nothing will go wrong.'

They kept out of the way and accompanied us to the Guardhouse where we said our goodnights. Mother retorted.

'Goodnight to the pair of yer's. I know where you two Boyo's are heading to the Mess, for a quiet drink Eh?' Jack, with a huge grin creasing his face said.

'Well only for one Mrs. Cunningham?'

Of course we knew once in the mess they would make a night of it! With a parting shot mother retorted.

'Go on away with the pair of yus. I'm warning yus. Don't be late at the Church to-morrow. Or I'll be looking for you Boyo's

CHAPTER EIGHT
A SOLDIERS WIFE

Wednesday March 13th. Our wedding day arrived with the early morning sun shining and that's how it remained throughout the day. Very early, Mother, left the house and while she was out, Nellie arrived to get ready, when Mother arrived back later I asked.

'Where have you been?'

'Decorating the church then onto to the Camp to see everything was Okay.'

Father and I left the house with plenty of time, outside the church joined up with Nellie and Lena. We entered the church to the sound of quiet organ music. As we walked slowly down the aisle towards the alter rails, there was no sign of Jack or Percy, only Father Joseph stood gazing down at his bible. Father squeezed my arm in reassurance, I wasn't fussed. I looked around admiring mother's handiwork, the flowers were beautiful, the organist played another hymn and as the last note of the hymn died away, the church fell silent, only interrupted by a few coughs. Impatiently Father Joseph kept on clearing his throat. We must have been standing there for five minutes or more. Unusual? Yes, the Bridegroom was late! When a slight commotion at the back of the Church, set my heart fluttering. Father, glancing back squeezed my arm gently they had arrived. Down the aisle they marched, Father Joseph signalled to the organist who unaware of the situation triumphantly played. "Here comes the Bride." To the sound of Army boots clumping on the stone floor, the pair of them trying not to make too much noise that was to no avail. A so called muffled Left, Right, Left, Right, advanced towards Father and me until the clumping halted beside me. Jack turned a huge grin on his face and winked, in return I smiled sweetly back at him. I wondered. *"How on earth could they be so late? Could it be to do with the night before?"* The last strains of. "Here Comes the Bride" died away then silence prevailed as Father Joseph proceeded with the marriage ceremony. Percy produced the all-important gold ring and the formal words of marriage were uttered. To my delight we were officially married. Father Joseph then continued with the Nuptial Mass until it finished with the blessing.

Outside the church congratulation was poured upon us. Mother disappeared, she had business elsewhere. After some photos were taken, the Battery Trap our means of transport back to the wedding breakfast was covered with garlands of flowers, throwing my posy of flowers over my shoulder it was caught by Nellie she being the tallest. Jack helped me into the trap, taking hold of the reins clicked horse into motion, we moved sedately away before turning off the road towards the Curragh.

Once out of sight Jack stood up and urged the horse into a gallop. As we sped over the Curragh road I held onto my hat. Still stood up Jack galloped the horse through the camp gates to the roars and shouts of approval from the Guards. Wheeling the trap right went down between Beresford barracks and the old Women's Legion huts towards the married quarters. Arriving outside brought the poor horse to a halt, it was lathered all over and snorting. Jack jumped down taking me in his arms, kissed me, carried me towards the door, which as if by magic opened, carried me through into the threshold, passing Mother stood by the doorway who shouted...'WELCOME MRS PLANT'.... on through into the parlour, the room looked splendid there were flowers everywhere, mother's handiwork again. Gradually the limited number of guest arrived to pack the then crowded quarters to overflowing before the festivities began. All day long, members of the Field Batteries squeezed in and out of the crowded quarters until they decided to set up a bar in the parlour. Our host's, Mother and Father had a wonderful time. Father played his fiddle whilst Mother with tears in her eyes was overcome with the event. As for me I cannot remember when the last of the Artillery contingent left but it was well into the early hours of the morning. The next day, our quarters were a mess. Rice and confetti was everywhere, empty glasses and left over food littered the table. Near to midday Bridget arrived to help with the clearing up, she exclaimed.

'My God Sarah! This place is like a war zone!'

'That I do know and to make all this mess, there must have been hundreds of people here. I don't feel like it but we had better make a start.' Jack grinned and made a stupid comment.

'Well they must have enjoyed themselves. Watch out Percy has turned up in the trap we'll get cracking clearing away the debris and get rid of the bar.'

Between the four of us we made light work of the debris. When all was clean and tidy. Jack and I were left in peace together for the remainder of the day in our first Army quarters. Number 4 B Block. It was small with a parlour, kitchen, small sitting room, and two small bedrooms, along with outside facilities yet comfortable and very basic. How we came to get the quarters I shall never know, but by some wrangling we did. With me a soldier's wife, it was my turn to receive goods delivered at the door by the provision man, a wizened old fella if ever you did see but, I was aware of all his tricks. Five days later Jack's Battery did leave for gunnery training.

On a cold and damp day, early in the morning, I left our quarters and made my way up to their Lines to see them off. I stood shivering as the battery of six guns pulled by snorting horses, emitting plumes of hot air from flared nostrils. The sound of their shoes clopping against the hard surface of the road mixed with the jingle of traces and metal against wood, mingled along with the grating of the steel tyres on the wheels, carrying the heavy load of limber and guns. Astride his horse Jack sat bolt upright, the strap of his peak cap barely visible under his chin covered by the collar of his greatcoat. He nodded to me as he went past towards the main gate. They would be away three weeks. When they returned I was delighted to see him but after a little while he politely informs me.... 'Sarah love! I will be away with the Battery for a few months, possibly once every month I will be able to get a thirty –six hour pass.'

I knew from then on what to expect as a soldier's wife, to be separated and left alone for long periods of time, something that eventually I came to terms with. To keep me occupied whilst Jack was away, I decided to seek work for any casual domestic work, so long as I would be at home upon his return (which did not materialise). At home in our quarters I spent my evenings writing letters to Jack, Mary in Bristol who was then pregnant and Kathleen in Wales, keeping them informed of what was happening in and around Kildare, that was not much. The regular dances at the messes had almost ceased, so my entertainment was curtailed. On the weekend I went to Mother's. Taking heed of mother's advice, I kept myself to myself, with the exception of the Gunners wife next door, who was expecting a baby. She seemed such a nice young woman. It became a very lonely existence,

Before he had left, Jack had arranged passes, for Mother, Bridget, Lena, and Eilish and most important permission for the use of a Trap and horse for me. It was Eilish who became a regular visitor to my much wanted company, she spent many nights' sleeping at the quarters, she driving there and back in mothers Trap, leaving it in one of the stables. One evening we overheard the husband of the young woman next door arguing and fighting with her. Eilish disturbed by the row whispered to me. 'Some soldiers are not nice to fight with their wives. I hope your Jack never fights with you Sarah.' Thinking back to mother's warning, I whispered.

'I hope not.'

One weekend, I was at mothers when she produced a letter from Mary, informing her that the labour force had gone on strike in England, and like a lot of the other reservists, Bert had been recalled to report to Aldershot. Mary's news about the strike in England bemused me, over there it appeared just as bad. As she was due in a few weeks-time to giving birth, she also asked Mother if, she could come over and stay there to give birth to her baby? Babies very close to Mothers heart and the prospect of having their first grandchild born back home really appealed to her, of course her answer was. 'Yes.' The following weekend Jack was on leave. I informed him about Bert's recall and Mary's scheduled stay at mothers. He was pleased at the snippets of news, including Mary's return, as she would be good company for me. I was at mothers along with the rest of the family to welcome Mary home. She heavy in pregnancy, felt very embarrassed by her condition. Nevertheless, it all appeared very natural within the household. But Mary was not happy with the sleeping arrangements she quietly asked me.

'Sarah please can I stay in your quarters with you?' I was more than happy at her suggestion.....'Of course, you can have the spare bedroom. But there are two problems you need a pass and another thing, you can explain it to Mother.'

While she explained her position to mother, who accepting the situation thought nothing more of it. I left mothers to return to the Camp stopped at the Guardhouse and requested to see the Officer of the Day, who after some time appeared and he listened to my request. Showing my pass I explained to him I was Sgt. Jack Plant's wife, gave him details about Bert's recall, that he had been stationed at the camp less than a year before. The officer said he did remember Bert playing football. He listened as I explained Mary's condition and she like me had been in the QMAAC. Could he please get permission for a pass for my sister Mary. After I had relayed all my reasons for the request, he asked me Mary's married name and other details that fortunately I could answer without too much problem. He wrote down the details, advised me to wait outside his office. It was sometime later when he returned stating.

'Mrs. Plant having discussed your request and due to the unusual circumstances. A pass will be granted for use only by Mrs Mary Batten.'

Promptly he signed the pass handing it to me. I thanked him, then returned to mothers. It was late in the afternoon when Mary and I left for the camp. Eilish always eager to help, she wanting to get away from doing the outside chores at mothers, decided to go with us to assist. Taking Mary's suitcase loaded it on the trap, then assisted her as she struggled to climb aboard, her face red with embarrassment, much to the amusement of our younger sisters that I sent away. Our drive to the camp was slow, arriving at the camp Guardhouse, showed our passes then proceeded to our quarters. We helped Mary down through into the parlour, where gratefully she sat down quite exhausted. Eilish and I prepared her bed for her stay, then the evening meal. Eilish stayed had something to eat before returning home in the trap. I was always pleased to accommodate Eilish as most of the time she provided me with company, even after her school day was over. The next day I re-arranged our quarters to make Mary more comfortable, before taking her to the camp hospital for examination, that proved all was well. On the Saturday Jack arrived home on leave, pleased to see everything was all going well with Mary. Nevertheless, on the Sunday Mary became ill. Jack un-fussed by the turn of event was a Godsend. Immediately he left to collect a battery trap and the pair of us got Mary into the trap with me sat beside her, whilst Jack with urgency clicked the horse into a fast steady trot towards the hospital where the Nurses took over. We went straight to mothers to advise her of Mary's hospitalisation.

Very early Monday morning I was up with Jack, he went to the hospital. He returned back to tell me the good news, Mary had given birth to a baby boy. He had also organised a wire to be sent to Bert, gained permission for me to take the battery trap to collect mother and father and bring them back to the hospital. Even before Jack left the camp I was already on my way to Mother's. Returning with them to visit Mary and their new baby grandson. They were overjoyed at the birth and after their visit I took them home. Returning back to our quarters I busied myself preparing the quarters for Mary's return with her baby boy. After all my previous experience with babies I was fully conversant with midwifery and more than capable to look after and teach Mary how to care, look after her new son. Later that week she received a letter from Bert, bearing good tidings and news that the strike was over. He would be over on leave in three week's time. At this news Mary decided to have Raymond (a name they had already chosen) christened in our parish church. Letters were being sent backwards and forwards to Jack to see if he could obtain leave to coincide with Bert's arrival. They both arrived on the Friday in time for the christening on the Sunday. Bert's brought more news to Mary that he had been requested to play for Plymouth Argyle, which meant they would be going to live in Plymouth. What a reunion it turned out to be, several of the football team arrived to drink the health of the new born baby. After the celebrations, Mary and Bert returned back to Bristol.

My Quarters returned to that of the quietness I was used too. One day I was busy baking when the Quarter Masters wife Mary Higgins called on me. Mary was rather robust and very forward in her manner with a heart of gold. I was glad of her company and invited her for a cup of tea, she accepted. Noticing I was making a cake mixture began to talk.

'Sarah I have just come from a discussion with Mrs. Lowrey-Corry, the major's wife about a forthcoming sports day event, she is organising to coincide with the return of the Brigade. She has suggested that all the cakes and sandwiches for the buffet should be made by all the married women. So Sarah, the purpose of my visit is to ask all the wives to help out. I can see that you are a handy cook, would you like to help out making cakes?'

Little did she know that Mary had only taught me my so-called cooking skills over the last few months, so I offered my services.

'Yes I would be pleased to.'... 'Good! I'll add you to my list. Thank you for the cup of tea I will be back in touch with you later about further arrangements.

A few days later Mary knocked on the door and handed me an invite to attend a meeting at the Majors Quarters. It was an invitation I could not refuse and she offered.

'I will come and pick you up and introduce you to Mrs. Lowrey-Corry and some of the other wives.' I did go and was introduced to the Majors wife and some of the other wives. It was during the meeting that Mary spoke up and recommended.

'Mrs Plant has kindly offered to make jam sponges!'

When I heard this, I nearly died of fright. I had no alternative but to accept the task, at least I would be doing something useful. Jack sent me a letter informing me that their training was over and they would be back in camp soon. However, I already knew the date and whilst writing a reply was about to inform him about my cake making duty, instead left it as a surprise for his return that made me ponder on the thought. *"Putting all the time together since we had been married. I doubt very much if it was a full month"*

The Brigade arrived back with grating wheels jingling of the harness's and the usual sound of snorting horses, mixed with orders being shouted out, all added to the excitement of their return. Later that same day Jack was back at the quarters, now was my chance, eagerly I told him about me getting involved in the forthcoming event. Obviously he was very pleased.

'That's very good news Sarah, now you have been accepted as a soldiers wife. You probably will get invited to do more things like that in the future?'

How right he was, on the day at the sports I received wonderful praise for my sponges and was invited to run in the women's racing event, much to Jack's pleasure and approval the icing on the cake. I won the race!

CHAPTER NINE
MOTHERHOOD

The ongoing talks for a truce in Ireland eventually came to a head with agreement by both parties, resulting in a few restrictions being lifted in the camp. To our great joy I find I am expecting a baby. I was more than delighted, with the thought of a baby in my arms, I would become fully occupied looking after the baby and my loneliness would cease. I waited awhile before I told Mother, naturally she was delighted. I wrote to Mary and Kathleen telling them our good news. I was not too bad at dressmaking so I spent most of my time making a layette. Meanwhile, Mary Higgins a regular visitor, had become a worthwhile friend to me. Whilst having tea and cakes and chatting about many things, she offered to help me make the layette. Very soon it was finished, then we turned our skills to making baby clothes, we were getting on just fine when I started to feel very ill. The symptoms would not go away. Jack decided to call the Doctor who advised me. 'It was due to being pregnant and not to worry about it.'

I became constantly sick with heavy bouts of sickness, which always occurred when on my own. With none of my family close on hand, I became very frightened, vulnerable and lonely, although Mary was a brick she could not spend all day with me. I just had to soldier on. In the evenings Jack on occasions would go and read 'Company Orders' then proceed onto the mess. I think he got it into his head that if he stayed at home with me the older married Sergeants would say. *"He was tied to his wife's apron strings."* When he did return home I enquired.

'Where have you been?'

'Just called in at the mess. So and so, a friend from somewhere had arrived and the time just slipped by.' I said nothing about his excuse.

It was the start of the football season Jack was picked to play in the team, so began his training. I attended possibly two of the matches, but feeling unwell with my constant bouts of sickness, I began to decline the invitations. Win or lose at football Jack still continued to celebrate in the mess. On those nights Eilish would come up to stay with me, therefore I didn't object at his staying out so late.

The Truce created by the Irish Treaty had somehow failed, nevertheless, further discussions on the future of Ireland were under consideration, therefore any meetings between Lloyd George and Eamon de Valera brought forth good signs, that maybe the possibility of the recent troubles were about to come to an end. However, rumours in camp began to rumble around, that a number of Army Brigades and Regiments located in Ireland were to be posted to different parts of England. Whether founded or not, I began to worry at the mere thought of being posted away from home before my baby was born. I sought Jack's assurance that we were not going to move? He just shrugged his shoulders saying.

'Sarah yes. There are rumours going around, don't worry your pretty little head they are just rumours. I have not heard anything to confirm our leaving Kildare and if we are to move, so be it.'

It gave me the reassurance I was seeking. I need not have worried the rumours were unfounded nevertheless, the Troubles between the North and South continued, various murders and incidents were a daily occurrence. Rioting in Belfast brought out the troops. Just before Christmas the talks ended with the future of Ireland agreed and finalised as divided, North and South. The six states of Northern Ireland would remain under British Rule and Southern Ireland was to become a Free State. Maybe this latest agreement was to be the end of all the troubles?

By Christmas time I was well into pregnancy, and due to my size found it difficult to travel, to and from mothers also like Mary very embarrassed appearing in front of my sisters, therefore spent less time visiting Mother. I still enjoyed the company of Eilish who regularly visited. On a bitter cold day just before Christmas, she arrived in the trap all wrapped up against the cold with a present from mother. A turkey, a much welcome gift that I would cook myself as it was to be our first Christmas together. Well we certainly were not alone, many visitors from the mess arrived, placed a kiss on my cheek exclaimed.

'Just popped in to wish you a Merry Christmas Sarah.'

They would stay for the rest of the afternoon. Our quarters became full of Sergeants, I don't think there was anyone over in the mess. It was also to be repeated on Boxing Day. Furthermore, the same performance happened on New Year's Day. By which time I was quite tired and glad that a week of festivities had finished.

January, apart from a few isolated incidents, all appeared to be quiet and a good indication that the troubles were almost over? Yet the previous rumours about Regiments moving did happen at the end of January, when the Duke of Cornwall's Regiment left. All the information I received was by word of mouth. Jack would come home and mention one or two things that had happened. The sale of equipment from Camps stores. Not very unusual as those sales were always going on, but as the rumours of moving had ceased, I became more relaxed with the situation and the knowledge that I would give birth to my baby at home. However, I was at mothers when she informed me.

'Allahnah. Do you know that the new provisional Irish Parliament in Dublin are at loggerheads themselves, over the so called 'Treaty with Britain.' Eamon de Valera has resigned and Michael Collins has taken over to become the new head of the Irish Government, and Allahnah. If the treaty was agreed, the British Army would withdraw from Ireland. Do you know that crowd could not agree amongst themselves, so what good will a parliament do?' All I could say was repeat Jack's advice.

'Mother it's early days yet. Don't worry about it, just wait and see.'

Then more trouble, violence and riots broke out in Belfast. Then a serious incident hit the Royal Field Artillery. Whilst carrying the soldiers pay one of their Lieutenants was held up at gunpoint, he refusing to hand it over was shot dead by his assailants who got away. This murder did not go down too well with the local population. March, time was closing in on the date of my giving birth and I was too preoccupied to worry anymore about what was going on in the outside world, and as Mother always did. I decided to have the baby at home. Mother assured me that she would be alongside the midwife to assist with the delivery. On the March 7th the weather turned nasty, the winds started blowing a hooley and my labour pains began, I struggled next door to get the young Gunners wife to go and fetch Jack. When he arrived I Immediately sent him to fetch Mother. I was sitting in the parlour in great pain unable to move, it seemed ages before they eventually arrived. Mother with ruddy cheeks aglow from the winds outside. Her windswept hair was all over the place, Mother just looked at me her experience told her.

'Jack, get the midwife.' Much later Jack arrived back with Sadie the midwife , she just as windswept as mother was muttering about. 'Tis a bad time to call out someone on a raw night like it is.'

With all the pain I was suffering, I could not give a damn what was going on outside. The pair of them shoved Jack out of the room and prepared for the birth. Then mother, having seen and done it many times before, made a cup of tea, then they sat there talking, whilst I was in agony with my pains. During the night outside the winds were howling away with me inside howling away in the throes of delivery. I eventually gave birth to a lovely baby girl. The following Sunday after a very rough time I remained in bed whilst mother took our baby to Mass to be fussed over by the Nuns at the Garrison Church. Jack and I decided to name our baby 'Caroline Mary' after our mothers. Later we had her baptised in the parish church in Kildare.

The announcement that both Irish and English parties had agreed, to the terms of the Treaty, meant that the British Army would be leaving Southern Ireland, which instigated more rumours about the camps interns. Along with other Regiments the Brigade would be withdrawing and being posted back to various locations in England. Fully recovered and back to normal size. I ignored them, I had a baby to look after. I was willing and quite happy, going backward and forwards to mothers in the trap with Caroline Mary. But it was not long before more trouble flared up. Civil war was about to break out, an Army Brigadier General was murdered, followed by more trouble in Dublin. The Brigade, which included Jack's battery, was sent to assist in the fighting in Dublin. They left without as much as a goodbye. I was not happy. It had become a daily routine for me, to walk out and read the Company Orders at the Company office. They had not been gone a week when I read on Company Orders.

"All soldiers' wives in married Quarters are advised to be ready and prepared to leave for England in April."

It came as a shock to me as I read that news. Then faced with the nagging thought of parting from Jack, leaving my hometown and family behind, to lead a new way of life with a baby somewhere in England. The previous notice was soon followed two day later by another one which stated.

'All Married Quarters personnel.
Departure: Saturday April 15th.'

Although by their own personal experience Mary and Kathleen, had many times before reassured me "That England, wasn't as bad as everyone makes out." I got in such a state with my nerves I became ill a week before we left. Jack arrived back from Dublin just to say his farewell. Tenderly he kissed me goodbye saying.

'I love you Sarah and our baby Caroline. You'll be all right you're a Soldiers wife now.' I said nothing then he was gone, back to the fighting in Dublin.

Then my tears did flow. I sat and wept buckets all I could think about was: *In all of my twenty-six years, apart from the short period in Dublin, then Cork. I had not left the surrounding area of Kildare.* I spent the rest of the week crying, reflecting upon my past life, my schooldays in Ballybrittas. Properly dressed I in charge of my sisters would set off with plenty of time to arrive for assembly. With no transport, it was a case of 'Shank's Pony' a two and a half mile walk to school. During wintertime not very good but spring and summertime's were pleasant. Picking wild flowers along the way, arriving late despite the peace offering to our teachers, received a good telling off. In Monastereven our schooling was at a little convent school, a short walk up the street, our teachers were very nice and pleasant Nuns. Education was my greatest joy. I was eager for it and became an exemplary pupil, grabbing at knowledge waiting for whatever the Sister chalked on the blackboard like a starveling for every morsel of bread. I ran to school knowing full well, when I was in class, my father would be at the school asking

'Sister Thomas will you send Sarah home to take care of the children. She is away in the trap to Dublin market. The lives of the children are in your hands.' Sister Thomas, told my father off saying.

'I had good brains, but he would not give me the chance of using them?'

Father would leave the school without me. Unfortunately, I would be sent home in tears. I was more at home than at school. However, Sister Thomas taught me after Sunday school, they

64

were my lessons. I often wonder what I could have been had I been better educated. My Grandmother had been a nurse (apparently the first Nurse at the Rotunda, to qualify as a midwife). She had made sure that my mother received a good education. In turn Mother ensured her children followed on with that practice, were provided with a catholic education. There were of course Aunts and Uncles. Some of whom I do not remember very well. On father's side there was: Tom, Joe, Ellen, Peter, Riter, and Theresa. The eldest three Tom, Joe, and Helen sought their fortunes by emigrating to Canada and America. The latter three looked after my ageing Grandparents. I remember Lar, father's cousin, who owned a Grand Union Canal boat transporting coal and such like heavy goods from Dublin. He would take us children for a trip up to the next lock, let us off to walk back home, a treat we all thoroughly enjoyed. Father's day off was confined to the odd Saturday, He would take a boat trip down to Athy, to his brother Peter's home, stay overnight and return on the Sunday by train.

They were memories of the past locked in my brain nevertheless, with those memories whizzing around in my brain, I had my baby Caroline Mary to look after. Be prepared they had said, but I had little or no luggage to speak of, and on the day of our departure from the Curragh Camp, all the married wives and families were taken by G.S wagons across the Curragh to Newbridge station, there to entrain for Dublin. At the station I had a surprise waiting for me, the whole family had made the trip to see me off. Mother last to say her farewell, provided another little bit of advice.

'Now Sarah Allahnah. You're leaving home with a young baby. I shall worry about you, but it brings joy to my heart, that you had all that training when you were caring for your younger sisters and brothers. You will be all right. God be with you.'

On April 15th. 1922. Sadly I left Ireland, a born and bred Irish Colleen, about to enter into a completely different way of life. Little did I know that my whole future would be drastically changed and enhanced by the forthcoming sequence of events?

CHAPTER TEN
ENGLAND – ALDERSHOT

I shall never forget that day. Unceremoniously, with my baby in my arms, I had been bundled into a carriage and sat in a corner seat. I was the only young married woman in the party with a baby of barely two months old. Other mothers had children ranging in ages from one year and upward. I was weeping buckets. The lady sitting next to me placed her arm around my shoulders and politely asked.

'Is this your first time for leaving home duck's?' I was unable to answer her, so just nodded.

'There you are ducks you have a real good cry. It will soon be all right just you wait and see, we've all experienced the parting from our husband's before'...turning to the others in the carriage loudly announced ....'It's her first time you know.'....this was followed by a chorus of: - 'Aah.'- 'Shame.'- 'Never mind.' Their comments of concern directed at me still sobbing, I turned my head into her shoulder and thought: *"Maybe, it was all right for them, they were going back to their homes in England."* They turning their attention away from me, continued with their excited chatter. I gradually ceased my sobbing composing myself, turned to the lady muttered.

'Thank you.' Placing her hand on my arm she squeezed and said.

'Don't you worry yourself ducks? You'll be alright; you just take care of your baby.' Then carried on with her conversation.

I sat there thinking about her advice: *She had reassured me a little, they apparently had all been through the same experience before.* Glancing down at Caroline Mary who was fast asleep, more to console myself I began rocking her. My eyes were dry and my sorrow had subsided yet, I had more to concentrate on the next part of the journey, something I was dreading. The sea journey crossing to Holyhead. The train journey did not take that long, as it slowly pulled into Dun Laoghaire station and stopped. The lady sat beside me said.

'C'mon duck's, ups-a-daisy we have a ferry to catch.'

Again I was bundled out of the carriage and swept along with the tide of families towards the ferry. Whilst their light-hearted and excited chatter filled the air, they struggling with cases, boxes and children, with me holding my baby in one arm and in the other a small case with my worldly chattels. We were pushed and shoved through to the quayside, there waiting for its next cargo of human beings was the ferryboat. It looked enormous. Immediately I became terrified of crossing the sea stopped, but the friendly woman who had stuck by me with her free hand grabbed hold of my arm and helped me up onto the gangway urging.

'This way up ducks. You keep tight hold of your young nipper there.'

Arriving at the top, my heart was in my mouth. Memories of my little sister Josephine, petrified of water leapt into my mind and they were certainly not helping me to board this boat. I was forced through a door in the side of this ship and swept along with the tide of women and children, through another doorway into a large room. Once inside the women dispersed in all directions. I was left standing with my baby in my arms tightly holding my small suitcase. Glancing around the room saw rows of seats fixed to the floor, some were already occupied by women urging their children to sit down and be quiet, whilst others milled around with their luggage jostling to get seats. A woman passing by me urged.

'Grab yourself a seat young-un before we sail.' I muttered.

'Thank you.' Do you know who's in charge?' She quickly replied.

'Yes. That Royal Artillery duty Major over there.' Pointing across to the other side where an Officer stood surveying the melee before him. As I navigated through the women towards him he watched my approach questioned.

'Uhm! Mrs?'

'Plant.' I answered.

'Aah. BSM. Plant's wife. How can I help you?' Obviously he knew of Jack. Here was the person who would understand my plight. I asked him politely.

'Excuse me Sir.'

'Yes. Mrs Plant.'

'Could I stay behind as I am not strong?' His reply, a typical Army response.

'You are a soldier's wife Mrs Plant. Yes. You are strong enough. Now this is your big chance to get quarters over in England. You are aware your husband is not entitled to them. Under your circumstances of being posted back to England. You might be lucky? Here let me carry your suitcase'....Taking hold of my suitcase grasped my arm and guided me through the melee of women... 'Excuse me ladies. Officer coming through. Excuse us please.'...Then we stopped in front of a Sergeant, stood with another woman and a little girl. The officer turned towards me, speaking loud and clear...'Mrs Plant. In order to keep your mind off things. I'm putting you in charge of another party.'...I was confused? This Major has found me a job to do. He then ordered...'Mrs Plant this is Sergeant Galloway, his wife and daughter. You will look after them on the trip over to England.'

With that curt introduction he turned about. Barked out another order to an orderly going past then marched briskly away. Leaving me and my assigned party, to pick up the pieces from there onwards. I clueless as to what I was supposed to do specifically with an Infantry Sergeant. Then I remembered: The two young Ox and Bucks soldiers detailed to Bridget and I in Cork. I looked around, spotted some empty seats on the other side of the room, sternly I ordered.

'Er. Sergeant. Go and reserve those seats over there for us please. We will follow you.' Looking at me he grunted.

'Uhm! All right then.' He drifted away carrying their luggage. As we followed I asked his wife.

'What regiment are you from?'

'Hampshire's.' was her frosty reply?

'Where are you going?' Just as frosty.

'Aldershot!' I answered.

'Sorry I can't help what has happened. I don't want to go either.'

'Oh it's not your fault. It's him in front'... adding...'I'm going to leave him when I get back home?' I enquired.

'Why? Whatever for?'

'Drink. Bloody drink.'

Remembering mother's advice. Don't get involved. I hesitated before answering.

'Oh.' I see.'

Sitting down in the seats, I changed the subject to the usual women's talk, about Caroline Mary, who exhausted by crying was fast asleep in my arms. Being distracted by our conversation, I had forgotten about getting off the boat and had no idea it was some way out of the harbour heading out to sea. The bar opened up Sgt. Galloway getting up from his seat headed straight for it, his wife didn't say anything. I did not know what to do? The movement of the ship made me heave I thought: *God help me*. He must have heard my plea. As another Infantry Sergeant in the same regiment approached me, quietly he whispered into my ear.

'Come on little lady, I'll give you a hand. I'll sort out Sergeant Galloway while you stick close to his wife.' Obviously he knowing about their problem having noticed my plight offered his assistance. That I was truly grateful for, making his way to the bar stood next to Sgt. Galloway.

I sat there for hours petrified by the ships motion, fighting off the queasy feeling, praying to God to get this boat to the other side without sinking. It was getting dark and other women began to settle down for the night where they sat or, some attempted to lie on the floor. Mrs. Galloway drew her little girl close to her wrapping her arm around her, they were soon asleep. As for me I stayed where I was in my seat bolt upright, clutching my baby and remained wide-awake throughout the night. It was still dark when Sgt. Galloway's wife stirred herself. Getting up, took her little girl to the toilets. When she returned she suggested.

'Mrs Plant, this is a good time to go and sort out the baby, there is nobody awake yet and nobody in the toilets.'

Taking her advice, changed Caroline Mary and freshened myself up before returning to sit down next to her, she muttered.

'Won't be long now before we reach Holyhead.'

It was getting light when the sleepy crowd of women began waking up. With the children refreshed from sleep, began rubbing their eyes stretching their arms, before the shouting and playing began, running around seats in and out of the doorways, being told off with a cuff around the ears, followed by the noise of crying. Above all the hubbub somebody yelled out.

'We are approaching the harbour entrance.'

This caused more commotion. Then Sgt. Galloway put in an appearance. Standing in front of us he swayed (not to the movement of the boat) grunted a sheepish.

'Good morning ladies.' That was met with frostiness from his wife.

The docking of the ship seemed to take ages before, with a final bump the ship stopped. Soon, an announcement advised. 'Gangways. Ready to disembark.'

In the mad rush to get off down the gangway. Much to my relief I lost the Galloway's. Accordingly I had performed my duty but what duty? That was a mystery to me. With my chattels in one hand and Caroline Mary cradled in my arm. I followed the party down the gangway and stepped onto the wet quayside of England. It was raining. Like one in a herd of lost sheep, I was swept along with the tide of women, still chatting merrily away making their way towards the waiting train. Jack had advised me. *"Do not worry yourself Sarah. Army personnel will be in charge during the crossing and the train journey to London, where GS wagons would transport us across London, to another station called Waterloo, then another train would take us on to Aldershot."* If said quickly all very simple. I had made the sea crossing, now for a long journey on the train stood waiting for its passengers with wide open doors.

An Army Orderly took my arm and ushered me to a carriage. Clambering up stepped in. Unfortunately I had not lost the Galloway's. There as large as life already sitting in the carriage, was Sgt. Galloway. He looked terrible, with a sheepish grin on his face, moving back from his window seat, he called out.

'Here Mrs Plant. You sit yourself down by me.'

This was the person I was supposed to be in charge of. But grateful for his presence of mind, thanked him. Other passengers behind pushed and shoved their way into the carriage. I was physically pushed into the seat by some youngsters, eager to get to the window, someone trod on my foot. Bodies were heaving luggage up into the string racks above our heads, before dumping themselves down in seats. Caroline Mary began crying with the pangs of hunger, she needed feeding. Taking no notice of others, I busied myself to feed her. After a while she satisfied fell asleep.

With a huge jolt the train left Holyhead station. it was quite misty and raining with streams of water running down the glass windows as we sped through the countryside. Seeing the fields pass by, warmed to the fact that it was much the same as back home, hilly and pleasant but not so green. Sgt. Galloway, who appeared to have sobered up a little, turned to me and with a beery breath informed me.

'Mrs Plant the next station we pass is a tiny station, but it has the longest nameplate in the world.' As we came into the station he nudged me. 'This is it.' He seemed an authority upon the subject. 'There you see'…He pointed to the start of the station nameplate.

LLANFAIRPWLLGWNGYLLGOGERYCHWYRNDROBWLLLLANTYSILCOGOGOGOH

He was right, passing through this tiny station, its nameplate stretched from one end of the platform to the other. (Apparently only the Welsh can pronounce it), continuing said...'Now the next point of interest is the Menai Straits Bridge. We have to go over that before we get into England.' I was baffled.

'Oh. I thought since we left Holyhead. We were in England?' He laughed.

'No Mrs Plant. Holyhead is in Anglesey. I'll let you know when we are in England.'

The only thing I knew about Wales was Frank Lewis was Welsh and lived there somewhere. The sound of the train's wheels changed to a low continuous rumble prompting Sgt. Galloway.

'This is the Menai Bridge.'

Looking out of the window all I could see far below was a great expanse of water. I became uneasy, my knees began shaking as we crossed the bridge. The hills behind us were getting further away. I turned to him and asked.

'What was that place back there then?' He replied.

'Anglesey. It's part of Wales.'

I was none the wiser. (Just shows how much I've travelled!) Apart from snatches of conversation between us. The strained silence between the Sergeant and his wife did not help the passage of our journey. Whilst others were sleeping I resorted to gazing out of the window. For miles and miles on one side it was coastline, with mountains on the other, until finally approaching a built up area. Sgt. Galloway, who had done nothing but snore woke up, with his elbow nudged me and said.

'Hey! Mrs Plant. This is Chester. We are in England now.'

The train made a brief stop then continued. I looked out of the window, seeing nothing of interest as it passed through dirty stations, whose names I can't remember apart from Crewe where it did stop. Sgt. Galloway got out and brought back a welcome cup of tea. After Crewe the scenery became large black hills, which Sgt. Galloway informed me.

'Those Mrs. Plant are slag heaps from the coalmines.'

Later on passing large round brick shaped objects with many tall black chimney's billowing out black smoke? I was informed.

'Pottery Kiln's. Where they fire pottery pieces.'

My impression of England was, it looked nothing like the green fields of Ireland, I was already missing. At one stage I lulled off to sleep, only to wake with my head, leant against Sgt. Galloway's shoulder. Who had woke me up with his snoring, fit to wake up the dead. Shaking myself awake, tended to my baby before resuming my gaze out of the window, my thoughts drifting over what Jack had told me: *He had written to his mother advising her of the time the train to Aldershot would leave Waterloo. She had advised him she wanted to meet me there. It would be my first time to meet anyone of Jack's family, and it would be very brief at that! Jack had only shown me a photo of his parents, so I did not know what to expect.* I became concerned and apprehensive, about the forthcoming meeting. With a start I came too, I had fallen asleep beside the snoring form of Sgt. Galloway. Realising I had no hold of Caroline Mary.. Immediately Mrs. Galloway said.

'It's all right Mrs Plant. I took her while you slept, she too has been asleep what a good little girl she is.'

She had Caroline Mary cradled in her arms. Relieved I began to rouse myself and thanked her for her kindness, however much to my gratitude she kept hold of her. Worn out from the train journey I eased my aching body as best I could, my arms ached from constantly carrying my baby since the Curragh. After a while Mrs. Galloway, passed her back over the snoring form of Sgt. Galloway. Again I thanked her for her assistance.

69

As we approached London, all I could see were brick walls, dirty windows blackened from dust and smoke, not a pretty sight to my eyes. Some of the other passengers having already heaved down their cases, stood impatiently waiting to get off. The train slowly clanked into Euston station and came to a gentle halt. Like a stampede of horses, they surged toward the carriage door, barging into each other as they dragged their suitcases and other chattels out. I waited until the last person was clear of the door, then moved myself, hesitating at the door looked out upon a spread of women children and in amongst them some soldiers. Looking up I was taken aback by the sheer size of the station, with the black smoke almost cutting out the daylight filtering through the glass canopy above. The smell of acrid smoke and steam filled the air amidst the noise of chuffing trains banging doors and the clanking of moving trains had me thinking: *My God this station is huge whatever is London like?*

Taking a firm hold of my baby I stepped down onto the platform. Immediately engulfed in the tide of humanity that swept me along towards the far end, where stood by a barrier. An Army orderly shouted out instructions that I did not hear as we were herded into some formation, and at a quick pace we moved out of the station towards a line of waiting GS wagons. A Sergeant barking out orders, instructed all to climb into them.

I with a young baby was singled out and allowed on first and sent to the front to sit on some boxes, others clambered in behind and settled down for the next part of the journey. When all appeared to be on board, the motor stuttered into life and the wagon moved off into the streets of London. As we trundled through its maze, now and then I had fleeting glances of its streets. People were everywhere, horses and carts mingled with Omnibus vehicles, sights I had never seen before. We crossed a bridge and someone shouted. 'HURRAH FOR OLD FATHER THAMES.' It was greeted with more cheers. I did not have a clue what they were cheering about. When we came to a halt, I enquired.

'Why have we stopped?' Somebody answered.

'Waterloo duck's. All get out.'

First in last out, a young soldier helped me down. Aghast I looked at what confronted me. Waterloo station was no comparison to Euston. It was clean, almost new with a wide stone flight of stairs ascending up to an enormous stone arched entrance. With little chance to admire it, someone grabbed my arm guided me up and through the entrance of the archway into a vast concourse. The noise. A repeat of Euston with the smell of acrid smoke tainting the air. The person guided me across a roadway under a rather large four-faced square clock suspended from high above. It's hands pointed to twenty-five past ten. The orderlies ushered us onwards, passing many gateways to other platforms before we joined a group of people, apparently waiting for us. More army families with children and dogs on leads. Where they came from I did not know? But some carried birdcages. The orderlies barking out orders got us on the move, herded like cattle to another platform and onto a waiting train. During my guided tour through the station. I had tried to spot anyone I might have recognised not that I had a clue who I was looking for? It would have made no difference, we were. 'En-Route. No stopping for anyone. I was bundled into a carriage, quickly glancing around saw no Galloway's. I had finally lost them, the other passengers were families we had just met. The train jolted into motion and we were off, next stop Aldershot. My baby began to cry so I fed her en-route from Holyhead, apart from some snacks our refreshments had been meagre. However this group were more organised they had more food than I had seen for two days, and it was generously offered around including me. With reluctance but thankfully took a sandwich, I was famished, the lady next to me took charge of my baby, while I ate some buttered bread then handed her back commenting

'Lovely little ducks ain't she?' I replied.

'Yes. She is quite good.' She questioned.

'Your Irish ain't yer?'

'Yes. Just over from the Curragh Camp.'

'Humph! Don't talk to me about the Curragh. My ole man spent all his money over there? Backing the bleedin' Gee Gee's. Now we're on our way out to India. Where I'm told they haven't got any horses only bleedin' elephant's! I can't see them racing them bleedin' big things around can you? So I'm thinking, my ole man can't spend his money out there can he?' I offered a reply.

'Oh. That would be wise then.'

She didn't respond and continued her conversation with her friends. The journey to Aldershot did not take long, by the time we arrived I was really feeling the pangs of hunger. Amid shouts and the constant banging of carriage doors the platform began to fill up with families and hordes of children, most of who were crying. I glanced around and once again it appeared that I, was the only one with a babe in arms, and after the tedious journey from Ireland I was rather dishevelled and very sorrowful. We were herded out of the station, where several GS wagons and an ambulance were parked waiting for us. Someone was put into the ambulance and that left, whilst the other families we had joined up with were ordered into the GS wagons. Leaving the Irish contingent stood waiting for some instructions. Nobody seemed to know what was happening. I thought: *This is a good start.* Then an Officer drove up in a vehicle. Getting out began speaking with someone in the Indian party, before singling out a Sergeant in our party. Had a brief conversation with him then got into his vehicle and drove off, followed by the GS wagons in line.

We stood there waiting for something to happen. The families getting very agitated, we still waited. A women's voice shouted out.

'WHAT YOU LOT OF SERGEANTS DOING ABOUT IT THEN?' Back came the reply.

'Waiting for transport. It will be here shortly. Just be patient.'

Half an hour later the same GS wagons returned, orders were shouted out and we climbed into the GS wagons and set off on our way to the Garrison Camp. When we arrived the wagons stopped beside a parade ground, we got down and huddled into a group of about forty-five women and dozens of children. By then all the children appeared to be screaming their heads off, with my baby adding her pitiful squawks to the chorus, before she too started screaming her head off. She was in need of feeding. Stood amongst the group of Sergeants. I spotted Sgt. Galloway. He spotted me, escorting his wife and daughter they approached me. His only comment was.

'Sorry Mrs Plant. We got separated at Waterloo. By the way my wife is called Rose.' Nodding to Rose. I assumed I was back in charge of what? All I could say was.

'Oh! Don't worry about it.'

Two Sergeants left to sort things out. After a while they returned. One of them spoke.

'Ladies! There appears to be a mix up. No one knows anything about this Irish party coming to the Garrison Camp. They are trying to sort something out. Just be patient.'

Word began to filter through our group of the pandemonium in the Orderly Room, caused by our arrival. Sometime later a Quartermaster appeared and politely informed all.

'Attention please! There has been a mix up somewhere. We were not informed of the Irish party arriving at camp. Unfortunately there are only four quarters available for all of you!'

We stood there dumbfounded unable to do anything about our treatment. Now there was something to talk about. The women were far from happy, their chattering turned to concern and anger. Some of the children were playing up, only to receive a swift cuff around the ear from a frustrated mother. I too was worried for our keep. Little did I imagine the problems I was to encounter during my stay in Aldershot. I shall never forget it as long as I live. Arriving with no accommodation for me and a baby. Stood alongside a Barracks square, somewhere in England. I prayed something would happen. Just then a QMS came marching by, he halted shouted.

'GALLOWAY!' Taken by surprise Sgt. Galloway walked towards the QMS. Like two long lost brothers, they greeted each other. His wife Rose bitterly muttered.

'Oh my God! Not him? He hasn't seen him since France. Bloody typical. A drinking mate.' Anyway Sgt. Galloway and the QMS came back to Rose, after exchanging pleasantries. The conversation changed to our present plight. Sgt. Galloway asked.

'Is it possible to find two quarters?'…Almost in a whisper they conversed before, the QMS spoke quietly to us.

'Stay where you are. I'll go and investigate the situation.' Leaving us marched away on his errand of mercy towards some buildings in the far distance.. We waited for hours, until some Army Orderlies came along, began grouping families into fours, including us. Sgt. Galloway approached one of the orderlies told him.

'QMS Satterly. Is sorting something out and we are to wait for his return and further orders.'

They accepted what he said and moved the rest of the families away to be accommodated. Caroline Mary had not stopped crying. I had tried to nurse her, but she needed more than feeding. From out of one of the dwellings. A woman appeared carrying a tray with a teapot and cups, she walked purposely towards us and when close enough said.

'Here drink this, I've been watching you lot all afternoon, but could not bring tea out to the whole party. But I can manage with your little party.' "What an Angel."

With my baby finally asleep, I sat down on the ground to drink the tea. The Galloway's were not talking. Furthermore we had become homeless, as we waited for the return of QMS Satterly. It seemed that nobody cared, it was none of his or her business. I was positive that Jack would never have let this happen. He would have sorted it out. Even then it never crossed my mind, for the next six years the pattern in my life was to follow a similar course. First the rumours then at a moment's notice, moving from one place to another. It was a case of either before or, after Jack but never together. With the addition of a second, followed by a third child, always living out of a suitcase. Now, reflecting back if, I had had an easy life in the Army, I would not have been able to relate to these incidents. It was almost twilight, when QMS Satterly returned. Only then was I formally introduced to him.

'Look. I have managed to find two separate quarters. But be warned. Nobody is to know. It's best you keep to yourselves and for God's sake. Do not mention where your quarters are.'

Handing a key to each of us, he led the way towards some quarters, stopping outside one, he said.

'Mrs Plant! This is yours. Bill, yours is the very last one further down.'

Thanking both of them they left me. Turning the key in the lock I entered the forbidden quarters. In the gloom of the fading light saw a little entrance hall, very grateful to be inside I put the suitcase down and quietly shut the door and laid my baby on the floor. I needed light and the best place to make for was the scullery at the rear. In the gloom I groped towards a doorway and spotted a white sink, at least there was water something I needed. Turning on the tap, a few dribbles came out with a gasp of air. 'No Water.' Puzzled, I began groping around for matches, but did not find any, what a predicament. No lights, no fire or water, but at least a roof over our heads. In the looming darkness, I felt really depressed at the outcome of my first night in Aldershot. Groping my way back to where I had left the baby. Suddenly a knock on the door. Hesitating, I thought the QMS was back? Avoided the little bundle on the floor, in my haste nearly fell over the case. Opening the door a woman's voice said.

'Hello in there. I know you have no lights or water. Take these.' Three candles and a box of matches was thrust into my hands the voice continued… 'You have a baby in there as well. Haven't you?' Cautiously I replied.

'Yes. I have.'

'I'll fetch you some hot water to bath the baby. I suppose you could do with something to eat? I have made you some tea and a sandwich. I'll fetch them along as well.'

'I certainly could, thank you so much your very kind.'

The mysterious person left and I closed the door. In my haste to light a candle, fully opened the box of matches spilling them onto the floor. Immediately down on my knees, I groped around for a match, finding two struck one and guided it towards the candlewick, which spluttered into life. From its faint glow saw my baby lying like a rag doll, the case I had knocked over was lying close to a staircase. Standing up, returned to the scullery making for the sink, turned the tap again nothing. The woman was right. With the candle as my only source of light, I gazed around in its flickering light. Another knock made my heart jump, leaving the scullery hurried back to the front door and opened it.

'Hello. It's me again. Here you are, a cup of tea and a sandwich, I've put another kettle on, it won't be long. Then you can bath the baby. Back soon!' She echoed as she left.

I took the steaming cup of tea, the plate with two sandwiches. Closing the door sat down next to my baby and like a gannet, gratefully devoured sandwiches and tea. Another knock on the door had me struggling to my feet, the mysterious woman, returned with a bowl of warm water. Gratefully I took it.

'Oh thank you. You're an angel.' A quick reply.

'No. Angels are made in heaven. See you tomorrow morning.'

Puzzled by her last remark. I placed the bowl on the floor away from the door and closed it. In the glow of the candle I saw the other two candles lying on the floor amongst the scattered matches. Needing more light picking up a candle lit it from the other flame, as it spluttered into life, gathered up the matches put them in the box and into my coat pocket. Returning to the scullery, spilling wax onto the washboard, set the candle in position. Returning to the front door for the third candle and the case took them to the scullery, then the bowl of water, sorted out a towel and some clean items of clothing laid them ready on the table. Last thing retrieving my baby, bathed and dressed her and had a cats lick myself.

With a lighted candle I ventured upstairs and found a bed without blankets, spilling wax left the lighted candle on the floor returned downstairs to pick up my baby. Blew out one of the candles and ventured back upstairs, where having wrapped her in a nappy gently placed her on the bed, taking off my coat laid down beside her, drawing the coat over both of us. The last thing I remembered was extinguishing the candle. I slept the sleep of exhaustion.

Someone trying to knock down the front door woke me. Daylight was seeping through a window covered by net curtains. I lay there wondering where am I? Then I remembered, we were not supposed to be in these quarters. As the banging continued, I was terrified to go down to open the door. In the distance I heard a woman's voice.

'Hello. Coooee. Hello in there.'

Swinging my legs over the edge of the bed, knocked over the candle before creeping to the top of the stairs, hesitating. I looked down towards the door, a chink of light was shining through the open letterbox. Another couple of bangs then the rattle of the letterbox, a voice yelled.

'HELLO IN THERE I'M YOUR NEXT-DOOR NEIGHBOUR. WOULD YOU LIKE SOME TEA AND WATER TO BATH THE BABY?'

Thinking: *It must be the mysterious woman from last night.* That made me move still dressed but barefooted, I made my way downstairs opening the door.

'Hello. I'm Elizabeth by name. Just call me Betty! Everyone else does. Can I come in?

'Er. Yes. Please do.'

The crying from upstairs had me tearing back up again, found her snuggled under my coat, she was Okay, just hungry, picking her up carried her back downstairs to re-join 'Betty.' Stood inside the doorway with a big welcome smile, her blonde hair tied back into a bun, wearing a flowered pinafore she was far taller than me.

'Aah. Baby all right?' I suggested.

'Just hungry.'

'Look. I've just made a pot of tea. Do come next door it will be more comfortable.'

She was already out of the door. In bare feet I sheepishly followed her into her house and through to her scullery, where she sat me down at the table poured me a cup of tea, she asked.

'Mrs? What's your name?'

'Plant. Sarah Plant'

'Look. The other sergeant's wife moved out of there two weeks ago. She is off to India with her husband. Everything was turned off so I knew nothing was on. I'll prepare you something to eat while you wash and feed your baby?'

'Oh. It was you. I wondered who the mysterious lady was. Thank you so much. I don't want to cause you any trouble.'

'No trouble, use the sink, hot water's on the stove.'

We both set too on our chores, she preparing food while I bathed and fed my baby, satisfied she fell asleep. The smell of cooked food had my stomach aching. Betty placed a plate covered with bacon tomatoes fried egg and bread on the table in front of me, she suggested.

'Here let me take her and lay her down in the next room, while you eat.'

I looked down at a full plate, I did not know where to start, but did. Having not eaten for two days I was famished attacked it with knife and fork, by the time she returned back had almost eaten half the contents,.

'She's fast asleep. You enjoy your meal. Would you like some more?'

I ashamed to admit it did, but shook my head. Hospitality is one thing, greed is another. She prepared another plate and sitting opposite me began to eat.

'Where did you come from?' I thought: *Here we go, question time.* I related all the facts to her, She was aghast as I relayed my problems. She asked.

'Who is your Quarter Master?'

'I don't know. We are not supposed to be in these quarters.'

'Not entitled? Well.I won't say anything, what are you going to do then?' I answered with some misgivings.

'I'm not really sure. But I will go down to see Rose the other lady and see what can be arranged.'

'That sounds sensible. Look all I can offer is water, lights and bedding, if you want anything else, just knock.' I thanked her and asked.

'Betty may I ask you about your comment last night. Angels are only made in heaven. It's Irish isn't it? '

'Oh that. The catholic priest here in Aldershot gave me that one. I questioned.

'I take it you're a catholic?'

'Yes. I go to mass on Sunday in Aldershot.' An opportunity not to be missed stated.

'I would like to attend mass.'

'Well. Next Sunday I will take you.'

'Thank you. Do you have children of your own?'

'Yes two. A boy and a girl but they are at school now.' Deciding to find Rose, I excused myself and thanked Betty.

'While you're gone. I will sort out the bedding I promised you. Just pop in on your way back.'

Taking my sleeping baby returned to my hovel, to collect my coat and shoes, quietly left. Turning right I walked to the last house knocked. Waited. No response. Bending down I called through the letterbox.... 'Rose are you in there? It's me, Sarah Plant.'...I looked through the letterbox at a pair of eyes glaring back at me....'Rose it's me.' she opened the door slightly.

'Quick come in.' I entered like a dose of salts, she shut the door quietly...'Am I glad to see you. Come through to the scullery, I have tea, Bill went out for some.'

It was obvious to me Luck was on her side they had the essentials. I told her I had nothing in the quarters. No light, fire or water. Telling her about Betty's kindness. Rose was concerned suggested I share her accommodation, but sleep in my own quarters. I did not have a choice and offered to do the cooking. Both agreeing to keep quiet about our illegitimate quarters until a QM began asking questions.

Next on our agenda was shopping in Aldershot. To avoid any prying eyes, which might report us to the authorities. As inconspicuously as possible Rose, her daughter, I with Caroline Mary in my arms (as I always did) went into Aldershot. .However, Caroline Mary was getting heavier and awkward to carry, the answer to buy a cheap pram, so I bought one. We purchased all other goods, returned pushing the pram with Mary and Rose's little girl Sheila in the pram, surrounded by shopping. Back at the quarters, like a pair of fugitives quickly unloaded the provisions and took them inside including the pram, leaving no evidence outside. We sorted out the provisions packing them away. A quick tour of her quarters proved they were the same as mine, two bedrooms upstairs but her beds had piles of sheets and blankets on top, which Bill must have acquired. Downstairs was a small sitting room, a scullery well equipped with cooking pans, plates, knives and forks, with privy outside including lights, heating and water. Comparing their quarters to mine they were well off. I cooked lunch after which, I decided to return to my hovel to prepare for the night. Whilst pushing the pram out of her doorway, I noticed a curtain behind a window fall back into place. Like a fugitive in a strange world, with tears streaming down my face I ran pushing the pram back to Betty's. Knocking on her door she opened it.

'Whatever's the matter? What's happened?'...I stood there sobbing. She urged...'Come on in, I'll make a cup of tea.'

Ushering me inside, she took Caroline Mary out of the pram gave her to me, guided me to the scullery, sitting me down at the table she made tea as I composed myself, then blurted out my soul, disillusioned and distraught with the new quarters, with nobody to turn to and nowhere to go. Betty, having listened to my tale of woe, reassured me that something would turn up. I eventually left her, to take the bedding with me next door to prepare for our night's sleep, whilst she looking after my sleeping baby, having finished returned next door to wash change and feed my baby before returning to a silent house. I too was very tired and ready for sleep. It was still light when I lay down next to my baby, slipping in between crisp sheets was asleep in no time. I woke in darkness with no idea of the time, as I lay thinking: *Of the dire situation I was in, I had to change my outlook, look on the bright side, it would soon be resolved?* I began to sob. eventually succumbed to sleep.

The crying of Caroline Mary woke me up. Outside it was light the start of another day of being a fugitive. I could do nothing in the quarters except sleep, make up my bed, keep the place tidy, and with water from next door use the meagre washing facilities relying on candles for lighting. Betty was a real. 'Brick' She even washed the bed linen and babies clothes for me. I did the cooking down at Rose's and between the three of us, we developed a bond. No doubt on her part, Betty had spread a good word amongst the neighbours, they nodding to us. We appeared no longer classed as fugitives. Obviously, there was little interest in us, even in the eyes of the Army!

On Sunday Betty suggested, I accompany her to mass, we walked into Aldershot, I pushing my new pram was quite happy discussing my life back in Ireland and my own time in the services, she surprised, showed great interest. In the meantime Sergeant Galloway had made contact with Jack in Dublin. Had informed him that: *"I had been fixed up with quarters."* Obviously did not tell the full story as he handed me a letter from Jack, which had arrived at the office. Jack was happy that I had "quarters?" Informing me of the mix up with his mother who along with his sister did make the trip to Waterloo. They waited two hours at the station before finding out our party had left on an earlier train. Responding, I wrote back and told him the full story of our "quarters."

Thursday was allowance day, I arrived at the Paymasters office to receive my allowance. The Paymaster produced an official looking document, I think it was 'Married Quarters Allowance Statement of Payment.' He asked who I was, where my husband was serving? I gave him the correct information, he passed over the sheet muttered.

'Dublin Eh? Just state your husband's Name Number and Rank sign there please.'

That was it. I received my pay, nobody enquired about anything else. Another letter from Jack informed me the on-going fighting in Dublin was more skirmishes than anything else. Nothing was mentioned about my predicament in my squalid quarters, instead he warned me. *"Not to say a word to anyone about the quarters?"* As far as he was concerned I had a roof over my head and could manage, anyway Jack knew I should not be in Quarters

On the third Sunday, upon returning from our trip to mass, Betty left me to take Caroline Mary out of the pram, when a voice hailed me.

'Hello Sarah Plant.' Alarm bells rang, fear gripped at my stomach. Guiltily I turned around looking up to see the friendly face of Mary Wright.

'Sarah. I've found you at last. What a job I've had. No one knew who or where you were. Or if you had turned up.'

My fear turned to pleasure. At last something good had happened. I was so surprised all I could say was.

'Mary. How did you find me?'

'Oh. When I was at the last Sergeants Mess social. I overheard a certain Sergeant Galloway's conversation, talking loudly about another Sergeant's wife. A little Irish lady who cooked their meals and what a fine cook she was. I interrupting his conversation asked him what her name was?' Suspiciously he queried.

'Why do you want to know?'

'Sergeant. I'm trying to find a Mrs Plant.'

'That's her name. Mrs Plant.' When he mentioned your name I just knew it had to be you.

'Where can I find her?' Sergeant Galloway became suspicious at my questions and declined to reveal where you were. Anyway I persisted until reluctantly he told me. Betty returned to interrupt our brief conversation. Introducing them I stated.

'Mary was a QM's wife back in the Curragh camp.' Betty, seeing my visitor was not a threat suggested.

'Sarah. Why don't you invite Mary into your quarters. I will make a pot of tea and bring it in. I thanked her asked.

'Mary. What a delight it is to see you. Do please come inside for a chat.' I beckoned her to follow me through into the scullery. She obviously noticed the 'Bare' state of the place. She shocked at the state I was living in immediately started to question me.

'Sarah. Who's your Quartermaster?'

'I don't know?'

'How long has this been going on? '

'Since I arrived here.' I then explained what had happened and how we had come by the quarters.

'Right leave this to me. You stay here. I'm going straight down to the mess. To see the Quartermaster Sergeant. Number sixty-six Centre square. Isn't it?' Cautiously I replied.

'Yes. But please Mary don't upset anything.'

Mary left in a right old paddy. I sat there waiting for Betty to return trying not to worry about the outcome. Returning with the tea Betty asked suspiciously.

'Where's that other lady?'

'Gone down to the Mess. To sort my problem out.'

'You should not have told her anything. '

'No. Mary is a good friend of mine. She is just like that.' We sat and drank the tea, Betty, obviously concerned asked.

'Are you sure she'll do the right thing Sarah?'

'Yes. I'm sure. If anyone can sort it out. Mary can.' We waited drinking tea until much later Mary returned.

'I've spoken to the RQMS. Mind you outside the mess. I told him about your plight. You with a tiny baby without water, heating, lighting, generally without anything. Would he kindly do something about it? The RQMS was totally unaware of any problem and assured me he would arrange for something to be done that day. So Sarah. Just sit tight something will happen today.'

We continued talking until she bade me cheerio, she would return later. Grateful for her help I offered my 'thanks.'

After she left I went straight down to Rose, to explain what had happened and to tell her, she would have to cook the day's meal. I returned back to my quarters, not attempting to go out, waiting until something happened. It was about six o clock in the evening, when a knock on the door had me jumping out of my skin.

'Who is it I enquired.'

'Mrs Plant . Open the door please.'

Cautiously I opened the door to be confronted by a soldier with a barrow load of coal and wood. I let him in. He turned the water and gas on, before lighting the fire he questioned.

'Why didn't you complain about your situation earlier?'

As it was too complicated, I didn't go into any details, but thanked him from the bottom of my heart. My immediate problem had been solved but not for long. News travels fast. The other women in the Irish party. Still living in their cramped quarters had somehow found out about my change in circumstances. They aggrieved, created a fuss. The following Thursday. I went to the Paymaster's Office to collect my allowance. I received my pay together with a bonus.

'Aah! Sergeant Plant's wife. You are not allowed quarters and as of now you have two weeks notice to get out.'

Shocked and dismayed by this latest order. I pleaded... 'But I have nowhere to go.'....It fell on deaf ears....' Mrs Plant.Orders are Orders..'

I wish I had kept quiet about the whole affair. Mary Wright had tried to sort out something better for me. It wasn't her fault, but the damage had been done. Although Jack could do nothing about my situation I sent him a letter and one to Mother, who sent me five pounds for my fare back home. Even Mary took up my case to no avail, she could do no more. I had heat light and water but no other necessities, just a roof over my head. As far as the Army was concerned. I was not officially in quarters. The Galloway's had been granted permission to stay in their quarters. Knowing my predicament they hoping I would also eventually be granted permission to stay. We continued with our previous agreement. I put in a request to be posted back to Ireland, which was refused. The Army's excuse was. 'The men will soon be posted back to England'. The only good news I received was from mother. My sister Mary, then living in Plymouth, had given birth to her second child, a little girl named Patricia.

It became a regular occurrence, every two weeks I received a verbal. Notice to Quit. Four months passed, until one pay day the RQMS finally gave me one week's notice. He had orders to evict me out of the quarters on to the street to find alternative accommodation. I sat there flabbergasted, I did not know what to say. I scratched away at my signature to receive my weekly dues then left the office. Outside my mind in a whirl, the only thing I could think of doing was going along to the Admin office to see if they would send a wire to Jack. The duty orderly wanted to know what message. He told me to write it down on the piece of paper he handed me. I scribbled a brief note and passed it back to him. Looking at it quizzically he said.

'I'll get this away as soon as possible.'

I was in no fit state to argue anymore with anyone. With a week's notice tucked under my belt I returned to Betty's with my dreaded news. Over a pot of tea we discussed what I could do. 'Nothing!' Just wait for an answer back from Jack. I informed Rose of the morning's happenings. She too did not have an answer to give me. While shopping in Aldershot I sent another wire to Jack.

COME OVER TAKE THE BABY AND ME BACK HOME TO MOTHERS STOP

Returning to my quarters. I stayed in waiting for a wire, which came late in the afternoon.

APPLIED FOR COMPASSIONATE LEAVE LETTER TO FOLLOW STOP

At last something was happening. I might be going back home. That final week found me at my wits end, in anguish I was biting my nails until they were down to the quick, unaware of what the future held for us. Living in accommodation outside the security of a barracks. Monday, Jack's letter arrived, but it was not the news I wanted, same old story. The Army would not allow it, he was refused. Instead they allowed him a measly weekend's compassionate leave. To travel over from Ireland, collect me along with Caroline Mary and take us to his mother's home in Putney. Then return straight back. With this latest bit of news. I went next door to speak with Betty who offered to let me stay with her the last couple of nights. At least I had somewhere to stay. My biggest worry was the answer I would get at the Paymaster's Office. Whether I could remain in the quarters, until Jack arrived? Wednesday I received a wire from Jack.

ARRIVING EARLY SATURDAY BE READY TO MOVE IMMEDIATELY STOP

Thursday I duly reported to collect my allowance and was told to hand over the keys. The QM in charge looked crestfallen but the Army is the Army and Orders are Orders. An Orderly was handed the keys to accompany me back to collect my possessions. I really felt much more like a fugitive, having to walk back accompanied by this young Orderly, but at least he had the forethought to walk beside me. I blamed it all on Jack's age which had turned the tide against me. The Galloway's remained insitu. It was I who had become the scapegoat. I took my meagre possessions and moved in with Betty until the Saturday. Betty provided breakfast and I was ready by nine. Mary and Rose arrived to say their farewells, then Jack arrived in a GS Wagon. Jumping down his face creased in a grin, as if he had not a care in the world. I burst into tears taking me in his arms kissed me saying.

'Sarah. Stop your weeping. On your feet soldier. C'mon climb up. Let's be off.' He was in no mood to dawdle about. While I said my farewells, he loaded the pram, and my meagre possessions onto the wagon. Within five minutes we were off on our way.

Aldershot not to be forgotten.

CHAPTER ELEVEN
LONDON - PUTNEY

Once on the train, Jack fussed over me then took hold of Caroline Mary, making a great fuss over her. After a while he suggested.

'Look Sarah, her names a bit of a mouthful why don't we just call her Mary?'

'Well if you don't mind? I suppose it's okay.'

We had been separated for five long months and had much to talk about. We discussed, the misery and anguish I endured over the past months with no prospects of returning home. He briefed me on news from mother, the on-going unrest in Ireland, Consequently Jack had written to his mother about the unfortunate situation we were in. She had invited. *'Bring her home here.'* That was where we were bound for right then. However, when I showed concern about meeting his parents for the first time he reassured me.

'Sarah, please do not fret, you will all get on well together. It's a big house and besides Ma and Pop's, there is only Rose and Len at home. Alf when on leave from the Merchant Navy is an infrequent visitor, so there's ample room for us. Don't worry you'll be fine you wait and see.'

We were still deep in discussion when the train arrived at Waterloo, where we had to change. Jack pushing the pram had us running, from one platform to the next to catch the train to Putney, with no time to spare we just made it. Once on our way, I made a comment about the size of London.

'Jack. I'm flabbergasted with the size of London. I thought Dublin was big.' He just laughed.

'Sarah ducks. You have not seen anything of London. I was born in Limehouse, about four miles from here, it's on the other side of the City.'... As he chatted on about London, the train stopped at a few stations before we arrived at Putney...'Here we are Sarah, nearly home. You carry Mary, I'll push the pram.'

Slinging his small-pack onto his back, he placed my chattels in the pram, opened the door and manouvered the pram out down on to the platform. With Jack pushing the pram, with me doubling to keep up with him, we followed other passengers down a long covered ramp, through a barrier out onto the main road. He stopped, taking Mary away from me placed her in the Pram arranging my chattels around her.

'C'mon along Sarah, It's only a short walk. You push the pram.'

With no experience of walking along a London Street, people rushing about like demented things. I quickly became aware of the noise of the traffic, the hustle and bustle of London's way of life. As horses and carts leisurely moved along the road, their owners shouting out their wares, With me pushing the pram I was almost running, my little legs going like pistons trying to keep up with Jack, as we careered along this road (Putney High Street) joining an army of men walking in the same direction, wearing suits, boots and flat caps. Above the noise Jack shouted.

'FULHAM MUST BE PLAYING AT HOME?' I responded.

'FULHAM? I THOUGHT THIS WAS PUTNEY. PLAYING WHAT?'

'FOOTBALL SARAH, FOOTBALL, FULHAM'S MY LOCAL TEAM BUT WE'RE IN PUTNEY.'

Mystified, I kept running until Jack, taking hold of the pram's handle guided it into a side street, away from the crowds. Pushing the pram down along some other streets into another main road, which I found out later was Putney Bridge Road. Careering along he finally stopped outside a large house.

'Here we are Sarah, this is home.' He went up and knocked on the door, turning to me grinning knocked again. A pause.... then a woman opened the door.

'JACK'...The woman shouted then shouted into the depths of the house...'POPS, JACK'S HERE WITH HIS MISSUS AND BABY.' I assumed she was his mother.

Lots of hugs and kisses, then Jack's father appeared, handshakes were now in order. I the bystander observed these formalities and took Mary out of the pram. Jack's mother was similar in build to my mother, with a cheery face wearing glasses, her wispy greying hair was pulled back in a bun. She had a flowered coloured blouse with the sleeves rolled up, a black skirt and wore a long white apron. His father was reasonably tall with a shock of greying hair smartly parted in the middle. Beneath his broad nose was a big grey walrus styled moustache. Black trousers and a

collar-less shirt wearing a waistcoat that he was busily trying to button up, Jack turned and came back to me taking Mary away from my arms said.

'C'mon Sarah, don't be shy come and meet Mum and Dad'...Taking hold of my hand he almost pulled me towards them, grinning all over his face muttered.... 'Mum, Dad, this is my wife Sarah, and our baby Mary, your Granddaughter.'

They both welcomed me with open arms. My new Mother-in- law wrapped her arms around me, kissed me on the cheek said. 'Sarah at long last. It's so lovely to meet you, please call me Miria. You're very welcome to stay with us. Now don't you worry, Jacks told me all about the problem. You'll be happy and safe here.' Then father -in -law took my hands and said.

'Welcome Sarah you're just as Jack described you, beautiful and petite. You just call me Pops like everyone else. ' Bending over kissed me on the cheek.

I noticed both had blue eyes, his father's more piercing than the smiling blue eyes of his mother's. At a guess they were both about the same age as my parents. By this time Miria had taken Mary from Jack.

'What a lovely baby Mary is. No baby like Jack's baby. Come on inside the pair of you.' They were obviously delighted to meet Mary and me.

Warmed by their lovely welcome, my previous fears disappeared. After eighteen months I had been stupid to worry about meeting such nice and welcoming in-laws. Miria led the way into the house whilst Pops closed the door behind us, Jack holding my elbow guided me through a hallway to a kitchen. I was sat down at the table, entering behind us Pops ordered.

'Tea Miria.'

'I was just going to do that. I'm sure they both need one.'

Pops took up a stance in front of the stove, his waistcoat now undone displayed braces and a belt around his middle, a gold watch chain dangled limply out of a side pocket. There were creases in his trouser legs, which stopped short of a pair of well-polished shiny boots. Jack began talking to his father as Miria passed Mary back to me and busied herself making tea, pouring water from the already boiling kettle into a large teapot before placing both back on the stove top. Miria spoke to me.

'Sarah Jack told me about the problems you had at Aldershot. I'm afraid I did not understand all of it, can you explain what did happen?'

I began to relate my tale of woe from when I first left Ireland. As Miria poured out the tea and handed them out. We all laughed about our so-called meeting at Waterloo station. Just then a loud banging on the front door made me jump. Miria said.

'That will be Jack's sister Rose, back from shopping. Jack you go and let her in. That will surprise her.' Jack dutifully left the parlour.

There was a small commotion in the hallway, before Jack returned carrying two shopping bags, with his sister behind him. She was about the same height as me with fairish hair and a warm smile. Placing the shopping bags on the floor he said.

'Rose' this is my wife Sarah.' Getting up I said.

'Hello. I'm very pleased to meet you Rose.' Grinning she just like Jack greeted me.

'At last and about time too, it's very nice to meet you Sarah. In his letters Jack has told me all about you.'

I warmed to her hospitality and we were to get on well together. When we had finished tea and eaten some food. Miria took me and showed me where everything was. I was to share the room with Rose. A little crib was placed close to the bed, which Miria said. 'She had borrowed from a neighbour.' Then further banging on the door had Miria saying.

'Oh, that will be Len back from watching Fulham. Now then Sarah don't you take any cheek from Len, give him a clip around the ear. You come down with me and I'll introduce you to him.' Leaving the bedroom we went down to a noisy commotion in the parlour. As we entered Miria said.

'Len, this is Sarah Jack's wife.' With a cheeky grin he muttered.

'Nice ter meet yer Mrs Plant.' He was the same height as me and thought: *He's tall for his age*. Turning back to Jack he continued talking. Miria took the baby from me, bathd and changed her, then handed her back for feeding. Afterwards she took her from me and cradled her in her arms. She looked so like Mother as she carried her upstairs to sleep. I felt very comfortable and conscious that here I had no worries. Unfortunately, that night Jack had to return to Ireland, we had spent little or no time together. Len left, whilst Rose disappeared upstairs, Pops taking hold of his watch glancing down gruffly said.

'Jack. Time for a wet before you go.' (Men's talk)

'Right o' Pops. I won't be long Sarah.' They left as Miria re-entered and said.

'Now Sarah, Jack told me all about the way your Mother took good care of him, whilst he was visiting, Now please tell me more about your home life.'

I talked about my home in Ireland, my mother, father and the rest of the family. Miria listening quietly to what I had to say, obviously understanding the way of our life, she said Sarah.

'If you need anything do not be afraid to ask. I understand you go to church on a Sunday don't you?' Surprised, I felt my heart was in my mouth. I was expecting trouble.

'Yes. I do.' ... 'Right don't worry yourself about it, I will take you along to the Catholic Church to-morrow morning. I'm sure you would like that wouldn't you?' ... 'Yes thank you I would, but I don't want to cause any trouble.'... 'Not a problem don't you worry your pretty little self about it.' We were interrupted by the return of the men Jack said.

'Sarah I'm sorry ducks. I know it was short but I have to leave now it was just to get you settled in with Ma. It won't be long before we leave Ireland for good I promise.'...Slinging his small pack onto his shoulders said his goodbyes to his parents adding...'Take care of Sarah for me.' Miria replied.

'Don't you worry about Sarah. We've already had a nice long chat, now you look after yourself and come back home safely to her.'

He bade me an affectionate goodbye and was gone. My heart went with him as I welled up, tears began rolling down my cheeks. Miria handed me a kerchief adding.

'Sarah take no notice of us. You have a good cry.'

Wiping the tears away I composed myself, fed Mary again, changed her, carried her upstairs and placed her in the crib. We talked for the rest of the evening, before I was packed off to bed. That night I slept contented with the knowledge another hurdle had been crossed. Early next morning Miria woke me .

81

'Come along Sarah if you want to go to church, get yourself ready. I'll see to the baby.' Lifting Mary from the cot took her downstairs. Quietly I dressed, left the bedroom with Rose still asleep. Downstairs a cup of tea was on the table. Whilst I drank it Miria said.

'So you won't get lost the name of the church is. St. Simon Stock in Hazelwell Rd, but I'll walk with you to show you the way.' I thought: *So I wouldn't get lost? Which was very generous of her.* We left a sleeping house, as we walked Miria was full of information identifying certain land marks. The names of streets were all displayed at both ends, house numbers odd one side even the other.' We turned into the main street...'This is Putney High Street.' Gone was the hustle and bustle of the previous day, it was all but deserted. On the opposite side of the road a few people were walking along. We crossed over and she chatted about the shops in the street, I recognised the railway bridge we went under. A little further along, pointed to the street sign...'Sarah, Hazelwell Road, the church is over there.' Other people were heading towards it, I assumed were going to Mass. We entered the church, together, Miria sat down beside me she stayed throughout the mass. I was truly grateful for her presence, she understanding it was my very first day in London. On our return journey we walked past the house.

'Sarah I'll take you to Wandsworth Park it's by the river. That's it over there. Len plays football here and you'll be quite safe to bring Mary along here for a walk and sit down when it's sunny. As you can see our house is just across the road, so it's no distance for you to get lost. While I go back to prepare the dinner. You can walk around with Mary.' Not liking the idea of being alone in this park, in panic I offered.

'Can I come back and help with the dinner?' Surprised she asked.

'You can cook?'

'Yes a little bit.'

'Oh my word that's good. Come on then you can help me.' Much relieved I went back.

From then on I assisted to help with the cooking to pay my way. After that first outing, each morning Miria would take me to the park leave me to sit with Mary in the pram, whilst she did the shopping. I would stay there returning home only to feed Mary, then return in the afternoon and watch the boats on the river, eventually Len would turn up on his way home from school with his pals. Greeting me he would take off his coat leave it on the pram. As I watched Len and his pals would start playing football. Len seemed a good player.

Life at my in laws was to be quite peaceful, certainly different from the regimented ways of Barrack life, which I certainly did not miss. They looked after me very well and I did not impose on their generosity. I found Putney was a lovely little place, with all the hustle and bustle of everyday life, everyone went about his or her business without much fuss. This was the first place, I had encountered with so many new exiting things such as Cinemas. The Mirror Picture Theatre, the Electric Picture Palace, a Music Hall, and Hippodrome, places I wished to go to see one of the variety shows. One day a letter arrived addressed to me. Opening it found a   book containting tickets for my army family allowance with instructions to take it to a Post Office to draw my allowance. It wasn't much but I did offer Maria some of it for my board and keep, the rest I would use to pay for Mary's necessities.

Jack's family went about their mundane way of life. Pops was a Pot-man in a local Public House, Rose worked in a Draper's shop somewhere, Jack's elder brother Alf, had returned home from sea for a brief stay. He was quite the gentleman and always had time for a chin- wag with me. Miria took me for walks across Putney Bridge, pointed out various places of interest. Life in Putney passed me by, I had no worries, with little to do. Nevertheless, I could have done all the chores myself, but there was no way Miria would allow me to take on more than she saw fit for me to do. The letters from Jack and mother I took to the park to read, maybe two or three times over, when not reading I walked around the park watching the oarsman rowing with the tides along the Thames, they fascinated me with the ebb and flow, as back home the canals were tide less.

Unexpected, Jack arrived home. He had managed to get a few days leave. He didn't talk too much about the troubles, just mentioned the RFA had temporarily become the Royal Artillery Mounted Rifles, in support of the civil authorities. After the death of Michael Collins in August, the granting of an amnesty to the rebels had caused a lull in the fighting. However still no news of the Brigade's return to England. We had little time together just went for walks in the park or to sit and talk, cautiously, I asked.

'Jack why is your mother called Miria? When her name was Caroline?'

'That's Pops pet name for her.'

'Another thing, when she takes me to Bishops Park she sits beside me with a cabbage leave on her head, it's funny but embarrassing. I've heard people remarking about it.' He laughed.

'It's her way of keeping cool, she says it helps calm her nerves avoids headaches. Next time you try it, sit beside her with a cabbage leaf on your head, do your nerves some good. He laughed. I retorted.

'Not me! I'm silly looking enough now. Anyway what news about married quarters?' He could not give an answer.

'Sarah I don't know, we will be there until the Army sees fit to bring us back. Only then can I ask the question.'

One thing was certain to me, I never ever wanted to go back to Aldershot. We spent a lovely few days together however, that was the only time he came home on leave.

One November afternoon in the park, the signs of autumn lay all around. A mixture of various golden leaves covered the ground like a thick brown carpet. There was I sat on a park bench wrapped up against the chill breeze off the river, with one foot resting on the wheel of the pram, with Mary wrapped up nice and cosy fast asleep. I was watching Len and his pals playing football, when suddenly a big thick brown dense cloud swept in enveloping us. I could not see my foot on the wheel of the pram, it terrified the life out of me. I thought: *The end of the world had come.* Not knowing what to do I stood up clutching the pram handle tightly listened? Not a sound could be heard there was no whistling or shouting from any of the boys playing football. I listened intently for any sound of Len calling my name. Nothing. I began to shout out.

'LEN. LEN.'...No answer, frantically I again shouted....'LEN. I'M OVER HERE. LEN.'

I kept on shouting in this brown cold damp cloud swirling around me. Nobody had mentioned anything about what I was about to experience. A London fog. As I bent down to cover Mary's face with the blanket, its smell made me cough violently. I do not remember how long I stayed rooted to the spot shouting. There was not a sound to be heard. Nobody called out, no footsteps, nothing except an eerie silence. My efforts of shouting increased my inhaling this horrible brown cloud making me cough even more. I decided the only thing to do was to retrace my steps back to the house. I bent down to see if Mary was still breathing with the blanket covering her. I could not see her but she appeared all right. Tucking her in more tightly I turned the pram around to face the other way, slowly I pushed the pram forward, thinking about where I was going. Bang, the pram ran into something. I exclaimed in fright.

'Holy Mary Mother of God who is it, you gave me a scare.'....silence...'In God's name is anybody there?'...I questioned pushing the pram but it would not go. I pulled it backwards, no problem, pushing it forward again. Bang, something was stopping it, edging my way along its side felt the front wheel then a little further past I found cold metal. Discovered it was a park bench. I stood there thinking: *How many park benches did I pass on the way in? Never noticed, but did remember at the edge of the grass was a small wire fence. If I could follow that for guidance to the next park bench, then onwards I could get to the gate.* I negotiated the pram past the seat, found the wire fence and kept the side of the wheel scraping against the fence before it bumped into the next bench. Making slow progress I proceeded forward, to keep my courage up began to sing out aloud. **Take me back to dear old Blighty.** Maybe someone would hear me and come to my rescue? I counted five seats before the wire stopped at a post, now what could I do? I tried to feel for any more wire but there was none. The only thing I could think of was the park gates must be around there somewhere, and the awful brown cloud appeared to be even thicker. Once again I shouted.

'LEN-LEEEEN.'...without any response. Very aware I might bump into something, I inched forward but nothing happened. I appeared to be in the middle of nowhere and the feeling of panic began. In between fits of coughing I began to sing again, then I did bump into something soft, bushes and remembered on the left at the park gates, was clumps of bushes. Therefore the park gates must be on the right. Turning the pram to my right pushed it slowly forward. Bang, again I hit something, thankfully this time it was the park gates. I guided the pram out of the park and onto the road, I thought: *Was it the main road? It has got to be. Once over it I would be able to find the house more easily. But where's the traffic?* I decided to cross over there. I was then hoarse from coughing, shouting and singing. After another barking spell stopped to listen intently, then cautiously in a straight line crossed over until the wheels bumped into the curb on the far side. Levered the pram up onto the pavement and pushed it forward until I bumped into what I thought were the metal railings in front of the houses. Turning the pram in the right direction, gradually inched my way along the railings to a gate opening. To make things worse it was twilight and light filtering through the brown cloud was failing fast. To get my bearings I left the pram and felt my way to the front door, feeling the number on the door worked out how many houses I was away from home. Then slowly pushing the pram proceeded towards the house, noting the spaces at each house until the right one. Leaving the pram by the steps I went up banged the knocker heavily on the door. From inside I heard Lens voice.

'Is that you Sarah?'...Then the door opened...'I couldn't find you, Ma and Pops are out looking for you.' Thankful to be back home I coughed.

'Please help me with the pram Len.' He came out and together we manhandled the pram inside. I unwrapped the shawl from around Mary, took her out of the pram and into the kitchen, she appeared okay except for a runny nose, which was all. I went to get a drink of water, whilst Len apologised.

'It happened so quickly. I couldn't find you and didn't hear any noise, so I came home and told mum and dad. They left to find you and they are not back yet.' I croaked.

'Len, I too did not hear a sound it was eerie. How I found my way back I don't know? I'm so glad to be back safe indoors.What is it?'

That's a London fog we do get then in the winter months,but that was a real bad one.'

Much later Ma and Pa arrived back. Miria entered, a scarf wound about her face, unravelling it she exclaimed.

'Thank goodness you're back safe and sound, I was frantic with worry but as soon as I saw the pram in the hallway. I knew you were home.' Pops, wheezing and coughing behind her agreed adding.

'We hate those fogs. They come from nowhere, we only go out if we have to.' The fog that day was the worst they had ever had in London to that date. To me a memorable experience for the future.

Christmas 1922, my first in England. I prayed Jack would get leave for Christmas, no such luck. A letter from him bore tidings but not good news. Leave impossible. Sometime in the New Year, the Brigade would leave Ireland heading for Larkhill Salisbury. No quarters available, still too young. Oh, how I wish he were twenty-six like me.

On the nineteenth December Edith, the wife of Jack's elder brother Harris gave birth to twins. Two days before Christmas day a turkey was delivered to the door, it was from Mother. Miria was thrilled with the gift and the thought behind it. However she was well provided for by Alf, having more than ample supplies any surplus food she gave away to her married son's wives. With the new additions to the family, the house at Christmas was full of brothers and sisters (some known, others introduced). All very understanding about my situation, I was made more than welcome but for me, a lonely Christmas.

March 1923, Mary's first birthday, I baked a little cake. It was then eight months I had been living with my in-laws, and I had only seen Jack twice during that period of time. Although the Brigade had returned to Larkhill just before Christmas, there were still no quarters for us. I resigned myself to stay at Miria's, assuming Rose was happy with us staying there. Only by chance one day, I overheard her talking to her mother in the parlour, making remarks about how tired she was of seeing nappies everywhere. I did not eavesdrop but took the hint. Rose was not alone with her thoughts, I too was not happy and wanted to be out of there, but with nowhere to go I was stuck there. As usual I went out and spent the morning in the park sitting thinking: *What I could do to ease the situation*? The thought of Mary living in Plymouth crossed my mind*: It had been two years since we were last together, possibly an opportunity to pay her a visit, maybe for a couple of weeks to ease the situation.* I decided to send her a letter. A week later I received her answer "Come and stay?" I asked Miria would she mind if, I went to my sisters for two weeks. Her answer was positive.

'No Sarah. That will be a break for you. We will see you when you return.'

Pops kindly sorted out my train journey and they both escorted me to Paddington Station. On the journey up, they kept reassuring me that everything would be all right and I would be most welcome to have the room when I returned back. I was truly grateful for their hospitality, thanked them from the bottom of my heart, but I knew what Rose had said and did not want to outstay my welcome, nevertheless had the comforting feeling that I was part of their family. Arriving at Paddington station once again to my amazement it was yet another big station.

The train journey was uneventful, long tedious but much more scenic, rolling hills and green pastures. In the distance on the side of a hill, I spotted the shape of a big white horse and thought: *It was a carving of a famous racehorse, like back on the Curragh.* I ate the small snacks, which Miria had provided whilst Mary slept all the way. At Plymouth I got out with my case. A kind gentleman helped me with the pram, then I pushed it towards the opening of a flight of stair going down, bumping it down into an underground passage way, pushing the pram joined the melee of other passengers making their way towards another flight of stairs at the far end as I got there, a Sailor said.

'Hold on Missus. I'll give you a hand up the stairs with your pram.' Grateful of his assistance thanked him.

'Oh. Thank you you're so kind.'

Between the pair of us we managed the stairs, and he placed the front pram wheels on the floor for me to push it forwards towards the ticket Barrier. Handing in my ticket pushed it into a large ticket hall.

CHAPTER TWELVE
SALISBURY

I spotted Mary stood at the exit beside a pram. Bert was holding little Raymond in his arms. After such a long period apart it was delightful meeting Mary once again. We chatted so much I do not think Bert got a word in until he questioned.

'Sarah how and where is Jack?' I truthfully replied.

'I don't really know, somewhere in England? I haven't seen him in months.'

'Well that's the Army for you.' With that answer Bert swung Raymond up onto his shoulders and said.

'Look our house is not too far away, it's nice and sunny, and with two prams it's far quicker to walk than bother with two taxis.' I thought: *It sensible to abide with his suggestion*. So we followed behind him pushing the prams, and to be honest it was not that great a distance before we finally arrived outside their house.

Their home had spacious accommodation, a room was provided for Mary and me. Having settled down for a quick spot of tea, It was not long before we began discussing the events of the past two years of our separation. Then my subject cropped up. Mary and Bert were both very receptive. Bert was more than helpful, understanding Jack's situation with its restrictions. Nevertheless, I thoroughly enjoyed my stay and their company so much so that the two weeks flashed past, it was time for me to prepare myself for the return journey. Then Bert came up with a suggestion.

'Sarah why don't you stay longer? We are both more than happy to have you staying with us as something might turn up for the better?'

An open invitation, which I had no objection too, gladly accepted. I sent a letter to Miria informing her that I would be staying a little while longer and another one to Jack, explaining the plight of his sister Rose. It wasn't fair on her if we return to his mothers but Berts suggestion of my staying longer with them had been a welcome blessing, concluded that it was not in our own interest to be separated, we desperately needed quarters, please try and do something about it.. Unfortunately his letter of reply was bleak, he was constantly applying but the reply was always the same. I was not very pleased but there was nothing I could do or say on the matter, it was all down to the Army.During the two months of my prolonged stay, Mary had taught me more about cooking and I must admit I became used to my unscheduled overstay. On occasional week-ends Bert was away playing football until one night Bert informed me.

'Sarah, its the end of our football season, I'm sorry to say Mary and I, have decided to take the children back to mother's in Ireland for a holiday. We plan to leave on the Monday after the FA cup game to be played at the new Empire Stadium at Wembley, it will be the very first game to be played there. I know it does not help you in your current situation, but I hope you do understand.'

'Of course not Bert. You'll have a good time back home.'

I had no alternative but to accept. It appeared I was heading back to Miria's. Mary and I discussed what I should do and agreed to her suggestion we all leave the same day. I sent a letter to Jack explaining what was going to happen, could he find somewhere outside their camp which could accommodate us? As the weeks dragged by soon it was mid-April. A time I was not looking forward too, preparing myself for a return to Miria's, for the right reasons something I was reluctant to do. It was my only option open, until a letter from Jack informed me, he had found a single room in a place called Durrington, not far from his camp. He had already accepted the Landlady's rent as 10s per week was it Okay? Was it Okay? I told Mary and went straight down to the post office, sent a wire.

TAKE IT STOP

Back at Mary's waited for his re[ply it came by mid day.

GOOD NEWS STOP   RENT PAID STOP LETTER TO FOLLOW STOP

Jack's letter arrived with details of how to get to Larkhill. I did not understand where these different places were? Gave the letter to Bert to sort out and arrange for the tickets on the same day as agreed. Bert did what was required, handed me a sheet of paper with the arrival and departure of each train en-route. He even showed me on a map where Plymouth was and where Durrington was, he was a great help. I sent a wire to Jack. Stating the time of my arrival at Tidworth. I also sent a letter to Miria explaining and. our good fortune, and thanks.

Sunday the day after the Cup Final whilst we prepared lunch, Bert read all the reports in the newspapers about the game. I went upstairs to my room to pack my meagre belongings When I returned back to the kitchen found Bert and Mary reading one of the newspapers spread out on the table, Bert hailed me.

'Here Sarah, take a look at this picture of the crowds. There's only one policeman on a white horse controlling over a hundred thousand spectators. What a sight Eh Mary?' Looking at them I remarked.

'They remind me of the crowds going to see Fulham, not as many though, they had mounted policemen there as well. Jack's young brother Len says he wants to be a professional footballer like you Bert.'

'Well if he's as good as Jack, he might well become one. But I'd like to play a game at that new stadium, that's for sure.'

We had lunch then. Bert took the papers, disappeared into the other room. We all retired early ready for the next day's travelling and I ready for a new venture.

Monday morning with two prams we boarded the train at Plymouth station, which was to take them to Reading where they had to change whilst I had to change at a place called Devizes, where we said our tearful farewells, Bert helped me unload the pram with Mary.

I was left on the station to fend for myself. I found the right platform for the train bound for Southampton. I had plenty of time, so bought myself a cup of tea while waiting. It arrived five minutes late. Boarding it was soon on our way. At Ludgershall, I got off to change onto the train for Tidworth, the last leg of my journey and the end of the train line. That journey took no time at all. It was late afternoon when it finally arrived puffing and wheezing its way into the station, passing by Jack this man of mine who I had not seen for many many months. He spotted me and with a big grin all over his face waved in greeting. I was so impatient for the train to stop. I opened the carriage door and shouted.

'JACK HERE' He came running up to the carriage doorway took me in his arms and swept me out of the carriage, kissing me. Oh the joy I felt.

'Sarah you made it okay then. It's wonderful to have you and Mary here together with me.'

'I didn't think I could do it. It's taken all day to get here, but it was worth it now I'm here with you.' He seriously asked.

'Have you had anything, food or drink?'

'Well, only what Mary made up, and a cup of tea at Devizes station'... I coyly said. 'Jack do you think you could put me down, people are watching.' But there was nobody else on the platform, only the stationary train quietly chuffing away... 'Oh. Sorry Sarah. But it's been so long.'

Gently he lowered me, Jack busied himself getting the case and pram with Mary still sat in it out of the carriage, down on the platform, he made a fuss of her, but she did not respond.

'Let's go and have a quick bite before we make tracks. I'm sure Mary will need something won't she?' Agreeing I enquired

'Yes she will. How far away is this place?'

87

'Not too far. I've got transport to take us there.'

Picking up our possessions he placed them on the pram in front of Mary. I grabbed hold of his arm so as not to let go, as we made our way out of the station, crossed over to a little Tea Room opposite. He asked.

'How's Mary and Bert and their two, Raymond and the little girl what's her name?'

'Both very well, so are their children, the little girl's name is Patricia, they call her Patsy. They send you their love, and hope to see you again sometime.'

We entered the Tea Room and sat down at a table. The waitress came over, Jack ordered a pot of tea, some cakes, offering the baby's bottle to the waitress I asked.

'Could you warm up some milk in the baby's bottle for us, please?

'Certainly Madam anything else.'

'Anything else Sarah?'

'No thank you tea will be fine.' Then he became serious again.

'Sarah, don't expect too much when you get there. It's the best I could find in the time allowed. There's very little accommodation available down here.'

A warning which went over my head. I didn't care we were together at last, that's all that mattered to me. The waitress arrived back with all our wants. I fed Mary while Jack poured the tea, offered me a selection of cakes. After my day of travelling I was rather hungry took one cake, it was delicious so I had more. Mary having finished her bottle fell asleep in my arms exhausted. Jack paid the waitress.

'C'mon. On your feet soldier. Time to go.'

Ushering us out he pushed the pram as we made our way back across to the station and to the transport he had arranged. Tethered to the railings a horse drawn GS Wagon, something I had not noticed. Surprised. I thought: *This is novel.* Taking Mary from my arms he urged.

'Come on, up you get Sarah.' He gave me a hand up to the seat, passed Mary up to me, placed our meagre luggage and pram in the back, un-tethered the horse clambered up alongside me. Muttered.

'Hold onto your hat, it won't take long?'

With that huge grin all over his face clicked the horse away, cantered out of Tidworth into the countryside. Within a short time we were going along lanes through flat plains of grasslands, then he clicked the horse into a gallop, I had to hang on tight to Mary. (Blow my hat) I looked at him grinning like a Cheshire cat.

'Just like old times eh Sarah?'

'Steady on Jack, you're not in a race back at the Curragh you know.'

'It's all right Sarah. I thought you would prefer this than anything else. Don't the plains remind you of the Curragh?'

He was standing upright holding the reins drawn tight in both hands, a look of sheer pleasure on his face with the horse at full gallop in front of him. I shouted.

'YES THEY DO AND I DO APPRECIATE YOUR THOUGHT, BUT PLEASE LET'S GET THERE IN ONE PIECE'....I was enjoying this trip far better than any train journey....'ANYWAY HOW FAR IS IT?' He shouted back.

'ABOUT FOUR MILES AS THE CROW FLIES ABOUT SIX MILES ROAD WISE.'

As we approached a village, he sat down slowing the horse into a canter, passing through clicked the horse into a gallop shouted.

'SARAH JUST UP AHEAD IS DURRINGTON.'

Slowing the horse to the trot we entered this village, the horse clopping quietly up the street halted outside a group of cottages.

'This is the place. I'll see you settled in before I take the horse and wagon back to camp, don't worry it's quite close. I'll get someone to bring me back, so I won't be very long gone.'

88

He jumped down, took Mary from me and then helped me down handing Mary back. I just had to go and pat the horse, in response it snorted, scraped its shoe. Jack urged.

'C'mon Sarah.' We walked up to the door, he knocked. A woman opened it. Jack spoke up.

'Mrs. Downey.' She looked straight past Jack, at me holding Mary in my arms exclaimed

'OH! When you took the room, you didn't say anything about a baby.'

Abruptly she turned about grumbling, we followed her upstairs to a small landing where she ushered us into a small room.

'There you are.'

She abruptly turned and left us looking at each other. Jack saw the concern on my face.

'Cheer up ducks. At least we are together at last, I'll fetch in the case.'

It was basic. In the corner a small sink, a tiny gas ring, a tiny table with two chairs, a cupboard with a mirror on the door and the bed. What a bed! Jack re-entering placed the case and boxes on the bed, which almost collapsed.

'Sarah, she's just told me to leave the pram outside.'

'But Jack.'

'Look I'll go now, I'll be back soon'.

Laying Mary down on the bed, I investigated what was hidden inside the cupboard, just assorted crockery. The landlady entered the room carrying a basketful of pieces.

'Hello' I cheerfully said thinking there's more.

She looked at me, promptly exchanged everything including the crockery and cutlery, with a grunt and no reason why, she left. I just stood there, very dismayed at her antics, knowing it was because we had a baby. Much later Jack returned with some essential provisions. I blurted out.

'Jack, Mrs, whatever her name is came back and just exchanged everything. That's a good start, and if she won't let us have the pram inside, where do we sleep Mary? Can't you do something about her.' He urged.

'Let's get settled in and sort it out after.'

I made up a makeshift dinner, we ate and deciding to sleep Mary along with us, then settled down for the night. During the night half the bed fell apart, I just saved Mary from falling onto the floor. Somehow we propped it up, then Jack had to leave. After he left, I dozed off. Mary crying woke me up. I fell out of the bed, prepared food for Mary and myself, washed and changed her. Constantly thinking, of the insults, which had been hurled at us, I was working myself up into a right paddy. With Mary in my arms went downstairs to confront the landlord and told him what I thought of the place.

'I'm going out to find somewhere else. That room is terrible and not worth the rent.' He replied.

'Don't bother you can go now.' Angrily I retorted.

'My husband has paid you for the week. And we will stay the week. I'm going to tell him what you have said.'

I was so angry. I stomped back upstairs, got Mary and myself ready to go out. Stomped back down the stairs out through the door banging it shut behind me. I was determined to find an alternative. With Mary in my arns I hurried to a little shop, which happened to be the Post Office, entering the tinkle of a little bell attracted the lady's attention. Before I even got to the counter I quickly asked.

'Excuse me. Do you know of any local board and lodgings available?' Looking me up and down looked over her glasses and said.

'Mrs. Brampton she might. It's the little house opposite, that one there.'

'Oh thank you very much.' I left the shop and once outside I calmed down. If this woman didn't, something else might turn up. I knocked on the door and a tall woman opened it.

'Mrs. Brampton?'

'Yes'.

'The lady from the Post Office sent me to you. Do you have any rooms to rent?' She too looked me up and down taking note of Mary then asked.

'What does your husband do?'

'He's a sergeant in the royal field artillery at the barracks up the road.'

'Um. I do have a room to let but not until next week. Rent will be Ten shillings (50p new pence) per week in advance. Would you like to see the room?' She offered.

'Please, if it is no bother for you.' She beckoned me to come in, showed me the room. Compared to our one, it was heaven.

'I will take it. If it's all right with you, I will get my husband to come down this evening after his duty and pay you the rent.' She nodded.

'That will be acceptable thank you.'

I left her house and spent the rest of the day walking around Durrington, a small pleasant little village. I found a little teashop, had something to eat and drink. In the afternoon, returned back to this hovel to wait until Jack got back. When he arrived I blurted out my confrontation with the Landlord. I had gone out and found other accommodation, but had to pay up front. I could see he was pleased.

'Sarah, that's great news, you are a clever girl. C'mon take me to this house.' Leaving the hovel went to Mrs. Brampton's knocked on the door she opened it.

'Aah, is this your husband?' Jack answered.

'Yes I'm Sergeant. Plant and this is my wife. Mrs Sarah Plant, this is our baby Mary, I've come to pay the ten shillings rent for next week, is that correct and acceptable?'

'Yes correct ten shillings in advance.' Jack took out some silver coins.

'There you are, rent in advance. When can we take the room?'

'If it's all right with you Sergeant, it will be vacant on Saturday.' Jack prompted me.

'Sarah.'

'Yes that will be fine. We will be here Saturday.' Business concluded, we returned to the hovel, Jack said.

'You stay in the room Sarah. I've got some words to say to someone downstairs.' (Which I was not party to) We never heard another peep out of the them throughout the rest of the week.

On Saturday we left the hovel, moved into the new flat, more spacious clean with **a nice** Landlady. She and I were to get on well together.

Larkhill barracks was about two miles from Durrington, so Jack acquired an army bicycle to get back and forth. One afternoon he came in said.

'Sarah. Maybe some good news. A little birdie told me there was a chance of quarters, the snag is they are in Windsor.'

'Where's that? I haven't heard anyone mention Windsor around here. Not that I see many people to talk to.'

'I know that ducks. It's not in this locality. It's about forty miles away, nearer to London, unlike Aldershot it would mean being posted to a Territorial Unit.'

'Don't you dare mention Aldershot to me again Jack Plant.'

'All right Sarah I won't. The quarters would be rented from the Territorial's. Windsor is the home of the Royal Family and there will be much more to see and do there.' Intrigued by his eagerness, I was in the middle of setting up his evening meal suggested.

'Let's get Mary settled down and talk during our meal.' Then Jack explained.

'Look Sarah I have the right qualifications and a good soldier's record, but with the wrong age, still cannot get quarters for another two years in the army. But if, I apply for the position of

Senior N C O in the Terriers, assuming it was granted. A transfer would be good for my career. Alternatively, it would mean staying just like we are now.'

I mulled over this and knew he was right. The next day Jack applied for a transfer.

Two months later he got his transfer with immediate effect, it was our chance to leave Durrington and move into new quarters. Only there was a problem! The allocated quarters in Windsor were still occupied for another month. If it was acceptable to Mrs. Brampton, I would stay on. Jack paid Mrs. Brampton a month's rent in advance. Two days later Jack left for Windsor. However, four months later I was still at Mrs Brampton's, until I received a wire from Jack.

PACK YOUR KIT- BAGS STOP GET UP TO WINDSOR IMMEDIATELY STOP

When Jack said immediate he meant immediate! I informed Mrs. Brampton and she went out of her way to help, finding out about the train times and the route to take, she even organised a friend of hers Mr. Sweeney, to take me in his car to the station. After she informed me of the train times, I sent Jack a wire with the time of arrival at Windsor. I was on the move again, little did I think this was to be my future way of life, all the time Jack was in the Army. Either he went before me or I followed after. Moving on my own, loaded up with baggage and children from place to place. All I ever got from him was nothing but orders.

'On your feet soldier. You're in the army now.'

CHAPTER THIRTEEN
WINDSOR

Early on a September morning the sun was shining brightly when Mr Sweeny arrived. He put the pram and luggage in the car whilst I thanked Mrs. Brampton for her kindness and hospitality. Nevertheless she did embrace me warmly her parting reply was.

'Sarah, if you and Jack are down this way again you're welcome here.'

Mr Sweeny drove me to Pewsy station, assisted me putting the pram into the Guards van before with my thanks bid him goodbye. I had only one change of train to make at a place called Slough where I nearly forgot about the pram, only spotted it isolated along the platform by the guards van. Standing beside it waited for the next Windsor train to arrive then with the help of the guard put the pram into his guards van, with Mary in my arms got into the next compartment. At Windsor Jack was waiting on the platform. This time with Mary in my arms there was no grabbing hold of me and swinging me off my feet. Nevertheless he embraced both of us, kissing me affectionately making me blush, the Guard hailed me to collect the pram, Jack let go of us to take the pram off the train, placing it on the platform, securing Mary in it he said.

'Sarah outside I've got a cab waiting for us. The quarters are in the centre of Windsor.' (Very up market) Just wait till you see the quarters Sarah. They're the best we have had so far.' I had to laugh at his point of view then retorted.

'Quarters, what quarters? We haven't had any.' Nevertheless I was excited with the prospects of seeing them for myself. In the taxi Jack took hold of Mary on his knee and commented.

'My you've grown up haven't you?' A smile creased her little face, as I said.

'Mrs. Brampton's invited us back if,we ever return down there again,'

'Well that was nice of her, but I don't think I'll be returning to Larkhill.'

When we arrived Jack beaming like a Cheshire cat, helped me out, paid the driver, unloaded the pram and cases, then with hands on hips questioned.

'Well. Sarah. I was only given the keys this morning. What do you think?'

I could not believe my eyes. I was in total agreement our very own quarters including a small garden as well.

'This is something to behold Jack. I like the look of this place.'

He took me inside and showed me around. It was just right, small and comfortable. A sitting room, a spare room, a kitchen with outside facilities, there were two bedrooms upstairs, but no beds? I questioned.

'Where are the beds Jack?'

'Don't worry I'll sort those out tomorrow.'

'But what about tonight, where is the bed?'

'I'll get some bedding from the stores for tonight. Mary will be all right sleeping in the pram.' My immediate thought was: *We'll be sleeping on the floor tonight that's for sure*....unconcerned Jack had moved across to the window.

'Sarah come over here'....Moving towards the window, stood beside him to see a big building with a large flat stone in its brickwork, upon which was engraved. DRILLHALL. I taken aback enquired.

'Is that the barracks?'

'Yes. There opposite is where I report for duty.' it certainly is handy, no early morning bike rides for me. What do you say ducks?'

'Well you won't have to leave before the crack of dawn that's for sure.'

I was warming to this new avenue we had found ourselves in, and as we walked around getting the feel of the place. On the table in the parlour, lay some provisions Jack had bought so they would come in handy. I looked in cupboards to find lots of useful items, which the previous people had left behind, but my main concern was the beds I exclaimed!

'Beds Jack. Beds?'

'No problem, now you've seen the place. We will decide what to do on a permanent basis. Just for tonight though. I get some bedding I won't be long.'

It wasn't the first time I have slept on the floor and I was sure it would not be the last. While he was away I fed Mary and got her to sleep in the pram. Soon after Jack returned armed with mattress's and took them upstairs. I could hear him clumping about in the empty room above, coming down he left for more bedding. When he returned I followed him upstairs, in the bedroom the mattresses were in a heap with the bedding slung on top.

'Sarah, you make up the bed. I'll go and fetch some more provisions.' I suggested.

'Well I used the milk so we need more milk, bread and eggs and bacon for tomorrow.'

'Well I'll get what I think is necessary for a couple of meals.'

Away he goes, while I set too making up a bed from four biscuits, sheets and blankets. I busied myself downstairs sorting out our meagre chattels. Jack returned with additional provisions to make up some meals and placed them on the kitchen table. He stood there, with his hands on his hips looking, spotting the tiny little stove said.

'That's got to be lit, I'll pop over and get some kindling to set it alight.'

In two shakes of a lamb's tale, he was back with wood, a bag of coal, laid the fire and set it alight, then filled the kettle for a brew.

'Right Sarah I'll have one cup of tea and then go back to my duty, I'll be a couple of hours. Now will you be Okay while I'm gone?'

He had, as far as he was concerned, done what was necessary. With the bedding, provisions, water and gas on and stove alight. No Aldershot here. It was now up to me.

'Yes I'm quite happy, I'll prepare a meal for you.'

After the meal we spent the evening trying to settle Mary down for the night, but she wasn't having any of that. It was late, when we discussed our future plan before retiring to bed. (Did I say bed?) I slept very well, but it was a few days before we eventually got a regulation bed. Jack, assisted by one of his store men, assembled the bed upstairs, before he took the other biscuits back with him Jack said.

'Sarah, that's the bedding fixed. Now be warned, I've been informed. At some time I could be transferred back into the Army. And we would be given quarters'....

I listened but was not too sure of what that really meant, as he had transferred into the Terriers to get this far, replied.

That's got to be taken with a pinch of salt. You know yourself these are not true allocated quarters. If, you do get transferred back? You're still too young to qualify, and according to the army, it still would be another two years.'

'Well I'm just telling you. I've been warned not to get a lot of personal possessions together.'

His last statement was not good news to me, we had only just moved in a week ago. Disregarding his warning I continued to buy odds and ends to make the place look nice and homely. We had not been there long before I discovered that I was expecting another baby. When I told Jack he was delighted. Once again it was the start of the football season. Jack was picked to play for the Terriers team, also the Windsor and Eaton football team. Heh-Ho! It was back to celebrations in the Drillhall. On Saturday morning, Jack was up bright and early for muster parade duty then football. He would be away at one p.m. until twelwe or one o' clock the next morning, whilst I sat indoors worrying in case he had been hurt, all he said was.

'Sarah bad news travels fast. Very soon you would be told.'

When he eventually arrived home, I gave him a piece of my mind, but he never seemed to mind just told me not to be silly. Jack was feeling fit and well. It was all right for him, he had spent a good night up the mess celebrating with the boys. He assumed it must be the same for me, but I was expecting another baby Most of the time I felt ill and sick, a repeat of my previous pregnancy, half of my illness was brought on through my constant worrying. When we moved in I was not aware he was in charge of and responsible for all the married quarters, including their occupants. Something he had not informed me about. Most of my time in our quarters was spent on my own, which became a lonely place. If Jack forgot to shut one of the front windows, I feared I could hear someone breaking in. The sound of the doorbell would frighten the life out of me, creeping out to open it only to find it was a Policeman, politely telling me to close up my front window. I would thank him and go out and struggle to shut it up, in the end I would go next door and ask Sergeant Preston an Infantry Instructor to close it for me. By this time Mary, was growing fast she full of mischief, much to Jack's mirth but not mine. One day a gang of painters arrived to paint the woodwork of all the quarters. Whilst I went about my chores, Mary instead of running about stopped and intently watched them through the window. It was sometime later when I was at the sink filling a saucepan with water I heard an almighty crash from outside. Fear gripped me immediately thought: One of the painters has fallen. Dropping the saucepan ran out through the open front door to find it was not one of the painters, they were nowhere to be seen, it was Mary lying in a pool of green paint. It was everywhere, on her face, hair, legs, her dress and shoes. I nearly gave birth where I stood, I screamed.

'What in god's name have you done?'

She just lay there grinning like her father. I ran back inside to fetch paper and rags, only to find I was paddling in water the kitchen floor was awash, I had left the tap on. Panic set in as I splashed over and turned off the tap, grabbing rags from under the sink, splashed my way through the water, ran outside to where Mary, was still sat in the paint rubbing her hands everywhere. 'NO.' I screamed pulled her onto her feet, trying to clean her up wiped some of it off her legs, carried her inside, removed her clothing and shoes, then paddled through the water to wash away the paint. Fortunately with a lot of soap got rid of it, put on her nightwear gave her a good smack, packed her off to bed. I threw her clothes in the dustbin. Only then was able to mop up the water, by which time I was exhausted and had to sit down. A knock on the door had me struggling up to go and open it. There stood a Painter and his mate. Who retorted.

'Hey Missus what's happened out here then?' I related the episode. Too my annoyance, they just laughed.

'Okay Missus. We'll clean up and make sure to put them away in future.'

I thought: *Too late now*. Little did I realise that little incident was her first of many. Another day, I was doing the washing and it was all too quiet, I called out.

'Mary.'...no reply...'Mary.'...nothing. I searched all over the house for her, even down the coal cellar, as I emerged. I noticed the front door was ajar, assuming she had got out, I ran outside, there was no sign of her. Still wearing my rubber apron I knocked on the neighbour's door, when it was opened asked.

'Have you seen Mary?'

'Mary. No, she not here.'

I ran up the high street stopping outside the Castle Hotel where some builders were standing, quickly asked.

'Have you seen a little girl?' Shaking heads informed me.... 'No.' ....In panic I began shouting at everybody.

'HAVE YOU SEEN MY LITTLE GIRL?' I'm sure everyone thought I was demented.

'Don't know luv.' A lady suggested.

'Maybe you're running the wrong way.' I stopped.

'Oh my God, which way should I go?'

'Heh Missus. You there.'

Turning my head saw a man stood by a motorcar pointing upwards. Following his motion glanced up to see Mary stood one storey above me, balancing on a window flower box. I nearly passed out at the sight of her. Thank God she never saw me. Not caring I was about to enter the men only Workingman's Club. I ran through its doorway barging through up the stairs to the top where I was out of breath, breathing heavy carried on running towards the room, shoving open the door saw her still in the same place at the window. The room was in silence apart from the clicking of billiard balls, its occupants intently watching the game. To attract anyone's attention frantically I began waving my arms about like a mad thing. A man stood by the billiard table looking up, frowned, quizzically stared at me, before slowly making his way around the table came towards me, he asked.

'What's up luv?' Pointing, I whispered.

'My Mary's standing on the window box.' Turning around quickly summed up the problem and whispered.

'Oh. Okay luv. Leave it to me.' Quietly approaching the window, he put his arm around her waist and pulled her back inside, carried her back to me.

'There you are luv. You should keep a hold of that little one, or you might lose her one day.'

'Yes how right you are. She is a handful. Thank you.' Much relieved I took her in my arms agreed with him. I was shaking exhausted, my nerves in tatters. Back home, I gave her such a good hiding she never went back to the club. It was where her father played billiards.

Jack had bought bedding plants to plant in our small gardenat the rear, spending a lot of time placing them in rows. No sooner had he left the house, when Mary would run out and pull them all up, so constantly Jack was replanting or replacing new ones he had bought moaned to me. 'Sarah can't you control her?' To which I retorted.

'Jack. You should be here. I can't watch her all the time, I need eyes in the back of my head.' To that he had no reply. Our next door neighbour Mrs. Preston in passing conversation said to me.

'Your Mary is more bother than all my four boys put together, with you in your condition expecting, and your husband-staying out late at night. Mary must be the bane of your life. We as soldier's wives, really have something to put up with. What we all should do is just leave them. All you do is only walk to the Copper Horse in the Great Park, that's you finished for the week.' Defensively I retaliated.

'When we get married. We take them for better or worse.' Quickly she retorted.

'More worse than better.'

I thought: *That one had an answer to everything.* Consoling myself with Jack's good points. To me he was still the gallant soldier I loved and married. I would forgive and forget his staying out, until the next time.

The Terriers held dances in the Drillhall every month. Jack always asked me to go. I refused, but that didn't stop him, it was his duty to be there. It is a woman's job having a baby not men's. I must just get on with it. I wasn't worried about him dancing with anyone else, he still couldn't dance a step furthermore he never would. Living directly opposite, the band's music was quite audible for me to listen to downstairs. However, it woke Mary, I could hear her moving about upstairs. Creeping upstairs I would find her jigging up and down in the cot. Tried to settle her until she fell asleep, then I would leave her, creep back downstairs. Within five minutes I heard her jigging about again, every five minutes heavy in pregnancy I struggled upstairs until I got an idea. Before the band struck up at the following months dance. I stuck cotton wool in

Mary's ears, then settled her down to sleep, which stopped her jigging about and gave me a little bit if respite.

Nevertheless Christmas 1923. An opportunity did arise, the Terriers held a Christmas Party. Jack insisted he took me and Mary. To me, a welcome blessing to be out socialising with the other wives. They very polite invited me to go out more often. Thanking them all declined. I preferring to keeping myself to myself.

On Christmas day, whilst I went to mass Jack took Mary off my hands to visit one of his Sergeant pals. On my way back home I was much more at peace with the world, when passing a couple I wished them a Merry Christmas. They looked at me as if I had two heads. Taken aback by their response, which shattered my peace so much, arriving home with the place empty, alone miles away from the hospitality of either Mother's or Jacks home set me off, I sat down and had a good cry before I rallied round to prepare the dinner. A turkey from Mother, which Jack had dressed ready for the oven, once it was cooking, started on the vegetables but was still upset when Jack arrived back, related what had happened.

'Sarah don't be silly. People are not as friendly and easy going as they are in Ireland. That couple didn't know you from Adam. You being so courteous most likely surprised them.' Unconvinced I snapped back at him.

'I don't care, they could have said Merry Christmas to me.'

Sometimes he amazed me, he was so down to earth, nothing seemed to bother him. Now I don't bother I've just become like one of them. In the afternoon Jack's pals arrived, everyone had a good time. On Boxing Day Jack goes off playing football, stays out half the night. The New Year another short celebration welcomed in 1924. Windsor was a very lovely place but I was lonely, as time passed by, worried and concerned with a new baby on the way. I became more anxious wishing I had mother to see me through the latter stages of my pregnancy. I sent a letter to Kathleen in Wales explaining to her my worries. I received her reply, asking if she could stay a couple of week to keep me company. Jack reading her letter suggested.

'Sarah that is a good idea. We could make room. I'll pay her fare.'

What a man he was, such wonderful good ways about him, as long as you didn't ask him to stay in the house. Kathleen arrived on the Saturday, Jack met her at the station. What a joy it was to see her and as we reminisced, I forgot all about my pains, never sat down, but continued with doing my normal household chores, although Kathleen offered I told her.

'You'll have plenty to do when I'm in bed.'

The next day Palm Sunday, the beginning of Holy Week. We had a wonderful Sunday, we attended Mass and I was more at ease with myself. Monday we prepared the quarters for the forthcoming birth, which did occur on Holy Thursday to a baby girl. It was not an easy birth. I really suffered, anyway we decided to call her Kathleen Patricia. Jack sent wires to our mother's about the new arrival, whilst Kathleen went to the Priest house to arrange the Christening. Returning she informed me.

'The christening has been arranged for Saturday morning, the Priest told me. "A child born on Holy Thursday and baptised on Easter Saturday, received blessings with Holy Oils and Water.'

That Saturday morning, still confined to bed, was unable to attend. In the afternoon, Jack left to play football, by the evening time I felt strong enough to get up, when Jack returned with a few team mates to celebrate the birth, who he brought into the quarters, during the evening Kathleen deciding to stay longer to take over the household chores and look after Mary, as I nursed Kathleen until I was fit enough to do my own chores. She stayed two more weeks and was preparing to leave, when I received a letter from mother informing me, our younger sister Margaret, would soon arrive in England to start a job in Reading, not too far from Windsor, had me thinking: *With the prospect of Margaret working not far away, she would provide the company I so much sought* .That was good news for me, talking this over with Kathleen she came up with a plan suggested.

96

'Listen Sarah. Instead of me going back to Wales. I will go over to Ireland for a short holiday then bring back Margaret with me.' .

Jack seizing on the opportunity, agreed to Kathleen's plans. Three weeks later the pair of them arrived. I had not seen Margaret for three years, she had out grown me. Far taller and much bigger. The three of us had a good chinwag before Jack arrived home, delighted to see Margaret asked her.

'Where's this new job in Reading then?'

'It's working in a hotel as a domestic, which includes accommodation. You probably would not know ever since the Curragh Camp was taken over by the Free State troops. A lot of people lost their jobs and jobs were hard to find including me. But a friend of mothers recommended the job in Reading, so I had to come over here. I start working there next week.'

Having listened to Margaret's answer, remembering the problem the four of us had to find employment I could have told her that myself. Jack suggested.

'Margaret please stay here until you start your new job, then I will take you there.'

'Jack if that's all right. I would love to.'

The next day Kathleen left on her way back to Wales, Margaret stayed for the week during that period, we had many chats about the old country, Mother not realising how close Margaret's job was to us, had lectured her on what she should look out for? The week flew past and it was time for Margaret to leave. As Jack had suggested he escorted her to the new job. Returning said to me.

'Sarah don't you fret yourself about Margaret she is settled in okay. I've spoken to the manager and checked it all out. The Hotel is a good one, its not in Reading but on the outskirts to the town.'

I received a letter from Mary bearing good news. Bert's team Plymouth Argyle, were to make a tour of Argentina, he would be away for three months while Bert was away she was going back home to stay with Mother for the summer. I wished that I could go with her but that was not to be. A few weeks later Margaret got time for a weekend off her duties, arrived Saturday mid-afternoon, she stayed overnight, returned on the Sunday evening. It was a journey she was to make whenever off duty. During those weekend visits, she helped me with Kathleen and provided me with more freedom to see Windsor and its Great Park. On Sundays we would go to Mass and then take long walks in the park with its woods full of oak and other varieties of trees, and visit its various gardens. The one in particular that I liked was the one called the Seville Gardens, which had every conceivable flower growing that you could think of, what a delightful array of colours they produced. I even got to visit Windsor town, very quaint and old, its tiny back streets cluttered with old buildings, which held many secrets and stories that could be told. We ventured up to the castle with its big round tower a feature in itself. With the springtime over and the weather not too bad. We walked the long walk, it was tiring but worthwhile and enjoyable. However, Margaret on her week-ends became tired of travelling backwards and forwards by train to Reading, she decided to buy a bike. I was against it but she, being the head strong one, bought one. Started me worrying about her being out late, riding along country roads in unfamiliar surroundings. Explaining to Jack of my concerns, pestered him into riding a bike on Sunday evenings with her to her lodgings. Just to please me he agreed. I think he would have been quite happy and settled to pay for her fare, nevertheless she did not want to travel by train.

Out of the pair of the two girls, Kathleen the placid one, was growing bigger every day. She would sit in her high chair for hours without a word, a smile on her tiny face surrounded by a mass of lovely blonde curls. For some reason? I had to see Mrs. Preston next door, warning Mary not to get into any mischief, I left. A shock awaited me upon my return. Sat in her high chair, Kathleen with a tea towel around her neck was practically bald. Stood on a chair behind her was Mary, wielding a pair of my scissors, chopping away at Kathleen's remaining beautiful curls the rest lay dormant on the floor. I let out a shriek.

'MARY. NO'...Grabbing the scissors out of her hands, dragged her off the chair, she still grinning like a Cheshire cat, until I landed a good smack on her behind making her cry out with pain. Shaking with rage I shouted at her...'NEVER DO THAT AGAIN.'

Hearing me shouting, Mrs. Preston came running in, stopped and burst out laughing. I must admit I seeing the funny side of the incident, quickly turned my head away to laugh. Restraining my laughter I warned Mary.

'Just you wait until your father comes home.'

Kathleen sat in her high chair, several large bald patches with small tufts of hair sprouting out of her scalp. She oblivious to her predicament was grinning and gurgling, I shook my head in disbelief, there was nothing I could do with her hair. Whatever could I do with Mary this child so full of devilment? When Jack arrived, home and saw the state of Kathleen's hair, he had to leave the room to compose his mirth. Little did we know at the time, Mary had a wild and fearless streak inside her, nothing vicious just full of devilment, which neither her Father nor I would ever control.

We had other visitors come to stay with us. Jack's brother Harris his wife Edith, Percy the surviving twin boy born at Christmas two years before and little Dorothy. Somehow we managed to put them up. At that time, being that twins had been born on both sides of our families. I was very conscious of the fact, that there was a strong possibility of me giving birth to twins, however it never was to happen.

They were good company and as the weather was good. We spent most of the time pushing the children around the town in prams and out into the Great Park. They stayed for a week. One evening Jack arrived home and informed me.

'Sarah I've just received orders. I'm being posted to London, to join the sixty-third London's as a Gunnery Instructor. Sorry duck's but we were warned.' I exclaimed.

'That was months ago, I thought they had forgotten about you.' Jack's answer.

'The Army never forgets. They just take their time.'

'What about quarters?'

'Er no. We have to find them.'...Sheepishly he added...'But we do get a subsistence allowance.' Then I was annoyed.

'There. Didn't I tell you so? As far as they are concerned you're still too young. More to the point . When do you leave?' .

'I.m afreaid. Next week is my last week here at the Drillhall.'

'What! Holy Mother of God. Here we go again, looking for a place to live. What about these quarters?'

'Don't worry about that, we're still allowed to occupy them.'

I resigned myself to the next few months of being separated again. The following week Jack left to join his new unit and to find accommodation for us. As far as I was concerned the sooner the better, which was not to be the case. A letter from Jack informed me. The accommodation situation in London was no better than anywhere else. At the mere mention of children it was closed doors. Possibly in the first place, it was the reason why we could not move into these quarters, the occupants couldn't move out. It was going to be a slow process. I thought: *I'll keep myself busy and pack as much as I felt necessary for a quick getaway.* The Adjutant of the Terriers frequently visited to ask, When we were moving out? I would just show him all the packed cases and reply.

'No but I'm all packed and ready to go.'

I even stopped Margaret from using her bike, so she came every third weekend. My sister Mary appeared to be in the same boat as I was. Now back, Bert was playing away some weekends, after being away for a few months in Argentina on a tour that had been successful, apart from one game when a riot broke out she had informed me. With Kathleen in Wales and Bridget somewhere in Scotland. It appeared to me that the four of us were scattered over the four corners of Britain. Then the best news I had been waiting for. A letter from Jack informed me he had finally got two rooms. Move next Friday. Catch the ten thirty train from Windsor to Waterloo, he would meet me there. To me it became a difficult way of living out of a suitcase. At the drop of a hat, move. What a life a soldier's wife had to put up with. I should become a snail with my house on my back

CHAPTER FOURTEEN
LONDON – BRIXTON

With no time to waste, I immediately went to inform the Adjutant of my moving date. I did notice a sign of relief on his face, obviously to him my news was good news. Back in the quarters I dressed my two, left the quarters and went down town to order a taxi.

Early on Friday morning the Stores Corporal arrived to check the inventory. With everything correct, he helped me carry my chattels that had by then increased to two suitcases. I handed over the keys for him to lock up. After he had gone, keeping a firm hold of Mary's hand I said my farewell to Mrs Preston, who had come out to see me off just as the taxi arrived. The Taxi driver got out loaded all my chattels including the pram. As I with little ceremony shoved Mary into the taxi, holding Kathleen in my arms climbed in, quickly shut the door behind me. At the station the driver got out and was more than helpful, he put the cases on the pram and pushed it up onto the platform, placed it in a carriage on the waiting train, Tipping him well climbed into a carriage. During the journey, I mulled over the thought: *Of once again living in London. Miria had always sent me letters, her last one had invited me back. That I was not sure about, but certainly would pay them a visit. I was too eager to meet up with Jack again, wished the train journey would end.* At Waterloo the train ground to a halt. I was up gazing out of the carriage window to catch a glimpse of Jack. I spotted him near the barrier stood with hands on hips looking for us. Waving my arm aloft I yelled out.

'JACK. JACK. BACK HERE.'

He spotted me, waved grinning came running back opened the door. Greeting me with a hug kissed me. With Kathleen in my arms he helped me down, lifted Mary out. Removing the pram from the carriage loaded with our meagre luggage. He asked.

'Is that the lot Sarah?'

'I'm afraid so.' In the pram he sat Kathleen and Mary opposite each other placing one case in between them.

'Right Sarah. You push the pram. I'll take the case. Let's go.'

'Where are we off to Jack? Putney?'

'No. Brixton.'

'Where's Brixton?'

'About six miles.'

'Oh is that close to Putney? '

'Not really, it's in the opposite direction, but Putney is easier to get to.'

I followed Jack through the barriers, under the hanging clock and out through the big front entrance. He grabbed hold of the front of the pram, we carefully carried it down the long flight of steps. Once on the pavement we crossed the road, with Jack at his normal fast pace, proceeded forward. On the way he pointed out places along the river embankment.

'That's Westminster Bridge, behind that, on the other side are the Houses of Parliament , that's Big Ben.' At some wide steps we came to an abrupt halt. Hauling the pram up to the top, stepped onto the Bridge, where the noisy traffic was going both ways, as normal everyone rushing along. Jack turning left led us down the slope then stopped. Lifting Mary and Kathleen from the pram gave Kathleen to me, removing the case Jack folded up the pram. With a resounding crash Big Ben struck the notes of twelve 'o' clock. Mid-day. I watched as a curious conveyance coming to a grinding halt, stopped in the middle of the road. I looked at this contraption with steel wheels, a train running on rails in the road. I remember its number was thirty-three behind it . The horse drawn carts, Omnibus and other traffic stopped. Jack urged me to push the pram towards it. 'C'mon along Sarah this is the tram we want.' As we approached the boarding steps the conductor said.

'Hoi Soldier. Take that pram and cases around the front. There's more room up there. Don't forget to tell the driver where you're getting off. C'mon Ma. I'll give yer 'and, wif those nippers of yer's.' Whilst Jack disappeared with the pram and cases, the Conductor grabbed hold off Mary's arm and guided her up the two steps. Taking Kathleen out of my arms he asked.

'Now you ducks. C'mon ups- a- daisy. Wher's yer going duck's?'

'Brixton I think.' With a big smile across his face he asked.

'Dant cha naw wher yer going then ducks?'

'No I don't. But my husband does, he'll tell you.'

The Conductor held Mary by the hand, until I was ready to take her and move inside this tram to sit down. Jack got on and sat down beside me. A ding ding sound of the bell and we were off. My very first ride on a tram.

'Fares please.'

'Two singles to Brixton.'

'Oh yer do's wants Brixton? Yer Missus din naw where she wher going. Did yer duck's?' Jack laughed.

'Well she only knows Putney you know.'

'Putney. Gor Blimey that's the ovver end o' town ain't it mate eh?' From a ticket holder he removed two tickets. Placing each one in a little machine attached to a belt around his waist, punched a hole in each one, handed them to Jack.

'That'll be three pence each mate.'

Jack handed him the money, he dropped into a leather moneybag. Jack struck up a conversation with the Conductor, who happened to be ex-Army, so they had something to talk about. They broke off when a lady further up, pulled a long cord hanging from the roof. Ding. It sounded. The conductor called out.

'Anyone for the North Lambeth?' The tram stopped, some people got off and some got on. The conductor pulled the string with a Ding-Ding, which started the tram in motion. As the tram trundled along, Jack pointed out place and their names, which went over my head, but the tram fascinated me. Mary stood on the seat watched everything. A noisy clanging sound attracted my attention to the driver at the front of the tram where our pram and cases were. Now and again the driver would stamp his foot down making this clanging sound. After about an hour of swaying about on the noisy tram, it went through a big shopping area. Jack turned to me ordered.

'C'mon Sarah the next stop is where we get off. We have a little walked before we get to the flat.' I thought :his *Little walk! His idea of little walks, always seemed like miles.* Jack helping us down, went around to the front to retrieve the pram and luggage, pushed them onto the pavement, where I joined him with the girls.

'Now Sarah. This is Brixton and we go that way.' Pointing across the road. So began our little walk. Half an hour later he said.

'Here we are Sarah. This is the place, just leave our luggage there. I'll sort them out.'

Opening the front door with a key, we followed him up a flight of stairs, onto a landing he opened the door in front of usn, the door next to it was ajar, which revealed a toilet and sink. I entered the room, it was tiny with not much in it. A big bed, a couple of chairs and a small table. No stove asked.

'Where's the stove to cook on?'

'That's in the room next door, there's also a sink and toilet in there as well. We share it with the other people. There are also three other lodgers in the house. But no children. Unfortunately, we are the last in line to use the gas stove.' Mystified I exclaimed.

'Gas. What gas?'

'Yes. Ma and Pops have got it now. You light it with matchsticks.'

I was gob-smacked. What a life. What a let down after Windsor. Determined to find another place. I just knew this was only going to be a temporary move. Nevertheless, I was to have another shock. When I first saw one of the other lodgers coming up the stairs, he was a Blackman. I nearly died with fright. The strange thing was I found out he had an Irish name. Mr. Maginty. I thought: *God help poor old Ireland.* Mary used to call him Mr Blackman, which the landlady did not like. Early one morning I was about to get Jack's breakfast. Leaving the room I took the frying pan and to my great surprise. Mr. Maginty was already in there washing in the sink. Immediately I dropped the frying pan ran back into the bedroom, jumping onto the bed disturbing Jack, who gruffly said.

'Whatever is wrong with you woman?'

'Mr. Maginty is still in there.' Sitting up replied.

'He should not have been using it. It's not even six yet.' I retorted.

'I wouldn't mind, but he never shuts the door. So anyone else can just barge in.'

'I'll speak with the landlady, to see if we can get a better arrangement sorted out.' He did speak with her. *"She said it was the best she could do."* Everyone had to share, and we would have to put up with it. If we did not like it, we knew what we could do. Get out."

We had no option. Knowing with children, accommodation was not easy to find. However to get away from the flat, with the girls in the pram I would push it all the way to the market in Brixton. A big shopping area with many big stores, two outside markets, two shopping Arcades containing small shops, and there were many more shops within the railway arches along the Atlantic Road. It was a shopper's haven. The outside markets, so reminded me of the Kildare market back home, the shouting amongst the costermongers was quite exciting. Nevertheless, during my visits, I had another purpose in mind. Looking at all the little advertisement boards in the local shops, searching for another flat. Finding one, enquired inside for direction and went to see if they were available. Only to be told. 'No children.' Jack tried through his contacts, but it was much the same. Neither of us was happy with our abode and desperate to find other lodgings. Nevertheless, I was determined to find somewhere in the vicinity. On a Sunday leaving the girls with Jack, after mass I went on my own to another address, when they enquired. 'Any children?'

'Yes two girls.'

'Sorry. No Children.'

A letter from Margaret informed us, she had changed her job, she was working and living in at a Hotel in Victoria. This good news made my shattered spirits rise again, but it was three weeks before she visited us. We spent a pleasant afternoon together, before she caught a tram back to her hotel. Another letter from Mother informed us that my younger sister Eilish had been obtained a receptionist job at Doctors in Gresham Road Brixton. She requested Jack to check it out, also informed her time of arrival at Euston. He did as requested. 'No problem.' I instructed him.

'Jack. Can you get time off to meet Eilish and before you take her to the Doctor's House. Bring her back here to see me.' On the Saturday afternoon they arrived at the flat, to a warm welcome and a good chat about things back home, and I being inquisitive asked.

'Eilish. How did you get the Job?'

'It was advertised in a Dublin newspaper. They accepted my qualification and I got the job I have a room in his house for my accommodation.'

As Jack was on duty that night, it was convenient for her to stay over and go to the Doctors the next day. With Margaret already established in the Hotel, the recent arrival of Eilish, it turned out to be a blessing in disguise. With all my searching for a flat. I suggested the pair of them should share a flat, which they both agreed to do. Fortunately I found a suitable flat for them within walking distance of our own flat. They moved in. In return they offered to help look for a new flat, on their afternoons off. However, one afternoon expecting them two knocks on the street door heralded their arrival. Hurrying down to let them I got such a fright. Three black men stood on the step I let out a shriek turned around and ran, pounding up the stairs I lost one of my slippers and hopped across the landing into our room, slamming the door behind me frightening my two girls. I stood with my back to the door my heart racing. I heard the landlady shout.

'MRS PLANT. IT'S ALL RIGHT'....Cautiously I opened my door to hear her shout.... 'MR MAGINTY LIVES AT THE TOP.' I shut and locked the door, suddenly a knock on the door made me jump. I unlocked opened it to see a giant Blackman who said.

'I'm very sorry Ma'am. I did not want to frighten you. I think this is your slipper'... handed over the slipper. I was flabbergasted muttered...'Thank You.' When my sisters eventually arrived, I told them about the incident, they laughing their heads off retorted.

'Your daft to worry, Sarah.'

Worrier I maybe. But even greater than looking for a flat, I find I'm expecting once again. Nine months of sickness, illness, the inconvenience of sharing a toilet. I was forced to use the guzunder in my bedroom, then emptied it when no one was about. I explained my concern to Jack, his reply was.

'You know Sarah God is good. Don't worry so much. Something will turn up.'

One afternoon my sisters were paying their usual weekly visit, when two knocks on the street door, heralded the arrival of someone to see us. Margaret, leaving the door open ran down to open the door. I heard the landlady shout out.

'HEH! YOU THERE. THAT'S MY RESPONSIBILITY. WHO DO YOU THINK YOU ARE?'

'These letters are addressed to Mrs Plant not to anyone else.'

Margaret coming back into the room, banged the door shut exclaiming

'It was the Postman. He handed me two letters.'

Just then the door was flung open, in barged the Landlady. Wagging her finger at me, angrily said.

'You and your family are on a week's notice. Out you go in a week's time.' Stomped back out slammed the door behind her.

Forgetting about the letters, the three of us sat there aghast, trying to sort out this new problem. I did not want to return to Jack's parents and knew my sister's flat was not big enough to swing a cat in. Quietly they left before Jack arrived back leaving me to tell Jack. When he did come home I blurted out.

'Jack bad news. The landlady's given us one weeks' notice to get out.' Standing, with hands on hips I could see he was annoyed he just said.

'Oh no Sarah. Okay.Now what are we going to do?'

'God help me Jack, I don't know what to do?' He stood there thinking.

'Neither do I Sarah. Well I can possibly sleep in the Drillhall store room, which leaves you expectant with the two girls. We will just have to sleep on it.'

With Jack snoring his head off beside me, I thinking: *Of the prospect of finding something in one week was impossible.* Could not sleep. Getting up, sorted out the two letters sat down to read them. By the stamp, one was from mother the other from Kathleen. I read both of them, thought a while before deciding what I should do: *Kathleen was a possible option?* Being already up, I jumped the queue for the stove, had Jack's breakfast cooked ready. I woke him, while he ate I said.

'Jack I've being thinking. I could visit Kathleen for a couple of weeks, while you, Margaret and Eilish find some accommodation. What you think?'

'Well Sarah, that's a short option, but a good one. Yes send her a wire.'

103

I was the first in the queue at the Post Office to write out the wire and send it. Late that afternoon the Landlady knocked on my door, with a curt nod she handed a wire to me. I shut the door in her face and tore open the yellow envelope.

COME STAY WITH US STOP YOU ARE WELCOME STOP

I was elated, when Jack arrived home I gave it to him.

'Good that's settled. With you in your condition the quicker the better if that's possible? Tomorrow I'll sort out tickets and trains. Just sort out your very basic needs for the three of you, all the rest, I'll store in the Drillhall until I find another flat. I'll start looking tomorrow, you mark my words. You'll be back in London before you know the time of day.' He said, but without a grin.

The next day Jack sent a wire to Kathleen. I sorted out the clothing, packed our meagre needs for a short stay? Saturday we left the flat. Jack took us to Paddington, bought our tickets, settled us into a compartment, already occupied by another lady and gentleman, he bade me farewell said.

'I will send a wire to Kathleen. She will meet you at the station, I'll see you in a couple of weeks. Okay duck's.'

The train had only just left the station when I felt very sick, I had to get to the toilet. I tried taking the two little ones with me however, the lady seeing I was not well looked after them for me. Which was just the start of a terrible train journey, how I ever completed it I shall never know. I had no sooner returned, than I rushed out again I must have looked dreadful, I certainly felt it. The gentleman observing my trips to and fro, standing up from his pocket produced a hip flask, held it out towards me and offered.

'C'mon Missus take a sip of this brandy, it will settle your stomach.' A kind gesture but unaware I was pregnant. I mumbled,

'No thank you very much I don't drink.' He insisted.

'Look Missus, the state you're in, it must do you some good.'

Obliging him, I took the flask, a sip, swallowed the fiery liquid, then beat a hasty retreat to the toilet. It was occupied, instead I opened the door window. Apart from nearly getting me head blown off I nearly lost my false teeth. Fortunately for me, the couple helping me remained on the train until three stations before my stop. I thanked them from the bottom of my heart.

It was close to evening time when the train arrived at Machynlleth, Kathleen and Frank met us. Seeing me they must have thought. "I was about to die". Whereas I thought: *I had already died a thousand deaths*. No time for niceties, they got us to their home, where I promptly retched into the flowerbeds. Inside they put me on a bed to rest. It was about an hour later before I was able to get up and face the world! Kathleen by this time had fed my two, suggested I have something to eat and drink. Still feeling like death warmed up declined her offer, I was not in a fit state to consume anything, but it was time to put my two to bed that chore I did carry out, whilst Frank and Kathleen had their tea. When Kathleen had been pregnant her first, a little girl was born in Ireland, unfortunately died three weeks after her birth. Her next birth was a boy who lived a few months. It was obvious that they were delighted to have our two stay, made quite a fuss of them. I was exhausted, excused myself to retire. I slept soundly. Next morning I woke to Mary's chattering, feeling much better, so as not to disturb Kathleen and Frank I shushed them to be quiet, got up dressed myself then dressed them in the bedroom, before I ventured out into the other room to find Kathleen already, cooking breakfast.

'Sarah. How are you? You certainly look a lot better?' I truthfully answered.

'Much better now I've had a good night's sleep and rest.'

Frank arrived back dripping wet, outside it was pouring down with rain.

'Good morning Sarah how are you this morning?'

'Much better, I did sleep well.'

I was so hungry I ate the breakfast laid before me, which made me feel better for it. After breakfast we sat down to relate the plight of my recent saga. Kathleen saw the funny side and could not stop laughing.

'Sarah. Nobody should get in a tangle with Margaret, she can give as well as she gets.' Her opinion, I did agree upon.

Late in the afternoon the rain subsided, occasionally the sun emerged from behind the dark clouds. Again I slept peacefully, knowing that at least if I needed to be sick I would not be locked out of a toilet. The following day I awoke to the sun shining through the windows. As I had done the previous day I got the two girls dressed ready for a day outside. Breakfast was eaten and then I took the girls out to see the surrounding area. Their house had ample rooms to accommodate us and did not cramp their living style. It was located in a delightful setting half way up a hillside, in the distance you could see the sea. Walking around in the sun it was quiet, peaceful and very pleasant, but I knew the quietness could not last? Over the following few days Mary was in trouble, doing everything she should not do. She was into everything. Most of her time she constantly pulled up all Frank's flowers out of his garden, she climbed out of the upstairs window that frightened me, she was never still for one minute, she tired me out just watching her.

To keep her out of their way I would take her to the top of the hill, where there was a seat and stay there as long as possible. My stay of two weeks flew by and there was still no news from Jack about a flat. They continued to make me welcome, but after a month I overheard Frank complain to Kathleen about Mary's antics. "That he spent more time in his garden replanting flowers than indoors." I could tell that Frank was getting fed up with having us around. Neither of them knew anything about high-spirited children. I overheard Frank remark to Kathleen that after seeing Mary's tricks, he certainly did not want any more children. (But they did later, produced three boys. They too were to turn out as little devils). Jack's letters regularly informed me 'No Rooms.' He had been competing in athletics races, swimming galas and was then playing football. I was in two minds as how to take his news. How could he be looking for accommodation and doing all those other activities? While I was stuck in the middle of Wales, worried silly about my future accommodation. Then Frank would start ranting on again about Mary's antics. I could not make any comment. I knew Mary was a handful, often wondered what I had done to deserve such punishment? I persevered for six weeks, then decided enough was enough. I did not care anymore. Leaving the two girls with Kathleen I walked into town, straight to the train station found out the times of the trains, bought a ticket, went to the Post Office sent a wire to Jack.

LEAVING MACHYNLLETH SATURDAY STOP
COMING HOME ON THE FIRST TRAIN STOP
ARRIVING 5:30 AFTERNOON STOP
MEET ME AT PADDINGTON STOP

CHAPTER FIFTEEN
LONDON - IN- BETWEEN

The train journey back to London was without any incident. Arriving back at Paddington with absolutely no place to live. Jack met us. Obviously very pleased to see us. I more than pleased to see him. We went into the buffet for a cup of tea, a sandwich with cakes for the two girls. We sat down talking. I explained how my stay had ended with such a quick departure. Jack not saying a word looked sternly at Mary, she just grinned.

'Sarah last Sunday I met your sister Lena at the station, she's has come over to work in Victoria near Margaret, they have all moved into a larger flat together. I did ask their old landlady if, we could have their flat? You guessed it. She said No Children. Not good news for us. I've looked everywhere. Our only chance is a one room flat in Holland road near the Drill hall, the landlady said. Yes only if I would promise her, we would leave in two months, which I couldn't promise so refused.'

'Jack. Another possibility gone, Mary in Plymouth can be ruled out, in her letter to Kathleen, stated, Bert had been picked to play for England touring Australia for the next six months. She had decided to go back to Ireland.'... A sharp reply....'Well good on Bert.' We were stumped as to what we should do?... 'Jack what about Harris? He might know of something?'....'Sarah, we have no options left. They live in Putney not far from Ma and Pops, it's worth a try. C'mon, let's move.'

Late afternoon we arrived on their doorstep. Delighted to see us invited us in. Their home was small, comfortable and just adequate to accommodate them. Over a pot of tea, we poured out our tale of woe with me in my state of health. After listening to this, Harris said.

'Jack. Ma's taken in lodgers, so don't go there. All we can offer is a roof over your head while you find something quick.'

I could not thank them enough. Somehow they arranged beds for us. Jack returned to the Drillhall and I cried myself to sleep. I helped out with the washing and cooking. Visited my In-laws, who welcomed me like a long lost child. They too began the search, while I pounded the streets looking for somewhere to house us. However, Miria found a little flat near Wandsworth Park, nothing much but I took it. Leaving Harris and Edith with my grateful thanks, took what I had and moved in. I was constantly being sick worrying myself silly, about our bleak prospects, only venturing out to get what provisions and necessities we required. After his duty Jack came everyday riding to and fro on an Army bike. We shared our evening meal together, bathed the girls and put them into the meagre bed we shared. This was a desperate time for both of us. He was very concerned about how we could obtain any accommodation. It was during the third week of our stay, that Jack arrived with a big broad grin spread all over his face, indicating something had happened, he announced.

'Sarah good news today. The lady in Holland Road was in touch. We could have the room from tomorrow for two months. I've seen her and paid for the flat. We move tomorrow. What do you say about that ducks? '...Physically, I breathed a sigh of relief, broke out in tears.... 'C'mon duck's it's going to be all right. On your feet Soldier.' I composed myself.

'Jack that's the best news I've heard in months, at least we will be together for two months. What about after? Did she say anything?'

'No, I think we already know what she has in mind. Those theatre people are coming back. In the meantime it's somewhere closer to start looking around.'

The following day I gathered my meagre chattels up to move. Jack was allowed time off to collect me and take us to this new flat in Holland Road. Before we left I made a courtesy call on Jack's parents as well as Harris and Edith. When we arrived at the other flat I found it was quite

106

close to the Drillhall and Jack could stay with us. The Landlady greeted us and advised us what the arrangements in the flat were. They were the same as the one in Brixton. Last tenant in last to use the facilities, the rent included the use of the gaslights and stove. It was inconvenient but we were together, we just had to grin and bear it, whilst we continued our search. It was within walking distance of Brixton, therefore was able to spend as much time as I had searching. Nevertheless the constant worry, each passing day was one day closer to being out on the streets. My three sisters were also searching and were able to resume their visits to me on their afternoons off. Their company gave me a little peace of mind. With their coming and goings, the landlady had the cheek to ask me.

'Mrs Plant how many more sisters have you got?' When I politely told her.

'Nine more and they will all be coming over soon?' I immediately realised I had said the wrong thing. She exclaimed.

'Oh my God.' She nearly died with the thought of it. She took exception to the thought of a whole gaggle of women taking over her house. Every week thereafter she reminded me.

'Mrs Plant. When the two months are up your out.' One week away from the last day of the two months, the Landlady informs me.

'Mrs Plant this is your final week. Next Monday you're out.'

I was well into pregnancy, praying myself stupid, in a terrible state with nerves. When Jack arrived home I relayed her message.

'Jack the landlady insists we go next Monday.'

'Well Sarah you know, I've being trying all over the place, I don't know where we shall go. The only thing I can do if the worst comes to the worst. Is to take you to the local police station. They would not leave you on the street with two babies and expecting another one.' I cried out.

'Jack Plant. I do not want to spend any time in any police station no matter what our circumstances are.' Jack just shrugged his shoulders.

I was poorly, at my wits end, twisting the wedding ring on my finger, biting finger nails that I did not possess, with a cry of anguish I wailed.

'What are we to do?' I decided to face the music and have a talk with the landlady to explain our circumstances. I tried to pacify her saying that my sisters would not be allowed to visit me. But she didn't want to know, it was an excuse for her to get rid of us.

Two nights later Jack arrived home from duty grinning. Sullenly asked him.

'Hello. What have you got to be so cheerful about?'

'Sarah. I think I have solved our problem. One of my sergeants Bert Thomas who is aware of our needs. Has an old lady staying upstairs in his house, she has lived there during his Mother's time and according to Bert. Not the best of tenants, as she was always fighting and arguing with his wife. He had tried on several occasions to get her out without success, she would not go. After the latest of these bust–ups. Bert has had enough and given her notice. This time it's worked, she's leaving her flat next Monday, the same day that we have to get out of here. I curiously asked.

'Well what does that mean?'

'Look, Bert has said that it's not much in the way of accommodation, but he and his wife Dolly are willing to offer it to us. I've already taken it. I've met his wife Dolly on a couple of occasions at the Mess. I think you will like her.' My spirit's soared at this news.

'Jack that's wonderful news. Thank God my prayers had been answered. When can we see it? Where is it? How long can we stay?' I full of questions, was impatient to get moving again.

'Hey one question at a time.' Number one we should not go until after twelve 'o' clock on Monday, after the woman has moved out. It's not too far away, its in conderton road the other side of Loughborough Junction.'

'I don't care how far away it is, so long as we have somewhere to live, rather than having the threat of being put out on the street and finishing up in a police station.'

'Well you can stop worrying, that threat has gone away. Bert said we can have the flat for as long as we like.'

Jack celebrated our success in the Mess with Bert, stayed out until the early hours of the morning. Not on that occasion I took too much notice. Nevertheless on the other hand I was too worried with thoughts of: *In case this other woman changing her mind and it all fell through!* I did not sleep well, I must have said the rosary twenty times. Slowly the days crawled by.

CHAPTER SIXTEEN
LOUGHBOROUGH JUNCTION.

Monday morning together as one family, with all our worldly goods left the flat without a word of goodbye. We had not done anything wrong, except just one chance of a wrongly worded remark, which did not justify her reaction. We left in good time to walk to Conderton Road. On our way we picked up some provisions for the next two days, as we were buying some vegetables Jack made a remark.

'You know Sarah, I think lady luck is on our side at last. We should be all right here.' With apprehension all I could say was.

'Jack. Let's wait and see. Only time will tell?'

Well before mid-day, we arrived outside Bert's house. Jack lifted Mary up into his arms I took Kathleen up in mine, followed Jack up the steps. He banged the knocker on the door, after a short time a women opened the door wide. She appeared to be in her late twenties, a little on the plump side, clinging to her pinafore was a little boy, dressed only in a vest hanging below his navel, he was bare footed with a runny nose. Jack greeted her.

'Hello Dolly. We've arrived is it okay to come in?'

'Hello Jack, and I take it this is your good lady wife Mrs Plant. Hello there ducks. Just call me Dolly, there's a ducks. Welcome to our house. Bert's told me all about you. Your pregnant I see'...Mrs. Thomas a cheery type of person continued... 'The last lady left only just minutes before you arrived. (A chuckle) Between you and me I was really glad to get rid of her. C'mon in just follow me.'

She with her little boy clinging to her pinafore walked down a passageway towards the stairs closely followed by Jack, I closed the door behind us following the procession up the stairs, whilst she talked on.

'C'mon up ducks. Sorry for the mess she left it in, but you will understand. I haven't had time to clean through.'...At the top of the stairs she still carried on...'Here you are ducks, through this doorway.'...She led the way into this room...'There's a sink over there and a stove. Your meters on the landing just outside. I will show you how to work it. It takes pennies and sixpences it's easy to use. Now toilet arrangements. There are no other tenants except Bert and me, and of course young Bertie here. Bertie. Say hello to Mrs Plant there's a good boy.'...Little Bertie cowered even further behind his mother's pinafore....'As I was saying. It's there whenever you want to use it. We don't stand on ceremony in this house. (followed by a chuckle)...'Anyway if you'll come this way, I'll show you the rest of the flat.'...still chatting we followed behind with little Bertie scrambling up another small flight of stairs exposing his little backside to the world. As they disappeared into another room I looked at Jack, with a huge grin spread across over his face. He certainly was quite happy with the situation, which made me feel this would be all right. I hissed at him.

'She hasn't stopped talking yet and I haven't even said hello.'...To hide his mirth, he turned away as I entered the bedroom where Mrs. Thomas was still talking...'Now as I was just saying?' Then I spoke my first words to her.

'Err. Sorry what were you saying? I didn't quite catch what you said?'

'If there's anything you want. Just give me a shout. I'm only downstairs and I'll be up in no time at all.'...Her last statement was the truth, that very soon I was to find out about...'Look there's another room next door, which we can make available to you. I'll sort that out with Bert. Don't you worry about a thing? I'll leave you two to sort yourselves out. I'll go and make a pot of tea for all of us. Do you take sugar? One or two spoons?' A chance to reply.

'Err. None for me. Thank you Mrs. Thomas.'

'Oh. Not a sweet tooth just like me. Okay ducks. (another chuckle) I'll give you a shout when it's ready. Come along Bertie.'

They left with Bertie still clinging to her pinafore. I turned to Jack and all we could do was burst out laughing, the tension of weeks of worrying had gone.

'My God Sarah. She does like her tongue. Bert said she was a chatterbox, now I know why.'

'She's harmless not like the other landladies I've encountered. I do like her.'

We surveyed the bedroom. "It was filthy and smelly." The bed was un-kept and possibly full of bugs. Still holding the girls in our arms we retreated back to the kitchen, which was just as filthy as if it had not been cleaned in years. I noticed the windows were wide open and exclaimed.

'My God Jack. This place will need to be scrubbed from top to bottom. We will have to buy some carbolic.' Jack stood there shaking his head muttered.

'By the state of this place. I can understand why Bert and his missus wanted the woman out. It is not healthy.' I was dismayed at the prospects of cleaning through.

'Well. The main thing is. We now have a roof over our heads. We will just have to clean it up. I'll start with the sink, then the cupboards.'

'Sarah. Before you start I'll bring up the boxes for you to unpack. Then I'll go to the stores to get some cleaning materials to get rid of the grime. I shan't be long.'

'Don't be silly Jack. I'm not unpacking anything until it's all cleaned up. You can't put anything clean down in this pigsty of a place. I'm certainly not letting these two run around.' A shout from downstairs stopped our discussion.

'COOOEE. CUP OF TEA READY DOWN HERE FOR THE PAIR OF YOU.' WHAT ABOUT THE TWO GIRLS? DO THEY WANT SOME AS WELL? COME ON DOWN WHILE IT'S STILL HOT.' Her string of questions ended as the sound of her voice receded. I remarked.

'She's real funny Jack. C'mon, let's oblige the lady and take tea with her. Only one mind you. We have a lot of work to get through up here.'

We proceeded down through a passageway into her kitchen. I was not surprised, it was very clean, tidy and comfortable. We had tea. Jack finally interrupted her on-going conversation.

'Excuse me Dolly. But I have to go. I have to get some cleaning stuff from the stores. Sarah and I want to get the place cleaned up before we.'...Jack did not even finish...'Oh you go on Jack. Once I get chatting it's the devil's own job to stop me.'...Then burst into a peel of laughter. I joining in her mirth, excused myself but she still carried on...'While you sort out upstairs. Leave the two girls down with me, they will be okay playing here with little Bertie.'

During her marathon conversation with us, she never mentioned, she had any time to clean up the flat upstairs. I made a mental note that neither had she offered to help. We both left her kitchen, with a word of warning to Mary,

'Now Mary. No trouble understand.'

As Mrs. Thomas continued chatting nineteen to the dozen to little Bertie. Jack left me at the bottom of the stairs to collect the cases. I went up the stairs to the kitchen, once inside shook my head in disbelief, removing my coat and hat, placed them on a chair, rolled up my sleeves about to start with the job of cleaning. Jack returned said.

'Sarah. I've left the cases in the hallway. Don't you do too much until I get back. I won't be long'. I thought: *Regardless of my condition. The quicker we got all this done the better I would feel.* Looking around, it all needed attention. I went over to this gas cooker. A tiny little thing with three gas rings on the top and a cupboard oven. Opening the door, found it contained two jugs of soured milk, immediately closed it shut and retched. *God. I thought I was going to be sick.* I turned away to the table where a few dirty plates lay in a heap. The sink was no better. In its deep depths lay two cast iron pots, their handles pointing at me in defiance at the cleaning they were about to get. A tin teapot lay drunkenly on its side, as was a small kettle with no lid. I stared

110

at the pile of utensils in front of me I thought: *Of all the places we have stayed they were nothing compared to this place. This must be the pittance! But cleaned up it would look very nice.*

I turned on the tap at the sink, as water trickled out partially filled it with water before swishing it around, emptied it. Taking hold of the kettle filled it up and placed it on the stove out of the way. The pots were disgusting. I needed rags. I looked under the sink, nothing it was a job for hands only. I had to make a start somewhere. By the time I had removed some of the grime and dirt from the sink, the sound of clumping footsteps announced Jack's arrival. He called out.

'Sarah.' I turned around to see Jack stood in the doorway with another Sergeant, who with his bulk almost filled it and was head and shoulders over Jack. A rather robust figure of a man with ruddy cheeks and a pleasant smile...'Sarah this is Sergeant Bert Thomas. Your landlord.'

'Hello Mrs Plant. Welcome to this humble abode. I've come to help Jack and you clean it up. I'm so terribly sorry for the state the old woman left it in. It's more like a pigsty. She was so dirty we have been trying to get rid of her for years.'

My first impression of Bert was another cheery soul just like his wife. I warmed to his hospitality, offered my wet hand saying.

'I'm very pleased to meet you. That's very kind of you.' Firmly shaking it he said.

'Already getting stuck in cleaning I see.

'Sarah, we can't sleep on that bed up there. So Bert and I have brought two mattresses plus a load of bedding, some cleaning material from the stores, it's outside on a hand barrow. Bert says he's got a cot that we can use for Mary, temporarily Kathleen can sleep in the pram. It's emergency time at the moment until we get sorted out. Is that okay?'

I was pleased they had thought about those immediate things.

'Well anything offered, would go a long way at this time.' Bert added.

'Any other bits and pieces you need, I'm sure we can help out with.' They retreated downstairs, returning with the bedding left it outside on the landing further up the stairs, another couple of trips, brought in the cleaning materials, mops, brooms, buckets, with jars of something. Bert coming into the kitchen stated.

'Mrs Plant. Let me take you downstairs to Dolly. She will make you a cup of tea and you can have a chat while we clean through.' I thought. *God another one way chat.* I stated.

'I'd rather be up here cleaning out.' But Bert insisted taking me by the arm ushered me out of the kitchen, back downstairs into her kitchen entering he said.

'Dolly put the kettle on. Mrs Plant wants a cup of tea while Jack and I clean through the flat.'

'Oh that would be nice, sit you down Mrs Plant.'

Bert retreated leaving me with Mrs. Chatterbox. After the cup of tea I excused myself and retreated back upstairs with the girls, only to be promptly ordered back downstairs again. Hours later when I eventually did get back upstairs, my ears were ringing from the onslaught of her chattering. Our possessions in boxes and cases, were on the landing. Jack was on his own at the sink, there was no sign of Bert. The kitchen reeked of carbolic, the table was scrubbed white with bleach, with our provisions stacked upon it.

'Aah Sarah. We've cleaned the floors, tables and chairs, the bedroom is cleaned out ready for use. Bert has taken the barrow back loaded with rubbish, to bring some other things, I've just finished cleaning the pots. Maybe you can start getting something to eat?'

The transformation from a pigsty to a liveable kitchen was evident, I pleased with their result, sat the girls at the table while getting on with the dinner. I had nearly finished when Bert arrived back with cutlery and crockery. After the meal I cleared away, Jack brought up the bed, cot the pram then made up the beds, whilst I bathed the girls dressed and bedded them down, before we got stuck in cleaning the kitchen cupboards. It was getting late and Jack tried to get me to rest, he gave up and went to bed around one a.m. It was three a.m. before I finished, being used to it, preferring to do my housework after the girls were asleep. I could not live in a dirty place and within a short period of time, we had the flat looking spick and span. Much to the approval of Bert and his chattering Missus. This fortunate break was a turning point in our luck. I was so grateful and happy to have a flat of my own without the prospect of sharing.

Their house was very old, in constant need of repair. After the First World War it had been condemned? From time to time the roof in our kitchen leaked, workmen would just patch it up. Nevertheless, our flat became a very happy one. We both thought Dolly was the best landlady we ever had, apart from her chattering and she was very forgetful. Often when washing up would leave the tap running soaking her kitchen. Dolly, God bless her. Could not care less, you could invite as many visitors as you liked and dance all night, it never mattered to her. She along with young Bertie, a year younger than Mary would pay me a visit in the morning stay for lunch, and the rest of the day. I gave up thinking: *She might go down to her own flat.* I just carried on with my usual chores and kept our flat spotless. Nevertheless, Dolly was a constant companion and became a good friend to me, a big strong girl, but the thought of doing too much work she would delay it for a later day. Every Friday, I would bake Irish soda cake, three dozen-fairy cakes and a sponge for the weekend. Dolly would sit there watching me, telling me how marvellous I was. On those occasions with me in my condition, in frustration I could have told her to make her own but it was pointless getting upset. She could cook cakes but it was far easier for her to watch me. Bert was pleasant placid and the Units mess Bar Sergeant. Jack was in his glory, he could stay out as long as he liked, when the Bar closed, then the pair of them came home. On occasions Bert would come up and ask.

'Hello Sarah how's everything?' Dolly sat at our table would ask.

'Hello ducks, just come up for a cup of tea with us?'

He would just shake his head, shrug his shoulders and go down again. On some occasions, Dolly would ask, if I wouldn't mind looking after young Bertie, whilst she went to the mess to have a few drinks with Bert. Dolly did not drink very much, but did talk with the other wives. The only drink she did partake was to lubricate her vocal chords. On those occasion when I was looking after Bertie, after a while Bertie would wake up terrified bawling his head off. apparently his bedroom was supposed to be haunted? I would go down carry him up and put him in bed with Mary. Upon her return Dolly would check Bertie's bedroom find he was not there come and collect him from Mary's bed, On her way back down with Bertie fast asleep in her arms would whisper to me.

'God Bless you duck's. Nightie-night see you in the morning.'

Dolly and I had a mutual understanding. I loved her ways and her company. I was totally happy living in her presence, upon looking back, one thing I can say is Dolly is always on hand to distract me from my sickness. From a store in Brixton we bought a lovely gramophone with some records, so I could relax and listen to the music in the girls bedroom, however when my sisters arrived, the gramophone was put to good use, they dancing to the Irish Jigs and Reels. It wasn't long before Dolly would come up pop her head around the door and say.

'Is it all right Ducks? I've only come up to say hello to your three sisters. I'll be off in a couple of minutes.'

She would stay for hours and join in the fun that went on well into the evenings, whilst they carried on I got Mary and Kathleen their food ready for bed in our bedroom. With Dolly's assistance and a little bit of shifting about, we would accommodate my three sisters for the night. A new dance the Charleston became the rage, which changed our selection of records, so the three of them would practice dancing for hours. I thought: *If only I was not pregnant, I could show my sisters a thing or two about dancing.* It was on one such day I had received a letter from Mary, to say Bert had returned from Australia. the England team had won all of their twenty-five matches, Bert was their top goal scorer. When Jack read this he was highly delighted with the team and Bert's performance, so much so, he and Dolly's Bert went down the mess, came back

112

very late the worst for drink, yet with the football season beginning had Jack out playing football at the week-ends. Autumn arrived. Mary the bane of my life, was constantly teasing the life out of Bertie, chasing him up and down the stairs. I would scream at Mary to stop it, but she would not give in. Dolly would take no notice of the racket they caused if, she had stopped young Bertie, then we could have sorted each one of them out, there appeared to be no point in it. I gave up. A couple of weeks before Christmas, I received a letter from mother. She was sending us a big turkey, warning me. "Don't be out, gallivanting about when the postman arrived." (In heavens name, what gallivanting was I going to get up to? With me heavy in pregnancy, I would only shop with the two girls down as far as Loughborough Junction). She also mentioned that the English and Irish Governments, had finally agreed about the border issue between the North and Southern States of Ireland, which would remain as before in the Treaty of twenty-one. It appeared that finally there could be a settled peace? The Postman did arrive with a big turkey, enough to feed a battalion?

Christmas that year was very cold without snow. The turkey was big we decided to have a joint Christmas dinner with Dolly, Bert, my three sisters to the festive dinner. On Christmas morning a table was set up downstairs in Dolly's front room. Whilst Jack dressed the big turkey, it was so big he had to cut off its legs. The four of us with Mary and Kathleen went to early Mass at our local Church, upon returning found Jack had left the turkey carcase and legs on the table, he and Bert had disappeared to the "Cambridge" pub for a pint leaving us to prepare the dinner. Eilish attempted to get the carcase in our oven but the door would not shut, we took it down to Dolly to cook it in her oven, the legs we cooked in our tiny oven When Jack and Bert arrived back, ten sat down to a lovely meal. Afterwards records were played on the gramophone to dance to the Jigs, Reels and Charleston records. I think we spasmodically carried on throughout that week, my sisters going to work then returning back home including the New Year, to me it the best I had enjoyed since I came to England. The arrival of 1926. Was quickly followed by another celebration. Bert's birthday, he invited us all to the mess for a drink. I politely refused. On the other hand Dolly came up asked.

'You don't mind looking after my Bertie, do you Sarah?' I didn't refuse.

After Bert and Jack had left. I began polishing down the stairways, having done the upper stairs, started on the landing where a tiny sink was located in the corner, quite happily polishing the floor, suddenly I came up banging my head under the sink with such force, knocked a chunk out of it which fell down onto my fingers, ripping a fingernail off. Apart from knocking myself senseless I nearly passed out with the pain of my finger, tightly gripping it trying to stem the flow of blood, getting up staggered downstairs to Dolly who was just about ready to leave exclaimed.

'Oh my God Sarah. That is a silly thing to do polishing.' She fussed over me, bound it up with a clean handkerchief, gave me a cup of tea and an aspirin... 'Are you all right now Sarah? When I see Jack in the Mess. I'll tell him about your finger.'...Then she left on her mission of mercy. The pain in my finger was bad, so I made my way upstairs to lie down. I lay there for an hour or more with no sign of Jack however, the pain of my finger eased, then to my horror the labour pains started, they were bad. I asked God to grant the baby would not be born with no one to help. The labour pains eventually did ease. It was about one o'clock in the morning when they arrived back. When Jack came into the bedroom he stupidly asked.

'Sarah Ducks. Whatever have you been up to? Dolly told me you had cut your finger, sha said she had wrapped it up and it was okay. How is it?'

I removed the bloody handkerchief that had stuck to the open wound making it bleed again, then I got him to feel the large lump on my head. All he said was.

'What a silly girl you are. In your condition you were silly to be polishing at that time of night.' I gave up, sleep was the answer, a disturbed one.

It was with some difficulty that I rose early, so long as I didn't knock my finger, it would be all right. I sorted out the two girls, got Jack his breakfast before he left. Later, keeping myself busy, trying to make a meat pudding for the dinner found it difficult keeping my finger straight, then the labour pains began again. I called down to Dolly to come and take the girls down with her, as I wasn't feeling too good, she came up.

'Don't you fret yourself, they will be all right with me. You lie down for a little while. It must have been that bang on your head you had last night.'

As the labour pains had eased I didn't argue. I went to bed, when Jack arrived home at lunchtime I was still in bed coming into the room he asked how I was? I told him about the labour pains I was getting. Then he politely informed me, he had to go over to the other side of London to get some important papers signed. That did annoy me.

'Never mind the damn papers. Go down to the post office and send a wire to Margaret to come immediately. She promised me she would look after the two girls.' Taken aback by my outburst he said.

'Right, I'll go now, send the wire before I return to barracks.'

I lay there unable to move, the pains had become more frequent, cursing my luck with nobody at hand. It was sometime later when Margaret did arrive. I sent her to get the nurse. Dolly brought in the three children, washed and fed informing me.

'Margaret has gone for the nurse, she said I should come up and see you. Now don't you fret yourself Ducks, I'll look after them.' Two bangs on the front door downstairs had Dolly leaving to open the door. Margaret puffed her way in stated.

'Nurse will be here soon.'

When the Nurse did arrive she ordered all out of the bedroom before examining me said.

'Mrs Plant your baby will not be born for some hours, probably tomorrow? Now I have to go and see someone else, I will return in an hour.' She left then Jack, came into the bedroom to inform me.

'I just got back, the nurse told us the baby will be born tomorrow. Sarah seeing you have Margaret on hand who by the way is cooking a meal for us? Do you want anything to eat or drink? Maybe a cup of tea?' Wearily I said.

'No. I am not in any mood for any food or drink.'

'Oh. Okay after I've eaten I must go and get these papers signed. I'll be as quick as I can Sarah.' He left then popped back in to inform me.

'I'm just away Sarah I won't be long.'

A couple a bangs on the door took him back down. Just then the labour pains began again The Nurse appeared in the bedroom, dumped her Gladstone bag on the floor, with not a care in the world, sat on the bed as I continued with the contractions. By eight-thirty that evening I'd had enough. I was in terrible pain, I pleaded with the nurse.

'Please get the doctor.' She felt around my stomach.

'No need yet. All in good time. You are not bad enough.' Not bad enough? I was in agony. Then Jack put in an appearance he came back in to ask.

'Sarah how are you? I thought it might be all over. I've got the papers signed.' I shouted.

I DON'T CARE A DAMN ABOUT YOUR DAMN PAPERS. NURSE. IF YOU DON'T GET ME A DOCTOR NOW I WILL SCREAM THE PLACE DOWN.'

'If you insist. When I'm in trouble I send for a lady doctor down the road.' I shouted at her.

'WHEN YOU'RE IN TROUBLE. IT'S ME WHO IS HAVING THE BABY NOT YOU.' She taking umbrage, ordered Jack.

'Hoi you. Go fetch Doctor Smythe. Her surgery is down the road on the corner of Coldharbour Lane. Do it immediately.'

114

I was more than screaming. Both Margaret and Dolly had disappeared. Soon Jack did arrive back with the Doctor.

'Mrs Plant isn't it? You are lucky, your husband is very concerned. He caught me just before I was going out with some friends, he insisted I come with him. Is it your first baby?'

'No.' my third.' With the Nurse in attendance she proceeded to examine me thoroughly murmured. 'Uhm.' Taking off her coat remarked.

'Nurse no time to waste. Forceps needed. Mrs Plant I'll give you an injection to ease the pain.' In agony I blurted out.

'I've been through hell since three 'o'clock this afternoon. I hope and pray that it will. The nurse told me it would not be born until tomorrow.' It was an becoming an effort for me to speak.

'Mrs Plant shush don't speak. I have only minutes to save your baby's life. By six tomorrow morning. I would not have given much hope for you or the baby.'

That really frightened me. In a state of forced delivery with the agony of my pains, I heard the Doctor tell the nurse off. I could not have cared less. At nine-twenty in the evening I gave birth to a boy and passed out. Coming round I faintly heard a voice.

'Mrs Plant can you hear me?.... still fuzzy I heard a raised voice. 'Can You Hear Me Mrs. Plant?' I was so fuzzy weakly whispered.

'What happened?'

'Aah Good. Mrs Plant. Your back with us listen to me. You had a bad delivery. Your baby wasn't breathing, we took turns to breathe life into him. But now he is fine, I've weighed him and he is nine pounds four ounces in weight. How do you feel now?'

'Weak very weak.'

'What happened to your finger?' I mumbled a white lie.

'I fell down the stairs last week.' Surprised said.

'Fell down the stairs I cannot believe that Mrs Plant. What other damage did it cause?' When I showed her the lump on my head, she erupted.

'Mrs Plant, that was stupid, very silly. You must remain in bed for a week. I'll tell your husband and let him in.'

Jack came in with that big grin all over his face, kissed me and touched his new baby son muttered.

'Well done Sarah. He looks very healthy, but how are you?' The doctor called in Margaret.

'It's all right, it's all over now, bring the two little ones in to see their new baby brother.'

They came in, the Doctor put them on the bed beside me. No more tears just smiling faces. Born on the 20th January, we decided to name him, John James after his father.

I thanked this angel of a Doctor. 'Janet Smyth' by name, for having saved the lives of my baby boy and myself. Before she left she said.

'Until I see your fit and well enough to get up. I will be in every day to see you' She bade us all goodnight.

From that day on she became our family doctor. However my saga didn't end there. After being told off by Doctor Smyth, this damn nurse took more than umbrage with me. I became the very last on her list of visits. It was past midday on a Saturday, she still had not arrived. Margaret fussing around me said.

'Blow her I'll bath and change John James.'

In doing so she pulled off his umbilical cord, he screamed, nothing would stop him wailing, which started the other two off. When the nurse arrived, the three children were wailing like a load of banshees, seeing John James less an umbilical cord she turned on Margaret , venting her anger shouted .

'DON'T YOU DO MY JOB FOR ME.' Margaret retaliating.

115

'YOU'RE NEVER HERE ON TIME AND CERTAINLY NOT FIT TO BE A NURSE.' They were at each other's throats, I had to get out of bed to separate them I too shouted.

'MARGARET GO DOWNSTAIRS TO DOLLY.'...Made the nurse smile so I said to her.

'You. You Should be ashamed of yourself the way you have carried on.'...'I'm sorry Mrs Plant.'

I climbed back in bed. As she attended to John James. In my mind I believed this mishap with his umbilical, was the cause of his constant crying over the following three months. It nearly drove me mad. However, on the Saturday as he always did after duty Jack had gone off to play football. Margaret had had enough of looking after the children, had gone out looking for another job. Kathleen being tantalised by Mary, was bawling her eyes out, as was John James In the cot beside me loudly airing his lungs. When I heard two knocks on the front door. The knocking became louder and more urgent. I did not know where Dolly was? I just had to get up. In my nightdress I gingerly crept down the stairs along the passage to open the door. On the doorstep stood Pops and Miria, she questioned.

'Sarah. What are you doing out of bed?'

'My sister has gone out.' Pops demanded.

'Where's the landlady?' I pointed to her kitchen, he stomped off whilst Miria helped me upstairs back into bed. Pops came in demanded.

'Sarah where's Jack?'

'He's playing football Pops.'

That did it. He was in a towering rage about Jack. They had only come to stay for an hour nevertheless Pops waited. Well after six, Jack returned. I heard raised voices mainly Pops as he gave Jack the wrath of his tongue. Even I winced in bed as he received the dressing down of his life from them. Miria came into the room her face was not smiling she said.

'Sarah. I'll cook the evening meal. Jacks got to wash and get the children ready for bed. Sarah you have spoiled Jack you let him get away with everything and anything, and by the look of it, you cannot do anything with him.' She left. Even I did not get away with it. I felt very guilty, but what could I have done? Dolly kept well out of the way, I lay there until Miria brought me up something to eat. The atmosphere in that flat was more than unbearable, you could cut through it with a knife, Jack came back in followed by Pops and Miria to say cheerio, they about to leave as Margaret came into the room, having come back from her searching, she walked straight into it. She having never met them, it did not matter to Pops, she got roasted. Gob smacked she was unable to retaliate. Then he turned on Jack again.

'Jack, You my lad had better mend your ways or, you will have to look out for me.'

The pair of them very enraged left. With the wrath of his Father thrust upon him Jack was more than subdued by this threat. Jack did improve his ways and became better.

On the twenty-eighth of January, eight days after young John's birth I was allowed to get back up and take over again. It was also Jacks birthday, the day he was officially twenty-six years old, then entitled to married quarters. We had several more visits from Jack's parents, by the tone of their conversation, the dust had settled down. After the previous months of upsets, a few days after Kathleen's second birthday. The Duchess of York gave birth to a baby daughter Elizabeth, followed shortly after by Lena's twenty-first birthday. I suggested to Jack.

'Can we throw a party for Lena's birthday?'

'Leave it to me. We'll get her a special birthday present for her to remember it by and throw a party.'

We bought her a gold watch, what a party we had, much to everyone's astonishment the three children slept right throughout it. A few days later saw the start of the General Strike, causing wide spread unrest. Jack came in one night to state.

116

'Sarah. Due to the strike Dick's been re-called to the Army. His Edith's very annoyed about that.' Immediately concerned asked. ....'Will you get involved?'.... 'No. I'm going on a course next week to Larkhill.' Surprised retorted...'Oh that's new.' ....'Well I only was told today. Anyway it's only for a week.'

Jack went away to do his course. At least he did not have to do anything during the strike. Living in the flat with our three children, became more orderly and as time passed it progressively got better. The worries and restrictions of our past ventures had long past gone, but still the daily visits from Dolly included Bertie, so with four children three running around screaming and shouting at each other, with John James quite content to cry, all the time Dolly taking absolutely no notice just continued talking. What she jabbered on about I shall never know? She certainly could - 'Talk the hind leg of a Donkey.' Every now and again as appropriate I just quipped. 'Yes.', No.' or, 'Oh you don't say.'

The Terriers Unit had won quite a few trophies and of course Jack had participated in most events. To celebrate they arranged a dance to be held at the Drill hall. Jack had invited all of us, nevertheless for obvious reasons I had refused. On one of their afternoons off my three sisters along with Dolly in attendance, were discussing theforthcoming event in the kitchen when Dolly

Bert sat second left Jack second left back row Dolly suggested.

'Sarah it's about time you got out c'mon along with me to one of the mess dances.'...Lena taking note added....'Yes Sarah. You are the one always stuck indoor looking after babies.'...Dolly added...'That's right ducks, on the occasions when I go out, you look after my little Bertie.' Her last remark stopped any further comments, silence descended. I had to say something.

'No, my place is at home with the children and besides. I do not have a nice dress to wear.'

The whole subject was dropped until Jack arrived then Lena asked.

'Jack would you buy Sarah a dress so she can go out to the Drillhall Dance?' I for one was not pleased about her raising the subject again.

'It's about time too. I'm always asking her but it's the same old story. I've got the children to look after! I don't see that as a problem, as I do know there is a room where other mothers take their children at the dances.' Eilish suggested.

'We three could all take turns to look after them.'

That was it. I did not have a say in the matter. Sarah was going! Maybe, I did need to go out on occasions. We went to Brixton and chose a lovely black and red dress.

On the Saturday, it was a lovely summer's evening. I had the children washed dressed up fit for the occasion. With us in our finery, we arrived at the Drillhall well before the start of the dance. It was my intention to arrive early, stay awhile, then leave early. Jack and Bert greeted us and showed us into a room where a few other mothers and children were. Eilish took the first watch. Jack escorted us to a table, requested our orders then joined Bert at the bar, talking to another tall Sergeant dressed in Blues. Dolly said.

'Look Sarah that's Wally. Bert's brother.'

Bert carrying a tray of drinks came over to our table followed by his brother. Dolly pointing to Margaret and Lena suggested.

'Bert aren't you going to introduce Wally to the ladies, these two are dying to meet him.'

They both blushed, with introductions over it was obvious to me from Wally's glances that Lena had caught his attention. The band struck up. Wally asked me to dance, he was a smashing dancer, we had three dances before he asked Lena. During the evening we were introduced to other Sergeants and I was asked to dance by two other Sergeants. The shorter of the two was

Sgt. George Ralph who had a walrus moustache he was a good dancer, he introduced me to his wife Peggy, a Scottish lady extremely nice and pleasant, with such a broad Scot's accent I could hardly understand her. Margaret left the group to relieve Eilish who came in whispered in my ear.

'While I was in the powder room, two other ladies were talking about you. Jacks wife with three children. They thought you were an old lady? Instead you were such a lovely little person and such a beautiful dancer. What do you say to that Sarah?

I was abashed, but rather pleased. Then other Ladies came over introducing themselves, and made a fuss of me. It was embarrassing nevertheless it was a change and I must admit I really did enjoy my evening out. The children behaved themselves and after a few hours I decided to leave with them, so accompanied by Margaret we left, leaving Lena, Eilish and Dolly behind.

Since his father's telling off lecture, Jack had certainly changed his ways although it did not stop him playing football and competing in sports. He helped me doing the shopping, which was another great help, also when Mary started her schooling he took her to and from school. However by then Lena was openly courting Wally, with early indications pointing to the sound of wedding bells. Christmas came and we received Mothers traditional turkey. Again it was too big for the oven and Christmas dinner became a joint affair. This time with more bodies to sit down.

1927. Not the beginning of a very eventful period, with little work available to the struggling mass of the civilian population. After Dick's recall to the army during the General Strike, he had found a job working for the London Omnibus Company. They had moved into a flat a few doors down from us, so it was convenient for me to spend some time with Edith. However, a crisis had arisen in China. It was the Government's intention to dispatch an Army division of twelve thousand soldiers to China in order to quell some rebellion. Harris (but known as Dick) had been back to sign up again, which had Edith very worried that he would be accepted, anyway he was told he was far too old. Whereas Jack having completed twelve years in the army, after his forthcoming last training session with the Terriers he was due for discharge. But with the working situation as it was, our future prospects did not appear too good. We sat down to discuss his forthcoming departure from the army.

'Sarah. If I sign on, I haven't a clue where I shall be posted. I know you don't want to leave this flat, and now I am eligible for married quarters, it's worth thinking about.' With that statement he did have a strong point.

'Well Jack. You're the breadwinner and I'm just a mother and housewife.'

'Sarah. I think we should wait and see what options there are in the Army. Then we can decide what we are going to do.'

'Well let's face it. Because of your age we have never had quarters officially assigned to us. Our first quarters were done unofficially. The next illegal one I was cast out onto the Barrack Square. Evicted from one, had two reasonably stays of execution, before being evicted from the next two in Brixton then threatened with sleeping in a Police Station. During all that time, had long separations from you, given birth to three children. One who drives me up the wall. Now we are well and truly settled in this flat. I do not know what to say.' Having said my piece I shut up. He could see I was annoyed.

'Sarah while I'm away, why don't you take the children over to Ireland to stay with your Mother for a holiday, how about that?'

I think he was trying to smooth the way with his offer, nevertheless I relished the thought of going back home even for a short stay to see Mother.

'Jack I really would like that. You know its four years since I last saw Mother. '

'That's settled then, you're going. Leaving this Saturday I'll sort the fares out.' I wrote to mother to tell her my good news.

118

On Saturday, with sufficient money to stay for four-weeks. Jack took us up to Euston to catch the boat train for Ireland. After a fond farewell we are off to Holyhead. Settled on the train, no sooner had we left the station when, I began worrying about the sea ferry trip. The train jouney was uneventful. At Holyhead when we boarded the ferry, fear swept over me, my stomach was churning nineteen to the dozen, but with three children to look after, outwardly I composed myself. Fortunately the crossing was very calm so all was well. At Dublin boarded the train to Kildare then a taxi to mothers. What a welcome we received. Mother her eyes bright with tears, Father delighted to see us, who had not changed still grumbling. Even old friends had turned up to welcome us. It soon became apparent that my other younger sisters had intentions of finding work in England, that would leave mother and father alone. I suggested to Mother the possibility of her thinking of them coming over to live in England as well. Her answer was positive.

Sarah ?, Kathleen & Mary

'Ah away with yus Allahnah.' In God's name what would I be doing living in England for?' Whereas Father interrupting said.

'To be sure. You're be far better off over there living with the girls than over here.' Jack will see you are all right, nither you worry.' I sensed, she wasn't convinced but just added a little more invitation.

'Mother, if and when Jack has decided to sign on. We will be entitled to married quarters, therefore will have to leave Dolly's. If I get Dolly and Bert's agreement to let you take over the flat and everything in it. What would you say to that?'

She didn't. So I forgot it. I stayed for seven weeks. Mother fussed over John James and somehow he became known as Jackie. Mother taking note of Mary's antics remarked.

'Sarah that one has a wild streak in her. You'll niver tame dat one.'

Our last week, Jack arrived on leave much to mother's delight. However when we were out walking Jack questioned me.

'Sarah. What's been going on? Your mother has asked me. If I sign on something about

Jack, Sarah Jackie

her taking over Dolly's flat. We have not even discussed that or, even decided anything yet.' Surprised at what he had said replied.

'Oh that was something that was mentioned weeks ago. I've forgotten all about that, when I suggested it, she ignored the subject.'

'Well she must have thought about it since. As I told her everything would be alright just wait and see.'

On the journey home, we had further discussions about our future plans. If everything fell into place, with the possibility of Mother coming over to take over the flat. It should work out okay. When we got back into our flat. It did not take Dolly long to come up for a chat.

'Coooee Ducks, time for a cup of tea.'

Life at the flat resumed its old routine. One Sunday Dolly, seeing me go to Mass stopped me and said.

'Sarah. I too am a Catholic, but I had a big row with my family over marrying Bert in a Registry Office. I did realise that according to the Catholic faith, I am not married, so I gave up going to Mass.' Her confession took me by surprise. All I could say to her was.

'Dolly can we discuss this later when I get back.'

I was totally unaware of her situation. On my way to church her admission worried me, had me thinking: *If it was Lena's intention to marry Wally she too would be faced with the same problem. How or what could I do to help her situation?* When I got back I broached the subject with Dolly, only to find out she too had the same concern about Lena and Wally's pending marriage. However Lena, would approach me when she wanted too. But in the meantime with a little persuasion on my part, I eventually got Dolly to come with me and meet our Priest. He suggested.

'If it is your desire. You can obtain the churches blessing. That I could arrange for a suitable time in the evening, if both you and your husband are willing.'

On the way home she thanked me for solving her problem, she would discuss the matter with Bert. Bert did agree, two evenings later they received the Blessings of the Church. Jack was Bert's best man and I Dolly's Matron of Honour. At least I did one good turn, whilst I lived there. Nevertheless, a year later Bert became a Catholic.

Early one afternoon having managed to get Jackie to sleep, I got on with mixing up the Irish Soda Bread. When it was all mixed, proved, ready and in the oven I cleared away as I knew as soon as Dolly smelt the aroma of it seeping downstairs, she would enter ask. *'What are you baking?'* That meant a cup of tea and a chinwag as she called it. More like a marathon gossip. I was just wiping up the last item when I heard her coming up the stairs. I thought: *Good I've finished, I'll be one step ahead of her. Fill the kettle.* I was at the sink filling the kettle when in stomped Jack, surprised by his sudden appearance.

'Jack whatever's the matter. It's just gone two 'o' clock. I thought you were Dolly and I was ready to put the kettle on for tea. ' He came across the room and kissed me.

'Sarah. I'll have the tea instead. I have some news to discuss with you, before going back to the barracks. Where is everybody?

'Mary and Kathleen are at school , Jackie's asleep in his bed. '

I went across and opened the oven door, the aroma of cooking enveloped the room.

'That smell always reminds me of your Mother's, a real homely smell. Is it ready yet?'

'Not quite, you'll have to wait.'

Anxious to know what his news was. I made the pot of tea, without a word said. Jack placed two cups on the table, muttered.

'Dolly won't be up for a while. Is that Soda bread ready?' I sat down at the table before I replied.

'Maybe in five minutes, have some tea first and tell me your news.'

We sat, Jack poured out the tea Jackie came in rubbing his eyes.

'Hello son you been asleep Eh?'...Jackie stifling a yawn...'Come here, have a mouthful of tea.'...Jack sat him on his knee and gave him a sip...'What about a slice of your mother's bread?'...'Please.'...'There you are Sarah two pieces please.' He was evasive, so his news was not going to be bad, but he was beginning to aggravate me.

'Jack, are you going to tell me or not?'

'All in good time Sarah.'

I gave up, went over to the oven took out the bread, placed it on the table watched by two apprehensive faces staring at the new bread, their tongues hanging down around their ankles. Both lost in a world of little boys, Jack questioned.

'What do you think of that Jackie? Yum Yum.'

I paid no attention to their craving. The bread knife didn't need washing but I thought: *Two could play that game.* Taking my time I wiped it, deliberately folded up the cloth turning to the table asked.

'Now Jack are you going to tell me or not?'

'Yes. Yes Sarah there's a ducks, cut two slices, I have to be going back soon.'

I took his word for it. As I cut two slices its aroma filled the room, smering butter over them them its warmth melted the butter, placing them on a plate pushed it in front of them. Jackie took a heel. (the crusty end).

'Thank you mummy.' Jack taking a bite remarked.

'Yum that's good eh Jackie?' No reply, he busily eating his own share. Pouring out another tea for myself I sat down, only then he spoke.

'Sarah you know that within a few weeks I will have completed my time with the Terriers.'

'Yes. I know that. But why are you here now? This could have waited till after you finished your duty. Then we could have discussed it properly.' He went on…

'The reason I've come home is to discuss our next move.'…I thought: *Here we go again*…'Go on.'…'I was ordered to the office this morning to see Major Craddock who had my papers in front of him. He was impressed with my service record and enquired whether I was prepared to sign on and stay at this unit or, return to the regular Army?'

'Can I have another piece please Mummy?' Knowing what Jack really wanted, without exploring the alternatives I could not agree. But grateful for Jackie's interruption, I cut and buttered another slice, gave it to him before I answered.

'I don't know? What do you want me to say? Oh yes! But see it from my point of view. All the time since we married, only by foul means did we get quarters with me watching my back to evade being discovered, along with being shunted from pillar to post.'

I could read his mind. He had already sorted it all out before he came home to discuss our future, and wasn't surprised when he replied.

'That's right Sarah. I did discuss this with Major Craddock. According to him, we would be entitled to quarters immediately upon my re-engagement and would not lose any rank or service time.'…. 'Have you signed on in the Terriers then?' … 'No-o. he suggested I discuss the matter over with the good lady of the house first. That's why he allowed me time off.'

'No Jack. I'm settled here, besides Mary and Kathleen are settled at school, and it won't be long before Jackie starts his schooling. Anyway where would you get a posting to?' I should not have asked that, he had won his argument.

'That's something I can't tell you because I don't know. But I would assume somewhere down here in the south. Aldershot or Salisbury. That's where all the training camps are located.'

'Well if you're positive we will get quarters and it's what you really want. So be it, but certainly not Aldershot. I am not under any circumstances going there.'

I was not giving in, but had to accept the situation. Where he goes we go. I had said my piece and was glad to get it off of my chest.

'Thank you Sarah, if it's all right with you, I will sign the transfer paper tomorrow. Another piece of bread Jackie?'

That familiar grin creased his face. As far as he was concerned another crisis solved. Army routine once again.

'Yes please.' Putting Jackie down, he stood up took another slice of the bread and said.

'Sarah, I'll be off now, got to get back to my duties.' I casually asked.

'Jack, if you sign on tomorrow when do we move? '

'Oh first things first. I have to have the medical etcetera., and be accepted. I don't think there will be any problems there. Posting, it's not going to be immediate, that's for sure.' A knock on the door.

'Coooee Ducks. Oh hello Jack your home early, not interrupting anything am I? Could you oblige me with a cup full of sugar? I've just ran out of it.' Jack responded.

'No Dolly. I'm just on my way back. I'll see you later then Sarah and talk a bit more.' I politely enquired.

'Like a cup of tea Dolly?' She already knew Jack was up here.

'Oh. I wouldn't say no to a nice cup of tea. Is that your Irish bread you've been baking I can smell downstairs?' Jackie chimed in.

'Yes.' 'Yum yum it's warm.' I interrupted.

'Would you like a slice with your tea Dolly?' Dolly laughing said.

'You know Sarah. I thought you would never ask, I'd love a piece if it's all right with you?'

I thought: *Mother of God here we go again. Give me strength.* At that moment all I wanted was time to wrestle with my thoughts. I made a fresh pot of tea.

A week passed before Jack had his medical and was declared A1 fighting fit, as he said there was nothing the matter with him. He had signed all the necessary papers. for all intents and purposes was transferred back into the Regular Army. All he had to wait for was a posting. Not long after the necessary brown envelope arrived addressed to 1033111 QMS Plant J.J. I placed it on the mantle shelf to wait his arrival home. He enquired.

'Any mail Sarah?'

'Yes Jack on the mantle shelf.'

I watched him. He went over took the letter, looked at the address, opened it up, reading the contents a big grin crossed his face, then handed it to me. I scanned the words until. "*Report to Royal Artillery Depot at Woolwich twenty-sixth July. The following week.*" Briefly my eyes misted over, he had got what he wanted. Now I would have to wait and see what would be in store for us. I looked up at him standing there, hands on his hips a huge grin on his face. How could I ever stop loving this man of mine, nothing seemed to worry him. I'm sure he left all that to me?

'That's wonderful news for you Jack, but where's Woolwich?'

'Oh Southeast London, not far from here a couple of tram rides or, one if I walk into Camberwell Green and catch the number forty tram.' This news perked me up, a London posting. Maybe we could stay where we are.

'How long will you be at this place Woolwich?'

'Sarah I haven't got there yet. But I should think a few months or more depends on whether there is a posting available for me to go too. We'll have to wait and see won't we?'

'Is Woolwich a training barracks?'

'Hang on. You sit down. I'll make a pot of tea while we talk it over.'…. Whistling a tuneless note. To his delight he was now officially back in the regular Army. Another celebration down at the mess loomed? Tea made enquired… 'Where's Jackie and the girls?'

'I sent the girls to the corner shop to buy some sweets, they'll be home in a few minutes. Jackie's down stairs with little Bertie'… He continued… 'Woolwich barracks is the Royal Artillery Depot and Headquarters. I was sent there when I first joined up in 1914. I doubt if I will stay there very long, until I get a posting to a gunnery-training depot, so it may be two or three months away. Anyway you won't have to worry about packing up and moving yet. Don't forget as far as the Army is concerned. My records show I'm now eligible for married quarters.'

I pondered over his last remark, hoping they were in short supply suggested.

'Maybe. I could stay here. I'm settled, happy and Dolly bless her, she has her heart in the right place, she does keep me company with all her borrowing of cups of sugar, it's her excuse to come up for a chin -wag.'

We both saw the funny side of this and laughed, a light-hearted moment, interrupted by the sound of the children running up the stairs and bursting into the room. End of our conversation on our future plans.

122

CHAPTER SEVENTEEN
ON THE MOVE AGAIN – LONGMORE

The next few days quickly passed by. Jack, together with all his old cronies celebrated in the mess. To say the least his stay at Woolwich was to be very brief, on the second Friday, having already arranged with Eilish to come and stay over the weekend. Unexpected Jack arrived home dressed in his FSMO (Full service marching order) full of the joys of spring, grinning all over his face, dropped his kit bag down onto the floor. Mary, Kathleen and Jackie leapt at him to greet their father, Jackie fell over the abandoned kitbag. He came over to me pressed his cheek to mine. A fond greeting.

'Hello Sarah, I'm home for the weekend, I've been posted to a place called Longmore Camp near Liss in Hampshire. You'll like it, and duck's we do have quarters. I report there Monday morning. Isn't that good news and to top it all. The unit is being posted to India. Any tea going?'

India! At the mention of India my heart dropped into the pit of my stomach exclaimed.

'India Jack.'

'Er yes, I'll make a pot.'

This last piece of news had me shaking. *Oh my God what do I do now?* He forgetting about making tea, began removing his webbing saying.

'Mary Kathleen, take the kitbag and put in our bedroom theirs good girls.'

The pair of them struggled to lift it, giving up they dragged it out of the room. Jackie helping, lifted the small packs over his shoulders, their weight too great for him he too dragged them outside. I sat down at the table with my hands clasped together, my immediate thought: *India?* I began twisting my wedding ring. Jack noticing this, he knew whenever I did that something was up asked.

'Whatever's wrong Sarah?'

'India. That's what's wrong, do we have to? What about the children have you thought about them?'

'Yes, they will be all right. Other families have been posted to India before our time. How about that tea, is it ready?' He wasn't the least bit concerned. I made the tea, poured and gave him a cup as he continued... 'Anyway it won't be for a few months yet so don't start worrying yourself silly.' ....'I do not like the prospects and would prefer to stay here in England. Can't you get another posting?' ... 'Don't be silly Sarah. I'm back in the Army now. You go to wherever you get posted, you know that yourself. You cannot choose. Where I go the family goes. Anyway you'll enjoy it, all those servants to do your work for you.'... 'Servants! I don't want any servants! I'm quite capable of looking after you and the children thank you very much.'

The three coming back into the room ended the conversation. I sat there supping my tea then I got up, to busy myself with preparing the evening meal, while Jack occupied himself with the children before Eilish arrived. After the meal he and his old partner in arms Bert, spent another evening down the mess, celebrating his good fortune and again on the Saturday. However, Dolly co-ersed me to go as well, and as Eilish had agreed to stay looking after the children. At the Mess the number of people who acknowledged me and wished the family good fortune surprised me. Any thought of India was gone from my mind. I enjoyed the evening.

Jack was away to his new posting. Leaving me on my own to organise and pack up our things. Jack had only been back in the Army five weeks, when he sent a letter informing me our quarters were ready to move into. I was on the move again, I was very sorry to leave the flat, that had provided the best and happiest times I had spent since leaving Ireland in 1922. We had pre warned Mother of our plans, she herself having decided to move was now preparing to leave

Ireland. Before we left Dolly organised a little party to say our farewells. The following Monday I was on the train with three children, packs and bags. Jack met us at Liss station with a horse drawn wagon, loaded up our bags and cases. Jack took the reins and with Jackie sat between us with Mary and Kathleen stood behind, peering over our shoulders we were on our way... `Sarah the quarters are small but they will do for the time being.' Alarm bells rang in my head I asked... 'Why do you say that?' He responded.

'India of course. It's not worthwhile unpacking, as we are not going to be there very long.' I exclaimed.

'Where have I heard that remark before?'

Shrugging his shoulders grinned. We approached the camp gates and drove in past the Guardhouse, arriving at the married quarters we moved in. They were similar to Aldershot's nevertheless, this one included all fixtures and fittings. Jack had already got some provisions that were laid on the kitchen table. Whilst I sorted out the children, he returned the GS wagon. I made an evening meal, before starting unpacking the items of necessity, before all retired for the night. The early morning bugler woke us up. It was back to normality. Jack was away for muster parade. Resigned to my lot.- 'Once a soldier always a soldier' I began again preparing my new quarters the way I wanted. Jack was in his element back in barracks and in the mess every night, meeting up and yarning with old comrades. With me the dutiful wife, back on my own with the three children. I sorted out all the items I needed and left the rest in the cases. We had a very good neighbour, Mrs. Stone and soon became great friends, typical of all Army women she lent me anything I wanted. I did not like bothering her but it was no trouble to her. We hadn't been there very long and I had got myself settled in, when Jack came home.

'Have you seen Company Orders on your trips today Sarah?'

'No why should I be bothered with those? Particularly today?'

'Well all army families going to India are advised to report to the MRS at fourteen hundred hours to-morrow, to be vaccinated.'

'Oh no Jack. So soon?'

'I did warn you.'

This was the time I was dreading. I had tried to put the thought of India to the back of my mind, which was not easy. I had no one to advise me on the whys and wherefores of life in India, all I knew was it was a boat trip of at least four weeks and thousands of miles from England. Apart from Bridget's husband Peter whom I had not seen since he went to India and according to Bridget, he had enjoyed his period of time out there. Since his return they had three children born, Michael, Peter, and Mary and they had been posted to Scotland. Nevertheless, I had to show a brave face. I had to tell our three, we were all going to India and had to be vaccinated. I said to myself. "Come on Sarah on your feet soldier." After their evening meal I did explain their next day's visit.

'Tomorrow, we have to go to the medical reception station and be vaccinated. Your father has a posting to India and we are going with him.' Mary chirped in.

'Where's India?'

'It's a long way away and very hot in the sun.' Kathleen's turn.

'Do we have to go?'

Then the questions flowed. I made a point about the voyage on board a big ship. That captured their imagination, stopped all further questions. However I still had to get them down to the MRS the following day. I took Jackie and on the way collected the two girls from school, I said.

'Come on.' Marched them down to the MRS. Never having been given vaccines before, I did not know what to expect. I was not happy and they, like lots of other children did not like the jabs. Nevertheless, we were in a queue, some children even started screaming at the sight of a

124

needle. That particular night Jack was Orderly Officer. What a night I had. The three of them were feverish, seeing men on the wall, first one then the other, until all three shouting at these men. Believe me I got frightened so much that I too began thinking I could see men myself. When Jack arrived home next morning, I told him about the feverish night.

' Don't be silly it's all imagination.' So much for that.

'Okay If we have had jab's, when are we leaving for India?'

'Not for some weeks yet, but we will be moving to another holding camp first.' That had me going....'What another move?' A weak response.

'Well I did warn you.' I thought: *That is great news, yet another move and more packing.*'

The weeks slipped by. Mother arrived with Eilish to visit. It was wonderful to see them again. Mother had decided to come over and did entrench herself in Dolly's flat, however father had decided to stay in Ireland. Mother had settled in with Dolly and according to Eilish she would have no truck from Dolly. Autumn football time. Jacks time. Christmas, Springtime all the flowers are looking lovely. We had been at Longmoor four months with all our possession packed, living out of boxes and no sign of moving. Then Jack gets the nod. We say our farewells and we're off travelling by GS wagon to a place not far away called Deepcut. I found out why it was so called. In the old days when they were digging the trench for a new canal waterway, a village was created for the workers, but they had to dig the trench far deeper than elsewhere so they named it Deepcut.

CHAPTER EIGHTEEN
DEEPCUT

When we arrived I could not believe our luck, real new quarters. This time fed up with being told. "We would move within weeks" I unpacked all our things, determined to get my quarters looking lovely. I soon made friends with some of the soldier's wives. Delia, the wife of one of the cook's, lived next door and had four little children. Delia was very pleasant, polite and always ready for a chat. Unlike Dolly not a marathon talker.

In accordance with the summer sunshine, the athletics competitions took place, of course Jack competed. His talents as an accomplished sportsman always went with him. Very soon in our married life I took it for granted, if a soldier had a talent for any sporting activity, he would be expected to train and take part in whichever sports event he was good at. The trouble with Jack was not only was he a Professional Soldier, he was also an all-round athlete. He had to compete in all these activities, when any of these things were getting on my nerves, it wasn't for me to grumble, he often used to say. *'If you do not like my way of life you know what to do.'* Unless it was to pack up and go home to my Mother, which in Mother's eyes the worst thing I could have done, as Jack could do nothing wrong. She used to say to me. *'He is a father to your children.'*

His only bad fault he loved the army and he, was the only one in the family who needed a break in the mess after a day's work? But I was the fool. Every time he invited me to a function, I chose not to, instead look after the children. I too had loved my time in the Army but I had been forced to give up that way of life many years before. Now as an army wife and mother I could see both sides of the coin. Nevertheless, I felt so loving and proud of him. Jack arrived home one evening and casual as you like said to me.

Mary Delia Kathleen

'Sarah, I have to go on a Quartermasters course in Bordon camp, it will last three months. Then I will be posted to the twenty-fifth brigade. Who are being shipped out to India in the spring?' Surprised retorted. ...;'India! I've forgotten all about that. I'm quite happy here. I like Deepcut. Now I have the prospect of India.' Jack retorted...'I've got to pass first.'

At that moment I remembered the married quarters in Kildare camp and the brass souvenirs I had admired so much. What lay ahead was an opportunity to get my own. So be it, yet there were more moves ahead for us? Towards the end of July, Jack was at Bordon. when one morning, Delia came in with her four children holding her youngest one in her arms, they all had large red swelling with yellowish heads on their legs and arms, the youngest even had it on his face, she was near to tears.

'Sarah just look at my lot, other children have got it too.'

'Delia that looks bad take them to see the MO immediately.' She did and returned crying.

'He said its Impetigo, very contagious apparently picked up when they were playing in the sand. He gave me ointment to apply twice a day wrapping bandages around the infected parts, even my baby has to have his face covered up. I don't know how I will cope?'

But I knew that was not her only problem, she had a contract to do laundry for the families of seven Officers. I knew as soon as the Officers found out, they would stop sending their laundry to her. Immediately I knew I could help her suggested.

'Delia don't worry. I'll help out with your laundry.' I did the washing and ironing of the laundry until after a week the four of them were clear of Impetigo. Funny enough none of mine caught it. Nevertheless, I discovered I was expecting. I wrote to Jack, his reply was. Delighted. But I was ill again with the pregnancy, the fingers of my right hand developed painful whitlows, gradually each fingernail came off. The MO said. ...'I was run down and needed a change?'

Where on earth was I going to get that? Maybe in India, but certainly not there. Delia returned my favour and helped me with the children. A letter from mother asked. Could she (Francis and Julia both new arrivals from home) come and stay with us? I thought: *In my condition they could help me and relieve Delia of her extra assistance.* I sent a wired.

COME IMMEDIATELY STOP

Their letter informed me of the time of their arrival at Brookwood station I went to meet them, they all looked well. Francis and Julia had settled in with Mother living with Dolly Thomas thay both loved the life of London, Mother said.

'Allahnah. Dolly does not spend all day chatting with me, like she did with you. I soon told her what time of the day it was.'

However, whilst they were there Mother did all the ordering about. My two sisters who had come down for a holiday, spent most of the time washing, cooking and doing general housework. The week went by very quickly, Francis left on the Friday to return to work, whilst mother and Julia stayed for another seven weeks, until a letter from Frances demanded Julia's return, she was missing school. Three weeks after they left. I was taken ill miscarried lost the baby. Delia was a tower of strength, a great help. She took over, relayed the news of our loss to Jack through the Admin Officer. Jack arrived back with two days compassionate leave. A much needed relief to me. I had a day in bed then had to get up and carry on as before. Seeing I was up and reasonably steady on my feet. ('On your feet soldier. Once a soldier always a soldier.') Which in his eyes I was supposed to be. Jack returned on the Saturday. The following week he came home, beaming all over his face and announced.

'Sarah. I've passed. Good eh? I've been promoted to Battery Quartermaster Sergeant. With a posting to Bordon. What do you say to that ducks?' I kissed him. ..'Congratulations on both account's, that is good news. I suppose we will have to move again?'...'I'm afraid so Ducks, it's all in preparation to go to India. I'll find out from standing order's on Monday.'

Back together with the children, we enjoyed a pleasant weekend. I was gradually getting fitter after our misfortune. On Monday evening Jack came back home to inform me.

'Sarah not good news I'm afraid. I'll be leaving Wednesday to take up my new posting. Unfortunately there are no quarters for us in Bordon. They are still occupied. You will have to stay here in these married quarters.' The same old story. I could have wept buckets at this news. But I was happy to remain in Deepcut. Come October I was still on my own thinking: *I might have to wait until Christmas, before Jack would spend his leave with us?* Then I received a letter from Eilish saying she wanted to come and stay with me. A blessing. I write back and invite her. She arrived on the Friday. The following Wednesday the telegram boy arrives with a wire from Jack.

BE READY TO MOVE FRIDAY STOP

Two-days notice. ' Oh my God Eilish. I'm on the move again. You'll have to help me pack all these things up and get organised.'

I arranged with the QM stores for some packing crates to pack our few chattels away. Early Friday morning sadly we say our farewells to Delia, just as the army lorry arrives, the driver loaded all the luggage followed by the children to sit on the cases, then we were off to Bordon. As we drove into the camp it was raining buckets, stopping at the guardhouse Jack clad in his groundsheet jumps up onto the running board, gave the driver directions. When we stopped he got us quickly inside the quarters out of the rain, that was still pelting down. The driver unloaded our possessions, once he and Jack had got them inside stacked in a pile Jack said.

'Sarah I've been informed we shall be moving again soon. So don't unpack too much. I've heard that they are shipping out to India in January.'

I thought: *How many times has he said that?*

127

CHAPTER NINETEEN
BORDON - BOUND FOR INDIA

Exploring the interior of our quarters found they were very old, small, furnished with the bare essentials. As Jack had said don't unpack much, once again we lived out of packing cases. Eilish had come down for a week's holiday, about to return to London, before she left I said. 'When the dust has settled come down for a proper rest.' She just laughed at my suggestion questioned ... Sarah knowing Jack will you still be here?'

The following weeks were miserable. The girls went to the Army school, so they were out of the way most of the time. Young Jackie was only happy when they returned home from school. The weather turned cold, the only bit of information I was informed about was, a posting to India was for six years, also I understood that once in India, there were many postings one could be sent to. To me a disturbing thought: *Six years was a lifetime and would we be sent to various posting as we had been over the past few years?* With time on my hands I did nothing, but ponder and worry about what lay in store for us. However a distraction from my worrying lay next door. The next door neighbour was a Mrs. Beckett who was heavy into pregnancy, during her confinement time, I became a willing helper to assist in the delivery of a fine baby boy, after the birth, I spent my spare time caring for her and her baby, doing the cooking, cleaning until she was up fit enough to take over. Thanking me said.

'Sarah. I'll never forget you. Would you and Jack be our sons Godparents?'

We were. I even took our christening robes out of the storage box to lend to her. Our last Christmas in England was upon us sooner rather than later, the schools holidays began. Mary came home with a bad cold, Kathleen catches it, then Jackie, it did not get better but turned into bad cases of whooping cough with all of them croaking with sore throats and fits of coughing, confining us to a very quiet but croaky Christmas, not a pleasant time that lasted through into January 1929, which brought news His Majesty the King's condition has worsened. The Government announced if His Majesties condition deteriorated further. They would form a Coalition Government. Under the circumstances I could not have cared less. My three were just as bad. I sent a letter to mother about their whooping cough. I received a wire from her telling me

COME IMMEDIATELY STOP

BRING THEM STOP

MOTHER STOP

I showed it to Jack who said. 'Go. It will possibly be the last time for a visit.' So I pack up, wrap up, and take the train, with all the children whooping and barking away, at least I would have my mother's together with Doctor Smyth's help to get the children over the whooping cough. When we arrived. Dolly her usual chatty self, was shushed up by Mother. Somehow we were bedded down including sleeping down in Dolly's, who then appeared to be an extension of the family. A week later Jack turned up for a weekend visit with news.

'Sarah our posting has been confirmed. We are on standby orders, departing, the third week in February.'

So the rumour had turned into fact, and our visit turned into a farewell parting. On Saturday, we visited Jacks parents and to celebrate Jack's forthcoming birthday an impromptu party was held at Mothers flat, which left all very jaded the following day. Jack returned on the Sunday evening, we stayed for another week and a half. Gradually their whooping cough subsided. Having already explained my fears to Mother, she said.

'Allahnah. You have already broken the ties with your native homeland. As I have done myself. I too feel the pangs of homesickness. But my reasons are different than yours. Marrying into an army way of life. You are expected to travel with Jack just like any other service wife.

128

Anyway, the Army always looks after their married families'... I thought: *They had overlooked our case with all the trouble I had endured since leaving Ireland*... 'Look to the future, your time out in India will soon be over. Take each day as it come,. when you come home, you will look back with good memories and forget the bad times.'

I was warmed by her advice but still wary of the forthcoming prospects. That last few days quickly slipped by. Margaret and Eilish had decided to return with us to our quarters. It was time for farewells. Tears flowed. Back at the quarters Jack arrived home grinning welcoming us back .

'Hello you three. Preparing for the voyage. That's my girl. Look Sarah. When I was at your Mothers something happened. I decided not to tell you until you arrived back here.'...Immediately flashing into my mind I thought: *Orders had come through it had been cancelled. No such luck*... 'When I arrived back. I noticed someone had broken into the quarters. I did a search and the only thing missing was the chiming clock. I had been presented with from my last Battery. I reported the theft to the Military Police, who had an idea who the culprit was. The Army Cook's family next door, who had moved that weekend to Colchester Barracks. They asked me. Did I know anyone at Colchester, who they could contact? I could only think of Quartermaster Johnson. I left them to sort it out. On Tuesday I was ordered to go to Colchester. I met QM Johnston, we reported to the Duty Officer. I briefed him with all the facts. He issued orders for the Cook to report to his quarters immediately. The three of us arrived there, knocking on the door, the Cook's wife Mrs Beckett opened it. What a surprise she had to see me! Of course it was an official visit and let us in. I identified the clock and when questioned she said. They had won it in a raffle at Bordon. When the cook turned up, seeing me. He confessed. He had broken in and taken it, nothing else. The Officer asked me if I wanted to press charges. I said No. Any trial would have delayed being posted to India. She broke down in tears stating. When her child was born. Sarah had been so good to her. She sent her apologies. However the Officer tore a strip off them Gave the husband extra duties and dismissed the case. The clocks over there.'

The day before we left, Jack had already left for duty. The three of us were preparing breakfast when the scullery water pipes burst, water flooded everywhere. There was no stopcock key to be found. I sent Margaret up to the company office, whilst I took the three children next door. Then Eilish and I went along to each neighbour to find one. Six doors away we found it and rushed back to turn off the stopcock. The whole of the ground floor area was awash with water. The packed boxes were sodden, all needed to be unpacked and repacked into new boxes, we got those up onto the table. Wading in freezing water, we used brooms to sweep the water out. I was in floods of tears. Eilish, who saw the funny side of everything, was in fits of laugher said.

'Sarah. Stop crying your eyes out. You're filling up the water we are trying to brush outside. You should be laughing. You're getting away from all this cold. It will be lovely and hot for you from now on.'

I never did like Bordon. Losing a baby, the children's illness, the theft, snow everywhere finally to cap it all a flood! I could not wait to leave. Margaret arrived back with a plumber. She began to help with the mopping up. We acquired more boxes, repacked those sodden with water. The plumber mended the pipe, filled up the kettle and made us all a cup of tea. Jack arrived seeing the state of the place stood hands on hips, exclaimed.

'What on earth has happened here Sarah?'

'You may well ask. It's all over now bar the shouting.' He could see I was upset. So didn't press any further comments about the flood, but cautiously mentioned.

'Sarah ducks. I've read Company orders. We have to be on the square at o nine-hundred hours tomorrow morning. We are going by train to Southampton.'

Margaret and Eilish left us in the afternoon, they were going to stay overnight at a hotel in Southampton. Late in the afternoon our packing cases were collected, leaving us with our personal luggage for the outward passage. With my mind in turmoil, I could not sleep. About three 'o'clock I left the warmth of the bed, slipped on a cardigan, quietly left the room, going down the stairs to the tiny kitchen, the smell of dampness was everywhere. Turning on the gas mantle which hissed, striking a match lit it popping it produced its stark white light. At the gas stove I turned on two gas taps striking a match ignited the hissing gas into fierce blue jets of flames, a welcome glow of heat. I busied myself making a cup of tea, sat down at the table alone in the silence, amongst the gentle hiss of the gas mantle and pleasant roar of the gas jets, in the distance upstairs the rumble of Jack's snoring provided a comforting sound. How on earth he was able to sleep, with all the worry of taking his family out to God knows where? Nothing seemed to worry him. I was the complete opposite. Everything was packed ready, only one suitcase remained open, I wondered what time it was. I thought: *I've been sitting here for ages, thinking about nothing.* However, my mind began to focus on everyday questions. Washing? What happens to dirty washing on board this boat? I started to twist my wedding ring. I got up, made another cup of tea before preparing Jack's breakfast, ready for him before he left at four 'o' clock. He, as we did, had a busy day ahead of us. I heard Jack coming down stairs entering the kitchen came to the gas stove whispered.

'Morning Sarah. You're up bright and early, looking forward to it Eh? I'll just go and do my ablutions.' He gave me a peck on the cheek then soon returned dressed in his uniform ready to walk out the door exclaimed.

'Tea. That's all I'm after. No time for all that breakfast Sarah. Thank you very much.' I ordered him.

'Jack. Just sit down and eat something before you go out.'

Grudgingly he obeyed my demand, but didn't finish it all. He left me with last minute instructions, adding he would be back later. I picked at the remnants then cleared away the,remains washed up ready for the next sitting. A good breakfast to fill them up. Then in the peace and quiet of the early morning. I took out my rosary beads sat down to say the rosary. I had just finished a decade, when Mary appeared in the doorway, rubbing away the sleep from her eyes. She came in yawning and snuggled up beside me.

'I'm tired Mum.' I quietly told her.

'Go back to bed then. We all have a long day ahead of us.'

She stifled another yawn. Then Jackie, followed by Kathleen arrived, I thought: *This is the start of their day.* I cooked their breakfast. Too nervous to eat myself, drank tea and more tea. Dressed myself in the bedroom, returned back into the warmth of the kitchen where they had finished eating, clearing away, I washed up putting the crockery neatly away in the cupboard, ready for the inventory to be taken. Jackie was crying Mary had hid his toys. Near to the end of my tether. I got hold of Mary and shook her until her finger nails almost fell off. Made her promise me she would be good for the rest of the day. With that grin of hers she promised.

I made the three of them sit at the table. Outside dawn was breaking it was nearing seven. Still a couple of hours to go. I finished off the packing and got the three of them to sit on the bulging suitcase, with them thumping up and down. I managed to secure the clasp, however this burst of activity started them fighting again. I ordered them back to the table. Making certain that everything that had to be done was done. About an hour later Jack arrived back accompanied by a Store orderly.

'Okay. Says he. 'Well done Sarah. Your better than most of the gunners.' He was thoroughly enjoying himself, I kept them sat, while the orderly done his rounds. Jack took the luggage outside. The Orderly completed his checking, requested my signature. My last chore. I handed over the keys. Jack called.

'C'mon out you lot.'

I ushered them out, the raw coldness made me shiver. The Orderly banged the door closed behind us. Jack organised his little squad with their packs on the road. We carrying the suitcases he said.

'All set then. Come on you three. Let's march up to the square like soldiers.'

Leading his squad, with me in the rear. Off we marched trying to keep in step. We must have looked a funny sight, Jackie striding out with his father, a few steps then breaking into a trot, the girls happily chatting to each other. I unsure of what was going to happen next? The only way was to put on a brave face. We marched to the square to join other families gathered close to platoons of soldiers. The RSM his pace stick stuck firmly under his arm, stood aside as he surveyed the scene. A line of G.S wagons was parked behind him. Jack left us to parley with the RSM. Jack began shouting out orders to the troops they began boarding the wagons. The RSM walked towards the families and barked out.

'NOW THEN LADIES. CAN I HAVE YOUR ATTENTION PLEASE. Ladies please only keep what you require for the train journey. Leave any luggage for the voyage beside you, which will be loaded onto a wagon. Now we all know you're off to a wonderful holiday in India? But before you depart. Please make sure you don't leave anything behind. That includes your children. I know some of you would be quite happy to leave them in my charge. Well Ladies. I have enough of my own babies to shout orders to. (A ripple of light-hearted laughter). Will the ladies to my right. Ah! Mrs. Samson. When I say, lead off. Would you start boarding the third GS wagon over there. Thank you. One last word before you depart. I myself have served in India. I can assure you. It is quite a pleasant and interesting place to be posted to. So Good luck to you all and Bon Voyage. Thanks to all of you for your attention. Mrs. Samson. Lead off.'

Following behind all headed for the wagon. The driver and another soldier, helped us climb aboard, the children were swept off their feet up onto the wagon. The remaining luggage was removed from the area and placed in a wagon. When everything was cleared off the square. The tailboard was locked in place the driver started up the engine and with a sudden jolt the wagon moved, that threw everyone about. All trying to hang on to anyone close enough, apologies came thick and fast. Being close to the rear of the wagon, I caught my breath as we passed the Guardhouse. The journey was short and brief, the wagon stopped, we were helped down, ushered along the pavement through the station gates to mingle along the then crowded platform. The train with its carriage doors wide open waiting for everyone to board. Jack emerging from the crowds came towards us.

'Now then Sarah. I see we haven't lost anyone. Good. It won't be long before we board the train. I'll be in with the rest of the troops. So I will see you at Southampton. Don't you worry now you'll be all right.'

Everything happened so quickly. A Royal Engineers Colour Sergeant was shouting for everyone to board the train. Walking up and down, ushering everyone on. Jack saw the children and me settled into a carriage, before he went back to the troops. So began the slamming and banging of carriage doors. We had hardly sat down, when the sharp shriek of the train's whistle deafened all, as the train jolted into motion, slowly pulled out of Liss station. We were on our way to India. In the carriage the chatter was India. No one had been there, knew anything or what to expect, but all had the same opinion. Lions, tigers, crocodiles, elephants and snakes. I'd never seen an elephant never mind any wild animals. These topics of conversation sent shivers down my spine. However, all the children were either looking out of the windows or playing in the corridors, they were happy going on a holiday.

We had been travelling for about an hour, when somebody called out. 'Southampton Docks ahead.' The children stopped running around and rushed to a window. At Southampton Docks station the train came to a grinding halt. Everyone eagerly got out and down onto the platform to

131

join the excited jostling crowd being ushered forward, passing the luggage being loaded onto a trolley for our collection elsewhere. Jack coming up alongside me said.

'Right Sarah. I've not seen any sign of them yet. Oh. There they are to your right.' Raising his arm waved it about. Then I heard them shouting. 'SARAH. JACK. OVER HERE.'

Jack guiding us to the right, In front of us people parted to let two mad Irish girls run through them. Each grabbed hold of my arms we walked towards the ship. Their presence eased my anxiety, as in the distance the faint sounds of a band played. Progressively it became louder as we rounded one of the warehouses, to come in full view of a large white ship. Far larger than the Irish ferryboat. Its single yellow funnel emblazoned with a wide blue stripe around its top. I

 physically shivered as we made our way towards it. The surrounding chattering mingled with the music of the band and above all. The shouts of Sergeants barking out instructions, where to pick up luggage before embarking. Proceeding forward, we passed the band, merrily playing a medley of military tunes. Eilish said.

'Sarah that's the Irish Fusiliers. They've come especially to see you off.'

I was not, impressed by her remark. We stood by a gangway, Eilish and Margaret took a case each from Jack, leaving me holding a small case in charge of my three. Jack seeing all was in order said.

'Sarah. You can go aboard now. Your cabin is on B Deck. Eilish its cabin number two hundred and thirty seven remember that. I will catch up with you later.'

He left us to get on with his duties. Margaret went up first followed by me pushing my three in front of me, with Eilish behind, we climbed up the steep gangway. At the top, a Steward was directing families to their cabins. Eilish spoke up.

'Cabin Two-three-seven 'B' deck. Please.'

'Go through that doorway there, down two decks Madam.'

We trooped after Eilish, through a doorway down four flights of stairways, Eilish pointing at a notice. Affixed to the wall indicating the cabin numbers. Exclaimed.

'Here we are. 'B' Deck. Your cabin is that way.'

It certainly made our search easy. Like lost sheep we followed her along a corridor with cabins on both sides, some were already occupied. Eilish called out in triumph, as if she'd won a £100.00 'Here it is.'.. She disappeared through a doorway, a small notice on the cabin door. Stated.

Mrs Plant. & Family.
Mrs. Porter.

Entering this cabin, it was so small we filled it up. Either side were two bunk beds, two small ladders provided access to the top bunks, in between and half way up the steel wall was a large glass porthole, it was closed. On one side beside the bunks was an open storage space. Eilish closing the cabin door exclaimed.

'Sarah what's behind this door?' She opened another to reveal a tiny room. The toilet and washbasin. She exclaimed. 'All home comforts. Eh Sarah?' Disillusioned I remarked.

'I thought that we would have a cabin to ourselves. But there's another lady sharing.'

We sorted out our berths, me on the bottom, Mary above me with Kathleen and Jackie on the opposite top bunk, leaving the lower one for this other woman. Much to Jackie's delight he was up and down this ladder like a monkey. I stood and surveyed the cabin that was to be my home for the next four weeks. I thought: *God Help me*. Someone poked their head into the cabin and asked.

'Is this the Jamieson's cabin?' A chorus of voices.

132

'No. It's the Plant's. Sorry wrong cabin.' Margaret suggested.

'C'mon you three. Lets' go and explore the ship.' I intervened.

'No. We'll shall all go.' I was not going to be left alone, being just as interested to find out other places. Leaving the suitcases on the bottom bunk entered the corridor where other families were lugging suitcases, trying to locate their cabins. It was strange but exciting. At the end of the passageway a rather stout woman who appeared to have given up was sat on her case, which was giving way under her weight. She hailed us.

'Where the bleeding hell is 'C' deck?' Eilish quickly answered.

'Next one down.' As we edged passed her she moaned.

'Thanks Luv. That's all I need.'

Climbing the flights of stairs to the next deck. We located the dining room, with rows of polished tables laid up for the next meal. Eilish counted twelve place settings per table. Jack found us on 'A' deck he retorted.

'I've been all over the ship searching for you! I've already been to the cabin, saw our suitcases there and wondered where you could be?' A gong sounded and a voice over the Tannoy called for everyone's attention.

'The Nevassa will sail on the mid-day tide to-morrow the twenty-sixth February. Tea will be served for all seagoing passengers in the dining room from seventeen hundred until eighteen thirty hours. Thank you.' A loud click, then silence.

With the excitement of being on board a ship, we had forgotten all about food. Only then did we realise it was half past four, Margaret suggested.

'Eilish we have to go ashore. Jack. Do you think you can you get off the ship before it sails? We've already booked a table at the hotel for a farewell breakfast.' Jack hesitating answered.

'I don't think it will be a problem. But I will check anyway. Thank you very much, we shall be there. What's the name of the hotel?'

'It doesn't matter. We will come back in a taxi for you.'

With bye byes from the children, me wiping away a tear, they proceeded down the gangway. Jack said.

'Come on Sarah. Pull yourself together. It's time for eating. I'm sure we are all hungry.'

In the dining room we sat down at a table. Two smartly dressed stewards served us, one placed an oval plate of sandwiches on the table, the other poured tea from a large silver teapot and milk from another jug. I was thirsty, the tea was a welcome drink. Jack served out one sandwich for each of our three, they were very quiet as they watched everything going on still eating their sandwiches, furthermore, as we had not eaten hardly anything since breakfast, the pile of sandwiches was soon consumed as was the tea. Jack called the waiter over and asked for another helping. The noise and excitement of others around us, was justification of their needs. We had plenty to eat, when satisfied, we left the table to return to our cabin to settle down for the night. Our cabin was in the same state as we had left it. However, seeing that the other lady had not arrived. We decide to use the four bunks. Jack left to make arrangements to stay with us for the night, which in my eyes was a godsend. I had not been looking forward to our very first night alone in a strange cabin on board a ship. Whilst Jack was away I just unpacked our night attire, there certainly was not much storage space available. Jack arrived back said.

It's okay and we can go ashore in the morning. Apparently the other lady Mrs Porter will be arriving in the morning.'

With the cabin door shut it was quite warm and cosy, the three of them were soon fast asleep. I could hardly keep my eyes open, soon we too succumbed to the necessity of sleep. I slept well, early next morning I woke the children. The little washroom was ideal with its hot and cold water and small lavatory. Jack left us to watch out for my sisters. Soon after we followed him up to the deck to find him standing by the gangway, he called out.

'Sarah. Hurry up. Eilish has a taxi waiting down on the quayside.'

As we went down the steep gangway onto the quayside, quick greetings were said as we climbed into the waiting taxi. Eilish gave each of them a small green flag, which Margaret had bought to wave us off later. Then we were off to their hotel for a last breakfast. it was Sunday, a grey overcast day threatening rain, as the taxi manoeuvred its way out of the docks through empty streets it began to rain. At the hotel we had a wonderful tasty breakfast, then all too soon, it was time to get back to board the ship. We hired two taxi's, by the time we arrived back alongside the boat, I was already welling up full of tears. I got out ran towards the gangway, then for the very last time leaving the shores of England behind, stepped up onto the gangway, bound for India too who knew what lay ahead of me? Margaret and Eilish followed up behind us to say their final farewells. The steward at the top of the gangway hailed Jack.

'Excuse me sir. While you were ashore. Everyone has been issued with Tobies, and guess what? Someone started a rumour. Without Tobies on your head In no time at all you are dead from sunstroke.'

They laughed, but this little snippet of information, did not inspire any confidence in me. Down in the cabin we met the other lady. A pleasant looking fair-haired woman, about five feet eight tall, she towering above me introduced herself.

'Good morning. I'm Mrs. Nora Porter, my husband Bill is bedded down with the troops.'

Introductions were cordially made followed by a brief chat. With all the bodies crammed into it, the cabin was almost bursting at its seams. The Gong of the Tannoy interrupted our brief conversation. A voice crackled.

'This is the final call for visitors. Will all visitors please leave the boat immediately.' A sharp click. Silence.

The time had come, when I was to be finally parted from my sisters. With a lump in my throat as big as a walnut, we returned to the gangway. With hugs, kisses, floods of tears, we parted company, it began to drizzle with rain. The band playing military music had assembled up towards the front of the ship, we found room by the ships rail to look down on the well-wishers gathered on the quayside below. Everyone seemed to be waving a small Union Jack, in amongst them, Jack spotted Margaret and Eilish wildly waving two green flags. The shouting of bon voyage was drownded out by the ship's siren blastihg out two eerie notes, as its echo died away. The band struck up. 'Auld Lang Syne.' Voices sang the words, as more floods of tears came from everyone, their voices drowned out by the ship's siren sounding out three long blasts.

Leaving England on the twenty-sixth February nineteen twenty-nine. I thought: *My heart would break. I never wanted to go to India and I had hoped, the doctor would pass me unfit.* Remembering my mother's words. 'If you have to go, go with a good heart.' But I did not know how too. With the ship's siren wailing from above, me wailing buckets of tears from the deck below. Through the haze of the drizzle, gradually the quayside began to get farther away, sailing slowly down the river around a bend into the Solent. Nobody left the deck, all too eager to catch their last glimpses of England. My three quite happy playing around with other children on the deck. Someone behind me mentioned.

'This side of the ship where we are standing, is called the port side. The other side is the starboard, and quipped POSH. Portside Out. Starboard Home.'

Passing the end of the Isle of White watched the Needles slip past us, reassuring me Jack had his arms around me and murmured.

'Don't worry everything will be Okay.'

I shivered. Very much aware of the ships movement sailing through the grey sea. We crossed over to the other side. At the ships rail with the wind blowing strong against my face, I did not dare look down at the sea far below, instead turned away to watch the children running around the deck. We remained on deck until the sight of England became just a fuzzy line on the horizon, having seen that last fleeting sight, feeling extremely vulnerable I left broken hearted, urged.

'Jack. I want to go down below to the cabin.'

'Okay ducks. C'mon you three. Down below.'

Jack placed his arm around me, which provided me some comfort as we proceeded below. It was then that the Tannoy bleeped to call us to a meal sitting. So changing course went and had the meal before going back to the cabin.

In the cabin, the lady Mrs. Porter was standing beside the bunk with another Sergeant behind her. Jack immediately said.

'I take it your Mrs. Porter. Who is to share this cabin with my wife and children.'

'Well yes. I just about made it. This is my husband Bill.' Jack shook hands with him and asked.

'What Battery are you with?'

'The Forty-second. Going out to India. Look it's a bit cramped in here, and we need to have something to eat. We will leave so you can sort out the children. We will come back later.' I answered.

'Why thank you. I do not think it will be too long before they are bedded down.'

They left us, to sort out our accommodation, as I had predicted the three were soon in their night-ware tucked up and fast asleep, by the time the Porter's returned. After small talk Jack and Bill left us to go back to their sleeping quarters. Then Mrs Porter and I sat there quietly talking about where we had been, just general chin wagging before we settled down for the night.

As I lay there thinking: *About the rather hazardous experiences I had endured, with all the different postings Jack had been given in the past, then to find myself on a long voyage to India. Just what would it be like in India? Would I be put in some horrible place amongst a lot of natives?* The gentle motion of the boat lulled me into sleep. I was woken up by the excited chatter of Jackie. Mrs Porter's bunk was empty. I heard the lock of the toilet door rattle, she stepped out exclaimed.

'Good Morning Mrs. Plant. Did you sleep well?'

Somewhat shocked to see her up already, maybe she had been woken by Jackie's chattering, I answered.

'Mrs. Porter. I'm sorry you were woken up by the children. I'm normally wide awake by five thirty.'

'Oh don't you worry about that. It's just gone six. I too get up early. Mrs. Plant please call me Nora, and your name is Sarah is it not?'

'Yes that is correct, I think it is right that if we are to be so close. Christian names would be an honour.'

We soon agreed that the washing facilities were cramped, decided to have a roster. In the mornings, I would be first into the small room, to wash, dress the children, take them to the dining room for breakfast, leaving the cabin free for Nora to carry out her own ablutions in private. In the evenings Nora would leave the cabin, so I could get the children ready for bed. A routine that was to work quite well throughout the voyage. Jack arrived back at the cabin with five Tobies, one for each of us. They had to be tried on, much to the enjoyment of all in the cabin. Jackie's was far too big for him and kept falling over his eyes, however when it was set properly on his head. Mary would tip the backup causing shrieks of laughter. Jack stopped that malarkey.

'Enough of this. I'll exchange it for a smaller size.'

Fun and games over. I put the Tobies away under the bottom bunk ready for India. Another must on board no shoes or boots were allowed, plimsolls only that made me look even smaller.

Jack had made sure we were kitted out with suitable attire and whites to wear later. As time progressed I found Nora to be very kind and loved the children. She used to call Jackie - Jim, why I don't know? Although his second name was James. She tried hard not to laugh at the antics of Mary. Lying in the bunk that night I tried to sleep, unsure if I was ever going to get used to the movement of the ship, nevertheless, later in the voyage our cabin became a retreat for both of us. The second day at sea, the motion of the ship became more pronounced, as it sailed through the Bay of Biscay, giving one the queasy feeling of seasickness. Our stewardess advised…'Lie down, get used to the motion of the boat.'

This we did but the motion steadily got worse. The children lying on the top bunk thought it was good fun until. Jackie puked up down on me, which started them puking onto the strip of carpet between the bunks. That sight started me off, very quickly treading in puke I headed for the lavatory, I didn't make it. Up it all came, progressively I became worse, I could neither stand up nor lie down. With Nora the same, Jack looked after the children until their stomachs settled down. Out of the five of us, I was the worse. I thought: *I would die.* After days of seasickness, I felt very hungry. I got Mary to ask the Stewardess to bring me something to eat, she turned up with. "Tripe and Onions." The thought and sight made me feel ill again, but I was so hungry I devoured it and asked for more. By the fifth day, the weather improved and so had my stomach.

Life on board was regimented with rigid timetables. All were kept in informed by the ships Tannoy system, at the sound of a gong all listened to what was going on. Mealtimes: Breakfast at 08:00 hrs. Lunch at 12:00-hrs. Dinner at 17:00 hrs. Everyday at 10:00 hrs including Sundays the Captain would inspect the whole ship, which lasted anything up to an hour and caused concern for everyone. Bed linen was changed every Monday. It was our job to ensure our cabin was clean, ship shape and tidy. After breakfast, Jack would look after the children, whilst Nora and I cleaned out the cabin. Before 10:00 hrs. Jack and Bill would return to stand along with us like everyone else in the corridor, to wait the Captains inspection. After our bout of sea sickness, when we were all fit. Captain Steadman, accompanied by a couple of his Officer's inspected the cabin,coming out into the corridor stopped in front of the two men, stated.

'Not good enough. I'll be back to re-inspect this cabin. Look in the washroom.' Jack being the senior just grunted.

'Sarah. Get it sorted out.'

Nora and I checked and found, discarded lavatory paper behind the lavatory, I removed it. He did return, left with a grunt. The rest of the day, we could within reason do what we liked. Lifeboat Stations were more exciting and had people scurrying around to their designated lifeboat number. Upon my very first sight of the Nevassa, I briefly noticed its Lifeboats, hung double-banked from the upper deck, called the Promenade deck. The call. 'To lifeboat stations.' Sent shivers down my spine. I could not swim and the thought of the ship sinking, and me unable to save the children, made me feel sick again. But they certainly enjoyed the confusion. Whooping around like Indians, as everyone made their way to the lifeboats. The very cumbersome Life jackets all the same size, with the ungainly blocks of cork in the front and rear upper torso, were donned, by winding the loose tapes around your waist then tied tightly secured the jacket to one's person. I made a mental note to do the children's first. We carried out this palaver only to stand about but, it did take up some of the time and broke up the daily monotony. On the second of March, stood at lifeboat stations with the sun shining we sailed into the Mediterranean Sea to see our first sight of land, the famous Rock of Gibraltar, even the colour of the sea changed to blue. So the saying was true.

The days on board were tedious. Church services were held every day at 07:00 hrs. As my three were always up at the crack of dawn, so as not to disturb Nora I got them out of the cabin to attend Mass before breakfast, that kept them quiet to pass another hour by. In the afternoons in our cabin, Nora and I began to hold an afternoon. "Tiffin Party." Having acquired a few cups and saucers together with a small tea pot from the galley, purchased some tea and biscuits from the ships shop, the hot water from the sink tap that was no good, however we found out that one of the soldiers working down in the boiler room, was willing to fetch us a pot of boiling water to our cabin, so for his trouble we gave him a few shillings. We thoroughly enjoyed the little luxury those Tiffin times provided us throughout the voyage. During one such Tiffin time I politely asked Nora.

'What do you think of the devilment of my three?'

'I would love to have them, as unfortunately I am unable to conceive.'

I did not make any further conversation on the subject. Apart from Nora, I knew very few other women, but did pass the time of day with others attending mass, amongst them was a little girl about eight years old, who always followed us into the dining room and sat at our table. Mary called her Bridget. A few days after we were way past Gibraltar, she politely asked.

'Please may I play with Mary and Kathleen?' Surprised I responded.

'Yes. Of course you can. Your names Bridget isn't it?'...'Yes.'... 'Is your mother in the dining room then?'...'No she is ill in her cabin.'...'How long has she been ill then?'...Bridget hesitating answered...'Since we came on the ship.'...'What's the matter with her then?'...'Just sick in bed.' I thought: *The poor woman might need help...*'Bridget. Do you think your mother would mind if I visited her in your Cabin?'...'No.'...She seemed pleased at my interest...'Which cabin is it?'...'B deck number one-hundred and sixteen.'....'Right Bridget. You go and tell your mother a Mrs Plant will be along to see her tomorrow morning.'

Jack who had been listening to our conversation enquired.

'Sarah what do you intend to do?'

'I don't know. All I can do is see what the matter is with her. After lunch will you come with me and help find her cabin?' We found their cabin on 'B' deck. The following morning, we carried out our usual early morning mass then breakfast along with Bridget, when we had finished. I left my three with Jack, then took Bridget down to their cabin to introduce me to her mother.

'Mum. This is Mary's mother.'

The poor woman lay in a dishevelled berth, white as a sheet, very haggard looking with dark rings surrounded sunken hazy eyes. She looked as if she had been pulled through a hedge backwards, her hair had not been combed for days. It was obvious she had been very ill.

'Hello. I take it Bridget has already talked with you about us. I'm Sarah Plant, how are you?' In a weak voice she replied.

'My names Elaine, Bridget has told me that you have been looking after her.' I thought: *Looking after Bridget! All Bridget had done was sit at the table and play with my three. Leave things as they are!* I enquired.

'How long have you been ill?' Weakly she replied.

'I caught flu just before we left England. I've been laying in this berth since we sailed from Southampton. I have had a terrible time, what with the flu and the seasickness. The ship's Doctor had been treating me. he says I'm on the mend. The way I feel I'm lucky to be alive. I'm going out to join my husband in Bombay.'

'Well that's encouraging news. I'm only too pleased to help out as much as I can. Are there any others in the cabin?'

'Yes two ladies, as the stewardess looks after me. They just ask me if I'm all right then leave.' I was a bit mystified at her remark asked.

'Is it all right if I come and visit you?'

'Would you? That would be very kind of you.'

It appeared my visit had perked her up a bit. The arrival of the stewardess interrupted our brief conversation. I left them together. Later about to visit her, I met the stewardess she stopped me in the corridor.

'Mrs whoever. Thank you you're a Gods send. I understand you look after Bridget? I do not have the time to look after her as well as her sick mother. and the other two women don't help.'

Four days later, Elaine was fit enough to get up on deck. I got her to sit in a deckchair alongside me, whilst keeping our eyes on the children playing. I invited her to join our Tiffin time, which too Nora an I was a treasured feature of a tedious day. Later in the evenings after the children were fast asleep, Elaine and I spent the time on deck, sat talking and gazing at millions of stars. Elaine was a good source of information telling me of what her husband had written in his letters, all about the heat of India, its food, the married quarters with many Indian servants. These little chinwags, although hearsay gave me some assurance as to our future. At least once a week, a dance would be held on the rear promenade deck, which were quite delightful. During the daytime plenty of deck sports, were organised for the troops. Jack knew everybody and they him, possibly for his football and sporting activities he participated in all of them. He said that was part of his job, mine was to look after the children. Nevertheless a boxing tournament had been organised. Jack took us all up onto the promenade deck, to watch the boxing bouts going on down from in a makeshift ring on the deck below, surrounded by soldiers, all shouting and booing encouraging the two boxers. This was Mary's cue to start shouting, so the other two joined in. A bell started the round. Coming into the middle of the ring they sparred about, exchanging a few cautious blows, then a flurry of blows had blood pouring from one's nose, making me feel ill. Jack laughing said.

'Come on Sarah. It's only a bit of fun. They don't mean any harm.' I retorted.

'God. What could they do, if they did mean it?'

'The trouble with you Sarah. Is you're too soft-hearted. C'mon. I'll take you back down to the cabin.'

One of Jack's Bombardiers came up to him and said.

'Sir. I thought you might like to know. There is going to be a burial at sea. One of the native seamen has died.' Jack said.

'Change of plans. Sarah. C'mon we shall see this burial and you can say a few prayers. You will prefer that more than the boxing.'

I remembered Jack's brother Alf had told me he only had one lung, he was a butcher/cook in the Merchant Navy, someone had locked him in a freezer room. He was in there for hours before someone let him out, taken into the ship's sick bay to be transferred to a shore hospital, where doctors removed his lung. I retorted.

'No. I feel bad enough about this boxing.' A soldiers wife alongside us quipped.

'Don't be so soft Mrs Plant. It was the native's last trip. He was going back home to his eight wives or, whatever number they have? What a lucky break for him.'

Her remark caused a ripple of laughter amongst the other bystanders. Reluctantly, we went to the burial where other passengers had gathered at the ships rail. I overheard someone say.

'Those sharks have followed the ship all the way. They know when someone will die on board a ship.' That remark made me feel worse so I shut up.

Six natives arrived carrying the body on a board, covered by the Union Jack, rested it on the rail. The Captain arrived cap under his arm, holding the Bible recited some words. I closed my eyes and prayed for the poor man's soul. I heard the Captain say...'to the deep...Amen.' Amid the Salaams and wailing of his shipmate friends. The natives lifted up the end of the board, and with a rasp of canvas against wood, the body slid over the ships side. With the ceremony over, all dispersed. Before I had attended funerals where it was the custom to hold a wake. This burial was definitive. Whilst on the upper deck, the two boxers were still knocking hell out of each other. I couldn't get away from it quick enough. Such is the way of life at sea.

A day before we arrived at Malta, as it was the ships first Port - of-Call. All passengers had been invited to a Military Parade ashore in Valletta. Elaine and I had decided to wash the

138

children's hair, having done that, we took them up on deck where their hair would dry quicker in the sun, while they played together. With the sun and sea breeze their hair quickly dried, but had the four of them looking like hedgehogs. At the sight of them we were in tears with laughter. Applying spit to my hand tried to smooth down their spiky hair did no good. The soldier who provided us with the hot water arrived, with a bucket of warm water, suggested.

'Ear. Mrs. Just rewash their hair in this water, what you did was used sea water. That's why it's made it spiky. I'll collect the bucket later.' We soon did what he suggested. and got rid of their spikey hair. The next day during breakfast Elaine mentioned.

'Sarah I don't feel well enough to go ashore I am staying on board.'

I not wanting to go ashore myself agreed to stay with her. Although Jack and Bill were on parade, Nora decided to go ashore. After breakfast we stood by the ships rail together with a few other families who had also decided to stay on board, to watch the soldiers being ordered into columns. All looking very smart in their Tropical kit and Tobies. With the bands playing along with the skirl of the pipes, the order. 'Quick March'! Rang out, the columns departed from the quayside. With their departure over, we returned to our cabins to prepare for Captain's inspection. A rather informal inspection and completed without too much ceremony. We almost had the ship to ourselves. Up on deck we kept the children out of mischief, just content looking over the ship's side, watching what was going on in the harbour. A constant change as flotilla's of small boats went about their everyday tasks, anchored farther out into the harbour was a Royal Navy ship. At 11:30. The little shop on board opened its shutters. As usual, Mary was first one to be served, asking for one thing then she would change her mind. It appeared to be a game with her, copying what she did Kathleen and Jackie did the same. I'm sure the shopkeeper, who was very patient with the children, was more than pleased when we all left the ship in Bombay. The sound of the Tannoy gong announced lunchtime. Taking much longer than normal over our lunch, it was the children who began too moan and groan about sitting still all the time. Returning back on deck we lazed in deckchairs, with fewer children on board the children had a great time playing deck quoits though not without a few squabbles that were sorted out by Mary. We were unsure about our Tiffin time hot water, until we without Nora who was still ashore returned to our cabin, fortunately the soldier was waiting, I asked.

'Why haven't you gone ashore?' Winking he said.

'I got extra duty Ma'am.'

I did not bother to ask why? I was about to make the tea, when through the open porthole the sounds of the band could be heard. The Army was back. Jackie in his excitement, eager to get up on deck and see his father return fell through the doorway. Mary hauled him up to his feet the four of them quickly disappeared, hurriedly we followed behind them to get up on deck by the ships rail . On the quayside below the troops were already halted and stood at attention. The band stopped playing. The troops were dismissed to march up the gangways, their Khaki tunics soaked with great damp patches showed evidence of the heat. I'm sure all were very pleased that the parade had finished. Jack found us on deck. Rivulets of perspiration ran down his face, Jackie leapt into his father's arms knocking off his Tobie.

'Whoa. Steady on their son. Sarah. You should have attended. It was quite something. on parade along with the ships troops there were soldiers from the Maltese Army garrison, the Royal Navy and the Band of the Royal Marines joined the Irish Band. It took longer than anyone had thought. But it was a real good turn out.'

'It certainly looked good from up here, but we had a peaceful day and besides look at the state of you, the same as the troops.'

I had noticed his KD was more than damp, his Sam Brown almost melding in with the damp stains.

'Yes. It was quiet hot down there. No sea breeze to cool us down. We had one or two of the troops faint from the heat, but they are all right. Look you'll have to excuse me I must have a sluice down and change'...About to leave checked his stride turned around again...'Oh by the way Nora has gone straight back to the Cabin. I thought I'd better inform you. Let her have some privacy.' I acknowledge his comment.

'Okay.' It was just as well. Tiffin forgotten.

That evening ship's orders: Tropical dress and headwear. Will be worn for Captains Inspection. After the evening meal the cabin became a hive of activity. Out came the whites. Blouses, and skirts for the women and little girls, white shorts, shirts for the little boys and of course more joviality. 'Tobies.'

Next morning, the ship well out of the sight of Malta, en-route to our next port of call, Port Said. Breakfast time looked like a tennis convention. Inspection over, on deck there were some funny sights to be seen. Tobies worn at rakish angles. Not so my three, constantly knocking them off of each other's heads. This game started all the other children doing the same. All you could see was some little body scampering around the deck, chasing a rolling Tobie. The shrieks

of Mothers running after it before it disappeared over the side. Mary arrived back with the other two, all minus Tobies. I asked.

'Where are your Tobies'? Mary answered.

'The wind has blown them over the side.' Aghast I said.'What all three?'....'Yes we tried to stop them but.' A grin spread across her face. I thought: *What's she up too?* Angrily I retorted.

'Well we can't get any more. So you'll have to go without.'.... 'Didn't want them anyway.' They chorused as they ran away. However a mother approached me indignantly she shouted.

'YOUR MARY. SHE LAUNCHED HER TOBY OVER THE SIDE, AND SHE PERSUADED MY TWO TO DO THE SAME. WHAT ARE YOU GOING TO DO ABOUT IT?' All I could say was....'I'm sorry, their father will sort out some more.'

Another problem for Jack to solve. However it was getting progressively hot, the Tobies although light and comfortable, did not stop the heat of the body. It was quite stifling inside the cabin but we still held out Tiffin time. Once the tea was drunk one perspired freely. The following day during our lunchtime. An argument broke out between Mary and Jackie. I told them to be quiet, they stopped for a brief second then it started again.

Jackie...'Yes we are'...'No were not'...responded Mary...'Dad said we are'...responded Jackie...'Through clenched teeth Mary retorted...'No were not.' I intervened.

'Will you two stop squabbling. Mary I'm warning you.' Ignoring my threat Mary asked her father.

'Dad. Will you tell him.' I was beginning to lose my patience with this squabbling going on between the pair of them and demanded.

'Jack. Do you know what these two on about?'

'I don't know. Mary what are you arguing about?'

'The map you showed us Dad. Jackie thinks we are getting off the ship at the next port and take a train journey across land. I said we weren't. I'm the right one aren't I Dad? Tell him Dad.' This was news to me and questioned.

'Jack. What's this about a train journey? I thought we were going all the way to Bombay on this ship.' He laughed.

'Now then Sarah. Don't you start. Mary is right Look you two, I will explain it again. That will stop this arguing. Is that alright Mary, Jackie?' They both nodded agreement.

After lunch we were all standing gazing at the map of the world. Before I had not taken much notice, but was intrigued by what this map revealed. Jack pointing began his explanation. 'See that little dot there. That is the island of Malta we have just left.' Moving his finger in a line said....'We are about here.' Interrupting I asked... 'Okay. Where's this next port they are arguing about.'...'There. That is Port Said.'....Tracing his finger in a long line over the land....'See that long line there. That is the Suez Canal all the ship sails down it to Suez there.'...

'Oh. Now I can see what they were arguing about. Jackie do you understand what your Dad has said?'

'No. I want to go on the train.' ...'What train are you talking about?' He wasn't happy sobbed....'Dad said when we get off the ship, we get on a train.' Jack interrupted....'I know what he's on about. I told them when we leave the ship at Bombay here, we get a train.' I looked at it.

'Where's England then?'

'There'. I compared the three places.

'Well according to the map, we are only half way there then?' Jack agreed adding.

'That's right and Jackie was right about a train. They did do that before the Canal was built in the 1800s. All ships took the route around the bottom of Africa, right there where the Boer war was fought. The Suez Canal is only about one hundred miles long now ships take that route, which cuts out thousands of miles from a sea journey.'

This to me was most interesting, not only did this map captivate me, but also the children. England appeared so tiny and Ireland was even smaller. My mind wandered back to my childhood enquired. 'Where was the Boer War again?'

'There why?' He questioned

'Oh nothing special. What you said about the Boer War, reminded me of my Grandfather. It was around about the turn of the century, he would occasionally visit us on Sunday evenings. Mother would read to him, from the correspondence sheets about the latest news of the war. I never did know where South Africa was until now. After that war was over I remember seeing a couple of the soldiers from Ballybrittas, returning home had been out there in the fighting. To me they all looked very old and weather beaten, the colour of bronze.'

'Well it was a hard fought war out there. Nothing in comparison to the 14 -18 war that was for sure.' Jackie had lost interest nevertheless I, would take more time to study it.

The day before we were due to arrive at Port Said. Ship's orders stated:

Breakfast: Serving at 06:00 hrs.

Beginning at 07:00 hrs. All passengers will leave the ship to be taken ashore.

During the evening meal Elaine protested.

'Sarah I still do not feel well enough. I'll speak with the Purser to see, if I can stay on board?'... She informed me later. 'He's allowed me. But I must stay in my cabin, something to do with loading coal.'

On the morning of the ninth, during the early hours, the sound and rattle of anchor chains had Nora and me awake. The hum of the ship engines stopped, all was quiet. Nora exclaimed.

'What was that, where are we?'

'I don't know.' Arousing myself from out of my bunk, I felt for the little ladder to the top bunk, climbing up a couple of rungs, peered through the porthole. In the distance I saw twinkling lights, going to the washroom, whispered.

'Must be Port Said. The ship will dock later?' Having done my ablutions, I switched on the cabin light that woke the children. Jack arrived at the cabin.

'C'mon Sarah its five forty. Hurry up. Breakfast.'

We joined the melee of passengers going to early breakfast. I noticed Jackie's plimsolls were on the wrong feet. Stopping changed them over and asked.

141

'Jack. Why has the ship stopped offshore?' Nonchalantly he answered.

'Well. They park offshore ready to join the convoy going down the Suez.'

'Okay then. How do we get ashore?'

'No problem. They provide boats to take us there and back.' Alarm bells rang in my head retorted.

'What do you mean boats?'

'They bring small boats alongside the ship. We all get in them, they ferry us to the shore. You'll soon see after breakfast.' That answered me. Water again?

With the breakfast finished. We went down to the dispersal point on 'C' Deck, Starboard side. Jack with Jackie, Kathleen in front, then me with Mary behind. Dark skinned Coolies wearing a bandanna and a dirty cloth wrapped around their middles, padded passed us, jabbering and gesticulating to each other. The queue moving at a snail's pace, stopped every now and then.

'What's the holdup Jack?'

'The ferry boats can only take a certain number of passengers at a time.'

A Steward counting heads allowed the queue forward an appropriate number, we all just made it through the doorway, into the deep orange glow of the rising sun. Through the haze noticed dark outlines of buildings, stepping onto a small platform, immediately stopped. Far below saw the sea. Panic set in. I gripped Jacks arm and pulled him back towards me.

'C'mon Sarah keep moving.' There was only one way. Down. The ships officer said.

'You'll be okay ma'am. Just follow the others down the ship's ladder.' Jack instructed.

'Sarah just hold onto the rail you will be alright.' Cautiously I followed step by step, behind me Mary screeched. 'Isn't this good Mum?'

The stairway swayed as we stopped halfway, I watched as one full ferryboat left, another took its place. We were on the move, stopped again I clung on. Mary, provided a commentary.

'Next boat will be ours Mum.'

Reaching the bottom, stepped onto a wooden platform full of square holes, through which little spurts of seawater came up with the swell of the water, I froze. Jackie urged.

'Mum get in.' I was about to say. *'I'm not going.'* When two burly seamen took hold of my arms, to help me on my way propelled me towards the bobbing boat, I landed in the boat.

Jack unceremoniously grabbed me and sat me down. Mary followed me. We were the last to get on. With a stutter the engine came into life moved away towards the shore. I clutched my three close to me, as the boat yawed, bobbed up and down on the open sea, passing returning empty boats causing waves I shrieked as splashes hit my face. In panic I grabbed hold of Jack's arm. He just laughed. Nearing the landing stage, a Coolie sent a rope flying through the air, caught in mid air by another Coolie on the boat we were pulled in. Other coolie's grabbed hold of us, pulling each one onto the steps. I was more than grateful when we docked to get off this little boat onto dry land. I had landed in the land of ancient Pharaohs. It was about eight 'o'clock, the yellowing rising sun was then well above the buildings, even then it was hot, here there was no cool breeze from the sea, perspiring freely. The quayside was dirty covered in sand, there were boats of all sizes tied up along the waterfront, some had strange sails up or unfurled their boatmen some half dressed with turbans on the head went about their chores. I was not impressed by the land of the Pharaohs, exclaimed.

'What now Jack?'

'Well we have a full day to waste. I suppose we just follow the rest of them, to that roadway in front of us. Mary you grab hold of Jackie's hand. I don't want to lose him before we start.'

Walking over the powdery sand, I was aware of a strange shaky feeling in my legs exclaimed.

'Jack my legs feel funny.' An echo sounded.

'Mine too.' Even the children felt it.

Jackie play acting wobbled around, which started the other two off, a game of slipping and sliding began. Jack provided an explanation.

'Sarah. The sensation in the legs is just a case of sea-legs getting off the ship and onto dry land. It'll wear off.' I thought: *It was bad enough when we first started the trip, here we had the reverse.* Along the front, the buildings were strange box like hovels, five stacked one on top of the other, separated by a wooden lattice balconies. A sloping canopy supported by long vertical beams to the top, finished off the structure. On each balcony was a tall doorway, louvered shutters covered the narrow windows. Along the roadway the trees were tall, strange looking with a long straight trunk and massive spider looking leaves beneath which, hung bunch of yellow pods, sheltered under their shade, were a long line of horse drawn Landau's. As we drew level Jack selected one. Its driver swept his red hat off his head offering us his greetings.

'Plenty plenty capitan. You take ride all over Port Said. Me show you everything?'

'What do you say Sarah?'

'Jack our priority is to find a shop to get Tobies for the children, not go gallivanting all over Egypt sightseeing. Ask the driver does he know such a shop.' My comment brought an immediate response from the driver.

'Tobies. Tobies, Misses. Sun hat from blazing sun. I take you my brother, he has finest Tobies in Said, shop in Bazaar not far.' I was amazed this driver spoke English. I looked at Jack he nodded to the driver.

'Okay. Take us to the Bazaar.'

'Yes capitan. Now.' Quick as a flash he replaced his red hat. We clambered into his landau. With a shout at the driver in front, probably saying get out of my way, With a crack of his whip, the poor horse jolted into action veering into the flow of other landaus. Picking up speed along the sandy road of the harbour, got the horse into a steady trot, headed towards the town. The breeze caused by the motion of the landau, cooled us down, our three were really enjoying the ride, but I had to ask.

'Jack. Do you think he knows where he's going? '

'How do I know Sarah? It's his town. Of course he knows where he's going.'

We turned off the waterfront into direct sunlight.

'Look Sarah, that's the Suez Canal.' To our left was a wide expanse of water with large concrete banks. A monument with a figure overlooked it.

'Jack do you know who built the canal?'

'A Frenchman called Lesseps. That's his monument there. It took ten years to complete and a lot of Arab coolies to dig it out. It was a good thing it was built, it's been a God send to shipping.'

We passed by a white building with many high arches. On its roof were three green ornate domes, the middle one had a flag flying from it.

'Hey capitan. This building suez canal bosses.'

'What's he saying Jack?'

'I think he is saying. That impressive building is where the suez canal bosses work. They control the ships going up and down from there.' Pointing across the roadway. Jackie let out a screech.

'Look what's that?'

'That Jackie is a camel, a ship of the desert. Oops! I should not have said that Sarah. wait for his next question.' Jackie asked.

'What's a camel?'

I was just as intrigued. I had never seen one either. It just stood there, a gangling looking animal with long spindly legs and big paws. Supporting its bloated body. It had a large curved

143

neck and funny shaped head. Some sort of saddle rested on his humped back, from which draped red bags with multi coloured tassels. A woen band around its head held more coloured tassels that moved as its huge mouth chewed on something? Sat below in the shade of its huge body was its handler, completely shrouded in a white robe. All you could see was a black face. We were past it before Jackie retorted.

'That's not a ship. We were on a ship.' Jack laughed.

'There Sarah what did I say. Now I have to explain why? Jackie it's called a ship of the desert, because camels are able to go right across the sand, carrying all the goodies from one place to another. As there is no water in the desert. Did you see his hump on his back?' With the saddle on top, that's where it can store water in, so that he won't get too thirsty.

'No.'

'Well the next camel we see I will show you its hump okay?'

We began to slow down and came to a stop alongside a dirty looking building, with a mass of people outside. That I assumed was a Bazaar. Jumping down the driver, extending his hand to me, took hold of my arm.

'Down misses. I Mohammed show you finest tobies in said.'

I was almost dragged away from his Landau. I wasn't too pleased with his attention. I turned around looking for support from Jack following behind. He just grinned shrugged his shoulders, my three were all giggling. We entered a narrow street. Arabs were everywhere. Dressed in flowing white robes, red hats or some form of turban, all shouting, 'Backshee's' pointing at their shop. The driver shouting and waving away other sellers, guided me into a tiny shop, cried out.

'Ali. Ali. Tobies for misses family.'

At the rear of the shop through a beaded curtain. A very fat greasy looking Egyptian appeared. I was introduced.

'This Ali. My brother misses.'

'Tobies. Misses. Finest in all said! You and little ones. Yes?'

'No three.' I waved my hand around the three children. Casting an expert eye over my three. From a rack full of Tobies, he selected different sizes, gave them out, they tried them on, fitted perfectly. Jack said.

'Three Sarah.'

'No Jack Five? Two the same size as Mart's'... 'Why five?'

'Yes five. Don't forget the other women's two children are about the same as Mary's size.' Then asked. Five how much?' Ali said something. Jack shook his head.

'No too much.' Ali said something else.

'No.' Ali rolled his eyes upwards. Muttered something about Allah, muttered something else. I intervening said. 'Pay the man Jack. We have what we want. Let's get out of here.'

Jack paid Ali. Mohammed hovering in the background, led us back outside into the noisy street. The air smelt of a pungent sweetness. I waited for Jack to decide what we should do. The driver tugging at Jack's sleeve.

Capitan capitan. Take's family to see sights. Yes?'

'No. Not yet'. We walk through Bazaar.'

'I wait you outside Capitan.' Jack cocking his head shrugged.

'C'mon Sarah this way.'

We walked through the throng of people. There were all kind of shops selling, bangles, beads, jewellery, brass and many souvenirs, all on view. One seller caught hold of my arm, attempting to make a sale, I shrugged him off, clung onto Jack. Mary inquisitive as she was, picked things up, walked away, a very indignant Arab shouted.

'No. Bacshee's. You pay.'

I got Jack to pay. I told her off, Jack just laughed at her antics.

'Sarah look. Over there.'

A group of Arabs sat on stools sipping from small bowls of black liquid, one was sucking a long flexible pipe attached to an ornate glass jar half filled with water within which bubbles gurgled. Puffing smoke out of his mouth he passed it on to another. I thought: *That's not very hygienic.* Questioned.

'What is that Jack?'

'They are smoking hashish, can't you smell that sweet smell, it's nothing like pipe tobacco.'

The only women I noticed were covered from head to foot in black dresses, even their faces were covered except for a wide slit to see through. We saw strange looking vegetables. Large yellow coloured beans, tiny peas, lentils, I recognised onions, salad, potatoes and carrots. It was all so new and fascinating. It must have been an hour or so we had spent walking around this Bazaar. I did not like it, so dry and hot. I was saturated with perspiration. Jack asked.

'Anyone like a drink?'

'Yes.' Was the urgent response, He bought glasses of orange juice from a vendor. It refreshed parched throats and revived my flagging body.

'Come on. Let's take a ride to see the sights.'

Meandering towards the entrance and exit. We came across another drinks seller, carrying in front of him a large vessel with a long thin spout, hanging from a wicker basket were small glasses. Passing by him, the strong smell of liquorice hung around him. The instant thought of drinking liquorice made me shudder. About an hour later we were back outside.

'Capitan. Capitan.' Jack exclaimed.

'I don't believe it. The driver is still here waiting for us.'

We got into his landau Jack said.

'Mohammed. Take us a round, see sights.'

We drove off to enjoy the sights of Said. Facing the sea there was a big array of buildings, we passed some ornate looking tower with a balcony close to the top, where someone was wailing out prayers. The Driver took us to a Mosque, their religion's church. He took us to other Bazaars and invited us to go and see them, but we declined his offer. Camels, donkeys the beasts of burden. You name it they were there, hauling heavy loads of produce, piled high on their backs, others pulling carts. The camels were the funniest they being so tall, the shafts of the carts they were pulling were so long they looked ridiculous. The blazing sun was so fierce and extremely hot. We saw large date palms laden with fruit. Under the shade of the palm leaves, stood many Arabs. The driver drove back along the banks of the Canal. We had spent best part of an twos hours riding around, there wasn't much to see, so back to the waterfront, this time Jack paid the driver without any haggling.

'Good Capitan. Good. See you again soon.' Saluted us and rapidly turned to his next customer… 'Mister Mister. Me take you see sights of said.' We were out of his mind.

At the landing point Jack bought tea from a Wallah.

'Sarah, time for a quick tea.'

I can still visualise the tall and very fat Egyptian Tea Wallah, with an enormous head and a small bright red fez perched on top. He looked so silly stood in his white gown that hung around his sandaled feet. When he handed out the glasses of tea, it was so hot to the fingers, that I nearly dropped mine but managed to hold and take a sip. It was extremely sweet and very tasty and funny as it may seem. It cooled me down. Jack purchased a hand of bananas for the children to eat. During our period sight-seeing. Out In the bay there was plenty of activity going on, with the Ferryboats and coal barges, going back and forth to the ships. I noticed other ships had arrived and anchored out at sea. Our ship the 'Nevassa' stood out like a sore thumb, it was then I realised how far out she was anchored.

145

'Jack she is out a long way, has she moved?'

'Don't be silly. She's where we left her this morning. That's not far.'

Having finished, along with other passengers, we boarded a ferryboat. It was not so bad getting back on from the quayside. With shouts and yells from the coolies, we finally left the shores of Egypt. Gently the boat swished through the calm sea and within a short period of time, it drew closer to the ship. Looking at the ship's ladder suspended down the side of the ship and the height we had to climb up. I thought: *My God! The quicker I get back on deck the better I would feel.* The boat engine stopped chugging, the boat started drifting towards the ship. I shrieked.

'Jack we've stopped.'

'No we haven't Sarah. Just wait and see.'

The boat gently swung alongside the small wooden landing stage, where two Seaman stood waiting. As the boat rose and fell with the swell, one minute we were above the landing stage the next well below it. I thought: *I'm never going to make that wooden platform. I'll be in the sea.* I cautiously watched as Jack with no problem at all helped our three onto the landing stage. Then turning to me urged.

'Come on Sarah. Your turn. Up you come.'

He grabbed me under the armpits, the next thing is I'm in the air, as two pair of hands grabbing hold of my arms and pulled me onto the landing stage, Jack said.

'There you are. The children did better than you.'

I followed my three up the stairs, with both my hands tightly clutching the rope rail. Half way up I had to stop for a breather, Jack came up alongside me urging.

'C'mon Sarah. It's not going to fall down. Look at the children they are nearly at the top.' Irritated I retorted.

'I've only stopped to catch my breath Jack. Going up is far more taxing.' Still he urged me upwards...'Just another flight and you can take as much rest as you like.'... I carried on upwards as Mary too urged...'C'mon hurry up Mum.'

Thankfully I reached the top, entered through the doorway back onto the safety of the deck, and received a round of clapping from them. Jack laughed,

'There you see. That wasn't too bad was it?' Not amused! Then it was my turn.

'Right. You three back down to the cabin for a wash and clean up.'

I ushered them in front of me downwards, upon opening the cabin door found, a fine layer of coal dust had settled everywhere while we were on shore.

'You three. Do not touch anything. Get into the toilet. Jack when I've finished washing and dressing them. Take them back up on deck. Then I will dust and wipe this mess up.' It baffled me how this coal dust got in? I was just finishing off when Nora arrived back flushed and perspiring enquired. 'What on earth are you up too Sarah?' ...'Well you may ask. When we got back everything was covered by black dust. It needed to be cleaned up, otherwise the children would make a bigger mess.' Nora suggested....'I agree with you. But if you had waited I would have helped.'....'No. It needed doing urgently, anyway it didn't take long. I've finished now. If you don't mind I'll use the little room to wash myself and prepare for lunch, then I'll leave you in peace.'

Back up on deck I found them playing deck quoits together with Bridget and Elaine who said. 'I should have gone ashore, I was bored silly stuck in my cabin. All you could hear were the shouts and rantings of the coalmen. I gave up and came up and stayed on deck.'

The Tannoy bleeped for lunch. The dining room was practically empty. Quite a few of the passengers were still ashore. We spent the rest of the afternoon, keeping well out of the blazing sun. A warm sea breeze wafted around that did little to cool us down. We could make out the formation of a convoy ahead of our ship. Took Tiffin in the cabin to talk of our trip onshore. The evening meal. What an evening meal that turned out to be. Listening to everybody chattering about his or her trip ashore.

That evening on deck we watched the sun set in the west. Astounded by its suddenness. One minute it was a large red ball of fire, the next it disappeared below the horizon, leaving the sky a mixture of bright yellow, orange, red, purple and fading into deep blue black. But news filtered through about a Sergeant's little boy who had caught a fever on the boat. He had been transferred to a shore hospital by the ship's Doctor. It was then that the ships engines began to throb, the anchor winches up forward started up, slowly the anchors were hauled out of the water. After a little while, the ship slowly began moving forward. In the semi darkness of twilight we counted four ships ahead of us, each one had a large light mounted at the front of the ship its beam shining forward. Slowly we sailed past the twinkling lights of Port Said to enter the Suez Canal. In contrast from the heat of the day a slight breeze caused a chill in the air. It was time to get the children down into the cabin for sleep.

That night lying in my bunk, I felt exhausted, aware of the sleeping sound of the occupants. With my mind going over the events of the day ashore in a foreign land: *The likes of which I did not find attractive. The unintelligible language mixed with the unbearable heat of the day. We had only eaten fruit, sipped tea, to cap it all it had turned cold at night. I was half way to India, what was India really like? Was this what I really wanted or, was I prepared for the start of a big adventure?* I lapsed into the sleep of exhaustion.

Day-break saw us passing the southern port of Suez, into the Red Sea towards Aden. After the Captains inspection, back up on deck we watched the ship sail on down through the Red sea, in between on the port side the Arabia desert and the Egyptian desert on the starboard side, very uninspiring. Nevertheless, the sea was blue with a red haze like a mirage over the water. In the fierce sun Tobies were necessary, yet Mary was at it again, tipping or knocking them off other children's heads, much to their Mother's annoyance. Once again I would have to grab hold of her and sit her down beside me, two minutes later she would be off again teasing someone else, even after Jack had warned her. No flinging them over the side. My God she was a handful.

On the second day sailing through the Red Sea. The ship's orders stated. "The ship had been placed in quarantine. Due to the possibility of fever on Baard." News soon got around that, the little boy having caught the fever on board and taken ashore in Port Said had died. The news of this set my nerves on edge. We were at our Lifeboat station on the Port side of the upper deck when the Soldier in charge of our boat station, stood at ease with his rifle, called for our attention. 'Heh you ladies. Look across the sea towards the land. You can just make out Mount Sinai where Moses took the tablets to the top of the mountain.'

It was something to take your mind off the recent news and a tedious exercise. Through the haze in the far distance I could just see the outline of some mountains that was all nothing really to see. The ship passed Aden then sailed into the Arabian Sea. Our daily routine carried on, but more people caught the fever whatever it was? I prayed like mad that my children wouldn't be struck down by it. As each day slipped by Elaine was getting more excited, she would soon meet her husband for the first time for some years.

The day before were docked in Bombay. The yellow fever flag was hoisted. That same night the Captain had arranged a final dance on the last evening, I think everybody turned up. What a night that was. We spotted the children in their night attire, hiding in their usual place, but decided not to put them back to bed, so they enjoyed watching us all dance the night away. As a finale the band played 'Auld Lang Syne' followed by the National Anthem. It was a memorable but sad time for all of us. We had made some friends, yet nobody knew where in India they were to be posted. We could only wish that we would be near to each other with the chance of meeting again. Jack and I put the children back into bed then went back up on deck to stroll around the deck. We were not alone, others couples were doing the same thing. One thing was

147

for sure I had grown used to the regimented settled way of life on board a ship, I was content what more could I want? I had just enjoyed a lovely dance. Jack had been my escort throughout, however I did dance but not with Jack, he still could not dance. Upon reflection it had been a most relaxing entertaining evening. But it was my Jack arm in arm here beside me, walking me around a ship's deck. In the cool night breeze he guided me over to the ship's rail stopped, leant over kissed me, then whispered.

'Sarah you've settled down to ship life haven't you?'

'Well yes. I suppose I have. But I certainly didn't at first. Mind you, I've enjoyed the company of Elaine and those little Tiffin times we had in the afternoon with Nora.'

'Yes. We heard about those little tea parties. You two started something off. Other cabins started doing the same thing, the boilers nearly ran out of water, but no harm done.' We laughed.

'Jack. Tell me. What is it really going to be like in India?'

'Sarah all will be revealed to-morrow, when we arrive at Bombay. The Gateway to India.' I thought: *He knows something I'm sure but he won't let on.* We stayed a while longer gazing at the stars, then he escorted me back to the cabin bade me goodnight. All was quiet as I prepared myself for my last night on board the Nevassa. I must have lay there for what seemed hours, my mind going back over the past weeks and my thoughts of landing in India. I did not sleep well that night. The rattle of anchors running out woke us. Silence descended as the hum of engines faded away, what was going on? We were all wide-awake. Outside it was still dark, Nora got up and switched on the light. I told my three to try to go back to sleep. It must have been an hour or more before the hum of the ship's engines started again, the muffled sound of chains was heard. We were moving again. Dawn was breaking as we eventually eased our way into Bombay to tie up at the new Ballard's Pier. There was to be no breakfast served that morning the 20th March. News filtered through, why we had stopped earlier? It was to transfer the sick to a hospital boat and taken ashore. Up on deck everyone was lined up against the ships rail, eager to see the shores of India and watch the activity below. Bare footed coolies, wearing remnants of a sheet around them, with ragged scarves tied around their heads were shouting at each other, as they manhandled gangways to the ship side, ready for disembarkation. The most disturbing factor was flies, thousands of them, they were everywhere. It was a sheer waste of time brushing them off they just came back again, they seemed to have made a beeline for the ship.

With gangways in place. An official looking Indian, in a white suit with white Tobie perched on his head, accompanied by two nurses and a European gentleman came on board. I guessed that they were Doctors. At 08:00hrs the Tannoy bleeped. "The order for Disembarkation" began.

A steady flow of troops descends from the aft gangway. Whilst some visitors boarded the ship by the forward gangway. Amongst them many husbands were reunited with their families, creating many happy reunions. Elaine came along with her husband an Infantry Sergeant, to introduce us and say our sad farewells before they disembarked going to a place called Poona?. Jack and Bill were engaged with their duties, so we all stayed on deck and watched the Irish troops disembark, with Sergeants barking out orders. They marched away to the tune of. 'When Irish eyes are smiling.' A large lump rose in my throat. As the strains of the music faded. A strange moment of silence descended upon the families gathered on deck. At 09:30 Jack and Bill returned, Jack said.

'Sarah. We are not disembarking from the ship till mid-afternoon. This morning we will leave the ship and go ashore to the Taj Mahal Hotel for breakfast. Afterwards we will see some of the sights of Bombay before returning to the ship to collect our luggage.'

I thought: *Breakfast in a hotel. Was this to be what India was really all about? I would just have to wait and see?*

148

"THE ADVENTURES OF A SOLDIERS WIFE"

BOOK II.

THE MEMSAHIB'S INDIAN EXPERIENCE.

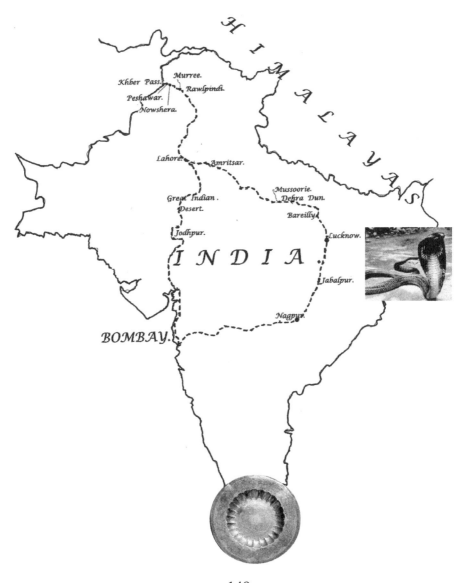

CHAPTER ONE.
INDIA. 1929.

Hesitating at the top of the gangway, brushing the flies away I looked down onto the quayside far below to see a hive of activity. Indians scurrying here and there like ants had me wondering: *Was this to be a new chapter in my life? Somehow Elaine had assured me army families enjoyed the comforts of many facilities during their stay in India. Here I was about to enjoy breakfast in a Hotel and after what Jack had said, it certainly seemed that way nevertheless, I was soon to find out.* With Mary and Kathleen in front of me, to avoid any recurrence of Mary's antics with Jackie's Tobie, I took hold of his hand as we made our way slowly down the gangway. Hesitating again at the foot of the gangway I thought: *Twenty-four days earlier I had left the shores of England now I was about to step onto the shores of India.* Stepping down onto the quayside, walked to where the others were standing, then as a seasoned traveller, much aware of the strange sensation in my legs, knew this would soon pass.

A dirty black hand was thrust at me, glancing sideways saw a filthy beggar sat cross legged moaning something or other, veering away from him I shoved the children out of his way. Flies in their abundance were coming from all directions, settling on our clothing and exposed skin, a swift movement of the hands sent them away but rapidly they returned for another attack, making all of us wave our hands about like some demented persons. Standing in the heat of the morning sun, it was very humid and stifling; beads of perspiration seeped out of the pores of our bodies I could sense that it was a different type of heat than Port Said. Jack shouted at a soldier on duty.

'Trooper. Where are the Tonga Wallahs?' He called back.

'Round behind those sheds just outside the dock gates Sir, you can't miss them, more than likely they won't miss you Sir. '

'Right. C'mon let's make tracks to the Taj Hotel.'

Trying to keep in stride with Jack marching in the direction of the dock gates I asked.

'What's a Tonga Jack?' He replied.

'A Tonga is the Indian version of a horse drawn trap, you hire them out like a taxi.'

As we rounded a warehouse in front of us we saw the dock gates. Jackie let out a whoop, pointed to a large animal. Immediately I asked.

'What in God's name is that Jack?'

'That Sarah is an elephant?' I thought: *So that is an elephant! That is a large beast!*

We stopped to watch this large beast with long curved tusks, its long trunk hanging down to a curled tip. Surrounding its dark eyes were black circles as if it had been crying. Sat astride its neck was a near naked little Indian boy holding a long cane, its big ears flapped slowly over its upper legs as it pulled a laden wagon attached by taut chains to a harness around its neck. Moving ponderously forward its huge feet hardly left the ground. Jackie excitedly asked.

'Dad can we go and see it?'

'No we haven't got time. Anyway you will see many more in India.'

'Please dad.' It fell on deaf ears.

We continued through the gates to a line of Tonga's, (carts with halve moonshaped covers) The Indian drivers were all dressed in loose fitting white trousers, with long loose shirts down to their knees, a white cloth forage cap sat squarely on their heads, they rushed towards us each one holding a whip. I cowered back pulling my three closer to me. They all began shouting.

150

'THIS ONE SAHIB. THIS ONE.' Jack called out.

'Two.'

Beating the others two drivers herded us towards their Tonga's; we clambered up onto one with Nora and Bill in the other. Our driver questioned.

'Kahan sahib?'

'Taj Mahal Hotel. Jahldi'... adding...'That means quickly Sarah.'

'Taaj otal Sahib. Jaiye velli achchha. ' *(Taj Hotel Sir. Go very Good)*

We set off at an alarming pace in this swaying cart, hanging on for grim death as it entered a stream of bikes, bullock carts, coolies either pushing or pulling laden handcarts, whilst others carried huge sacks across their shoulders or on their heads. The area was filthy with a terrible smell. We slowed down into a melee at a crossroads it seemed chaotic. Somehow the driver got through. Then getting his steed into a steady trot veered away from the traffic and went along the waterfront, where funny looking boats were tied up, gently bobbing about with the swell of the water. Up ahead of us was a large ornate archway. Jack informed us.

'That is known as the Gateway to India, and the long building ahead I think is the Taj Hotel...poking the driver Jack pointed...Taj Hotel.'

'Ji hai Taaj Sahib.'

The Taj Mahal Hotel had a beautiful grey stone front. I counted five floors with many windows, white columns supported the balcony above, even the red roof was very ornate, with one large red dome in the centre and four smaller ones at each corner. At its entrance a large automobile was just driving away with its passengers. The Tonga driver crossing the road, pulled up the horse alongside the white steps of its main entrance. Jack jumped down, in my attempt to get down I grabbed hold of the offered white-gloved hand. Startled I looked at an Indian dressed in a white suit, bright red turban adorned in the centre with two white feathers, I looked up to see his face covered by a well-groomed grey beard, through parted lips pearly white teeth indicating a smile, his eyes like black coals looked down at me as he gently assisted me down.

'Memsahib salaam alekum.' I murmured.

'Thank you'...Automatically I wiped the palm of my hand on my dress, as he helped my three down, moving his arm in the direction of the entrance he murmured.

'Sahib. Memsahib. Ji han.'

With an air of authority he strode before us up the few steps. I noticed attached to the back of his turban were two red sashes laying neatly down the back of his long white coat, which finished just above knee level. His white tight fitting trousers clung to his legs with ornate sandals on his feet, moving to one side, permitted us to pass him into and through a large arched entrance leading to a grand reception area. Where a line of servants dressed in smart white Indian style uniforms, wearing red turbans and white gloves, stood each with a silver tray tucked underneath their arm. The gentle ringing of a tiny bell, attracted my attention to a young boy servant in similar attire, calling out the name of the person he was seeking, placed in the middle of a silver tray he was holding was an envelope. Nora who had come up alongside me whispered.

'Isn't this grand Sarah? Look at all the servants?'

One of them leaving the line came towards us. Joining his hands up in front of his face owed. 'Salaam alekum. Memsahib's plees.'

Assembling my three in front of me, we followed him into a vast room. It was the dining hall, at the far end was a long table, where some of the senior Officers were already sat, whilst others

151

stood talking amongst themselves. Waiters dressed in white suits wearing a blue and red coloured turban were busy serving other people at the many individual tables. Jack said.

'Sarah. Bill and I are on the top table for breakfast. There's a table laid up for you.' Jack addressing the waiter said...'The Memsahib's and children will be taking breakfast at the tables.' Bowing deeply to Jack murmured.

'Bahut achchha sahib.'

The waiter guided us through rows of tables to one close by the window with four place settings. I sat down with Mary and Kathleen either side of me, Nora sat opposite with Jackie. The waiter handed the pair of us a menu, clapped his hands. Two waiters arrived, they poured tea into two cups, from a pitcher poured orange into gasses for my three. Nora said.

'Sarah, I require something substantial, but I cannot make head or tale of this, someone told me the best thing to eat in India is fish and chips. At least you know what you're getting.' A unanimous decision, we ordered.

'Fish and chips for all.' I waved my hand in a circle.

'Ji han achchha Memsahibs.' Bowed leaving us.

Surprisingly the room was quite cool and by far the grandest place I had ever eaten in. We would have to watch our P's and Q's here? We made small chat about its decor of high ceiling with ornate gold chandeliers, its polished marble floor. Amongst the quiet use of cutlery the level of noise was a murmur. The two waiters returned, one holding a large silver tray balanced on his right shoulder. With ease brought it down to table level, whilst the other waiter laid plates in front of us, before serving our fish and chip breakfast from the tray. Nora being served first looked closely at hers pointed. I noticed on her plate tiny black things crawling around its rim. I thought: *There's a nice start for you.* As mine and my tribes were placed down I did not see anything amiss with those. The waiters left, Nora whispered.

'Sarah. I think they are ants? What do you think?'... Well they might be but they are so tiny I don't see any on our plates'... Look Sarah, you're better at talking to them. Would you go and speak to them about these ants? I will see to the children. I wondered but flattered by her remark got up, approached a waiter serving at another table who bowed.

'Memsahib.'

'Sorry. the ladies breakfast, it's got little black things in it.' Pointing in Nora's direction.

'Memsahib.' Frowning put out his arm to guide me back to our table. I pointed to Nora's plate, taking note, turned away clapped his hand jabbered something to another waiter, who came over with carrying a big silver tray. Taking each plate placed them on the tray, took them away. The waiter beckoned me to be seated...'Memsahib.' Gently pushed my chair under me. Fresh dishes were quickly served at the table. I'm sure they were larger portions, we were served a far better meal than anyone else, even my tribe ate everything. They entranced by the activity going on around them, when something different caught their eye they would only confide with each other. More tea was provided before Jack arrived back to inform us.

'Sarah we have to stay to receive further briefings, also our train will not leave till late this afternoon. Why don't you all spend this morning seeing the sights of Bombay, when you come back we will return to the ship for lunch? Is that okay?'

Having no option agreed, however all wanted the lavatory, possibly the right time before our next venture. A sightseeing tour of Bombay? We joined Jack in the vestibule and proceeded outside where Jack spoke with the Doorman.

'Tonga for the Memsahib's. See Bombay.

'Ji han achchha. Sahib. Ji han achchha.'

Bowing he approached a line of Tonga's, shouting out instruction to one of the drivers who began to rant and rave as the doorman pointing towards Jack. he started yelling at the Driver.

'SAHIB. ZURURAT BOMBAY.' The driver with hands wide apart shouted.

152

'BAHUT. BAHUT ANNAS.' Beckoned us to his Tonga. We helped the children up then clambered up ourselves, with a jolt left the Taj Hotel at a leisurely trot. Passing by the Gateway to India that was not unlike the Marble Arch in London. This time able to take in the splendours of its honey coloured structure, with three archways, one large central one adjoined by two small ones on either side. On the top at each corner was a small round tower, similar to the Keep at the Tower of London. The Tonga joined into a stream of traffic, Tonga's, bicycles, cart's, animals and hordes of people dressed in all sorts of coloured clothing. I saw beggars with various disabilities grovelling about on the ground pleading with outstretched hands clutching a small bowl. The sight of them disturbed me but we carried on passing a very large ornate fountain with gushing water and a few more large buildings, the Tonga driver turned around pointed to one building it was long with yellow coloured stonework adorned with dirty white window arches and a clock tower, its hands pointing to eleven o'clock, grinning muttered.

'Memsahib's. Steshan.' Nora exclaimed.

'What's he saying?'

'Don't know? Something about steshan.' Suddenly it dawned on me- It reminded me of St. Pancras station in London. 'That's what the driver is telling us. It's a railway station.' Turning around the driver responded.-

'Ji han achchha. Memsahib. Ji han steshan steshan. Qween Wictoria velli goo man.' Nora exclaimed.

'Whatever is he talking about now? He thinks Queen Victoria was a man?'

We laughed at his response as we weaved, stopped, started in amongst the melee of assorted traffic going around a massive round temple, passing a garden full of blossoms and swaying palm trees. The air was laced with the overpowering sweet scent of flowers (I later found out were called Frangipani's), along a roadway close to a sandy beach with overhanging palm trees. It was such a beautiful and exciting place. We came across a tall square ornate clock tower, its hands pointed to nearly twenty past twelve. I noticed a beggar woman spitting out blood, poor wretch! However, my tribe were loving it, waving to everyone. Jackie's excited shouts at seeing a camel then we were back in amongst the bedlam of Bombay traffic. The air filled with strange smells of filth, spices, cooking, burning wood and the flies. The quicker you fanned them away dozens more replaced them. Leaving the melee behind we went along the harbour road, the driver must have taken us in a complete circle around Bombay before we were back to stop at the Taj. We had no money, the Indian footman approaching us bowed.

'Memsahib.' - Pointing towards the Taj entrance with halting words I spoke.

'Find. Army. Officer. Sahib. He. Pays. For. Tonga.'

He clapped his hands - almost immediately an Indian boy came running out, he jabbered away to him. I wondered. *"How on earth was this little boy going to find Jack?"* He scampered off He shouted something at the Tonga driver, who just shrugged his shoulders? Within minutes Jack appeared at the entrance, placing his Tobie on his head strode towards us.

'Hello. Sarah, Nora. Had a good trip? We have finished our briefing were just drinking tea. Would you all like tea out on the veranda?' - He paid the Driver...

'Ji han achchha Sahib. Ji han.' - I answered Jack...'Yes we all would, we are so parched even a drink of water will do.'

Back inside Jack motioned to a waiter said something, gestured with his hand towards our little group, then returned to the gathering of Officers. The waiter ushered us outside onto the veranda, bade us to sit down at an ornate Indian table. Two small boys dressed in white jackets and breeches with green turbans served tea, biscuits, cold drinks, with a deep bow they left. We sat there, amazed at the speed of service, we had not even ordered! As we sipped the tea we talked about the sights of Bombay. The children were quiet, which was a godsend. Jackie sat on the floor beside me watching the activity on the veranda. I had been very dubious of what lay ahead of me but judging on that morning's introduction, I had been pleasantly surprised. However, still had reservation on what lay ahead, but willing to trust Jack's judgement? Bill and Jack arrived back. It was time to get back for lunch collect our luggage before disembarking. As we walked out of the Taj I turned to Jack and said.

'You know Jack whilst we were on the Tonga ride. I saw a beggar women spitting blood. She must be awfully ill poor soul.'

'Oh don't take any notice of that Sarah, they are not diseased they chew a red nut called beetal which dyes their mouth bright red, it cleans their teeth.'

So ended the first lesson about India. We hired two Tonga's and left the grandeur of the Taj. Passing by the Gateway to India Jack informed me.

'Sarah we built that gateway in 1911 when King George the fifth and Queen Mary visited India. Did you know, after the Suez Canal was opened. It was here in Bombay along with other places in India, the English built all the large civil buildings laid the railway tracks to connect the various places using trains instead of the old fashioned cart transport. With the strong British influence that we brought to India it become known as Raj Country.'

'I can see that, as we passed one station, which looked like Saint Pancras in London. The Tonga driver said it was a station and he said that Queen Victoria was a very good man. That had us roaring with laughter. Now Jack. Will you please tell me where are we going in India?'

'I'll tell you over lunch Sarah.' He wasn't giving anything away I dreaded to think where?

Finally the Tonga drew up at the foot of the gangway. We got down, helped our three down to begin our last upward climb to the deck. Jack paid the driver, we went straight down to the dining area for sit down for our last meal. Seeing that many families had already left the boat leaving just a few already seated to be served a light lunch, after our large breakfast, it was just sufficient to satisfy our needs. Only then Jack informed me of our posting.

'Sarah. During our briefing the Brigadier informed us that after we leave the ship we were to be entrained to a place called Nowshera up in the North West Frontier Province of India'...I thought: *My God. Where in heavens name is the Northwest?....* He continued...'According to him it will take four days to get there'....carefully he watched for my reaction. My willingness, suddenly went out of the window.

'God almighty Jack. You can't be serious? Four days in a train? London to Ireland is only an overnight trip. What are we going to do in the train?' - I didn't know what to say anymore but he continued...'We are to be provided with rations for the train journey.'....'What about Nora?'....'Yes she and Bill will be on the train, going to their posting.'

I sat there twisting my wedding ring, mulling over what he had just said. *Four day's in a train. That's almost a week to God knows where. I couldn't believe it. I started off with a train ride then it seemed I was going to end it with another train ride. This was not what I had expected. I* sat there with nothing to say. I didn't have the stomach to finish off my meal. My tribe having eaten well were eager to go and play on deck, but this was not the time for gallivanting around. Leaving the dining room, we collected our travelling rations in paper bags. I had a sudden desire to see the big map.

'Jack. Can you show me on the big map just where, we are supposed to be going? '

'Yes. Okay. But I don't think it will show you much, only the area.'

At the map we met another sergeant with his wife studying the map, obviously Jack knew him called out to the sergeant.

'Looking to see where we're off to then Harmon?'

'Yes I've just found it. But not much detail' - I nodding to his wife, turned my attention to where the sergeant was pointing – 'It's about there. We're off now see you later.'

Jack pointing at the map said. 'Sarah. Look here is Bombay.' With my three stood gawking at the map as I was, sharply retorted.

'I know that, where's this other place? I'm more interested in that.' Jack studying the map traced his finger upwards, impatiently I demanded.

'Well. Where is it?'

'Hold on Sarah, the writing is so tiny. I've found Rawalpindi, there's Peshawar. Ah. There we are Nowshera. It's in between the two. Look there.' His finger indicated a spot at the top of the map. to see it properly I needed a chair. Looking at the distance on the map, it did not appear that far, from Bombay. I asked.

'If it takes four days on a train, how many miles is it from Bombay?' Bending down spreading out his fingers he took a measurement from the scale of miles. Mary asked.

'What are you doing Dad?'

'Right. You see that little scale there, it tells you how many miles to the inch, what I am doing is making a guess at the distance from Bombay to Nowshera where we are going to.'

Now they all wanted to do it. As Jack placed his thumb on Bombay with his extended fingers gradually marked out the distance to this place Nowshera, then exclaimed.

'About twelve hundred miles.' I sharply retorted.

'God. Twelve hundred miles? No wonder it's going to take four days. '

Whatever, I was not pleased with the thought of four days on a train, did nothing to raise my spirits as we made our way back to the cabin, where Jack left us to collect his own equipment. As he left Nora came in holding her paper bag of travelling ration, indigently exclaimed.

'Did you hear the latest Sarah? A four-day train trip to some place called Rawalpindi.'

'Where? It's not what Jack told me. He did mention another name, where's that place then?' Cautiously Nora added.

'Rawalpindi. Well wherever it maybe? It's a long way from Bombay.' Sitting on the bunk dejectedly I replied

'Jack said it is about twelve hundred miles away.'

The cabin lapsed into silence. I think the pair of us were depressed at the thought of a long train journey. Outside the children were playing in the corridor so they were out of the way. Jack returned to the cabin with a few coolies to take our baggage ashore. Oblivious to my concern, he cheerfully asked.

'All set then Sarah?' Without much enthusiasm I responded.

'Ready as I'll ever be.' Jack beckoned the coolie's in.

'Jahldi Jahldi.' - Effortless they lifted the suitcases up onto their heads, picked up other cases quickly departed. I took one last look around the cabin to see if we had forgotten anything, a feeling of nostalgia overcame me, for what it was, I left its comfort for the last time. Nora said.

'I'll see you on the train Sarah.'

For the last time of our long voyage I walked along the deck towards the gangway with my three skipping ahead. Very aware of the oppressive heat, which had replaced the cooling breeze, caused by the forward motion of the ship, not to forget the constant invasion of the blasted flies. Lined up on the quayside below was a long line of Tonga's waiting to transport the families to the station. Just before 14:00 hrs we all disembarked to catch a train to the Northwest Frontier of India. In the tense atmosphere I did not know what to say, perspiring with the heat and constantly swotting flies in their droves, made me feel more miserable. After a short frustrating journey in the Tonga with hardly a word spoken, we arrived at the same station we had passed in the morning, Jack said.

'Sarah this is it. Victoria Terminus.'

155

We had not even got down off the Tonga when several Coolies besieged us, as we got down they grabbed hold of our cases swinging them up onto their heads stood waiting, then our little party set off marching right through the station out into the blazing sun towards the conveyance I was going to be on for the next four days. A train waiting in a siding. It did not look too inviting The brown painted coaches were dusty and dirty, there were no carriage doors like the coaches back home, instead   at each end steps with a handrail led up the door to the carriage. Metal bars protected the windows that had no glass, instead white painted wooden slats. On the roof of each coach sat on his haunches was an Indian surrounded by several large bowls, I wondered what the bowls were for? Each one had a cloth draped over their heads, you could just about pick out the whites of eyes against the dark shadows of faces; lazily they watched the activity going on below. At the far end its large engine intermittently puffed out plumes of black smoke.

The scene alongside the train was that of intense activity. Soldiers were loading their equipment, into the carriages at the front end, whilst down at the rear stood in the meagre shade of the train, agitated mothers with their children waited to be advised where to go we joined the tail end to stand and wait along with the Coolies with our luggage balanced on their heads passively waiting for instructions. Beggars with their hands outstretched moved slowly up and down the families, muttering something or other, hopeful to attract some coins but nobody cared. Then Jack led us to the second rear carriage, I got my three up into the carriage then followed behind. Inside its interior heat hit me, it was like an oven, very quickly took note of what comforts lay inside. Four seating compartments, two on each side separated by a wooden partition then another four, a small aisle led to the exit door at each end. Some of the compartments were already occupied by families, busy sorting out their luggage. Jack stopped at the far end called out. 'This one here Sarah.'

Pushing Jackie in front, we came to our allotted compartment. On my right two women were already sat down, I nodded to them, ushered my tribe into the left compartment.

'C'mon you three. Go and sit down just look out of the windows. While we sort out the luggage. - Jack the luggage?'

'Right Sarah. Come with me and tell me which cases you want for the journey.'

Back I went to the exit, to find the Coolies still stood with our luggage on their heads. where we had left them. Jack jumping down requested.

'Point out which ones?' I pointed to two cases for the compartment.

'Jahldi. Jahldi in carriage.'

One climbed the steps, jabbering away to the others, took two cases from them, I let him pass by, Jack pointed to the remaining cases said...'Back there last carriage Jahldi. The others scampered away with the rest of our luggage. I turned my attention back to the coolie stood behind me with two cases, ushered him into the carriage where he put the cases down by our seats. I followed him out to find the other coolies had returned to receive their dues from Jack. Seeing money was being handed out, beggars with outstretched hands approached Jack screaming. 'Baksheesh. Baksheesh.'

Jack threw a handful of coins over their heads, which I did not think was helpful, as they scampered after the coins, hitting, pushing, shoving, grovelling in the dust just to get a coin. On the outskirts of the mob I noticed a skinny woman in a dirty so called white Sari. It was grey with grime, sat astride her hip she held an equally filthy naked baby; many flies were crawling about its eyes. It was pitiful to watch as she desperately tried to grab some coins from amongst the other fighting beggars. Taking pity I told Jack.

'Jack give her a sixpence.'

'Sarah, forget pounds shillings and pence, its anna's and rupees from now on Okay. Look this is a quarter of an Anna the equivalent to a farthing. If you give them one of these, they will

156

think they are rich.' He handing it to the woman, she bowed and almost scraped the earth in front of us. I turned away, then Nora came walking towards us she called out.

'Sarah. I've got a seat two coaches in front, it's only for women without children, but I will see you on the train.'

That was not good news to me; I climbed down to talk for with her for a while until she departed, however climbing back up found our coach was then full of families and luggage. We put our luggage away under the seats. Jack returned up to the front saying we had some time before the train departed, but he would be back. I thought: *Right no point in sitting inside.* I got my tribe off the train to await his return. The activity of people had subsided, some stood in small groups chatting and laughing, but still on the prowl were the beggars, amongst them was a blind one. Skinny as a rake, burnt black by the sun, a small cloth was wrapped around his waist his open eyes were just white, not a pleasant sight. He leant on a long stave, a young boy clad in the same fashion, grasped the blind man's hand, in his other outstretched hand he held a bowl. I shuddered, Mary said.

'Mum. Look at that man.' My tribe stood there gawking at this poor unfortunate wretch. Turning them away said.

'Don't be bothered by those things.' Hopefully wishing Jack would hurry up, when he did full of the joys of spring prompted.

'Alright Sarah. Ready for the train journey?'

Reluctant to talk about anything ignored his question. Further up the track a few soldiers stood outside the coaches about to get on. We got back up into the carriage and our compartment, the two women on the opposite side had already settled in, one had two little boys, the other a baby in her arms, they acknowledged my greeting. The wooden slatted seats were just wide enough for two people to sit down; to avoid any fights I sat Jackie next to the window, with Kathleen and Mary sitting opposite, Jack and I sat down next to Jackie. There was absolutely no air circulating in the carriage, even with the wooden slats of the window fully open it was hot and stifling. Whoever had opened them need not have bothered as my cotton dress was soaking wet and clung to my body, I asked Jack.

'What about sleeping are the beds in the next carriage?'

'No. The beds are here, above these seats you lower the two top ones down and secure them, these seats are the other beds, you lay on the cushions behind you, Mary can sleep on this one and Jackie and Kathleen on the top ones. In the morning just put the top bunks back in place. Simple.'

'What about lavatories and washing?'

'At each end of the carriage you can use either and there is water for washing. Look I have to report back up front, I will come back later.'

Leaving the carriage I saw him through the window slats striding past. His remark about washing did not help there certainly was not going to be any privacy on this journey, I gave up as beads of sweat ran down my cheeks, brushing my forearm against my brow took out a hankie from the sleeve of my dress and wiped my face. The woman beside me fanning herself with her Tobie said.

'My God it's so hot. I wish we were back on the Nevassa, at least you had a cool breeze all day long.'

I smiled at her, a much tanned young auburn haired woman about my age, her two little boys sat motionless beside her. The other woman, her black hair swept up and pinned on top of her head was a bit on the plump size, she cradled her baby, constantly fanning it with her Tobie, as sweat dribbled down her glowing red cheeks, I did not think the fanning was doing anything. Casually I asked.

'Where have you been posted?'

157

'Rawalpindi. Our husbands are Sergeants in the Royal Field Artillery. They are up with the rest of them.' I assumed they were from another Battery? She enquired.

'Where are you headed for?'

'Some place called Nowshera.' - The other woman interrupted.

'Oh. Nowshera. That's farther on than us.' A shriek from Jackie frightened the life out of us. 'Mum look.'

The three of them were peering through the slats of the window, at a pack of monkeys scampering on all fours across the railway lines towards the train. Grey in colour with little black faces and long tails, they leapt up onto the train climbed onto the roof, we heard the patter of feet as they padded about. A shout from above had them screeching, as they swung down passed us to the ground, from above we heard another torrent of language possibly from the Indian? Maybe that was his job? But the arrival of the monkeys excited not only my tribe, but all. This broke up the tension in the carriage. Jackie shrieked as a monkey grabbed hold of the slats of the window, a hairy arm was thrust through the slats, a black furry hand grabbed hold of Mary's arm. Laughing she shouted.

'GET OUT.' Two tiny black faces their big round eyes peered through the slats, they slid their hairy arms in between the slats, almost human like their black hands tried to grab hold. Mary slapped one shouting. 'GET OUT.'

With loud screeches, their arms were quickly withdrawn, they were everywhere. Someone at the doorway threw out some fruit. Immediately it was pounced upon by a large grey bearded monkey resting on three legs he gorged the fruit in his hand, he looked menacingly at the rest as they sat around waiting for some small morsel. None was given, he gorged the lot. Then my tribe decided they wanted the lavatory, so I got up with them to see where it was. I let them go in and waited until they had finished, I heard them giggling then Mary shouted. 'GET OUT.' I knocked on the door.

'Mary. What's going on in there?'... A shriek then peals of laughter... I demanded.

'Mary what's going on in there? Open this door now.'

'Can't mum the Monkeys will get you.'

Another fit of giggling. I froze, monkeys, they had monkeys in there. Oh my God banging on the door I shouted.

'MARY. OPEN THIS DOOR. MARY. NOW.' The door was opened a little way. Mary's head cautiously poked around the side.

'It's all right Mum they are outside.'

'Come out the three of you. Now.' Pushing open the door wide looked in. My first sight was little black hands waving about through the slats of the window I shouted.

'YOU THREE GET OUT NOW.' They ran past me back to the compartment, pulling the door shut ran back myself. The three of them were sat on the seat giggling. I shouted at them.

'DON'T YOU DARE GO NEAR THOSE MONKEYS AGAIN? DO YOU HEAR WHAT I AM SAYING?'

There was no response except giggling amongst themselves. I was sweating freely not with the heat but fear. I flopped down in a heap thinkng: *Oh my God. What am I to do? We haven't even started yet. They do not have an ounce of fear between them. What happens if one of those big elephants charges them?* The mere thought of a huge elephant charging around set me on to them again.

'You three promise me you won't go near any wild animals again.'

Mary grinned, Kathleen put her hand up against her mouth, Jackie just dropped his head downwards. That was the real response I got. The dark haired woman spoke out.

'You have a handful there.'

158

'I don't know what to say? Mary is their leader. What she says they follow her. She has got me in a state of nerves now and we haven't even left the station.' The other woman added her pennies worth.

'They look like three grinning monkeys themselves'.

I looked across at the three of them all-smiling very sweetly I thought: *Little do you know what my tribe can get up to?* Jackie let out another shriek. As another hairy arm came through the slats. Quick as a flash Mary gave it a whack with her Tobie shouted.

'GET OUT AND STAY OUT YOU LITTLE PEST.'

With a screech it dropped to the ground, it sat there chattering before it moved away to join the others, her action seemed to stop the rest of them. Much relieved with no further attacks I decided to inspect the bunk above to see how it worked. As I stood on the seat the auburn haired woman said.

'Hold on I'll help you. I want to know how it works too.'

She being much taller, reached up and undid a strap in the centre of the bunk, it came down easily, two straps at each end held it in place, the two big bolsters fitted on top as the mattress. We got the other one down, I thanked her for her help. She asked.

'Do you want to put them back?'

'No. When the train moves. I'll get them up there hopefully to sleep.'

I had not done much but in the sweltering heat of the compartment was perspiring freely, it was strangely quiet. I glanced around to see everyone frantically fanning themselves with Tobies trying to keep cool. I sat down to see the beggars outside sat or lay in the dust where they were, they too had given up begging. The incessant chattering of the monkeys continued as they sat in a cluster or squabbled, then one would run off and climb onto the carriage roof. In the still silence you could hear it padding about above, until with a short shriek of the train's whistle followed by a long piercing shriek. The train jerked into motion, sending the monkeys running on all fours scattering across the railway tracks screeching abuse.

.As the train gathered speed the air entering through the slats was warm, just about sufficient to stir the existing stifling heat. I thought: *This journey is not going to be enjoyable.* With their adventure with the monkeys over, I got my three settled into the bunks, they just content to lay there to watch the passing scenes. On the outskirts of Bombay we passed by what you could only refer to as a village of hovels, There were no streets just walkways of flattened mud with a some sort of running drain in-between the hovels. It was crowded with dirty Indians, I noticed the men wore only a cloth around their middle, the women in some dress that covered their heads and the children, nothing. What a totally different scene to what we had seen in Bombay. Slowly the train went over a long bridge crossing a very wide river, then gathering speed travelled along the seashore overlooking the Arabian Sea, where further out at sea there were plenty of ships and boats. With envy I sat there thinking: *At the comfort of the Nevassa we had left earlier compared to the confinement in a train.* As the rays of the sun quickly began to fade, the sky coloured to a pink hue then deep red, in what appeared to be minute's, darkness descended. With nothing to see the children were soon rocked to sleep by the motion of the train, sitting there dabbing my forehead with my hankie, my eyelids began to droop, oblivion overcame me.

A slight disturbance had me awake, I was sat half-twisted as I had slumped over, I heard whispering from the opposite compartment, but my senses were not with me. Laying down on the seat I dozed off until disturbed by a few bumps on the floor, a short period of quietness, then the sound of a man's heavy snoring below me. Fearfully I put my hand down to feel cloth, quickly withdrew it, I was wide-awake, I wondered. *Whoever is it? The whispering before must have been one of the women. Listening intently I heard two different snoring sounds.* A glow of light distracted my thoughts, rising into a sitting position. I glanced up and down the aisle. Hanging from the roof three oil lamps provided some meagre lighting for the coach. Gradually I got accustomed to the shallow light and looked down to see the forms of two soldiers sprawled fast asleep on the floor. I thought: *Don't mention a word.* I was very pleased to know in case of trouble there were two men about. I returned to a restless sleep. Next morning they had gone. The next night they returned and every night thereafter.

In the morning I went to the little lavatory, when I got in there, the lavatory was a hole through which you could see the sleepers below, perched in the corner was a tiny hand basin and beneath it on the floor a pail of water for washing. To wash oneself in such a tiny space was going to be a real chore. I decided to loosen my clothing and wash as best I could. Then quickly fetched the children, got them washed, more of a cats lick, anyway there was not that much water available. With the four of us jammed in this tiny lavatory, I did the best I could. As for me I never took my clothes off throughout the journey. I wore the same clothes I had left the Nevassa in, and by the time we finally arrived I was to feel very dirty and unclean.

When we went back into the carriage, lying slumped at an awkward angle on the bottom bunk was the dark haired woman, laid behind her was her baby waving its arms about. The other woman having just woken up was stretching. On the top bunk her two little boys, lying on their bellies were awake staring at us? I motioned to my tribe to be quiet not disturb them. The rays of the rising sun shone through the slats casting shafts of light on the floor. In the next compartment a couple of women were moving about, further down a baby was crying. Through the slats of the window only the open countryside could be seen, Jack's entry into the carriage woke up the other women. Above the noise of the rumbling wheels Jack quietly asked.

'How did you all sleep?'…I nodded, I wasn't going to let on about the other two soldiers, he continued '… There is a chai wallah (Tea seller) on the roof of the carriage. He will be along soon. So you can have some tea with your rations. I've bought some small raffia fans, so instead of using the Tobies you can fan yourselves and keep cool.' I enquired.

'On top of the roof. What do you mean?'….Then remembered the Indian adding... 'Oh that one. I thought he sat up there to shoo the monkeys away. You missed all the commotion we had with them. These three were having a great time. I've now got them to promise me not to go near any wild animals in future.' Jack looking at their grinning faces instructed.

'Listen to what your mother has to say and behave yourselves. Monkeys you say. No we didn't miss them, they were all over the train on the rampage for tit- bits, they are so funny and so agile with it. You'll see a lot more of them in future'….So much for his concern as he continued... 'That chai wallah attends to the water in the lavatory and the lamps at night-time. He like the other entire wallah's on each coach, brew the tea up on the top of the carriage, they walk along the top to the front of the train to get hot water and you don't have to pay.' Jack noticed the two women were preparing to get up, having ensured we were all okay added…. 'Sarah. I'll come back later.' I accepted his excuse without any comment.

For breakfast I shared out some of our rations before the chai wallah arrived. He beaming showing a set of pearly white teeth, his black hair was greased and parted on one side, his long white shirt covered a cloth type skirt. In one hand he carried a sack with a yoke across his shoulder, suspended from either end were two large pots, one was surrounded by glasses. He placed the sack on the floor and by the sound it made must have been more glasses. As he sat down on his haunches, a strong waft of scent emitted from his person, he prompted.

'Memsahib's. Chai, velli goo chai.' - He motioned to my tribe who had gathered around to watch the proceedings. - 'Memsahib, missy baba's nimbu ras. Leemon?' I nodded.

'Lemon. Yes please three.' I put three fingers up.

'Achchha. Memsahib. Achchha. Velli velli goo, velli hot, drinky penty chaiji han?' Speaking almost in brocken English, turned his head towards the two women, they in awe, nodded. Arranging eight glasses in front of him poured the tea, served me and then the other women.

'Achchha. Memsahib. Achchha. Chai velli goo. Dena baba's Leemon ras. Ji han.'

160

He nodded at Mary who nodded back, as he began pouring out this whitish liquid into glasses, gave one to each of my gawking tribe and the two little boys, saying.

'Velli goo leemon '…Indicating sipping at the glass to Mary, she took a dubious sip, by her expression he could tell an instant success….'Aah baba's. Velli goo velli goo'- Clapping his hands in front of his face bowed…'Achchha. Memsahib. Soo back.'

The tea was very welcome thinking: *It tasted better than the tea at the Taj.* Having consumed some of our rations, I glanced through the slats of the window to see green shrubbery, tall trees, not very inspiring. The temperature in the compartment was gradually increasing, above the noisy clanking and rumble of the train wheels, it was difficult to hold any conversation. For the children there was nothing to do except watch out of the window or play in the narrow aisle between the compartments. Watching the countryside pass by, most of which appeared to be some agricultural farming land. I saw an Indian farmer in a waterlogged field wading through muddy water, wearing a cloth around his waist and a white cloth wrapped around his head, he was black from the sun, in front of him he guided a funny looking plough with a long pole at the other end a yoke was rested across the necks of two scrawny looking cows with strange humps on their backs, from their bellies up they were caked in dried mud, as very slowly they dragged this plough through the water. At that time I was unaware it was a rice paddy field. On the edge of the water the swaying fronds of the palm trees cast shadows on the parched vegetation below, I recognised fields of flax, which reminded me of my days in the flax field back home. In an effort to keep cool we fanned ourselves frantically with the raffia fans, which in turn made you feel exhausted. At midday the arrival of the Chai Wallah broke up the monotony, bringing some form of a meal, fruit, flat bread and sweet cakes, which made you drowsy in the afternoon. From time to time Jack would come and see how we were getting on. The train sped past one or two small stations then a big town, it did not stop to pick up other passengers soon it was late in the afternoon the sky was turned to blood red from the setting sun, it was nearing dusk when we made our first stop at a place called Ahmadabad. However that was only to take on coal and water. Jack arriving outside at the compartment window shouted up to me.

'SARAH WE WILL BE HERE FOR AN HOUR, DO YOU WANT TO GET OUT AND STRETCH YOUR LEGS AND HAVE SOME TEA?'

'Not really, but I would like some tea.'

'Okay. I'll get some do you want something to eat.'

'Yes lease see if you can get some fruit.'

Some passengers taking the opportunity to stretch their legs, were getting off the train to stroll about in the setting sun its light just sufficient enough to cast their shadows into long shapes. I noticed our Chai Wallah was talking with another Chai Wallah who was sat next to a large single wheel barrow laden with fruit and other morsels. A few Indians were either sat on their haunches smoking or lying in the dust presumably asleep. Lights from oil lamps cast a glimmer of light from the station building. Jack returned with the tea, lemon drink, then went to collect some other food before getting on and sitting with us. He handed out bananas to or three, handed me some more rations to eat later. Our Chai Wallah had returned and was busy lighting the oil lamps in the coach. The long whistle of the train had the remaining passengers scurrying to get aboard. Then with three long blasts it jerked back into motion. Jack left us, venturing to cross from one carriage to another. Better him than me. I pulled down the bunks and got my tribe settled to sleep. Later the Chai Wallah returned sat on his haunches to pour out a glass of tea, passing it to me with a wide grin he murmured.

'Memsahib. Chai velli goo tu slep.'

Silently he moved onwards to serve whoever wanted chai. It was pleasant just sitting there sipping a nightcap of chai, finishing it off placed the glass on the floor in the aisle. After the full day of many bodies lounging about perspiring freely, the air I was breathing was rather humid and stank. As my lids slowly drooped I too was ready for sleep. I woke up with a start laid curled up on my bunk. That whispering again the soldiers were back, I thought: *Must be their husbands?* I curled up under the window gradually sleep came. I woke up; it was still dark but in the warm glow of the oil lamp noticed their husbands had gone, but the monotonous drumming of the trains wheels did not send me back to sleep. I sat up shivering guessed the time was about five 'o'clock, decided to say a few prayers. Not having my rosary beads handy I counted each Hail Mary on my fingers. The crying of the baby opposite stopped me. The dark haired woman woke up to feed the baby looking across at me she whispered.

'I'm sorry did my baby wake you up?' Moving across the seat towards the aisle, whispered.

'No it's all right I was awake. I must say your baby is very good, it's very quiet and placid'...we continued to whisper... 'It must be the heat, she has done nothing but sleep, but she has a fine pair of lungs in her I can tell you that for nothing. Would you be kind enough to look after her while I go to the lavatory?'

'Yes of course I will. I was about to start my morning ablutions myself but give her to me.'

'Oh. I'm sorry. If you don't mind, when I've finished, before you go in, can I use it to wash and change her?'

'Okay I can wait.'

I sat there cuddling this little baby, it fell asleep, she soon returned and carefully took her baby from me whispered.

'You must have a way with babies?' I thought: *Little did she know? I had been looking after babies practically all my life.* She whispered her "thanks" then I went to the lavatory to carry on with my own ablutions. By the time I had done mine with my tribe awake and washed, it was almost light outside. One thing for certain they did sleep. As the dark haired woman had mentioned. 'It was the heat.' The rays of the early morning sun lit up the inside of the coach, the activity of other people too-ing and fro-ing, provided some form of interest to my tribe and kept them quiet, until everyone had settled down for another day of sweltering in the unpleasant sweaty atmosphere. I looked out through the slats to see not green vegetation but a flat arid rocky, sandy countryside for miles. Through the slats on the other side I saw a range of mountains in the far distance; the scenic view would not be very interesting that was for sure.

The arrival of the Chai Wallah was the start of the day's attractions. When Jack entered he stood up and saluted, it was comical to see this Chai Wallah stood at attention like a ramrod in a long white shirt, white skirt and bare feet with one arm at the salute. The other straight beside him, his pots of tea and lemon drinks arranged in order around his feet. It had me stifling a laugh behind my hand. Jack nodding smiled and sat down next to me. The Char Wallah resuming his position began pouring. I laughed

'What was that all about Jack?'

'Oh they all do that. If they see a Sam Browne you're an officer. I don't take any notice but I must say all the Chai Wallahs are experts in making tea they don't tire of travelling on these trains maybe its their home?'

Jack stayed for some time before he returned up front. As he said even on the train he was still on duty. The two little boys along with my tribe and some other children were all-playing running up and down, where they got the energy from God knows? If I told them to sit down and be quiet once, I must have said it a dozen times. Dinnertime came and went. The scenery changed to scrub land with sandy patches somehow the heat of the breeze from the trains motion appeared to be getting hotter increasing the heat in the coach into that of an oven. Then Desert, (an area I later found out as the Great Indian Desert). It was flat for mile after mile, disappearing into a shimmering haze in the distance where the blue sky mingled with the sun burnt land. We passed a line of camels tied one behind the other, their handler sat astride the lead camel bedecked with bangles and tassels. Other handlers sat astride the ones behind, all laden with bags and boxes. So that was what they called a Camel train? The sight temporarily halted the children's play and they began counting out aloud.

'One Two-Three. Thirty. That's a lot of camels.' Jackie shouted.

Travelling across this desert was extremely tedious and baking hot. Without any physical signs, the temperature suddenly dropped, howling winds drowned out any noises of the train, whipping the sand up, rapidly it swept in through the window slats, we struggled to shut them, even that didn't keep any sand out. Through cracks and gaps it blew in, it was everywhere. We were covered in sand, it was horrible, it stuck to the sweat of our exposed flesh. Just as quickly as it had started the storm stopped. Choking and coughing in the dust-laden air we opened the slats of the windows, shafts of sunlight showed minute particles of dust floating about in the air. As best as we could, we spent the rest of the day with our hands, cleaning out sand and dust from the compartment. On a distant hill a huge fort came into view, as the train got closer the size of this fort was huge, looking like a giant sandcastle, its smooth walls the colour of the desert, square turrets and arches dotted its top, everything appeared to be square. Signs of civilisation came into view as the train entered a town, coming to a halt at what they called a station. Jack entered the coach accompanied by two sergeants, both taller and older than Jack; the two little boys greeted them. As they sat down beside the women. It was my first sight in daylight of the two men who slept on the floor. Jack enquired how we had been in the sandstorm.

'Not very pleasant but we managed.'

'Sarah this place is called Jodhpur. We've stopped just to change engines.' He purchased tea from the Chai Wallah and lemon for the children.

Jack was right about the short stop, three short shrieking blasts of a whistle and we were off once again, travelling into the countryside that I thought: *Was just barren desert.* Jack stayed with us for quite a while, when the Chai Wallah entered the carriage to light the lamps. Jack and the two sergeants left to return up to the front. That was when daylight rapidly turned to dusk then blackness, bringing with it the coldness of the night. The only clothes we had were those we wore, no overcoats or woolly jumpers at time ones shivered with the cold. The Chai Wallah, having completed his chore returned to serve chai, that was at least warming for me, then the two sergeants returned to sleep on the floor, so I curled up in the corner of the seat to spend yet another restless night, listening to the snoring and other sounds of a sleeping carriage with the endless noise of the train wheels, lulled me into a form of sleep. I was so very pleased when the rising sun providing some warmth, the Chai Wallah came around early to serve warming chai.

Outside we were back into green plains, rich with vegetation and rivers meandering through the lush undergrowth. Occasionally we saw some beast lazing up to their necks in water, their large curved horns almost horizontal with the water swirling about their necks. We saw the occasional herd of elephants, which brought whoops of joy from the children. Late in the afternoon we arrived at a place called Lahore for another brief stop with a welcome glass of chai. Jack sat with us and watched what was going on in the station siding.

There were many women in dirty Sari's doing manual work with wicker baskets filled with coal, balanced on their heads, they walked to and from a huge heap of coal, to an engine where they would pass the basket up to another woman, she would empty it into the tender then hand it back. It fascinated me the effortless way they did the job. Jack drew my attention to another stationary locomotive, where more women were cleaning out the old ash remains from the fire bottom. They were filthy dirty, their bare skins grey from the ash stuck to them through sweat, but I did notice the red gash of their mouths, some constantly spitting out this red stuff. Whilst all this activity was going on the Indian men sat on their haunches or, lay in the shade, a few cows wandered around or just lay in the dusty sidings. Watching all this activity helped to pass the time. I asked Jack.

'Why do the women do all the work?' Grinning said.

163

'Sarah we are in India now, this is the way they live. During your time out here, you will see stranger goings on than this.'

Little did I know how true that was? A shriek from the engines whistle shattered the everyday sounds with a jerky startwe were off heading for a place called Rawalpindi. Throughout the night it remained cold, I woke up the following morning cold and damp with perspiration, the two sergeant's had left. I did my ablutions, came back, and sat down to finish my decade of the rosary. I woke up my tribe for ablutions, then back in the compartment they sat yawning and shivering against the cool breeze entering through the slats, Jackie fell asleep again. The other two women sorting out their things were getting ready to get off. I bade them good morning. The Chai Wallah came in served chai, sat sipping it, I watched the rugged countryside rushing past. In the far distance the large range of mountains seemed to go for miles. The rays from the early morning sun lit up many peaks that glistened white with snow against the blue background of the sky, as the train got closer they became larger until they filled the horizon. The Officer of the day, a Major accompanied by a Sergeant entered the coach. He addressed the families in each compartment.

'Ladies could I have your attention please. For all those families detraining at Rawalpindi, Please be ready with all your luggage. Now how have you all enjoyed the train journey?' I said.

'Well apart from the sand storm reasonably well.' He nodded and said.

'Yes that storm was unexpected. But they do happen very quickly like that . That desert was the Great Indian Desert. I can assure you that nothing like that happens in the North West Province. We are now crossing the plains at the foot of the Himalayan hills, those are the range of mountains you can see to your right.'

Mary listening to what was going on chirped in on the conversation.

'Mum couldn't take her clothes off, the whole of the time because of the two sergeants who slept on the floor.' The Major surprised exclaimed.

'Is that right?' I butted in.

'Well. Yes but.' He turning to his Sergeant ordered.

'Go and fetch them at the double. I'll come back when I've seen the other families in the carriage.' He moved away from us. I looked across at the two women and shrugged my shoulders. I turned on Mary and told her off.

'Mary you had no right to mention anything like that.'…She just glowered at me. I turned to the other two women saying… 'I'm sorry their presence did not bother me.'

Very soon the two Sergeants arrived in the carriage and stood waiting. The major returning, gave them both a blasting and put them on a charge, however I intervened.

'Major. It's been all right, there's no need to charge them. I took it more as a security action than anything else, there was no harm done.'

'Well. If that is the case. I'll say no more about it. You two sergeants return up the front of the train.' They were dismissed, the Officer and sergeant followed behind. The two wives thanked me for speaking up in defence of their husbands.

Cool breezes replaced those of ones we experienced in the heat of the desert, making the interior much cooler, I sat there wishing that we were on our final leg to our destination. Then as the sun disappeared it became very overcast. Without warning down came the rain, descending from the sky like stair rods, the noise on the top of the coach sounded like sticks beating down, within three minutes the deluge stopped. Out came the sun shining on the leaves of the trees washed clean of any dust still dripping with rain drops. The sudden deluge had made the air very fresh and so much cooler, which was a welcome blessing. During the rest of the journey the train laboured up slopes and hillocks, until about nine thirty in the morning in the shadows of the Himalayas, we arrived at Rawalpindi. Jack had already said it would be a long stop. When it finally ground to a halt, beggars of all description besieged the train reaching up to the slats of the

164

window, it was quite disturbing. The other two women said their farewells and good luck before they got off along with many others. Their departures left the compartment almost empty. Jack arrived with chai and fresh fruit for the children, spritely he said.

'Next stop is Nowshera. We get off there, not long now, should arrive about noon.' I wished it was right then and replied.

'Thank goodness for that. I'm worn out sitting in this compartment.' He suggested.

'Why don't you get out and stretch your legs for a while. The train won't be moving off for some time yet.' Rather irritated at his suggestion, I replied …

'No I'm stuck in this train and I don't want to be bothered by all those beggars outside. I'd like some more chai if you can get some.'

Off he went. In the meantime my tribe was going mad running around in and out of the aisle towards the end opening, a shout from Mary.

'Hey that's ours.' Had me running towards the three of them stood at the entrance I questioned.'What's happened?' Mary standing there with her hands on her hips said.

'Jackie lost a sandal, it fell down onto the track and one of those beggars has run off with it.'

What in heaven's name did he want with one sandal was beyond me?   When Jack arrived back with the chai. I informed him of the latest mishap, he retorted.

'Well! Not enough time, cannot get to the luggage, as we're about to leave for Nowshera.'

That kept Jackie quiet for a little while. With a whistle and a few jolts the train resumed its final stage of our journey. Sipping the chai I sat in the near empty carriage thinking: *Within a couple of hours we would arrive in this damn place called Nowshera. Casting my mind back to when we arrived and left Bombay .Realised that day was Sunday 25th of March. The Feast of the Annunciation. A very special day in the Catholic Church.* I blessed myself and began to say a decade of the rosary. Only to be disturbed by the sound of the Chai Wallah quietly calling out.

'Chai. Memsahib. Leemon?'

I nodded having served the drinks, he stood up clasps his hands together in front of him muttered words. It must have been another hour later the train came to a clanking stop. We had arrived at our final destination "Nowshera."

I took no notice of what or how the station looked. I was unclean and stinking, to me the air in the compartment was becoming more stifling second by second. My immediate thought was: *Getting off this stinking train, into our quarters. Thinking back to our quarters at Deepcut doubted if our new quarters would be anything like them?* Jack came into the compartment.

'All organised Sarah? Good I've got our other luggage outside.' Taking the cases, with my three in front followed Jack to the carriage doorway climbed down onto this dirt track of a platform where our other luggage lay.

'That's all of it Sarah, just stay here and wait. I'll be back soon.'

We stood alongside the train, our luggage all around us, like others all rather dishevelled waiting for someone to give us some directions, with the children not knowing what to do, all extremely hot in the blinding heat of the sun, further along a little baby hungry for food was screaming its head off, whilst Jackie with one sandal on was hopping about had the other two doing the same plying hop-scotch, which due to the heat did not last very long they stopped. Jack came striding up.

'Sarah not good news. Quite a lot of the children in the next coach have been taken to hospital with mumps and some wives with heat stroke.' I thought: *Possibly exhaustion.* - 'Er another thing. I've been just been informed that we are to live in tents.' His last remark really threw me.

'Oh no. Holy Mother of God" Jack. Not tents. I've just survived a train journey I'll never forget. Now tents.' The story of my life, however hearing this news, my tribe started hopping around whopping like Red Indian. This was the last straw? Whatever will happen next?

CHAPTER TWO.
NORTH WEST FRONTIER
NOWSHERA - PART 1.

TENTS? I could have screamed aloud. Standing on this so-called railway platform, the earth baked hard by the relentless sun, surrounded by luggage and three listless children, unable to keep them cool in the searing heat, deprived of privacy for four sweltering days and sleepless nights on a stinking train. There was I eagerly looking forward to get into quarters, have a good sluice down, rid myself of accumulated sweat, dust and sand to change into fresh clothing. However that was not to be, instead frustrated very unhappy at the prospect of being forced to live in tents. With the reality of the situation, below the brims of Tobies, instead of smiling faces, it was signs of irritation and frustration. I thought: *How on earth did I get myself into this situation?* A group of filthy looking beggars with hands outstretched were constantly moving amongst us muttering. 'Anna's. Baksheesh. Baksheesh.' I did not know what they were saying, gathered my three in close to me. Jack seeing my displeasure uttered.

'Sarah. Hold on. Let me see what I can arrange.'

He marched off towards the front of the train, where the detrainment was a state of orderly pandemonium. Officers and Sergeants were bellowing out orders. Soldiers further up the track were unloading ammunition and stores. A B.S.M. (Battery Sergeant Major) at a smart gait arrived on the scene, shuffling behind him was a coolie with an ammunition box balanced on his head. The BSM came to a smart halt, the coolie dropped the ammunition box on the hard earth. Stepping up onto it, the BSM with rivulets of sweat streaming down his red face, in a booming voice addressed the waiting families.

'LADIES. LADIES. YOUR ATTENTION PLEASE. WELCOME TO NOWSHERA STATION AND THE NORTH WEST FRONTIER. WILL ALL THE FAMILIES MAKE THEIR WAY ALONG TO THE FRONT OF THE TRAIN. ON YOUR LEFT YOU WILL SEE A LARGE WHITE MESS TENT. PLEASE MAKE YOUR WAY INSIDE AND BE SEATED AT THE TABLES PROVIDED. A LUNCH WILL BE SERVED. PLEASE LEAVE ALL YOUR POSSESSIONS WHERE THEY ARE. DON'T WORRY THE COOLIES WILL LOOK AFTER THEM AND BRING THEM ALONG LATER.'

With his short and sweet orders over, the BSM stepped down. The coolie retrieved the ammunition box, swung it back on top of his head began his shuffling gait behind the retreating figure of the BSM as he continued to bark out another order.

'THIS WAY LADIES WITH YOUR CHILDREN. FOLLOW ME THROUGH THE STATION.'

Listening to him I wondered. *"What station? A dirt track road with railway lines running along it".* The touch of cold against my hand startled me. Quickly snatching my hand away I glanced to my left. A coolie dressed in a long white shirt, a large red turban wrapped around his head, his lips coloured red showed through the unshaven features of his black face, he grabbed hold of the small case in my hand. Salaamed spoke.

'Ji han. Memsahib tu jao! Okay.' Not understanding a word he said replied.

'Oh all right.' The grinning coolie salaamed again began to gather up our luggage, shouting out to another coolie in a torrent of words who came over to assist him.

Like a load of sheep, we fell in behind the retreating figure of the B.S.M. Jackie, half walking half hopping held my hand, whilst Mary and Kathleen walked in front with the coolies following behind. The families were quickly ushered through this station, as we approached the locomotive Jack saw all the families going past, spotted us *came* over to speak with me.

'Sarah. They have got some food laid on for all of you, after I've got all the stores sorted out, I will see you later. Don't worry, I'll sort something out. Oh by the way Nora and Bill said

166

their goodbyes when they left the train at Rawalpindi. Okay'. He returned back to carry on. I was annoyed I had even missed Nora, this was not a good day called out to him

'Oh that is a pity. I would have liked to see them before they left.'

A wave of his hand acknowledged my answer. I was disappointed at not seeing my friend Nora but that wasn't to be. As we passed by the locomotive, lying across the track in front of it were two cows with big humps on their backs. The engine driver instead of shooing them away, just stood there with his head bowed, clasped hands in front of him, as if he was praying? We continued on towards this big mess tent, with rolled up sides. I assumed, to let the air circulate and keep it cool. Upon entering a somewhat scramble broke out as families sorted out a suitable place to sit down. I ushered my three to one table with four place settings sat them down. In the middle of the table a plate covered by another plate revealed slices of bread, obviously covered to keep off flies. My tribe dived in, taking a slice each, they were happily eating keeping quiet.

Then more bare-footed coolies dressed in white tunics, trousers, swarmed from all directions of the tent with plates of scrambled eggs, more slices of bread were given to everyone, there was plenty of it. Other coolies brought pitchers of chai and drinks for the children. It was the first reasonable meal we had since leaving Bombay, it was delicious. I think everyone, ravenous with hunger, devoured all that was edible. Just like the scrawny-necked vultures we had seen outside. More chai was served, after everyone was satisfied. The general hubbub of chatter was again interrupted by the booming voice of the red faced BSM calling for quietness.

'QUIET PLEASE. Well, I see everyone has had their fill and had a good lunch. Now to other matters. All senior ranks families fall in outside. You are to be taken to the Sergeants mess further up the lines. All other ranks families will remain here until further orders are issued.'

Standing up, I got my tribe moving outside where we joined a few other families, now much reduced in numbers. The BSM bellowed.

'PLEASE FOLLOW ME.'

We followed, leaving the spasmodic chuff of the stationary train behind. By this time Jackie had abandoned his other sandal had handed it to me to carry. I did not like him walking in bare feet, but it seemed the most practical thing to do. I was not feeling too happy about a lot of things. No quarters, Just tents. I was dirty, smelling, definitely in need a sluice down and change of clothes as were my three. Having missed Mass on this special day just added to my anguish, so I said a few silent prayers to myself as we walked. By the time we got to the sergeants mess I was soaked in sweat. Just as we were about to enter the mess, a short way behind us, I caught sight of Jack marching his troops along. Inside, the cool atmosphere and gloom of the interior hit us, trying to accustom my eyes from the glare of the outside sun, a figure advanced towards me, his booming voice surprised all.

'Is it private Sarah Cunningham I see before me. Isn't it? Must be all of ten years. It's lovely to see you.'

I recognised the voice, then in front of me loomed the familiar face of Regimental Sergeant Major Jimmy Townsend. It was more than ten years when I first knew him. I was in the W.A.A.F. at the Curragh Barracks and many years before I knew Jack. Taking hold of my hand Jimmy shook it violently with surprise all I could say was.

'Jimmy of all the people I was to meet. It had to be you. I never thought I'd ever see you again.'...'Who is your husband?'... 'Q.M.S. John Plant.'...'Ah you did right their Sarah. He's a first class soldier and a good athlete. I've seen his records. These your three then?' ..'Yes this is Mary, that's Kathleen and the one behind me is Jackie. He's not usually this shy.'

He said hello to all of them. I had been taken completely by surprise, at this sudden reunion in such an outlandish place. Nevertheless it was so pleasant to see someone you knew, it bucked me up so much I temporarily forgot about my immediate problems. We spent quite a long time yarning about the old days. I was telling him about Victoria Barracks in Cork, being demobbed, meeting Jack, getting married and finally getting posted to India. He made a great fuss of me and gave me many good tips on, what and whatnot to do in India. But I did notice some strange glances by other ladies, obviously very curious about the attention I was receiving. Jimmy explained that, as it was too hot on the plains, his Brigade was being posted up into the hills. Jimmy had stayed behind to hand over to the incoming Brigade. I thought: *That's very funny. We just were arriving from the cold winter of Blighty he saying. "That it was too hot for them to stay on the plains and they were used to it."* He continuing... 'Anyway your husband's Battery should have been out here ages ago before the start of the monsoon season. It would have given you more time to get acclimatised. But that's the Army for you.' Roaring with laughter he added ....'Sarah. After four days in those confounded trains you must be worn out. Let me take your two lovely little girls and little boy off your hands. A couple of the orderlies can look after them for a while.' He hailed two young orderlies over and spoke to them. My three were gone... 'Sarah. Please excuse me as I have to do my rounds and welcome everyone. I will be back shortly. Don't worry about your three. They're in good hands. I'll see you later Sarah.'

He left me to sit down next to one of the other Sergeants wives, with a young lad of about fourteen years old. As a matter of courtesy, I explained to her about the unexpected welcome and surprise I had just received. That seemed to justify the situation, no doubt this tit-bit of information, would soon circulate and be accepted as a friendly reunion. Most of the families I spoke with were from other batteries, as we had nowhere to go stayed in the mess until late afternoon, when a light buffet was to be served. Hopefully Jack would have come back to collect us and take us to "The tents." In the meantime my tribe had returned to sit beside me. Jimmy returned and sat with us, making a quiet comment on.

'What a handful you have in Mary?'

Jack arrived in the mess, spotted me, came across with his Tobie tucked under his arm, coming to a smart halt in front of the R.S.M. Spoke up.

'Q.M.S. Plant. Reporting in sir.'

I noticed rivulets of sweat running down his face into the neckband of his tunic top, quite stained from sweat.

'You got your men and stores sorted out then Plant? '

'Yes Sir, all in the lines now Sir.'

'Good you'll find it a bit warm out here. I've just been telling Sarah about India and giving her a few tips. We are old friend's way back from my days at the Curragh Camp.'

'Thank you Sir. I'm sure they will come in handy.' Jack looked quizzically at me. I winked as Jimmy added. ...'I hear you are bit of a sportsman Plant?'

'Yes Sir. I try and do my best.' The R.S.M. went on usual Army talk, exclaimed... Aah there they are? Let me introduce you to Q.M.S. Burton and his wife. The Q.M.S. you are replacing.' He called them over. Jack replied.

'We have met sir. Down in the lines.'...Turning to me he added. 'Er Sarah. You won't be sleeping in tents. I've got things arranged.' Jimmy retorted.

'There you are Sarah, nothing to worry about. Your husband has solved your problem. Elizabeth has come up from their quarters to meet you and your children. When they move out, you will take over their quarters.'

Immediately I thought: *What a relief, possibly Jimmy knew all about the situation as well. But did not let on.* Standing up got my tribe to stand beside me for introductions to Elizabeth. Fair of hair with a roundish face tanned brown by the sun, a medium sized lady dressed in a loose fitting flowered frock. I was aware of a very strong smell of eau de cologne. Introducing my tribe I could not hide Jackie's feet almost black with dirt. She bade me to be seated.

'I've been told about your problem of sleeping under canvas until we move out. Only too well do I remember when I first arrived here, that arduous train journey from Ahmadabad? Well

168

as you are about to take over from us, tonight your family are most welcome to sleep in our quarters. It will be a bit makeshift but we will manage.' Thinking to myself: *What a God send.* Quickly replied.

'Thank you very much, that is most kind of you. We don't want to be of any trouble.'

'No trouble it's the least we can do. Please call me Elizabeth and you're Sarah?'

The afternoon tea of chai and biscuits with cold drinks for the children was served. We returned to our discussion the usual chitchat about families. I discovered that she was a Catholic and had three children of her own, who were being looked after by their Ayah's back at the quarters, questioned.

'Ayah's who are they?'

'They Sarah are Indian servant women who look after you and the children. I have four you won't have to do anything yourself. They do it all for you?'

We didn't get much further with our conversation. Jimmy came towards me.

'Sarah, it's been wonderful meeting you again. Pity it wasn't at a dance, no matter in case I don't see you before I leave. I'll say goodbye and good luck.'

I, flattered by his compliment, bade him farewell. It was time we made our way back to their quarters (our future abode).

Outside, temporarily blinded by the fierce rays of the sun, quickly placed my Tobie on my head to provide shade to my eyes. Two Tonga's had already been ordered, one was stacked with our luggage, we clambered up onto the other one, Jack and Bill mounted two horses moving ahead Bill called out something to the Tonga Wallahs who got the horse into motion leading us away from the Sergeants mess. My mind concentrating on what our future accommodation was like? desperately wanted a sluice down to rid myself of four days of privation. As we passed various places by, Elizabeth mentioned what they were, apart from the lines of Bell tents the troops sleeping quarters, I did not take much notice, thankfully those were not ours, The journey did not take long, Jack and Bill led the way into an open compound. In the middle raised off the ground by many wooden supporting legs was a Bungalow, with four steps leading up to a long veranda covered by the overhanging roof made of corrugated sheets, stood on the flight of steps was a reception party. On the lower step stood to one side was a tall turbaned Indian, dressed in a long white shirt type coat, white trouser wearing sandals on his feet, on the next step stood three children, two boys and a little girl all dressed in white with large Tobies on their heads, stood on the veranda behind them were four Indian women dressed in various coloured Sari's, whom I assumed were those Ayah's Elizabeth had mentioned. My first impression, a strange set up totally isolated without any neighbours, but it appeared adequate. Two small Indian boys came running from around the side of the Bungalow to take the reins of the horses as Bill and Jack dismounted their horses, the Tonga wallah pulled up by the steps.

The tall Indian stepped onto the baked hard ground, quickly followed by the children who stood beside him. Elizabeth got down first the Indian salaamed in greeting. I got down and took Jackie in my arms as Mary and Kathleen jumped off, we stood together. Elizabeth's three eyed up my tribe. Bill pointing to our luggage shouted. 'Utana Jahldi.' The Indian clapping his hands shouted something, other servants appeared to remove our baggage from the Tonga, carried them into the bungalow. While this was going on, formalities were in order Elizabeth introduced her three to us these are my tribe namely. Freddie, Matthew and Matilda, I responded with our introduction with those over, we were ushered up the steps onto the veranda out of the blazing sun, invited to sit down at a table, still eyeing up my three her three children stood to one side. Elizabeth clapped her hands together, gesturering to us she spoke to the Indian.

'Memsahib.Sahib. Dhona pani. Jahldi jahldi'.....turning to me said. I've just told them to bring some water for you to freshen up. I'm sure you would like that before we have chai. Come along you three go and play off the veranda. '

169

From around the side of the bungalow, two servants appeared carrying bowls of water with a cloth draped over one arm, coming up the steps walked to the far end of the veranda, placed the bowls on a small table then stood to one side. Elizabeth urged.

'Sarah please use the water to freshen up. Don't you worry about the servants? Chai will be served very quickly you will see.

I didn't want a freshen up, I wanted more but a least it would clean my face and hands, we all carried out some primitive way of splashing water over our faces and hands. It was refreshing but not what I really wanted. The servants offered us the cloth. With these ablutions carried out we returned to the table, where drinks were already placed on the table, they were quickly drunk by all of us. Mid way through his drink Jackie stopped asked.

'Can I go to the lavatory please?'

'Lavatory. Oh yes the lavatory facilities... she called out...'Matthew, show young Jackie where the lavatory is. Sarah. They are very primitive, but you soon get used to them? Just be careful when you go into them, make sure the Bearer he is the one standing at the foot of the steps or, one of the other servants check them out for snakes? Don't worry I've never seen one in there before and we have been here two years. The night-time's facilities are indoor chamber pots. Nobody ventures out during the night?' I hung on her words, cringing at the thought of snakes.

After an evening meal of tinned Bully Beef salad fruit and more drinks. Elizabeth set about making arrangements for the sleeping. She put Mary and Kathleen in a bed with her little girl. Jackie in with her two little boys. With the children settled, we all sat out on the veranda, Oil lamps were lit and in the warm pleasant light we continued talking It was obvious, they were eager to find out what was happening back in Blighty, so our discussion was more about England. Two hours later I stifling yawns realised just how exhausted I was. Elizabeth noting my yawning had her servants prepare a makeshift bed in the inside front room, possibly their dining room. The bed laid out on the floor was made of bolsters filled with heaps of coir matting (The hair of the coconut and something I was to get used to very quickly). I could have slept on a heap of stones I was so tired. Jack and I without night attire, partially undressed, lay down covered ourselves with a couple of army blankets. I fell asleep before my head hit the bolsters. Early next morning I woke out of a deep sleep, not knowing what time or where I was? Jack was already moving about whispered.

'Come on Sarah it's getting on for six. There is a lot to be done today up in the lines. Your job to sort out with Elizabeth, how the running of this bungalow goes.'

Reluctantly, I rose to get myself sorted out. It was still dark, I shivered my shoulders with the cold of the morning. One of the servants quietly entered with glasses of chai, placing them on the floor next to me. I had a raging thirst, gratefully taking one of them drank thirstily. Although it was hot the chai brought me back into the land of the living. Another servant entered with a bowl of water and cloth for an early morning wash. More refreshed, I slipped my dress back on, ready for something to eat. The four of us sat down at a table out on the veranda, to be served breakfast there were plenty of boiled eggs, flat bread and more chai. Two horses already groomed and saddled were brought around to the foot of the veranda. Bill and Jack left us to mount their horses and rode away to report in. As the early morning sun began to rise it was peaceful as Elizabeth and I chatted, More chai was served, I sat shivering in the chill of the early morning until the sun brought forth the heat of the day. At the clap of her hands an Indian woman appeared, Elizabeth ordered.

"Baba's. Jahldi. Sarah after the children have got up and eating breakfast. I will show you the Bungalow and its facilities.'

Within minutes we heard muffled noises from the back rooms, eventually they all came out rather dishevelled, my tribe still half-asleep could have spent another hour or so in bed. However they were up, it was the beginning of a new way of life for them and me. They were sat down at the table, the servants provided them with breakfast. Elizabeth took me on a quick tour of the quarters. The Bungalow was spacious with five rooms, two large at the front, and three smaller bedrooms at the rear. The bungalow walls were made of panelled wood whilst the inside walls were made from thin panelling with doors. We discussed the sleeping arrangements of the quarters. I liked the way she had hers with one room for the servants. I decided not to change anything. As she was leaving later that day, she explained many other things, with me trying to make a mental note of do's and don'ts. It was confusing. I sought her advice about the servant's.

'Where or who do I see about getting replacement?'

'Oh don't worry about that. Bill and I have decided to leave all the servants behind. Sarah, I can vouch for all of them, they are all good and trustworthy. Their problem is they only speak Urdu yet, somehow they do seem to understand English. Apart from the language barrier, you shouldn't have any problem with any of them. Unless Sarah. You want to change them?' Very quickly with much relief I replied.

'Uhm No. If they are that good and you have had no problems with them. That's fine by me. Thank you very much'... (Later I found out, normally the servant's go with the family to the various postings). Anyway fortunately, she was handing them over to me. So I didn't have to worry or bother about looking around for new servants, I asked...'How do they understand what you want them to do?'

'Oh. That's a point. I was in the same boat as you but gradually learnt using a sharp tongue with a few words of command in Urdu, gets them moving. By the sounds the children are making, they have finished their breakfast. Now after they have got dressed. I think I had better introduce you to the servants as their new Memsahib. I don't know all their real names and can't even remember most of them, so I call them by their duty names. Come along now Sarah. We haven't got that much time before I leave.' We joined the children playing on the veranda. I ordered.

'C'mon you three, let's get you changed into clean clothing.'

'No Sarah, that's the Ayah's job. Leave it to them, they will dress all of them. All you have to do is show what clothes you want them to change into. Your luggage is in the children's room.'

'Oh that's no problem. I can manage without their assistance. I've been doing it all their lives and I don't think an Ayah's going to change the habits of a lifetime.' She roared with laughter at my answer.

'No Sarah. They are the servants of the household. They all have individual jobs to carry out. That's what they get paid for and their job is sacro sanct. In other words no one else interferes with his or her duty. Just let them carry on.' Startled I quickly responded..

'Well. If they do it all for me. I'll have nothing to do all day?'

'Yes I know. I found it very strange at first, but very soon you will accept this lazy way of life. Now. What you can is sort some clothes out for them then leave the rest to the Ayah's. Come along.'

Bewildered by this news followed her into the back bedroom where the Ayah's were already sorting out Elizabeth's three as my tribe watched I found the case I had put aside for the train journey, sorting out three sets of crumpled clothing laid them on the bed. Elizabeth urged.

'Right. Come along Sarah leave them to it.'

Reluctantly I followed her out. I was more concerned what Mary might get up to? Returning to the veranda we sat down, with a matter of minutes they all trooped out fully dressed.

'There you are. See I told you so. Now the servants. Let's get organised. Sarah you stand on the bottom step with your three'...I moved down the steps...'Come along you three down beside your mother.' She ushered them into place, then moved to one side. In line we stood in the sun wearing our Tobies. Elizabeth clapped her hands.

171

'Bearer. Jahldi jahldi.' She mumbled something to him, gestured to us.

'Achchha. Memsahib Buron.' He clapped his hands, in a loud voice called out.

'JAHLDI. JAHLDI. MEMSAHIB. BURON.'

A host of servants including young boys appeared from all directions of the quarters. The Bearer said something and they all lined up facing us. Elizabeth pointing to me.

'Memsahib nam Memsahib Plant.' - placing her hand on Mary's shoulder. 'Missy baba Mary.'...then in turn....'Missy baba Kathleen.'...'Sahib baba Jackie.'

All the servants with hands together, bowed and touched their foreheads salaamed us, murmured. 'Salaam alekum.' Elizabeth translated.

'Sarah they are greeting you, 'Salaam alekum which means peace be on you. And you should always reply. Valekum as salaam, which means. and also on you.' I responded.

'That's nice of them.'

'Well that is the normal way of greeting anyone out here. Just say achchha which means good.' One by one she beckoned them forward, the first one...'This is Abdullah the Bearer. "Munshi". But just call him by the English word bearer. He is the headman he is very good. Nobody does anything unless he approves.'

He stood in front of me. A tall proud looking man, beneath bushy greying eyebrows his eyes seemed to look into my brain, under his prominent hooked nose was a nearly grey walrus styled moustache. Very similar to Jack's father. Pop's moustache. His white tunic coat was buttoned right up to a tight white collar. He was the only one wearing a turban with a different coloured spiked cloth stuck out at the top. I was about to ask about his turban when Elizabeth interrupted my thoughts.-...'He's wearing a pugri on his head. It's a local head dress. You will see many different types of head-dress up here in the province.'... In greeting he bowed deeply towards me then walked to one side to stand close by me as Elizabeth introduced the others informing me what their job was. The rest of the male servants dressed in long white shirts covering white trousers some wore sandals, some wore Pugri's but none so elaborate as the Bearer, following one after the other. "Khansama" (The Cook). I hesitated on this one. A man for a cook?. "Dhobi Wallah".(The Washman) "Mussaul" (The lampman and washer of plates)."Malee" (The gardener). "Chowkidar" (The night watchman). "Bheestee" (The Carrier of Water). Then the little "Syce" (Who cared for the horses). Followed by the four women. "Ayah's." Each stood there all about the same height as me. "Tiny". One dressed in a white Sari, was introduced as. Number One "Ayah" whilst the other three wore various coloured Saris.' As each one was introduced, their eyes met with mine. I noticed a soft and caring look in each of them, with a gentle smile they placed the palms of their hands together in front of their faces bowed in greeting. Their jobs: to look after the children and me. I counted sixteen little boys (Chico's). Typical little boys some with shirts, all were barefooted, giggling and shoving each other. Their black cropped hair shining in the sunlight. I think they had all used Lavender Bryantine to smooth their hair down. Most of the time they did whatever the elders ordered, the rest of the time they played with the children. A sharp order from the Bearer brought them to stop their antics. They all bowed salaamed, in turn I nodded with a smile with a murmured. 'Achchha.' Introductions over the Bearer clapped his hands, they all dispersed. Never having servants before. I had now been pitched into having counted a grand total of twenty-eight. Such was my inheritance. Elizabeth Laughed.

'Memsahib Sarah. Let me show you the outhouses.'

We walked across the open space towards a shack, through the open doorway into the gloom of its interior. Immediately, the heat struck me along with the smell of wood smoke.

'This Sarah is where all the cooking and brewing chai is done, it's then brought to the bungalow, which is only used for eating and sleeping in.'

Surveying the interior it was very primitive. Laid on the floor in a tidy manner were some funny shaped pots, a pile of wood was stacked in one corner, the cooking was done on a sort of open range with fire holes, beneath which flames from the burning wood licked the sides of a few cooking pots blackened by smoke and flames, the smoke rising from the fire curled upwards and out through a hole in the roof. The cook, sat on his haunches was busily cutting up vegetables on a wooden board supported on some rocks, placed around him in raffia baskets were the vegetables cabbage, potatoes, carrot, onions, tomatoes, funny looking cucumbers and a lot of green foliage of some sorts, there was also fruit lemons banana and some other types I did not know. The Cook looking up smiled at me, standing up salaamed. Elizabeth spoke half in Urdu, half English something about, I was an "Achchha Memsahib." he was to do everything for me, as he had done for her. He turned towards me and salaamed again. I returned the gestures.

'Achchha.' I thought: *This is a great start. A cook that knew no English and I knew no Urdu. The only thing to do was somehow to get him to do it my way.* He sat back on his haunches and carried on cutting. Elizabeth commented.

'He is very good he understands more than you think he does'…adding…'He buys all the food.' … 'Oh where are the shops?'… No shops, the various wallahs bring their goods here.' I thought: *Oh my. There goes another job.* We left him to it, moved outside into the searing sunlight she gestured to the Bearer - 'Jahldi pakhana. Sarah that means lavatory.' - He led the way to another shack, opened up a door. Peering inside he muttered.

'Achchha. Memsahib.' Stepped aside.

A shack with a deep hole in the ground? I thought: *Charming.* I did not linger, onto another little shack beside a chicken coop, as we approached the chickens began squawking in fright, half a dozen scrawny chickens pecked at the dirt, a cockerel glowered menacing at us. Opening a small door revealed a few gardening tools. We left the chickens squawking to walk around to the rear of the bungalow. – 'This is the washhouse the Dhobi Wallahs domain.' From inside I heard the methodical slap of something going on, through the open doorway I saw the Dhobi Wallah stripped to the waist, with a towel wrapped around his middle, like a madman was beating and flaying some clothing against two flat stones in the middle of this washhouse. Large bowls full of water were laid ready for his use. The flagstone floor looked quiet slippery, in the middle of the floor a small stream of water flowed down a gully into a hole in the far wall. At that second I was aware of two things. One: The strong smell of Elizabeth's eau de cologne, Two: Our unclean smell, neither my tribe nor I had washed since Bombay. The events of yesterday had overtaken any ablutions. I turned to Elizabeth and requested.

'Would it be possible for me and the children to get a sluice down?'

'Oh I am so sorry Sarah. Excuse my manners, of course you can. I should have given you the opportunity last evening, but you know how that turned out. Look the Dhobi Wallah will get the washhouse ready and after we have finished the tour you can take a sluice down, whilst I get ready to leave. – Dhobi. Pani. Memsahib. Babas, saf. Jahlil. Jahldi.' She indicated pouring water over her head.

'Achchha. Memsahib.'

We continued onto a stable where I assumed Jack's horse would be stabled, Elizabeth informed me….'That's where the Syce's sleep.' …'What's a Syce?' ….'Oh. They currie the horses and look after the tackle, very useful they are too.'

We walked around the other side of the bungalow, passing along a garden of beautiful flowers their scent hung in the air. Then back to the cookhouse Elizabeth instructed.

'Memsahib Sarah. No time like the present. You tell the cook to bring us. Chai on the Veranda.' Fear overcame me. I peered inside saw the cook still cutting vegetables . I blurted out.

'Chai on the veranda please.' He grinned salaamed answered.

'Ji han Memsahib. Elizabeth seemed pleased.'

'There that's the way. Not such a big problem after all. I was just the same as you until I got the hang of it.'

173

We gathered the children around on the veranda floor. We had just settled in the chairs, when the Cook arrived balancing a tray on one shoulder, having served us salaamed left.

'Sarah you'll find that tea, chai as it's called is always on the go. A pot of boiling water is permanently on the fire. So don't worry about asking for it.'

We talked on, as she explained that Bill was in an Indian Army Artillery Regiment and had been up in Nowshera for two years. A small but very hot dusty town teeming with all kinds of tribesman. Abound with the usual Bazaars the biggest one being the Sudder Bazaar close by the camp,...'Never go alone into the town.' I thought: *No fear of that I'm staying right here...*'Nowshera it's about fifteen miles from Peshawar quite close to the Khyber Pass. Where most of the Army activities are taking place. We are very close to a river called the Lundai? That runs down from the Khyber Pass and meets another river further down on the way to Rawalpindi. I keep my three well away from the river.'...She talked of a hill station near Murree. Where married families spent at least, three to four months away from the heat of the plains...'We are now going back down south to Almadabad. Another four-day horrible train journey.'... With the chai finished Elizabeth turned to me...'Now Sarah let's get you and the children spruced up with that sluice down.' She clapped her hands the Bearer standing at the foot of the veranda steps, came up towards her salaamed. 'Memsahib.'

'Dhona Memsahib Plant and Baba's. Jahldi.' He salaamed walked away from the steps...'Sarah. Dhona means wash. Take a change of dress when you go for a sluice down. While you sluice down keep your soiled dress on, it will preserve your modesty. Dry yourself and change into your other dress. You'll soon get used to it. By the way I've got the servants to move your entire luggage into our room. Oops sorry your room. So you can sort out your own things to wear.'

I was dripping with perspiration itching uncomfortably. A splash of Lavender water earlier in the day had not helped, realised the only way to cool down in the heat of the day, was a complete sluice down. Grateful for her suggestion, I went into the bedroom to sort out changes of clothing for all of us. The number One Ayah was hovering about watching me. I nodded, gathering up the clothes in my arms and a bar of soap. I made my way out, she bowed as I went past her and returned to the veranda. Placing the pile on the table stood there wondering what I had to do next? The sound of the children playing came from around the side of the bungalow. Elizabeth's voice called out.

'Sarah go over to the washhouse. The Dhobi Wallah is waiting for you?'

Gathering up my change of clothing, I went down the steps towards the washhouse then stopped and thought: *What was he waiting for? I did not want any servants to wash me. I was quite capable of doing that on my own.* With some hesitation, I walked towards the washhouse where outside the Dhobi Wallah was sat on his haunches waiting for me, as I approached he rose up salaamed. 'Memsahib.' Opened the door and then scuttled away leaving me alone.

Relieved I went inside, draped over some stones were a couple of towels. On the floor was a line of large pans full of water, one had a large ladle partly submerged. I supposed that was the one to use. Doubting if I could have managed lifting one of those pans, placed my clean clothing out of the way, leaving my dress on began my ablutions, taking the large ladle of water poured it over my head, although the water was tepid it made me catch my breath. Ladle after ladle followed, the wet dress clung to my very person as I soaked myself, washing thoroughly with the soap. I rinsed down again ladle after ladle followed, until I was clear of soapsuds. Very much refreshed, with the sheer joy of being clean revived me no end. I took off my wringing wet clothes, leaving them in a pile. Drying myself left my hair long to dry in the sun. Dressed into the clean clothes felt more than dressed. Now for my tribe, I went outside and called them. They came to me and I told them they were to have a sluice down, when Elizabeth's voice halted me.

'Sarah. Leave that to the Ayah's they will handle them.' Bewildered by all this malarkey I answered.

'Oh all right, if you say so.'

She clapped her hands, three of the Ayah's appeared – pointing in my direction she said something. They disappeared inside to return holding sets of clothes for my three. They approached us each placing a hand on my three took charge of my tribe, as Elizabeth's three stood to watch. I told my tribe to go with the Ayah's. Interested, I too followed them in to watch. Expertly they were sluiced down washed, dried and changed without any fuss. I was amazed at the speed with the quickness of the operation. The Ayah's took the wet clothing placed them on the top of several stones. As we left the washhouse to go back to the bungalow, the Dhobi Wallah returned went back inside, very soon the sounds of slapping erupted from its interior. No doubt he was re-washing all the wet clothing. As we approached the bottom of the veranda steps. The servants were busy carrying out her luggage to lie at the foot of the steps, Elizabeth with her Tobie cocked at a quizzical angle on her head, was ready to leave. She enquired.

'Well Sarah. How was that?'

'Oh I feel so much refreshed and totally clean. Now I have got rid of five days travelling. I must say the Ayah's are experts with the children.'

'Yes that's one chore that they respond too quite willingly. You'll find that they themselves are constantly washing. Now it's time I made a move myself. But before I leave would you like some chai to quench your thirst.

'Yes please'….Clapping her hands she continued….'You know Sarah your three will be away to the army school for the first part of the day until noon. Then they will be home for the rest of the day. The army school is on the other side of the camp'…A servant arrived and served the chai…'The Ayah's take them there and bring them back in a Tonga. So that's another thing you won't need to get involved with.'

The arrival in the compound of two Tonga's created a stir from all the servants. Coming out of the shade the Bearer went down the steps clapped his hands called out.

'Memsahib Buron joa jalhdi.' The servants arrived to form a line. Elizabeth murmured.

'Here we go Sarah. Something I don't like doing that is saying. Khuda hafiz. That's goodbye. They have all been very good and faithful to us. It's your gain my loss. Pity I can't take them with me. But I have all my old servants to go back to in Almadabad. Take my advice. You treat them well, they will respect you for that, and you won't have any problems.'

With that she got up and went down the steps of the veranda followed by her children, as we watched she started her goodbyes. The male servants bowed deeply took hold of her hand. The Ayah's gently pulled their headscarves across their faces, possibly to hide their emotions. I don't know? All I wanted to do was take her place. Her final goodbye was to the Bearer she bowed to him took his hands and murmured.

'Shukria Abdullah Shukria.' With this ceremony over she came back up the steps wiping the corner of her eyes.

'Don't mind me Sarah, I'm just being stupid. I just thanked the Bearer he is the one in charge of them all. But mark my words. You will find they simply love all these ceremonies and parades. They think they belong to the army and join in. It's all a great charade, do not forget Sarah you must carry that on. Well it's time for our goodbyes. I wish you well and a lot of luck. You will become lonely, homesick and dare I say with all these servants to wait on you. Bone idle. Eventually you will come to enjoy your stay in India, it grows on you. Bill has a further two weeks here and will stay in the sergeant's quarters. He will see you before he leaves. We are getting on the train you arrived on yesterday.'

I had known her for less than twenty-four hours, a person I warmed to and her advice. She went down the veranda steps climbed into the Tonga with her three. The Tongas drew away out of the compound, with a final wave they were gone. I hadn't noticed before, but the servants were all still in a line. The bearer clapped his hands the ceremony was over they disappeared.

Alone I stood on the veranda with my tribe still sat on the steps wondering what was happening. Stood In the middle of the compound was the Bearer, hands behind his back no doubt deep in thought about: *How to come to terms with this new family?* Likewise I struggling to understand the predicament I was now faced with. Some of the Chico's dressed in coloured shirts no doubt for the ceremony, approached my tribe, smiling in friendship joining their hands together, salaamed, sat down on their haunches in front of my three. Began pointing at each other, chattering away. Mary stood up pointed to Jackie said.

'Jackie...Kathleen...then herself. I'm Mary. Number one the oldest.' She salaamed to them. Astounded I watched thinking: *My God they are talking to each other.* I noticed the Bearer was also watching the scene unfold before our eyes, made me think: *There would be no trouble with the children but my biggest problem would be myself. Trying to run a household with servants I didn't want and whom I could not understand. What the Bearer was thinking? I would never know or understand?.* I stood there looking down at Mary, she in full control of the situation, I looked out at the Bearer. Maybe he was waiting for me to tell him what to do. What was it that Elizabeth had said? Chai is always on the go, don't be afraid to ask. I called out.

'Bearer.' He spun around.

'Ji han Memsahib. ' He came towards me a tall proud figure of a man before he got to the bottom step I ordered.

'Chai please.'

'Ji han Memsahib achchha.'

He turned walked towards the cookhouse, I watched as he disappeared in through the door, almost immediately he came out followed by the cook carrying the chai, walking across the open space, came up the steps up onto the veranda salaamed. The cook placed the chai on the small wicker table, poured the chai into a glass turned towards me salaamed. I did likewise and murmured.

'Good.' Immediately thought: *That's English.* The cook returned back to his cookhouse, whilst the Bearer salaamed me.

'Achchha Memsahib.' - I'm sure he was prompting me, thought: *Oh that's the word.* Unsure responded.

'Achchha. Bearer.'

Sitting down at the table. He moving to one side stood there. Taking hold of the glass sipped the chai, it was refreshing, but my mind was a blank I did not know what to do next. The midday sun was at its highest point, the heat of the day was unbearable, everything was still except for the scratching of insects the constant whirring sound that crickets made. Such was my concentration I didn't even take in what was going on outside. It wasn't long before my tribe came around from the back asking for a cold drink. Beads of sweat were evident on their little faces, Mary excitedly said.

'Mum were playing with the chico's.'

'Oh that's good you have made friends.'

'Yes they're all right.' I called out.

'Bearer.' He approached me from the other side of the veranda salaamed.

'Ji han Memsahib.' I nodded and waved my arm in a big circle.

'Drinks for the children.'

'Ji han Memsahib achchha.'

Again he salaamed. Leaving the veranda went across to the cookhouse, entering, a pause, then came out followed by the cook with glasses of water on a tray perched precariously on his shoulder, quickly he swayed across to the bungalow. As the bearer stayed at the foot of the steps, the cook continued up onto the veranda towards my tribe. Taking each glass from the tray, gave one to each of them and offered me one. I didn't want it but out of politeness took it. It was cool and rather milky coloured with bits floating in it. I declined his offer and placed it on the table. He frowned.

'Memsahib nimbu, shaking his head... ji nai?' Jackie had already drunk his and said.

'That was nice can I have some more please?' Intrigued I asked.

'Mary what's it like.'

'It tastes good very sweet'...'Kathleen?'... 'Yes I like it too.'

If they liked it, picking up the glass I ventured to taste this concoction. It was good strong very sweet lemon, took another mouthful. The cook, who had been watching all this, quizzically looked at me. I think he wanted a response.

'Uhm. Achchha. Achchha.' His face lit up in a smile.

'Achchha Memsahib nimbu jai han achchha.'

The ice had been broken, knowing that he had pleased the Memsahib salaamed, returned to his cookhouse. Much later I was to learn that he made up the lemon drink himself. The children went back to play, leaving me sat at the table alone mulling over what I was going to do with myself faced with doing absolutely nothing all day? I was lost, all I could hear was the sound of the children playing around somewhere. Jack was up in the lines, hopefully he would soon be back here along with me. I gazed out onto an empty compound, its heat from the sun radiated in towards me, it was deathly quiet punctuated by the noise of insects, the cawing of some crows in the trees farther away mingled with some other strange sounds of birds or chattering of whatever else that were sounding off. I sat there with nobody to confide in thinking: *What I should do next? I was so lonely, desperately homesick and very far away from home. My thoughts went back to Aldershot. That terrible time I had there, at least then I had neighbours.* Overcome with my thoughts of desperation, tears welled up into my eyes. I began to cry, quickly buried my face in my hands, wept with anguish. *What was I going to do with myself in this God forsaken hole?* A quiet voice disturbed me.

'Memsahib. Memsahib.' I looked up to see the towering figure of the Bearer standing in front of me, silently he had approached me. With a tear streaked face I looked at him. In a gentle voice he quietly spoke.

'Memsahib Inshallah'...

He motioned with his fingers to my cheeks, traced his fingers down his own cheeks... 'Achchha Memsahib achchha.' I think he was telling me. It was good that I cried? Pointing to the sky, clasped his hands together murmured...'Allah Achchha.' I did not understand him just nodded with sobbing voice murmured. 'Achchha. Achchha.' With the back of my hand wiped the tears from my eyes and face. The bearer clapped his hands, shouted a torrent of something. Within a few moments the Cook and Dhobi Wallah appeared. The Dhobi Wallah carrying a bowl with a cloth over his arm came up the steps of the veranda, placing the bowl at my feet, the Bearer indicated to me to sluice my face. Bending down scooped the water into my hands, immersing my face in the cool water, which I did a few times. The coolness of the water-cooled downs the puffiness of my eyes. A cloth was handed to me to dry my face, handing it back to the Dhobi Wallah, he took hold of it along with the bowl of water, bowed and hurriedly left the veranda. I began to take stock of the situation; somehow they appeared to understand my predicament. I said.... 'Bearer chai.' He beamed salaamed.

'Ji han Memsahib achchha.' The cook who had been standing beside the Bearer salaamed then ran, within seconds he was back with the glass of chai handed it to me, I took a sip placed it on the table. He stood there besides the Bearer waiting what for I did not know? I looked up at their faces to see concern on both of them, the Bearers eyebrows furrowed close together, the cooks much younger face, the softness of his eyes squinting at me. All I could think about was nodding saying 'achchha achchha, thank you thank you.' In return they both salaamed murmured. 'Salam al akum Memsahib.' The bearer moved to one side as the cook left the veranda., leaving me ashamed of my outburst of crying, nevertheless it had relieved the tension of a tense moment I .sat there sipping the chai sweating freely gazing out at nothing. Sometime later a Wallah arrived conversing with the Cook having sold something left. I sat there thinking: *Even shopping had been taken away from me, was this a forerunner of what my life would become for the next seven years? Whatever you do don't cry something will turn up?* It did, sometime later the Cook arrived with a glass of chai, I grateful of his interruption had a gnawing feeling of hunger in my stomach needed something to eat. 'Cook I need something to eat.' Indicating to him with my hands, imitating cutting with a knife and fork for something to eat, he responded saying.

'Ah khana. Ji han Memsahib achchha.' He salaamed left.

Sat sipping the chai, decided not to be silly about all this, it was about time I rallied around and got things moving. After a little while, the cook returned followed by two of the Chico's, each carried a tray bearing two large plates of salad, placed them on the table with other plates and cutlery, salaaming they left. I called my tribe in to eat. Satisfied after their meal they were drowsy, so I ushered them into a bedroom to rest, soon they were fast asleep. It was early afternoon and I was tempted to lay down myself but shrugged it off, I had to get started. I went into our bedroom to sort out our clothing for that night I noticed the Ayahs were stood watching me, I did not know what to do with them. I emptied all the cases of soiled travelled garments, dumped them on the floor, then called the Bearer, when he came in I pointed to the pile of clothing imitated scrubbing muttered. 'Dhobi.'

'Ji han Memsahib achchha.' Salaamed he disappeared. I stood there thinking: *No. What I wanted was he to take them out and do the washing. That's what he's for.* Then walked out to call him back, but he was already on his way in walking towards the bedroom followed by the Dhobi Wallah, both salaamed. The Dhobi Wallah walked past me. 'Memsahib.' - Gathered up the pile of clothing left. First lesson learned. If you want anything done. Get the Bearer to arrange it. The rest of the clean clothing I laid out flat on the bed to get rid of the creases. I would sort them out later. I had come across my writing paper pen and ink, decided to write a letter home to mother, taking them out to the veranda where the table had been cleared, sitting down in the quietness I heard the melodic singing of the Dhobi Wallah, accompanied by the slapping sound as he beat hell out of our washing. I ordered chai. It was served before I had even started my letter.

Taking a sip composed myself, began writing my woeful tale about: The boat trip, our arrival in Bombay, the flies heat, smell, the magnificence of the Hotel Taj, the illusions of forthcoming grandeur, followed by four days of purgatory on a train, also inheriting an already made family of twenty-eight servants placed at my disposal, that I did not want and could not converse with them. I literally poured out my heart to her. It was mid-afternoon before I finished the letter. By that time my tribe had woken up, arriving on the veranda they slumped down in the chairs, in the heat of the afternoon they were all wet with sweat, as I was too, I drank a mouthful of the cold chai, then ordered the Bearer to bring cold drinks for them. Quickly the cook arrived with the drinks including one for me. This time I was glad to take a glass of this lemon water. It was so refreshing and quenched the thirst. My tribe moved down onto the veranda steps not knowing what to do with themselves. The heat was not going to go away and neither were we. I decided to go into the bedroom and sort out the clothing. To my horror everything had disappeared. No boxes or suitcases, the bedroom was neat and tidy, the double bed had the counterpane drawn back and the netting hanging from above was neatly draped ready for use. I went over to the cupboard beside the bed, opened the double doors, an over powering smell of mothballs wafted out, but all the clothing was hanging from coat hangers closing the cupboard doors turned around, to be startled by the presence of number One Ayah stood in the doorway, salaamed towards me. I returned the compliment I spoke to her in English using my hands to try and communicate.

'You put the clothes away?' Nodding she smiled at me.

'Ji han Memsahib ana ji han'...spoken softly her words were full of warmth, she beckoned me to follow her; I followed her into the children's bedroom. Along one wall stood the other three Ayahs all were barefooted they salaamed. Number One Ayah murmured...'Ji han Memsahib'.... clapped her hands. One of the Ayah's moved across the room, it seemed as if she floated she stopped at the chest of drawers, pulled open the top drawer. Number One Ayah beckoned me to go over to see. All Mary's clothing neatly folded, the drawer was closed; the second Ayah came across, pulled open the middle drawer to reveal. Kathleen's clothes all neatly folded, the drawer was closed then the third Ayah floated over, bent down pulled open the bottom drawer to reveal, Jackie's clothes neatly folded, that drawer was closed. The four of them bowed salaamed. I returned the compliment but did not know what to say. How on earth did they get the different clothing right? Jackie's was easy but the girls? As I racked my brain to say or, do something. My tribe came scampering in from the veranda to see what was going on. Instant smiles came onto the faces of the Ayah's. Number One Ayah came over, taking hold of Jackie's hand guided him over to the third Ayah's, stood him next to her, she came over taking hold of Kathleen's hand took her over to the next one, last in line Mary was taken across to stand beside the third Ayah. Then number One Ayah came over to me salaamed, standing next to me took hold of my hand, whereas the other Ayah's each took hold of my tribes hand all murmured.

'Salaam alekum Memsahib. Missy Babas.' All bowed. I now understood what number One Ayah was saying. My tribe had been put under the care of individual Ayah's, which included me. I bowed and said.

'Achchha.' Everyone was smiling. I motioned to my tribe to smile back at their Ayah's say Hello. That they did amid giggles, it was a new game to them. I motioned them to follow me outside onto the veranda, they all followed including Number one Ayah. I sat down at the table all six stood in front of me I addressed my three whilst the Ayah's, stood watching what I was doing with my three.

'Look. What happened in the bedroom was each one of the Ayah's were saying hello, by holding your hand from now on, they will look after you. Of course I will be in charge but they will become your servants to wash and clean you, lay out your clothes and things like that. I don't like it but that's what is going to happen from now on. You have to be good to them and do what they tell you to. If you don't. I will sort the three of you out. Do you understand what I am saying?'

They stood fidgeting in front of me, Mary chirped up.

'Mum. You mean they will look after us?'

'Yes that's right. As they looked after Freddie, Matthew and Matilda. Like all the rest of the servants, who will do all the work around the house. The problem is we don't speak their language and they don't speak ours. I don't know what to do. We will wait and see what your father has to say about it. He got us into this mess.'

Quickly their attention was averted to the sounds of a galloping horse. I followed suit spotted Jack galloping toward us. Pulling on the reins he pulled up the horse at the foot of the veranda steps, jumped down. A Chico appeared from nowhere, taking hold of the horse's reigns, snorting to its self, led it away. With whoops of joy in greeting to their father, my tribe leapt down the steps.

'Hello you three. Sarah this is a lively horse I have here.'... Jack bounding up the steps enquired...'All settled in then Sarah? I saw Elizabeth down at the mess, she said you have met all the servants and you are ordering them about already.'

179

'Yes she might have said that, but I can't for the life of me remember their names. I've just been explaining to these three about the Ayah's and the rest of the servants.'

'Well. Now seeing as you have done that you will have to introduce me to the servants.' That did it. I retorted...'Jack I can't. You got us into this mess. You just do it yourself.'

'No. This is your domain, so come on get on with it.'

'Jack. I can't do this. Leave it till next week.'

'Yes you can. Don't be silly.'

There was no way I was going to get a chance to delay it anymore, so I stood up and moved over to the top step of the veranda. I called the Bearer, with a wave of the arm ordered.

'Bearer. Go and get the other servants please.'

He salaamed, moved down the steps to stand at the bottom clapping his hands and called.

'Memsahib Plaan. Jahldi.'

All twenty-eight servants arrived, fortunately they lined up in the same order. Much to my embarrassment, my tribe sat down on the veranda steps, giggling away as I began to introduce Jack. Waving my arm in his direction muttered.

'This is the Sahib. Do everything he says.'

That was all I could say, which was not very convincing. Jack looked at me shaking his head grinning; he went down the steps walking along the line, salaamed to each servant saying.

'Salaam alekum.' They returned the honour with big smiles on their faces. Then Jack came to the Bearer, who stood to attention saluted Jack he addressed the Bearer.

'Achchha Bearer Achchha'...He returned to the veranda retorted ....'There that wasn't bad. You'll have to do better than that Sarah. Now take me around the compound and show me where everything happens.'

Ceremony over the Bearer dismissed the servants. We all trooped down the steps, the Bearer fell in behind. I following the same route, Cookhouse first, I called upon the Bearer to check out the lavatory. I spoke knowingly.

'Always do that because of snakes'... into the washhouse, the Dhobi Wallah had all our clothing laid out in the sun to dry, Jack exclaimed aloud.

'Aah this is what I want. A sluice down to get rid of all the dust and sweat of the day. I had a sluice down up in the latrines early this morning. You should do it as well Sarah.' I retorted.

'I can't do that. With all these servants about. I've already had one, with my clothes on.'

'Sarah love. it's natural to them, just wrap yourself in one of those big clothes like a tablecloth, nobody will take any notice of you. C'mon on I show you how, then the tribe can do it.

'What about the rest of the outhouses then, don't you want to see them?'

' Oh well yes. But let's be quick about it.'

We completed the rounds, the last place was the stable where Jack went in and inspected the horse. The little Chico was still grooming it, he stopped what he was doing salaamed to Jack. His eyes wide open as he followed Jack inspecting his horse. He came around the front of the horse looked down at the Chico smiled murmured.

'Achchha.' A grin broke out on the Chico's face, he bowed again and carried on with the grooming. Leaving the stable Jack said.

'That Chico is called a Syce. He tends to all the horses needs and looks after the tackle. I think there is one more amongst them. I'll find out.' ...He motioned to the Bearer, pointed to the Syce... 'Two Bearer. Two.'

'Ji han Sahib Ji han do.' Jack said.

'Sarah yes there are two. Ji han means Yes. Ji nahm, means No, Do means two, remember that.' We returned to the veranda he called out to number One Ayah.

'Sahib Memsahib go nahana pani.' He made out he was pouring water over his head, pointed to the washhouse, then to my dress adding ... 'That Sarah means bath with water Okay.'

180

'Ji han Sahib. Achchha.'

She entered the Bungalow, whilst she was away, we sent the children to play with the Chico's. Arriving back with some large folded clothes, she beckoned us to follow her back to the washhouse. In her sing song voice she called out something, the Dhobi Wallah came out to open the door, she handed the clothes to us. We carried out our ablutions in private. I must say that the experience was very refreshing. Whenever I found it necessary to freshen up in this heat it became a daily routine. Changed into clean clothes, we left the confines of the washhouse returned to the veranda to sit down at the table. Jack ordered chai. I ordered the Ayah's to take over, get the children sluiced down in the washhouse. That chore became a game with them, from the sounds of the screams and shouts from their sluice down, there was more water thrown at each other than tipped over from the pans. When they finally emerged the Ayah's were soaking wet with their hands covering their mouths hiding their laughter. My tribe never refused bath times. The cook served a meal then to bed. My first and very eventful day in my new quarters over.

The next day we attended the hospital. The MO passed us fit, administered more jabs and in case of accidents, issued an emergency medical kit. Bill came over for an evening meal and explained the rudiments of India.

'Sarah like Elizabeth. You will become accustomed to doing nothing yourself, the servants do everything.'... He informed us, in his spare time was a keen gardener, had created the paradise of colour at the side of the bungalow....'Sarah out here, if you throw seeds on the ground with a drop of water they will take root and flower in no time...The chickens, besides eggs and eating, are a good alarm system when disturbed by Loose Wallahs.' (Thieves). After a pleasant evening, Bill returned back to the Mess.

After three days, all my bits and pieces of home comforts were in place, which pleased Jack and he assumed everything was all right. But it wasn't. Once the breakfast was over I had nothing to do. At the table on the veranda I would sit like a dummy, I would call for chai, it would arrive, I drank, looked out, for fear of snakes would not venture out, instead for hours pace up and down the veranda. The servants carried on as if I wasn't there, they would salaam say something to me, shrugging my shoulders would say either. 'Ji han or Achchha.' They would salaam go away. Jack would arrive back for lunch, talk awhile return to his duties, my tribe would sleep in the afternoon but not me, just a catnap on the veranda. Jack would arrive back home. We would sluice down followed by dinner then bed. A full day's activity, which continued day after day.

On the day after Elizabeth had left I was aware but unconcerned at what was going on around me. With nothing to do, my days became long and drawn out. I sat down got up paced up and down the veranda. I walked through every room, rearranged the furniture several times, but finished up the way it had been. My tribe were quite happy playing around the bungalow sometimes with the Chico's. The following week my tribe were to attend the army school, I dreaded the thought of being on my own. Yet, most of my time, sitting on the veranda perspiring or pacing up and down, thinking of nothing but home. On occasions I paused with my pacing to watch and observe the daily activity that went on. The arrivals of the milkman with pots of milk hung from a yoke, agreeing a price the Khansama, would approach the Bearer, the Bearer would approach me, ask.

'Memsahib. Bahut anna's Dudh'...pointing to the milkman.

I was clueless. Did not understand what he wanted. He went over to the Khansama, brought back a pan of milk, handed it to me holding out his other hand, muttered.

'Anna's Memsahib. Anna's.'

Then I understood money. It was the same with a greengrocer pushing a strange looking hand barrow, with fruit and vegetables in raffia baskets, he would visit the cookhouse. He and the cook would argue fiercely about the price, no doubt the normal practice, then the Bearer would approach me asking for money. Jack had left the housekeeping money in a special tin in our bedroom, which I went and fetched out, handed it to him. He opened it took out some Anna's, handed the money box back, returned to the waiting Khansama gave him the money. In turn he paid the milkman, the same palaver happened with the greengrocer. On occasions, an Oilman arrived done his business with the Mussaul. What a palaver that was however, the same ritual occurred with every Wallah that turned up. At the beginning I was not interested in what they were up too and thought: *Leave well alone. I would learn in time?*

I was terrified of the lizards which clung to the walls or ran across the ceiling catching flies. Jackie, tried to catch them but they were too quick for him. Watching Jackie's attempts made me understand they were there for a purpose, and would not harm us. Then there were the big black beetles that would run around the floor, using the walls as if they were the sides of a racetrack, those I believe were cockroaches they did not bother me. Crows would fly past to roost in the trees croaking noisily, a flight of long legged birds with long necks with big beaks would rise up from the river further away. The horrible looking Vultures hovering high in the sky, would swoop down land, then hop about with a strange gait, the mere thought of snakes made me shudder but I saw none. As the days went past. I gradually became use to them. The only familiar sounds of Blighty, were the infrequent shriek of a train's whistle, the sound of it's puffing as it clattered along in the distance. During the night, I lay awake thinking and listening to the tiny buzz of the mosquito's trying to get through the tiny holes in the netting, to bite and pass on malaria, for which we had to take a daily dose of some foul tasting liquid called, Quinine. That was the devil of a job to get my tribe to take it. Every night I went into the children's room and made sure the netting covered them. The Ayah's had done it, I wasn't even wanted there. I heard strange howling sounds they were not dogs.

The night-time seemed endless, until in the distance the duty Bugler blew Reveille to herald the start of another Army day. This would stir Jack he would be up, quietly moving around, I lay pretending to sleep, listening to his limited chat with the Bearer and Chowkidar (Night watchman) Later I found out from Jack that the Chowkidar always had a glass of chai to offer. I lay there wide-awake knowing much more secret activity was going on behind my back. I was not getting on very well with the servants, furthermore, did not understand what they wanted, somehow I had to learn the language. I got up, slipped on my dress, which had already been laid out, ablutions, then breakfast, saw my tribe off to school, that was that another day lazy lay ahead I sat there with my thoughts: *There was I, having never had servants to wait on me hand and foot. In the past it was I, the servant to sisters and brother, my employers, the Officers in the Army. Then I had inherited a full family of servants. It was alien to me.* These thoughts never went away and began to get on my nerves. I realised that the plain simple truth was, I was the person who employed them. The unexpected arrival of Bill on his horse broke my day's frantic activity.

'Good morning Sarah. Hope you don't mind I've just came to see how you were getting on?'

I was only to grateful to be interrupted from my inert activity.

'Good morning Bill. It's very thoughtful of you. Getting on well? Not good, I'm not used to this way of life, the natives scare me, I can't communicate with them, they are always enquiring to do something. I do not understand what they want. I just respond with a shrug of my shoulders.'

Obviously he saw my agitation and was concerned of my situation. Dismounting he said.

'Right Sarah. Leave this to me. I'll converse with them in their own language.'

He left me, sitting twisting my wedding ring like a demented soul, wondering what was going to happen. Bill returned.

'Don't worry Sarah you will be okay. I've just told them, do what the Memsahib Plant tells them to do, as Memsahib Burton had done. Just you tell them what you want. They can

182

understand more English than what you think they can, they will do it. Anyway apart from saying hello. I just came across to see the garden. How's it doing?'

'I don't know. As far as I can see from where I'm sitting, I suppose it's doing okay. I don't dare go out there because of the snakes.'

'Oh. Don't concern yourself too much about them. They will only strike if you disturb them, always have a stick handy and make a noise, they usually glide away. Come with me for a walk in the garden. I'll show you some of my special flowers.'...Uneasy I left the veranda, walked with him around the garden. 'There see those, Columbines and those there are Poppies.'...Having spent about half an hour talking about his garden he said...'Sorry Sarah, but I must get back to the lines.'

I was more than grateful for his little chat and his reassurance. Although still unsure about the snakes. He refused chai before he left. Back on the veranda I ordered it for myself and sat there mulling over our recent conversation. Jack arrived at mid-day, so I told him about Bill's visit and his chat with the servants.

'I'm sure you will overcome this fear of yours, to me they are more than capable of doing all the household chores. That's what they are paid for. Please don't worry about it.' His answer. I worried all night.

Next morning at the first sounds of Reveille. I was up with Jack to see what did go on. My excuse the Bugler woke me up. Before first light I padding about in the background. In the dim light of the oil lamp the Chowkidar with a blanket covering his shoulders, approached me salaamed handed me a glass of chai. His Pugri almost covered what I could see of his dark face, the rest was covered by a huge white beard, his engaging smile revealed a set of gleaming white teeth, salaamed walked back to sit down on his haunches next to the Bearer and sip chai. Jack was busy shaving by the light of the hurricane lamp, having finished used the cloth on his face. The sound of a horse snorting outside drew my attention to the steps, as the Syce arrived with Jack's horse. Taking the hurricane lamp Jack went down the steps and handed it to the Syce who carried it high, while Jack inspected his horse, a magnificent animal curried and groomed ready for the day's inspection, Jack muttered.

'Pukka.' Gained quiet response from the Syce.

'Teek hia Sahib.'

Jack came back up as the Bearer stood ready with Jacks jacket, Sam Browne, Tobie, pulled on his jacket buttoned up, then put on his Sam Browne buckled up, adjusted his jacket, he was ready fully dressed he came over and kissed me saying.

'Sarah I'll see you at lunch time.'

With that he went down the steps took the reins from the Syce mounted the horse rode quietly away. I was still in my nightgown with a shawl around my shoulders, there was no sign of the Chowkidar. I ordered.

'Chai Bearer. Chai'...

'Ji han Memsahib.Teek hia.' And so the cook arrived with the chai as he placed it on the table murmured.

'Salaam Alekum Memsahib.' I accordingly responded.

The dawn chorus of many birds singing their way into the daybreak heralded the dawn of a new day. Noticing the chattering of Magpies I thought: *They must have them out here too.* Sipping my chai watched the dark shape of the mountains in the far distance begin to lighten up by the rays of the rising sun, casting many shapeless shadows onto the mountains alongside. The unexpected arrival of the Dhobi Wallah carrying a bowl of water came up the steps onto the veranda, distracted my moment of solace. Normally he did this later after I had risen, with the usual salaaming he placed it on the table. Leaving the chai I stood up and took the bowl back

183

inside to our bedroom. Number one Ayah had already laid out my dress and clothing. Washed dressed I was prepared for the day. They all knew the Memsahib was awake.

Back outside on the veranda I stood watching the still rising sun, the long shadows had visibly become shorter, the dawn chorus of the birds had subsided, to be replaced by the sing song chatter of the Ayah's inside as they got my tribe up ready for their day at school. The cook brought me another chai. I sat down, sipping it slowly, made up my mind come hell or high water, today was the day I took over. I was going to be in charge. Finishing my chai, I got up and went back inside to sort out my tribe. I needn't have bothered the Ayah's had done it, they salaamed as I went in I responded.

'Achchha.' Jackie's first thoughts to start his day.

'Mum I'm hungry.'

'Okay. The cook will be serving it shortly hurry up.'

On my way out I clapped my hands and called out.

'Bearer. Breakfast.'

They followed me out and sat down at the table, just as the cook arrived with a couple of Chico's carrying their breakfast of flattened bread, milk, boiled eggs and a sweet rice dish. They all ate, drank with satisfaction. The Tonga's arrived, they climbed up with the Ayah's, with a wave they departed. The remnants of breakfast were cleared away, the Chico's returned armed with brushes entered the bungalow to carry out their chore, yet another chai was served. I drank this nectar to give me courage. Brushes appeared in the doorway as the Chico's clearing before them some remnants of the previous day's activity swept the veranda. My time had come. I stood up, went down the steps, quickly followed by the Bearer, walking with purpose, unannounced entered the cookhouse.

Inside, the Khansama, the Mussaul and two Chico's were horrified at my presence. The Khansama got up with a knife in his hand, his Pugri was orange in colour, he shorter and much younger than the Bearer, with a small black moustache, he salaamed. The Mussaul, wearing a clean white cloth around his waist was tucked up so they looked like short pantaloons, he was thin barefooted with a white sort of cap on his head. He the washer of pans and other things was the one to ensure everything was constantly washed and spotless. The two chico's stood near the fires with frowns across their foreheads. Addressing the Khansama, with much difficulty I explained what I wanted. The way things were cooked, the cleanliness that I was concerned about, which I need not have been. After their immediate surprise they settled down to carry on with their chores, as I took note of what was in the cookhouse.

A meat cleaver, sharp knives, copper pots, there was four fires alight, one of the Chico's was adding wood to keep them burning, whilst the other one blew through a hollow piece of wood to catch the new wood alight, the smoke from the fires billowed up into the wooden rafters then out through a hole in the roof, a large copper pot full of boiling water was sat on one of the fires, that I remembered was only for chai. The Khansama made some, passed a glass over to me. The heat generated by the fires within together with me sipping the chai made it very unpleasant. I perspired freely but I was not leaving. In the far corner on a large round flat stone a long round stone lay on top, had me wondered what that was for? I soon found out when the cook begun making dough, possibly making that flat bread? I had nothing to do, so, stayed there all morning just watching as they carried on preparing the lunch, the Chico's fetching and carrying as ordered. Constantly the cook would glance over at me shake his head mutter in Urdu, no doubt. *"At the madness of the new Memsahib."* When I saw the dinner was ready I left with the Bearer beside me walked back to the veranda sat down drenched in sweat.

When Jack and my tribe arrived back, lunch was served. He returned to the lines and my tribe were sent to rest. For me a return visits to the cookhouse to watch the preparation for the evening meal. Late in the afternoon Jack arrived back to find me, still in the cookhouse.

184

'Sarah, whatever are you doing?'

'Making myself useful. '

'That's their job not yours.'

'I know it's something I've got to do for myself.'

'C'mon back to the bungalow have some chai. Bearer. Chai. Veranda.'

I followed Jack out like a lost sheep, shading my eyes from the sun, sweat running out of every pore of my skin. We had chai. Jack murmured with concern.

'You're going doo-lally, with the sun Sarah. Let them do it.' I shrugged it off.

We had a sluice down, something I badly needed. Then the evening meal, children put to bed. Jack when we were sitting on the veranda raised the subject.

'Sarah what's this all about you doing the cooking? That's what I pay the cook for.'

'Jack I am not cooking. Only watching. Besides I have nothing to do and it worries me. So I've decided to learn all about their ways.' He roared with laughter.

'How are you going to do that by watching? There's other things besides cooking.' Having started on my quest I retorted.

'Other things? Those I do not know. But it is a start.'

'Your right as usual. How long are you going to stay in the cookhouse?'

'I don't know a couple of days.'

We discussed other things before retiring. Whether it was the heat of the cookhouse or, peace of mind. I slept well, was up the following morning with Jack.

A week later, after Bill had talked with the servants. He paid a visit to bid us farewell, We were eating lunch on the veranda when he rode up.

'Hello you two. I hear Jack's got you doing cookhouse fatigues now Sarah. What have you been up to then? It's all right Sarah I'm only joking.' I blushed as he mentioned my trips into the cookhouse I had to respond.

'No Bill. It's what you said that started me off. If I have to control them I have to know how they work. It's a simple as that. I cannot sit alone on this veranda forever and a day. That will drive me doo-lally. Besides the children are at school until the afternoon. So I made up my mind. Once I'm in charge then I'll be happy. You wait and see, then you'll both agree.'

They both nodded applauded me for doing it my way. That satisfied me. Before he left, Bill carried out his inspection said his goodbyes to his old band of servants, as we the spectators watched. The next day I was back in the cookhouse!

It was desperately hot, apart from a sudden downpour that chilled the air before it became a steam bath. In the cookhouse the heat was appalling, but I stuck it out. By the second week I had found out what the Khansama's name was. I took to saying.

'Good Morning Abdul...He would salaam bow deeply mutter...'Namaste Memsahib Plaan.' That I assumed was. '*Good morning*.' My visits to the cookhouse lasted two weeks. I took to taking a paper and pen in with me to write down the names of the vegetables and fruit I was familiar with. *"Alu."* (Potatoes) *"Gobhi."* (Cabbage) *"Matar."* (Peas) *"Palak."* (Spinach) *"Pyaz."* (Onions) *"Tomatur."* (Tomatoes) *"Sag."* (Lettuce). *"Lehsun"* (Garlic) *"Mirch* "(Chillies) --- Fruit: *"Seb."* (Apple) *"Kela."* (Banana) *"Nimbu."* (Lemon) *"Am."* (Mango). *"Aru"* (Peach). I watched as he made, *"Chapatti"* (Round flat bread) cooked very quickly in a dish with a little oil, turning them over to cook on the other sides, he made plenty of them. Naan Bread heated in an oven and Rotis plus other breads. *"Chawal"* (Rice) and *"Anda"* (Egg) he even demonstrated different ways of cooking them spoke the word, *"Ublahwa Anda"* (Boiled egg) a fried one was *"Anda frai"*. He took my hand with the Bearer walking behind, led me to the chicken coop to show me where the egg came from the *"Murgi"* (Chicken). That I laughed at, he not understanding I already knew laughed with me. The words I would try to learn them later in the evening time. I would ask Abdul how to say them? He was helpful would grin when I pronounced it wrong or, more so when

185

he didn't understand my accent. We progressed slowly before one scorching hot day, I all but fell out of the cookhouse. The Bearer shouted the Ayah's appeared, grabbed me, took me to the washhouse they stripped my soaking clothing dressed me with a sari, poured cooling water over me then dried and half carried me back to the bungalow then laid me down to rest. The four of them, clucked around me like mother hens. I had never been so cosseted in my life, like a fool I started to cry. They kept everyone away even the children, let me sleep for hours.

The next day I did not go into the cookhouse, instead after breakfast I sat down at the table on the veranda ordered chai, to relax and contemplate what I had achieved. Initially all the servants sought my advice or agreement, which I did not know what they were on about? Then after my past two weeks of madness, learning the limited words of Urdu, it appeared to have paid off, there was a subtle pleasing difference in their attitude. Between us we were then able to understand what was going to happen. Apart from breakfast and lunch (khana) in between times was spent doing absolutely nothing, yet in the afternoons I could spend time writing letters, however, they were limited. All in all, any day was not very active, potentially a life of idleness that I did not want, my visits to the cookhouse had proved useful but I could see no future in those. However, pleased with myself, began to think more of how I could spend my periods of idleness. Remembering Elizabeth's parting comment. "*On keeping up the ceremonies.*" Provided me with an idea: *Casting my mind back to the daily muster inspections we attended back at the Curragh camp. I could start my own inspection. Tomorrow was as good a day as any, furthermore was not prepared to tell Jack about my idea until I had established a routine.*

Next morning, after breakfast after my tribe had left for school. I put my Tobie on my head ordered the Bearer to follow me out to the cookhouse. I noticed him shake his head, no doubt thinking: *It was back to the cookhouse.* But I stayed put outside. I spoke waved my arm backwards and forwards.

'Bearer Jahldi Jahldi. Servants line up.' Quizzical he looked then understood clapping his hands shouted.

'Memsahib Plaan. Jahldi. Jahldi.'

Out they came from all various places. The Bearer waved them into a long line, they stood there, in much the same order as before, they wondering what was going on? I moved along to the end of the line where the Khansama Abdul was. I stood in front of him and bowed my head looked at him. 'Abdul.' he responded and smiled. 'Memsahib.' The next one the Dhobi Wallah. I bowed to him. 'Nam?' he smiled and responded. 'Haseem. Memsahib.' Then I heard the Bearer mutter.

Haseem Dhobi Wallah) - Abdul (Khansama) - Abdulah (The Bearer)

'Bahut Achchha Memsahib. Achchha.' I turned looked at him, he was beaming; his dark eyes were twinkling with appreciation. His Memsahib was inspecting her servants. This I found funny, back in camp Jack was inspecting his troops with me back at the quarters inspecting my little band of servants. With my Tobie perched on my head I stopped at the next one The Massuall. 'Nam?' he responded smiled 'Kaseem. Memsahib.' Walked along in front of the asking the same question they responded by which time I had forgotten their names, then came to the Ayahs. Number One. 'Nam?' 'Indu. Memsahib.' The next one Mary's. 'Nam.' 'Nannu. Memsahib.' Kathleen's. 'Rhuma. Memsahib.' Jackie's. 'Indri. Memsahib.' I think they liked the idea of my madness. When I had finished, knowing full well, there was no way I was going to remember all their names. However the Bearer. (Elizabeth had told me his name). Out of respect. I would never call him by his name. I nodded to the beaming Bearer.

'Achchha Bearer. Pukka.'

186

He clapped his hands for them to disperse, they went away giggling. A silly idea, but it eased my mind to think I had wasted another half-hour of my tedious day. But that was just the beginning. Once they understood just how I wanted things done we got on famously. I did regularly visit the cookhouse, where the Khansama showed me how to cook Curry. I'd never eaten curry before, found it very hot, nevertheless, found I enjoyed the taste together with all the condiments that went with the meal. Sliced apples, tomatoes, limes, bananas and coconut. The Khansama showed me the different spices and leaves, that went into making it. Speaking in broken English he stated their names, indicating with gestures and rolling eyes, which spice was good for the various parts of the body. Chilli, he would thump his chest, something to do with the heart. Ginger, pointing to the veins on the back of his hands, then following them up his arms around his body. I gathered good for the circulation. *"Lehun"* (Garlic). I discovered was the reason that their breath was so rancid. He showed me how he mixed them to make curries *"Garam"* was Hot *"Tanda"* was cold *"Pani* " (Water). *"Dudh"* (Milk). *"Gosht* " (Meat) He used coconut and bananas in his cooking. I always thought: *Something used only as fresh fruit.* He cooked different curries using meat, chicken, mutton and even egg. I became fascinated by the way he cooked and the quickness he produced the meals. I was much later to become a very good curry cook. It became clear to me out of my initial two-week period of madness, the respect they gave me and likewise me to them. Unrecognised at the time I had created something more important to me. I became active, instead of just being waited on hand and foot had something to do. The early morning inspection became a daily routine, without prompting from me, the Bearer had those all lined up ready for my inspection. Only when it rained was there was no inspection, however that was very very seldom.

Taking in Bill's suggestion, I became confident of going out into the garden, always aware the Bearer was behind me. I took out number One Ayah, got her to pick some flowers to decorate the house, much to the annoyance of the. *"Malee"* (Gardener) a wiry old fellow with a whispery white beard against the black colour of his skin, from years of exposure to the sun, he was always in bare feet with a long shirt that was miles too big for him, he carried a long stave no doubt to ward off snakes. His Pugri was extremely large with many yards of cloth wrapped around his head. He would rant and rave at this insult, it was his job to pick flowers for the Memsahib, and the Bearer muttering 'Kharab.' with other words that I enquired, what it was all about? Through our ways of communication I discovered that. *"Achchha"* was good and *"Kharab"* was bad. The Malee had no right to question the Memsahib's wish. We were finally getting somewhere. I decided to make amends and ordered the Malee to cut bunches of flowers for my table, that satisfied him. The Dhobi Wallah wasn't left out, I inspected his washhouse needless to say it was spotless, like the Khansama he was fully occupied every day, continually washing, drying soiled clothes more from sweat than dirt, he too was helped by a couple of Chico's, and the *"Bheestee"*, the Water carrier, who provided the endless pans of water to both the Dhobi and Khansama Wallahs, using a yoke to carry the water from a well a distance away from the Bungalow. I found the Dhobi Wallah was the happiest one at his work. Before he began his Dhobi-ing he removed his Pugri revealed a head of jet black hair tied in a knot on top of his head, pulling up the legs of his trousers, tied them into a sort of shorts whilst he threw pans of water over the clothing, before twisting the article into a long thin shape. Holding the garment in one hand swung it over his head, to beat it against the flat stone, keeping up a steady rhythm provided the familiar rhythmic slap as cloth hit stone before unravelling It, hand it over to one of the Chico's, to flatten the garment out and place stones on it to keep it taunt to dry in the sun. Jacks uniform would get the same treatment; however, he would crease and starch both tunic and jodhpurs before laying a board on top with stone weights, no such thing as a flat iron. I never understood how our clothing stood up to his merciless beating, but it was always crisp and spotlessly clean with no creases, yet I was forever sewing on a new button in place of the half broken one. I visited the stables, but I really left that to Jack to deal with his Syce's but it too was always just so.

We had been there a month and I had not ventured outside the confines of the Bungalow, only to visit the MO. whilst eating the evening meal I said to Jack.

'Elizabeth said they went to mass every Sunday at the Church close to the sergeants mess, can you find out the times of mass, I want to go next Sunday.' I think he was pleased that I was finally attempting to venture out.

'Yes I'll do that tomorrow. It's not far to walk.'

At lunchtime he told me the times. On Sunday after breakfast. Jack ordered a Tonga to take us there. We all climbed aboard started off. To my surprise all the servants walked behind the Tonga. This was too embarrassing, they being of a different faith, it had never crossed my mind to ask them however, they were all grouped together hurrying to keep up with the sedate pace of the Tonga. After Mass the priest standing outside welcomed us, thanked us for attending, When Jack introduced me to some other wifes, two prevailing smells became evident, mothballs, which strength would catch your throat making your eyes water, the other was lavender water or, coconut oil, however one did not stay too long in conversation, whilst over in the shade of a large tree stood all the servants patiently waiting. I was so pleased with their effort I said.

'Jack let the Tonga go. We can all walk back to the bungalow.' He grinned.

'Okay you're in charge my girl.'

We slowly walked back to the bungalow in an orderly fashion, with the servants behind. Every Sunday after that first church outing, we were accompanied by the servants dressed up in their best whites, coloured cummerbunds and Pugri's, the Ayah's in their lovely coloured saris. We hired two Tonga's, one for us, one for the Ayah's. It was Mary who said she wanted to walk with the servants, which was quickly followed by Kathleen and Jackie. I threatened my tribe with extinction if they did not behave themselves properly like the servants. So she walked alongside the Bearer with the rest following, all appeared to love this Sunday outing as a great treat. Rain or sunshine it had to be done. When it rained the servants would hold old black umbrellas above our heads. Without being aware of it. I discovered that with all these new events I had formed my servants into a unit to run the house as I wanted it.

During our first four weeks in Nowshera, four of the Batteries young soldiers had died with fever, with another one in Peshawar including one of the Sergeants little boys. Jackie became ill with sand-fly fever. He was very bad, I was up with him night and day, keeping him cool, administering medicine the MO had prescribed, it took a while before he got better. Then I discovered I was pregnant, making me wonder how will the next nine months affect me in the dreadful heat of India,? But took solace in the fact that I had just survived seven weeks and could congratulate myself on not having done too badly so far. I just had to get on and continue my daily routine. One morning I was in the washhouse explaining what I wanted washing, suddenly I came over very faint slumped onto the stone floor. Before blacking out I vaguely heard the Dhobi Wallah scream out.

'MEMSAHIB.' When I came too the Bearer and Ayah's were leaning over me.

'Memsahib Kharab.' I tried to raise myself up but he gently pressed down on my shoulders.

'Kharab Memsahib. Sahib. Jahldi. Jahldi. Sahib.'

He said something to number One Ayah then ran off , whilst number One dampened my forehead with a wet cloth the other Ayah's surrounded me, jabbering away I heard her saying Memsahib many times. Unable to understand, I just lay there constantly being attended to, I gave up, lay inert until Jack arrived on the scene. He knelt down beside me.

'Sarah. What on earth has happened?'

'I don't know? I just came over faint, they won't let me up. You get me up.' Lifting me in his arms, carried me into the bungalow, laid me on the bed.

'Sarah. I'll get the MO to come and check you over.' Calling out loud.

'BEARER. JAHLDI. M.O. FOR MEMSAHIB.'

The Ayah's were constantly dampening my forehead, clucking like a lot of hens with their concern. The Khansama pressed a drink of water to my lips. It seemed like everyone was in the bedroom. The MO duly arrived, ordered everyone out, checked me over.

'Mrs Plant, stay in bed for a few days. You need rest, possibly in your condition. Heat exhaustion.' Then left. Jack came in.

'Right Sarah. Bed for you, plenty of rest. No more of your malarkeys. Doctor's orders. I've got to go now. I'll be back at lunchtime. No excuses from you. Bed.'

I was confined to bed, when the children arrived home from school, they began running from room to room playing, screaming and shouting. My poor head was splitting with a headache, it was better to get up than to stay in bed, so I got up staggered to the veranda and sat down, there to survey the beauty of the garden, which helped me to pull myself together. It was times like this when I wished Jack would stay at home. Whenever the children or I were ill, he refused saying. "He was more trouble than he was worth in the house." Which he was, he did not have the patience or know-how to organise the household. He was a good husband and father to the children also extremely kind, but his job was the Army and a wonderful soldier too. I loved him dearly, likewise in his eyes. I was a soldier as well but my job was the home front. However within two days I was back carrying out my daily routine, much to the delight of the servants.

Apart from the Sunday social chats at church any opportunity of socialising I avoided like the plague, yes there were opportunities for me to go to the Sergeant's mess or other functions and although the servants were trustworthy, I was scared and reluctant to be away from my own household. My motto was: where I go the children go. Instead content to be in our own company, relying on infrequent visits from Jack, due to his army routine. After the mornings activities I would take solace in sitting alone sipping chai, listening to the droning of big bumble bees amongst the flowers, the crickets busily sawing away, the birds singing and the shriek of a Mynah bird not un-similar to that of a blackbird, the calls of other bird's cry of Kooh Kooh or another with a metallic note, all new to me. The panoramic view across the river In the far distance, provided a picture of the foothills covered with dark green trees in the background, their slopes formed into mountains, high above their peaks covered white in snow gleamed in the sunlight, whilst puffs of woolly clouds lazily drifted over, casting a dark shadow on the slopes below. Idyllic, but if only if I were back home in Blighty. At lunchtime my period of solace shattered and welcomed by the arrival of my tribe home from school, then after lunch, a short period of solace maybe with a cat nap ended by the arousal of my tribe. It was time for play.

However, one Sunday after we had returned from Mass, Jack decided to take us to the Sudder Bazaar He ordered a Tonga, we set off and trundled past the camp, the hospital, passing many Tonga's carrying army families out for a Sunday jaunt before lunchtime, quite a few hailed Jack as we trundled along the dusty, rutted pot holed road bumped over the railway tracks, passing other strange looking carts, the driver's sat inside a large raffia hooped cover pulled by two white hump backed cows, their curved horns painted in different colours including around their eyes. We crossed over a bridge spanning the fast flowing white waters of a river that Jack informed me.

'That's part of the river Lundai. It starts in the moutains of Afghanistan, runs east down through the Khyber Pass towards Rawalpindi, where it joins the river Indus, to continue flowing down to the Arabian sea , which must be a thousand miles away. I bet you didn't know know, most Indian rivers are sacred.'... I didn't. To me they were just flowing water. Arriving at the Bazaar we clambered down, entering into the tiny streets crawling with people of all creeds, mainly men with large beards dressed in various styles of tribal costumes, some wearing a flat woollen hat (Pakol) others with coloured cotton Pugri's like a twisted rope wound about their heads. What women I did see, were covered from head to feet in a black gown, a black veil hid their face with only slits for eyeholes. I thought: *What a way to live.* The first thing I noticed was the different smells. Pungent spices, sweetness of fruits, fragrance of incense, coconut oil, lavender, introduced by the English ladies, who splashed gallons all over ones person, those were the smells of India. Amongst the vegetables on sale I recognised Banana's, Coconut's, Lime's Apples, Mango's, and Papaya, the latter two the Khansama had introduced me to, they were very refreshing, tasty but there were other vegetables and fruits I did not recognise, there were shops selling a multitude of different cloths stacked high to the roof, which gave me an idea, I could buy some to make clothes for my tribe. I suggested to Jack I wanted to buy some. I chose some white cloth, the wallah measured it out to my hand signals then added a few more yards, I bought cotton thread as well. Jack haggled with him, before he handed over a few Anna's, a very cheap purchase. I was happy then I had something to occupy my idle hours. The Bearer carried it for us. We saw Indian pans, pottery and best thing of all my brass. We stood to watch a couple of the men beating sections of brass with hammers, as they made tables and little ashtrays. It was fascinating to watch their workmanship. Sat on their haunches sipping chai, argueing amongst themselves was a group of tribesmen surrounding a Chai Wallah. Having finished our tour, I was more than happy to get back outside into the Tonga and return back to the safety of our bungalow.

I had not received any letters for nearly twelve weeks, although each week I wrote home to Mother and Eilish. until one lunchtime, Jack came riding up on his horse waving letters in his hand shouting. 'MAIL'S ARRIVED FOR YOU SARAH.'

Jumping down from his horse, bounded up the steps handed them to me. Excited, eagerly took them questioned.

Eilish   'Why did they take so long?'

'C'mon Sarah, look at the time it took us to get here it, five weeks. You sent your first letter a few days later, which took the same time to reach Blighty, their return letter would take another five weeks. So twelve weeks is about right, you might get your next mail in a months time.' He provided a detailed reply. I was not interested just murmured.

'Uhm the boat trip.'

I quickly looked at the writing, two were from Mother the other from Eilish. Lunch was served but I carried on opening the first letter from Mother, it was full of the "cold weather, blizzards in London" passing it across to Jack, I opened the one from Eilish enclosed was a photo, I looked at her features as pangs of homesickness had me welling up before I started to read her words. Again full of the weather her job, . "Don't tell Mother?" she had met a nice young man, I gathered she did not want me to mention it in my letters. Mothers second one mostly full about the constant chattering of Dolly Thomas, at the end of the letter a P.S. "Women were now allowed to vote when twenty-one, with her own comment. We four sisters must have helped, by volunteering for the army." We read the letters making comments to each other taking longer than usual over lunch. After the tribe were asleep, I sat with a glass of chai to re-read them three times, although I had sent one the previous day. I wrote another letter about their receipt nevertheless, happy with the realisation, lines of communication had been restored.

We had been in Nowshera about three and a half months. One morning, with the cloth we had purchased in the Sudder Baazar, began making clothes for my tribe. Very aware that I had an audience watching what I was doing. The sighs and clicking of tongues from the watching Ayers was amusing to me, as I measured items of their clothing, rolled out the white cloth allowing extra for loose fitting dresses shirts and shorts for Jackie, marked out each one, cutting them accordingly to size, then sew them up on my Singer sewing machine on the veranda table. I

190

was in the bedroom sorting out some dresses, I was making, when the Bearer came into me. – pointing to the veranda waving his hand spoke.

'Memsahib ana, Missy Coolie Memsahib veranda ana.'

I got up and followed him out thinking: *What does a Coolie Memsahib want with me? I don't want to hire any-more Ayah's I've got too many already.* Instead got a surprise to see stood on the veranda the so called Coolie Memsahib. Was the school teacher Miss Tait, wearing a long loose fitting white frock with her Tobie firmly placed on her head she spoke with firmness.

'Mrs Plant. I've come to talk to you about Mary.'

I thought: *God what has she been up to now?"* Quickly sizing up the situation, I asked.

'Would you care for lemon water while we talk?' Nodding curtly.

'Thank you that would be pleasant. 'I ordered.

'Bearer. Nimbu pani.'

'Ji han memsahib.'

We sat down at the table to begin our conversation...'Yes. What's up with Mary?'...Lemon Pani was served....'I don't know. But it's worth a try'...taking a sip...'Thank you this is most refreshing. You know we have a rest period, so that the children can sleep between classes.'...'Yes.' [*When I had visited the school, I had noticed there was a canvas covered lean too, underneath were some Charpoy's (rope beds)*]....'Well, when we break for the rest period with the children settled and asleep, Mary being the live wire that she is, can't sleep herself so she decides if she is awake, everyone else has to be. She gets Kathleen and Jackie up then the three of them go round tipping the cots over. I've scolded her on several occasions but too no avail she still does it when I'm not around. Can you get her father to speak with her please? Otherwise we won't allow her into the school.'...I thought: *Well that was straight to the point. But what could I do I'm not there in charge.* With a hint of exasperation I answered.

'I'll see what I can do.' We talked small talk until she was ready to leave.

'Thank you very much Mrs. Plant. I must say Mary is always up to something. She must be a handful for you.'... Little did she know the devilment Mary did get up to, with true honesty I replied.... 'Well miss Tait I can only try to keep up with her antics. I can't watch her twenty-four hours a day.'

When Mary arrived back from school. I gave her a good telling off and got her to promise me she wouldn't do it ever again.

'Yes mum.' She promised, but with that grin again.

Another day, I was on the veranda, busy at the machine making a dress, when I heard the sound of children crying, looking up saw about five Indian children walking towards the bungalow, as they came up the veranda steps noted that they were all little girls, with tears streaming down their brown faces presenting little slates in front of them they shuffled up to me. I did not know what they wanted? The Bearer spoke with them, whilst they mumbled away through their tears, he turning to me tried to explain their problem.

'Memsahib. Missy baba Mary. Kharab.' He took hold of one of the slates, imitated writing with his hand, then imitated rubbing out said...'Memsahib. Coolie.'.. I understood it was to do with school yet still unsure what it was all about, but. "Mary Kharab." What has she been up to? I decided to give them a quarter of an Anna each. That would shut them up. However this occurred the following day and throughout the week. Every day they would turn up crying their hearts out, the Bearer took no notice just smiled. I became suspicious. Were they beggars? So decided to watch what did go on. By Monday I had forgotten all about it. Wailing Indian children shattered the stillness of the afternoon, again the same procedure. Enough was enough tomorrow was the day.

The next afternoon, as usual I carried on making dresses. At their appropriate school leaving time, I saw the little girls on their way home, their slates balanced on their heads. Lying in wait behind a small group of trees I spotted my tribe. With caution the Indian girls approached the clump of trees, then veered away. That's when my tribe pounced. Kathleen and Jackie snatched the slates, passed them to Mary, who spat on them rubbing them clean. It must have been the Indian children's homework. I watched in awe, as Mary handed the slates back to Jackie, inturn he handed them out, then they ran off to hide. Mary the clever one had organised the other two. Then I understood what all the commotion was about. Once again the wailing party arrived at the veranda steps. I paid the dues. Called for the Ayah's, sent them out to find and bring back my tribe. The Ayah's arrived back, herding along the lost sheep. I stood them on the veranda in front of me. I noticed the Bearer move behind the Ayah's to watch, heard him mutter. 'Missy baba Mary. Kharab.' He was not pleased, neither was I taking notice of his remark. I had to make a show of firmness with my actions.

'Mary. I have watch what you three did to those little Indian children's slates. What have you got to say for yourself?'...silence reined...no comment...'Well'... More silence...'MARY.'...'It was only a game nothing else, we didn't do any harm.' Jackie giggled,so did Kathleen, a smirk appeared on Mary's face. I shouted ordered.

'OH SO YOU ALL THINK ITS SO FUNNY DO YOU? RIGHT OFF TO BED. NO TEA. NO IFS OR BUTS. AYAH'S JAHLDI. MISSY BABA'S DHONA THEN BED. NOW.'

I saw a faint smile appear on the Bearers face, but could not be sure?...Obeying, the Ayah's hung their heads. It was early afternoon, which meant the Ayah's had to stay with them as well... 'Go on. Off you go. I'll speak with your Father about your little game. You won't do that again that's for sure.'... They left the veranda, number One Ayah made a sucking sound with her teeth. "Memsahib was wise." That was the last I saw of them that day. When Jack arrived back he enquired about the silence of the bungalow. I retorted.

'Bed.' Then I told him the full story. All he did was laugh. At least once a week he used to take them horse riding up the lines, the Mule handlers would allow them to ride on the ammunition pack mules, they loved those rides and it took them away from causing trouble around the bungalow. Yet on another day sat at peace taking chai on the veranda, when all hell broke loose from behind the bungalow. Quickly fearing the worst stood up, called the bearer to follow me down the steps towards the rear. Where we were met by the sight of an ensemble of my tribe, the Ayahs, servants and Chico's, all gathered around an old disused lavatory, it's open door hanging by one hinge, a few of the servants were shouting as they heaved at something, whilst the Dhobi Wallah grasped hold of a long tail. Then I saw what it was, the rear end of a donkey. In amongst the Chico's my tribe were stood shouting encouragement to the heaving servants, all I'm sure swearing shouting in Urdu, along with the echoed braying of the unfortunate Donkeys, from inside the lavatory, obviously trapped it desperately trying to reverse out, with the servants trying to help by pulling it out. The Ayahs unable to help stood watching and I'm sure laughing with my tribe who thought this was extremely funny. The Bearer and I stood watching the pandemonium in front of us. The Khansama seeing us pointing at my three shouted.

'MISSY BABA MARY, MISSY BABA KATHLEEN.' I lunged at Mary grabbed hold of her.

'How did that get in there? Where did it come from?' She explained.

'We brought it back from the Bazaar. It was running loose, so we decided bring it back to keep it in the shed then we could take rides on it. We pushed it in there and tried to shut the door. Now it can't get out. It's swollen up.' Looking back at the rear end of the Donkey I could see its extended belly, I shouted.

'GO AND GET YOUR FATHER QUICKLY. I'LL SORT YOU OUT LATER.'

I stood there watching as the efforts of the servants continued until later Jack rode up with Mary sat behind him. He swung her down before jumping off, he strode towards the Donkey, stopped, with hands on his hips stood surveying the scene before him. With a big grin all over his face he enquired.

192

'What's going on here Sarah?'...He already knew, Mary had told him.

The servants stood back, as he walked closer to inspect the donkey....'Well Sarah. like you It's pregnant. She's in foal and stuck fast. To release her without causing any damage, we'll have to knock the walls down. Leave it. I'll go back for some help.'... I cried out....'Oh my God Jack.'... He swung back onto his horse rode back to the lines. As the rest of the audience just stood gaping at the Donkey's rear, its tail swishing to and fro in anger in its confined state, its echoed braying still continued. Ten minutes later, Jack arrived with a posse of three of his gunners, big hammers slung over their shoulders. Sitting astride their horses looking at the strange sight before them, seeing the funny side, they all roared with laughter. Jack shouted.

'C'mon you three. Let's get this poor thing out of there.'

Jumping down they carefully began to knock the walls down until the donkey was surrounded by a big pile of debris, she with her rather distended belly stood her ground. Jack ordered.

'Bearer bahut bahut pani Jahldi Jahldi'.

Indicating to give the donkey a drink and plenty of water to sluice it down. I ordered chai for the soldiers before they departed back to the lines. Half an hour later, the Donkey was able to walk groggily away, none the worse for her inflicted trouble. They were all in it together. Mary got a strapping, as did Kathleen and Jackie then sent to bed screaming the place down. It was all quiet when Jack arrived back all he said to me about the incident was.

'Sarah it is time I taught the children how to ride properly and to care for horses.'

Jack hired three donkeys he stabled them up the lines. On Saturday and Sunday at five a.m, he took the children together with two Syce's and three Chico's, to the stables. I told the Bearer that the Ayah's would stay behind. Jack explained to me, he taught them without saddles only quilted blankets, to ride the donkeys around in the cantonment (enclosure) he showed them how to harness feed, currie and stable them properly. It was all done for a good purpose.

Progressively, I was showing my pregnancy. All the time number One Ayah fussed and clucked over me. Gentle saying. 'Memsahib ummid se acchacha.' (pregnant) I could do practically nothing for myself, at the least opportunity she held onto my arm. One evening, we were sitting on the veranda taken chai. Jack said to me.

'Sarah. Today's company orders stated. You're on the move again.'

After four and a half months in this bungalow. I'm just getting acclimatised to this place and in he walks as bold as brass and tells me this. I retorted.

'No Jack. Not again.'

'No Sarah. It's not that bad. You're only going up to the hills for a rest period. Away from the heat of the plains. Now it's your turn to spend time up there along with some of the other married families of the Brigade. Indignantly asked.

'Where is it?'

'A place called Khanspur up in the foothills. We leave Monday morning.'

'Monday morning! How long will we be up there?'

'Oh about three months or so. '

'Three months don't you know I'm preganant? What about the servants?'

'I do know that you will be all right, You can take them with you. Mind you not all, some will stay behind to look after the bungalow. Besides I won't be up there. I have to stay behind.'

'Oh God. That mean's I'll be on my own again. You can't do this to me Jack.'

'Sarah don't start getting worried now. You'll have the other families around you up there. It will be great and with you in your condition the temperature will be good for you?'

I certainly was not happy at the prospect. Pregnant, about to start a journey to God knows where? With only four days-notice, typical. He had said it would be cool, so I sorted out the warmest clothes. Decided which servants should stay behind with Jack. I spent the next days worrying about the forthcoming trip. On the Saturday Jack arrived home with four letters.

'Mails arrived Sarah. Now you'll have something to read and write back.'

'What about the mail up there, will we receive any?'

'Don't worry about that, up there are several Army camps and a Hospital, the mail gets delivered to them regularly.'

From the time we told the tribe after school on the Friday, they were going on a holiday up into the Hills, they had done nothing but run around like a bunch of wild Indians. On Sunday we all went to mass, that night we were all packed up and ready for the early Monday morning start. How we settled them down on the Sunday night, I just don't know. I was exhausted as I'm sure they were.

CHAPTER THREE
THE MURREE HILLS - KHANSPUR.

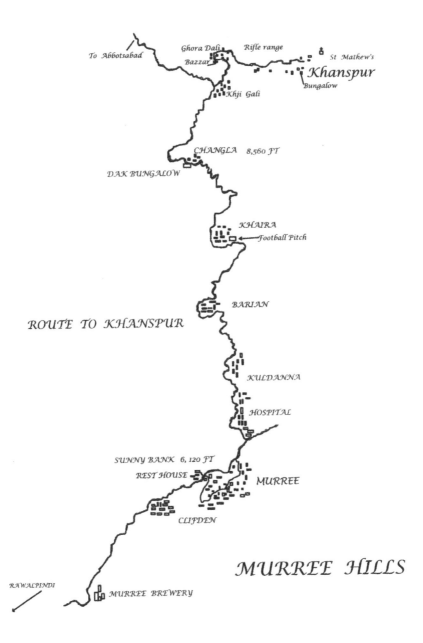

To Abbotsabad

Ghora Dali Rifle range

Bazzar

St Mathew's

Khanspur

Bungalow

Khji Gali

CHANGLA 8,560 FT

DAK BUNGALOW

KHAIRA

Football Pitch

BARIAN

ROUTE TO KHANSPUR

KULDANNA

HOSPITAL

SUNNY BANK 6, 120 FT

REST HOUSE

MURREE

CLIFDEN

MURREE HILLS

RAWALPINDI

MURREE BREWERY

Monday morning before the crack of dawn we were ready. I noticed waiting in the compound besides the Tonga's, in the light of a hurricane lamp, the Bearer along with other

195

servants had blankets covering their shoulders, I assumed it was to keep them warm in the morning chill. We climbed into one of the Tonga's with the Ayah's in the other, the rest of the servants walked alongside uttered quiet cries of Khuda hafiz (Goodbye), as we set off on the first part of the journey to the hills. Dawn was just breaking when we arrived at the station, where other families, their servants had gathered. Polite greetings were exchanged; there was no one I knew. Half an hour late the train from Peshawar arrived, even at that unearthly hour, it was quite full of people, a mad scramble began to get on the train and occupy some form of seating. At least the army families were lucky, theirs were reserved. Then with a blasting shriek of the whistle we were off.

I was sure that the mess that littered the floor was the very same as we had left it, but how could that be? However, this was different. A trip of only few hours to Rawalpindi, an uneventful trip although I did notice different varieties of trees covered in blossom, pinks, white,some deep red. Well into the journey Jack brought my attention to a huge impressive fortress we were passing, I had not noticed it on our inward journey. Its battlements went down into the depths of a gorge right to the edge of a river.

'That's Attock fort, the river is the Indus, this flows all the way down from the Himalayas, the other river I told you about at Nowshera, flows into it.'

'Not much of a river there Jack, looks more like a stream?'

'No. Maybe not at this moment. But after the Monsoon seasons, the waters turn into a raging torrent. It's the same with all the rivers from the hills.' I asked.

'Who built the railway then?'

'Well I did briefly mention it when were in Bombay at Victoria Station. Years ago the British began building the Indian railway, roughly at the same time as we started ours, amongst the many new ideas we brought too them. Its one thing the Indians can be grateful for.'

With idle conversation we continued our journey until the train pulled into Rawalpindi, stopping with a shudder, we clambered down onto the dirt platform. Jack left us to talk with an Officer. He returned to say.

'Right Sarah I have my orders I'm in charge of the party.' I grabbed hold of Mary and said.

'Mary you're in charge of Kathleen, Jackie and the Ayahs. So you stick to them and I'll stick to you.' It was one way of keeping her out of mischief as the servants gathered around us. Orders were being barked out. 'Please take your luggage,children, servants and form up alongside the transport, lined up by the railway track.'

In the searing heat, we followed other families towards the long line of Tonga's, at the rear was an assortment of bullock carts for the luggage and servants along side them was a group of mounted soldiers, I assumed they were from the nearby army camp at Rawalpindi each one held the reins of spare horses. Jack along with a number of soldiers, joined the mounted group. I noticed Jack patting a beautiful white horse, taking hold of its reins he quickly mounted it, the other sergeants and troopers mounted their horses. They gradually moved along the line of transport organising everyone on to the Tonga's. Our little group came to a halt near the front of the line of Tongas Jack riding up towards us called out.

'Sarah follow me right up to the first Tonga's.'

Following Jacks instruction we walked further along the dirt road up to the first Tonga, we clambered up on to it, when we were all settled, .Jack swung his horse around cantered off to the rear. Just then from behind us the train's whistle shrieked as it began its onward journey. I heard Jack shouting out orders.

'MOUNTED ESCORT PARTY. TAKE POST BE READY.'

The other sergeants and soldiers moved their horses into positions alongside the convoy, a Sergeant came riding up towards us to stop beside us. I heard Jack shouting to proceed. The sergeant ordered the driver. 'Jao Jahldi.' We were on our way up the hills, to a place called

196

Murree. Moving slowly down the dirt road, the sergeant indicated to our driver to ' 'Jao dahina.' He turned the horse off to our right. "The road to Murree". We went through another Army garrison town called Islamabad. Our progress was very slow due to the bullock carts at the rear. Trundling onwards through a huge park called "Shakespeare Park" with a large lake in the centre, some officers were playing Polo on the *"Mydam"* (Field). Leaving there we entered flat gorse land as the hills in the distance became closer, then the inevitable climb. Onwards and upwards the dirt road was very rutted with bumps and ridges, so it was quite a slow lurching bumpy ride much to the delight of my tribe. Jack came along side to give each of them a ride astride his horse's neck. The dust created by the cavalcade of carts in front, made those behind, cover their faces with handkerchiefs or scarves. At a place called Ghora Gali, we stopped for lunch before continuing upwards with the hillsides covered with trees and gorse, there was little shae from the sun which beat down relentlessly on our exposed skin. although a slight breeze which cooled us down. Jack came along side to inform me.

'Sarah. That building on the right is the Murree Brewery. Murree is about three miles further up where we will stay overnight.'

Slowly we continued upward. Now and again we caught sight of bungalows partly hidden by trees, then a cluster of them. Until just below us, through the gaps in the trees we sighted Murree. The Sergeant ordered our driver. 'Jao bayen.' The driver pulled the horse reins to the left and continued on through some sort of a small Bazaar, by which time it was late afternoon the sun had disappeared behind the hills, it aso had become decidedly chilly, eventually we stopped outside the Army Rest House. Clambering down off the Tonga was a delight to stretch our legs. Jack rode up dismounted handing the reins to a Syce before saying.

'Sarah c'mon, I'll take you inside where you can sit down have chai. A couple of the Ladies, farther down the line have been taken sick. I have to organise some medication for them, so I won't be long.'

He took us in to be greeted by the QM. (Quarter Master) in charge. I overheard them briefly discuss the matter about the sick ladies. The QM. Barked out some orders to other soldiers, they left with Jack. A welcome brew of chai was served. A little later the QM approached me.

'Mrs Plant would you follow me with your children please.' We got up followed him along a corridor, he conversing…'it's not much but it's only for your overnight stay. Refreshments will be provided at eighteen hours. Nothing to write home about. But it will be nourishing, Mrs Plant, these two rooms please. I'll speak to you later alright.' He left us.

Laid on the floor was four coir biscuits to make up a bed, apart from that the two rooms were empty and there was only one blanket on each bed? Nobody had informed us to bring blankets, besides if, they had it was impossible to get them from our luggage. I selected one room for my tribe leaving them to run around, Jack and I would sleep in the other. I found out later the other families were provided with the same accommodation. All the servants were sent to sleep around the back of this hostel. Jack came clumping back along the corridor entered with a glass of chai ,questioned

'How are you feeling Sarah?'

'Not very well I'm afraid. There's only one blanket each and it will become colder I'm sure'.

'Um'…He was stumped….'We'll sort something out don't worry.'…His answer to everything…. 'I've sorted out the ladies they were just sick due to the days travelling up into the hills alog with the drop in temperature. They appear to be okay.' Another problem solved.

With nothing better to do, my tribe together with the Chico's were now racing backwards and forwards from one room to the next. Looking through the window everywhere outside was in shadow, whereas still bathed in the setting sunlight, the opposite side shone bright with the hill tops covered in snow. Jack murmured.

'Quite a sight eh Sarah?' Shivering in the chill air I replied.

'Yes quite a sight. What about more blankets for the night and some food?'

'Yes. Okay food first. It's on the go outside.'

Jack rounded up the tribe along with the Chico's we went outside where a small canteen was laid ready to serve the food. A queue had already formed, the food of thick spicy soup with wads of Naan, was quickly served along with Chai fresh fruit to follow and plenty of it. As the QM had mentioned. 'Fit for the purpose.' The freshness in the air together with the day's arduous journey left me and I'm sure the children very sleepy. Jack had acquired only one more blanket, so we had to do with what we had not much. Jack went outside brought in two of the Ayah's, who came in with their blankets to stay in the room with the tribe, it was then I realised why they all carried blankets, they had been up the hills before knew of the cold. We settled the children down covered them up with one of the blankets and our coats, they were exhausted and were fast asleep in no time,

'C'mon Sarah, let's go and speak with the QM and find out about Murree and this place called Khanspur?' QM Baxter was quiet a nice man, small thin faced and very bronzed? As he related He had only been posted up there the week before from the Rawalpindi Garrison, he was only getting to know Murree.

'You are the first group of families I have had to look after? Murree is about six thousand feet above sea level. It was built about seventy years ago as a Hill Station for army personnel and their families. Other Hill Stations had been built about the same time, like Simla. I've been there; it's very quiet and can get very cold of a nighttime. Sorry about the blankets, not had time to sort out the winter stores requisitions. I am sorry. I cannot tell you much about Khanspur have not been there but its the Galis area, maybe another two thousand feet above Murree. It's another twenty miles further up. It is the last hill resort in the area furthermore, at least another two days travel. I've been told a lovely area but full of wild animals?'... I sat there yawning, this talk was going over my head. I was so tired.... 'You should go to bed Mrs Plant. The air up here makes you very tired.'

Jack excused us. The Hostel was silent; all were asleep as we crept in to see our tribe fast asleep, with the two Ayah's wrapped in their blankets curled up on the end of the mattress. Jack pulled the covers over our three. In our room we both cuddled together covered by one blanket, it was cold, unable to sleep, catnaps were the best we could achieve. After several hours we got up, wrapping the blanket around us, we spent the early hours, quietly walking up and down in the corridor. The sound of birds twittering outside was a sure sign dawn was breaking. I was never as pleased as I was on that occasion to be wide awake. The rising sun brought forth a blaze of orange, which rapidly changed white. We gazed out of the window at a magnificent picture. As the sun slowly rose, illuminating the brilliance of the snow caps of the whole western range of the Himanchal Pradesh. Its glorious green slopes, streaked with silver where rivers cascaded down into exotic valleys far below us. We warmed to the glory of the dawn, decided to rouse the children from their sleep, to enjoy this magnificent sight. All stood looking, my tribe unsure of why they had been disturbed, gazing through sleepy eyes and stifled yawns totally unaware of what they were looking at. We stood awhile as we shivered then quickly got the children washed and ready. We left the rooms returned to the reception room where chai was being served. As Jack was not travelling with us, he left to get his troops ready for their downward journey. A little later he returned said everything was prepared, ready to leave. Outside the Syce's arrived with their horses. I said my sad goodbye to Jack. Mounting his horse he ordered the two separate troops to mount, one to return back down whilst the other with two Sergeants along with a number of soldiers were to remain with the cavalcade.

With a final wave, Jack along with his troop set off back down the track. I myself was not feeling too good, without my Jack I was very alone in a strange world, going somewhere into the unknown. As I stood on the veranda of the Hostel, I could not help myself, unashamedly had a good cry, with the back of my hand I wiped the tears from my eyes. The cold air of the early morning brushed the wetness of my cheeks physically made me shiver. My tribe were gathered around me, with Jackie clinging to my leg, we watched the retreating figure of Jack and the troops disappear from view. Out in the sunlight. our servants stood huddled in a group their blankets covering their heads, visibly they shivering with the cold, their exhaled breath became wisps of white vaporous cloud, as they quietly talked amongst themselves. Neatly piled beside them was our luggage. Looking towards us, the Bearer extracted himself from their midst purposely walked towards the veranda. Salaamed. Pointed to the sun said.

'Memsahib. Garam Memsahib Jahldi'...muttered something else in Urdu...'Memsahib Baba's handa?'

Pulling the blanket tightly around his shoulders. I understood what he was trying to say. The Baba's were cold. To keep warm stand out in the sunlight like them. There's sense for you. I ushered them off the veranda, down into the open sunlight to warm them up. We joined the servants to accompany them shivering with the cold, but at least the heat from the sun was warming. Taking notice of our example, more families moved out of the shaded area came down to stand in the warmth of the sun. An occasional chattering of teeth interrupted the quietness and stillness of the cold morning air, tinged with the smell of smoke from burning wood. The silence was soon shattered by the rasping bark of QM Baxter shouting.

'GOOD MORNING LADIES.THIS WAY FOR CHAI BISCUITS.' A BIT OF NOURISHMENT FOR YOU ALL.'

The chai I could murder for, it seemed to have powers to liven me up. We trooped back into the Hostel, formed an orderly queue to be served chai and biscuits. Making the most of the opportunity. I took more biscuits, put them in my pockets, they would come in handy later on the trip up the hills. We returned outside into the sun to wait for somebody to tell us what to do. Our escort, the mounted party of soldiers arrived on the scene. It was then I recognised two Sergeants Atwood and Collins, as the ones who slept on the train's carriage floor. They must have recognised me, as they both rode up to me greeting me.

'Morning Mrs Plant. It's nice to see you once again. Sorry about the little incident on the train, but much obliged for your prompt action. How are you finding your stay in India?'

'Very strange but I'm settling down to the life now. How's your wives? Are they in this party?'

'No. They have already been up here, they all enjoyed their stay up here. They are back down in Pindi.'

'Oh. I thought after seeing you two. I might have some company up here.'

'You'll be all right, it's very lovely and much cooler further up, the quarters are comfortable.'

A Military Policeman. "Red Cap" approached interrupted our somewhat brief but pleasant conversation casually mentioned.

'We are waiting on the Dandy Wallahs they are going to carry you up the hills to Khanspur.' I immediately thought: *What on earth am I doing here in my condition? Now I have to be piggy backed up this mountainside*...He did not finish, as a posse of these so-called Dandy Wallahs arrived in front of the Hostel. A scruffy lean bare footed looking bunch, each wearing a hat of some sorts? A jumper, shorts or some form of a skirt, pulled up between their legs. A large blanket was slung over one shoulder. They gathered themselves in front of us, eyeing up their new customers. As they waited for a word of command. I wondered what they were going to do. One of the MP's shouted.

'JAO JAHLDI.' (Go quick)

En-masse these Wallahs came running towards us. Several making a beeline for me. There was much shoving tripping and general fights before eight Wallahs won the day. They gesturing for us to follow them, leading us away from the other ongoing fights behind us. Rounding the corner of the Hostel, another two MPs were stood in front of a line of these "Dandy's."

I nearly died when I saw what they were. Shaped like a canoe, made from cane and wicker, attached on either side were two long poles, at the end of those poles, two smaller poles  were lashed across like yokes. The Wallahs gestured for us to get in, with me and Jackie in one. Mary and Kathleen in the other. Four Wallahs took up their positions around this contraption, two in the front and two behind. Whilst this was going on, their other customers were being coaxed into other Dandy's. When everyone appeared to be settled in their Dandy, one of the MPs shouted out something, immediately our four Wallahs each took hold of the extended yokes. Bodily they lifted the Dandy up off the ground up onto their shoulder. In terror I yelled out grabbed the sides to steady myself, terrified screams from others proved I was not the only one yelling. Sgt. Atwood who had spoken to me was apparently in charge of the calvacde. Maybe through a guilty conscience he ordered our eight Dandy Wallahs to take the up the lead position shouted. 'Ab.' He and the Wallahs moving at a slow pace, walked onto the dirt track continued along then stopped. As the cavalcade of Dandy's formed up in line at the rear were the servants with the luggage, the other escorts took up their positions along the cavalcade with everone

Sarah & Jackie in the Dandy ready. Sgt. Atwood shouted.

'JAO' (Go). Amid more shrieks from the women we moved off. I gripped the sides for dear life as we were jostled about, until the Wallahs got into a steady gait actually they started to run. Then I realised why they had all made a beeline for us. They were looking for lightweights to carry, rather than the heavy weights that stood around. I said a silent prayer that we would live through this journey. In time together the Wallahs got into a steady trot the jostling became quite an even steady movement and was not uncomfortable. Certainly better than walking or riding piggyback style as I had originally thought. Behind us the children loved it. Mary and Kathleen were calling out to Jackie, shouting all the time at the Dandy Wallahs 'JAHLDI JAHLDI' ('faster faster'). Much to my surprise we made good progress, unfortunately for them, a further twenty odd miles carrying us at the trot.

At a junction, the Wallahs turned left onto the cart road, overlooking Murree below. In the middle of the whole area, in amongst a few large buildings, I noticed a square towered church, scattered around on various surrounding levels were other bungalows, giving the impression of an English village. A group of trees obscured any further sight of Murree. We passed a lake and after about another mile turned off the cart road. At a steady pace we progressed, there was a slight breeze to cool us down from the rays of the sun, riding up alongside me, Sgt. Atwood informed me we were about to go through the Kuldanna Garrison Army lines. We passed the Officers lines, a long building with some nurses walking about, indicated it must have been a Hospital. Farther along we passed the soldiers lines. When we were out of the sight of Kuldanna, the track became steeper, one side was the hillside lined was full of trees and shrubs, on the other side it fell away to whatever was down below. The cavalcade came to a halt for a rest, the necessary lavatories were taken in amongst the shrubs above, back into the Dandy's, with a heave-ho up continued on our way again. These regular stops were to become the pattern of our journey all the way up to Khanspur, Sgt. Atwood coming along side informed me.

'Mrs Plant. Three miles further on there is a place called Barian. We shall stop there for something to eat and drink.'

200

I was none the wiser but warmed to his attention and information on our progress. Barian was nothing like a village. Just a few bungalows scattered about in amongst trees, A shout of 'ROKNA', brought the Dandy Wallahs to a halt and lowered the Dandy to the ground. I was grateful to get out walk about to stretch my legs. I noticed a couple of the families leave the cavalcade farther back, made their way to some of the bungalows. Their journey was at an end. The Chai Shop, well four upright posts supported a tin roof plus a table with glasses, below was a fire stove with a rather enormous kettle on top, the Chai Wallah came out with an urn and glasses, served chai that was welcomed by all. Next on the menu was some light refreshments of curry and rice with fresh fruit. Although the sun shone brightly, it was much cooler quite bearable while eating the meal beside the dirt track. We soon were on our way upwards, where the cart track became narrower and much steeper, which slowed the Dandy Wallahs down to a walking pace, therefore more stops were necessary, each time I gave them a quarter of an Anna each to cheer them up. As a gesture for the gifts they salaamed me like idiots. At one such stop Sgt. . Collins suggested.

'Can I ride Jackie on the horse in front of me?'

I readily agreed giving me the opportunity to relax without Jackie fidgeting and turning around. As he lifted Jackie on to the back of his horse, a howl of protest came from Mary and Kathleen. Sgt. Collins roared with laughter at this outburst, called out to them.

'Next stop one of you can swop with Jackie and so on. Take it I turns Eh?' That seemed to pacify the girls who nodded. As the track progressed up the hillside, it twisted and turned causing us to be bathed in sunlight for periods at a time, traversing a bend we would be in the shadows of trees, then through a clear space would briefly reveal on the track far below us, the tail end of the cavalcade. Apart from the cry of some birds all that disturbed the quietness was the creaking ropes of the Dandy as the Wallahs took the strain. I thought. *"What a miserable life they had."* With the gentle movement of the Dandy coupled with effects of my previous sleepless night was taking a toll on my senses, my eyelids would not stay open forcing me into a false period of sleep. Mary's shouting woke me with a start.

'MUM LOOK, THERE'S A FOOTBALL PITCH AHEAD.'

I was lying on my back in the Dandy. Embarrassed gathering my senses, quickly sat up. Jackie was kneeing up one arm pointing forward, over his head I saw Mary sat astride the neck of the Sergeant's horse waving her arm as they rode back towards us she pointing back up the track. I could not see anything, Sgt. Collins pulling up the horse said.

'Mrs. Plant. Up ahead is the Army post at Khaira, we shall make a stop there.'

We must have only travelled another three miles from the last camp. As we went round the next corner, the football pitch came into sight. I thought. *"If Jack was up here, it wouldn't take him long before he was out playing football."* A little way past the pitch, we passed some bungalows then a line of army huts, before coming to a halt by a little Bazaar. Everyone got out of the Dandy's. I noticed more families leaving the cavalcade, making their way into the Army camp. We sat down to take chai and some fresh fruit. I was so weary wondered how much further we had to go. During the last mile or so, the sun had disappeared behind bring forth menacing dark clouds with a distinct chill in the air, it was apparent rain was not far away. Soon we were on our way once again It was Jackie's turn to ride up with Sgt. Collns.nevertheless, we still had another overnight stay and tomorrow a further trek upwards I was so weary of this endless trekking thought: *The sooner the better for me.* Further along we came across more bungalows, then a larger bungalow with a notice board outside stated OFFICERS MESS. Our Bearer came alongside our Dandy his blanket secured around his shoulders, salaamed smiling down at my tribe gestured to me, muttered something in Urdu. He as ever aware of what was going on around us. I was grateful of his presence and concern. I suppose he was seeing how we were fairing on this journey? I did not know but responded saying.

201

'Achchha Bearer Pukka.' He responded by shaking his head something was up? By then the clouds above were much denser but no rain. However, from the rays of the hidden sun, the colour of the opposite hillside had changed to a bluish purple. After a few more short stops, it seemed as if we were going up a steeper incline, making me grasp the sides of the Dandy. Then suddenly a mist descended to swirl around us briefly to clear only to come swirling back again. It was quiet eerie, my concern grew we would not reach the next place before twilight set in. Anxiously I began twisting my wedding ring when I called out to the Wallahs to.

'Jahldi Jahldi.' The Bearer who had grasped the side of the Dandy said something in Urdu; they appeared to respond increased their steps. Going over the top of one incline we went down onto more level ground. In the swirling mist we could not see much in the gathering twilight did not help. It was almost dark when we made our final stop. It was difficult to see anything but noticed the shape of a large bungalow, I assumed was where we would spend the night. Coming to a halt the Wallahs lowered the Dandy we got out. The Bearer disappeared I drew my tribe in closer to me, then out of the mist loomed the figures of the Bearer with the rest of our servants. 'Salaam Alekum's to each and every one. The place was fast become a hive of activity, voices in the mist were being raised in anxiety above which a Sergeant shouted.

'LADIES PLEASE TAKE YOUR TIME. THOSE THAT ARE READY. PLEASE ENTER THE BUNGALOW OUT OF THE MIST AND CHILL.'

The Bearer had taken care of our cases so I led my tribe into the bungalow. The glow from hurricane lamps revealed a very large room; this certainly was not a Hostel. Bare boards with a pile of coir biscuits in one corner, in the centre of the rear wall was a large fireplace. The sergeants organised the servants doing various chores, whilst all the Khansama's were set the task of lighting the fire and preparing a meal for everyone. It wasn't long before the fire was alight with the dry wood crackling and blazing merrily away. Chai was made, served in the warming light from the blazing fire warmed everyone up, soon the smell of cooking wafting around the room it was not long before the dish of the day hot soup with naan bread served to all sitting on the floor was devoued with relish. Coir biscuits with one blanket were issued out to the families to pick out a spot and settle down for the night. Covered by two blankets the four of us snuggled up close however, even with the fire blazing away it was still cold. Our sleep was disturbed when one of the mothers who after we left Murree had been ill she vomitting brought up blood. Both Sergeants along with two other wives looked after her until the morning.

Before first light of dawn arrived. One of the Sergeants left the bungalow to make arrangements for this unfortunate woman to be taken to a Hospital. Its whereabouts in this God forsaken hole I did not know, but I did find out that the so called Hostel, was a communal rest place called a Dak Bungalow. I could not have cared less; I was not feeling too bright myself. I was very queasy and short of breath. Someone came in from outside with more good news to announce. 'It's snowing.' I thought. *"My God and this is India. Let me get down to the plains."* I rallied around. With the small amount of water made available, gave my tribe a cat's lick. Chai was handed out then breakfast was served, more hot soup with naan bread. Sgt. Atwood came up and sat down with us.

'Mrs Plant, this place is another small Army camp called. Changla. Its smaller than the last one but do have some married quarters dotted around. A few of the families are to stay here, unfortunately for you Khanspur it's about another two thousand feet above Murree. Mrs Plant, my advice to you is wrap up well.'

'Can we take a few blankets with us to wrap up in?'

'Sorry can't do that. Not allowed they are part of the bungalows inventory.' He excused himself, as the other Sergeant arrived back, accompanied by two Medical Orderlies carrying a stretcher. There was much concern for the poor woman, who was as pale as pale could be, the incident provided a talking point amongst other wives. Ignoring that situation I was more dismayed at the prospects of snow, busied myself sorting out extra clothing to wear, that wasn't much. Taking his advice got the children to put them on over their existing clothes. Meanwhile the woman was stretchered away. The two Sergeants then began organising the departure of the remaining reduced cavalcade. The Khansama's smothered the dying embers and, with the last hope of warmth extinguished, we left the bungalow.

Outside flurries of snow had covered the ground. Covered in their groundsheets both Sergeants were already mounted on their horses; at least they looked prepared for the journey. Stood waiting alongside their Dandy's were the Wallahs with blankets around their shoulders. Once we were all settled in the dandy's, out came the "Black Umbrella's" for some protection against the intermittent flurries of snow. We resumed our journey in the same formation. This time with the flurries of snow it was decidedly colder and quiet miserable. The Wallahs were like mountain goats carrying us up these steep inclines without slipping. Now and again through the flurries of snow, we would see a number of Bungalows, which would raise our spirits of getting into their warmth only to carry on past. What a journey, it seemed endless.

The cavalcade was progressively getting shorter, I was now able to see the tail end behind amongst them were our servants with and Sgt. Collins. Although slight the snow began falling steadily I thought. *"How much further had we to go? Khanspur must be the "back of beyond". I was not a very happy person. How did we ever get involved in such a journey. The Army of course. You take orders and go where you're told to go. No Ifs or Buts.'* I reflected on my first Ferry crossing from Ireland, I did not want to go but go I did. Now thousands of miles away from home I'm suffering from near frostbite and could not do anything about it. Just soldier on.

Late in the afternoon, we finally arrived at Khanspur with thick snow everywhere. The Dandy was full of it, my legs blue from the cold were numb, my body wasn't much better either. The Wallahs had all but turned white with the cold. It was freezing as were my tribe with running noses shivering bodies and chattering teeth. Sgt. Atwood barked some directions to the Wallahs. We left the cart track, heading towards a bungalow. Emerging out of its doorway came a kilted Scots Sergeant. Shouting at the Dandy Wallahs, they came to a halt lowered us to the ground. The kilted Scot greeted us.

'Huwaa thurrr. Deese rr yee yon quaaters.'

I was so cold, I could hardly get out. He seeing my predicament came striding through the snow, slipping two hands through my armpits helped me get out then said.

'Mam yons a wee one. I've jist carreed som woood inte yon bungalow fir Te fire, yon Khansama Wi soon hae it aleet un roaring. ' I could not reply.

As my shoes touched the ground the coldness of the snow bit into by already numb feet. This was no place for summer sling back shoes. The sergeant picked up Jackie and carried him towards the bungalow. I turned around and called Kathleen and Mary both covered in snow.

'Quickly you two get inside.' They did not need a second command, as we stepped into the imprints of giant footsteps he had left in the snow, quickly followed him into this Bungalow. Jackie was plonked down on a chair. The Scot addressed me.

'Mam. Ye luggage wal ba alang latar. Mabe temorra.' Exasperated I retorted.

'What do you mean tomorrow?'

'Wi yon fall of snow tis wee bit difficult far te mules.'

'What will we do tonight then?'

'Make dey te best ye con.'

What with his broad Scottish accent and my Irish brogue, we weren't getting very far. I had a suspicion that he thought we had been up there before. He left us to our own devices. I looked around surveying our quarters with dismay. One big room, a table with a hurricane lamp placed on it, some chairs, a stone fireplace with unlit wet logs, in one corner lay heaps of coir for bedding down upon, my tribe were all shivering crying with the cold. The Bearer and servants, carrying our

203

cases and their chattels, entered through the door, their blankets draped around their shoulders were encrusted with snow, all were shivering with chattering teeth. The Khansama thoroughly miserable with the cold, set down his baggage from his back, stared glumly at the empty fireplace an expression of defeat on his face, the first thing he had to do was to try and get a fire going. I pointed to the fire place ordered.

'Bearer. Jahldi Jahldi. Garam.'

He clapped his hands shouted at the Khansama, who immediately set too trying to lighting it with a box of matches, blowing, fanning it only produced smoke. I watched until he was half way through a box of matches. I stood there in dismay shivering, wondering how to get this wretched wood alight, when the door swung open, looming in the doorway was a figure covered with a blanket that was quickly discarded as a tall woman entered followed by a servant with a large jug and a Chico carrying glasses with a cheery.

'Hello there. I've brought you some chai.'...Salaams from the servants...'I saw you arrive during that last fall of snow, just knew that a drink of chai would liven you up. You're new up here aren't you?'

'Yes. My God thank you. You're an angel, were freezing.' This woman told her servants to put the chai and glasses on the table saying... 'Just help yourselves. I'll fetch some more until you get your fire going.'...'That's the trouble. We can't, the wood is too wet. The Khansama has tried to no avail.'... 'Hold on I'll fetch some dry wood.' Covering herself with her blanket she left with her servants What a Godsend she was. I moved across to the table called over the Bearer.

'Jahldi Bearer. Chai all.'

I waved my arm around for everyone to share this jug of chai. I looked upon them as being part of our family and justified to have it as well? They grateful to be inside out of the cold, not only that, but to take chai with the Memsahib, this was more than they could wish for. As we stood at this table sipping the chai, warmth seeped into cold bodies. The bare boards were wet from the melting snows we all had brought in. The door swung open, in came the woman followed by her two servants, one holding some smouldering smoking branches, the other with an armful of dry wood, shutting the door behind them, she exclaimed.

'There you are, that will get it going.'

Immediately the Khansama was there with them jabbering away to the other two. One of her servants threw the dry tinder into the fireplace as the other waved the lighted one to and fro to make it glow, causing smoke to drift around the room. I thanked her for her kindness.

'Oh don't mention it. I've been up here four weeks, it's the first snow we have had. What a time for you to come up here.' -pointing. - 'That bungalow over there is mine' Opening the door about to leave hesitated.... 'Anything else you want just gives me a shout.' Her two servants left with her... 'Thank you.' I didn't even know her name.

By this time the Khansama had got the fire going the flames licking around the dry wood as he coaxed it with more of the wet wood causing more smoke before it was soon ablaze. I sat my tribe down in front of it out of his way. Covering themselves with blankets the Bearer, Khansama went outside, to make more chai I got one of the Ayah's to go outside with a pot, indicating to fill it full of snow, that done placed the pot on the fire. The other two returned with more wood covered in snow, going backwards and forwards a few times to stock up for the night, when they had finished, I got both hunched down in front of the fire to thaw out, gave them another brew of the fresh chai. Salaams after salaams. The door burst open in strode a Quarter Master in charge.

'Hello to the Plant family. Here are two blankets for the night.' He handed over two very large double blankets. I complained about the issue. He replied...'Sorry that's all I can do this storm was unexpected. Two blankets for each family.' Very quickly he left.

Lighting the two hurricane lamps the Bearer hung them up. In their warm glow I took a quick look around, my tribe sat in front of the fire, their Ayahs stood behind them shivering trying to dry their personal blankets, a damp atmosphere filled the room. I decided due to the prevailing conditions, that night all would sleep in the big room, keeping the fire alight and they with their personal blankets dry, it would be more comfortable for all. Stacked at the back of the room were our cases, looking at them and the two blankets gave me an Idea: *"Find darning needle and cotton."* 'Number One Ayah.' Pointing to the cases, with my hands indicated a sewing action explaining to her what I wanted. Understanding, she got one of the Chico's to help her rummage through the cases, whilst I spread one of the blackets open over the table, folded it length ways. Having found the sewing items she handed them to me. I sorted out two darning needles and cotton, gave her one with a length of cotton, showed her what I wanted her to do; stitching two ends of the blanket together along one side, whilst she did that I did the same with the other blanket, with both finished, I got a couple of the Chico's to stuff then full of the coir, which always seemed readily available to make any mattress. Gradually we were getting organised.

By this time the dampness smell of the room was replaced by the smell of burning wood a lttle smoke mingled with the magic smell of cooked food, curried soup,the Khansama had done his bit served in dishes he had found accompanied by naan bread, no doubt he had picked up at the hostel.. We sat down in front of the fire eating sparingly but sufficient for that evening. Warmed by the blazing fire the curry soup, had everyone ready to sleep away the arduous journey of the day. I arranged sleeping places in front of the fire, one makeshift mattress for the Memsahib and three Babas covering ourselves with our coats, the other for the servants with their blankets. With the sound of the whistling wind outside I assumed we were better off than most.

The crackling sound of a fire woke me, putting aside my coat I sat up, illuminated in the glow of the fire the Bearer was adding more wood to the fire sending sparks up the chimney. I glanced towards the window, outside it was still dark even better, no sound of the wind, hopefully the snowstorm had eased. The Bearer aware I was awake looked over at me murmured quietly.

'Salaam Memsahib.' I roused myself.

'Salaam Bearer Achchha.'

Slipping my arms into my coat got up. From a chatty bowl the Bearer poured out a glass of chai passed gave it to me, It amazed me how chai was always available. The Khansama was quietly sorting out his stock in readiness to prepare breakfast., muttering his salaams joined us sat in front of the fire quietly sipping chai. With no idea of the time I could not wait for dawn to break, gradually the room showed signs of daylight, a few coughs and sneezes indicated there was some stirring of bodies from sleep. Getting up went to the window looked out. Outside lay a deep carpet of snow. Nevertheless, at that moment I would gladly have given "The Bank at Monte Carlo" to be back home with Mother, but scanning the outlook what a splendid sight met my eyes, as far as the eye could see the mountains of the Himalaya's covered in snow. There was not a cloud in the sky, the light coloured blue of the early morning emphasised the stark sharp contours of the mountains right down to the snow-covered foothills below, and possibly as far down as Murree where the greenery lay untouched. Diverting my attention away from the scenery, there were much more important things to sort out. More chai was on the brew along with something to eat, Where he got it from I did not know furthermore did not really care, that was his department. Telling my tribe to stay where they were, finding my shoes pulled on my coat left the bungalow to go and thank the woman.

Outside the freshness of the air pinched my cheeks, aware of my shortness of breath, someone had informed me. *"Until you become acclimatised the higher you go the more difficult it is to breathe."* I was not sure how long? However nobody had said anything about snow. Stood on the small veranda of the bungalow I took stock of our surroundings. Almost at the top of this hill, above us was another bungalow tucked in the wooded slopes, I noticed indents of footprints in the snow partially covered by a fall of snow led towards a bungalow a little way below us, she had said she was next door. In my sling back shoes. I steeled myself for the walk to this bungalow, the snow was not deep but its coldness penetrated my feet, squinting against its glare I slowly crunched my way down the sloping path, without slipping over safely got to the bungalow. Knocking on the door, it was opened by a servant. A voice from inside bade me.

'Good morning. Welcome come on in. Would you like some chai?' I entered into its warm interior laid out the same as ours a blazing wood fire provided its warmth.

'Good morning to you. Yes thank you that would be most welcome. I've just popped over to thank you for your help last night. I don't think we could have managed without your assistance.'

'Oh that's all right don't mention it.' - Chai was served. - 'My name is Grace Gould. Just call me Grace. I'm an Indian Army Sergeants wife stationed in Pindi.'

'Sarah Plant, wife of BQMS Plant. Twenty-fifth Royal Field Artillery stationed in Nowshera, just call me Sarah. I prefer that. Pindi. Where's Pindi? 'I asked.

'Pindi. Oh that's short for Rawalpindi, everyone calls it that. I take it you have settled in alright.'

'Oh no, not that quick. We had little or nothing for the evening, our luggage never arrived. We all slept on the floor in front of the fire. A Scots Sergeant told me, the luggage would be arriving this morning.'

'Oh him Macgregor. He's all right he's just been posted up here. Most of his time he spends going up and down to Pindi. He keeps us up to date with all the news of what's happening down on the plains.' I ventured to enquire.

'This place Khanspur. It seems like it's on top of a hill and miles from anywhere. Is there any life up here?'

'You can't go any further up than Khanspur. It is the last of the Galis. It is beautiful. I have always enjoyed my stays up here, this is my fourth stay. Down the hill there is a small schoolhouse, a little bazaar for provisions. You passed it on your way up, its not far away. Most provisions are brought up from the plains, they are meagre but sufficient to meet most meals, if you venture further up the track there is another bungalow and a Church. Like a top up of chai?'

I was conscious of the time I had been away from our bungalow, with the children on their own in a strange place, albeit a short stay, I. refused.

'No thank you. I should return back to wait the arrival of our luggage. I will speak with you later, once again Grace many thanks for your assistance. It was gratefully received.'

I left the hospitality of her bungalow. Outside the warmth of the morning sun was thawing the snow, the crisp crunching sounds underfoot was gone retacing my steps entered the warmth of our bungalow, the fire was blazing away, with my tribe still sat on the makeshift mattress, watching the flames as the Khansama busily prepared scrambled eggs and Naan, what a gem he was. The table was already laid with plates found from somewhere. The rest of the servants were moving about, the Ayah's clucking and sighing at the state and what the bungalow provided. I had a quick tour of the accommodation that appeared to me, ample for our stay. Khana was served, we sat down to ate with relish, then I had to get things organised before the luggage arrived. I got Mary and Kathleen to put their coats on, noting their coat sleeves finished half way up their arms, obviously they had grown. I sent them out, together with the Chico's, to forage around outside collecting wood. With the wood party going in and out stacking up the wood. I said to Mary.

'I'm going to find a little Bazaar the lady told me about. I'll go with the Bearer and Khansama to buy provisions, we won't be long.Mary, you're in charge you continue collecting the wood and don't you dare wander off.' Putting my coat on leaft the bangalow accompanied by the Bearer and Khansama, they wearing sandals had their blankets covering their shoulders. The

Khansama was highly privileged to be taken by the Memsahib on such a shopping spree. Outside the sun was very warm, the sky was as blue as could be, underfoot the snow had almost gone therefore it was not going to be a slip and slide journey. We had not gone very far when we came to this little Bazaar, a couple of shops with a Chai place, locating the provision store we entered. Inside three Indians were sat on their haunches arguing, they stopped stood up salaamed, salutations over it was down to business. With the Khansama I looked at what provisions they had laid out in wicker baskets. Very basic, cabbage, potato, carrot, onions, there was milk, chai, sugar, a selection of fruit - the usual selection.

'Achchha.' I indicated to the Khansama to sort out what he required. He fingered the goods muttering to himself or, tutting with a quick intake of breath a shake of the head, having made up his mind he began shouting, bartering for everything he picked up, turning to me a huge grin on his face salaamed.... 'Achchha Memsahib. Bahut Achchha Pukka.' I produced some money, gestured to the Bearer to pay for the goods. Whilst I stood to one side, he started bartering at the price. When all was done and dusted, they saw I trusted them both salaamed. I returned their compliment....'Wa Alekum as Salaam.'...The shopkeeper looked crestfallen at his diminished sale, but shouted instructions for two of his Chico's to carry the goods. On our way back little evidence remained of the previous day's storm. By the time we arrived back my tribe were playing outside with the Chico's, all chores had been completed.

The Khansama happily went about preparing and cooking the midday meal. All we had to do was wait for the rest of the luggage. It wasn't long after we had lunch, when a soldier arrived with coollies carrying our big wooden boxes. Whilst the soldier sat drinking chai more Anna's were paid to the coolies. Unpacking the first box found all the glass in the pictures and photographs were broken. I said to the Soldier.

'I don't mind the broken glass in the photos, so long as my sewing machine is safe.' He apologised saying.

'Sorry about the broken glass Mam, we had an accident further down, one of the mules slipped over the side. We had a job heaving it back up again.' I enquired.

'That mule, was it injured?'

'No it just lost its footing just, slid about five feet down the hill good job it was reined to the others, obviously with the damage caused, too far.' Leaving his chai he helped me sort out the sewing machine intact. I would be lost without that. You could not buy a sewing machine out there for love nor money, they were like gold dust. Finishing his chai the soldier muttered.

'Well I must be off now got to make Khji Gali before its dark.' Hurriedly he left, just as the QM arrived to hand over more blankets possible why the soldier left. With the help of the Ayah's, we unpacked the heavy stuff. I found our own blankets and mattress covers, giving the job to the Ayah's, they busied themselves stuffing the remaining coir into the mattress covers for the other charpoys. That night it would be decidedly more comfortable than our previous night's escapade sleeping on the floor. The large empty wooden boxes were taken outside out of the way. Leaving the main room full of smaller boxes. I was now able to get the quarters more comfortable. We had not completed the unpacking before the fading light of dusk descended upon us, the rest could wait until the morning. The Khansama had prepared spicy hot filling soup. With ample pans of rice and hard-boiled eggs. The different flavours he produced in his meals always had everyone drinking pani, nevertheless, acceptable and delicious to our palates we enjoyed it. With the fire crackling and blazing away, the whole of the bungalow was completely warm. After the sumptuous meal it was time for bed, this time spread out in the rooms.

The following morning everyone woke up much refreshed. That day we would finish off the unpacking. I would sort out the daily routine of chores to be carried out. I looked out through the window to see a heap of wooden boxes where the servants had left them, they would have to be moved around to the back of the Bungalow. I called the Bearer to follow me outside, walking around the rear found a wooden shed, it was an empty stable. I ordered the Bearer to move the boxes inside the stable, they would be re-used again. I went back inside to resume the remainder of the unpacking, which was completed by mid-afternoon. My tribe were quiet happy playing outside, after a hectic week of packing trekking and unpacking I took a break to take chai sitting on the small veranda to survey our surroundings.

It was obvious that many years before. The area in front had been cleared, flattened to allow the Bungalow to be built. The track continued on upwards to disappear into an avenue of tall Pine, Oak and other trees I didn't recognise. Indeed the whole of the hills were covered with trees shrubs and wild flowers that provided a blaze of colour. In the distance the mountains peaks were covered in snow. It was so quiet and peaceful in the hills, the only sounds one could hear above the rustle of the wind in the trees, my tribe's voices in play close by, only occasional interrupted by an shriek of birds high up in the trees. Sat in the sunlight the temperature was still very hot and mused at the thought: *At least you could walk around in the cool air without perspiring, which left you like a damp rag down on the plains.* I had more chai brought to me, I must have stayed out there for a couple of hours resting and taking in the tranquillity of my surroundings, before the setting sun together with a rapid drop in temperature had you shivering, it was time to go inside. Night times descended very quickly. I went to bed early.

The following morning I woke up quiet ill. I was sick with a temperature, with number One Ayah's insistence, she confined me to bed, where I stayed for two whole days until I thought: *I was fit enough to get up and get back to normal.* There was no need the Bearer, the Ayah's had everything running like clockwork, exactly as I would have done down on the plains. I warmed to the thought of. *During the prevailing weather condition I had extended our hospitality to all of the servants. It alone had merged into an understanding of trust and respect between us, which became more evident.* In the morning the children would attend the local classes further down, so they were out of the way for a few hours. With absolutely little to do, except go for walks with my tribe, always accompanied by the Bearer and Ayah's. In the afternoon on some occasions I would write a letter, as there was no mail times, I would spread them out to take up the time. With the abundance of wild flowers everywhere, I got the Ayah's to cut bunches, put them in vases to create colour and a scented smell within the bungalow. In the evenings I used to sit in front of a roaring fire relaxing with the children, reading their books, nevertheless all I could think about was Mother and home. In bed lay there too frightened to move, listening to the noises of the wild animals in the surrounding woodlands, yet very aware that the Bearer was vigilant at all times. At some point I would inevitably doze off into restless sleep. Suddenly I would wake up to the sound of the Khansama quietly brewing up early morning chai. A Chico would bring me a glass of chai, get up to prepare for the days routine such as it was. Slowly the days passed by, after a few weeks I was getting more used to our new quarters. For me it became as they say. "A Life of O'Reilly".

Along with Grace's bungalow opposite, we appeared to be the highest in the area, with other bungalows dotted around on the slopes below. With no Mess do's to attend or any socialising, I still preferred my own company apart from Grace Gould we would spend time sat on the veranda, she told me about the little Catholic Church further up the mountainside which only opened for six months during the year for the Army's married families. Then well enough decided make a trip up there to find it After the children had finished their school had lunch together with the Bearer we left the bungalow haeding upwards, for me in my state the going was heavy, after we had stopped a few time to catch our breathes, we found a narrow step footpath led up to it on the summit of a hill, hanging onto the shrubs of trees alongside the pathway we pulled ourselves up. Whoever thought of building a church so high up with such a treacherous way to get to it, must have thought: *It would be good penance for everyone attending.* Built entirely out of wood it was beautiful, outside a notice board stated. "The Church of St Matthew's."

Unfortunately it was locked, disappointed I read a notice on the door stating the times of mass each Sunday. Twelve 'o'clock, however, after the trek we made to get there, settimg off early would give us sufficient time to climb up the hill in time for the mass.

The following Sunday we set out early to attend mass with the servants at the rear, eventually puffed out we finally arrived at its doors to find them open. A mule was tethered at the corner of the building. I walked forward peered inside. A priest with his back to us was stood close to a small alter, alongside him was a Chico helping him, he must have heard us entering he turned around.

'Ah parishioners. Please come in'…He left off what he was doing and walked towards us. An old Grey haired priest wearing glasses, with outstretched hands and a warm smile approached me taking hold of my hand….'Welcome to you all. I take it you all have come to hear Mass?'

'Yes Father. Just the four of us. Not the servants outside. They always follow where we go.'

'Ah well. Never mind. They have their own religions to follow. I am nearly ready to say mass. It will be so pleasant to have someone in my congregation for once. It's such a trek to get up here. Now you're here I shall proceed. Then we can talk afterward.'

The inside of the church was small with wooden forms for seating, it was one step up through a gap in the wooden alter rail on to the alter made out of wood with a simple sheaf of cloth over its top with two unlighted candles. To one side the priest donned his garments, as did the little Chico who then lighted the two candles. When all the preparations were complete. The Priest proceeded with Mass, which was simple and quickly delivered, at the offertory the Chico rang a little bell, with his final blessing the Mass was over. I was very grateful to have attended. We left the church to wait outside. It wasn't long before he came out closed and locked the door. The Chico had hold of the Priest's small attaché case, which he fastened securely to the saddle on the mule. The Priest came over to where we stood along with the servants.

'My you have a lot of servants. Mrs?'

'Mrs Plant. Father. These are my three Mary Kathleen and Jackie. The servants well this is most of them, we left half of them down In Nowshera, my husband is still down there.'

'Oh I see. Which bungalow is the one you're staying in?'

'The very last one past the little Bazaar.'

'Ah yes. I know the one. I don't past that way. I take the other path.' I ventured.

'Father. This is a lovely little church you have here.'

'Yes indeed. It was built many years before by an Irish regiment. I think it was the Connaught Rangers, when they were stationed in Pindi, they used the Galis as their hill resorts. I have been the Parish priest here for many years, when not up here at Khji Gali. I stay at the convent in Murree. You may have spotted a church from the main cart road that is Holy Trinity Church. There is a saying. Mind you, a very curious one about a grave on one of the hilltops. It is the grave of the Blessed Virgin Mary? However, we all know different don't we.'… Adding… 'I always hold Mass each Sunday and if you could make the trip, I shall be pleased and delighted to see you all.'

He bade us farewell and left on his mule. We followed behind him back down the treacherous path. He went one way we continued back towards the bungalow. Now I had heard Mass for the first time in weeks. I was much more at peace with the world.

During one of my conversation with Grace. I found out I was the only RFA sergeants wife living in the surrounding bungalows, the rest of the women were wives of British Indian Army Sergeants. On some afternoons Grace would go to visit them, obviously word does get around. One morning sitting outside on the veranda enjoying the sun and tranquillity of the area, I heard the sound of a horse snorting, turning my attention in the direction of whence it came saw a horse come into sight its rider was a woman, riding towards the bungalow, to see who it was shielded my eyes from the glare of the sun, then Immediately recognised Nora. Unable to believe what I was seeing, got up to greet her I shouted.

'NORA IS IT REALLY YOU?' She responded shouting.

'YES SARAH. IT REALLY IS.' She reined in, swung herself down off her horse. I met her at the bottom step, delighted to see each other we embraced.

'Sarah how good it is to see you. Wherever did you finish up?'

'Nowshera. Where did you get posted to?'

'Pindi. Where's your three lovely children?'

'Oh they are down at the schoolhouse they should be back soon'

'Can't wait to see them all again.'

'They haven't changed, got more boisterous you'll see. Will you stay for lunch then you will meet them again.'

'Well let me see. Up here my engagement book is quite empty. So I suppose I could fit that in.' We both laughed at the mere thought of having an engagement book. Chai was served.

We exchanged gossip filling in the gaps since we had last parted on the station at Bombay. At least now, whilst I was up in the hills I had someone I knew to converse with. She told me she had been up there for a month with a further two months stay before returning to Pindi she was staying in a bungalow further down at a place called Khji Gali she told me about the different Galis. The little Bazaar was at Ghora Gali a little further down was Kaji Gal further down were Changla Gali and Khaira Gali then Murree.' I enquired.

'What's Gali mean?'

'Gali is what we call back in Blighty a Hamlet. Well that's what I've been told.'

I had no idea of these places. We had not seen any coming up, but there again we had stopped some families had left the calvacade and it was in the middle of a snowstorm. Anyway if we did go past them I would not have taken much notice of them. When my tribe arrived back from school. Nora was overjoyed to see them all. They all made a fuss of her. According to her they had grown, apart from their coat sleeves I hadn't noticed. It was about mid-afternoon we were having chai on the veranda when I reminded her.

'Nora it's a long time since we had Tiffin on the Nevassa how about we continue doing it of course not everyday but when its convenient to you?'

'What a good idea Sarah I can bring a couple of the other wives I am sure they would be pleased for the opportunity of something different. I'll speak to them when I get back.'

She left promising that she would return the following week bringing along some other wives all riding horses. So began our Tiffin party's just like on board the Nevassa. Likewise on different days I was invited to their bungalows. As everyone lived some distance from each other, travel on horseback. If you wanted a horse you just used to inform the QM.

'Ponies or Donkey?' Either would arrive accompanied by a little Syce. In Khanspur it was to be my first time, I had the opportunity to ride a horse since back in Ireland in nineteen twenty. It was natural to me even in my state of health it was fun. Every event whether visiting far away neighbours or, going down to the Bazaar, was an outing. My tribe would ride donkeys with the Chico's running beside them. At the Bazaar Mary noticed some of the local men wore little circular embroidered hats like a pillbox, trying one on asked.

'Mum can we wear these? Instead of Tobies all the time?'

'Well. I suppose so.' They all had to have one. Then she suggested.

'Mum. Buy all the Chico's one as well. Then you will be able to recognise us at once.'

Great idea, much to the pleasure of the Bazaar Wallah including the Chico's who had something of their own to be proud of. They wore them all of the time, Tobies were cast aside only to be worn for Church or special outings.

Since the meeting with Nora, my pattern of sleep had greatly improved, I tended to sleep well. However one night, a terrible shriek outside had me sitting bolt upright. Wide-awake in a cold sweat, I listened, but all was quiet. Instinctively I buried myself under the covers laying there quivering, frantically trying to say a prayer. Gradually calmed myself, removed the covers from over my head concentrated on listening, apart from the sound of snoring bodies the bungalow was quiet I relaxed, slowly I began to doze off, a slight movement outside had me pulling the covers up to eye level listening something was being dragged along the veranda towards the window, a thump followed by a deep cough the low growl of an animal, warning me and anyone else not to move. I lay in fear of my life, hardly breathing intent on listening. Thoughts of: *QM Baxter comments of wild animals flased into my brain.* As outside the sound of gnawing, cracking of bones, tearing and chomping continued, they seemed to go on forever, they were dreadful before the feast stopped then the sound of heavy purring took over. I lay there not daring to move listening to this purring, it must have been a big cat or something else? Abruptly it stopped, a movement, then the sound of renting, scratching, followed by a thump. This time the sound of contented purring like an express train, it stopped. I heard the sound of padding about going on it stopped under the window replaced by the unmistakable sound of liquid being sprayed over the veranda as whatever it was it left its scent before leaving to vanish into the hills, in the quietness I lay there frozen with fear, my heart pounding away. I prayed until I fell asleep.

Next morning, I woke to the sound of sweeping outside and water being splashed about. I got out of bed to looked out of the window. The Bearer and Chico's were cleaning up the mess on the veranda. I slipped a shawl over my shoulders went through into the main room. The Khansama salaamed, pouring out chai handed the glass to me. The Bearer came in from outside, a wide beam of a grin spread across his face, proudly presented me with a large switch of fur. "The Trophy." 'Memsahib. Bara billi. Pukka Memsahib.'

Handing the piece of grey and white fur to me, indicated a four legged beast with big teeth and a long tail, unaware of what it was, the Khansama clucked his tongue muttered. 'Aaii'. The Ayah's seeing the switch tutted sucked on their teeth pulling their veils across their mouths. I none the wiser of what it was, later showed the piece of fur to Grace, she remarked.

'I heard that shriek as well. My God! Was it on your veranda? By the colour of fur, it must have been a snow leopard. That's its territory now; no other animal would attempt to go near it. You're very lucky. That's for sure?'

Lucky! *I was petrified at the thought of this wild animal coming anywhere near the Bungalow, let alone eating its kill on the veranda.* This "Trophy" a good luck charm, was tied above the entrance to the bungalow, something I would rather not have had. But from then on it was taken with us all over India. One good thing every other wild thing gave us a wide berth for the rest of the time we were up there. a small mercy I was little aware of at the time.

Nora! A friend indeed. I became ill. I thought: *With all my recent activity of walking and horse riding I might lose the baby.* I badly needed her help, I sent the Bearer to fetch her. Returning back with him she saw I was quiet ill, confined me to bed. Sent the Bearer with a note, Explaining my condition. Rrequesting Jack's presence, back down to the Officer in Charge at Khiji Gali. Nora stayed all day, until late in the afternoon the Bearer returned with a message that contact had been made. Nora then left saying .'Sarah remain in bed. I'll come back tomorrow.'

She did and the following day she informed me. Jack was on his way up, I struggled out of bed went out onto the relax on the veranda in anticipation of Jack's arrival. Nora left giving me strict orders.

'Sarah. Take it easy, stay in that chair, from now on there will be no walking, no horse riding or, going to Church. I'll be back to morrow.'

Three days later it was warm with drizzling rain I was sat on the veranda. Jackie came running up towards the veranda shouting.

'MUM. DAD'S COMING UP THE TRACK.'

He was away like a shot running back to greet his father. Struggling up out of the chair I moved to the front of the veranda, spotted Jack emerging through the trees he was soaked through. Jackie, was sitting in front of him astride the horse's neck, with Mary and Kathleen sat astride the horse flanks. Trailing behind was a packhorse laden with cases. What a delight to see him with that big grin. The servants appeared from everywhere. The Bearer got them lined up, He at their head waiting to greet their Sahib, stopping all salaamed murmured.

'Salaam Alekum Sahib.' He bent his head and indicated a salute.

'Hello Sarah, what have you been up to then?' Mary Kathleen move a bit so I can dismount.

Letting Jackie down, dismounted then returned him up onto the saddle before bounding up the veranda steps to kiss and embrace me. Nonchalantly I replied.

'Nothing much. You know I'm having a baby. I've been overdoing it that's all.'

'How could you overdo it? In such an idyllic place like this?' I lied.

'Don't know. Just have.'

'Well. You look fit enough to me. Anyway I've been given ten days leave. I'll be here for four days before I return.' Delighted with this news.

'C'mon Jack inside and remove those wet KD's and change.'

'Whoa back Sarah. One thing at a time. Before I change, chai would be nice.' Clapping my hands ordered.

'Chai Bearer. Sahib jahldi. 'Inquisitively I asked.

'Jack what have you brought with you on the back of the mule?'

'Oh just some few odds and ends, mostly food for the Khansama. A case of tomatoes and other items to eat. (Tomatoes! Very scarce up here and in great demand). 'Bearer. Khana baks for Khansama jahldi jahldi.'

Jack went back to the horse, helped the children down, then to the mule to untie the holding straps around the boxes. The Bearer standing beside him motioned him away.

'Sahib. Chico's jahldi.'

'Okay bahut Achchha.' He left it to the Bearer to sort out. Back on the veranda chai was served by a beaming Khansama. No doubt overheard that the Sahib had not forgotten him.

'By God Sarah. This place is beautiful don't you think? What a lucky girl you are, and there's me sweltering down on the plains'…Little did he know about the wild animals up here…'C'mon inside to see the rest of the bungalow'….Jack viewed each of the rooms commented.

'Well-done Sarah. You have made this comfortable and homely, what with that fire in there. Oh I have four letters for you, they arrived just as I was leaving. Have you received any up here?'

'Yes. two weeks after we had arrived. I received three from Mother and Eilish. Quickly scanned the letters to see whom they were from…'You can read these and the others after you've changed out of your uniform.'

'Yes that would be good, apart from yours. I haven't seen any from Blighty since you left to come up here, before I change I'll see the horses are settled is there a stable here?'

'Around the back with a lot of boxes stored.'

Jack through and through, the Syce would have cared for the horses but he had to check. I followed him out onto the veranda, he went down the steps to be presented by a line of servants, ready for the Sahib's inspection, immediately behind him, my tribe in line followed mimicking their Father, the servants all grinning as he walked passed each one, Jack nodded in approval.

'Ji han Bearer. Pukha. Syce. Jahldi jahldi'.'

'Ji han Sahib. Pukka Sahib.' Salaamed saluted to Jack, my tribe copying started saluting everyone. I had to smile at their antics, a big grin appeared on Jack's face. A clap of the hands the servants dispersed, laughing at my tribe's antics went about their chores. The mock inspection over. The Syce came up to Jack salaamed.

'Sahib.'

'Ghora. Jahldi jahldi.' The Syce took hold of the horses reins and led them away Jack followed him with the rest of the tribe in tow. They disappeared to the stable to the rear of the bungalow. It wasn't long before they returned Jack satisfied that all was in order.

'Chai Bearer.' Chai was served by the grinning Khansama murmured.

'Pukka Khana Sahib.' (A splendid meal for Jack this evening). Obviously more than pleased with what the Sahib had brought him. Typical of Jack he thought of everything. The Khansama provided a wonderful curry with a side dish of fresh tomatoes, during the rest of Jack's stay he was treated like a Lord, a compliment paid to me from Jack.

'You certainly have them well trained Sarah, and it sounds like you're learning Urdu.'

'Not much, it's only general words.'

We sat down to catch up on all our news from down on the plains and to read the letters.

'Sarah, nothing has changed, the servants are looking after the Bungalow and garden. Unfortunately whilst I was away, a Chico left the door into the chicken coop open, something had got in and ravaged all the birds. When I returned this little Chico was paraded before me. You know Sarah; I didn't have the heart to say anything, he stood in front of me crying crocodile tears. I gave him money to purchase more. I spent most of my time going too and from Peshawar or to another place called Mardan. North of Nowshera. I ate mainly in camp. By the way, I'm playing football again. So Sarah how was it up here?'

I related our trip up, the incident with the snow leopard, which he passed by. These things do happen out here in India? The surprise meeting with Nora, the Tiffin parties. That he was pleased about looked forward to seeing her once again. After that chat, we read the letters by the light of a lamp. Mother's first letter informed me of Mrs. Pankhurst death in June, a Miss Amelia Earhart flight in an aeroplane across the Atlantic, she had landed in Wales? Knowing mother's feelings about men in their flying machines, we had a good laugh about her little comment. Her latest letters mentioned some trouble out in India. About riots in a place called Kharagpur between Sikhs and Muslims. Was it anywhere near where we were? Jack informed me that he had not heard of any rioting, so not to worry. Another snippet that she mentioned would interest Jack. Was a Treaty paper had been signed by America, Great Britain and other countries including Germany? About the Renunciation of War would provide Peace in Europe?

'I know about that Sarah. It has been the topic of discussion in the Mess.' He just shook his head.

The next few days, he helped looking after the children, generally keeping them out of trouble taking them for rides on the horses. After hours being away they would come back to the bungalow,running in to tell me what they had done or seen during their day's outing, the pheasants, which I had seen myself wild goats some deer or big eagles, always something different to report back on. One good thing it stopped me worrying about what Mary got up to in the surrounding hills? I was still very wary of what wild animals would be lurking about in the area. On the third day of his stay he was out with my tribe when Nora arrived, she was disappointed but there would be another time

We had a most enjoyable four days respite. That provided me with the time to rest recuperate enabled me to get back on my feet, before Jack had to return back down the hills. Jack left saying that he would be able to make another trip up to the hills, for me not to overdo things. We said our goodbyes. I watched from the veranda as he started back down the track. Mary Kathleen and Jackie were given a final ride on his horse before he put them down. With a final wave was gone from sight. After he left life returned back to the normal daily routine. Tiffin time had now become a daily occurrence, but with a difference. The visits would be made to me, all the wives agreed. It would be better for my sake. An arrangement that I was happy with. The wives asked me if Jack would mind bringing up this or that on his next time up, I conveyed these requirements in my letters to him. Although I had recovered from the last bad bout, I was still getting unwelcome symptoms. I did not feel right, there was not much I could do about it, very aware to be careful. Some Sundays I would miss going to Mass.

The following month Jack came up. He had two Donkeys in tow laden with the supplies of the women's requisites, which they all were delighted to receive, before he returned back to Nowshera there was a pleasant reunion with Nora. Not far off was the end of the Monsoon season it was much colder in the daytime and the torrential rains were sparodic, during the night, falls of slight snow had occurred laying like a white carpet on the ground in the morning. It would soon be time for us to return down to Nowshera, although I was well developed in pregnancy, I still did not feel right. In my letters to Jack I told him to save his leave until the end of the season, when he would be able to return to Khanspur with us, it suited him he could delay his leave as the Battery football team were doing well in the Charity Football Cup competition. As normal Nora arrived with one of the other wives for Tiffin, it was to be their last visit, as they both had to return the next day to Pindi. We said our fond farewells.

A few days after they had left, once again I became ill. This time Grace came to my rescue she went to the QM who sent a message to Jack to come up immediately on compassionate grounds. Three days later he arrived late in the afternoon, when he saw the condition I was in, he was concerned. We talked about it decided not to wait to go down with the rest of the other families but leave Khanspur with haste. To my relief I did not want to be stuck up in the hills miles from anywhere giving birth to a baby. Jack immediately set about the packing, to lighten our load arranged to have the big luggage carried down later with the other family's luggage.

On the second day after Jack had arrived the early morning sunrise saw the arrival of the Dandy Wallahs, heralding the end of our stay in Khanspur. We said our goodbyes to Grace and some of the other women who came to wish us well and a safe trip down. With Jack astride his horse, and my tribe with the Ayah's all settled in the Dandy's we started on the downward trek to Murree. Going downwards was much faster and easier with the Dandy Wallahs making great haste the jostling I was experiencing was not good for me. We stayed overnight in the Rest House leaving early in the morning on the way down I progressively got worse, it was earl afternoon by the time we reached the Hostel in Murree. I was so ill Jack decided not to stay overnight, so set about hiring a private car to take us all down. The car turned up, the driver seeing all these passengers, arguing with Jack said he had no room in his car. Jack got the Bearer to agree with the driver. He, the men servants would ride down by horse, with the Syce astride Jack's horse and the Chico's behind the other men. When all was finally agreed we climbed in the car, Jack made me sit in the front passenger's seat, somehow most of us got in this car, with a couple of the Chico's clung onto the roof or stood on the running board. Led by Jack the horse party galloping full tilt down behind us. We made quick progress on the cart road down to Pindi, as we rapidly descended down towards the plains. The temperature steadily increased, in the late afternoon we arrived at Pindi. My stomach pains seemed to have eased. Jack paid off the Driver, met the horse handler who was already waiting to take charge of them.

We were lucky, as the train to Nowshera had been delayed by almost a day it was due the following morning. We had to spend the night at a hotel in Pindi. I was grateful for the break in our journey. Up at the crack of dawn down to the station. Much to the delight of my tribe the Station had installed flush lavatories. So the three of them did nothing else but keep pulling all the chains. I wasn't in a fit state to chase them left Jack togetner with the Ayah's to chase them all over the station; they thought it was a huge game. The train duly arrived we climbed aboard.

214

Jack commandeered seats for us all, we were off headed back towards Afghanistan. Half way through the journey just before the railway bridge crossing the gorge at Attock the train stopped. Jack was up like a shot; put this head out over the top of the open slatted window to see what the trouble was. He stood there. I noticed his hand on his holster ready for action, outside there was a of lot shouting and waving of hands going on. I immediately took fright my heart was racing. After a few moments he called to me.

'It's all right Sarah. It's only the railway authorities holding up the train. Apparently everyone must get off, something's wrong on the bridge. C'mon you three we have to get out. Sarah you stay close behind. I'll help you down.'

This was something I hadn't bargained for; I just wanted to be back in my bungalow. All the passengers were standing alongside, a commotion at the rear of the train was holding everything up, some Indians on the roof were reluctant to come down, were forcibly persuaded by the Guard. The empty train slowly moved forward with its passengers walking behind, none appeared to be concerned as if it were an everyday occurrence. When we arrived at the bridge its span was quite long, laid over the sleepers were a couple of narrow boards to walk on. I grabbed hold of Jackie and Kathleen hands, one in front and one behind, assuming behind us Jack had hold of Mary, joining on the end of the line proceeded cautiously forward, I did not look down through the open sleepers until we reached the other side. Harrowing but we made it to the safety of the waiting train however Mary had disappeared, we couldn't find her, Jack said she was behind him all the way. I was frantic with worry, she was fearless, had she fallen through or not? Then from in amongst the crowd she just turns up grinning. She got an instant lashing of my tongue from me. She promised to be good (which lasted a day.) My anxiety along with traversing the bridge started the pains off again. We all climbed aboard. I sat down in agony with these spasms of pains the train continued on the rest of the journey. I tried to relax in this crowded compartment, but the pains were back again. It wasn't long after that we arrived back at Nowshera. I had no strength left in me I was worn out from the effects of the journey. Jack organised the Tonga's settled me as comfortable as one could get in a Tonga for the short journey home.

CHAPTER FOUR.
NOWSHERA - PART 2.

I was so relieved when we arrived back, even before the Tonga had stopped, the remaing servants came out to greet our return, smiling wth much salaaming Salam alekum's greetings quickly turned to concerns as Jack and number One Ayah helped me down. I did not have the strength to go through all those greetings, without their help I could hardly manage the veranda steps, guided to a chair I flopped down exhausted. Immediately Jack ordered chai, whilst the Bearer organised the servants re-opening of the quarters. The Khansama came up the steps looking very concerned, served me chai, taking a sip, could see all appeared pleased to be back in the warmth of the plains. Feeling mentally drained and physically sick, could not even stomach the chai, which normally revived me. Jack came out onto the veranda holding some letters, quietly murmured.

'You feel any better Sarah? I have some Mail that's arrived.'

Handed me six letters to read. left them unopened on my lap, the pains were so bad then vomited. Jack lifting me out of the chair carried me into our bedroom laid me on the bed. His voice full of concern asked.

'Sarah.What is the matter you look as white as a sheet. I'll send for the MO immediately'....He went outside I heard him call the Bearer... 'Jao Jahldi Jahldi MO. Memsahib bimar Jahldi.'

The Ayah's came in with bowls of cold water and towels, quickly followed by Jack, the look on his face was great concern, he stood watching as they administered the damp towels to my forehead and neck, in an expression of their concern all clucking, sucking at their teeth. I screamed as a large pain seared through my stomach. Panting I perspired freely, slowly it subsided, quickly followed by another fierce one, instant fear took hold of me as I began to give birth to the baby I miscarried. The Ayah's took control, shooing Jack out of the room. By the time the MO arrived there was nothing he could do except makes me comfortable, do the necessary and confine me to bed.

Five days later, I could not get over our misfortune. I lay there weak struggling with my thoughts: *All about Jackie's birth, a time when I had nearly lost him. I never seemed to carry babies well, always being sick and ill but to me for some reason this pregnancy never seemed right? Maybe it was not meant to be. Something I was never to know?* Jack was very concerned and would spend a lot of time consoling me sharing his responsibility with me, he was most unhappy with our loss, even our household had lost the mood. Gone was the singing, for what it was their chattering was confined to a whisper. On the sixth day, nobody had asked me or told me to get up I just had to. I managed to struggle out to the veranda sit in the chair like a dishevelled wreck. The Ayah's came from all angles to fuss over me pulling me up to get me back to bed urging.

'Na han Memsahib. Bima bahut bimar.' I resisted, shooing them away saying.

'Ji han Memsahib pukka.' I repeated this a few times shaking my head. Smiling put my hands together bowed my head. Still looking very concerned at my being up, shaking their heads, they gave up. Number One Ayah quietly asked.

'Chai Memsahib.' I nodded she clapped her hands called aloud. 'Chai Memsahib.'

The Bearer, Khansama came running up the steps, seeing me stopped. Both possibly shocked by the sight of this dishevelled wreck of a Memsahib sat before them, number One Ayah called out.

'Chai Jahldi.' The Bearer salaamed, the Khansama was already running. I sat there looking out at the garden it was pleasing to my eyes. I became aware that quite a few servants were standing on the veranda, staring at their Memsahib with concern. Chai was placed in front of me, together with a plate of small pieces of fruit. A nice thought and gesture, nodded my thanks, Number One Ayah shooed them all away as I took hold of the glass sipped the chai tasting its goodness that quenched my thirst, sitting there feeling the heat of the day, realised I was back down on the plains. I enquired.

'Kahan (Where) Missy Babas?' Two Ayahs spoke up.

'Coolie. Memsahib coolie.' That was a signal for them to disappear, salaaming they left the veranda. Number One Ayah looked at me knelt down took hold of my arm and placed her hand in mine she stroked my arm in comfort.

'Allah achchha memsahib. Inshallah'…I didn't know what she meant, I looked into her soft deep brown eyes, saw sympathy, I smiled she smiled back I murmured'Shukria (Thank you).' Making movements of washing her face and hair quietly asked….'Memsahib dhona sanp e pani ji han?' I nodded…'Ji han number One. Shukria.'

She raised herself and went into the bungalow, quickly returning with a washing robe and some clean cloths. In her sing song voice called out.

'Dhobi. Pani nahana Memsahib.'

She took hold of my arms gently pulled me up. I realised now she wanted me to take a sluice down with soap (nahana and sanp) not a face wash. I hesitated but she insisted pulling at my arm.'Memsahib nahana achchha.'

I gave up, I did not have the strength to fight her off. I knew she was right I had not had any ablutions for days. The Bearer walked over, took my other arm, both eased me up slowly took me down the steps. The Bearer began growling instructions to the Dhobi Wallah. As we slowly made our way across the open ground, the hard baked earth was very hot under my bare feet. About to enter the washhouse, the Bearer let go of my arm. I felt her arm around me to support me, as slowly we walked forward. Inside the washhouse many pots filled with pani lay waiting on the floor, she guided me forward, stood in front of me taking hold of the washing robe draped it over my head so that it hung from my shoulders. She nodded for me to slip my night-dress off, which I did, Lifting up a pot gently poured pani over my head although cool had me taking an intake of breath, as she poured pani over me I stood there, then another, followed by more before she handed me soap to wash, feeling the suds slide easily over my body having finished, she doused me with fresh pani again and again. Holding a cloth out for me to dry, then another one to dry my hair, finally she handed me a clean dress to wear. Ablutions over I did feel much better leaving my hair long I took her hands in mine squeezing them together thanked her, she smiled held her head down, I'm sure she blushed she exclaimed. 'Memsahib pukka ji han?'

'Memsahib ha pukka number One. Bahut Achchha.'

Revitalised, she helped me out back to the bungalow where the Bearer helped me up the steps on to the veranda into the chair, he bowed salaamed. I bowed muttered.

'Achchha. Bearer.'

'Memsahib chai?'

'Ji han Bearer.' I responded as he called out.

'Chai. Memsahib.'

The Khansama with a forlorn look on his face arrived to serve the chai quietly murmured.

'Memsahib. Chai Achchha.'…I smiled at him, which brought a grin to his face, he waited for me to taste. I obliged… 'Ji han achchha pukka.'

Then beaming bowed was off back to his kitchen. The faint sounds of him singing could be heard, he was satisfied the Memsahib was getting better. Number One Ayah appeared with a big bunch of flowers, arranging them in a vase on the table.

'Memsahib sunghana khushbader…She smelt the flowers.(Smell fragrant) I leant forward and smelt their fragrance was beautiful and fresh, it was very thoughtful of her.

217

'Achchha number One achchha.'

She knelt down beside me, stayed there whilst I drank the chai. I watched a green lizard scurry across the table towards the vase of flowers, instantly stopped. I watched what it was going to do. A fly came whizzing around with quick flick of the tongue a gulp it was gone, the Lizard scurried away that was their way of life. After the sluice down I sat there feeling quiet refreshed. I was missing the noise of my tribe running around, but had to wait until they returned from school. I took stock of the situation understanding, not only Jack and I had lost a little life, the servants too had great feelings about the tragic event, such was their concern for us.

My hair was still damp but drying in the warm air. I decided to get my hair sorted out make myself presentable, with the help from number One Ayah I made it back in my room cooling down my forehead with Lavender water, when I heard the noisy arrival of my tribe, patting my hair went outside onto the veranda. to be met by an onrush of the three of them running in. Mary the first to speak.

'Mum you're up are you well now?' Then Jackie.

'Hello mum. I'm hungry.' Kathleen.

'Mum. I'm thirsty.' Things were back to normal.

'Mary. Get the Khansama to fetch lemon pani and fresh fruit. Dinner will not be long away, so you can wait Jackie.'

When Jack arrived for lunch, he was surprised but very pleased to see that I was up, with concern asked.

'Sarah. Your up do you feel well enough?'

'Yes. I'll manage.'

'The MO. spoke to me he will be around this afternoon to check you out. I told him that you were still resting in bed, but he insisted on coming over. So you can expect him later.'

'Well I don't mind, I feel much better now I'm up, had a sluice down, but if he insists all well and good.' We had lunch and sat talking together for a while before he left said.

"Sarah. I'll leave now, don't forget the MO will be over later this afternoon bye the way you never read those letters I gave you, they are still in the bedroom. Maybe you can spend some time reading them this afternoon.

'Erm. OK.' Getting up kissed me got on hi horse and rode away.

The remnants of lunch were cleared away my tribe were still sat at the table Jackie eyes were near to closing, I called the Ayah's to take the children into the bedroom for their rest. I sat there and must have dozed off. The next thing I knew, someone was shaking my arm.... 'Mrs Plant....Mrs Plant..'... With a start I jumped, opened my eyes saw the MO stood in front. of me. ...Aah, Mrs Plant. I'm sorry to disturb you. I did inform your husband I would pop in to see how you were coping?'

'Oh I'm sorry I must have dozed off. Thank you Doctor, I do feel much better. I just could not stay in bed any longer, I have been up for some hours now. Being up is what I needed. Would you like some chai?'

'That's the ticket. I'd love one.' He then started to talk to me about my health, the recent happenings. After we had finished the chai, he gave me a brief examination. A bottle of red iron tonic to take, three times a day with meals. Mounting his horse said he would visit me again in a couple of days.I watched him ride away, looked at the tonic and wondered, should I take a spoonful now or leave it till the final meal of the day. I chose the latter. I thought about the mail Jack had left inside, I could spend a quiet half-hour reading the letters. I got up collected them from the bedroom, returning to the veranda sat down, a quick scrutiny of the letters revealed they were from Mother and Eilish. In addition were three Christmas cards, realised we were only a couple of weeks away from Christmas, which would be our first one in India with the sun beating down on us. It was so unlike the season of good will, besides at that moment in time, I was not

218

in any fit state to contemplate anything to do with it. However the children did matter, I would have to discuss the event of Christmas with Jack when he came home. Before my tribe stirred themselves and came out onto the veranda, I had read each letter twice, they ready for afternoon playing. Daily routines were definitely back to normal. When Jack arrived back that evening. Immediately he asked if the MO had called to see me. I told him he had, gave me an examination and gave me a bottle of tonic to take and ordered me further rest. I mentioned about the letters and Christmas cards. Those he said he would read later after the tribe were all in bed and asleep. We had khana, I did not eat very much tired by the toll of my day's inactivity intending to go to bed, at the same time as the children, leaving Jack alone on the veranda reading the letters by the light of the oil lamp.

Next morning when I woke it was daylight. I got up slipped on my dressing jacket. The bungalow was unusually quiet, number One Ayah came into the bedroom salaamed parting her hands.

'Memsahib. Baba's challiye coolie.' Children at school. Surprised at her comment heard the chimes of the clock strike eight 'o'clock. I thought: *I must have slept undisturbed for hours, maybe it was the red tonic? What would we have done about the time, if Jack had not retrieved the clock from the cook in Colchester.* I wandered outside on to the veranda the Khansama salaamed, there on the table was a glass of chai. I went over taking hold took a sip, glanced out at the flower bed, all neat and tidy with an abundant of coloured flowers. The old Malee was tending to them, glancing up saw me, began cutting some flowers then brought them to me, grinning he smrelt them handed them over to me.

'Memsahib Phal kusubaarji han.' (Memsahib flowers fragrant)I responded.

'Ji han. Malee. Ji han.' That was a nice gesture of him. I handed them to number One to put in a vase. Finishing off the dregs of my chai, after my full night's rest I felt much stronger went back inside to carry out my ablutions get dressed ready for the day, thinking: *"On your feet soldier things to do."* Picking up my Tobie I walked purposely out towards the veranda steps clapping my hands called out.

'Bearer. Inspection time.'

The Bearer looked at me, immediately understood what I was up to. He in turn issued his orders, all came running to form up in line for the restart of our daily routine. I walked along their line, giving a nod and a smile to all. With inspection over returned to sit on the veranda ordered another glass of chai, noticed there was a change in the attitude of the servants. in the quietness of the morning, in the background the sounds of the Dhobi Wallah singing accompanied by the monotonous slap of beating him hell out of clothes, whilst inside the chattering of the Ayah's had begun again that added to the daily sound of work. After my forced six days of absence, just the Memsahib's Inspection had brought about the change, instead of moping about over the past. I had much to do to catch up, I would throw myself into occupying my boring day. I had the bungalow to sort out, letters to write. I wandered around the different rooms to see if anything had to be done or changed. I need not have bothered. My tribe arrived from school, the midday lunch was quickly over, soon resting in the searing heat of the afternoon, as for me I catnapped, woke took a sluice down sat down to write, as there were no greeting cards to send instead wrote brief words of seasons greetings. I still could not get used to the timing of letters, possibly in my previous letters, I had repeated events time and time again. However this time, I had bad news to write home about. In my letters I wrote of our misfortune, I never finished one letter, my tribe came out from their afternoon's sleep. The letters I would finish off later. That night I asked Jack what should we do about Christmas? I still was not in any mood for it, but for the children's sake, we should do something. He agreed saying.

'. I have arranged some presents for our three so under our circumstances just have a quiet Christmas dinner also, during the following week the Sergeants mess has organised a Christmas party for all the children and if you feel up to it Sarah you have been invited to a Mess Ball?'

I declined, as at that moment in time I was very far from socialising, Jack understood. We had a pleasant day on Christmas Day, a quiet one on Boxing Day the children went and enjoyed the Chistmas party, New Year was very quiet. Having got through an unwanted passage of time. I was sat idly watching the too-ing, and fro-ing of the Wallahs selling their wares. When it occurred to me back back in the Currah married quarters Mother and I had done exactly the same thinking: *Here was something else I could become involved with. Selecting and buying the vegetables, but one small problem, I did not want to upset the Khansama. In the past when I had been in to his cookhouse, he appeared to be upset but after a while he had accepted I was the Memsahib and he must do what I ordered. I decided the next day when the Sabzi (Vegetable) Wallah turned up, I should go with the Khansama and inspect his selection. Once he saw and understood what I was up to he would not get upset.*

Next morning, having completed my daily inspection, taking chai sat at the table I waited for one of the Wallahs to turn up, the first one arriving with a couple of Chico's pushing his funny one wheeled barrow festooned with pots and chatti bowls,was the Dudh (milk) Wallah. Intently I watched, as he pulled up outside the cookhouse. The Bearer hailed him, they began chatting away in Urdu then the Khansama came out, a few more words, laughter! With those formalities over. Normal procedure of purchase proceeded with the Khansama, watched over by the Bearer (an onlooker). Dudh was purchased. Then the Bearer (he the Banker) approached me, for Anna's to pay. I thought: *That was one thing; I would not get involved in, leave that solely to the Bearer.* I got up retrieved the money box from the bedroom, handed it to the Bearer, who taking out Anna's, proceeded to haggle with the Wallah, agreement made. The end of that saga.

I sat bemused by all this palaver. In the past I had let these daily occurrences pass me by, then my intention was. Let them get on with it. Nevertheless, I had made up my mind up to get more involved. I did not have long to wait the arrival of the Sabzi Wallah. He arrived pushing his funny wheelbarrow, hailing the Khansama he stopped outside. I got up, with my Tobie stuck on my head, I set off for the cookhouse followed by the Bearer. At my arrival, the Sabzi Wallah salaamed, unsure of my presence stood there, probably wondering what the Memsahib was up to? I looked at the array of vegetables and fruit on the wheelbarrow. The Khansama, already looking at the produce, looked at me puzzled. Deliberately I spotted some mealy-eyed onions picked them up, held them out towards him. The Khansama inspecting them shook his head. I replaced them he picked up a few good ones showed them to me. Looking at them I nodded, he grinned murmured something to the Bearer. Every time I sorted out a different item, I noticed the Bearer lift one eyebrow, whether or not it was a show of approval I did not care just carried on repeating my bad choice, until the Khansama understood. I was there for his guidance. I was getting rather hot stood out in the sun, removing my Tobie used it as a fan. Noticing this, the Khansama murmured.

'Memsahib garam?' (Memsahib hot)

'Ji han Khansama. Memsahib garam.' He murmured words to the Bearer, which I understood to mean. *"The Memsahib should be sitting on the veranda out of the heat of the sun."* Nevertheless, I still carried on picking up items, showing them to him, he either shook or nodded his head in approval. When each of the produce had been sorted out to buy, then the haggling began, then I left, dutifully the Bearer followed behind me as I walked back I noticed my action had attracted an audience, some of the servants had stopped what they were doing to watch, also stood in the doorway on the veranda so were the Ayah's. I took no notice as I went up the steps sat down at the table the ritual of payment was about to get underway. This little extravaganza on my part began a new chapter in my morning ritual. Giving me yet another

220

opportunity to get more involved to break up my monotonous day. For the next three days, I carried out exactly the same procedure, but on the fourth day the Khansama came out of the cookhouse and stood waiting for the Sabzi Wallah. I sat there waiting with curiousity as to why? The Sabzi Wallah arrived then the Khasama directed him to the foot of the veranda steps thoughtful as he had already pointed out 'Memsahib Garam'. I should stay on the veranda out of the sun, I sat there watching, as he began to sort out the vegetables, this time showing each produce to me, for me to approve with a nod or with a shake of my head disapprove, again I noticed everthing came to a standstill as the servants gathered to watch the pantomime and the finale the formal act of payment, carried out by the Bearer.

The following day was Saturday, my tribe would not be at school. After breakfast. We had the normal daily inspection, they joined in walking behind me giggling, then they would be off to play with the Chicos. Calling out his cry the Sabzi Wallah arrived pushing his barrow right up to the veranda steps, where the Khansama was stood. I was seated on my chair ready to agree with the Khansama each item on offer, the Chico's playing with my tribe stopped playing. came over to sit on the veranda steps their action encouraged my tribe to sit down alongside them, they casting glances at me to get my approval. I took no notice. I had other things to attend too. Automatically they became a willing audience. As ever all very watchful as the events of this pantomime of sorting, haggling, then payment unfolded in front of them. With all this going on I soon understood, what Elizabeth had told me. That Indians love to watch some form of a play or, actually become involved, they just loved to become part of it, as they did participating on our Sunday morning trips to Mass. As the days slipped by other Wallahs, were introduced to this daily morning ritual. Then the Bearer and I would check what had been saved with his haggling. By the end of the month, the savings would go to purchase a new coloured turban for him, a beautiful Sari for each of the Ayahs smart cummerbunds for all, for the family Sunday Parade. This was much appreciated by all the servants.

Through exchange of letters I had also kept in contact with Nora and Grace, both had been dismayed by our loss but very supportive in their words. Mail eventually arrived from mother and she expressed her deep sorrow at our loss but assured me that what must be must be. Just get on with life. Mentioned a couple of points in the paper, Eamon De Valera had been arrested and jailed for illegally entering Northern Ireland. It appeared the Troubles in Ireland had not totally gone away, about the series of riots that had taken place in Bombay hundreds had been killed, asked were we near them? When I queried it with Jack he retorted.

'Don't worry about those things; you know how far Bombay is away. Besides the riots took place in January. Those riots were between religious factors the Muslims and the Hindus; they take their religious beliefs very seriously in India. Up here in the North West Frontier the issues are far more tribal between the Pathans, Afridis and Mahsud the tribes fighting over land or water rights. The army was out here to keep the peace between all of them.'

I discover I am pregnant again. We are both overjoyed but wary of the consequences. This time I must take it easy! Not a hard task as I did not do anything. Replying to mother advised about what Jack had said about them, but too early to mention our good news. The Battery football team were in the final of the Charity Shield competition to be played at Risalpur, a couple of miles outside of Nowshera. The kick off was scheduled for nine thirty in the morning, having not been on any outing since returning from the hills, I decided to take my tribe to watch their father. Jack arranged transport for us the Bearer, Ayah's, and Syce's to accompany us. Saturday morning we set off early, the journey was bumpy we got the Tonga driver to stop under the shade of the trees with a good view of the pitch, even under the Tonga canopy the temperature gradually increased to a searing heat. The Battery team won the game. The Brigade Commander Lt/Col. Duke awarded the Shield. Jubilant with their victory we set off back to the Sgt.'s mess where a buffet was laid on in celebration of the win. For me it was a time that I was back in circulation in amongst the smell of mothballs and eau de cologne, generously dabbed on by all the women.

25th BATTERY R.A. NOWSHERA
Winners- The Charity Shield Risalpur

Standing: Grn. Martin. Gnr. Burns. Grn. Growat. L/Sgt. Harrow Grn. Ward. Grn. Hughes Grn. Wren
Sitting: Grn. McGee Lt/Col W. Green DSO MCRA. Grn.Dobson (Capt.) BSM Maley - L/Brd Slatter
Front: Grn. Coyles-   BQMS Plant

Easter came and went, before I knew it, Jack told me to pack my bags, we were going for a four-month rest up to Khanspur. Being pregnant again I was dreading the trip, this time just in case, blankets and warm clothes were packed for the journey. At Murree we parted ways, Jack returned, we carried on in the Dandy's, this time no snow instead favourably weather. At Khanspur we were in the same bungalow. I was to meet Grace and Nora both located in their old bungalows so began our Tiffin time. I did take to riding a horse but only for a few weeks. All went well for the first eight weeks of our stay, once again I became ill experienced the same feelings again, very unwell with vomiting, I took to my bed to rest. Jack arrived for a five-day leave, along with two ponies in tow laden with provisions, which were handed out to our scattered neighbours. Before Jack returned back, he left me with strict instructions not to overdo it. I became heavy with pregnancy, was too scared to move I did little or nothing, then was very unwell. The MO confined me to bed. Nora sent a wire to Jack, within the week he arrived. Very concerned of my condition, immediately decided that I must return down to Nowshera. He went and saw the QM, arranged for me to travel back down with him. The trip down was the exact same as my previous trip, Dandy's to Murree, a private car to Pindi. At Pindi we caught a train and arrived back at the bungalow early in the afternoon I was exhausted by the travelling thanking my lucky stars.sat down on the veranda chair, Chai the reviver was served. Jack handed me four letters to read, In amongst the letters was a blue envelope stamped with an aeroplane. It was by Airmail sent by Eilish, immediately thought *Communication between Blighty and India was getting better, I would not have to wait three months."* Quickly opened it took out the few paper thin pages, reading the first paragraph discovered the awful news two weeks before my Father had passed away, What a great shock that was. I let out a howl of anguish that had Jack bounding up the steps. His voice full of concern.

'Sarah what is it?'

'Father has died. God rest his soul I shall never see him again.'

That was all I could say I sat there weeping. Jack knelt down took me in his arms consoled me, letting me cry for a little while before he took the letter out of my grasp, read it murmured.

222

'No not Michael, what a good friend he was to me.' About to say something else. I cried out.

'Oh my God' I've started.' Immediately, thought the baby was going to be born there and then. Jack picked me up and took me into our bedroom laid me on the bed.

'Hang on Sarah. I'll go and fetch one of the other wives to come and stay with you. You just hang on. I'll sort out the tribe.'

Before I could say anything he was gone, he just didn't want to be around at that time. The Ayah's were more than capable of looking after the children. He arrived back accompanied by one of his sergeant's wives, who enquired.

'How are you Mrs.' Plant? Have you arranged with the MO to go in to hospital?'

'No. We've just arrived back from up the hills an hour ago and my pains have gone. Anyway like all my others babies I am having the baby at home,' Concerned she questioned.

'Were any of them born out in India?'

'No all back in Blighty.'

'Well, I would suggest that you go and see the MO as soon as possible.' She was very kind, and stayed with me, just before twilight she left told Jack...'Get in touch with the MO.'

'Okay, after I take you back to your bungalow. I do have to report back so I'll see him then. I must thank you for your assistance and advice.'

She bade me goodbye hoped I would be Okay. I never saw her again. As I lay there thinking: *Whatever was the MO going to say when he found out I was nearly eight months pregnant without visiting him?* The Ayah's came back in fussing over me. Chai was brought in, whilst I heared my tribe playing outside, sometime later Jack arrived back.

'You feeling a little bit better Sarah? The MO was unavailable? Anyway company orders states all families returning from the hills, are to report to the MRS tomorrow at ten 'o clock, you will see him then.'

During the night the labour pains began. I did not sleep very well. Next morning I was in no fit state to go anywhere, never mind the MRS. Jack arranged for the Tonga's to take us there. When we arrived, I must have looked a sorry sight. The Matron asked.

'Mrs Plant are you all right?

'No not really. We came back from the hills yesterday, When I was reading the mail, in amongst it was one of those new airmail letters informing me my father had died. I'm sure the shock of that started off the labour pains, they did subside but started again during the night. But again the subsided I have not had any since.'

Quietly she listened to all I was saying, before she began asking about the health of the children? Then she started asking questions about my previous pregnancies?

'Well as you can see I have three children. During those pregnancies I was never examined by any Doctor. I had a miscarriage about a year ago. Furthermore, I have no intention of going into hospital to have this baby either.'.... 'Mrs Plant. Did they not bother in England?'... 'Yes. They did, but I never liked hospitals I did not want them pulling me about. Anyway I had enough to go through when having a baby.' ..She ordered.... 'Mrs Plant wait here.'

Turning on her heels with a rustle of starch disappeared into the Doctor's room. After a short while she came back out and retorted.

'Mrs Plant. I have spoken to the Doctor, who has advised me to tell you. That he has no intention of pulling you about. You're just going to have a medical examination. In your condition you definitely need one. No ifs or buts about it. Stop worrying.'

Taken aback by the forcefulness of her remark, anyone would think I was going to be murdered instead of a simple examination. The Doctor examine me, explained.

'Mrs Plant, everything is all right you will go the full time with the baby, it will be a big baby when born? Certainly not now possibly just before Christmas. I understand you have just received some bad news. Most probable it was that shock that caused the pains. However all is quiet and settled down. Please convey my condolences to your family.' he proceeding to tell me off....'Mrs Plant. Even if I have to give up my own bed. My final word is.You will have your baby in hospital.'

Then proceeded to examine the children. As I watched my mind was in a whirl. *The thoughts of going into the hospital to have the baby, I'd never been in one before. What was I going to do about my tribe?* My fingers twisting my wedding ring at nineteen to the dozen. The Matron must have noticed my agitation, politely asked.

'Mrs. Plant are you feeling alright.' Venting my feelings sternly replied.

'No I'm not. What am I to do with my three children when I do go in hospital? I don't want to leave them at the bungalow. Is it possible they can come in during the dattime so I can be near to them? then they can return back to the bungalow to sleep. My husband could bring them and take them back.' Listening to my searching request the Matron said.

'Well Mrs Plant. Now we are faced with a problem! I don't think the army would be very pleased to have your husband neglect his duties do you? But don't you worry your baby is not due until Christmas, something will turn up.'

I wasn't convinced. The Doctor passed us all fit. We were about leave the MRS when the Matron came out behind us called me.

'Mrs Plant. I've been thinking about your problem. I too have a bit of a problem. My two children at the Convent will be home for the Christmas holidays. Maybe, I too will be on duty while you are in confinement at the hospital. How about the children playing together, surely that would solve both of our problems don't you think?'

It was a possibility. Therefore I agreed. That was one thing less to worry about, I thanked her. Back at the bungalow it was back to normality, the children quite happy playing, making the most of the day off from school, I sitting there sipping chai contemplating the day's events thinking: *About all the things I had to do? And the Doctor telling me to look after myself. What a hope with three wild and healthy children to run around after, actually they were quite stupid thoughts, I did nothing, what on earth did I employ servants for?* To take my mind off that subject, I began to read the letters I had not read the day before. When Jack arrived back I was crying as I had just re-read Eilish's letter, informing of Fathers death. All he said was.

'C'mon Sarah don't be silly. You have to be brave get on with it. Once a soldier always a soldier.'

I could have screamed at his remark but I knew he was right. He was very supportive spending as much time as he could back in the bungalow, except when playing football in the Punjab Cup competition, their next match was against the Royal Air Force team from Peshawar, his team won. But more illness Mary became ill, quickly followed by Jackie, then Kathleen. All with suspected Malaria the MO confined them to bed dosed them up with quinine, the Medical orderly came every day to take their temperatures, and give them the foul tasting substance, what a job he had trying to force spoonful's down their necks, nevertheless they became worse, neither I nor the Ayah's could cope with them. We had to call the Ambulance a large four-wheeled Tonga arrived to take them into hospital. I went with them. They were admitted, I was ordered to go home. Leaving my three behind, hired a Tonga. During my journey back, agitated by my future confinement in the hospital, I could not stop crying. Gone was the Matrons plan she and I had hatched up. Instead it was the opposite. I visited them daily taking a jar of sweets with me to entice them to take this vile medicine. Without their boisterous noise, the bungalow became silent. The Ayah's were lost with nothing to do, everything appeared too center entirely around my unruly tribe. I would worry pray and cry myself to sleep. Between Jack's duties he would come with me to visit the children, nevertheless my pantomime with the Wallahs ceased. As the days past they gradually became better. However Jacks football team had won their way into the final of the Punjab Cup at Risalpur, once again their opponents were the Royal Air Force team, to be played a week before my baby was due to be born; On the day of the match he said to me.

'Sarah with the baby due at any moment. I shall stay with you so that I can take you into hospital.' Apart from him taking me into hospital, in my heart I knew he could not help me any further; it would be down to the Doctor and nurses so replied.

'No you go win the cup and bring it back to all of us to see. But don't forget I will be here on my own waiting.'

Trying to reassure him that I was not going into labour, gave him my permission. He left the bungalow early. In the morning I visited my tribe, who were by that time resonding to the treatment, upon my return to the bungalow expected Jack to be back from the match waiting for me. Did he come home? No. I waited for hours wondering if he had been injured, my thoughts: *If I went into labour how was I to get to hospital without his presence?* I went to bed trying to keep awake I prayed before dozing off. About one a.m. a dreadful racket at the back of the bungalow woke me. The noise of the chickens and turkeys were squawking and gobbling, nineteen to the dozen. (We were looking after the turkeys for the Batteries Christmas Dinner all we had to do was feed them). Immediately thought: *Some Loose Wallah Dacoit or maybe Jackals were trying to get at them. No matter what happened. I certainly was not going outside.* Getting out of bed, found the revolver we always had ready for such an intrusion, taking hold of it checked the chambers, it was loaded. Climbing back into bed lay down to listen, holding the revolver in both hands its weight resting on my chest as I levered the catch back on the revolver I could feel my heart pounding. I started praying for whatever it was, to take all of the chickens and turkeys but do not attempt to come into the bungalow. It never occurred to me that none of the servants, particularly the Bearer or the Chowkidar had ever made any move whatsoever about the disturbance. I heard a noise listening heard a voice in a loud whisper called out.

'Sarah it's me. Sarah ducks. Open the door there's a good girl. '

At that moment I also could hear other voices. So that's why anybody didn't move. It was the Sahib of the house. To say the least relieved got out of bed, released the lever on the revolver put the safety catch on, laid it on down on the side table, turning up the hurricane lamp, slipped into my knickers, put on my dressing gown. Carrying the lamp went out to the door hesitated, whispered.

'Jack. Is that really you with someone?' Another whispered exchange.

'Yes Sarah. C'mon there's a ducks open up the door.'

I put down the lamp on the floor, lifted the wooden security bar from across the door, lifting up the lamp opened the door, in its glow saw the grinning faces of Jack and the rest of the team.

'We've won the cup Sarah! As I promised I've brought it home, along with the team. Sarah can they all come in for a celebration drink?' I retorted.

'Celebration drink? Yes bring them all in.' Jack beckoned them to follow him.

'Ssshoosh. Come on in lads don't make a noise.' I stood to one side, as they filed past me with the crates of beer they had brought with them filing past me all murmured. 'Thank you's. Sorry Mrs Plant. It was Jack's idea when we were up at the Mess.'

They all settled down to have a few more drinks, except the goalkeeper, who did not drink. Instead he chatted to me apologising for disturbing me so late at night. I told him I was already awake? They must have stayed for about an hour, as they were preparing to leave. Jack in his usual hospitable manner, invited the whole team around to have dinner with us later that day. I thought. *"Oh my God. They are all too drunk.I hope they don't remember."* They left quietly.

We retired, I lay awake. Jack snored. The rest of the household slept.

Early next morning saw Jack up and on parade as usual. The previous night's celebration was not even thought about. To him duty is duty. Before he left he reminded me.

'Don't forget Sarah. We invited them all around for dinner today about four is that okay?'

I did not respond just thought: *WE" What he really meant was. "HE" invited them all around, at least he has given me plenty of time to organise it.* He left on his horse quietly galloping away. This functional duty had been passed over to me.It was my territory I had to get this function organised before I went to visit the children.

Before dawn had broken, sat at the table on the veranda, a shawl over my shoulders sipping a glass of chai, in the glow of the hurricanre lamp I began preparing a list of vegatables for the meal to be cooked, it was light by the time finished. Then it was the seating arrangement at least twelve. I beckoned the Bearer to follow me around, with a lot of gesturing about the table settings, hand signals counting on fingers the numbers of men to lay out the tables places, the Sahib had invited. I gave him the list for the Khansama to organise Khana, The Ayah's to gather flowers from the garden to make a beautiful table centre, so that the guest could all have a wonderful party and enjoy their Celebration Dinner, thousands of miles from home. With all these preparations organised and underway. Accompanied by number One Ayah, we got a Tonga to the hospital there to spend time with the children. They were my worry and was certainly not going to concern myself about the dinner party until I returned later. I arrived back at the bungalow to find the Bearer standing impassively at the foot of the veranda steps waiting for me, he salaamed.

'Memsahib.' Helped me down from the Tonga up the steps to the veranda, then gestured for me to follow him into the sitting room, standing to one side he let me pass. What greeted me was the tables laid out with flowers decorating the centre piece, with each table setting correctly placed with my dinner service, the room was heavy with the sweet scent of flowers placed in all the nooks and crannies. I truly was amazed at the sight and nodded my approval.

'Pukka Bearer. Pukka' He salaamed, hastened me to follow him out across the veranda helping me down the steps led me to the cookhouse. As we approached I heard a hubbub of noise, standing aside let me pass through the entrance into the gloom of the cookhouse into a hive of activity. Immediately it stopped, quickly glancing around, it appeared that everyone was helping the Khansama. He stood up smiled at me, waving his hands shaking his head from side to side in that funny way they all expressed. Nodding my approval spoke aloud.

'Ji han Khansama. Pukha khana pukka.'

That gave the Khansama the right to shout out instructions. Clapping his hands for them to get back to their tasks and carry on. I was more than pleased at their efforts, with salaams all round I left them to it I had little to worry about on that front.

'Ji han Bearer pukka.' We left, I to return to the bungalow to lie down to rest before the next episode of the dinner party. I must have dozed off. A gentle shake on my arm woke me, number One Ayah whispered.

'Memsahib. Memsahib. Do bajeh.'

'Do bajeh?

'Ji han memsahib.'

'My God. Its two 'o'clock.' I must have been asleep for a couple of hours. Getting up moving like a carthorse in my condition, rallied around and could well do without all this palaver that Jack had brought upon me. I padded out into the main room, its sweet fragrance hit me. It truly was a lovely sight. I decided to have a sluice down before getting ready to greet our guest. With that done, found the Bearer and all the other servants had dressed up for their part. The men dressed in new whites with dark blue cummerbunds including the Chic's in white shirts dark blue cummerbunds, the Ayah's dressed in lovely multi- coloured saris. Only then did I realised, it was the very first entertainment that had been laid on by us as a family. The servants were in on the act, they had done me proud. I would reward them later.

226

There was little for me to do, so sat down to take chai on the veranda to await Jacks arrival. When he reined in, life at the bungalow appeared to be just as a normal day, Jumping off his horse, still holding the reins out for the Syce to take charge of his horse. He greeted me.

'Hello Sarah. How are you feeling?'

'Oh as well as can be expected.'

'Children okay today?'

'Yes. As well as can be expected.'

'Erm. Our guest will be here soon.'

'Yes I know.'

'Erm. Is everything ready?' Pointing inside I left him pondering retorted.

'Go and see for yourself!'

He came up the steps onto the veranda went inside to see what arrangements had been carried out. He was gone for a few minutes, coming out he came up to me bent down kissed me.

'You're an angel Sarah. The table setting looks really wonderful.'

What a compliment from him. We had chai then he got ready to receive "OUR GUESTS." Who arrived in a fleet of Tonga's, bringing with them the Trophy, crates of beer, banjos and mouthorgans? If only Mother could have witnessed this with me about to give birth. Jack and I entertained them with pre dinner drinks on a very full veranda. After a short while, I clapped my hands and called.

'Bearer. Khana ab. Jahldi.' In turn the Bearer went to the end of the veranda called out 'Khana ab.'... He ushered the guest into the inner room to sit down. The Khansama followed by a line of Chico's, carried the food inside to serve his specially prepared sumptuous meal. As it was a man's party I stayed out of the way on the veranda, to organise the servants with the different courses, whilst I re-read old newspapers. When the meal was over, Jack came out said.

'Sarah the team wishes to thank you and would like you to come in and take a drink with them.' Quietly I replied.

'Jack. You know I don't drink, certainly not in my condition.'

'C'mon just pretend you are, it will please them.' He insisted, taking hold of my hand helped me up. I don't know why I went in carrying a newspaper in front of me.

They all cheered, thanking me for the wonderful Celebration Dinner I had prepared. I was given a glass of beer as all toasted their success. I pretended to drink with them, wishing them success the next year thinking. *"Hopefully I will not be pregnant again."* Having had a wonderful time they left in the early hours of the morning. Jack who normally only drank beer, was very drunk. Someone had made him drink whisky, in his drunken condition, I had to get him to bed. He with a silly smile across his face lurching and staggering around trying to sing, managed to pull all the curtains off of the windows, before we finally made it to the bedroom. I tried three times to get him onto the bed, each time he fell off. The third time I gave up threw a blanket over him with a mosquito net on top left him to sleep it off on his own. The next morning he was back on duty, none the worse for his drink, later in the afternoon Jack informed me. When he related his previous night's escapades to the others.They all had a great laugh about it, started to celebrate all over again.

Still in hospital, my tribe were making good progress on their road to recovery. It was the third day after the dinner party I went to visit them, upon my arrival the Matron stopped me.

'Mrs Plant you're not allowed to see the children. They have been put in isolation along with others. We suspect its Black water fever. They are all with high fevers, it will be a period of crisis for the next twenty-four hours. Why don't you sit down?' In shock at the news I exclaimed.

'What all three? Matron. Please can you get word of this crisis to my husband Jack?'

As I sat there demented with worry not one but all three, praying like I had never prayed before. Just before Jack did arrive my labour pains began, he informed the Matron she got the

Doctor, result. I too was hospitalised, put into bed in another ward, on this occasion Jack was beside me. Only to be ordered back to camp by the MO. All his family were in capable hands. I was made comfortable pending the birth, which did not ease my worry of my tribe. I had a sleepless night. The next morning, I was informed the children had all safely got through their own crisis. It's amazing how children quickly recover, one minute at deaths door the next, happy as sand boys. Later that evening my labour pains really began just after midnight the twenty-fourth of December. I gave birth to a big strong healthy baby boy. Next day the MO arrived on his rounds with the Matron, examined me , the baby, gave me the good news that my three had been passed clear of the fever. With her rounds over the Matron stopped beside me remarked.

'That's very good news, all have been passed fit.' I'll get word to your husband.'

Before lunch I was moved into their ward, they were at the far end sitting up and waving from their so called isolation section. Later that morning the Matron came back.

'Mrs Plant your husband is here to see all five of you.'

Jack entered with his arms full of presents. Seeing his new baby son, his eyes full of tears as he bent over me kissed me and our son. He was obviously delighted, he lifted him up from me cradled him in his arms. With the Matron as escort, he carried the baby down the ward, to my show my tribe their new baby brother. I heard the Matron say.

'There you are. You three were so good taking your medicine. I kept my promise Father Christmas did bring you a baby.'

Jack carried the baby back to me and laid him besides me.

'Well-done Sarah. I love you, the baby and the other three terrors down there.' (Not a man of many words but everything was worth it just to hear those few words from him.) I urged him.

'Jack. send a cable to Mother.Let her know our good news. Write this down. Michael a baby Boy, born Christmas Eve, nine pounds. All are well.'

'Whoa back Sarah. I need something to write on. Matron do you have some paper and pencil to write on Please?'... The Matron went to get some writing material. Came back and gave him a plain envelope and pencil...'Thank you Matron. Now then Sarah what was it you said?'

I repeated it again as he wrote it down on the envelope put it in his tunic pocket. After a little while left to go down to the mess to break his good news and "Wet the baby's head." Christmas day was a miss for all of us in hospital. On Boxing day a soldier's wife was brought into the ward to have her baby. Accompanied by her young daughter, she was put in the next bed to me. She too was in agony, possibly she must have had the same worries as I leaving her daughter? A fair curly headed girl. Seeing my new baby she moved towards the bed exclaimed.

'Isn't he lovely? Can I come and see him and play with him when we get home?'

I thought: *Her question was funny as she had never seen us before but I acknowledged her question.* 'Yes. Certainly and you can also play with my other three down there in those beds.'

But she never ventured down there, stayed beside her mother who was thrashing about in her torment, until early in the afternoon; she was taken out of the ward. Complications had developed. She was transferred to the big Hospital in Peshawar.

Our little son was the first baby boy to be born within the Regiment. The Officers wives were wonderful, they came to visit me to see the new baby boy. First arrival Mrs. Green the Lt/Col's wife followed by the Adjutants wife, Mrs. Williams. Delighted to see my baby, enquired about the health of my other three still in bed in the other ward. After spending New Year's Eve in hospital, my baby and I were declared fit by the MO. The Matron told me not to worry about my tribe, who had still to stay in hospital for a while longer. Jack arrived at the hospital with a Tonga, to take me back to our quarters. When we arrived back at the bungalow, I was treated like royalty. All the servants lined up to greet the new baby and me. They all clapped number One Ayah placed a garland of flowers around my neck. Their fragrance was lovely, willing hands helped to escort us up onto the veranda where I sat. In turn all the servants were presented with

228

the baby. They all cooed, sighed at the sight of our new arrival. Inside in our bedroom Jack had placed a cot beside our bed to put Mchael in. The Ayah's had dressed it with white muslin and silk drapes, it really did look splendid. With the welcoming over all things settled down. Jack went back to camp leaving the servants to look after me, and so the household returned to its normal daily routine. With my tribe still in hospital their Ayah's had little or nothing to do, instead I had four Ayah's fussing and cooing over me, I wasn't allowed to do anything. Nevertheless I did insist on bathing the baby. In the mid-afternoon they brought the chatti bowls full of warm water into the bedroom, ready for me to bath him, I had just got his nappy off when the Bearer came rushing in excitedly exclaimed.

'Memsahib. Burrah Memsahib.' Pointing outside. I thought it was the Majors wife but no. In walks Mrs. Green the Lt/Colonels wife.

'Hello there Mrs. Plant. I've come to see how you and your baby are progressing.' I stuttered in reply.

'T-Thank you Ma'am.' Noticing I was about to wash the baby she rather loudly exclaimed.

'You shouldn't be up doing that. It's the Ayah's job.' I replied.

'No Ma'am. I prefer to do it myself.' Whereupon much to my surprise, off came her Toby and her loose white topcoat.

'Come along let me help'…. She bathed the baby herself, wrapped him in a towel, held him in her arms for a little while, before handing him back to me saying…'There you are all done. What a lovely little boy you have Mrs. Plant.'…The Khansama entered salaaming, served chai, quickly disappeared…She enquired. 'What are you going to call him? '

'Michael after his Grandfather, who has just recently died.' I replied as I began to feed him.

'A very suitable name Mrs. Plant. However with Michael being born on Christmas Eve, he brought his name with him. It has got to be. Noel.' I thought for a moment : *That seemed suitable.* Agreed with her…'We will christen him Michael Noel.' After I had finished feeding him. She left saying she would return another day. However my tribe had been in hospital for four weeks; before they were declared clear of illness. Back home they returned back to school, it did not take Mary very long to return to her devilment ways. On two previous occasions the teacher had been back to see us about Mary's antics. One afternoon she arrived I was sat relaxing on the veranda when she rode up. Immediately I thought: *Oh no here comes trouble again.* I greeted her served Lemon pani. Giving her and the teachers congratulation, it was down to business.

'Mrs. Plant. I.m afraid Mary has been up to her old tricks again. Her recent illness seems to have revived her enthusiasm. We the teachers have discussed the situation and I'm afraid agreed to cease the rest period forthwith instead, we can use the extra time to teach instead. So I will not be paying you anymore visits on that subject.' I was gobsmacked. Mary had won!. We passed more pleasantries before she bade me good afternoon.

It was later that we heard, the pregnant lady in the next bed to me, who had developed complications during childbirth had both died, even worse news the following day her little girl had caught a fever and died in the hospital in Peshawar. One minute she was all right the next down with fever. They didn't know what the fever was? For the young soldier husband father, a treble tragedy, that news set my nerves off worrying how I was going to cope with my new-born son out in India? I received my first air mail letter from Mother informing me she had not received the cable from Jack, until five days after his birth? When Jack read the letter all he said was, he had forgot to send it. I thought: *Good job I had not informed Mother about my tribes stay in hospital with the fever.* Mothers letters always contained her concern over happenings in India she had read out of newspapers. Her latest concern was about an Indian by the name of Mahatma Gandhi. Who was marching to the sea, followed by millions of Indians? Something to do with the British taxing salt. So I could write back and tell her not to worry. I asked Jack what this was all about?

'Oh him. Gandhi as he was known is an Indian lawyer. He wants India to become an Independent State with self-government and the British to leave India. His protests are peaceful with no violence. His latest one is against the salt tax imposed by the British. He began his march starting from Ahmedabad way down south of about three hundred miles from the sea. Trust your Ma to get it wrong. Not millions but a huge crowd. Do you remember what she said about Amy Johnston? In one of that flying contraption she's always on about.'

'G'on with you Jack, she means no harm.'

March 1930. We had been in India two years, By trial and error it had taken all that time for me to manage the household, by learning more words understood more of what the servants were trying to explain, progressively it had improved, however I would watch Mary ordering the Chico's (whose numbers seemed to have increased?) shouting to them in their own tongue. Somehow she had learnt the language, at her command she had all the Chico's running in all directions with peals of laughter, broad grins and flashing teeth on their faces, until the Bearer would come out with a clap of his hands, shout.

'JAHLDI. JAHLDI.' They would run away to continue with their chores. Mary would stand there place her hands on her hips cast a scowl at the Bearer, something he ignored. I would call her over.

'Mary. The Chico's have been told off by the Bearer, for not doing their duties. Would you please leave them alone.' To which she retorted.

'It's not fair mum we were having a good game then the Bearer just comes out and spoils it for all of us.' ...'You three go and play on your own. They will be out later when they have finished their duties you wait and see.'

With a scowl, she organised the other two it didn't make any difference the same thing would happen the following day and thereafter. Mary had a mind of her own. Yet for me they had been frustrating, traumatic, on occasions very eventful period in my life, I had come to terms with my drab daily routine, nevertheless with the arrival of Michael had change my day looking after our son. Invitations to attend Mess dos, particularly for the wives fell on deaf ears. For me no gallivanting about, I had a new baby and family to look after, with a routine revolving around them. The only inspection I carried out was the early morning, One afternoon whilst Jack and I were having Tiffin Jack said.

'You know B.S.M. Maley. I have invited him his wife and child over to have dinner with us next Saturday. Is that Okay?'...'Yes. I suppose so it's not a problem to me.'... 'Sarah have a word with Mary. Make sure that when they arrive. Mary won't say anything about their little girls colour.'...Discussion concluded. I knew that B.S.M. Maley had been in India many years. He had married an Indian girl. A subject not encouraged by the Army. Probably he was not the first and no doubt would not be the last. It was left to me to organise the dinner. I spoke with the Bearer to organise dinner for two couples and four children? It must have been hilarious to watch our somewhat muted conversation, to provide details for him. Using broken English a few words of Urdu. Gastrulating with fingers, arms, shaking and noddin heads. I finished up chuckling to myself, tears streaming down my cheeks at the antics of the pair of us, finally he would smile mutter.

'Ji han achchha Memsahib. Bahut achchha' (Yes good Memsahib. Very good) Salaamed went straight over to the Khansama, so I left them to it. When Mary arrived back from school. I had a little quiet chat with her on the very subject.

On the Saturday afternoon, the Bearer and all the servants once again had put on a splendid setting. Our guest arrived as the Bearer greeted them, before they came up. I noticed his wife, dressed in a beautiful white Sari, removed her footwear at the bottom of the steps. B.S.M. John Maley introduced his wife Indra, a young and most beautiful girl I had ever seen in my life. I would have given my eyes for her complexion, her long almost wavy dark brown hair

230

tumbled around her shoulders. Her hazel brown eyes sparkled with a pleasant smile on her lips. Their little daughter Rachel, a pretty little girl dressed in a white frock and white shoes, about the same age as Kathleen. Indra had brought a small gift for me. Drinks were served, the children were all playing quiet happily on the veranda, when in a loud voice, Mary asked Rachel.

'Rachel. Why is it? That you are so much darker than us?'

I froze with embarrassment. I looked over at Jack, who for once did not smile, however Rachel smartly replied.

'Mary we have been in India a lot longer than you have. You will be the same after a little while longer.' I thought. *"Good for you little girl."* That stopped Mary in her tracks? The matter was brushed over.

Once again the Bearer and servants did us proud dressed for the occasion served a splendid meal with the entire refinery. Indra thanked and complimented me on the meal and extended an invitation to their home, which we did accept nevertheless, I did not forget the incident with Mary. After they had left she received a good telling off. Jacks only remark was. "What can we do with her?"

It was about mid-morning one day when Jack rode up on his horse, surprised at his sudden visit got up from the chair. Reigning in he did not dismount instead politely informed me.

'Sarah ducks. Orders have been received for the Battery to immediately go to the troubles in Peshawar and the Khyber. The local authorities has informed the Army they cannot contain the peace. One of the senior tribe chiefs is aiming to whip up a war. We understand several thousand Red Shirts are preparing to advance on Peshawar. The camps on full alert. I've just come home to tell you I'm off with the Battery. I don't know for how long I'll be gone. But don't you worry Sarah. You're in a Garrison Camp. No harm will become you.'

Leaning over the vearnada rail pulled me towards him kissed me. Not a man of many words. Not concerned about himself, quite assured me being an army wife, no harm would come to me or the children. Anyway he was partially right. Away he goes galloping out of sight. I stood there taken aback by the occasion of that moment. For him this is what Army life is all about. For me another worrying time. In the past, sitting on the veranda I had often see in the distance, the Batteries leaving camp for gunnery practice or, some other incident. In the quietness of the day you could hear the distinctive jingle of horse's harnesses, the rumble of the gun carriage wheels, would notify anyone of their progress. Marching behind them creating a dust were the Gordon Highlanders in their kilts, along with the Khyber Riflemen with their brightly coloured turbans. They would be gone for a few days, then back to the camp for a short time, an endless too-ing and fro-ing. However, the arrival of Jack with this news was different.

Twenty miles away from Nowshera, was the town of Peshawar. It was the last major town before the barren hostile Khyber Pass. The British Army had a large garrison in Peshawar with a Squadron of the Royal Air Force located somewhere close by. Sometimes, I would spot a RAF aeroplane flying around in the sky overhead. With all the different tribesmen living within that barren area from Nowshera to the Khyber Pass it was a hot bed of unrest. In and around Nowshera amongst other local tribesmen, were the Afridi's known as the "Red Shirts" all wore a distinctive red shirt. They were very active in creating disturbances and unrest amongst the other tribesmen who all strongly objected to the presence of the British Army, would rather see them all leave the North West Frontier Province.

It must have been three weeks after Jack had left, when one day in the middle of the afternoon I came out onto the veranda with my writing pad, sat down about to write a letter. Casually looked out to see my tribe sat in the middle of the mydam (field), with two strange looking tribesmen wearing flat type woollen head-dress, their tribal blankets thrown over their shoulders. Extemely unusual and suspicious? I did take notice. Mary was deeply engrossed in conversation with them, with the other two looking on. These two tribesmen were making

231

slashing, thrusting movements, in the sunlight I saw the flash of silver, they were waving blades about cutting and thrusting, as their performance continued noticed the distinctive colour of red beneath their blankets both wore red shirts. This sight made my blood run cold, anxiously I stood up, I did not know where the Bearer was, number One Ayah was stood beside the doorway, I hissed at her, placing my finger on my lips whispered.

'Bearer jahldi jahldi.' From inside the Bearer pocked his head around the doorway. I pointed in the direction of my tribe. A look of concern appeared on his face he raied an eyebrow I sensed he was going to go out to confront them. God knows what would have happened? I moved towards him grabbed his arm, shaking my head whispered..

'Ji nahn Bearer. Army Chowkidar jahldi jahldi.' Pointing to the camp placed my fingers to my lips indicated. "Quietly go up the lines"...He nodded... 'Ji han Memsahib.' He quietly left running towards the camp. I went back inside, got the revolver returned back sat down with the revolver resting on my lap, I cocked it ready my full attention on the performance out on the mydam with Mary thrusting and jabbing talking, it seemed ages before a troop of mounted soldiers, raced up amidst a cloud of dust surrounded the little group pointin rifles at the two tribesmen . A soldier jumped down off his horse, took charge of my tribe ushered them away towards the veranda as the Bearer returned at the run he took charge of them, escorting them back up the veranda steps handed them over to me. We all stood watching, as two of the soldiers dismounted pointing their rifles at the two tribesmen still sat on their haunches, without any resistance a soldier took the knives from them. They were shackled, hauled to their feet. The troop Sergeant rode over towards us reining in said.

'Well done Mrs Plant. We've been looking for these two. They are leaders of one of the local Afridis Red Shirt gangs, who are causing all the trouble around here? Oh by the way, you won't need that revolver now. I suggest you put it away in a safe place.'

I still had hold of it, in the excitement of the incident I had forgotten all about it uncocking it replaced the safety catch, thanked him for his prompt action. He waved as they led their two prisoners away. I asked Mary.

'Why were you talking to those tribesmen? You have been warned not to talk with any strangers, whoever they may be.'

'They were only trying to sell their knives. I was haggling with them about the price, I had made the deal when the soldiers rode up and stopped it.' I thought. *"My God with their father up in Peshawar fighting against these tribesmen and my daughter is sitting here back at home haggling with them to buy their knives. What am I to do with her?* "After six weeks away Jack returned informed me.

'Sarah. I heard about your incident with the Red Shirts. Good Girl. More fighting and riots have started, we are being sent further up to the Khyber Pass. By the way, do you remember us talking about Gandhi? Well he was arrested and thrown into prison in Bombay. There are more riots down there but not to worry. I have been informed you are going back up the hills. You will be well out of it.' Then away he goes. The weather was becoming hotter information on Company Orders, stated married families were to go back up to Khanspur. Once again, I was dreading the journey, The following week we began the trip up to Khanspur, this time taking all the servants with us, a normal procedure but nobody told us how many. Not that it mattered, they would come anyway the0y were part of the family. But I wondered where they would all sleep? Leaving the Bungalow closed with only the Chowkidar looking after it and the chickens.

The journey was much the same as before however, this time I had a baby in my arms. The weather was good, the sun shone throughout the whole journey, it still took the same time, arriving in Khanspur the kilted Scotsman. "Macgregor" greeted us.

'Hello te ye al.' A cheery greeting which received the response it deserved. In that idyllic spot. With much clapping calls of 'Jahldi' the Bearer sorted out the servants. He soon has everything and everyone sorted out. To provide an extra room for the servants I decided to sleep with my tribe (a gesture much appreciated) some of the chico's slept in the stable they appeared quite comfortable well Indians would sleep anywhere.. The following day. We had to go back down to Kaji Gali to the M RS for a medical inspection. We are all passed fit but in the afternoon, the weather turned, the sun was obliterated by heavy black clouds quickly turned into torrential rains, it poured out of the sky, as if someone had opened up a huge tap. Confining everyone to remain indoors it was not a comfortable situation. That evening Michael became sick and very ill. I sent the Bearer for the MO. The MO arrived, states it's probably due to the altitude?

That night Michael develops dysentery I was up all night with him. Next morning I sent for the MO, who prescribes some medicine. The torrential rain continued making it impossible to dry nappies,whilst we tried to dry them by the fire, I tore up some sheets to use as nappies, The prescribed medicine did not work the dysentery was bad, then Michael began vomiting he was not taken any food. In constant attendance the MO stated that breast-feeding didn't suit him. From the Army shop I bought him Cow and Gate powdered milk, feeding him it immediately he threw it up. Down in Nowshera he weighed just over eighteen pounds, within eight days with his dysentery and the vomiting he lost six pounds. Michaels health was deteriating, the MO was concerned told me he did not hold out much hope for Michael? I was frantic with worry. I now had two major worries on my hand. Jack in the fighting in the Khyber Pass and Michael close to deaths door. I asked the MO would he send a cable to Jack to tell him what he had said, I wrote down the note.

LITTLE HOPE FOR MICHAEL STOP

WOULD HE PLEASE COME UP TO THE HILLS STOP

Jack cabled back to say.

KEEP MICHAEL ALIVE AT ALL COST   STOP

CANNOT LEAVE THE KHYBER PASS NOBODY CAN   STOP

This helped me no end. So I asked the MO, would he send a cable to my Mother advising her of illness and the trouble I was in. Again he obliged. Two days later the MO rode up with the cable reply from Mother saying:

TAKE HIM OFF COW AND GATE STOP

FEED HIM ON BOILED PEARL BARLEY WATER FOR A FEW DAYS STOP

THEN PUT HIM ON NESTLES MILK   STOP MOTHER STOP

Fortunately, we had Pearl Barley in our provisions. I left number One Ayah in charge of Michael; she was constantly beside him watching over him. Whilst the Khansama watched what I was doing, boiled up the Pearl Barley in a chatti bowl, when cool, gently fed Michael spoon by spoon, initially he brought up a little but at least kept it down. Mothers remedy appeared to be working so just fed him with the warm residue water until after two days his sickness eased, then began tp feed him little by little the Nestles Milk he did not sick that up. Day by day Michael became stronge, began gaining a little weight, much to the MO's surprise and delight, I wrote to Jack telling him of Michael's progress another to Mother to say that her remedy had worked. I was so relieved at one stage I thought: *My baby would not live.*

Sarah with Jackie Kathleen Mary & BaBa Michael

The rain had restricted any movement of visiting, Neither Grace or Nora were staying up there and there was only two wives staying in Khanspur who I had previously met. Our daily routine returned to normality although very crowded, but the daily torrents of rain that descended became more sporadic than not, consequently the bungalow becomes a madhouse with my tribe whooping around with the Chico's. I used to pray that nightfall would come early, so I could, pack them off to bed.. The improvement in the weather had my tribe wandering around outside and I did invite the two wives to Tiffin times at my bungalow. Whilst in the warmth of the afternoon sun, I sat lazing on the small veranda had me thinking: *Since the birth of Michael, particularly during his recent bout of sickness. Carefully watching all the servants I had noticed their deep concern. Number One Ayah had almost adopted Michael, I even allowed her to bath him. It was then I accepted the fact that they were completely trustworthy. I realised that neither the children nor me, would come to any harm from them. I was becoming to accept India.*

After a rather traumatic time, our stay in Khanspur came to an end. All packed up ready for the downward trek. It turned out to be a glorious day, the temperature was just right for walking. I put Kathleen and Jackie together in one Dandy with number One Ayah carrying Michael in another. Mary and I walked all the way down to Murree. It was no hardship, as we shared the beauty of the scenery, we had come to appreciate and love so much. It dawned on me that with Jack am posting to Nowshera; it had turned out to be, the longest period of time we had spent in any quarters since we were married. With the added advantage of being afforded shall we say? A retreat in the Hills. No wonder the English took to the hills with its scenic views and climate, it was almost home from home up there. For once Mary was good, happily conversing with me, having become quite good at speaking Urdu, she told me all the names of the servants. The Bearers name Hamedullah, the Khansama Abdul, the Dhobi Wallah Haseem. Number One Ayah Indu. Those I did remember from my initial inspections many moons before, the other names rolled off her tongue. We stayed overnight at Murree. Next morning the final leg down by Tonga's. At Pindi waiting the arrival of the train, in the intense heat we were dripping with perspiration, even entering the carriage it was like an oven, it took some time before the movement of the train cooled down the interior. Upon our return to the closed bungalow, all got down from the Tonga's. The Bearer stopped everyone from entering, until he had checked for snakes, scorpions or anything else hidden unwanted potential hazard? Armed with a long stick he unlocked entered the bungalow, he was in there some time before he came out onto the veranda called out. 'Ji Han Memsahib.' Then we entered the bungalow, it became a hive of activity. A shriek from the cookhouse had us all dashing out on the veranda. The Khansama with a big stick was trying to urge out of his doorway, a cobra its hood up waiting to strike. We all watched fascinated much to Jackie's delight. It was the first cobra or snake, I had seen since arriving out there. Stood still, the Khansama held the stick ready until the cobra settled down slithered away, scare finished. Towards the end of the day the MO rode up welcomed us all back, enquired about Micheals sickness, which he knew all about, before enquining about our health. He informed me Jack would be away for some time and advised us to be at the MRS the following day for our return check-up. We went next day all declared fighting fit. Two days later, sitting at the table on the veranda, I was reading the new mail for a second time, when I was disturbed by a Quarter Master riding up on his horse. I did not recognise him from the camp, reining in he remained mounted called out.

'Mrs Plant.' Immediately thought: *Something had happened to Jack.* I stood up, my heart went into my mouth, stumbled with my answer.

'Y yes!'

'I'm Q M Burns. Bobby Burns. I've been posted here. I'm standing in for your husband while he's away. I've just popped over to say hello and introduce myself. I hope you don't mind?' I noticed his Northern Ireland accent. Instant relief overcame me relaxing responded.

'Oh thank you. That's very kind of you. Would you care for chai?'

'Uhm. Well yes. Okay. Thank you that would be nice.'... I clapped my hands, as if by magic the Bearer appeared... 'Bearer do chai.'

Without any effort this little rotund QM swung down off his horse, removing his Tobie as he came up the steps onto the veranda wiped his brow with a handkerchief, striding towards me he held out his hand, we shook, he sat down spoke.

'Yes. Mrs. Plant. I've joined the Brigade. Just been transferred from Hyderabad down south. I understand your husband has been up the Khyber some time now? I was in the Mess when I heard you were the BQM's wife and had just returned back from the hills. I found out where your quarters were. So I thought I would pay you a visit.'

'That's right, we have only just returned from Khanspur, after three months stay. Its quiet pleasant up there.'

'Never been up these hills. We, that is Kitty the wife and our tribe of four. Were always sent to another hill station. Mount Abu.

'Oh is your wife out here with you?'

'Yes.'

'I can tell by your brogue you're Irish. What part of the emerald isle are you from?'

'Northern Ireland. Kitty and I come from Armagh, a pretty place. I can tell from your brogue you're from Southern Ireland. What part? '

The Curragh in Kildare.'

'Ah Yes. I know it well. I was they're myself in eighteen, spent two years at the Newbridge camp.' A bond had been struck. We talked about many things around and about the Curragh. Having finished his chai he said.

'Well Mrs Plant, it's about time I started making tracks back to the family. Thank you for the chai and the pleasant gup. Look would you like to meet the wife and family. Having just been posted here, the wife doesn't know anyone yet. I'm sure she would be pleased to see you.'

'That would be most pleasant. I'd love to meet them. Tomorrow would be okay with me. I'm not going anywhere furthermore don't plan to either.' He bursting out laughing replied.

'That sounds good. My tribe is about the same ages as your three children apart from your baby. So they should get on well together?' Having noticed the antics of Mary commented...'Mrs Plant your eldest. She's a handful, she should have been a boy. Where did you get her from?'

'From Ireland where all the devils come from.' Again he roared with laughter.

A sense of humour like my own. Bounding down the steps mounted his horse and with a quick wave rode away. Roaring his head off at my parting remark. I warmed to this new unexpected meeting and looked forward to meeting his wife and family. The following afternoon, after my tribe had woken up from their rest. They were sat at the table drinking lemon pani, I was standing close to the veranda steps with Michael cradled in my arms, when a Tonga arrived. Its passengers a woman with four children, her head appeared from the rear of the Tonga called out.

'Is this the residence of Mrs Plant?'

'Yes. You're speaking to her.'

'I'm Kitty Burns. Bobby came to see you yesterday. I'm here at your invitation.'

'Yes that's right. I had the pleasure of meeting him yesterday. Welcome please come on in.'

Mrs. Burns. (Kitty) climbed down from the Tonga, helping her youngest one down whilst the other three jumped down. She was not wearing the traditional Tobie, instead a fashionable light green Poe type hat. Followed by her four children this slim woman about my age, came up onto the veranda her hand outstretched. We shook she advised.

Marty Kitty Jack

'Kitty Burns. I'm very pleased to make your acquaintance. These are my brats. Young Jack, Andy, Marty and Kathleen.

235

'My name is Sarah. These are my four. Mary, Kathleen, Jackie and Baba Michael. She was slightly taller than I was (but there again everyone is taller than me) Very pleasant looking with a twinkle in her eyes. Dressed in a loose fitting long frock pulled in at the waist by a belt from which dangled a small riding crop. That I was very curious about.

'Now then you brats, no shenanigans while you're here at Mrs Plant's. Otherwise I'll swish you. Do you hear?' She spoke in a terse voice to her "Brats" as she called them. I noticed Mary staring at her eldest Jack. I gave Mary a warning shot across her bows.

'Now no nonsense from you Mary. Do please sit down.'

So began the start of our lifelong friendship. Right from the start we both had a good rapport going. Over chai we compared stories. Kitty a very easy going person with a good sense of humour. I told her as much as I could about Nowshera, which wasn't anything of great importance? We had shared the same experiences coming out to India, although they had been out there much longer, initially near Bombay before moving up to Nowshera. My burning question was, why she kept a riding crop slipped inside her belt?

'That Sarah Plant. Is to cut the backsides of my brats. They are too quick for me to smack them. So I use this, to crop them. You should use one. Particularly with that eldest one of yours. I've been watching her. She's got the match of my young Jack that's for sure.' The fading light of the sun, brought a halt to our Tiffin time.

'My God Sarah Plant. We have been gupping for ages. I must get back before it gets dark.' I asked.

'What's Gupping?'... Quizzically she looked at me.....'That Sarah Plant. Is what we have been doing for the past hours? Just talking.' We both laughed. Half an hour before sunset she left. As she went down the steps, shouting at the Tonga Wallah, which at that time was most likely asleep.

'JAHLDI YOU LAZY BUGGER. JAHLDI. C'mon on you brats get aboard the Tonga.'

I had to laugh. However my meeting up with Kitty Burns was to me a gift. By my own choice, totally isolating myself from other wives. With Jack away for God knows how long, I desperately needed someone to confide in. Just like me, when I first arrived. Kitty Burns was in the same situation. Newly arrived, lonely for the want of company. I wrote to Jack to inform him of meeting the Burn's family advising him I would keep him posted of all events as they transpired. Over the following weeks, Kitty became a regular visitor. Whilst engaged in our private Tiffin time, we would have long gupping sessions. She was the one who insisted I go down the Bazaars for shopping.

'C'mon Sarah Plant. You don't want all these servants holding your hand all the time. I will take you. They won't beat me with their haggling. I'll tell you that for nothing.'

When all the children were at school, we would go on shopping sprees for cloth to make dresses and purchase other little souvenirs. Always I might add accompanied by my Bearer, who insisted on coming with us? On one such occasion we were in the Sudder Bazaar. Kitty spotted a white fur coat made from a snow leopards skin hanging inside a shop, she exclaimed.

'Sarah Plant. That's for me.' I looked at the fur coat. Rather bemused by her suggestion questioned.

'What on earth do you want with a fur coat out here?'

'I like the look of it and it would cost a lot of money back in Blighty. Anyway if we get a chance to go up the hills, it will keep out the cold.' I retorted.

'I wouldn't buy that. Anyway it's bad luck.'

'Don't be such a daft fool it's not bad luck to buy a fur coat. I'm buying it and that's that. Now just you watch. I'll knock this bugger down with his price.'

She was determined to buy the coat. The Shop Wallah had not taken much attention to these two Memsahib's stood outside discussing things that didn't concern him. But when Kitty turned made her way towards the entrance he pounced upon her.

'Memsahib's wishy pay annas plees.' Grabbing both of us by the arms he led us into his shop. With an authoritative gesture, Kitty pointed at the coat.

'Vo wala. Kitna hai?' (That one. How much)

'Aah. Memsahib pukka. Memsahib try?' The Wallah got hold of the coat, thrusting it at Kitty, he began rubbing the palm of one hand over the fur.....'Velly goo, velly goo.' All his attention being poured on Kitty, I was of no interest to him, again she repeated.

'Vo wala. Kitna hai?'

'Beess (Twenty) Rupees!'

'What! You're a loose wallah. It's not worth das (ten) rupees.'

By this time the Wallah seizes a chance to make a sell. Had draped the coat around Kitty's shoulders she looked down at its drape. I stood there amazed but amused at her audacity. Earnestly the Wallah began lifting one of Kitty's arms inside the sleeve, quickly followed by the other, in seconds Kitty stood there wearing the fur coat, she looking totally out of place. She started parading back and forth asking.

'What do you say Sarah Plant? '

'I wouldn't buy it, that's for sure. Kitty it will only bring you bad luck.'

The Wallah looked quizzically at me, waving his hands about shaking his head he murmured.

'Memsahib pukka.' Kitty attempted to remove one arm from the sleeve retorted.

'Bahut zydda hai.' (That's too much).

Quickly the Wallah, pulled the sleeve back up. Obviously he did not want to lose such a valued customer muttering.

'Pukka Memsahib. Pukka.' Indicating she looked very smart in fur. Kitty wasn't having any of that. Then a struggle began between the pair of them, until the coat was back on Kitty.I watched with amusement at the tussle they were having. Kitty glowering at him made her final move stating.

'Panj Rupees dungi ji han anna zydda.' (I will give you five rupees not an anna more)

'Ni han Memsahib. Das rupee.' He had halved his price. She had him, still she shook her head. As she took off the coat she said.

'Bahut paise ahim hain' (I don't have much money) I don't want to buy.

'Memsahib. Ath (Eight) Rupaya's.'

Again he tried to induce the coat back onto her, instead Kitty succeeded in taking it off. Between the pair of them. It was like watching a boxing match. She shouted.

'NO BUY. YOU'RE A THIEVING BUGGER'... turning to me...'C'mon Sarah let's go.'

We went to leave the shop, as the Wallahs whining gave in offered.

'Memsahib. Panch rupaya's' She stopped turned.

'Panch rupees. Pukka?'

'Ji han panch rupaya's.' He salaamed. The deal was made. She paid.

Outside with her fur coat tucked under her arm she turned to me.

'There Sarah Plant. A fur coat for nothing. I knew I had him when he said das rupees.'

'You're daft Kitty. That fur will bring you bad luck. I'm sure.'

'Your daft yourself to think that way.' She was very pleased with herself.

It was about two weeks later she arrived at my bungalow for Tiffin. After chai had been brought Kitty touching my arm said.

'Sarah Plant. Erm you remember that fur coat?'

'Yes. That one I said would bring you bad luck.' With some hesitation she said.

'Well. It isn't a fur coat anymore.' With interest I asked.

'Why ever not?'

'Well. Today I went to the cupboard to admire it only to find it had moulted. The fur had dropped out leaving great patches of bare skin. You were right about the bad luck bit.'... I couldn't stop myself from laughing. Her thinking she had a bargain fur coat for nothing and finished up with a piece of skin... She added sulkily. 'Sarah Plant. It's not funny and certainly not a laughing matter. I lost five rupees over the deal.'..'Serves you right. I did warn you'...adding...'Good job you didn't pay twenty for it then.' Seeing the funny side of it we both rocked with laughter.

One thing that really worried me was Jackie's throat. For no known reason it would swell up, he would become hoarse without a cough. On one occasion before, one of Jack's friend's daughter Enid Broughton, who used to come to play with my tribe left us feeling unwell. That night she died of Diphtheria, was buried the next morning. On the same morning Jackie's throat was inflamed swollen, as a precaution he was taken straight into Hospital. If anyone died of fever Jackie was the first to be rushed into hospital and kept in. The MO had prescribed him to gargle with diluted Iodine. On the occasions when his throat flared up, he began whinging at the mere thought of this job of gargling, he was terrified but it had to be done. After all he was only a little boy. His mouth and lips would be stained yellow, he could only swallow lemonade with a little mashed mango. This routine happened three times a day, sometimes it took up to five days until his throat was cleared. Amongst other families it was common knowledge that Jackie was a carrier of diphtheria? Although unfounded, I did not want visitors. Nevertheless, it did hurt when people kept away as if we were classed as contagious. It was only very good friends that took it upon themselves to visit us including Kitty and Bobby. They made a point of visiting us with their Brats, so they could fight and play at will together. I once asked her.

'Kitty Burns. Aren't you bothered by the problem with Jackie's throat? '

'Sarah Plant if my brats haven't had it. It's about time they did and got over it.'

That's all she ever made of it. I loved her for her attitude; she made light heart of everything and thought I was a fool to worry. It had been nearly five months since I had last seen Jack and a lot had happened during that period of time. I had been back from the hills about two months. When Jack rode up one afternoon. Greetings all round; we were all delighted to see him. As normal the Bearer lined all the servants up, for the Burrah Sahibs inspection with my tribe following behind him.

'Pukka Bearer. Pukka.' Salutes and 'Achchha Sahib.' A beam of a smile, a quick clap of the hands the parade was dismissed. Chai was served by the Bearer. That brought a remark of surprise from Jack.

'What's this Sarah? The Bearer serving chai?'

'Well. He took it upon himself to do it. I did not ask. But it is a nice compliment don't you think?'...He just grunted...'Now then Sarah. What's your news?'

I brought him up to date with the local gossip, about Kitty Bobby and their family. He had already met Bobby and was pleased that I now had a friend in Kitty. He spent the first day reading letters and old newspapers. Three days later Kitty and Bobby turned up for Tiffin. After meeting Kitty, Jack's feelings were as mutual as mine. He too warmed to the pair of them like long lost friends. While the men gupped about Army matters, their brats and my tribe played, squabbled then fought. However after his seven days leave, unfortunately the Battery was recalled to the Khyber Pass to renewed fighting. As for us we returned to our normal daily routines.　　　*Bobby Kathleen Marty*

Four weeks later,one Saturday morning Bobby and Kitty

238

arrived for Tiffin, unfortunately for me they were the bearers of bad news. Bobby had been given another posting to Lucknow Central India. They were to leave the following week. This news set me back, I was about to lose a dear friend and confidant in Kitty. We had got on so well right from the start. I would miss her humour that readily came out at any sentence in a conversation. The dreaded day arrives and we all see the Burn's off at the Station. Tearful farewells were made between Kitty and I. Her parting shot to me was.

'Sarah Plant don't you worry now. We will keep in touch and get together one day back in Blighty?'

I agreed, but I knew that was in another five years' time. As the train pulled away I readily shed tears. I reflected upon the fact that after meeting Kitty the past few months had been some of the happiest I had spent out in India. Now alone to my own devices and tedious way of life, returned to the previous routine.

Sometime later I did receive a letter from Kitty, she had settled in to her new Quarters and complained that it was far hotter in Lucknow than in Nowshera. That I could not believe. Fortunately I was able to correspond with her. A couple of months went by and I received orders that once again we were to go back up to the same bungalow in Khanspur. This time for me our stay was to be much more enjoyable with no illnesses. The revival of Tiffin times took me out on horse rides to other bungalows. I never did see Nora again, but did bump into someone who knew her, they had been posted to Delhi.

A letter from Jack informed me that the fighting was at an end, furthermore he gave me the run down on a meeting he had with the new Lt/Col. Proberts who had replaced Lt /Col. Green. Having already visited the Battery emplacement he had called for Jack asked. "If Jack would become the Battery Sergeant Major?" Jack reply was..."No thank you sir. Forgive me for saying but it is in a hell of a mess"...."Well that's an honest answer. Due to your good conduct and devotion to duties, there is a Quarter Master's promotion available in another garrison in India. Would you be willing to accept it? "' Jack had accepted the offer. I kept on glancing at his letter, reading his words a few times, realised Jack was now waiting for a posting. We would be moving from Nowshera to God knows where? Another new start! A couple of weeks after his letter arrived. I was sitting on the veranda watching the sunset over the Khanspur hills. When emerging from the trees I saw Jack. What a wonderful sight he made riding up on his white horse with a packhorse in tow, the children went wild with excitement. Reining in jumped down greeted me.

'Sarah I have two weeks leave up here. You will be going back with me.'

What a surprise We were to spend a blissful two weeks. When it wasn't raining we went out for walks or, Jack would take the tribe, ride them around on horses and ponies. On other occasions sitting on his horse he would take Michael up in his arms, slowly walk the horse around. Very quickly those two weeks went by, it was time to pack up and leave, knowing it would be the last time I was to visit the tranquillity of Khanspur. I left with sadness, nevertheless, for all our problems I had endured up there, I really did like the place such a welcome retreat I would miss. This time Jack, Mary and I walked down to Murree. One thing that Jack had found out about were the origins of the Murree Brewery, which was once owned by the Dyer Family? The name made infamous by Brigadier-General Dyer who was responsible for the Massacre of women and children at Amritsar in 1919. I enquired.

'What happened there?'

'Well it's something to do with that fellow Gandhi. Who had caused a strike of some sort to do with businesses? After two days of rioting, it got out of hand. Three English people were killed. Then under the command of Dyer re-enforcements advanced on the riot and opened fire. In the panic that followed most of the Indian women and children were killed. Another matter that might be of interest is that the fighting up here in the Khyber Pass area has been going on since about the same time and I don't think it will end just yet. There is a still a lot of unrest throughout India.'

The very thought of it made my hair stand on end. The remaining trip back was uneventful and upon our return to the bungalow, Jack expected to hear of his new posting. As he understood it, possibly to Delhi? For me maybe a chance to meet up with Nora once again. A few days later Jack arrived home early, still sat on his horse said.

'Sarah I think I was wrong about Delhi. I've heard another rumour, it's to another Regiment scheduled to be returning to Blighty. I don't know when, but I did find out was they are located at the "Residency" Garrison in Lucknow.'

Blighty. Lucknow. Those two words were magic to my ears. Blighty? Yet we had not completed our seven years. But Lucknow Kitty and Booby were there. I just had to pray that it was true. A few days later Jack rode up with a huge grin all over his face, swinging down off his horse, came bounding up the steps, swung me off my feet said.

'Sarah. We are on the move again this time to Lucknow. You've been waiting for that my girl. It's been posted up in Company Orders. Don't tell the tribe about it yet Sarah. Wait until we are nearly ready to move, you know what they are like.'

That I did agree to. Oh what a relief I could not believe it clapping my hands shouted. 'CHAI BEARER.'

We sat and quietly discussed the next procedure. This time with three weeks' notice we will all travel together to a new posting as a family. How unusual that was? Apart from the passage out from Blighty. Nothing was mentioned at the evening meal. Next morning, the usual routine proceeded. During the morning inspection of the servants something was not quite right. I became very aware that of a change in the servant's attitude. All was quiet. That worried me and had me thinking: *Although Jack and I had been very discreet about the pending move. We had not even mentioned it to our tribe, perhaps somehow they already knew about the posting, but how? For me it would mean to start all over again with strange servants.'* I carried on finishing off my list, before I began thinking about the move. That morning passed quickly by, with the bungalow almost void of its usual buzz. Over lunch I quietly mentioned to Jack about the change in the servants attitude asked.

'What can we do? I trust them all, I do not want to leave them behind.' He replied.

'Don't worry it will be all right. I'll apply for permission to take them all. I'll do that to-morrow. If it's okay. I will inform them accordingly?'

A good suggestion I welcomed. Nevertheless the atmosphere prevailed, with me trying not to show I was preparing for a move, it was getting on my nerves. Three days later Jack arrived back after duty for lunch, swinging down from his horse bounded up the steps said.

'Right Sarah. You've got your wish. Permission granted for all of them. C'mon forget chai get the tribe on the veranda. We'll tell them first, then the rest of the family. This will have to be done properly.'

'Jack that's wonderful news. That's a load off of my mind!'

Jack called the tribe up onto the veranda, sat them down around him, whilst I held Michael in my arms talking quietly he began.

'Listen to me please. We are all going to leave Nowshera and move to a place called Lucknow.' Mary interrupted.

'Is that where the Burn's went to?'

'Yes that's right. Now we will be packing up everything, just like you did when you went up to Khanspur. But this time we will be going to Lucknow to stay there.'

With blank faces they looked at Jack as if he had said something wrong until Kathleen enquired.

'What about our servants? Will they be coming too?'

240

'That is what I have called you all together for. I have to tell the servants just that. Bearer.'
The Bearer appeared from inside the bungalow salaamed.
'Ji han Sahib.'
'Bearer. Chai. Lemon pani. Jahldi.'
'Ji han Sahib.' When he had gone Jack spoke again.
'We are going to take all of them with us. And when I tell them. I do not to hear one word out of you three, just you sit, listen to your father. Do you understand? I will address them myself.'

He got them all to promise him not to say anything. The Bearer returned with a Chico holding the drinks on a tray salaamed.
'Sahib'...he served the drinks...Sahib.' He shoed away the Chico stood back to one side. Jack ordered.
'Bearer. Wallahs. Ayahs, Chico's. Syces. Jahldi.' He pointed with his hand to indicate here in front of the veranda.
'JI han Sahib.'

The Bearer descended the steps clapped his hands hailing all to come to Sahibs Plant's instructions. While he did that Jack arranged us into a sitting order, according to him this had to be done properly, moving a chair to the top of the veranda steps he said.

'Sarah would you please sit on that chair with Michael on your lap. Now you three sit on the next step down. Jalhdi'...as we moved into positions he confidently adding...'This shouldn't take long.'

They all arrived stood quietly in line, with furrowed brows. Jack indicated for them to squat down on the hard ground in front of the veranda steps. The Bearer, understanding something important was going on, began organising them in rows in his or her rightful place, just like a military parade. He clucking and growling at the playful Chico's. What a finale this was going to be! Jack with his Tobie tucked under his arm stood up. Moved to stand beside me, then in broken Urdu began to explain and gesticulating with his arms.

'The Burrah Sahib. His Memsahib with the Baba's. We are leaving the bungalow and going to Lucknow'... This brought forth gasps, mutterings from his most attentive audience, they stared up at Jack with doubt in their eyes. A couple of the Ayah's pulled their Saris across their faces unable to contain their disapproval at such a drastic suggestion. The Bearer shushed the muttering...Jack continued...'And as all the servants had served the Sahib and Memsahib with excellent service'...he paused surveying his audience, who had almost as one bent forward, eagerly waiting for his next statement...'He the Sahib and Memsahib would like to take all to Lucknow. But only if they asked their families for permission. The Sahib would allow two days only for their answers.'

He stood there looking down at them as they all began clucking and chattering together. The Bearer talking above everyone, explained the situation in Urdu. More excited muttering went through the assembly. Then the Bearer pulling back his shoulders, bellowed for quietness in his ranks. Jack turned to me with a big grin.

'That's your influence on them. Sarah you've done well.'

My God what a compliment. I was flattered and proud. I looked down to see the Bearer move in towards the bottom step. Smartly stood to attention in front of Jack. Looking up saluted. Placed his hand on his chest. In broken English informed Jack.

'Sahib me go Lucknow. Sahib it would be honour go to Lucknow with the Burrah Sahib's family. Would the Sahib Memsahib accept this humble servants service. Take him to Lucknow with them?'

All this said in broken English, was a surprise to me. I didn't give it a single thought that any of them could converse, except in their own Urdu. Jack was taken aback by this immediate response, as was I replied.

'Teek aaha. Bearer.'

The Bearer saluted, turning addressed the assembled servants. Speaking in Urdu, obviously telling them of his decision. It was then that I looked hard at the number of servants sat before us. When we had arrived, we inherited twenty eight, by the number of rows, I'm sure there were more than thirty-six, sat down on their haunches. It was the number of Chico's that astounded me, before I could say anything Jack said.

'I think we're in for a shock here Sarah. Come stand beside me there's a good girl. This is a time I now need your support. This is your domain not mine.'

Again I was flattered by his request. I got up and stood proudly beside him with Michael fast asleep in my arms. Then Mary seeing what was happening organised the other two, shoving them to stand in line along side of me. Surprised as we were, all the servants got up moved into a single line filed before us, each one approached with a big smile on their faces salaamed, offered their service to us as a family. We salaamed in return. It was a good job it was late in the afternoon. The temperature of the day was cooling down by the time the last Chico had presented himself. The Bearer shouted at them they all formed up in a very long line in front of us all salaamed, we responded. The Bearer clapped his hands, they happily disappeared to their duties. The ceremony must have taken all of an hour then I was able to question Jack.

'Jack forgive me for asking. You did say we could take all of the servants with us?'

'Yes. Why did you ask?'

'Oh nothing much just making sure that is all.'

We had a sluice down, dinner was late but the Khansama did us proud. There certainly was a lift in their attitude, that of excitement of the forthcoming moves to a new place. I must say I was also very happy at the outcome. I sent a letter to Kitty telling them of our great news. Jack brought home a map showed me where Lucknow was. A very long way away.

'I'm afraid it will take about four days.'

'Well it took four days to get here and I'm getting used to the filthy trains.'

But at least I would have Jack's company on the journey, along with the rest of the servants. The trip would not be as daunting or, traumatic as our first trip. Wooden ammunition boxes were provided, the packing commenced. Jack had the usual farewell do's in the mess. I said my goodbyes to the few nice woman friends I had made at the church. We attended the Hospital and were all signed off as fit by the MO. The final day quickly came around; the quarters were checked I signed over.

Outside our packed possessions were piled high on the mydam, the four-wheeled Tonga's carts arrived. The Bearer ranting at the Chico's who thought this was a big game tried to help the servants load them. I turned away from the palaver outside. I took one last walk and looked around my quarters. Reflecting upon all the worries the happy times we had during the past two years in Nowshera. I moved out onto the veranda where Jack was stood watching the loading, standing beside him, looked out at the scene before me, the fleet of carts, Tonga's, the Ayah's along with my tribe already sitting in the Tonga waiting for me. I spotted the Chowkidar and the Bearer together saying their farewells. At that moment I felt extremely lonely and sad, I started to cry. Jack enquired.

'Sarah what on earth is the matter now?' Wiping away the tears murmured.

'Nothing. Nothing just memories.' Jack walking down the steps called.

'Come on Sarah it's time to go.' I went down the veranda steps for the last time. Jack helped me up onto the Tonga, climbing up alongside me we started off. I never looked back.

242

At Nowshera station I'm sure we could fill a carriage by ourselves. Not so, the train from Peshawar arrived full with the usual amount of people squatting on its roof. God knows what they did when they came to a tunnel. We had seats, the rest of the servants would ride wherever they could squat down, except number One Ayah, she would take care of Michael during the trip. There were plenty of Sikhs on the train, huge men with turbans of all colours with long flowing beards, they were going as far as Amritsar, where I understood was their Shrine of Worship. Seeing them I thought: *They too had somewhere to make their way to on a pilgrimage.* I could not imagine me doing that once I got back to Blighty. I would not venture out on any more escapades abroad. Jack could go alone. I had seen many other religious practices during my stay in Nowshera, with all their wailing and chanting at specific times during the day. The fasting that they adopted was all very strange but fascinating to me.

We left Nowshera with me thinking: *Of the trials that I might face ahead of me when we finally arrived in Lucknow. The only certainty was renewing friendships with Kitty Burns. She will put me straight on what it's all about in Lucknow.* We slowly pulled into Pindi stopped, more people got on the train. I didn't notice anyone getting off. The bearer came through stopped. Salaamed to Jack.

'Ji han Sahib. Memsahib. Chai pani Babas.'

'Ji han chukriya bearer.'

My tribe decided they wanted to go to the lavatories off the train. I thought. *"Oh no me bucko's, you only want to go and pull the Chains."* Curtly ordered.

'No. We will be off in a minute, I'm not running around the platform chasing you three.'

Jack looked over at me grinned but said nothing. I thought. *"Yes you can grin, remember the time before last we were here?"* The Bearer arrived wuth the drinks. Then we were off again, travelling South East across India. There was little or nothing to do except look out of the slatted windows. Jack would draw my attention to something of interest from time to time. Unlike a troop train it stopped at every station. More people got on; some were now riding on the running boards clinging to the windows. I turned my head away nobody seemed to care. Night came and we all settled down to get what sleep we could, the children were soon flat out with not a care in the world, I dreaded the thought: *We had a further three nights of this. At least on the Troop Train we had a reasonable amount of privacy amongst our own kind.* Morning came I dashed off to the lavatory compartment, this was the same as the other train so I knew what and how to go about doing the old routine. The Ayah was a blessing in disguise she took Michael did the necessaries. Jack came back grumbling about the amount of water he had to shave in. We had some form of breakfast before the next stop Amritsar.

About ten in the morning the train arrived in Amritsar. As the Sikhs were getting off I thought. *"This would allow more room in the carriages."* I was right in one way nevertheless, for everyone who got off two more Sikhs got on heading back home. So space got more precious than ever. The rest of the journey followed the same routine. With my tribe getting more and more boisterous with the lack of anything to do. I'm now wishing the train would go faster so that we could arrive in Lucknow sooner. I was noticing I understood words other people were saying, I felt that I had accomplished something without any teaching, even the station names I could pronounce almost immediately. India does grow upon you. We had just entered a station, I found the name very funny. I laughed drew Jacks attention to it.

'Just look at that stations name Jack. It must have been named after a drunken Irish man.'

'Bareilly. Trust you to think of something daft like that. Oh now I see what you mean that's a good one for the mess. You know Sarah, Lucknow is more in the central part of India and away from the Mountains. So you won't get any cooling breezes there. It will be just hot all the time so prepare you for the burning plains.' I remarked.

'Can it get any hotter? India just seems to be hot all over except for the hills.'

243

Back in Nowshera Jack had already told me about his new posting to the Residency Battery of the Twenty Second (the Double Ducks). Apparently they had moved back to Lucknow, from somewhere else in India. It was to be the first time the Battery had been stationed in Lucknow, since the siege during the Indian Mutiny in 1857. Much later, I found out more of their history.

I had received a letter from Kitty, just before we had left Nowshera. Informing us that they would meet us at Lucknow station. Jack had sent a message to Bobby of the scheduled time the train would arrive. I was looking forward to that meeting. On the fourth day we arrived in the middle of the afternoon. I was so pleased I could have shrieked with joy.

CHAPTER FIVE
LUCKNOW AN INDIAN SUMMER.

As the train began its slow down, I watched as one by one the faces of the Indians hanging on to the bars of the windows outside, began to drop off. I nudged Jack.

'Jack look those Indians will all get killed.'

'No Sarah. Don't be silly they won't. They are jumping off before they reach the main station. They've had buckshee's ride.' I exclaimed.

'To get a free ride!' Thinking: *Of the number of our servants riding the train...*'Oh so that's why they ride on the roof?'

'Yes of course. As you have already noticed, there are plenty of them that do.'

The open window became clear of hangers-on. My tribe having noticed this, became excited. got up from their seats at the prospect of getting off the train. I became concerned they would get lost in the forthcoming mad rush of Indians when the train stopped exclaimed.

'Jack make them sit down until the train finally stops. They won't get killed falling off the train; they will get killed in the mad stampede to get off.'

He turned, pointing at the seat sternly looked at them, quickly responding they sat down. He never chastised them just a stern look from their father was enough, well sometimes but not always. The train having reduced its speed to a crawl went over a railway bridge, spanning a wide river. Below on the riverbanks, I noticed Indians waist deep in water either bathing or beating washing to shreds. It always amazed me that any of the clothing still came back spotlessly clean and still in one piece. The train finally arrived at Lucknow station, then the mad stampede inside began as outside, more buckshee travellers clambered down from the roof, many pairs of barefooted legs dangled down, found foot holds on the bars quickly followed by a white Dhoti clad body, then a grinning face. Their luggage wrapped in a blanket was being flung down to whoever was ready to catch them? The heat inside the carriage increased minute by minute. Taking our time restrained our tribe from joining the heaving mass of pushing and shoving Indians, some with luggage balanced on their heads all eager to get off, we joining the tail-enders arrived at the carriage door climbed down onto the platform to join a mutltude of Indians. My first impression, not a dirt track this was more like a station. Jack gathered us into a little group. Number One Ayah had Michael in her arms for protection. Mary, Kathleen and Jackie excited at the renewal of friendship with the Burn's tribe were eager to move, somehow within minutes the rest of our servants found us and quickly encircled us. Jack got hold of my arm.

'Right Sarah. Now it appears everyone is here. You stay right here. Don't move. I'll sort out our luggage and claim it.'

He left us. Close to me the Bearer began shouting at the rest of the servants to do something or other. Within five minutes Jack was back.

'Right that's arranged, now let's get out and find the Burns family.'

With Jack leading the way, our entourage jostled its way to the exterior of the station out into the blazing sun, its heat was so intense it certainly was the "Burning Plains." On our way out the only thing I had time to briefly notice was the Indians of all sorts scurrying back and forth, of course the beggars with their ever-outstretched hands pleading for gifts. How on earth did they survive? We came to a halt, I checked to see if my tribe were all there then had time to look back towards the station building, noticing its features, which were quiet outstanding, made out of white brickwork with minarets at all corners, the entrances were Indian style gateways. Jack called out.

'Sarah. I've spotted Kitty over there. She's waving her arms about to attract our attention.'

'I can't see anything but servants'...making a pathway through the servants...said. 'Look over there. By the Tonga's.'

Through a pause in the constant movement of Indians I sighted a mad woman holding a riding crop in one hand waving her arms above her head, saw Kitty stood with Bobby surrounded by her brats. Kitty was someone special a delight to my eyes I led the way, as our entourage swathed a pathway through the masses of Indians going in all directions. Then Kitty spotted me and our entourage shouted.

'SARAH PLANT OVER HERE.'

We fell into each other's arms. Amidst the handshakes hugs and kisses all around, the two eldest of the brats and tribe met...

'Hello you Jack Burns... 'Hello you Mary Plant.'

Old adversaries had met, yet not to be left out, our servants in their own way of greeting grinned and salaamed, Kitty quickly surveying the servants, with a twinkle in her eyes exclaimed.

'Christ Sarah Plant. Have we got to put up with your tribe again? And I might add your family seems to have grown?'

Kitty, taking hold of Michael, began speaking with my tribe, whilst I spoke to Kitty's brats, who were as pleased to see us as we were them. Bobby, then with a new rank of a BQMS, had organised Tonga's but not enough to cater for our household hailed up a couple more. While the Tonga's were being organised I had to laugh at Kitty, like an Indian woman got up onto one Tonga with Michael straddled across her hip. I ushered my tribe up before I got up myself. Jack, Bobby, the Burns brats climbed up onto the second one. With the servants scattered amongst the rest of the Tonga's, at the rear a four-wheeled Tonga loaded with our luggage, with the Chico's sat on top. We set off on the way to our new quarters. Our line of Tonga's moved into the living humanity and clutter of carts, camels, bicycles, handcarts. I thought: *It was just the same as Bombay this place was definitely more civilised than the Northwest.*

Jackie whooped at the sight of two huge elephants their ears flapping against their shoulders, their eyes, all painted in garish coloured flowers, attached at the end of their tusks were little gold tassels. Astride their huge necks dressed in brilliant coloured silks, bright red turbans, were their handlers, behind they were howdahs draped in deep red and gold silks, as they manoeuvred the elephants through this mass of humanity and carts, to wherever their destination was? Maybe a festival or something? Kitty grabbed my arm.

'Sarah Plant. Look over there the ruins of the Residency.'...She pointed out a large derelict building... 'Get Jack to take you there to see it, he'll like that.'

She talked about different places, as we passed a dirty looking area ...'There, that's the Sadr Bazaar. I'll take you there to shop. Wonderful things to buy. You take my word for it. I joked.

'Any good fur coats on sale Kitty?'

She looked at me, we both broke into fits of laughter. We went through some Army lines, obviously part of the Garrison, tt had taken us about half an hour from the station to our new quarters, before she said.

'Here we are Sarah Plant. This is your place.'

'How do you know that?'

'Bobby looked into it.'

Stood on the edge of a compound, was a massive ugly looking tree, which I did not like the look of. Casting its shadows across the compound and partly over a bungalow's roof. I took stock of what our quarters were located in the middle of this compound. A galvanised roofed bungalow four steps led up to a long veranda which continued down both side. Its windows had wooden shutters, all very similar to the one in Nowshera. First impression. "Same old issue." Very basic but comfortable. Two black horses were tethered at the bottom of the veranda steps, their riders were stood at ease on the veranda. Two turbaned Indian Sepoy soldiers smartly dressed in their number ones holding their lances upright. They obviously were guarding the property. The Tonga's came to a halt by the main steps. One of the Sepoy's a corporal, came down the steps towards the party. Jack and Bobby got down; talked with him before following the Corporal up the steps onto the veranda towards the door the Corporal opened, they disappeared inside. Kitty asked.

'Well what do you say Sarah Plant? Much more civilised. Eh?'

'Yes it is, but this heat is sweltering hot.'... Beads of perspiration were breaking out on my face and arms, feeling quiet uncomfortable in the intense heat asked ...'Is it always like this?'

'Yes Sarah Plant. You'll soon get used to it.'

'I wish they would hurry up, so we can get into the shade. You know Kitty I've just realised that this is the first posting we have been given with quarters, that Jack has actually been with me to take the keys.'

' Don't remind me Sarah Plant. I know exactly how you feel.'

'Kitty where are your quarters?'

'Back down that dirt road we've just come from, not very far about a bike ride away.'

It seemed as if it was not as close as I would have liked. Eventually the three of them emerged from the bungalow. Jack hailed us.

'Come on up out of the sun.' He spoke to the other Sepoy. Who came down salaamed towards us, began speaking to the Bearer. Getting down off the Tonga's the two tribes went running up the steps into the bungalow, we leisurely followed behind. Kitty murmured.

'Sarah Plant. You're going to like it here. There's more to do, better Bazaars, more fun bargaining with the Wallahs. They like to try it on, but they don't get anything out of me, you'll see when we go shopping.'...With a quick swish of her riding crop she caught Marty a slap across the backside...'Now you stop running in and out of the rooms'...she yelled after him... 'get outside with the rest of the tribe. 'Er what were we saying Sarah Plant?' I had to laugh, she hadn't changed furthermore I did not want her to. I was sure what she said was true and looked forward to an eventful stay in Lucknow.

The Sepoy's, having carried out their duty, mounted their horses rode off. Outside it was a hive of activity, the Bearer ordering everyone around getting the luggage sorted out, having made a tour of the rooms, came to the conclusion it was much bigger albeit with the standard issue of furniture,and charpoys ready waiting to be put into use. At the rear of the bungalow another set of steps led down to an open space with what I assumed the stable, along with some other dwellings. Along the side and towards the front of the bungalow was a chicken run. The cookhouse, washhouse and toilet. By the time we had done the rounds we finally arrived at the cookhouse. The Khansama had already got a fire going.

The heat in Lucknow was totally different to Nowshera. I was wringing wet with perspiration; Michael was like a wet fish, although number One Ayah had all but stripped him to his nappy, she still constantly fanning him with a raffia fan. Chai was served on the veranda, before the Burn's departed. Kitty informing me that she would visit in a few days' time. Giving me time to settle in. My tribe worn out, listless had given up cavorting around, just sat on the veranda trying to keep cool. I said to Jack.

'We are all slowly baking to death with this heat. There is only one thing for it and that is to organise sluice downs.' He readily agreed, ordered the Bearer.

'Bearer. Sahib, Memsahib, Baba's nahana pani's.' The Bearer shouted to the Dhobi wallah. I went in to sort out robes, clean clothes from our luggage. After a while the Bearer arrived back to inform us.

'Sahib. Memsahib. Goa Pani.

In the washouse the Dhobie wallah had laid out plenty of pans of water for us to sluice down. Revived by the water, my tribe refused to get into cotton pyjamas, so I left them in knickers and pants and it was not long before they began to run around again. The evening meal was sparse, but sufficient for our needs. It was getting late I had to sort out night attire before, exhausted from the heat and a most eventful but tiring day, we all retired to bed.

The next day early in the morning we were sat eating breakfast on the veranda when the arrival of a herd of meatless raw-boned sore encrusted buffaloes slowly meandered past the bungalow onto the mydam, they were tended by two poor Indian women dressed in dirty white coverings, we sat watching this strange herd pass by and wander around the mydam. However we had other things to do. Visited the MRS. Declared fit for duty by the new MO. Who wanted to know everything about our ailments: Malaria, Black water fever, prickly heat, scratches, burns, bites, my miscarriage, Michael's birth his ailment? Not forgetting Jackie's ailing throat that at the time of examination was inflamed, so another dose of iodine was necessary. We visited the Army school arranged for their attendance the following week. The heat was something else by mid-day the sun blazed down leaving you like a damp rag. We drank plenty of pani, my tribe hardly ate their lunch but at least ate some fruit, early sluice downs temporarily revived them for a period of time, then tea-time and bed for all of us. Possibly a disturbed night through the heat.

The next morning Jack left for duty. Leaving me with Michael and my tribe finding out what their new abode held for them? The Bearer engaged in seeing that everything was just as I had it in the Nowshera bungalow was barking out his instructions to the servants, with all their gabbling and singing it appeared to me they were happy with their new abode. With our change in abode I had to change my way of doing things, it was late but first the daily inspection. I called the Bearer who had taken up a position in the doorway of the bungalow. He knew what I wanted. Clapped his hands hailed all the servants, I donned my Tobie walked to the steps waited until they had all formed in a line along the front of the bungalow, stepping down with somewhat at speed I quickly carried out my inspection nodding to each one. They responded clasping the palms of their hands together bowed their head. Inspection over the Bearer dismissed them. I went to the Cookhouse just to see the layout. The Khansama appeared more than happy salaamed grinning waved his hand around to show me his new abode. To me it looked the same with more room including a small work table and an extra firepot, I had already see the wash house so with the bearer beside me I took a look around the other outhouses the stable, the empty chicken coop I would get Jack to purchase some. Basically all our facilities looked exactly the same.

  Returning to the veranda I sat down at the table to collect my thought's, ordered chai, to watch the herd of buffaloes wandering endlessly over the mydam, I noticed their handlers would meander over to collect any of the buffalo's droppings laying on the ground, which almost immediately dried on the sun-baked earth like patty cakes, with a swift movement of the hand either one or the other women would deftly scoop them up and drop them into a basket balanced on their heads then gracefully continue on their endless walk. The old Malee appeared in front of me with his staff, salaamed waving his hand around the area, stamping his staff on the hard baked ground muttered something. I understood what he was saying. It *was going to be tough making a garden.* his tale of woe, salaamed went about his business.

I continued gazing around the area, gone was the view of distant hills. Instead that large forbidding tree with rising out of the ground like many serpents, were dozens of large gnarled twisted and coiled roots joining together at about four feet high to form its large trunk, thicker than an old oak with big shiny dark leaves, the tree next to it hardly had any foliage, perched on one of its upper branches, were two huge black vultures. Their scrawny necks tucked into the cavity of their broad backs. From the safety of the veranda I watched them as with a twitch of their heads, sharp eyes watched everything, with a rustle of feathers they stretched their red necks, ready to swoop down on any unlucky animal or, morsel of food that presented an appetising alternative to their normal dead meat diet. We did have them in Nowshera, but never as close to the bungalow. They frightened the life out of me. Jack told me not to worry they were more scared of me than anything else. My solace was disturbed by the early arrival of a Dudh Wallah, He was old, barefooted leaning heavily on a long stave as he shuffled along, while his two poverty stricken Chico's, pushed his barrow carrying a couple of large bowls and festooned with chatti bowls. The Khansama came out looking in my direction, to see if I was going to resume my participation? I was unsure of any of these new Wallahs. I would wait, observe, before entering in to any future transaction. I waved my hand to indicate. You carry on, however what was to happen did gain my attention. As he drew up, the two Indian women approached him holding out their chatti bowls, begging for some dudh. I watched as they being in charge of a hrrd of milk producing buffaloes found this amusing. Humbly they continued begging for dudh off the Wallah, who impatiently waved them away but they gabbled on pushing their bowls towards him, he gave up indicated to his Chico's who were systematically laying out pots and pans on the dirt road, the Wallah shaking his head, begrudgingly filled the Indian women's little chatti bowls, gave them back. They salaamed purposely they walked towards the forbidding tree, placed their chatti bowls in between the roots. They stood facing the tree with palms joined together salaamed deeply five or six times chanting prayers as an offering. Leaving the tree, not deigning to cast a sideways or backward glance at their benefactor, regally returned back to the Mydam to tend their herd. I sat there amazed at the shenanigans I had just witnessed as did the servants, watching the new pantomime evolving before their eyes, noticing that all chores had come to a standstill. One thing I had quickly learnt about Indians, regardless of age, caste or creed, would at the drop of a hat loved to be entertained. Any haggling and bartering, the norm of all transactions became a focal point of their daily entertainment. Then it was the Khansamers turn. I was the Dudh Wallahs first customer; no doubt he would charge me double to cover his loss, something I did not object to. Transaction over, he went back along the cart track away from the bungalow passing a large clump of trees, disturbed the tribe of monkeys with their long tails and white whiskered faces, cavorting about in the branches. We had seen those on our way in yesterday. Their noisy chattering, screaming and screeching carried on throughout the day. However they were everywhere in India, totally brazen always up to no good and would snatch anything and be away with it before you could utter a shriek. I ordered chai and resumed observing the new surroundings. The buffaloes had moved in under the shade of the trees surrounding the mydam, possibly a haven for snakes and birds. Amongst the various bird calls in the distance, I heard the sudden high-pitched shriek of a peacock, as it scratched around in the hard packed ground for some morsel of food. They were the most magnificent birds I had ever seen, with a deep blue-feathered neck tapering up to its small head encrusted with a crown of blue tipped feathers, as they strutted around proudly displaying their huge multi-coloured fantails. In total contrast between them the beautiful and the ugly vultures. Again I was disturbed by my tribe wanting pani. They came onto the veranda their faces running with beads of sweat. Mary blurted out they had been to see the monkeys. Immediately I told them not to go near them. But I knew regardless of my warning they would. The rest of the morning I just sat there mulling over the tedium I was faced with. Yes I had that in Nowshera, to pass the morning by I had found a way to employ myself in a slight way. But here the heat was stifling too much to just sit doing nothing. The morning dragged by Jack arrived back for lunch. I put my tribe them into rest, I myself cat napped, had a sluice downs, Jack and I relaxing on the veranda before the evening meal. In the fading sun of the evening these two pathetic women passed the bungalow driving the herd back to wherever they lived. My heart went out to them. Furthermore their arrival and departure was a regular daily occurrence throughout our stay. I also discovered the big forbidding tree was a snake tree (a Beepol well named tree) the cow pats, fuel for their fires. Nothing went to waste in India.

Much the same as in Nowshera, at meal times, each Chico carried the food in a chatti bowl covered by a cloth from the cookhouse to the veranda. But here they were to experience a new threat from the Vultures perched on the branch above they ever watching what went on below. Mary had nicknamed them. "Agog and Magog". His or her sole purpose in life was to snatch anything from anybody down below, who tried to run the gauntlet of the few yards of open space to the bungalow. After a few days they took courage with a flurry of feathers, they took off to circle around above waiting for something to be dropped, that made the Chico's run. Bearing in mind what Jack had said they were more frightened of us. I took no notice of this slight interruption. Unwittingly, much to our amusement every khana time, the servants were to act out another pantomime. I watched, as pairs of big brown eyes peered out from the cookhouse doorway to see the lie of the land, before venturing out with any khana. That gesture alone alerted Agog and Magog they began stirring on their perch. One big claw stretched out in front raised threateningly, black ghastly wings would spread open, its red-wattled neck raised its head, opening its great cruel hooked beak to its fullest extent the tongue fully distended, a quick shake of its head, one last ruffle of feathers the head would drop, this movement alone stirred the other one to spread it wings (indicating Try just try) Now their stage was set. We sat waiting at the table as if nothing was happening.

The Bearer would appear out of the cookhouse (pure importance) striding purposely across the compound, followed by the craving Khansama, who would shoot across like a startled rabbit The Khansama shouting abuse at the failure of the Chico's to follow him with the khana. The gibbering Chico's pushed one black umbrella after the other out of the cookhouse doorway. Under the black canopy assembled themselves with their chatti's ready to shove and push each other across. Moving as one screaming with fright if one should fall, talons would surely rip and tear at the fallen body. With a flurry, beating of feathers Agog and Magog rose in the air. Hovered ready to strike, four huge black wings blocked out the whole of the sky as they dived on this puny defence of umbrellas. Talons wrenched the umbrellas out of palsied hands tossing them high. Talons tore with claw, mercy for none. Fallen chatti bowls spilt out their contents as the Chico's gave up, ran either back to the cookhouse or towards the veranda, to run the gauntlet of the Khansama's fury. As he had to go through the gauntlet once again. Needless to say no breakfast that day, anyway breakfast was only porridge, which Jackie loathed. Sweet limes it was to be. We watched this pantomime with glee. It started the day off with a little excitement. Agog and Magog never seemed to win anything very much, only maybe umbrellas, which they collected and tore to bits with temper on their perch. This was their territory and you had better know it. The garden looked as if I cultivated shrouds with the bits dropping down. It cost me a fortune for umbrellas every month. But then lunch would come, which was curry of one sort or another that they loved. Sometimes we went for days without a bite; it depended on how active they were. One afternoon Jackie ran the gauntlet ignoring the skyward menace, ran to the cookhouse to get a slice of naan and jam, running back in triumph thinking he had succeeded, I shouted a warning.

'JACKIE WATCH OUT.' But he was physically bowled over as one vulture tore the sandwich out of his hands. He came crying towards the veranda his hand had some ghastly scratches on it, which had me administering raw Iodine. As I poured it on his wounds he screaming in pain of the sting sentation. Above Agog and Magog never ruffled a feather.

During that week, I continued with the early morning inspection. Each time a new Wallah arrived, the Bearer and Khansama looked to me for guidance. I indicated for them to carry on, together with the servants I was a bystander watching the transactions, quickly conducted and completed by about 9:30, leaving the rest of my morning idle. Within reason after a week or so, I became acclimatised to the intense heat. Although Kitty had not visited I had missed her company, realising she had left me to get organised in our new environment.

On the Monday after Jack and my tribe had gone. I carried out the daily inspection. Then the Dudh Wallah arrived, when all the palaver of the free duhd had been completed. This was my cue, he like those Wallahs in Nowshera would be introduced to our normal routine. With my Tobie on I left the veranda surprising him, stood in the blistering heat watched the on- going transactions. much to the approval of the Bearer and Khansama, they conversing with the Wallah explained the madness of the Memsahib. After he left, having returned from dropping off my tribe at school, the Ayahs were busy doing their chores, as were the Chico's, everybody was busy except me. I wasn't satisfied with what I was doing, each transaction was over far too quickly, leaving me with hours to just sit and melt away. That afternoon Kitty came riding up on a bike, I nearly fell off my chair with laughter at the sight of her. Braking to a stop, she retorted.

'Well. What's the matter with you Sarah Plant? I've got it to ride to and from the bungalows. Anyway it's quicker than those Tonga's. Look Sarah Plant. I think you should get one as well then we can go gadding about.' I thought. *"All in good time"* retorted.

'Kitty. I'm not venturing out, until I'm satisfied with my new surroundings, only then will I think about it.' *But a bike as she stated, was obviously an alternative method of transportation.* In the afternoon we resumed our Tiffin times, whilst our two tribes played and fought amongst themselves. After the third day when each Wallah arrived the Bearer and Khansama kept on muttering. 'Garam garam,' insisting I stay on the veranda as I did in Nowshera. On my part noticed the interest each new Wallah took to the pantomime they were introduced too during the battering for goods. Like they did in Nowshera our servants would stop what they were doing, to take more interest in the entertainment provided, standing, squatting down or, even lying in the dirt, I even noticed the two herdswomen would wander over, their baskets balanced on heads to stand and watch what was going on. That gave in an idea I thought: *Moving to Lucknow must have something more to offer? Developed a crazy idea that a playhouse had to be set.* Over the weekend I mulled over how I should approach this crazy plan.

On the Sunday, accompanied by our servants, we met up with Kitty and her tribe went to the Garrison Church to hear mass, then back to her Bungalow for lunch, chai and a gup. The two groups of servants conversing amongst themselves. No doubt, comparing the difference of their two Memsahibs? This became a regular feature in our weekly mundane program of idleness. By Sunday evening I had worked out my plan for my pantomime. I did not tell Jack of what I was about to do, he would think I was going Doo-lally. That night I lay thinking of the cast: *Me the Queen, the Ayahs Ladies in Waiting, The Bearer - Banker, The Khansama - Wiseman, The performers - the various Wallahs and the Audience - Servants....* The stage, My veranda and steps. I woke up to the sound of Jack moving about. My day was about to begin. Over the previous months I had had enough practice with the various Wallahs so it was simple to see how each performance would take place including the performers:

Week three staging my pantomime, after the morning inspection before the first Wallahs (*the Performers)* arrived I would take up my position to the side of the veranda steps. I the Memsahib (*Queen*) seated in splendour on my deck chair (*definitely the royal box*). The Ayahs of great importance (*Ladies in Waiting)* stood behind me, amidst great swishing of Saris, jangling of coloured glass beads bangles, the arranging of long plaits of hair all silent not a word was uttered. Other members of the household (*the Audience)* would then form themselves into a semi-circle to the side of the veranda steps, eager to watch the forthcoming attraction of the performers in front of the veranda steps, whilst the Bearer (*Banker*) the Khansama (*Wiseman*) stayed to one side. On the Saturdays my tribe would sit clustered on one side of the top step (*the Stalls*). Kathleen would come over and arrange my frock; she had to have things just so. The *Performers* would miss not a jot of this, appreciating that their *Audience* were there to be entertained by them, had to be in a receptive mood to be dazzled by the miracle about to be performed before them. The stage was set. All I had to do was trying and converse my wishes to the Bearer who was to be the main person to organise and allow the servants to watch.

The day began well Jack and my tribe left. I carried out the normal daily inspection. I sat on the veranda sipping chai waiting. It could be any one of the *Performers* arriving either on a daily basis or on their weekly schedule. But always the first one was the Dudh Wallah. With hand signals, waving arms and my help I manged to get the Bearer to organise the servants out front in a semi-circle the Chico's thought it was great fun, gradually got the others into some form of order. Before the bemused Wallah, took his turn in serving buckshee dudh to the two women. Then our performance began.

Silently enters *the Banker* wearing his beautiful pink turban, which was always used for business? A tall heavily moustachioed Mussulman, (His ancestors had been some of the greatest fighting men in India) challenging the Wallahs yelling at them to. 'Jao' (go). The *Performers* with their entourage salaamed to me dozens of times before *The Banker* demanded from them the nature of their business. (Though it was obvious, he sold Dudh or the other *Performers* sold their wares (their Chico's were their very own *Cast*). All this paraphernalia went on before they were allowed to enter and place their pots, pans, baskets or, whatever onto the bottom veranda step. Woe betide them if, a spot of dudh spilt or, provisions dropped during the forthcoming transaction, they the *Performers* would then receive the wrath of the *Banker*. Dudh bowls, dirty old shagalls and baskets were all carefully laid out on the steps. (Wonderful things would appear from them) to be observed and admired by the *Audience*. The *Banker* quietly turned facing me, with a firm but silent step up to the veranda towards me then another to stop salaamed, spoke in broken English.

'Memsahib, this miserable Dudh (*Performer* or whomever) wishes you to purchase his wares.'

I nodded that he might try. He salaamed again turned and roundly berated the performer shouting words for wasting my Memsahib's time… A clap of his hands brought forth the *Wiseman* entering from the wings…The *Banker* muttered.

'Get on with it. The Memsahib has much business to perform in Delhi.' Caused great intakes of breathe from the *Audience* at so important a Memsahib. With great jangling of bracelets the *Ladies in Waiting* sighed encouragingly. The Dudh *Performer* produced his wares, extolling its virtues one of his Chico's poured dudh from a chatti bowl into his cupped hand, the Dudh *Performer* fingered the milk as it swam through his fingers. He touched it to his lips and was in ecstasy as he explained.

'Memsahib. Dudh only from Kashmiri she buffaloes. Memsahib.' He sighed, offering to let me try. I inclined my head. 'No.' gesturing to number One Ayah.

Number One *Lady in Waiting*. Got up amongst heavy acclaim from her sisters, she descended past *Svengali*, two steps from the Dudh *Performer* (honour enough for him) she stopped turned salaamed deeply to me, then to her sister's they heavy kohl eyed, drew quick intakes of breath. I nodded my head in acknowledgement she turned to face the Dudh *Performer* he and his *Cast salaamed* deeply to her. She proffered an opened hand as dudh was gently poured over her fingers, not so fast as to hurt her, behind me the *Ladies in Waiting were* breathless. Number One *Lady in waiting kohl* eyed at me. I nodded. A hiss came from Jackie she turned slightly, so they could see as dudh was dribbled again over her fingers, as it sparkled in the sun intakes of breathe came from all of them. She turned back to me again salaamed. I nodded she turned to the Dudh *Performer* smartly she clapped her hands once, which always made me jump. The deed had been done but not struck, there was yet more to follow. The payment! The *Banker walked* ahead of her up the steps towards me stopped on the last step salaamed. I nodded. He moved to one side to let Number One *Lady and Waiting* pass. Salaaming deeply to me she joined the other seated *Ladies in Waiting* with much jangling of

252

bracelets and great pleasure from the cast at such a superb performance. *Svengali* salaamed I nodded. Ascended the last step passing the *Ladies in waiting*, who had all but passed out, at the honour. Quietly he entered the bungalow taking his time before emerging clasping a big green shiny moneybox, which he and he alone was entrusted to collect from the Burrah Sahibs safe (a shelf behind our bed). Two steps down he turned to me with a deep salaam, offered the moneybox to me, which I never touched, entrusting its keeping only to him. At best it never held more than forty rupees (the wages and food allowance for everybody for the month). He salaamed turned to the entranced *Cast* and *Audience,* all staring at this moneybox filled with gold. It was now his business to pay; he sat down on the step. Now the deal could be struck, with the payment made the whole audience would withdraw. The Pantomime was over. The *Wiseman,* who had been watching from the wings, collected the dudh took it to the cookhouse for boiling. End of that play.

I clapped. encouraging the rest (audience) to follow suit they did, the Bearer did his part and shooed them back to their chores, I carried on sewing until the next Wallah arrived, who would probably be the Phal (fruit) Wallah? The Bearer glanced at me, I nodded he smiled flashing pearly white teeth I do believe, he was really enjoying the madness of his memsahib. The play would be re-enacted all over again. Silly but we all loved every moment of it until all the day's provisions were purchased, It did break up my lazy morning. Nevertheless, towards the end of the week, Jack arrived back to inform me he had been picked to play for the "Double Ducks " the Battery football team. It appeared that wherever Jack went, he was included in any football team that was going. A Sergeant, by the name of Jackie Leask who organised all of the fixtures, became a regular visitor to our bungalow, obviously to discuss football, subsequently he became a close friend of the family. At the insistence of Kitty we did go to the football matches and she also coersed me in going to the odd mess dance although infrequent.

22nd. (The Residency) Field Artillery Battery Football Team Lucknow 1931

Dvr. Moore- Grn. Lockett – Sig. Skelding.
L/Bdr. Winstanley- Farr. Slade.- Sig. Cowgill
Grn. Southern – Bdr. Lambert –Sgt. Leask – B.Q.M.S Plant B.S.M. Jordan. Grn. Sutcliffe – Sig. Williams.

When we arrived there were hardly any garden flowers to be seen, I ventured out to see how the Malee was coping with the hard ground, he certainly had broken up the ground into flower beds, which had some growth of plants, Salaaming he got up began gabbling on in Urdu about this and that. A large scorpions scuttling about on the ground which was quickly killed by the Malee's staff. They were much larger in Lucknow than Nowshera, where Jackie used to walk around clutching an old Bourneville Cocoa tin. No one else was allowed to take it, until I saw the three of them together with the Chico's hunkered down in a group. Wondering what was going on I silently crept up to have a closer look, stood watching as each one in turn pressed a stick down onto a scorpion's head causing it to jab its tail, Jackie would then pinch hold of the tail sting jerking it up threw it on the floor to break off its sting, the scorpion minus its sting scuttled out across the ground. That was enough for me. With a swish of the crop I cut into all of them, sending them scattering in all directions, leaving the tin lying sideways on the floor. Picking up the tin to my horror counted six other stings inside. "Jackie's hoard." Immediately I dropped the tin and ran screaming after them. 'I'LL MACRO (BEAT) THE LOT OF YOU.' More letters of woe were sent to their father up in the Khyber Pass, not that he could do anything about it.

There were definitely more snakes in central India than in the Northwest. The children had been warned from the day of our arrival, that they were absolutely forbidden to go near the Beepol tree. No amount of ranting and raving on my part or lectures by Jack, seemed to be of any avail, they were drawn to the tree like a magnet. Snakes, Mary was rather wary, Kathleen was not sure and ready to run, but Jackie was fascinated, he being too young to understand the fatal consequences of a snake bite or the sting of a scorpion. Once I found him kneeling close to a tiny baby snake crooning to it as he gently ran a finger lightly down its back. I nearly died with fright as I recognised a Krait, I could not help myself, shrieked with fright, Jackie yelled at me.

'Mum you frightened it.'

I turned and grabbed hold of his arm dragged him up onto the veranda into the bungalow and thrashed him. Above his yells tried to tell him how dangerous it was. Pulling himself away from me, ran to the girls crying and complaining about how he had been beaten for nothing.

'You don't mind a hiding, if you have done something wrong, but to have done nothing, it's worse.' He sobbed, they glared at me. Mary exclaimed.

'She's just vicious don't speak to her.'

I grabbed hold of my riding crop, at the sight of that she vaulted over the veranda rail, whilst the other two leapt down the steps all running away. Oh! What was I to do with this tribe of mine? They have no fear of anything, whatever they are told not to do they immediately did it. I was more ashamed of thrashing him over nothing but it was for his own good.

Another day, all was quiet whilst I was sat out on the veranda catching the slight breeze filtering through. With my back to the window in my sewing area. At the other end veranda my tribe off school for some reason or other were playing together. Lunch was soon to be served. I was engrossed turning the sewing machine handle stitching a shirt, when something heavy seemed to fall beside me, wondering if it was one of the children's balls glanced down. A foot or so away from me, was a huge snake reassembled itself. I froze unable to move. Its head rose slightly, its flickering tongue tasted the air around. As its hood began to flatten. Its cold eyes seemingly inspecting me did not like what it saw? Slowly it lowered its head to the ground began to slide away towards the veranda steps. I watched as its tail slid away from me. I yelled out.

'DON'T MOVE. DON'T MOVE.'

The Bearer stepping out from the doorway, saw the snake, with one leap was on the top of a tin box located next to the doorway. Meanwhile my tribe running towards the veranda steps right into its path. Mary, quick enough to see what was on the veranda, grabbed both of their shirts to bring them to a stop. They had disturbed the snake, a Cobra about to slide down the steps, stopped in front of them. Its head began to rise up, its hood was not fully open, its forked tongue flicking in and out. I was frozen to the chair, frantic at what Jackie would do. I whispered to myself. "Oh dear God. Don't let Jackie put his hand out to stroke it. It was he who whispered.

'Mum look how beautiful he is.'

254

I watched in horror as it raised its head further, as it swayed flicking its tongue at them, its hood began to flatten. I prayed it would not strike. Extending its head further, it stayed like that for what seemed hours. its sole attention on them, ignoring the Bearer behind who was clutching his robes tightly around his legs. Fortunately my tribe had the sense to remain motionless, frozen to the spot. The Cobra, seeing that it was not in any danger, slowly lowered its head to continue on its journey off the veranda, effortlessly it slid down the steps as its tail disappeared, I did not know what it was to faint, but I wanted to do it right then. Instead in a stage whisper called out.

'Jackie, don't you dare move. Mary, Kathleen just stay still.'

Quietly it slid off the bottom step onto the baked surface of the compound, I watched as it snaked its way across to the snake tree. Jackie yelled to the others,

'Quick the vultures.'

They all grabbed balls, anything from the veranda, and ran back along the side veranda to the rear. I shouted after them.

'HOLY MARY MOTHER OF GOD, WHAT ARE YOU GOING TO DO?'

I had been keeping a watchful eye upon the cobra, that was halfway across the compound snaking towards the protection of the snake tree. The Bearer jumped down off the tin box spoke loudly.

'Memsahib. Sanp. Bara. Salaams.' (Snake Great Honour) He salaamed to me. Apparently, we were on the snake's territory, he just wanted to see who we were and we were gifted everyone must know. I couldn't have cared less, the last time I was honoured it had been a snow leopard. My heart was racing, I was pouring with perspiration. My tribe appeared around the side of the bungalow. Vulnerable in the open they ran towards the tree, where the vultures were perched. Yelling and shouting they began to pelt them with their missiles. Needless to say they never got anywhere near the vultures that, disturbed by their little onslaught rose into the air, giving the snake its chance to escape. Oh my God, if only Jack was here, whenever these things occurred to deal with, let me not be on my own I was in a panic. When they had finished shooing away the vultures and returned to the veranda. I grabbed hold of them told them off smacked each one of them, then threw them into bed, all my ranting had the Ayahs clucking and sucking teeth. It was my answer to all panics. The whole episode had taken less than ten minutes, it seemed a full day (Not such a good day at all, but a very bad day). Later, I was still in a cold sweat when Kitty rode up on her bicycle, with her tribe running along beside her. shouted out.

'WHAT'S ALL THE HULLABALOO WITH YOUR TRIBE? I HEARD THEM YELLING UP THE ROAD.' I explained to her the recent happenings, adding my own morbid comments on the occasion... 'All I seem to get are visits from wild animals, huge birds and reptiles all for some reason or another to honour my household and me.'...'Sarah Plant. You should be thankful that nothing happens on these wild occasions. It's far better than having been fleeced buying a useless fur coat.'

Her chance remark brought sanity back. That had me laughing once again. I went in to my tribe and got them up. When I informed Jack of the events of the day, he was concerned but praised me on remaining calm. Calm! I wasn't able to move with fear.

Amongst other dos and don'ts, my tribe had been warned about, was the sacred cow. I had witnessed stall Wallahs paying it a privilege salaaming, as the indolent creature, nonchalantly devoured everything on his stall, even a train driver would wait until it decided to move. One such incident really worried Jack. A sacred cow, which appeared not to be one of the scabby herd owned by the herdswomen, adopted us making its home in our compound. My tribe had been told just to shoo it away, even the Chico's would not do that. I was on the veranda, making clothes. Kitty arriving without her tribe getting off her bike said.

'Sarah Plant. I just popped over for some peace and quiet, I've quarantined my tribe to their beds, and I'm fed up with their fighting.' Chai was served. I continued to machine whilst we gupped.

'Sarah Plant, it's very quiet around here, where's your tribe? You sent them off to bed as well?'

'No they're playing on the mydam with the Chico's'

'Well, I can see you too want a bit of peace and quiet.'

'Yes. Don't often get much around here Kitty, what were you saying?'

Suddenly the Bearer followed by the rest of the servants, came running to me. The Ayahs were slashing the air with their arms screaming.

'Macro (beat) Missy Baba Mary. Macro.' Immediately I was on my feet. Kitty exclaimed.

'Christ Sarah Plant. What have your buggers been up to now? She must have done something dreadful, for them to want you to whip her.'

'Kitty. I don't know? But I'll soon find out. Follow me.'

I grabbed my Tobie, riding crop. Quickly ran after the servants, with Kitty shouting.

'SARAH PLANT. YOUR BIT OF PEACE AND QUIET, DIDN'T LAST VERY LONG!'

I could not care less, we ran around the outhouses only to stop dead in our tracks, at the scene not far away in front of us.

Astride a cow sat back to back were Kathleen and Mary. Kathleen holding a rope with her knees around its neck. Mary, her legs gripping its flanks pulling its tail up. Looped around its neck was a rope, its ends tied to a blanket laid on the floor behind it, with Jackie hanging on. Every time Mary pulled on its tail the stationary cow, lurched forward kicking with his back legs its hooves missing Jackie's head by inches. The three of them shrieking with laughter. Kitty Burns muttered.

'Christ. Sarah Plant. You're in the mire this time?'

I dashed forward, running through the middle of the servants. With a swipe of my crop caught Jackie on his backside, he never even looked up just slid off sprang up and ran to his Ayah, who grabbed his arm and raced off to the bungalow. Chasing the pair of them, stopped turned about ran back to the other two, unfortunately I had provided them a chance to jump down and run away in opposite direction. I ran after Mary whilst Kitty chased Kathleen. Both of us slashing the air with our crops, but they were too quick, we gave up the chase. My heart was pounding perspiring freely, I noticed the servants gathered together looking very unhappy but did nothing to help, Kitty running up to join me shouted.

'QUICK SARAH PLANT GET THE ROPE OFF ITS NECK, KEEP IT WITHIN THE SHADE OF THE TREE. NO ONE MUST SEE US FROM THE ROAD.'

As I moved towards the cow, I was shaking with anger. It tossing its head about quiet content still munching cud. It looked at me with doleful eyes. I patted its head whilst I dithered with this rope around its neck. I had to go around both sides, noticed its poor scabrous skin covered with sores. Then I spotted blood running from squashed leeches adhered to its neck and flanks, where my two devils had gripped with their legs. With both ropes untied dropped them on the ground, Kitty shaking her head watched me as the cow unharmed moved away. Nevertheless my temper was getting the better of me, leaving Kitty I turned around running towards the bungalow shrieking and screaming for them, the servants scattered as they ran ahead out of my way. They probably thought I was going to murder them as well, which made me stop. Returning back to Kitty stood watching the cow. Called out.

'Oh my God Kitty. What am I to do with them?'

'Sarah Plant. Am I glad their yours, not mine.'

To make amends, I picked up some cud and thrust it towards its mouth. It took it and munched on. I was speechless as we gathered up the ropes and pulled the blanket away dragging it behind us, returned to the bungalow. Kitty exclained.

'Christ Sarah Plant I'm shaking.'

'So am I. How do you faint Kitty. I'd love to do it right now.'

'Come on Sarah Plant. Pull yourself together. No time for fainting, can't let anyone see us like this. By God Sarah Plant my kids are bad, I know what they get up to, but your kids are ingenious. Who would ever think of treating a sacred cow like that? C'mon best foot forward.'

We entered the compound to find it deserted. This was a bad sign. Kitty's bike was propped up against the steps.

'Well Sarah Plant. There's a good sign they've got my bike ready? I shan't stay for chai; you probably will never be served by any of the servants ever again. I'm off to sort my tribe out. Batten the place down Sarah prepare for the worst. Hope to see you all alive in the morning.'

She got on her bike and quickly pedalled away. I waited in the cart road until she turned towards her home. I thought: *What a Jobe's comfort she is.* I walked up the steps slapping the crop against my dress, in temper muttering. 'I will make them feed that cow for the rest of their stay.' As I proceeded to beat hell out of the rail with the crop, yelling for the Baba's who I was going to kill...AYAHS, AYAHS. BRING BABA'S. JAHLDI JAHLDI.'

The Ayahs had hidden them. I had reached a situation that was no longer fright but anger, ceased using my crop. One by one their Ayah's brought them to me, they avoiding any contact with my eyes, as they ushered their victims to the slaughter. Kathleen and Jackie bawling their eyes out followed by a very sullen but defiant Mary, even Michael was brought out, held in number One's arms, she remained at the doorway alongside a very sullen Bearer. Six of them stood before me, raising my crop, indicated to the Ayah's to move away. They moved backwards no salaams, even before I could utter a word Mary exclaimed.

'It was only some fun mum'...I gave her a quick cut with the crop that shut her up. There was no excuse worth listening too I shouted.

'AYAH'S, STRIP THE THREE OF THEM.' They were too slow, in my wrath I grabbed Jackie and tore every stitch of clothing off of his body, then Kathleen's, moved towards Mary....'I can take my own clothes off thank you' I screamed...STRIP NOW.'

The three of them stood naked, their clothes in a dishevelled pile in front of them, waiting for my next move, striking imaginary matches. I screamed at the Chico's.

'JAHLDI JAHLDI. AG AG. (FIRE) IN THE COMPOUND. JAHLDI JAHLDI.'

Understanding the Chico's ran crashing into each other. As they gathered wood they too were howling, crocodile tears streaming down their brown faces. Memsahib's going to burn Baba's on pyre, adding to their fear the Khansama came out brandishing a burning stick shouting at them. The fire was quickly lit I shouted.

'CHICO'S. COME HERE. JAHLDI'

Whimpering they scampered up onto the veranda, their eyes wide with fright. Gesticulating with my crop I shouted.

'PICK UP EVERYTHING INCLUDING SANDALS. AG THEM.' They grabbed all the clothes and ran to the blazing fire. I shouted to the Dhobi Wallah.

'CHATTI BOWLS ARUM PANI SABUN FOR DHOBI. JAHLDI JAHLDI.'

In turn he screamed at the Chico's. Pandemonium set in, they left the fire fled into the washhouse. I'm sure they had developed wings. Each returned carrying a large chatti bowl of pani, their knees buckling under its weight. The Khansama and Dhobi Wallah, recognised as voices of authority were shouting at the whimpering Chico's, following each other up the veranda steps, the second in line managed to trip screaming in terror, threw pani over the first Chico, the third one fell over the second one, emptying his pani full of water over him. The veranda was awash, three bars of soap skidded across the veranda. To vent my anger, I screamed waved my crop at the Dhobi Wallah, it was his fault. He screamed abuse at the two sodden Chico's sending them wailing back for more. Determined not to laugh at this shambles, I kept my gaze fixed on my tribe. They in turn dare not break into any form of mirth. At that moment to avoid bursting into laugher I bit my crop if, I could have run into my bedroom buried my face in the bolster I would have done so. The two sodden Chico's returned still wailing, aware not to spill any pani slowly mounted the steps placing the bowls in front of Kathleen and Jackie alongside Mary's. Pointing my crop in the direction of the bars of soap, I spoke.

'Ayah's.' Each one picked up a bar began scrubbing their charge while this was going on I went inside to my medical treasure chest, took out the bottle of Iodine returned to the scrubbing area. Where three very soapy individuals were being doused. The Chico's running backwards and forwards brought more pani. I poured a good amount of iodine into each bowl, indicated to the Ayah's, more scrubbing had my tribe howling. With the endless water supply provided by the Chico's there was more dousing, they were almost drowned, I shouted 'BUS.' (Stop).

Then in front of all. With my hand thrashed the three soaking wet bodies, that had them stamping on the spot, their backsides red. I ordered.

'Ayah's. Pyjama's for Baba's.' The three Ayahs disappeared. I spoke.

'Mary when this is all over. I am going to have some very serious talking with you.'

The Ayah's returned, quickly the three were dressed in their pyjamas and sent to bed, howling rubbing their backsides. With me yelling after them.

'YOU'LL NEVER DO THAT AGAIN MY BUCKOS.'

No doubt their Ayah's glad to be out of Memsahib's sight. I turned on the wide-eyed Chico's waved my crop at the Chatti bowls, shouted. 'JAO.' Grabbing them ran disappeared, leaving me soaked with perspiration shaking with horror at the outcome of their mischief. I went to the dhobi house, quickly scrubbed myself down all over threw out all of my clothes to have them burnt. Wrapping myself in a towel shouting at the Chico's.

'AG. AG. JAO.'

I returned to the bungalow, the howls and sobs of my tribe echoing from within, I went straight to the bedroom changed, went to the cookhouse, shouted for the Bearer, who emerged looking very concerned.

'Ji han Memsahib.'

'Chai Jahldi Bearer. I must gup with you. Jahldi.' He salaamed.

I returned to the veranda sat down to compose myself, I was still perspiring. Just then Jack rode up, swung down off his horse.

'Sarah whatever is wrong? I heard the children howling from far away.'

'Well you may ask Jack? ...He came up stood in front of me...'The three of them were riding that cow under the tree. Kitty and I had a hell of a job undoing ropes. She would not stay.'...Placing his hands on hips, shook his head, he was worried.

'What did the Bearer do?'

'He and the Khansama went and hid themselves.' Jack shouted.

'BEARER.' The bearer emerged with the chai, brought it across, served it...'Bearer Baba's Kharab Memsahib Macro.' ...Jack indicated to the cow lying under the tree in the shade...'Ap Ji nai bolteh.' (You no speak) Placed his fingers against his lips... Ayahs, Khansama, all. Ji nai bolteh...Jack placed his hand on his chest, secrecy, tell no one, tell the other servants to do the same. The Bearer nodded and placed his hand on his chest. 'Teek heyh Sahib. Memsahib. Macro Babe's. bharut accha.' Pointed to my crop that was lying on the table pointed to the cow....'Pukka' and salaamed.

'Sarah, I think he is telling us, the cow excepts Memsahib's macro-ing our three. Being somewhat so isolated, apart from the Burns', who will not say anything, we will just have to wait and see the outcome.'

Jack spoke to number One Ayah... Mujhe chahiye Missy Mary.' (I want)

Mary came out in front of the Ayah. She stood in front of her father, a look of defiance on her face, her eyes screwed up nearly closed. As he proceeded to give her the dressing down of her life? He never chastised them that was my job, nevertheless Jack talking to her was the only way to make her cry, her tears began to flow, in between her sobs emerged the sorry's, begged to be forgiven... 'You tell your Mother you are sorry and will never trouble her again.'

She turned to me sullen as ever, her tears gone, grudgingly mumbled.

'I'm sorry Mum. I won't worry you again.'

I nodded as accepted, but deep inside knew it would not last. Quickly turning to Jack demanded.

'Why can't I have a pony like everyone else? Instead of stealing rides on donkeys, horses or sacred cows?' Jack let out a roar and went to grab her...

'GET BACK INTO YOUR BEDROOM MISS.'

I grabbed the crop but she leapt off the veranda running across the compound in her pyjamas. We just stood there looking at each other then laughed. You could not tame this girl. She just wanted a horse to ride. The chai was cold but drank it. We spotted Mary going around to the rear of the bungalow. We took no notice as I continued relating the full version. Kitty's chasing around the pandemonium when the Chico's lit the fire, the water, the beating, all of it. Seeing the funny side of the poor Chico's plight. He just roared with laughter Nevertheless, there was a serious side to it. Which he was very concerned about? The evening meal was served only to Jack and me. Fruit was sent into the other three in their bedroom. I hadn't forgotten about the talk I was going to give Mary. Whilst Jack read, I got into my nightdress. Had Mary brought to our bedroom. Once again to explain, the seriousness of her action.

'It was only a lark mum. I really did think it was a buffalo, I said I was sorry. I shall explain to the Bearer, I thought it was a buffalo. We will pay it great honour, huge salaams, feed it every day.'

'Well you do what you think is best. Apologise to the Bearer and all the servants. They have a right for an apology from you three. I'll leave that matter up to you?'

The next day she carried out her promise. For weeks after we worried about the incident, Mary was quiet, but not for long.

The beginning of the Monsoon season brought rain. Within minutes the weather changed from the searing heat of the blazing hot sun to freezing cold. Leaving us shaking grabbing blankets. The distant dark clouds would rapidly build up accompanied by the slow rumble of thunder with flashes of lightning. A cold wind would herald the onslaught of a downpour, a crack of thunder opened up torrential rain, its incessant drumming on the galvanised roof nearly drove me mad. When you thought it could not beat down any harder, a new blast of wind would throw large raindrops into the flooding torrents in front of the bungalow, causing spray to jump a foot high, whilst we watched every form of rubbish flow past the bungalow, long staves were kept handy on the veranda to push away piles of it, which could build up forming a dam that at times would soak the inside of the bungalow. By blocking off any route of entry I quickly learnt to stop any reptile or small animal seeking the safety of higher ground. The metal trunks that held clothes, were raised high off the floor so snakes, scorpions, or spiders could not hide in to bite or sting the unwary. Storing clothes in metal trunks was useless, insect's got in them. Huge moths six inches long or fish ants, something I'd never heard of, which were capable of devouring a coat in front of your eyes in minutes. Termites that just ate everything including the sides of wooden walls, even under the floorboards, which might give way and plunge you down below onto anything to bite you. Then, as suddenly as it started, the rain ceased leaving only the sound of dribbling water that turned into drips before it stopped and the sun came out. "Oh how I loved this country." It was our first Christmas in Lucknow, the Garrison held a Christmas party for all the children. On Christmas Eve to celebrate Michael's first birthday we held a party, inviting all of Jack's football team, they all turned up even Lt. Tucker who stayed for one drink then left. On Christmas day, Bobby provided a turkey for the two families to have Christmas dinner, The Khansama cooked the turkey to serve it cold with all the trimmings and place setting with a variety of salads, fruit down the middle of the long table the servant set up to seat the two families with presents for all. It turned out to be a most memorable one.

We had been in the quarters about 5 months, when Jack arrived back early from the camp. Calling me out onto the veranda. He stood there, his Tobie still under his arm, a subdued look on his face said.

'Sit down Sarah. I have a question to ask you. In the same breath he called... Chai Bearer, jahldi karo jahldi. With immediate concern I sat down on the wicker chair.

'What is it Jack?'

'What would you say if I was to tell you, that we have to pack up again, we are on the move.

'Oh my God Jack. Where to now? I've just got the bungalow the way I like it. We've not long been here. Don't tell me back to Nowshera?'

'No Sarah, somewhere better.' I retorted.

'Come on out with it Jack Plant. Don't keep me twisting my wedding ring until it falls off.' The Bearer arrived with the chai, placed it on the table, salaamed left.

'No it's not back to Nowshera, but to a place called Mussoorie.'

'Where on earth is that? Does that mean we're not going to return to England with the Twenty-second?'

'No. No. It's another hill station further north of here. About a day and half train journey.'

'Oh my God not another of those train journeys. Anyway what's going on up there that it's so important that they want you? Not more fighting?' He just stood there and roared with laughter.

'No Sarah listen. It's a hill station, we're all going up for a rest. I'll be up there for a couple of weeks leave. Also to attend a gunnery course at the Army camp they have up there. So I'll be with you for about six weeks. Of course you'll stay on after.'

'Jack I'll kill you. You've set my nerves off again.'

'Sarah. You should have seen the expression on your face.' He said with another roar of laughter. I retorted.

'I did not see anything that was funny. When do we go?'

'Well, it is likely that it will be tomorrow.' Irritated I asked.

'Come on Jack. When will it be?'

'Well. Maybe a few days.' I was going to give him as well as I was getting, indignantly replied.

'How often have I heard that? I'm always prepared. I've had good training over the past ten years as a soldier's wife.' That big grin appeared again.

'Well then. You know what it's all about.'

'Well I suppose it's something to look forward to. I'll tell our tribe later before they bed down for the night. Jack what about the servants?'

'Same as before.You choose who should go. Must say Sarah that you have done remarkably well in running the household. I do get complimented on the smart turn out you always present, now I'm passing the compliments onto you.' I aptly replied.

'You've always said. I was a soldier's wife, so under the circumstances I try to do my best. It's very nice to have good remarks made about one's self.'

260

That night we told the tribe about our forthcoming holiday up in the Mussoorie hills. That we should not have done. All that night they were restless. We could hear Mary whispering to the other two, plotting their next adventure.

The next day, after the early morning schedule had been completed, quietness reined upon the household, I worked out the number of servants going, called the Bearer to inform him.

'Sahib, Memsahib, Baba's jao Mussoorie.'

I pointed out with my arm raised upwards. A big beam creased his face; he understood where we were going. I again pointed to him Bearer, Ayah's, Wallahs and Chico's jao.' Then put up four fingers started counting, indicating the number four Ayahs'. The Khansama, Dhobi Wallah and Chico's that could go.

'Achchha Memsahib. Bahut bahut Shukria. Kitna jao kab?' He was thanking me and wanted to know when? I told him.

'Er maybe parson' (the day after tomorrow). Thanda garam kapre (cold warm clothes).' That he understood.

'Achchha Memsahib Pukka.' Teek aaha. Main jao sakte (I go speak).

Salaamed turned hurriedly moved off the veranda, shouting for the Khansama who came running out of the cookhouse, with an umbrella above his head, his arms white covered in flour from whatever he was making. I had to laugh at the sight of the Khansama, thrashing the sky with his umbrella, whilst shouting at the Bearer, for being disturbed. They stopped in the middle of the compound the Bearer began to talk to him, a lot of arm waving ensued. In a fit of temper the Khansama threw his umbrella on the ground started to rant at the Bearer. When he noticed me sitting on the veranda laughing at his antics he stopped, stooped, picked up his umbrella carrying it over his head approached me salaamed.

'Memsahib jao Mussoorie.' I firmly replied.

'Achchha. Jao Mussoorie.'

Now came the tale of woe. With arm waving towards his cookhouse, the veranda table, from what I understood of his antics and verbal dialogue he was explaining.. 'Memsahib, this humble Khansama has no time to prepare khana for today and parson journey.' I knew he was playing for time. I answered him with firmness.

'Khansama. Parson. Ath subah. Jahldi Jahldi.' (tomorrow morning eight o'clock.)

Crestfallen, a disgruntled Khansama salaamed, scuttled away ranting as he waved the umbrella above his head. The Bearer, having done his rounds, began to organise the household in preparation for the forthcoming trip. It erupted into a hive of activity now and again the Bearer would present something to me and mutter.

'Jao Memsahib?' Whether I wanted it or not replied.

'Ji han Bearer.'

My motto was be prepared I sorted out my important items, the medicines and cure all ailments that I would take with me and left them on one side, letting him get on with the rest of the preparations. By lunchtime all was but ready. Just before the children returned home from school Jack arrived back from Camp. His Syce, ever there to meet his master, took charge of the horse and ran it round to the stable at the rear. Jack exclaimed

'Sarah I've decided to take little Salem as well. He is very good, he can come back down with me when I return!' I had forgotten all about the little Syce.

'I'll tell the Bearer one extra to go.'

Regardless of the ranting and raving of the Khansama lunch was on time. It was pointless making my tribe have an afternoon sleep. Michael of course was no trouble. Early in the afternoon Kitty Burns turns up with her tribe in a Tonga, that was it, her tribe joined mine and immediately disappeared to play. She shouted at the driver 'INTEZAR' (to wait. I puzzled by her demand) she did not get down called out

261

'Sarah Plant. Leave the kids here to kill each other. I've come to take you down to the Bazaar. You haven't been out shopping since you got here. There are some great material shops to explore.' Then I knew why she turned up in a Tonga, not on her bicycle.

'Thank you Kitty, but I can't. We're all off up into the hills to some place called Mussoorie and after my first trip up the hills to Khanspur, I'm too concerned to go out gallivanting about shopping with you.'

'Fiddlesticks Sarah Plant. You are lucky. I hear only good things about it. It's a wonderful hill station. Even royalty have visited it, far better than mount Abu where we used to go and from what you said about Khanspur even better. Still Jack has been in the fighting in the Khyber Pass, he must be due for a spot of leave. I wish it were us, we shall miss you all. C'mon let's move. Maybe you will find something in the Bazaar for your trip up the hills. Bearer. Memsahib's jao Sudder Bazaar. Leave Baba's here with you. C'mon Sarah Plant Jahldi.'

She was determined I should go. I shrugged my shoulders it was pointless arguing with Kitty. I turned to the Bearer clenching my fist just said.

'Babas.' He understood what he must do, clapped his hands and shouted at two Chico's.

'Memsahib's. Jao.'

Two Chico's obeying his order ran to the Tonga climbed onto the sides, I climbed up after them still protesting feebly.

'Kitty this is not right.'

'Get on with you. With all their bodyguards they'll as safe as houses.'

Having sat down beside her we moved off. The Chico's' hung onto each side grinning at us. The Chico's they were supposed to be our interpreters, but with Kitty around one didn't need one, she did all transaction, the way she wanted them to go. It was just a ride for the Chico's. With reservations, on these very rare occasions, I was reasonably happy to leave the children with the Bearer. No harm would come to them and certainly not with the Ayah's around. On the way Kitty and I gupped. The Tonga did not take long to get to this Bazaar she was always on about, it was just past the Polo ground close to the army lines. My first visit to the Sudder Bazaar highlighted a different class of people. Not tribal or as menacing as those of the Northwest but dressed for the heat of the day. Men in whites or long flowing gowns women in multi coloured saris. However, thanks to Kitty, who guided me to a fabric Wallah she knew, I purchased some fabric at a knock down price to make clothes while up in the hills. I had no rupees to pay for the fabric neither did Kitty, but she had an arrangement with the Fabric Wallah owner. She would pay later I would pay her upon our return to the bungalow. Our shopping trip over and done, on our way back with a twinkle in her eye she said.

'Sarah Plant, You can ride a bike can't you?'

'Yes, you know I have one.' Well next time, you and me will take our bikes on a jaunt.'

'Oh. Where to?'

'Never you mind.'

As the Tonga pulled up outside the bungalow, our two tribes appeared from the rear. All was okay no problems. Kitty ordered the Tonga Wallah to stay, who promptly fell asleep. Kitty stayed for a quick chai. I paid her what I owed. They left she shouting at the Tonga Wallah.

'JAHLDI YER LAZY BUGGER...as they all clambered up she yelled....WE SHALL SEE ABOUT COMING TO THE STATION TOMORROW MORNING TO SEE YOU ALL OFF.'

Within the short notice given, everything had been packed for the trip. I like the children, was beginning to treat it as an adventure. The next day we left for the station. The servants remaining behind were not happy! All lined up, silently salaamed. "Maybe next time?" The journey by Tonga to Lucknow station was short. In the morning sun the station looked beautiful with its yellow and red stonework surmounted with tall Minarets located around on its top. Gathered in groups outside were the few families travelling to Mussoorie. As promised Kitty minus half her tribe at school turned up to see us off. Whilst Jack began talking with a couple of Infantry Sergeants, Kitty and I gupped alone before it was time for us to board the train. A journey that would go west back towards Pindi. This time we were getting off at a place called Dehra Dun.

The carriage had been requisitioned by the Army, so we had some form of privacy to hold conversations. We were to spend a restless night on the train, with Jack snoring his head off throughout the night. Just as the train pulled into Bareilly the first rays of the sun lit up the carriage. Jack promptly came alive yawning asked.

'Sarah, how would you like an Irish cup of tea?'

Not waiting for an answer stuck his head out of the window and shouted down to a Chai Wallah sat down on his haunches waiting.

'Tin Chai, tin nimba pani.' I wondered: *Was this just a coincidence? It seemed that all Chai Wallahs picked the exact spot to haunch down and prepares chai for the next train to arrive, which maybe could be hours away or even day. I had first noticed them at Pindi, they always ready to serve chai.* I heard the Chai Wallah mutter.

'Sahib.' Jack took hold of the glasses of chai gave me them, one for number One Ayah still holding Michael, then the glasses of lemon water for out tribe. A few sips of chai soon had me revived from an uncomfortable night's sleep. Whilst sipping the hot liquid I had a chuckle to myself "Irish tea indeed" He's like an elephant he doesn't forget! Having given our three something to drink Jack sat back to enjoy his chai. From the time we had left Bareilly the train had run alongside a wide twisting river that would disappear then reappear as the train crossed a few bridges from one side of the river bank back to the other, in places its banks narrowed as its muddy coloured waters changed cascaded over rocks to foaming brownish white. The surrounding countryside was lush green with clumps of trees along the riversides. Buffaloes trying to keep cool wallowed in its shallow muddy waters. Standing on one leg some Ibis birds ever watchful for fish, their long extended necks close to the water. We passed herds of, deer, antelope, many single humped cows. In the distance the familiar sight of the Himalayas dominated the horizon, its snow-capped mountains, rising high into a blue sky whilst below the hills covered in tall rising trees, setting the foreground scene. According to Jack, Dehra Dun was a small town at the entrance to the Dun Valley and over a century before it was in the possession of the Gurkha Empire until the British drove them out during the Gurkha war. It then became under the protection and possession of the Honourable East India Company. Everywhere we went there was always some historic attachment to the British hence the Raj Empire. He also informed me that there was a horseracing course at Dehra Dun, and for us. The end of the line, we would stay overnight before travelling up to Mussoorie the next morning.

CHAPTER SIX
THE MUSSOORIE HILLS- LANDOUR.

Finally we arrived at Derah Dun. According to him being the end of the line, there was no need for anyone to panic getting off. Jack left us to get off to check the arrangements for the families. A heap of sweating humanity began the panic to get off, joining in we were hustled and bustled along with other families to converge at the exit door. Untangling ourselves we managed to get down onto the track moved onto the road to find us, in amongst a melee of people, all wondering what to do next. Jack arrived back, called for everyone's attention.

'The Officer of the Day has ordered you all, to leave your luggage where it is at the station, to be loaded onto Bullock carts ready for an early start tomorrow morning, Please only take overnight items and make your way to the front end of the train where Tonga's are waiting to take you to a Hostel, where overnight accommodation has been arranged including meals. Would that party at the front? Please make your way to the far end of the train.'

Immediately,the order was carried out by a surge of families, there was even more confusion as they jostled to get on a Tonga. The cavalcade of Tonga's made a short journey to the hostel, there to be allocated a room for our brief overnight stay. It was reasonably respectable and comfortable, but alas another restless night. An early morning call, breakfast of scrambled eggs with chai. By 0730 hrs had all the families onto the waiting Tonga's on the road outside. Jack had been provided with a horse, along with other soldiers in the escort. At the rear were the bullock carts carrying the luggage. For the journey up to Mussoorie. Riding up Jack pointed up into the hills informing me.

'Sarah. Mussoorie is way up there, if we make good progress we will be there before nightfall. We're all set to move off now.'

Wheeling his horse around galloped off to the rear, I heard him bark out the order to move. I looked up into the distant hills covered in mist or clouds seeing nothing to inspire me. The Tonga jolted into motion. Once again we were off on another trip up into the hills. Would this new venture turn out to be similar to the first trip where we were so isolated? Only the end of the day would provide me with the answer. Very similar to the road to Murree, the ride took us along a flat cart road before it came to a gradual incline, becoming steeper as the cavalcade moved further up into the hills. On the journey up we stopped a few times to relieve ourselves. On the last one, Jack informed me. He was going to ride ahead to see what the arrangements were at this place called Rajpur. Slowly the cavalcade continued upwards. Sometime later Jack came riding back down the incline, pulling up alongside our Tonga informed me.

'So far we've travelled about ten miles up into the hills. Rajpur is about two miles further up, we'll soon be there. We will stop for lunch at the army hostel. The QM has informed me that after lunch you will change your mode of transport and take a shorter route known as the bridle path. Although it is steeper it's quicker, we will change our horses for fresh ones. I'll inform all the rest.'

He wheeled away riding back down the cavalcade. Around mid-day we arrived at Rajpur, the cavalcade came to a halt outside a hostel of some sorts, Jack rode up.

'This is it Sarah, take our tribe into the Hostel, they are waiting to serve us lunch send the servants around the side for their food. I'll join you inside. Mary you help your mother.'

He wheeled his horse around and cantered off to the rear. I ordered the Bearer to take the rest of them around the side. Retrieving Michael from number One Ayah, taking him in my arms, entered the Hostel with my tribe. Jack joined us for the meal of curry rice and chapatti's washed down with chai, through mouthfuls of curry began explaining our next mode of transport.

'They are called Jhampanies a form of palanquin, similar to the Dandy in Murree.' Frustrated at the thought. I exclaimed.

'No Jack. Not a ride in those Dandy's again.'

'Sarah were not talking about twenty miles, but only seven to Mussoorie. Anyway it won't be such an arduous journey. You wait and see. I'll get the rest of the party sorted out and then we can get moving.'

Not much reassurance from Jack, anyway how did he know? This was his first time up the hills as well. I resigned myself to the fact that another seven miles would soon pass, at least we would not have to spend another night in a hostel.

With everyone fed and watered. In two shakes of a lamb's tail, we were back outside, to stand around in the peace and cool warmth of the midday sun, waiting for further orders with time to gaze around. Rajpur appeared nothing special just a stop over place with a few bungalows dotted around. Located on the side of the hill overlooking the Dun valley with Dehra Dun just about visible in the distance. Looking the other way along the cart way, I noticed what must be the Jhampanies? Absolutely nothing like the Dandy. Still very strange looking, a seat supported by four poles, reminding me of somewhat like a medieval Sedan Chair. Standing beside each

 Jhampanie were four coolies, dressed similar to their fellows in Murree, patiently waiting for their human cargo. I pitied them, but it was a meagre means of earning some Anna's for a living. A short while later Jack came back and informed me that everyone was now ready, bade us follow him along the dirt road. Running beside his horse, my tribe were more than eager to try out this new mode of transport.

With number One Ayah carrying Michael, I ushered her into this contraption, got my tribe sat in the second one then got in beside number One. When everyone was settled in these Jhanpanies, Jack gave the order to move off. With much heaving and straining we were lifted off the floor and once again, after a few staggering steps the coolies got into their stride. I must say these were far more comfortable to travel in, sitting upright, as one does in a chair yet near to the ground. The coolies kept up a steady pace up the Bridle path that twisted turned like a huge snake up the hillside, until we reached the first staging post at a place called Jerapani Bazaar where chai was provided. Resting, taking in the view could really see the gradual slope of the tree covered hills where there were flat areas of ground. Many white painted bungalows could be seen, they were all shapes and sizes, a small pathway joined one to the other as it meandered through the wooded area to reappear either further up or down the hillside. In the distance a long straight road carved its way upwards to disappear behind a cluster of more white bungalows. Maybe that was the longer cart road up Mussoorie? As we sipped our chai, even though the sun was very hot, it was so lovely and cool. Back into Jhampanies we were on our way again, crossing over streams with gushing waters splashing their way downwards on their endless trip to wherever. Jack rode up, pointed out a building just below us.

'That's a college called St. George's. I asked.

'How do you know that?'

'I was provided with a survey map of the area by the Officer back in Dehra Dun.'

'Oh. I wondered how you were so well informed.'

Most of his time Jack was going backwards and forwards checking to see that everyone was all right. No one had been sick so it appeared everyone was okay. When he had the chance, he had taken each of our tribe up on his horse for a ride. It wasn't long after that we began passing other bungalows just off the track. On our right we passed a large building in ruins. Jack informed me was an old Brewery, evidence of the existence of British troops in the area. As we approached the top of the hills, we came upon a few large buildings it had to be Mussoorie. Half an hour later we entered Mussoorie. It was late afternoon and it had taken about four hours from Rajpur. The cavalcade left the incline of the Bridle path onto a more level man made road. I looked down at Michael cradled in number One Ayah's arms part of her sari drawn right across his body and face, its fine weave of silk acting as a protection from the rays of the sun. Since we had stopped at the last Bazaar he had slept nearly all the way. She herself had never got out of the Jhanpanies, her attitude totally protective. As we had ascended she had made conversation in Urdu, pointing out items for me to take note of a building, shrub or flowers, uttered with a sigh at her delight in seeing them. I doubt even when we finally stopped she would get out. I smiled at her, she responded with a slight nod and a smile. The cavalcade made its way along this wide stretch of road.

There were many English people walking about or sitting outside a chai shop, as we came towards an open space like a square with a very typically English styled bandstand with seats around it, a few Officers passed us on horseback. Jack rode up alongside with Jackie astride the horse's neck, eagerly watching all that went on, I looked back at the other two they also were engrossed in the ongoing proceedings. On the top of other small hills were some white brick buildings. This place amazed me, the whole area appeared so English. Definitely different to Khanspur. A large building dominated the area; it was a Bazaar of some sorts.

'Sarah.That I understand is the Library. This is much livelier than Khanspur isn't it?'

266

'Yes. Much more so. Jack are we staying here or, do we have we got to go further up? Like we did to Khanspur?'

'That I don't know? But will soon find out. My course is at the Army camp at a place called Landour. First we have to make for the Savoy Hotel, that large building just ahead of us. I have to meet a QM Quiggle. I'll get directions from there.'

Two large trees cast great shadows along the roadway providing an area of shade where the cavalcade halted. The coolies carefully laid the Jhampanies down on the ground. I raised myself up assisted by a coolie, got out very pleased to stretch my legs, number One stayed sat holding Michael. The two girls already out of their Jhampanies were running around on the grass lawn In front of us that separated us from a very long two-storied building, Jack pulled up the horse, jumped down leaving Jackie sat in the saddle.

'This is it Sarah. I've spotted the QM, they're standing in front of the hotel steps. Just hold on to Jackie while I go and parlay with him.'

Jack strode away across the grass. I moved over to Jackie lifted him down out of the saddle so he could join the girls. The coolies were crouched down on their haunches; most likely they were worn out after their recent exertion, their passengers were walking around, stretching weary bones from sitting idly doing nothing for hours. I stood beside the Jhampanies watching the children whooping about, on the open stretch of lawns. I watched the comings and goings of many English Officers with their lady wives arriving in Tonga's or just walking up from the direction of the bandstand we had just passed. I looked over to this hotel where Jack was deeply engrossed in conversation with the QM a tall figure of a man head and shoulders above Jack. A group of officers on their horses, rode up to its entrance, immediately two Syce's came out to take charge of the horses. Whilst Jack came striding back across the grass towards me, the QM headed in the direction of the other families.

'Sarah. QMS Quiggle has taken charge of the cavalcade. This is the dispersal point, for most of the families. We and another couple of families are to proceed onto Landour, where our quarters are located. Apparently, it's not far, about another three miles or so down that road they call the Mall. He said there is hardly any hill climbing to do and certainly not like the trip up to Khanspur. He's also provided me with directions and something else that will please you. Our bungalow is next to a catholic church. Quiggle has informed me we stop here at the Savoy for three quarters of an hour to take chai and biscuits.' That took me aback I exclaimed.

'Jack. We can't go in there looking like this, with all those officers I've seen going in and out!'... 'Why ever not? We're only going onto the veranda, were not staying there. This has all been arranged. All of our small party will be there. C'mon don't be silly. You'll get chai in china teacups for a change.' His finished his remark with that silly big grin creasing his face.

I called in the children, taking Michael from the arms of the Ayah, and then she did get out. I followed Jack across the lawn to the entrance, up onto the veranda; behind us close in pursuit were the other wives and children in our party. Jack ushered us along to a table on the veranda that was laid out with silverware for afternoon teas. We sat down surveying this grandeur of set silverware. My immediate thoughts went back to the Taj. This was something I had never thought of sitting in up in the hills aware of our surroundings I issued a warning.

'Now you three listen. I don't want any running around or any mischief out of you. Mary I'm warning you do you hear me?'

'Yes mum.' Came her reply with a hint of. "Just wait and see."

'What about chai for the servants. Jack?'

'Don't worry about them, they are being looked after.'

The hotel servants served chai. Sitting resting from the jolting we had received, we were joined by two sergeants.

267

'Jack Plant. we thought it was you. What are you doing in this neck of the woods? We thought you were still back up the Khyber.' shaking hands Jack introduced me.

'This is my wife Sarah. This is Sgt.'s Farrow and Slater. They were both up in the Khyber Pass with me. Where are you two posted?' Sgt. Slater replied.

'At the moment were both attending a gunnery course at the Army Camp up in Landour and billeted in the Sergeants Quarters, very pleasant indeed.'

'Likewise as I, but I've got a couple of weeks leave thrown in.'

Jack responded having found some old acquaintances, the three of them continued to gup, before they left they invited us to the Sergeants Mess.

'Nice chaps Sarah. I met them up the Khyber, there're from the 58th in Risalpur. We played football against them. Anyway we just have enough time before darkness to get up to Landour.'

I must say that the view from the hotel was magnificent. Far down below us the setting sun was already casting shadows over the slopes. The remaining few were ready to move off all left the hotel veranda as we walked over to the few Jhampanie's left facing the opposite way, the Coolies got up off their haunches. Number One Ayah was already seated in our Jhampanie; we set off back the way we came, passing this Library and bandstand. Noticing the lamp-standards along this Mall I thought: *They must have some form of lighting in Mussoorie would we have it where we were?* We carried on past a church, a Bazaar, a hotel called the Himalaya, small roads led up to bungalows located on the crest of a small hill. We began to move up an incline passing yet another church. Had me thinking: *It certainly was a little part of England. I warmed to it but still in doubt about our future abode.* In front of us a couple of families left the cavalcade. I thought. *"Just my luck. Our bungalow must be remote again."* As we went through an avenue of trees I heard a dog barking, emerging from them, the rays from the setting sun lit up a clearing dominated by another church with large colonnades. Jack called out.

'Sarah. That's the Catholic Church and behind it that's our bungalow.'

That cheered me up, living right next to a church. If it was open on Sundays? I wouldn't have such a trek to mass. The bungalow was located on a small hillock, a flight of stone steps led up to a long veranda there stood the dog growling. Coming to a halt the coolies placed the Jhampanie on the floor; one of them assisted me out. I gave each of them some Anna's, which encouraged many salaams. Jack swung down off his horse handing the reins to the Syce, walked up a pathway towards the steps, just as a Chowkidah (watchman) appeared from a doorway further down the veranda, obviously it was his dog stood eyeing Jack up as he mounted the veranda, with its tail down it, cautiously approached Jack extended the back of his hand allowing it to sniff then its tail wagged strongly. Jack stroked it, saying something in Urdu. With the dog at Jack's heels he walked down towards the Chowkidah who slammed, stood to one side to let Jack through the open doorway called out.

'Come on you lot inside.'

My tribe didn't take a second invitation scrambling out of the Jhampanie scampered up the steps, ran along the veranda disappeared through the doorway. Taking my time with Michael in my arms, walked up the steps along the veranda towards the end door, the servants all excitedly gupping in Urdu, followed behind me. I counted five separate doors before the last one where Jack and the Chowkidar were standing together, the children were exploring accompanied by the dog. Behind me the Bearer shouted. 'RUKIYA!' (Stop) Stopping the servants entering, they gathering around the doorway to look in. The Chowkidar about to leave, salaamed me outside spoke with the Bearer went down the steps leaving the dog behind? Jack called.

'Bearer. Chowkidar Kutta (Dog) Challiye.' Over the side of the veranda the Bearer shouted to the Chowkidar. I assumed a question the Bearer came in.

'Sahib kutta nam Soo, Rukiya!' (dog named Sue she stops here).

We had inherited a bitch Bull Terrier, much to the delight of my tribe who were patting it and making a fuss of her, she wagging her tail furiously they decided to take her outside, far more fun than looking at quarters. A quick look around the quarters revealed six separate accommodations, each had a sitting room with a bedroom at the rear. After surveying the accommodation, I sorted out who was going where, the middle one for us, the children next door and the servants in the others, the last one became the Kitchen, accommodating the Khansama and Chico's. Our luggage had yet to arrive, although still reasonably light outside the Bearer lit the hurricane lamps. Definitely no electricity here. Jack went out to tend his horse, whilst I went to the kitchen and found muttering to himself the Khansama trying to light a fire, I'm sure he was swearing in Urdu. As the fire caught he uttered a sigh possibly of relief? I requested.…'Khansama. Chai.'…'Ji hai Memsahib.'

Soon chai was served by the Khansama, salaamed left the bungalow heading back down the cart road. As I sat relaxing on the veranda watching the last rays of the setting sun begin to disappear over the hills, when the bullock carts arrived with our luggage, there sat on the back was the grinning Khansama, jumping off patted two wicker basket, called out.

'Sahib. Memsahib, pukka Bazaar.' Jabbering away in Urdu with the Bearer pointed down the hill carried the baskets into his domain. Jack roared with laughter.

'Sarah he's already got provisions. I wasn't expecting anything. Let's see what we get for khana, meanwhile I'll get the luggage unloaded.'

Jack along with Mary the Bearer and Chico's carried it in, Sue sniffed at all the box's to see if any goodies were there. Later we found her asleep under our charpoi Jack said.

'Leave her, must be her sleeping place.'

He was more than pleased she liked the children and would be a wonderful housedog, a warning of unwelcome visitors. With the fire crackling away warming the interior we sat in the main room of our section for our evening meal. Once again the Khansama had proved his worth with a filling meal. Sue disturbed by the smell of food came out and laid on the floor watching waiting for scraps. Soon the warmth of the fire had us all yawning and eager for our beds. Michael was asleep in my arms, in front of the fire Jackie was slumped fast asleep, Jack picked him up whispered. 'Mary, Kathleen, bed now.' Without any questions they followed him into their bedroom. We all slept the sleep of exhaustion.

With the light of day filtering through the window, I awoke very much refreshed after an undisturbed sleep, there wasn't any sound from my tribe and Jack wasn't in the room. I lay there wondering if it would it be the same as Khanspur with its solitude? Jack quietly entered the room, with Sue padding behind him whilst Jack sat down on the bed she slumped down on the floor.

'Sarah come out and see the view, I didn't see much last night but now in the daylight, there's much more to see and to do, you can plainly see Mussoorie below us. '

'How long have you been up?'

'About half an hour, you know me once awake I can't stay in bed.'

Getting up again went back outside followed by Sue. I raised myself out of the Charpoi slipped on my dressing jacket and slippers followed him out. He was standing down on the verge away from the bungalow, just in front of the church. I went down the steps and stood beside him. It was very still only the twittering of birds in the trees broke the silence. The early morning chill accompanied by a faint breeze had me shivering, the Khansama came up to us offered chai.

'Memsahib. Sahib.' Taking it thanked him.

'Shukria Khansama.'

Sipping the chai with the early morning sun on my back it was warming as I gazed across the horizon, which was very similar to Khanspur the Himalayas spreading from east to west, in front below sprawled the extents of Mussoorie, with dotted out around the hillside were other bungalows, below the Dun valley hidden by the early morning mist. It really was beautiful. Jack murmured,

'You will like it here Sarah. It's not as isolated and it is close to Mussoorie.'

'How far up are we?'

'Someone told me about seven thousand feet, not as high as Khanspur but about the same height as Murree. Today with the tribe we will take a trip down into Mussoorie, see what it's all about, what do you say?' I readily agreed.

As Jack was only up there for six weeks, on a gunnery course. I wasn't going to miss out on anything; I was going to enjoy what little time we had together as a family. From what I had seen in the hour we had stayed at whatever the Hotel was called, it appeared quite an exciting place.

'Right. After breakfast we will sort out the luggage, organise the Bearer and servants then walk down to Mussoorie.'

I turned around to look at the church; we walked over through its two central colonnades up to its notice board. "St Peter's. Roman Catholic Church" Jack ventured to open the door it was locked.

'Maybe another time Sarah, we'll find out later. C'mon let's have breakfast.'

'How on earth did they get these colonnades up here Jack?'

'I don't know, but it must have been by brute strength and a lot of swearing and cursing.' With Sue at our heels we returned to the bungalow. Inside the tribe was still fast asleep. By mid-morning the weather was good with a slight breeze as we started on our trip down to Mussoorie, , entering the avenue of trees shielded us from the sun, we walked past some army huts almost hidden by the trees, out in the open stopped by the church to read it was St Paul's. We passed four shops with a Post Office, a Bank and many bungalows with very English sounding names, Eva Cottage and Ivanhoe to name but two, before we came to Landour Bazaar, a long row of shops where no doubt the Khansama had been the evening before. Curiously I asked.

'Jack how did the Khansama pay for the provisions?

'Good question Sarah. Probably he had made an agreement. I noticed he spoke with the Bearer after he had returned.'

By the Himalaya Club we joined the main road, from then on it was easy going we passed another Bazaar called Kulri then the Himalaya Hotel on towards the Bandstand, the Savoy Hotel. Jack suggested we have lunch there. On the veranda he met another Sergeant from the Bengal Lancers with his wife and two little girls. I sent my tribe down onto the lawn to play as we engaged in conversation. His wife told me they had been up there for some time, before she went on to give me quite a lot of information about Mussoorie. It was a hill resort not only for the English but also for wealthy Indians. Typically English in Its style and presentation of the bandstand, Library Bazaar, Library and of course The Mall, obviously associated with the London Mall where everyone seemed to meet or walk along. There were British schools and Convents dotted around the Hills, the original school "Maddock's school", was burnt to the ground and replaced by a new school. The very same hotel we were taking lunch in was the Courthouse also a Theatre. As we talked a string quartet played soft background music. She directed us to several places of interest. As I listened to what she was saying I began to understand this was so different from Khanspur. A servant came around advising. 'Lunch was being served.' That as both families was having lunch that was most pleasant. They having finished their lunch bade us Cheerio.

So began our sightseeing tour. At the Bandstand we sat to watch the daily goings on of Mussoorie. There were Officers on horses also a few driving automobiles with their Ladies. A two-wheeled contraption with a wide seat, followed by second rumbled past us. A new mode of transport to see. The occupants in the first one, a well-dressed Indian in a white English styled

270

suit wearing a white Panama hat, in the second two Indian women dressed in Saris, certainly by their dress by the amount of gold bangles and earrings must be of upper Indian caste. Both these contraptions were pulled by two coolies in the front and two behind, "pull me push me" no doubt to help with the surrounding steep inclines. (We were to find out later that the contraption was called a Rick Shaw). Sat watching them I noticed Kathleen her mouth aghast in wonderment until they disappeared from sight. She exclaimed.

'Dad can we go in one of those please?'

'Later Kathleen later.' But I thought: *Those I would have to try later during our stay.* There were many other English and Indians pedestrians, the ladies held parasols above their heads; some were going into a very smart Bazaar opposite advertising Coffee as a beverage. We walked back to the Mall to the square Tower of the Church its notice board stated. "The Christ Church of Mussoorie" Built a hundred years before, we walked around its grounds and came upon a Plaque in front of a tree. Reading its notation, stated it was to commemorate our then present Queen Mary, planting the tree in 1907, when she was HRH the Princess of Wales. Kitty had said that Royalty had visited up here; I would have to tell her how right she was. I was thrilled at this discovery, during the 14-18 war, Queen Mary was the patron of the QMAAC. We continued our walk to an Observatory, located on the top of the Camel's back. At a viewpoint we stopped to take in the view of the numerous Himalayas peaks stood out sharp against the deep blue sky showing the almost horizontal line of snow. It was a breath-taking view. Below us wild Khuds (precipices) fell sharply away with small tributaries that appeared and flowed downwards and joined others to form the rivers far below us. We were surrounded by hills on our right where some sort of a building looking like a castle, beyond and upwards was Landour. We walked onto the Observatory then on to a place called Gun Hill. We had walked almost in a semi-circle when we joined the Mall again. Continuing onwards towards Landour I was feeling quite tired as were my tribe, sat astride Jacks shoulders Jackie was all but asleep. It was just as well we left Michael in the care of number One Ayah and the Bearer. We arrived at the place where the four shops with the post office and Bank were and stopped for chai to revive our weary bodies. We sat down on a small wall; the afternoon breeze cooled us down as we viewed Dehra Dun just visible in the

far distance below. The cart road could be seen at different levels cut into the side of the hills like long white snakes they lead to dwellings dotted across the hills. While we sat there and gazed out over the hills Jack remarked.

'It appears there is a lot of British history attached to Mussoorie. When I'm up at the Camp I'll try and find out a bit more about it.' I added.

'Well if Queen Mary was up here years ago she became Queen, it must have been discovered well before then.'

'That Sarah is a statement in itself. C'mon we had better make tracks for the Bungalow. It's not far now only about half a mile away. C'mon on you three. Jahldi. Jackie climbs up on my shoulders.'

Jack as ever could walk the hind legs off a donkey. Our last leg of our journey down onto the flat road then uphill. Jack discovered that a right fork off of the track led to the Army Barracks. Not far from our bungalow as we could hear the barking of Sue, as we came out of the avenue of trees she bounded down towards us, waging her tail in greeting, then I saw number One Ayah stood on the veranda with Michael in her arms. We were all pleased to get back and sip chai, a sluice down, eat Khana, then sit on the veranda watching the sun go down. I was more than content on the outcome of the day; even though we were away from most of the other bungalows it did not bother me. I was to like Mussoorie, little England as I named it.

In the early morning sunrise, I woke to find Jack was outside. Slipping on a dressing jacket I went out to him asked.

'What time did you get up?'

'The crack of dawn Sarah haven't got time to laze in bed. I've already taken Sue for a walk up the hill. There are two army huts beyond those trees but nothing else, except trees, shrubbery and large rhododendron bushes. Good hiding places for wild beast.'

'Jack don't say there are wild cats up here please. I had enough of them in Khanspur.'

'Well you never can tell. It's still India up here; there are plenty of walks you can take. This morning after breakfast. We will go up to Gun Hill. Oh! The other thing I found out was the height of this hill. There is a little marker just further up there. Its seven thousand five hundred and seventy-five feet, so were higher than Murree.'

The sound of the tribe waking ensured that our peace was to be brought to an abrupt stop. They emerged from their doorway yawning their heads off. After breakfast I had decided to take Michael with us, Jack told the Khansama we would be back for lunch, the Bearer and number One Ayah would accompany us. With Michael sat astride the Ayahs hip we set off down the track On the top of Gun Hill was the Observation post with a similar view as the Camel's Back, On top of one of the hills behind the Savoy was a very large building with round conical spires at each corner. It looked like a palace or something. There was a obelisk stating the height as 7,029, feet above sea level. We sat there for some time, just relaxing, Mary drew our attention to the little church next to our quarters, but the view of the Himalayas was something else. I asked.

'Jack how far do the Himalayas go east?'

'About two thousand miles or more, they certainly are a sight to see. Sarah on our way back why don't we pay a visit to the Mess?'

Well. Yes if we don't stay too long.'

We made a detour to the Army Barracks number One Ayah was finding it hard going carrying Michael. Jack took over carried him on his shoulders, had Jackie moaning, the Bearer took over lifted him on his shoulders. As we traversed the track Jack said.

'Sarah if you are going to go out for walks with the children, we should start thinking about means of transport. Horses, Donkeys or whatever. We'll have to arrange something better than this palaver.'

I was in full agreement at his suggestion. I was puffed out from the exertion of walking up these slopes. I called for a halt.

'Right a five minute stop to catch our breathe. '

As we stood or sat on the ground Jack looked at the Bearer quizzically before he asked.

'Bearer Baba Michael'…pointing to Michael sat between his legs, Jack patted his back to indicate Michael being carried enquired.

'Sarah what's the word I'm looking for? Backpack?'

'Don't ask me I don't know?' Number One Ayah observing our gup appeared to understand she smiled.

'Aah. Baba Michel.' Then broke into a stream of Urdu with the Bearer, she patting her own back and pointing to Michael, the Bearer nodded.

'Aah. Ji hai Coolie Wallah… standing up addressed Jack…

'Sahib. Coolie wallah baba Michel'…Tapping his shoulder with his hand they both understood what we needed for Michael. Jack responded.

'Bearer kali kal (tomorrow) ane wallah. (Coolie Wallah Quarters). Pukka. Sarah it looks like we will get transport for Michael. We'll see tomorrow what that brings along. Now that's organised for Michael, I'll sort out some horse transport at the camp. C'mon on your feet soldiers. Jahldi jahldi.'

272

We arrived at the fork in the track a sign indicated right where the Barrack Nos. 10 to 26. Jack hailed a passing soldier enquired... 'Where the Sergeant's Mess?'

'You've passed it back up the track, its Barrack number sixteen Sergeant's Mess. Can't miss it! It's in the trees just off the track.'... Retracing our steps we arrived at this wooden hut. Jack went in. within a couple of minutes he reappeared.

'C'mon inside Sarah, you're invited in. I've met Sergeant's Farrow and Slater.' I firmly replied.

'No thank you Jack. I'll stay outside with the rest.' *As far as I was concerned to me The Sergeant's mess was for men.*

'Okay I'll order drinks for all.' We sat down under the shade of a tree to be served with cool drinks and some fresh fruit for the children. Sgt.'s. Farrow and Slater came out paid their respects spending time to tell me about the Army compound in Landour. They informed me that there was a school for the children up a narrow track opposite the mess, there was an Army Bazaar further along towards our bungalow and a large Army hospital unit past a place called Lal Tibba, with two cemeteries just over the hill. As they put it. "Quite a nice little area." Jack came back out of the Mess joined us, Sgt. Slater asked

'Jack how about you playing football down in Mussoorie? We have a game set up for next Wednesday.' Without hesitation Jack took up the challenge.

'I'll be delighted to play.'

'Well there's a practice game arranged in the Army lines, you'll play in that.'

'Ok. But have you got any kit for me?'

'Not a problem.'

With football arranged, we stayed for an hour; it was pleasant the children were quite happy playing in and out of the trees. Jack had found out where he was to report to and the general lay of the land. He decided it was lunchtime so we left the Sergeants mess. Tomorrow was another day. Early next day Jack took Sue for a walk, however, overhead were dark threatening rain clouds, it was quiet chilly if the weather changed. For us it would be a day of rest. I was stood on the veranda holding Michael while watching the tribe playing, Jack was reading an old newspaper he had picked up in the Mess and Sue was lying at my feet, when suddenly she stood up and growled. I exclaimed.

'Jack someone's coming up here.' Getting up he stood beside me.

'Uhm, looks like some Wallah wants to sell something, That's your job Sarah.'

We stood watching as this Wallah got closer. Sue swiftly padded off the veranda down the steps, stopped then barked. The Wallah stopped as Sue stood her ground, Jack called out.

'Bearer Jahldi.' He appeared on the veranda walked down the steps and shouted at Sue.

'KHAMOSH.' (Quiet) Then spoke with the Wallah before addressing us.

'Aah. Sahib achchha Sahib Pukka. Coolie Wallah Baba Michel.'

Unbeknown to us the Bearer had sorted out some transport for Michael. They came forward stopped below the veranda, pointing to a big wicker basket strapped to this Wallahs back, the Bearer beckoned for us to come down.

'Sahib, Memsahib Coolie Wallah, Baba Michel. Pukka Sahib.' We left the veranda followed by number One Ayah, jabbering excitedly to the others waving her arms about. 'Jahldi Jahldi Michel baba Coolie Wallah.'

About what? I did not know possibly about the contraption we were about to inspect that looked like a giant ice cream cornet. Narrow at the bottom and wide at the top, secured by a leather strap around his waist with another one around his forehead, it didn't look too safe to me. Jack had a good look.

'It looks solid enough to me what do you say Sarah? Sit Michael in it see how he likes it?'

273

He took Michael out of my arms. I noticed all the servants appeared along the veranda rail to watch the proceedings of a new stage show, yet another feast of entertainment. The Coolie Wallah sat down on his haunches thus allowing Jack to place Michael into this basket, Jack started to talk Michael into getting in this contraption.

'Michael Baba, have a ride on the Wallahs Back?' No response. Jack repeated the question, no response, a few tears began to well up in Michael's eyes.

'He doesn't want to know Sarah. Wait I have an idea, take hold of Michael a minute. Jackie comes here.' He sat Jackie in this Basket facing backwards, a grin creased Jackie's face as Jack with some form of raffia rope secured Jackie into the seat.

'Utanha Wallah. Uthana.'

The Wallah stood up. Jackie let out a roar of laughter as the Wallah walked up and around in front of the church. Kathleen wanted a go, Mary stood silent a look of defiance on her face retorted.

'I'd rather walk than get in that thing. Dad can I ride a horse instead?' I thought: *There was no way she was going to be transported around in that thing?* Jack suggested.

'Mary we'll see, just be patient. Let's get Michael sorted out first okay?'

That satisfied her. Kathleen had a go. Having seen how it worked I coerced Michael into riding in the basket, we both made sure it was secured. The Coolie Wallah gently lifted his little burden up and started to move around. Jackie shouted.

'Hooray for Michael.' The Ayah's clicked their tongues clapped and sighed in approval the rest of the servants joined in the clapping. Michael, now the centre of attention at least no tears. The Coolie walked him backwards and forwards whilst we just stood there watching. If we were to take him out walking with us Michael would have to get used to it. Jack suggested we walk down to St Paul's church and back again. Michael was happy! Another problem solved. However, the threatening clouds had rolled away, once again the sun blazed down, Jack seizing the opportunity suggested.

'Sarah now we have this Coolie Wallah up here. Let's go for a walk?' I could see his reason for wanting to explore. I suggested.

'Well not down into Mussoorie, maybe a shorter walk towards the Army Hospital, Sgt. Slater spoke about.'

'Okay that isn't far through the Army Lines, it will give you a good Idea of what's around the Bungalow area, we can be back in time for lunch.'

At my suggestion. He was as happy as a sand boy, we were off down the track in crocodile formation, with the others in front when it became narrow I closed up behind Michael going through the Army Lines past the Sergeant's Mess. At least the going was quiet even. Until we got to this place called Lal Tibba, there the paths became closer to the edge of Khuds, almost sheer drop to whatever was below covered in gorse. The surrounding scenery was unbelievable, on top of each hillcrest sat large buildings and bungalows of all sizes. We carried on passing small groups of Bungalows on either side, then a fork in the pathway where a sign pointed to "Army Hospital" The path zig- zagged downwards to a large building far below. Jack said. That long building down in front of us must be the Army Hospital.' Further up. Jack saw a small obelisk, he climbed up followed by Mary, they came down to inform me.

'Sarah. Up there that obelisk states it's seven thousand three hundred and eighty-five feet above sea level it's called Prospect Point. Were about one hundred feet lower, than the one by the Bungalow.' I hopefully suggested.

'That's all very well Jack but do you think we should head back now.'

'Oh well if you say so. I thought we were doing great. We'll stop at the Mess.'

We about turned and began the trek back to the Bungalow. Michael was fast asleep on the Coolie's back. We came to another large wide fork, which led up to the two cemeteries over the brow of the hill Jack remarked.

'Must have been quite a few people buried who fell down onto those craggy rocks below.' I wasn't impressed by his remark. We arrived at the Mess and had refreshments brought out to us. Sgt. Slater informed me the building we had spotted on the crest of the hill below, was a Boy's school called St George's. I was concerned about the Coolie Wallah who was a great asset in transporting Michael around.

'Jack, can we manage to keep him, maybe let him sleep in with the rest of the servants?'

'Well it would be a good idea but what about the rest of the servants.' Sgt. Slater intervened.

'Look let me find out where this fellah lives. I speak reasonable Urdu. Some of these coolies have hovels up here.' He conversed with the Coolie, coming back informed us that.

'Your Bearer knew where the coolie lived. It was just down close to St. Paul's Church. He even agreed for a small sum of ten rupees, to become your Coolie Wallah all the time you're up here   How about that Jack.'

'That's suits me. Sarah?' Ten rupees for three months hire was not bad and he was not aware of the time period. That would save me a lot of heartache.'

'Yes I'll pay him when we go.'

Our first Sunday in Landour, sat leisurely sipping chai on the veranda, the tribe were playing in front of the church, when Sue got up growling, and we had visitors? Someone on horseback emerged through the avenue of trees. Sue bounded off the veranda ran towards our new visitor. By this time easily recognised by his dress a Priest walking beside him was his Syce. My tribe had stopped playing to watch the Priest, who continued riding towards the bungalow he called out.

'Greetings, Are your family the new occupants?' Getting up went down to meet him.

'Hello, I'm Father O'Hare and have come up to say Mass. You wouldn't be Catholics by any chance would you?' Jack shook his hand replied.

'Yes Father we are. We were not expecting a Priest to come and say Mass, we thought the church only opened six months during the year.'

'Oh no. I say Mass every week up here it's part of my parish. I normally arrive about this time, say mass then return to the Convent of Jesus and Mary down at Waverley, the other side of Mussoorie.' I enquired.

'Father was not dressed properly, but can we attend Mass?'

'Yes of course you can Mrs. Er. I didn't catch the name?' Jack apologised.

'Sorry Father we are the Plants. These four are our children. Mary, Kathleen, Jackie and Baba Michael, up on the veranda with the Ayah.' Jack indicated to the three now standing beside us. The Priest scanning the gathering exclaimed.

'At last I have the makings of a congregation, usually it consist of some soldiers from the barrack or, sometimes other families like you.' He beamed down at my tribe, I offered.

'Father would you like to take chai?'

'No thank you, not until after Mass. I will open up and prepare for Mass. Will anyone be taking the Sacraments?'

'Er no Father, we have already eaten breakfast so have broken our fasting.

'Oh that's all right not to worry. I must be a bit of a surprise to you all.'

He certainly was! We attended Mass finding the church inside quite plain and ordinary. A small alter the usual statues, pictures of the Stations of the Cross. Two Soldiers came in to swell his congregation to eight.   Afterwards we provided Father O' Hare with chai before he left downwards.

On the day of the football match Jack took the tribe, the Bearer three Ayahs and five Chico's to watch the match while I stayed behind to look after Michael. They arrived back full of the joys of spring. They had won! As Jack informed me.

'Sarah it was a good game and wonderful to play up here. It was just like playing back in Blighty, to cap it all we've been invited to a Dinner Dance at the Savoy Hotel on Saturday evening, we have to stay overnight' Hesitating I replied.

'No Jack you go. I don't want to leave the children.'

'Why on earth have I got these Ayahs's here for? If it was not to care for the children?'

With insistence Jack argued his case so, to keep the peace, I agreed to go. The following day we went down to a Bazaar in Mussoorie. Jack bought me a ball gown for the Dance, which had to be made but there was another small problem. I had no appropriate shoes to wear, they did not have my size. That was resolved by the Gown Wallah who knew of a Macht Wallah (Cobbler) that he would recommend, send him up to the bungalow to take my measurements. That afternoon we were sat on the veranda when a Wallah turned up Sue did her usual growling. The wallah approached a wide leather strap across his forehead, held his wares on his back. Sue growled that brought him to a halt, she was shushed by the Bearer who began ranting in Urdu with the Wallah. Possibly asking what did he want with interrupting the Sahib and Memsahibs rest? Anyway during this conversation all the servants came out and stood along the veranda, had me wondering was this the cobbler? The Bearer having found out what he wanted spoke out.

'Memsahib. Macht Wallah, Lib baazar.'

'Jack. Is he talking about the Wallah with the shoes?'

'I think so Sarah. Bearer Memsahib shoes?'

'Ji hai Sahib Memsahib macht. Pukka.'

'Right Sarah, let him up here and gets some shoes for the ball.'

Jack beckoned the Wallah up. Hesitating, looked at Sue stood watching, assured he was safe came up onto the veranda towards where I was sat; slipping his strap over his head dropped his sack down near me. Immediately the servants gathered around to watch what good things he had brought. The Macht Wallah looked at my feet, looked at me, with a quizzical look in his eyes, and held his hands up with open palms shaking his head exclaimed.

'Memsahib. Baba's jata.' Jack roared with laughter.

'Sarah. he's saying you have babies feet. Not baby's feet, bloody stumps.'

'Jack you can pack up that language in front of the children and servants.'

'Well Sarah, I doubt if he has anything your size. Let him get on with it. Ji hai Wallah.'

Pointing to my feet. The Wallah got out a piece of string with many knots in it, his "tape measure" began measuring my feet. Much to the clucking and intake of breath by the engaged audience diligently watching everything that was going on. Amidst the jangling of many bracelets I noticed the Khansama had crept up to watch over all the heads, once again another pantomime. The Mocht Wallah having finished his measuring, opened the neck of his sack began taking out one by one different pairs of shoes, laying them in line in front of me. to choose a style. As I pondered over each pair, a gasp came from the audience until I noticed a pair with a court heel with a strap over the front of the foot, which   I thought was appropriate to dance in, I pointed to them. The Wallah took hold of them put them on my feet gesticulating me to stand up. Bringing gasps of surprise from the audience at such a demand on the Memsahib, nevertheless I did obviously they were quite big and lower than I thought. The Mocht Wallah waggling his hands about pointed, his two fingers apart obviously indicating he knew the right size, but I was not happy with the heel, pointing to them indicating more height. Jack said.

276

'Sarah. You can't have those high heels that you usually wear. He doesn't understand that does he?'

'Yes I do understand, but I don't have a pair to show him. If he can higher the heel and possible the sole they will have to do. Otherwise I won't be going.'

'Okay it's your choice. Get him to do it.'

While this is going on the Wallah was listening intently, in broken English took up the shoe indicating suggested.

'Memsahib. Heely high and soley lit. Pukka Okay.' He understood I replied.

'Accha. Do (Two) Savoy shanivar (Saturday) Okay?'

'Ji hai Accha Memsahib Pukka.' I instructed the Bearer.

'Bearer Anna's. Do Mocht Wallah shanivar.'

The Bearer full of importance began the bartering for two pairs. With the deal done the Mocht Wallah gathered up his wares into his shop pulled the strap over his head left. The pantomime was over. That had wasted an hour and a half. Chai was served by the Bearer.

Saturday Jack had arranged everything for our trip down to the Savoy. He arrived back from the army lines trailing two horses a pony and two donkeys. He left them being attended by the Syce, to graze outside the church. Early in the afternoon we set off, Jack and I rode horses, Mary a pony, Kathleen and Jackie a donkey each. The Coolie Wallah carrying Michael on his back. With the Bearer, three Ayahs, the Syce, and four Chico's with baskets on their heads containing our change of clothes. The servants had no problem in keeping up with us. Arriving at the Savoy the Syce took charge of the horses. With our tribe around us we entered into a reception hall. Salaams all around. A porter gestured us to follow him through another entrance into a wide corridor with a marbled tiled floor that must have stretched from one end of the building to the other there were windows everywhere. High above us the ceiling was interlaced with criss cross woodwork everything was painted white. At various intervals big brass urns held shrubs and along the walls hung sets of antlers and various stuffed animals heads hung from the walls, it was all very ornate. The porter led us upstairs to our spacious room, with a large double bed and a chest of drawers with two seats thrown in, along with the usual washing basin and jug, and what a surprise electric light bulbs, the first we had seen in India. The usual order was uttered to my tribe.

'Don't touch anything.' My Ball gown was already hung in a cupboard. At the foot of the bed was my two pairs of shoes, those I tried on, they fitted perfectly. When we had settled in our room, I quickly took my tribe to see the Ballroom that they say, "It was large enough to hold a thousand dancers?" At the far end on the stage, was a huge grand piano, I thought. *"How on earth did they get the piano up here?"* Waiting for the orchestra was rows of empty seats. Hanging down from the high ceiling above were many electric light chandeliers. The dining tables laid out in rows with place settings were being attended too by the servants; they dressed in whites with red turbans and cummerbunds. My tribe was delighted with this small treat, before they left to return to the bungalow, we took them out onto the veranda sat them down for afternoon tea. Jack issued his instructions to the Bearer who was to be in sole charge of the Household? Mary filled with instructions from me about seeing all of them into bed. Michael now entrusted with number One Ayah. They all departed happily with plenty of time to reach Landour before sunset. I did not like to see them go, but I had sufficient trust in my servants to let it be for this once. We walked across the lawns to wave them off. Mary at last astride a pony was more than happy and put in charge of the other three. After they had departed we prepared for the evening's festivities.

We dressed fitting for the occasion. Jack was in his Mess uniform and I in a three-quarters length gown. We had a very pleasant meal before the dance. We joined forces with Sgt. Farrow and Sgt. Slater before we went into the ballroom for the evening's entertainment. Much to my delight the Orchestra played the Fox-trot Waltz and One Step. I had plenty of partners to enjoy the dancing; some were good others were not. Sgt. Slater was quiet good and good company; I praised Sgt. Slater on his command of Urdu. He laughed and told me he had been in India for over six years. They had been posted from Risalpur to some place north of Delhi. Suddenly all the lights dimmed before they came bright again. I thought. " *It was something to do with the dance but we found out that all the lights in Mussoorie were purposely dimmed at nine 'o' clock each evening as a time check. It was locally known as "The Wink".* I was quite fit and really enjoyed the dancing; Jack did dance the last dance with me, well stumble around. In the raffle Jack won a bottle of rum, I won a box of twenty-five strange looking cigarettes all different colours called Sobrano Cocktail cigarettes. I didn't smoke but thought. *"I would keep them as a souvenir; it truly was a wonderful night."* But I could not sleep fitfully, could not stop worrying about the children. Anxious to be getting back to the bungalow I was up next morning at the crack of dawn. We were down early for breakfast, Jack checked out retrieved the horses, with overnight luggage strapped to the saddles we were off back up to Landour.

Just before nine when arrived back at the Bungalow, in the early morning sunlight they were all out playing. I relieved, we swung down off the horses. They leapt at us in greeting Mary got up on her father's horse for a ride around to the stable at the rear, with all their noise the house sounded like bedlam. Jack went to the mess, I was quite content to sit on the veranda to think back on the tremendous night before. I realised I was really delighted I had been, everything was okay. We had a lazy afternoon, Sgt. Slater and Farrow turned up for afternoon chai, Sgt. Farrow informed me he had asked the Hotel Manager about its history so related to us.

'Many years ago it had been a Mr. Maddock's Mussoorie School, a fire burnt it down, and it was rebuilt as a hotel. An earthquake in Mussoorie had caused severe damage to the Hotel. It was repaired and became the Savoy Hotel in 1906, before Her Majesty Princess Mary stayed there. (hence our previous discovery of the plaque).Interrupting him. I told him about me being a Q.M.A.A.C., which surprised him, he continued... 'A hydroelectric power station was built about 1909, a new electricity supply was installed providing electricity to the inhabitants. The hotel itself was a favourite resort for Maharajas and Indian princes. And listen to this Sarah. The hotel is haunted by a Lady Gore Ormsby (Whoever she was).Who had died under suspicious circumstances? I thought: *If I had known that I would not have stayed overnight?* These snippets of information backed up what Kitty had told me. Jack opened up the bottle of rum he had won, and I offered the coloured cigarettes around, they stayed for the evening meal.

On the following Monday Jack began the Gunnery course. Now he had an open invitation for me to the mess, I refused but he attended. Night times became lonely and frightening. One night I was sat reading mother's letters when Sue began to bark, something outside had disturbed her. She would not stop and began leaping up at the windows tearing down the curtains to get outside, whatever it was went away then she became quiet settled down by the door very alert still growling. The Bearer entered, quickly closed the door, and so not to let her out, still disturbed her paced around growling. The bearer would not go near her, so I got up and stroked her to calm her down. The bearer uttered.

'Memsahib. Janvar bahar (animal outside).' He stood up pawing the air in front of him opened his mouth and snarled. That I understood.

'Oh my God. We have bears up here.' I broke out into a cold sweat, I was petrified at the mere thought of what was outside.

'Memsahib Janvar joa. Okay. Baba's Okay.' Reassured me that everything was all right, pointing to Sue he wagged his finger. 'Jinahm bahar.' (No do not let her out) Sue was laid down on her belly her ears pricked, listening for the slightest sound. I sat down to recover my senses. The Bearer left closing the door behind him, only to return a few moments later with chai, I took hold of the chai, and then with his hand he touched his chest   pointed towards the door and muttered.

'Memsahib. Joa bahar.' He would stay outside.

'Bahut achchha Bearer.'

I sat there shivering with fright. Where the hell was Jack? Some nights I would lie in bed shivering with fright at the least sound. The shriek of some poor creature reminded me of Khanspur. I just kept praying eventually when there wasn't a bead left on my rosary. I could hear Jack miles away, roaring with laughter as he rode home, drunk as a lord with his poor Syce, clinging on to his boot howling with fright as they all but fell down the Khuds to their deaths. Jack would still have laughed like a mad man as they both went over. He would not come in immediately. Oh no. That would be too easy; his horse had to be tended too. Meanwhile I was still praying myself silly. Jack would bound up the steps as sober as a judge, enters the bungalow.

'Oh Sarah there you are. '

As he gave me a quick peck. I had been promising myself to knife him in a thousand different ways when he got back. No need to worry about neighbours here. I had no idea if there were any within miles I angrily retorted.

'Where else would I be, at the Vice Regale's lodge at a Ball?'

'Come on there's a good girl help me to get these boots off.' I was a good girl and helped him to get his boots off he went on.

'Sarah you have no idea what sort of a day I have had.'

'No I have not.'

That fell on deaf ears. I helped him to undress as he continued on about his hard day.'How was your day Sarah?'

'Oh nothing much. We were visited by a big bear. He likes us.'

'Oh now. I am pleased you had a visitor. You could get lonely here. I'm glad people come around saves you moping. I worry about you.'

'So do I sometimes.'

My remark went over his head. I helped get him into his pyjamas and into bed tucking the mosquito net around him. By the time I got around the other side into bed and secured the mosquito net around myself he was fast asleep snoring his head off. Oblivious to the world or my problems, this was a good day. You must try the bad ones sometimes a bad day would start out as a good day. Then all too often everything would go wrong.

An incident that involved Kathleen had me concerned about cigarettes. One afternoon the Bearer came up to me, as I sat on the veranda salaamed, I could see he was troubled by something.

'Memsahib Baba's sigaret kharab.' He held his two fingers to his mouth and blew. I thought. *"He's telling me that my tribe are smoking."* I jumped up and followed him down the veranda steps towards the back of the bungalow. I began to question in my mind where on earth did they get hold of cigarettes up here. Behind the stable my tribe were all sat smoking, Kathleen with a pink coloured lighted cigarette dangling from her mouth, a wisp of grey smoke curling into the air, Mary held a blue one, Jackie coughing had a green one. the box of cocktail cigarettes and matches lay open at Kathleen's feet. I ran at them grabbing hold of Kathleen immediately she screamed, dropping their cigarettes the other two were off like hares. I was aware that the Bearer was watching. I snatched the cigarette out of her mouth stamped on it. I bade him pick up the box of cigarettes and matches. I tanned her backside. Then marched her back to the bungalow, calling out for Mary and Jackie, to come out of their hiding places. Not that they did. Back on the veranda I questioned her about where she had got them? I already knew, from the trunk. Through her sobs she told me she wasn't doing anything just wanted to try one. I looked down

279

towards the Church to see Mary and Jackie peering around a colonnade watching. I shouted at them to come back up to the veranda immediately. They came dragging their bare feet through the dust slowly up the veranda steps to stand in front of me. I told Mary that she wasn't to steal anything else in future; she should have had better sense than indulge in smoking cigarettes. Through clenched teeth she retorted.

'I did not take the cigarettes. It was Kathleen.'

She looked at me, her eyes screwed up in defiance. I knew she was telling the truth. Jackie began tittering that stopped the telling off. The three of them leapt down off the veranda and ran around the back of the Bungalow, I shouting after them.

'COME BACK IMMEDIATELY WAIT TILL YOUR FATHER GETS HOME.'

I was more upset that Kathleen had stolen them from our room. I did tell Jack about the cigarettes, with his hands on hips he said.

'Sarah get rid of them.'

It became a very lazy peaceful life, the weather ideal in the warm sunshine with a hint of breeze. During the daytime Mary and Kathleen attended classes, Jackie played with the Chico's, however as the Khansama obtained all provisions from the Kulri Bazaar, there was no visits from various Wallahs to provide some entertainment. After lunch I would take them for walks, Michael sat in the basket on the back of the Coolie Wallah who was bedded down along with the Syce and the horses. We would walk everywhere along different bridle paths, leading to hidden bungalows with English, Irish or, Scottish names. We visited the two cemeteries, just over the brow of the hill. Near one a Roman Catholic cemetery found a cypress tree with a small plaque

informing all it was planted by HRH the Duke of Edinburgh in 1870. Further evidence of visits in the distant past by royalty. On Saturdays with Jack we visited the Kempti and Mossy waterfalls, both picnic areas, of the two, Kempti the highest was rather impressive, my tribe bathed but not for long in its freezing waters. On other occasions during the afternoon, Jack would take Mary Kathleen and Jackie up to his camp for a couple of hours. On Mary's birthday he arrived back with a pony and two donkeys, to take them for a ride down the Khuds. I prepared a small birthday party for them all. She came back quite elated as were the other two, they had been up to something that I was not part of. But the party pleased her no end. Sgt.'s Farrow and Slater arrived, the cigarettes were dutifully got rid of. Sgt. Slater always had other snippets to tell me about Mussoorie. *Kemptee falls*

'Captain Young an Irishman was the first soldier to venture up into the hills. He established the army camp in Landour as a convalescence depot for British soldiers. He became the Commandant of Landour and built a house called Mullingar. Others followed Colonel Everest the Surveyor General of India he was the chap who named Mount Everest, he built a house in Mussoorie. More officers' bungalows were built along with schools and churches, as the hill station expanded Mussoorie with Landour became one British Hill Station. Every day at twelve noon at Gun Hill cannon was fired, its report could be heard for miles, until after a cannonball landing on people's bungalows far below, they stopped the firing. The building with the conical spires at each corner was called The Chateau Kapurthala the hill residence of a Maharaja.' I listened to what he had to tell me about Mussoorie and Landour that was so different to the wild of Khanspur. I warmed to this ideal place and decided to see more of it while we up here. Jack came back to the Bungalow early one morning and said.

'Sarah I'm leaving first thing tomorrow morning, so are Farrow and Slater. Orders have come through, some trouble involving rioting at a place called Cawnpore.'

280

He still had another week or so to go, before his six weeks would be up in Landour, our time together had flown by. The following morning we were up at the crack of dawn we all went down as far as the bandstand in Mussoorie to see them off. The party of eight mounted soldiers set off down the Cart track. Jack had his little Syce astride the horses back, clinging like grim death to Jack's Sam Browne. It was a very sad parting nevertheless; we would be soon leaving ourselves.

Sunday Mass became the high light of the week. Father O'Hare with his Syce would arrive, our presence provided him with his small congregation. I took an armful of flowers to decorate the Alter, whilst outside the entrance the servants would haunch themselves against these columns, quietly wait until the Mass was over. The priest would lock up. We all went down to the Char Dukan (the four little shops) to partake chai with Father O'Hare to gup about any news of various local happenings. Early one Sunday morning I was getting ready for Mass, I had plenty of time to waste, the tribe was outside playing when the bearer came running into the Bungalow shouting.

'Memsahib. Memsahib. Missy Mary. Kharab. Kharab. Pani.' I dropped the dress I was sorting out ran outside, The Bearer was stood pointing up the hill. I didn't notice anything... Pointing up he said 'Missy Mary Pani.' I glanced up to see Mary at the very top of the ladder on the water holding tower. I screamed at her.

'Mary. Come down slowly please.' Not moving she turned her head and looked down again I called her.

'Mary please climb down slowly.' she called back down.

'No.'

'Mary. If you don't come down I'll come up after you. Then you'll be in trouble.' There was absolutely no way I would do that!

'Come on Mary. Climb down there's a good girl.'

That made her move. Slowly she made her way down rung by rung, my heart was in my mouth as I watched her place a foot on each rung slowly she descended at the last few I moved closer. As she jumped down the last three rungs, I grabbed hold of her dragged her back to the Bungalow, smacked her backside so hard my hands were hurting. Then I got hold of a pyjama cord and tied her to the bottom leg of the charpoi. I shouted at her.

'NOW MY GIRL YOU'LL STAY THERE FOR THE REST OF THE DAY.'

I was ringing wet with perspiration, my heart was pumping ten times faster. She just sat there, rather forlorn with a determined look on her face. I left her there went outside to cool down and calm my nerves. With my attention concentrating on Mary, I had forgotten all about mass. Father O'Hare had already arrived, he emerged from the church walked up to the bungalow, he could sense that I was upset asking what all the fuss was about. Embarrassed I spluttered.

'It's Mary Father.'

'In heavens name what could she possibly have done Mrs Plant?' I replied.

'Nothing Father only climbed up to the top of the water tower further up. If she had fallen in she would have drowned, if she had fallen off could have broken her neck killed herself. I managed to coax her down, I gave her the thrashing of her life I've tied her to the foot of the charpoi. Her father only laughs at her escapades. But she terrifies the life out of me with all her antics.' Shaking his head he came up the steps offered.

'Now then Mrs Plant. Would you mind if I had a little talk with her?'.... 'Well Father a good talking too by someone of importance, just might put some sense into her head. Do please try.'

With me in tow, he entered the bungalow and went into the bedroom where Mary was sat tied to the charpoi. Sitting down in front of her quietly said.

'Now Mary you have not been very good have you?' A sullen answer....'No Father.' ...'Now then Mary will you promise me you'll be good to your mother.'...she nodded looked at him with "that" smile on her face...'Now Mary. You say it out loud to me. I will be good Father.' She dutifully answered.... 'I will be good Father.' I thought. *"Very little hope of that."* Father O'Hare began untying her enquiring. 'Mrs. Plant. Wherever did you get this devil from?'

'From Ireland where all the devils come from? laughing loudly replied

'Ho that's a good on.'

We artended mass and had chai at the bungalow. Certaily no trips for Mary that day.

Life up there didn't go without incidents and surprises. One morning rising from my bed, I placed both my feet straight onto a cold object, looking down it was a big skinned dead rat shrieking aloud, I jumped back onto the bed looked down to see Sue lay on the floor looking at me wagging her tail. She had killed it laid it conveniently out for my approval. The Ayah's came running in to see me clutching my nightdress around my knees. They could not hide their mirth. Another day opening the door to the lavatory was confronted by a huge bullfrog rearing up on his hind legs trying to get out. I let out an almighty shriek, slammed the door ran back inside. The Bearer removed it. Spiders we had plenty of them running around with white round things on their backs. I told one of the soldiers who attended Mass about these spiders with things on their backs His reply. 'Get rid of them, burn them they are females the white thing is their baby pouch.'

Mary being very attentive to this conversation of burning them, armed with a box of matches a bottle of mentholated spirits, together with the other two they searched every nook and cranny in the bungalow to incinerate them, it became a game.

Riding out on horse, pony, and donkeys with Michael in the basket, we trekked all over the hills, slowly riding to wherever, staying for a while, then back. Mary became a capable horse rider and fearless like her father, riding along the Mall she would gallop away then gallop back. Early one morning I was sat on the veranda when a soldier rode up on a horse and said.

'Mrs Plant. Q. Plant has requested you to return to Lucknow. Could you go to the company office for instruction please?' Curious to know what was going on asked.

'Do you know what's it is about?'

'No Mrs Plant. Sorry. I'm just the messenger.'

I took my tribe down to the Quarter Masters barrack room and met him.

'Yes Mrs Plant. All under control. You are on the return list. Transport has been arranged. You leave in two days' time.'

Two days' later early in the morning, the Jhampanies arrived followed by the bullock carts for the Luggage. The Bearer paid the Coolie Wallah, with many salaams he left. The Chowkidar arrived to take over. With the bungalow clean and tidy. My tribe hugged Sue almost to death we left her incessant barking echoed behind us all the way down past the lower church. We joined the cavalcade assembled outside the Savoy. In little or no time we moved off back along the Mall turned down onto the cart road that led down to Dehra Dun. Going down the hills was a great joy for the children. Everything was one great adventure for them, although I was pleased to be returning back to Lucknow. I had thoroughly enjoyed my stay up there. One thing I had not done was a ride in a rick-shaw, maybe next time? At Dehra Dun we were up early next morning for a quick breakfast before catching the train back to Lucknow. It being the starting point there were plenty of room in the carriages. The train journey was uneventful and went without any mishaps at the various stops on the way, more Buckshee passengers climbed aboard. At Bareilly station we were delayed by some holy cows, which lay in the middle of the track would not move. Nobody took any notice just let them lay there, for almost an hour we sat in the sweltering heat, before the train driver caused them to stir by letting his whistle off. Why he didn't do that earlier I shall never know? Nevertheless "This was India." I was exhausted by the time we finally reached Lucknow, thankfully got off the train, much relieved to get back safely.

282

CHAPTER SEVEN
SORE THROATS

In charge was the Bearer shouting out his orders, as we made our way through the mass of Indians ushered outside towards a line of Tonga's. There waiting to greet us was Kitty and her tribe all sat in a Tonga spotting us she got down and stood there, her Poe hat stuck on her head, her belt gathered in her light dress at the waist with her riding crop dangling down. Grinning like a Cheshire cat, she yelled out.

'WELL. SARAH PLANT. WHAT DID I SAY BEFORE YOU LEFT?' After the usual embracing and salutation I eagerly replied.

'You were right. Royalty has been up there, I have seen the evidence. How did you know about that?' ...'Your Jack told us all about it including you gallivanting and dancing at the ball. Sarah Plant you're a fraud.' ...'Well Kitty. If you could get up there with your tribe. You will see for yourself it really is a delightful place.'

The heat from the sun was intense, as the Bearer with the Chico's sorted out our luggage onto the Tonga's, we set off back to our bungalow, on the way gupped to Kitty telling all of our stay up there, the antics my tribe had got up to. All she did was roar with laughter. I wasn't going to get any change out of her. Arriving back at the bungalow all I wanted to do was to sit down with Kitty and take chai but no. The Bearer organised the rest of the servant to form up in line up to be inspected. Much to the enjoyment of the Burn's. I with my tribe following behind me made the inspection. They salaaming me with 'Salaam Alekum Memsahib.'...To each one in turn salutation.... 'Valekum as Salaam.' Their broad smiles left me in no doubt all were very pleased the family was reunited again, finally a quick word.

'Bearer bahut achchha pukka.' With a wave of my hand I sent them off to their duties, which did not go unnoticed by Kitty who exclaimed.

'By God Sarah Plant. You inspected them. That trip up the hills has given you a swollen head. I don't do that with my lazy lot of buggers. I just give them a lashing of my tongue. But I must say I might try your method, it certainly seems to work for you. C'mon let's have that chai and gup awhile.' She urged. I felt as if we had not even been away.

A week had passed by, we had all settled back into the daily routine. The two Indian cow handlers performed their act, even the various daily Wallahs seemed pleased that I was back, once again they could perform to an audience as normal. Nothing seemed to change the pace of life in India. In the afternoons at Tiffin time Kitty updates me with news of Lucknow and the recent riots in Cawnpore. A town not very far away that had developed into somewhat of an emergency, which recalled Jack back.

'From what I understand three agitators were hanged one day. In protest to the previous days hanging, a peaceful demonstration was held in the centre of Lahore, however some shopkeepers not wanting to join in, carried on working, sparked the Hindu's and Moslems fighting amongst themselves, which turned into a full-scale riot. Over two hundred people were killed including women and children. The Highland Light Infantry had to be called out to quell the fighting. It all subsided as quickly as it had started. Until it settled down to normality the authorities imposed a curfew on Lahore. Anyway your tribe were well out of it up there in the hills. Lording amongst the royalty.' Defensively I replied.

'Well. What about the big bear that visited us. I can assure you Kitty Burns he certainly was not royalty.' Teasing me she quipped.

'Jack did mention something about you loving wild animals.'

A very tearful Jackie interrupted our line of conversation, arriving on the veranda he sat down grizzling. I asked.

'What's wrong Jackie?' He croaked.

'Nothing, don't know.' His croaky voice worried me. Mary came up to him sat down beside him placing her arm around him. Jackie mumbled something.

'Mum he says his throat is sore.'

'Mary bring him here to me, then fetch me the medicine chest please.'

An urgent order, a sore throat could be mumps or his old trouble. Exactly when his problem started no one could remember. He, a little boy always in mischief roaring with laughter, then suddenly out of the blue he would be moaning and grizzling. Any of their aches and pains however trivial out in India was taken very seriously. At any moment in time anything could happen. Being miles from a Doctor unable to administer the right antidote or medicine, panic would set in. All Army wives were issued with an Army medical box, containing a thermometer, big bottles of mentholated spirits, surgical spirit, Iodine (for infliction of pain on open cuts), malaria tablets, a big jar of Conllies crystals for washing everything, a few rolls of bandages, cotton wool and splints. All these items were in constant use and would be replaced in this treasure trove of medical emergencies, which you had to combat all the ills that India could throw at you. There was no serum for scorpion stings or snakebites. Even if someone had the misfortune to be attacked by a panther or tiger, torn to ribbons by a bear, bitten by a camel, kicked by a mule or worse still, stamped to death by an elephant. Nothing in this box of treasures would cure those ailments. When I first saw the contents and complained to Jack all he said was.

'Sarah. All Army wives have had to cope in the past. So why should you be different? Why do you make a big thing about everything?'...With a huge grin all over his face, to finish off his charge added...'Anyway. I've never heard of anybody, being stamped to death by an Elephant.' Not letting him get away with it I retorted.

'You only need that to happen once. Then you'd be dead.' He didn't listen. It was too silly to argue about. Mary handed me the box of treasures. I made Jackie open his mouth to look down his throat, it was angry red and badly swollen with masses of white spots. I did not like what I saw. This was nothing like anything before.

'Kitty took a look.'

'My God. That looks bad Sarah Plant.'

I felt his brow he was burning up. I put the thermometer in his mouth reading it showed 104.

'We must get him to the hospital. Mary tell the Bearer Tonga jahldi jahldi.'

Within ten minutes a Tonga arrived. The Bearer shouting at the driver for more speed as it stopped turned about at the veranda steps. Helping Jackie up climbed up behind him putting my arms around him Mary and Kathleen had also joined us. Leaving Kitty in charge. the Bearer shouted.

'JAHLDI JAHLDI. JANA JANA ASPATAL.' We were rushed as fast as it would go to the MRS. The MO examined him and suggested.

'We will keep him in overnight for observation if, all is well? Collect him tomorrow.'

Having already visited the Doctor. All had been declared A1, nevertheless, just for the hell of it a nurse administered a few jabs against something or other, to the four of us making Jackie cry and cough with a hoarsely bark, We three left with sore arms. Next day at the MRS. We found Jackie sitting on his hospital bed weeping, covered in red bruises and wondered why. First I got him to open his mouth to inspect his throat, it still very red and raw. I questioned the nurse standing close by. I gasped.

'What on earth have you done to him?'

'Done with him? Jackie fought like a tiger. It took six of us nurses and the Doctor to hold him down, while we forcible swabbed his throat with glycerine and carbolic acid to burn away the ulcers.' Glycerine and carbolic acid a new one on me? Watched a weeping Jackie, I listened to

284

what she said as Mary and Kathleen sat with their arms around him in comfort, through his sobs Jackie whispered hoarsely.

'Mum please takes me home, they are worse than you.' I thought. *"Oh. God, he's only a little boy."* The starchy Sister arrived adding insult to injury announced.

'We cannot be responsible for his life. Next time his throat would close up completely.' Then the Doctor turned up, shaking his head said.

'Mrs Plant I have no idea what it is he has, but whilst swabbing his throat he broke off the end of the swab with his teeth practically swallowed it, he was blue in the face still bucking and kicking, the nurses had to hold him upside down. Very gently I had to force my fingers down his throat to retrieve the swab. Mrs Plant, if and when his throat starts to swell again. It must be swabbed immediately. Don't you bother to come in? I will show you how to swab his throat. You must swab the ulcers away, otherwise they will swell and he could die.' After what the doctor had finished his recipe. I explained.

'In Nowshera when he had it before, on those occasions it was never as bad as this. I was instructed to get him to gargle with diluted Iodine.What is this Glycerine and carbolic acid?'

'The iodine is not strong enough. The ulcers must be burnt out properly, using a mixture of glycerine and carbolic acid. It does work I can assure you. Nurse please. '

A nurse arrived carrying a kidney bowl with a green bottle, six long sticks some cotton wool and cotton thread. We all watched intently as she took one of the sticks, covered one end of it with a wad of cotton wool, winding cotton thread around it secured it. Then from the green bottle poured some of this clear syrupy mixture over the cotton swab handed it to the Doctor said.

'There that's how you make them up. It's quite simple. Now next operation, let me show you how you must do it. Jackie opens your mouth very wide for your mother'...obeying the Doctor with his mouth wide open, his eyes transfixed fearfully on the Doctor... 'There's a good fella. Look Mrs. Plant you see the deep red spots on the left side, that's where the ulcers were.'... I saw a lot of flamed red blotches but no white spots.... 'Now with the swab you must quickly rasp it up and down before he chokes. Mrs Plant, please make up another two swabs ready for your practice'...I did as shown and laid them in the kidney bowl ready, expecting to swab Jackie's throat however, to my surprise the Doctor said.

'Mary will you stand here while you're Mother practices on you. It won't hurt and it won't do you any harm.'... Without flinching she stood beside Jackie.... 'Jackie you hold one of her hands. Kathleen you hold the other.'

Mary stood close to the bed, holding their hands her mouth wide open stared straight into my eyes trusting me. I thought. *"By God just like your Father. Anything in the line of duty."* Three times I fumbled with this swab before I got it right. Mary retched but did not flinch, each time I had finished, she gagged coughed then spat into the kidney bowl. I was so proud of her. The Doctor and nurse who had watched the proceedings applauded.

'Mary you were very brave and you too Mrs Plant. Wonderful. Mrs Plant now you know how to administer the swab. Do this every time Jackie's throat become inflamed, the sooner administered the better. The nurse will provide you with the mixture along with some sticks and cotton wool. Anyway I am sure you must already have cotton thread, for sticks you can use any pencil or pen holder. Swabbing to be carried out three times a day until it subsides. Good luck.' After he had departed Mary said to me.

'Mum you didn't have to be that rough. 'Kathleen asked.

'What's it like?'

'Horrible she's a viper.' Just then the Sister arrived to inform me.

'Mrs Plant. We will keep Jackie in for another night.' Jackie wailed.

'No Mum takes me home. They will kill me?'

He got his wish. We all went home in the Tonga. Jackie, more than happy to be going home held a handkerchief soaked with cough mixture in his mouth. I with a green bottle of Glycerine and Carbolic, plus more cotton wool, to add to my medical treasure trove. It was now my job to administer this foul stuff on Jackie that transpired into a major task, it took the three of us to administer the swabbing. I would begin by stripping him down to his little shorts while Mary and Kathleen would wrap their arms around him, talking baby talk to calm him down. Mary quietly whispering.

'Come on now Jackie Baba. It's got to be done, come and sit on the bed with me.'

On the side table resting in a kidney bowl, was the implement of torture. A pencil with on one end a wad of cotton wool held tightly by cotton thread the cotton wool soaked in glycerine and carbolic. Mary would sit herself up onto the bed with Jackie between her legs to hold him down; her arms ready to grip him tightly, with Kathleen knelt beside them ready to pull his chin down force his head back. His eyes expressing fear, as I with my finger depressed his tongue and shoved the swab into his mouth then rasped the back of his inflamed throat. He would buck and choke squirming and twisting, we firmly held him down until it was finished. I grabbed him from Mary and held him face down, so he could be sick. Talking and cajoling him in case he died of shock. We would all finish upon the bed holding each other with Jackie sobbing where he lay. Little did I realise that this new wonder concoction, would be used by me for many a year to come in the future

I was only content on a few occasions to be away from the bungalow out shopping with Kitty, always back before the tribe arrived back from school. Fortunately, Kitty followed my  example of keeping ourselves to ourselves. On some mornings starting off at a leisurely pace. Kitty and I would ride our bikes out to see some of the sights of Lucknow. In the center of Lucknow the roads were littered with dung of every description. Having been raised with animals I ignored the mess. Joining the mass of transport of every description nevertheless, very fearful of the lumbering black water buffaloes pulling carts along, who might suddenly turn in to rip me apart with their massive big horns. We would get in amongst the hordes of bicycles, some with big wicker baskets tied on, I even saw an Indian with his charpoi strapped to his back, if he got tired of pedalling he could lie down and sleep. The two Memsahib's arriving at an intersection, would stop put one foot down to let the other traffic coming the other way pass, thus causing havoc behind us. Much ringing of bells shouts and curses, nobody stopped; they just carried on with not a care in the world. After a few times of this stopping lark Kitty suggested.... 'Sarah Plant. If we stop we are going to cause more accidents. So in future doesn't stop just carry on riding through?'... We cycled on following everyone's example weaving in and out of the carts until we found ourselves on the opposite side of the road? Not our intended direction. Kitty roared with laughter.... 'Sarah Plant. Quickly get back over the other side.' Somehow we succeeded in weaving our way through the mayhem.

We enjoyed our homely way of life, except as she used to say go gadding about. (Always upon her insistence), to see a change of scenery. I wanted to see many places of interest so we made trips to. 'The British Residency' with its holed and battered walls? A stark reminder of the Indian Mutiny many years before. The La Martinere School for young gentlemen. The magnificent 'Bara Imambara' Surrounded by walls with little mosque style pinnacles and its monster ornamental gates the

entrance to a giant Mosque. The 'Dilkusha Palace' The Kaiser Pasind and many more places of interest. Our trips out were unhindered, there was no animosity towards the British as we had experienced up in Nowshera.

The only other visitor to our bungalow was the daughter of BSM. Jordan and his wife. Desire Jordan a great friend of the girls, she without her parent's knowledge would arrive on her pony then Mary and Desire would take turns racing it over the Mydam. Mary sick with jealousy always asked.

'Mum when am I going to get a pony? We all had one up in the hills.' As far as Mary was concerned, the little donkey Michael rode never fitted the bill, small, unable to gallop and only fit for Michael to ride. One of the oldest Chico's holding him would just walk it around the compound and when the other three did climb astride it to ride it, the Donkey would not move just stand still until Michael was remounted, only then it would move. At times my tribe could all be very entertaining. Jackie dressed similar to the Chico's little cotton shorts with shirt outside his shorts, always contented he never seemed to want for anything. Mary only content to live in Jodhpurs, an old KD shirt of her fathers although shortened was secured around her waist by her prized possession, an old Scouts belt with a snake clasp a present from Jack Burns. In typical army fashion she drilled and bossed everyone, including the Chico's, always ready to argue with anything I had to say. Kathleen the opposite,.Someone amongst the army wives would receive a dressmaking pattern, it became red –hot, it was passed around to be copied. The Bazaars were scoured for some different patterns of cotton cloth. For a dress to be made, to show off at the high light of the social week. The Sunday Church Parade all wearing Tobies that did nothing for anybody, even with a new dress we still looked a dowdy bunch. all craved the attempt of "haute couture". Nevertheless Kathleen was never content with anything I had made for her, having taken days to sew it together, she would stand watching me soaked in sweat, trying to make three matching dresses for Sunday, if Mary had two pockets to her dress, Kathleen just to be different with her big blue eyes full of tears, would want one or none, the material might be the latest thing in the Bazaar but to her, looked exactly as a previous week's find. Having fitted it on would shout...'Mum just look at it.'.....She would tear it off, I had to agree with her....'Mum can't you buy me a Sari. They are beautiful they are yards and yards.'

For weeks she pestered me, until for a bit of peace I gave in. I wasn't too happy with the thoughts of the prospect of her wearing saris, for peace and quiet we went shopping in three Tonga's. In the first one me with Michael in my arms Mary, Jackie. In the second. Kathleen's treat, herself, number One Ayah, the Bearer in charge of the magic box, followed by the last one with the three Ayahs in. All the servants came out to see us off. "Katie Baba was going to buy a Sari." You'd think we were making a trip to China instead of a Bazaar to buy cloth at the best shop, playing Indian music on a gramophone with little girls outside dancing in the dirt. The sari's every colour of the rainbow was displayed, once Kathleen was satisfied, the sari draped around her all applauded such a fine choice. What a palaver over the purchase of cloth or indeed anything in India. It took hours then the deal was made by the Ayahs, babbling and gesturing, pointing at Katie Baba waving of hands, jangling bracelets, cuddled amongst them. Only when the Bearer opened the magic box rupees exchanged hands. Now we could get home and I get some peace. A little streamer of her sari fluttered out of the back of the Tonga, to get the last sighs of pleasure from everyone. (India could be so easily pleased then erupt into violence for no known reason.) Then back at the bungalow I had the unenviable task of making it up. Its wistful fine gauze slipping to the floor at every moment, I had to finish up with a piece of Buckram cut out of one of Jacks waistcoats. (He'd be very pleased about that when he found out later.)

287

Kathleen was delighted as were all the Ayahs. A Pan mark on her head (I forbade kohl eyes put on with spit). Glass bangles with little bells on her ankles and wrist, hennaed by the Ayahs, she could stamp her bare feet, weave the hands intricately all day long to great applause until Sunday, All nonsense put out of the way, dressed the same as everyone else. Tobie crammed on her head everybody cried. Kitty Burns always preferred to be gadding about, her excuse, she didn't have a baby to look after. Arriving by bike one Saturday morning her tribe running behind her straight up onto the veranda whooping like red Indians joined my tribe, then raced around the veranda out onto the compound. Chai and nimba pani was served, Jack Burns decided to teach Mary how to box. Everyone sat in a circle, the Ayahs sat on the veranda, sighing and clucking at the antics of these two as they squared up. Jack shouted.

'COME ON PLANT PARRY THE BLOWS.' Kitty encouraging.

'Sarah Plant. Let them get on with it, I have wonderful news for you. Oh by way a young soldier died of the fever, the MO will arrive to take Jackie to hospital.'

'Oh my God. God rest his soul.' Says I, watching the antics of Jack Burns sparring around Mary, gave her a few open handed slaps on the face before dancing away grinning. I could see she was tight lipped ready to explode I shouted.

'MARY. ' Jack turned round towards me, immediately Mary smashed him on the nose and knocked him flying. Up he jumps with blood pouring from his nose roaring with laughter he hugged her.

'Mary Plant you beat me.' Kitty Burns shouted.

'JACK BURNS COME HERE.'

Jack ran up the steps, grinning wiping the blood with the back of his hand. Kitty scolded him.

'You bloody fool letting a girl beat you.' Swiftly caught him across his shoulders, with her riding crop he shouted.

'MUM.' Kitty retorted.

'Take your shirt off and lay on the veranda.'

He knew better than to argue with his Mother, the others following behind knelt down beside him with Mary trying to stem the blood with his shirt sleeve she turned shouted at her.

'YOU'RE A VIPER KITTY BURNS YOU OUGHT TO BE THRASHED DAILY.' Kitty having dealt out her punishment, taking no notice sat down to drink chai, urged.

'Sarah Plant. Beat her.'

So far the day was going well, one bloody nose no broken bones until sounds of activity in the compound, as the young tall handsome MO rode up on his horse, we stood up he saluted us.

'Good morning Ladies. Mrs Plant. Mrs. Burns. So the Burn's and Plants are killing each other off once again. That's good news. Now maybe I can get some peace. What's this a battlefield? Lay still Jack Burns' He dismounted, took off his medical bag and came bounding up the veranda steps. Kitty stated.

'He banged into a door Sir.'

'No doubt Mrs. Burns. Pushed by Mary Plant I imagine.' The pair of adversaries looked up both grinned at him.

'But I didn't come to see you Jack Burns. I came to see young Jackie.'

Looking at Jackie, immediately Kathleen placed a protective arm around him. I thought. *"Oh God no. His throats not inflamed."*

'First. Jack Burns you're a fraud there's nothing wrong with you. Mary give that disgusting shirt to the Dhobi Wallah, get a towel soak in water and wring it out, bring it to me dry please.' Off she scampered returning with it knelt behind Jack.

'Put it over his head. Don't strangle him. That will stop the bleeding. Now. Jackie come on over here there's a good boy.'

Jackie stood up, with a wary scared look on his face, moved towards the Doctor stood in front of him who questioned.

'You don't like this swabbing do you?'... Jackie shook his head... 'Well I'm going to teach you how to do it yourself. You know. It is much easier if you do it yourself'... he urged...'I have a mirror here that is called a convex mirror that I use for shaving. Open your mouth wide, look in the mirror at your throat.' Jackie followed instructions... 'See but if I turn it over, see it's much different it's larger'...For Jackie's benefit he reversed it a few times until he was sure he had captured his attention...'See those white spot's at the back? Those we have to get rid of them by swabbing, then you'll get better and if I or, your Mother swabs you, it hurts and you hate it. Don't you?' Jackie nodded...'but if you did it yourself, you can do it for longer, and make a better job of it. How about, you do it to me, then I do it to myself. You will see I can do it better on my own. Shall we try?'...Jackie nodded in agreement. As we watched this discussion I thought: *Oh dear God this wonderful man was going to show my little boy how to do something to him, which very few people could even manage.* We were agog watching this new saga of entertainment, as there was an Officer present I did notice the servants were silently appearing to watch from hidden places. He went to his medical bag, removed the implements of torture, a kidney bowl, a green poison bottle containing the glycerine and carbolic, cotton wool, a reel of cotton thread a handful of long wooden skewers, then prepared the swab, wrapping a wad of cotton wool around the end of one skewer secured it with thread, taking hold of the green bottle poured the syrupy solution onto the swab, turning it spreading the liquid evenly over the cotton wool, a few drops dripped into the Kidney bowl. With the instrument of torture ready for Jackie to carry out the first part of this drama, he moved down onto the step below, knelt down he was ready!

'Mrs Plant can you please make up another four swabs.'... Whilst I prepared those The MO said.... 'Now Jackie, this is where you come into the picture. You stand on the top step in front of me. Mary would you be good enough to come and hold Jackie's shoulders. He needs support as he swabs me. Now Jackie I want you to take this swab. Hold my chin down push the swab right to the back of my throat and rasp up and down. When I say now. Okay.'...Jackie stood there looking terrified nodded, took hold of the end of the swab. 'Now. Okay.'

Jackie placed one tiny hand on the MOs chin pushed the swab into his open mouth down into his throat and rasped. Though the doctor's face went blood red, he stuck it for some seconds then choked, pulling out Jackie's hand holding the swab, turned about spat, wiping his face with his handkerchief exclaimed.

'By God Jackie, that's awful isn't it? '

Jackie stood there looking at the used swab in his hand nodded. Mary still holding his shoulders tightly was fascinated by the proceedings.

'Now. I'm going to do it to myself. Jackie, you see if I can do it for a longer period. The longer you take the better chance to get rid of the white spots; if you want to get better they all have to go. Now Jackie you add more carbolic on the next swab.'

Jackie took the already sodden swab; carefully tipped the bottle onto the swab twirling it around as he had seen me do it, then gave it to the Doctor, knelt down ready for the next demonstration?

'Here I go.' He pulled down his own chin pushed the swab into his mouth down into his throat rasped, he stuck it out for what seemed minutes, choked, gagged, spat, his face bursting as if he wanted to gag again red smears appeared on his handkerchief... 'By God Jackie, that was a good long rasp wasn't it?'...Jackie nodded. I think we all agreed.

'Now Jackie it's your turn, kneel on the step where I was'... Jackie did that... 'I'll hold the kidney bowl. You pour the carbolic on the swab, pull your chin down, push the swab in, and rasp up and down. Like I did.'

289

I was breathless, praying and watching all this. Jackie didn't hesitate just pushed the swab in and rasped... the Doctor encouraged...

'Good boy Jackie. Rasp it up and down. That's the way as hard as you can.'...he did and lasted out until he choked, jumped up ran down the steps spat, came back up grinning. No tears but his mouth were shut tight. The Doctor put his arms around him.

'To-day Jackie. You are the bravest boy in the British Army. Open your mouth and let me see. Mrs Plant come and sees what your Jackie has done.'

I moved, looked into Jackie's mouth. His throat was red with a little bleeding, almost clear, but the main thing he was grinning. However the Doctor had noticed some spots urged.

'There's just a little more down there, can you do it again Jackie? I did it twice and the next one will be your second. Okay?'

Jackie now grinning nodded and repeated the same procedure. He choked pulling out the swab ran down the steps gagged spat out saliva mixed with blood, grinning broadly came back up onto the veranda.

'That was excellent Jackie. Now let's have a look down your throat'...he examined the back of Jackie's throat turned to me and winked... 'There you are Jackie; you have swabbed them all away. You were very brave.' The Doctor lifted him up and carried him around. We all kissed him shook his hand congratulated him. They both sat down at the table, the Doctor ordered lemon pani to soothe their throats.

'Now Jackie I'm going to write a chit out to the hospital.'... Jackie looked startled... 'No. It's to tell them. Wait a minute, I'll write it down then read it to you.' He took out his notebook and pen and began to write. Finishing, he addressed Jackie reading aloud said:

"To-day this young man. Jackie Plant has swabbed his own throat and nolonger requires your butchering. Signed the Doctor." Jackie roared with laughter, the doctor turned to me.

'Mrs Plant would you kindly get the Bearer to take Jackie by Tonga to the Hospital. To deliver this note in person. They will look at his throat, all will agree he makes a better job of it himself.' The Doctor thanked us for the lemon pani stated. 'Hopefully Jackie had now solved his problem, mounted his horse turned to salute us. With all our outspoken thanks ringing in his ear he rode off. A Tonga was ordered. Kitty Burns who had not uttered a word throughout all this entertainment exclaimed.

'Well I'm damned. That's the best piece of surgery. I've ever come across.' A little while later the Tonga arrived, Jackie with the precious note grasped in his hand.accompanied by two Ayahs climbed up. Jackie croaked to the Tonga Wallah. 'Jahldi jahldi hospital.' We all waved him off. Then without further ado Kitty brought us all back to reality.

'Sarah Plant. Now that's over will we ever get to the Bazaar? I still have great news for you. Wait while I get rid of my brats, before yours kill them all. Jack Burns get your shirt from the dhobi Wallah and head for home out of my sight.'

Jack ran off to the washhouse soon to return grinning, as he pulled on his shirt over his head and chivvied his lot onto the road. 'Right double quick time now home.' With her riding crop Kitty aimed a swipe at Jack, he dodged, took a swiped at Marty the last in line he dodged the descending crop.

'Oh did you see that Sarah Plant. You have to be like grease lighting to land a blow on any of my tribe.' Jacks parting goodbye.....'I'll fight with you again tomorrow Mary Plant. '

In response Kitty turned on Mary.

'Now Mary Plant any lip from you and if your Mother won't. I'll thrash you for breaking my poor Jack's nose. Brazen piece.'

Mary just tossed her head at her, went inside the bungalow followed by Kathleen. I saw that number One Ayah was caring for Michael, so it was about time we left. We got onto our bikes and pushed off, nobody bothered to wave us off. It was an uneventful jaunt, we rode there and back. Kitty forgot to tell me what was so important. On the way back I left her at her quarters rode back on my own. However it was not the last time the MO visited us for Jackie, but he did for a very different reason. Mary. I was inside the bungalow when someone hailed me.

'Mrs Plant it's me the MO. Can I speak with you please?'

Leaving what I was doing, I went outside to find my tribe along with the Chico's stood sheepishly alongside the MO astride his horse. The MO sternly addressed me.

'Not many minutes ago, riding past, I nearly died with fright. I saw Mary with a stick over her shoulder, dangling from its end was a live snake, with the rest whopping and shouting behind her. I immediately stopped jumped down ordered Mary do not move, all the rest stand away. Where did you get that snake from?' she replied... 'It was hanging down from a tree. So I hit it with a stick until it was dead.' ...'Please Mary, carefully hand the stick and the snake to me. None of you children move. She did exactly what I told her. To kill it I dropped it on the ground drove the heel of my boot onto its head. Mrs. Plant if the snake had bitten her or any of the children, we do not have serum available that would have saved any of them.'

I could see that he was in no frame of mind to contemplate any reasoning from anyone. I too was very concerned about her latest escapade, I just muttered.

'Thank God you were passing this way at the same time.' However the MO was not finished.

'Mary. Never ever go near snakes again.' She promised.

'I'm sorry Sir. I'll never do it again.'

Satisfied with her response he rode off. In addition, she received another good hiding from me and sent packing to her room.

Another morning after the usual visits from Wallahs was over, my tribe was at school, I was sat sipping chai savouring the moment, just thinking about the brass ornaments I had seen in the

 married quarters at the Curragh camp, remembering how much I had admired them, thought: *Now was the time I could set about to purchase some as mementoes of India. Horse's, sacred cows, antelopes, camels, monkeys , peacocks, and many others not forgetting something special elephants, the first animals I had seen in the docks at Bombay. I decided to make a trip to the Sadr Bazaar to purchase some. I was sure Kitty would be only too pleased to be out shopping with me.*

The following Saturday I set off on my bike to Kitty's with my tribe running behind me. Kitty was all for it, so we left the two tribes playing together in her compound. Once we arrived at the Bazaar it took no time in battering for some items, with Kitty doing the business. Bought a magnificent pair of elephants made out of black ebony, with tapering ivory tusks and toe nails, a pair of antelopes a peacock with a coloured fantail that was the start of my collection. Just before we left I was rather thirsty and saw some ripe apricots on a fruit Wallahs stall. With one hand supporting the bike with my free hand picked up two. Offering them to the fruit wallah began battering with him. The next thing I knew a monkey swinging down from an overhanging branch snatched the pair out of my hand. I shrieked out in fright and shock at the quickness of the theft. But not Kitty she roared with laughter, seeing nothing but fun in every situation. The fruit Wallah did a merry dance demanding payment for his lost sale. I shouted back at him.

'BAKSHEESH BAKSHEESH.' Pointing to the monkey sat up on the branch of the tree, savagely ripping away the outside skin, oblivious to the furore he had caused below, in contempt dropped the skins onto the Wallah, who began hurling abuse at the wretched monkey. We left him to sort out his own problem. Pedalling on our way back Kitty suggested.

'Sarah Plant, before we go back to separate the tribes, let's have five minutes peace together at your place over a spot of chai.' I agreed.

'Okay, but not for long.'

291

I was always worried about what my devils could be up to. Pedalling along the track as we got nearer we heard a right old din going on. Awful screaming chattering and it was coming from our bungalow. Kitty shouted.

'CHRIST SARAH PLANT. WHAT THE HELL'S GOING ON?' I shouted.

'DON'T ASK ME KITTY. C'MON JAHLDI.'

As if it were the start of a race, we pedalled like fury. Covering the last few hundred yards raced into our compound, where hordes of screaming monkeys were running around in front of the bungalow. Their chattering, screeching was incessant they were everywhere, clambering up the veranda chicks, jumping up and down on the roof, even on top of the chicken coop. The chickens inside in an effort to get out from the onslaught above were beating their flaying wings against the wire netting. Some monkeys were trying to get in through the windows. I could see sticks being poked out from inside at the monkeys. As we rode towards the steps Kitty shouted.

'CHRIST SARAH PLANT. YOU SHOULD HAVE PAID FOR THE FRUIT. NOW HE'S GOT THE WHOLE TRIBE OUT TO GET YOU?'

We rode straight through the monkeys, scattering them in all directions. I kept going like I was on a charger shouted my response.

'C'MON KITTY WE'VE GOT TO GET INTO THE BUNGALOW.' Kitty shouting behind.

'GET OUT YOU BUGGER'S.' Had the monkeys darting everywhere, their mouths wide open showing horrible teeth as they screamed and chattered back. At the veranda steps we dropped our bikes run up the steps, the door mysteriously opened, we fell together in a heap inside the room. The Bearer immediately shut the door. Quickly looking around saw that everybody was inside. The servants along with my tribe were at the windows defending the onslaught, thrusting with the staves, all were roaring with laughter as they stabbed the monkeys, inciting them even more as outside they tried to tear down the chicks. They were to say the least, a very angry tribe of monkeys. I yelled at Mary.

'WHAT THE HELL ARE YOU LOT DOING HERE?'

She didn't answer just clouted another monkey. I peered through a gap in the chicks, outside in amongst the monkey tribe were mothers with their babies clinging to them. Constantly running backwards forwards, chattering hurling their abuse towards the bungalow, the noise was unbelievable. Kitty and I now joined in the affray grabbed hold of a stave each, thrusting them out through tiny gaps in the chicks. Kitty yelled at me.

'BY GOD SARAH PLANT, THIS IS GOOD EH? WHEN DO WE SEND FOR THE ARTILLERY?' I yelled back.

'NEVER MIND THE ARTILLERY, JUDGING BY THE SIZE OF THE STONES THERE IS THROWING THE MONKEYS HAVE THAT OUTSIDE. HOW IN DEVILS NAME ARE WE TO QUIETEN THEM DOWN?'

The answer came from an unexpected quarter. All of a sudden Gog and Magog came out of the sky. Whoosh, with talons outstretched, without landing successfully grabbed two of the baby monkeys, flying up into the sky landed on their roost and proceeded to tear the poor little things to bits. That stopped it. The siege ceased, all the monkeys screaming with fright fled up the road. The two mothers crying piteously, again and again dashed back towards the bungalow. To add to all this noise the crows joined in with their cawing. We stood back from our defence positions. I looked around everyone was smiling and laughing. Kitty and I ventured out onto the Veranda. There were heaps of stones strewn all about; which the monkeys had torn up out of the compound amongst the debris, were pieces of brass that had dropped out of the basket. The veranda chicks had been torn to bits. The chickens clucking in their coop were terrified could not be quietened. I cried out in disbelief.

'Oh my God. Look at the mess, how did all this start? What on earth have they done now?'

'Christ Sarah Plant. What was that all about?'

'Kitty I don't know. But I will soon find out.'

I went back inside. My three still holding staves stood grinning, as the servants were busy cleaning up the mess.

'Mary, tell me. Why aren't you at the Burn's. What the hell's going on here?' Mary began to relate what had happened.

'I had a fight with Kathleen Burns. Right. I shouted pack your bags, we are all going home and will never visit this tribe again. The Burns' shouted. Good riddance. So we set off to come home we hadn't gone far, when some monkeys descended from those trees started to pester us. I warned the others to keep going not to touch or encourage them. (They had been warned not to touch them or pick up their babies). When one of them grabbed hold of Jackie's shirt it hung on. I caught it a clout that sent it flying. That's when they ran screaming at us. I grabbed a stone and threw it at the leader hitting him. Then we grabbed Jackie's hands between us and made a dash for it. They came howling behind us. We got indoors and the servants closed all the Jalousies. (Chicks) For a little while the monkeys just stood outside screaming at us. I thought they would go away, then their leader threw the first stone. That did it they all started attacking the bungalow. They were hurling stones, anything they could tear up out of the garden. The veranda chicks were being attacked and pulled to pieces. Two of them terrified the life out of the poor chickens in the coop. Then you and Kitty Burns rode into the compound that's all.'

Kitty and I both listened to this wild story. I wanted to believe her, the preceding siege had been all too much for Jackie. He started to roar with laughter cried out.

'Oh Mum what wonderful fun.'

I was so annoyed, everything was just a great lark to them. I grabbed my crop tried to cut him right across his backside, missed he jumped down the veranda steps, turned around rubbing his backside, started to imitating a monkey stampeding and chattering his teeth at me. The other two began laughing at his antics, I raised my crop but missed them as they leapt the steps, joined him they too imitating monkeys. Kitty Burns and I turned to each other just roared with laughter. They could be so comical. Everyone was in fits of laughter, when their father rode up on his horse, he roared.

'SARAH, WHAT'S GOING ON HERE? I'VE JUST PASSED A TRIBE OF MONKEYS SCREAMING THEIR HEADS OFF.' I didn't get a chance to say anything. The children all ran to him blurting out their story. Kitty and I just stood on the veranda listening to a slightly different version. Mary shouted

'DAD THEY ATTACKED US.'

'You were told never to touch them.'

'We didn't until one tore Jackie's hand.'

Quick as a flash, Jackie showed a non-wounded hand, Jack swung off his horse, Mary grabbed hold of the reins was up on its back in a second. Jack took Jackie's hand.

'Right mister shows me this wound. All wounds are treated with raw Iodine Okay.'

Jackie tore his hand free, ran under the horse's belly. Looking under the horse Jack roared… 'Come here' …Only to see Jackie stampeding his feet at him gibbering like a monkey…. 'Sarah throw me that riding crop. I'll teach this lot some manners.' I slipped it off my belt and threw it to him he caught the crop in mid-air, bent down to find Jackie. Mary shouted… 'Dad he's away.' Jack straightened up as Jackie ran towards the Mydam, Kathleen ran after him, Mary kicked the horse and was away, all three howling with delight, Jack running after them roaring…. 'I'LL MACRO THE LOT OF YOU. COME HERE.'

As he went past, he caught the chicken coop with a clout of the crop, which sent those poor devils into frenzy? Mary galloped the horse in a wide circle over the Mydam. If her father was having fun, she was not going to miss a moment of it. He caught Kathleen and Jackie around the shoulders, signalled Mary over to join them. Got her to dismount marched the three of them over

293

towards the Sacred Cow beneath the shade of the trees, which could not have cared less. We watched as he stood them in front, wagging his finger at them gave them a lecture. They would take heed of but not for long. I was soaked in sweat wiping my brow, turned to Kitty Burns.

'So you see Kitty Burns. This is what I have to put up with.'

'Sarah Plant, You don't have to go to a theatre, you have your own one here. They are priceless. You will never have to say. You've led a boring life with your tribe.'

'No. But all I ever wanted? Is a bit of peace and quiet.'

Jack by this time was walking back with them all very subdued Mary holding the horse's reins. Jack called out.

'Sarah ask the Bearer to bring us some chai please. Then I'll ride along with Kitty back to her house.' Kathleen spotted the two vultures still tearing at the remnants of the baby monkeys began to cry, pointing up she pleaded.

'Dad can't you do something? '

'No Kathleen this is something else you will all have to learn. They are protected and must not be harmed, they are scavengers and clean up everything that's dead or, anything they can kill. The Monkeys live in the trees. They are very vulnerable on the ground, as you know they chased you three leaving themselves open to attack. They haven't got home safely to their own trees yet. I shall ride home with Kitty in case they attack her as she goes past.' Chai was brought; surveying the scene Jack called the Bearer.

'Bazaar. Karidna murgi, jalousies.' (buy chickens and Jalousies.) After chai, Kitty and Jack left, I had the tribe sluiced down and ready for bed. All in all. Not a bad day.

CHAPTER EIGHT
GYMKHANA

During the mornings, Kitty Burns and I had made many trips into the Sadr Bazaar. She had taught me how to barter, particularly for Tobies, as our two tribes spent a lot of time throwing them backwards and forwards breaking the rims. Every week she argued with the Wallah, that we would become his regular customers forcing him down with his price. Therefore with the amount of tobies we purchased, he did not lose out. While in the shop I was looking at rolls of silk, as I wanted to send some Indian silk back to the family in Blighty. Kitty quietly asked.

'Sarah Plant you're not buying more silk for your Kathleen again?'

'No Kitty. I want to send some back home.'

'Well don't buy it from here. I know a cheap shop in a Bazaar outside Lucknow. We will ride out there, just you wait and see how cheap they are, and also they have other cheap things to buy.'

'Kitty. What on earth would I want to ride outside of the army lines for, when I can buy it here.'

'Fiddlesticks Sarah Plant. We will go.' She insisted, reluctantly I gave in. We arranged with a Mrs Turner to oversee our two tribes until we got back.

The following day we set off on our bikes, riding away from the centre to God knows where. Passing the Governors House in the middle of the road I spotted a discarded horseshoe, stopping I picked it up for luck and hung it on my handlebars, much to Kitty's displeasure who retorted.

'Come on Sarah Plant we haven't any time for that rubbish.'

But I felt safer as we rode on along this empty cart track until all of a sudden she shouted.

'GET OFF SARAH PLANT, BEFORE YOU KILL EVERYONE IN SIGHT.' Totally surprised by her outburst. In panic I applied the brakes came to a shuddering halt, I got off shouted.

'WHATEVER'S WRONG? THERE'S NOBODY ON THE ROAD. YOU'RE BARMY KITTY.'

'Be quiet Sarah Plant, this is what I've been meaning to tell you. The good news first. You know the Indian Mutiny was seventy-four years ago?'... (I didn't)...'Well the Battery is to be renamed the Residency.'

'So what?'

'On the day of the Anniversary, there are to be great parades held at the old residency fort, with a garden party, balls and dances in every mess now listen to this Sarah Plant. A gymkhana and the "alarm stakes." what do you think of that? But wait there's more the icing on the cake.' ...dropping her bike she grabbed hold of me shouted...'THE BATTERY IS BEING SENT BACK HOME. ' I shouted.

'HOME WHERE IN INDIA?' She shouted.

'NO. ENGLAND YOU FOOL, BACK TO BLIGHTY.'

Immediately what she had said registered in my brain. I shrieked and yelled, we both hugged cried and danced a jig around our bikes, left lying in the middle of the track.

'Oh Kitty I think I'm going to die.'

'Don't be such a fool Sarah Plant. You have not got time for that. We have rubbish to buy at Old Babu's cheap Bazaar to make dresses for the Balls. C'mon.'

Remounting our bikes rode on, shouting in happinest, roaring with laughter, eventually we arrived at a small village, where I did notice a strange atmosphere about the place. We stopped outside a Bazaar dismounted. Odd that it may seem that even above our own personal excitement, many Indians were crowding around us not in a threatening manner but all the Wallahs were urging.

'Jahldi Memsahib's Jahldi Jahldi.' The surrounding atmosphere gave one an uncomfortable feeling. I grew tense muttered.

'Something's up Kitty.' She urged.

'C'mon let's get to Babu's. Then home.' We hurriedly wheeled our bikes towards his 'cheap' shop where he, Babu was standing outside, probably he knowing Kitty excitedly beckoned us.

'Inside Memsahib's Jahldi.' He ushered us into the back of his shop, his Chico's brought in our bikes and closed the shutters. The pair of us totally bewildered by whatever was going on? It wasn't very long before loud shouting could be heard outside, as it approached his shop it increased in volume. With a shrug a waggle of his hands, old Babu explained.

'Barbary Wallahs Memsahib's.' Beckoned us to be seated, offered glasses of chai, we sat there whilst outside the tremendous racket continued. The shutters rattled by what I assumed were sticks, stones and rocks, as whatever or whoever it was passed by his shop. I thought. *"Everyone was going to die, gradually the mayhem subsidedas it passed by."* The Babu explained in reasonable English.... 'Asti, (stay). Memsahib's rioting in village, two of their caste hung that morning. For murder of an army officer his memsahib, but his two children saved by Tobies'...shrugging spread out his hands as if he didn't know....'Memsahib's Asti'. He sent out one of his Chico's, meantime not wanting to lose a sale he almost sold us all his stock. We made our purchases arranging that our Bearer would pay for and collect them next day. After what seemed an eternity the Chico arrived back, jabbering away to the old Babu before he said.

Jahldi. Jao Memsahib's bungalow. Jahldi.' The Chico wheeled out our bikes; he let us out through the front entrance, outside his shop the Bazaar looked as if a bomb had hit it. Rubbish, sticks, rocks, littered the place; two of the shops were on fire, their Wallahs trying desperately throwing Chatti bowlfuls of water to quell the flames, in the far distance, the sounds of the mayhem continued. The Chico beckoned to us to follow him around the back of the Bazaar, through some back alleys onto the main road.

'Salaam Memsahib's'. He was gone.

'Salaam to you Chico. C'mon Sarah Plant we had better Jahldi, just walk your bike.'

A note of apprehension in her voice, until back on the empty track we mounted our bikes and pedalled like fury away from the riot. It then dawned on me the reason it was empty of Indian traffic. That was due to the hanging that morning. Sweat was streaming off me, as we pedalled like they were after us. Then in the far distance, we saw a cloud of dust as two horsemen were galloping towards us. Kitty yelled at me.

'JESUS CHRIST SARAH PLANT, NOW WE'RE FOR IT.'

Applying the brakes we shuddering to a halt. My heart was in my mouth, my throat was parched dry. Still these two horsemen came galloping nearer and nearer in desperation I shouted.

'CHRIST WHAT SHALL WE DO KITTY?' A frantic response.

'CHRIST KNOWS. I yelled.

'LET'S GET OUT OF THE WAY AND HIDE.' She yelled back at me.

'WHERE IN CHRIST'S NAME? YOU SILLY BUGGER, THERE'S NOT A BLADE OF GRASS IN SIGHT NEVER MIND A TREE.'

We stood there awaiting our fate with bikes ready, for a quick getaway to God knows where. Then as they got closer we spotted their Khaki drills, they were British soldiers. Kitty cried out.

'Oh thank Christ. Their ours.' Still galloping towards us as the two horsemen gradually came closer We recognised them. I shouted.

'CHRIST ALMIGHTY KITTY. ITS JACK AND BOBBY.' They galloped up, in a cloud they both pulled up their horses. Jack shouted down at us.

'WHERE THE BLOODY HELL HAVE YOU TWO BEEN?' I bleated.

'In the Bazaar back there.' Bobby roared.

'WHAT THE HELL DO YOU THINK YOU ARE DOING IN THAT BAZAAR? WHEN THERE'S A FULL-SCALE RIOT IN PROGRESS. YOU PAIR OF BLOODY IDIOTS.'

I could see the pair of them was furious with us. Kitty questioned.

'How did we know?' Bobby retorted.

'WELL YOU BLOODY WELL OUGHT NOT TO BE OUT OF THE ARMY BOUNDARIES. COME ON HOME YOU TWO. JAHLDI.'

We got blasted by both of them. They wheeled their horses around, from their recent gallop both of their mounts were lathered, snorting and foaming at the mouth. In between our escorts we set off sedately riding on our bikes. They both sat bolt upright in their saddles, they were not very pleased, Jack's face did not have that usual grin instead it was a look of thunder. He spoke down at us.

'We've been given special permission to come out and find you two pair of idiots. It's a good job you told Sergeant Turner's wife where you were going. The whole camp is on emergency stand by.' Kitty defensively answered.

'We did not know that the Brigade was on standby.' Jack angrily retorted

'Next thing. You two will be running the bloody Army.'

We rode on in silence back to the Garrison compound. When we got insight of our bungalow Jack shouted.

'RIGHT YOU PAIR GET HOME JAHLDI. SARAH. I WILL SPEAK WITH YOU LATER.' WE ARE OFF.'

They left us in the middle of the road, galloped back to the camp. Kitty rode back with me to collect her tribe, but before we got off our bikes, Mrs. Turner met us with a cheery message.

'The children have been all right. Your husbands are out looking for you two. I'm glad I'm not wearing your shoes.' I replied.

'Yes we've seen them thank you'…. she made a hasty retreat. her parting shot to us was. 'When the dust has settled. I'll speak with you both later.' Kitty laughed.

'Christ Sarah Plant, we're right in the mire now.' She shouted to her tribe and was away peddling fast with them running in front and beside her she shouted.

'I'LL COME OVER LATER.'

Jack arrived back for his evening meal. Still smarting from his day's event.

'Sarah the rioting has finished, all is under control. You frightened the life out of me. Please do be careful in future. Can't stay get to get back to the camp.'

After a quick sluice down, change of clothes, a quick snack he returned to camp. That evening, I was sitting on the veranda, when a grinning Kitty Burns arrived in a Tonga still sat on the Tonga, she called out

'Sarah Plant. It's all over. Those pair of silly buggers made a big hoo-hah over nothing. What did Jack say?'

'Not much. He was very short, said it was over and I should be more careful in future.'

'Is that all. Bobby blasted me so I blasted him. C'mon Sarah Plant, let's go up to the Sergeant's mess and hear all about today's events? Climb up alongside me. C'mon the Tonga Wallahs waiting.'

'Kitty Burns. No. I don't want to. I've had enough trouble from you for one day thank you very much.'

'Fiddlesticks. C'mon Sarah. Only for half an hour, we will find out more that's for sure.'

It was pointless she never took no for an answer. Once again I gave in. I gave the Bearer full instruction, I would be back very soon. Off we went, I made Kitty promise we would stay half an hour no more. She agreed. At the Mess she told the Tonga Wallah to wait for the Memsahib's. As we walked towards the mess she prompted.

'Sarah Plant when we walk in. Put on a brave face, smile as if nothing had happened.'

What audacity she had, once again I took heed of her words. Smiling we strode into the mess, there to be seen by a very surprised and embarrassed Jack and Bobby, who immediately came over, escorted us to a table. in a lowered voice Jack said.

'Sarah. What are you two up to?'

I just pointed at Kitty and shrugged. Just then the RSM came up, he had a quiet word with them, they stood back, he turned to us.

'Welcome ladies. This calls for the best drink on the house. For the bravest two ladies, who had been at the heart of the riot and had shown no fear.'

I thought. *"Shown no fear. Had I known I would have died with fright and certainly would not have been anywhere near that Bazaar?"* Nevertheless very relieved we stayed the half hour.

A week later news circulated that more rioting had broken out in the same Bazaar. Jack arrived home in the afternoon. It wasn't long after that a rider came and told him that he had to return immediately. Before he left he warned me.

'Sarah this new outbreak of rioting. Has nothing to do with our little problem. But Sarah please does not do any of your daft shopping sprees with Kitty. Leave it till these troubles are over. Just keep to the Bungalow and you will be all right. They won't venture into the Garrison area. Apart from any orderly officer duties and I'm sure there will be plentiful. I will be on hand.'

Having already been witness to what the riots were about, knowing that the rioters did not care for anyone, not even amongst themselves. We could all be murdered in our beds. The tribe had been listening to Jacks warning, when they were ready for bed, Mary wanted to know what it was all about, I explained.

'A riot has begun in one of the village Baazar's. That means everyone is confined to camp including us as well. Our bungalow will be closed up and secured for the night. You three will sleep in with me, Michael with number One Ayah. The rest can sleep in your bedroom and the other room. I have a revolver I will take turns with the bearer, to stand watch during the night.' I was taken aback when Mary responded.

'No Mum' I have a better idea. My Urdu is better than yours and Dad's. I have my own revolver it's under my pillow. '

'What do you mean? Your own revolver?'

'Dad gave me one for my eighth birthday. Do you remember in Khanspur when Dad used to take us down the Khuds? We just didn't collect wild flowers; Dad taught me how to shoot. Jackie and Kathleen had to reload one revolver while Kathleen held it, Jackie put the bullets in. I had to fire the shots off at a target pinned to a tree. Dad said I was quite good. Wasn't that wonderful! I did it again in Landour when he used to take us to the camp up there'…(I just stared in amazement at this new bit of information) 'Dad said if you were killed. There was to be no cowering under the beds. I had to get your revolver as well. Then get Kathleen and Jackie behind me and when I use one gun, they would reload the other and give a good account of ourselves. So you go to sleep, I shall lock up everything with the Bearer. The Bearer and I will do first sentry duty. Then you take over and I will go to bed. '

Oh my God I thought. *"This child of mine was priceless and she was probably right. The early part of night-times would not be too dangerous."*

'Mary that makes sense, now you two go to bed.' The other two looked at Mary for instructions.

'C'mon get into bed.' She got up and took them to our bedroom. Then returned dressed in jodhpurs and a jacket, as she went outside ordered me.

'Mum keep your revolver to hand.'

298

Outside I heard her talking Urdu with the Bearer. They both left the veranda soon returned with all the servants, who filed through to the rear. The bamboo slats (Chicks) were lowered all around the windows and for what it was worth. We were all locked up.

Happy that everything was locked up, I too retired fell asleep almost immediately my head hit the bolster. I woke up to a strange clicking sound. I was cold laying there trying to make out this sound but could not. Quietly I got out up and crept across the floor to the door. Number One Ayah was lying asleep by the doorway. Quietly I opened it peering around getting adjusted to the dim light of the low flickering light of the hurricane lamp on the table, I saw Mary sat in her father's seat unloading, reloading the revolver, she looked up grinned. Obviously the little devil had heard me and knew I was watching her. Stepping over number One Ayah, crept across the room to the slightly open main doorway, peeking through saw the Bearer with a blanket covering his shoulders holding a machete in his hand. He stood up silently salaamed; I nodded then went back inside. I sat down next to Mary.

'Nothing much Mum, three people came into the compound right up to the front. The Bearer and I were ready for whoever they were. Then we heard a cry I think it was fright, we heard the sound of running then silence. The Bearer said they were probably Dacoits. Probably Rajah bit one?' I whispered.

'Who's Rajah?'

'That the king cobra he's so large. Jackie calls him the Rajah he says he is the king of India.'

'All right Mary you're a very brave girl'... She looked startled but pleased... 'Now you go to bed I will stay up. You should have called me earlier.'

'All right. I don't think anything will happen now.'

Nothing did. The night passed quietly, near to dawn I dozed off. The bearer woke me with chai. Mary still in Jodhpurs came out holding her revolver. I motioned to the revolver said.

'Mary you can put that away safely now, take mine as well.'

Taking hold of it disappeared into our bedroom. Then more excitement was to happen, the Police arrived. A Sikh sergeant came in asked.

'Salaam alekum Memsahib. Have you reported the dead person lying in the roadway?'

'Valekum as salaam Sergeant. No. What has happened?' He just replied.

'Snakebite. Good Day Memsahib.' Then left. Mary next to me heard this and retorted.

'I told you mum. It was Rajah he got one.'

The body was unceremoniously removed taken away in a bullock cart. Now everyone gave us a wide berth however, the riots subsided, life quietened down again.

It was now getting closer for the great parade. Preparations were underway for a memorial stone to be dedicated at the Old Residency Fortress in honour of the fallen. After Kitty had told me about these future celebrations, I asked Jack what it was all about. He told me about the history of the Mutiny, who took part in it he suggested.

'Instead of you and Kitty gallivanting out to strange Baazar's. Visit some of the places of interest.' He still was not happy with the previous incident.

Next time Kitty visited we agreed to go to different places nevertheless, the next Sunday after Mass, Jack took us in Tonga's to visit the Residency while the Bearer decided to ride my bike rode alongside. It was blistering hot as we walked up an Incline to the ruin. I looked up at this old vast ruin, it reminded me of: *"The Big House." (its local name) back in Ireland, a burnt out building close to Rascal In the middle of Captain Adair's Estate who had been the Queen's High Sheriff. It too had vast grounds and green lawns where my*

Grandparents were employed as Estate Lodge-keepers. Walking through its vast grounds, I used to visit them as they lived in the Gatekeeper's cottage. I asked my Grandmother about the ruins to which she related its history. In 1861 during her first visit to Ireland, Queen Victoria was to stay at the Big House and my grandparents were honoured to open the gates to her Majesty. However, a few days before the Queen arrived, fires were set alight in every room to air them out, one of the fires set a room alight, rapidly the flames spread throughout until it finally burnt out leaving the house gutted. Obviously Queen Victoria remained in Dublin. Although derelict my Grandparents remained in the Lodge-Keepers cottage until they died. By the time we got near the ruin Jack informed me.

In two weeks' time on November twenty second, it will be the seventy-fourth anniversary of the ending of the Siege of Lucknow. The Garrison are holding a ceremony here to commemorate the Siege. You're all invited to attend. Regiments of the garrison including our Battery will be taking part. That old building in front is called the Residency. It is the last remains of the home of British residents and traders in Lucknow. Built about one hundred and fifty years ago Most Indian's didn't take kindly to their ever-increasing presence. In 1857. Some Sepoy's of the Bengal army decided to revolt in what is called the Indian Mutiny. Jackie interrupted.

'Dad there's nothing to see.'...Even I thought that, apart from grass lawns, flowers, its damaged watch tower with big chunks out of it possibly from cannon balls, creepers covered the walls and entrance....'Well Jackie that might appear to be the case, but around the other side are two big guns re-captured back from the mutineers. See all those holes in the walls; they were caused by cannon balls fired by the two big cannons. C'mon I will show you them.'

'What's a cannon ball?'

'It's a large metal ball loaded into the barrel of a canon with a charge of gunpowder. The gunner lights the fuse with a flaming torch and the ball is projected towards the enemy.' Mary retorted.

'There's must have been a lot of them.' Jack had caught their interest. As we walked through its main archway of a gate called Bailey Gate. I could make out different sized areas of ruins, probably rooms; in the silence it was very eerie as Jack went on.

'Yes the mutiny was quiet a battle, many people died as a result of it.' Kathleen questioned

'Why did they shoot at this place?'

'Well. Living in and around Lucknow were a lot of British families. When they found out about the mutiny, they left their homes and fled to the fort including sons of officers and soldiers from the La Martinere English school. To be protected by the regiments inside the fort, the Duke of Cornwall Light Infantry, the York and Lancaster Regiments, the Bengal Artillery Battery including the Lucknow Regiments. After the fierce battle they finally won.' He had now captured my interest.

'Okay Jack you've mention them. But how did the twenty-second become involved in the first place?'

'Well that's even a longer story. Way back in the mid seventeenth century, the original Battery was part of the Bengal Army Artillery Force known as the "Gunner and his Crew". They fought in many battles up till the time of the mutiny when the battery was part of the Oudh Field Force, under the command of Sir Henry Lawrence Chief Commissioner of Oudh? He ordered all the local British people to take refuge in this place. According to the records, a fearful fight in which he and many other soldiers and civilians were killed. The Battery was to become famous in July 1857. A VC was awarded to a gunner, another strange fact Sarah. was Sir Henry Lawrence's wife gave birth to a daughter during the actual siege. Mary asked.

'What's a V C?'

This story was becoming more interesting. The VC I knew about, but how could someone give birth in those conditions, I felt terrible just being in hospital under care. 'Jack continued....

300

'The Victoria Cross nominated by Queen Victoria for special valour and gallantly, was first awarded 1856? Mary eager to know everything asked.

'Who was it given to?'

'If I remember rightly it was Jacob Thomas a Bombardier. I will have to read up about him. Now Sarah back to your question. in 1871 the twenty-second became the 4/16th. Brigade Royal Artillery, they returned back to India about the same time as we came out here. In 1930 the Battery were awarded a new title. The twenty second (The Residency) Royal Artillery. So that's what the commemoration is all about...Jack pointed to a Cross...'That's Sir Henry Lawrence's memorial cross. The guns are around the other side.'

We walked around the hilltop, below us flowed the river Gomuti on the river banks you could see the Indians bathing and beating hell out of their clothing, furher along was the railway bridge, Jack pointed to a very Tall Clock tower.

'Sarah see that clock tower there apparently its the tallest clock tower in India.' I looked at it but noticed my tribes attention was elsewhere and boring.

'Jack, these places might be interesting to you and me, but look at them they couldn't care less. I think they will be better back at the quarters.'

'I suppose your right I thought they were interested in what I was saying, Okay lets take them to see where the ceremony is to take place and the guns. Come on you three around this corner are the two cannons. Look Jackie, there's the two Cannons.'

The three of them looked at these big guns. Jackie went up closer to see them; standing beside the wheel of the cannon his head was just about level with the axel of the wheel. Jack lifted him up carried him to the front of the gun.

'The cannon ball is loaded down this hole in the muzzle.'...Peering inside Jackie retorted.... 'Can't see anything?'

'I must say Jack, seeing the size of these cannons, adds to the atmosphere.'

'Yes, possibly fearful days during the siege. It started in May and lasted eighty-seven days. I take it you all have seen enough, let's get back to the bungalow.'

'Yes but I could murder a glass of chai.' We walked down the slope to the waiting Tonga's. Jack finished our tour with a suggestion.

'Next Sunday we'll visit the La Martinere School.'

The following Sunday after Mass we visited the school. We sat in the Tonga for about five minutes, looking at this strange building,Jack explaining what it was all about.

'Claude Martin, a Frenchman, worked for the East Indian trading company he became very wealthy and built this building as his home. When he died he left instructions his house should become a British Military school for Officer's sons in India. Mary. Last week you asked who the soldier who won the VC was. Well I looked it up he was Jacob Thomas, he dashed out of the Residency to rescue a wounded Madras Fusilier lying on the ground, he hoisted him onto his back and carried him back inside.' ...Mary enquired. 'But when did he do that?'.... 'I thought you might ask that question? All I could find out about him was it happened on September twenty-seventh.' Having seemed to satisfy Mary's curiosity, we returned back to the bungalow.

On the day of the commemoration the sun was just rising, when together with Kitty and her tribe we arrived early at the Residency at the roped off spectators seating area settling down we were close to the two big guns. In between them was the Commemoration Stone covered by the Union Jack. Within the hour the sound of the music from the Regimental bands heralded the arrival of the brigade leading the column was the Lancers on their horses, behind them marched the East Yorkshire Regiment (the Guard of Honour) - At the rear came the 3rd Kings Hussars, with the 22nd Royal Field Artillery and Indian Artillery. They all formed up to wait the arrival of the unveiling party. During this lapse of time Kitty became concerned about Marty and Kathleen; both felt unwell with a high temperature, some sort of fever? Kitty said.

'I don't like this Sarah Plant I'm going to take them home. Leave you to see the ceremony.'

Sir Malcolm Hailey

She get a chance about to leave when the dicnatories drove up in their cars, conveying. General Sir John Shear, His Excellency Sir Malcolm Hailey the Governor of the United Provinces and their wives. With much saluting and general pomp the ceremony began. His Excellency inspected the Guard of Honour, before taking his place at the Commemoration Stone. Followed by the Service of Dedication then the unveiling ceremony. A simple obelisk stone about four feet in height. The last post was sounded, two minutes silence then Reveille. The Old Residency Standard was handed over to Commanding Officer Major Haytor. Renaming the Battery by their new title "The 22nd (Residency) Royal Field Artillery Battery". With Jack barking the orders for the gun salute, each gun was discharged with a deafening roar; clouds of smoke drifting into the air, all were re-hitched to the horse teams followed by the March Past, the Dismissal of the parade and return march to barracks.

As we returned to the Tonga's, Kitty climbed up into theirs saying.

Sarah Plant. I'm taking these two back to the Bungalow I will see you later today at the garden party.'

It never happened. Jack who arrived back later with the old Union standard informed me that Kitty brats had been confined to their quarters, so they would not be able to go to any of the other forthcoming events, such was the life in India. Perfectly fit one-minute ill the next. We attended but did not stay long. The next day Jack was playing in the 22nd. Football team against the Lucknow Garrison team. In the morning my tribe were getting ready to attend the match. But trouble lay ahead. Kathleen came out dressed in a sari, which I soon removed amid showers of tears she was re-dressed properly. Mary did not like her dress so she dressed in her Jodhpurs and shirt. I ordered her.

'You're not going in that Mary, go back and change again.'

She ignored me and ran outside, following her out climbed into the Tonga sat down between a sulking Kathleen on one side and a jubilant Jackie on the other. Alongside of the Tonga the Bearer was leading Michael's donkey with him firmly astride it, at the rear, Mary had all the servants lined up like a platoon I called out.

'Mary, Go back and change into a dress now.' She just stared straight ahead. I gave up pointless talking to her. We were the first to arrive, chose a site in the shade of a huge tree. After the recent death of the young Soldier from the fever, we were ignored left on our own but very disappointed without Kitty's company. However I put a brave face taking no notice of their ignorance. However, Mary mysteriously disappeared and I began to wonder why? She was up to no good. The two teams came out to lined up on the pitch, BSM Jordan the referee blew the whistle to start the game. Every time Jack played the ball we all cheered, the first half ended goalless. After refreshments with a short interval. BSM Jordan placed the ball on the centre spot, the two teams lined up waiting for him to blow his whistle when all of a sudden he hesitated as two mounted horses galloped onto the pitch, wielding polo sticks, scattering a few of the players. Immediately I recognised the two riders, Mary with her friend Desiree Jordan, both swinging polo sticks, Mary leading with a resounding whack chuckered the ball off the centre spot. Wheeling her

302

horse away, as Desiree Jordan galloped after the ball with a sweep of her polo stick whacked it further away on the pitch. With daredevil skill the pair of them whacking the football, weaved the horses in and out of the players scattering them then hit it off the pitch as they galloped across the Mydam, the players running in hot pursuit after them, shouting their disapproval but all roaring with laughter, taking no notice, the pair of them kept on whacking the ball between them into a ditch, which they jumped over. It was so exciting watching the antics of the two riders and certainly not in the rules of football that had Jackie shouting.'Great sport.'   What a light-hearted way to start the second half. Everyone was cheering and laughing nevertheless, I noticed some disapproving faces around. Old Ma Jordan was glaring across at me, regardless of whose idea it was? Mary would definitely be in the wrong, certainly not her daughter Desiree, the pair of them was well matched. Her old man blew the whistle to abandon the match. The two teams were instructed to line up in front of the marquee, where a grinning Colonel addressed both teams over the loudspeakers.

2 Battery Teams taking part in a POLO match

Jack: Back row 3ʳᵈ from right.

'Congratulations to both teams on a great first half. Unfortunately due to the recent incident when the ball was taken out of play. I feel that would be a fair judgement to declare. The match a draw. BQMS Plant and BSM Jordan please remain standing. Remainder dismiss.'

The teams retired in more than jovial spirits to the marquee, whilst the Colonel quite audibly addressed the pair of them. Stood at attention sweating buckets both with faces of thunder.

'BSM Jordan. You were the referee in charge. Do you know the identity of the two riders?'

'No Sir.'

'BQMS Plant. Do you know who those two riders are?' Another abrupt reply.

'No Sir.'

'Well. For a moment I thought I had two riders from the Skinners Horse in my Battery. Beautiful riding don't you both agree?'

'Yes Sir.'…They chorused.

'Anyway congratulations. We shall wait and see.' Shaking their hands dismissed them, neither looking very happy. I thought. *"This one you can deal with."* On the way back we met Mary walking alone, a beaming Bearer gave her a big Salaam.

'Bahut achha bahut Missy Mary.' .

'Bahut khush Bearer.' She was very pleased, certainly not her father.

The rest of the day passed quietly, I put the tribe to bed before Jack arrived back.

'Sarah I shall speak to Mary alone please.'

He sat down in his Chair at the table inside, ordered the Bearer to fetch Mary. Meanwhile I stayed out on the veranda to listen to his lecture. He shouted,

'WHAT ON EARTH HAS GOT INTO YOU? IT WAS VERY TOTALLY WRONG OF YOU TO DISTURB A FOOTBALL MATCH AND PARTICULARLY THIS ONE, IT MEANT SO MUCH TO EVERYONE.'

Immediately I thought. *"Fatal. You've lost it. She'll beat you."* They all knew when he started to shout, he was about to roar with laughter.

303

'Ho. Dad did you see old man Jordan's face, when he recognised Desiree he nearly swallowed his whistle.' Jack roared with laughter.

'Mary you have no right to say that.'

'Dad he was blue in the face.'   Had both of them laughing aloud. That was not good I marched in to stop this frivolity.

'Mary goes to your room. You will not ride in the Gymkhana tomorrow.'

'Oh Mum.'

'You heard what I said. Go to bed.' She looked at her father, he looked at me.

'Sarah?'

'No Jack. Don't interfere. She does not ride to-morrow. I have had enough of her shenanigans this week to last me a lifetime.' She went to bed in a fury,

'Sarah. I've hired a pony and entered her for the race.'

'Jack. Don't interfere. She will not ride that's final.' We hardly spoke all evening.

Next morning Jack was up leaving early, as well as organising the Alarm Stakes he was riding in the horse race. I had them dressed in their best except Mary, wearing Jodhpurs and a shirt. I wasn't having any nonsense today I ordered her.

'Mary gets those off and put a dress on.'

She completely ignored me; throwing her head back in a sign of defiance went outside. The Bearer had the Tonga waiting. We set off to the racecourse to join the cavalcade of Tonga's heading that way. Followed other families into the reception area, after curt nods from one or two people, we moved over to the side of the racecourse to sit under a large Beepol tree. On the far side of the mydam were a row of tents where the teams were preparing with the Gun Carriages lined up, the horses tethered ready for the Alarm Stakes later. An event I had not seen before however, Kitty had explained what it was about. A contest between two gun teams, driving at speed dangerously close together, requiring expert handling of the team of horses, any veering horse might cause serious consequence. The start of the race had both teams in their tents feigning sleep. When a Bugler sounded the alarm. The gunners had to dress, harness up seven horses to the limber and field gun, race to a designated point, uncouple the horses load and fire off one round, reload. The first team to complete the action was declared the winner.

Having settled down, decided to take a walk around with my tribe. The Bearer walked behind with Michael sat on his donkey. I spotted Desiree Jordan nodding at Mary, she glowering shook her head. I just knew how much she wanted to ride, I thought. *"Just ask me."* But not a defiant Mary. We returned to the shade of the tree. Opposite us under the shade of another tree, were two Ponies, with their Syce's sat on a Persian carpet. The reins of the ponies were draped over one shoulder, gripped tight in the right hand, on the carpet beside them, were two polished saddles. They were in charge of the Colonels two Polo ponies. Nothing could have looked more perfect; the ponies sleek in perfect shape, something we admired but not Kathleen, her attention was concentrated on the Syce's. Totally entranced by their outfit of the regimental colours, sky blue turbans with a fringe of gold coins draped above their eyes, wearing little red jackets tight white-legged cotton Jodhpurs, with green and golden sandals curled up at the toes on their feet. Kathleen lost in admiration exclaimed.

'Mum aren't they beautiful?'

Just then echoing through a megaphone the M/C shouts... 'Please clear the course for the racing to begin. The first horse race is for the youngest age group. Come on all of you. We have to clear the course. Please.'

Looking around to see my tribe were out of the way saw Mary with her arms draped around the other two's shoulders, whispering earnestly. I called out.

'Mary come on out of the way.'

The race began; there was plenty of cheering and urging on by the parents for their young riders. The next race was Desiree's Jordan's age group, which Mary would have been in. I noticed Mary, appeared to show no interest whatsoever. So be it. Jackie cried out.

'Mum. Michael's being sick.' I immediately turned went over to where Michael was sat on his donkey. There was no sick, he looked perfectly all right, just a big grin on his face his answer to everything. The Bearer gesticulated to me; he would have to get another softer saddle for Michael BaBa. I thought. *"Why? There's nothing wrong with that one."* Whilst I was distracted by the Bearer. The M/C was shouting a final announcement for the line-up of Desiree's race. I turned to see my tribe had gone, they were on the opposite side of the course, stood in front of the little Indian Syce's. I called out to them.

'Stay where you are. The race is about to start.'

The Bearer came alongside me leading Michaels donkey, pointing towards it. Muttering something? Trouble was afoot, but what? Keeping my gaze firmly on my three, the Bearer kept on muttering, distracting my attention. There was nothing I could do? as I watched my tribe on the opposite side, Jackie sat down cross-legged in front of the Syce, Kathleen knelt down in front talking to both of them. One of them glanced up, shyly abashed looked down. Kathleen took hold of the reins out of his hand, enraptured by Kathleen's looks the Syce bowed deeply, the reins were passed onto Mary who quietly led the pony away lifted the rope led it onto the course. I thought. *"Oh my God, what is she up to now?"* About to call her, the sound of the starting pistol cracked. Mary leapt up onto the back of the pony raced off up the course after the field. I heard the noise of the crowd on the course as a surprise entrant raced past them. I thought: *Oh my God what's going to happen next?* Both Syce's jumping up began to wailing. Taking hold of the donkey's reins I ordered. 'Bearer. Jahldi Jana Jana, madid Syce's macro-ed.' Kathleen and Jackie had run across the course, appeared in front of me very guilty stood with hands behind their backs. I shouted.

'BY GOD YOU THREE PLANNED THIS LATEST ESCAPADE, DIDN'T YOU? DON'T YOU DARE MOVE FROM THAT SPOT EITHER OF YOU? WHAT HAVE YOU DONE?' Both chorused.

'Nothing Mum.'

By this time the riders were half way round the course, the Bearer was still on the other side talking to the Syce's minus one pony. As the riders came galloping around the course, in front neck and neck raced Desiree and Mary. I found myself yelling, 'C'mon Mary.' As they galloped past Mary tight alongside Desiree, just edging forward, they galloped towards the finishing line to win. The Bearer crossed over and took charge of Michael, Jackie and Kathleen ran onto the course towards the winning post, then I too ran to see Mary and Desiree rein in jump off their ponies. Hug each other shouting their pleasure. Jackie and Kathleen were cheering with them. Everyone was laughing and cheering. Mary and Desiree were stood in front of the Colonel. Everyone heard him say.

'Congratulations to the pair of you, wonderful racing.' I was so proud of her. He was almost drowned out by the voice of the M/C Bellowing out.

'Would BQMS Plant and BSM Jordan come forward?'

I thought to myself. *"This event I must see."* The Colonel had his hands placed on Mary and Desiree shoulders all were laughing as Jack and BSM Jordan came up to stand in front of them. Both boiling with rage as the Colonel addressed them.

'So these two are my mysterious skinners riders? Now Mary and Desiree it appears that both your father's don't seem to know you? Mary Plant you won but I'm afraid. I have to disqualify you for riding bareback. Desiree Jordan will receive the cup. Mary Plant. James my son is riding in the next race. If he rides as well as you did. I shall be more than proud and with my full permission. Every day I will have him ride over to your bungalow with my other Pony, for you to use. In addition to that I will get the polo team to teach both of you how to chukka properly, instead of with a football. Though I'm sure you both can probably show them how to do that. Now Mary Desiree stand to attention.' With huge grins all over their cheeky faces... 'Dismiss. Come up and sit alongside of me.'

Everybody clapped as the Colonel led them onto the dais sat them alongside his wife and son. We returned back to our places under the shade of the tree to watch the other events, Annoyed at the problem she had caused but really proud of her. the Colonels son win his race. Later I saw the three of them riding ponies together. I tried to catch Mary's eye, but she wasn't having any of that. She was in her element having a wonderful day at the races. Jack's race was about to start and had been nominated as favourite for two full circuits. Mary arrived back grinning, the other two joined their champion, all she said was.

'Mum.' I took her hand and kissed her, shaking my head.

'Mary I don't agree with what you have just done. It was a wonderful race. Congratulations we are proud of you.' The Bearer salaamed to Mary.

'Missy Mary, Noa Baba.' The Bearer was pleased and proud bestowing his ultimate accolade, which a delighted Mary accepted, deeply salaamed back. A pistol shot started the race. The shouting and urging on was something else as the riders thundered past, with Jack last. Puzzled I exclaimed.

'What's up with your father Mary?'

'Mum, he's playing fox.' As they raced up to us on the second circuit, Jack on the outside. Mary screamed out.

'NOW DAD. NOW GALLOP.' We were all yelling our heads off. Win he did. Kathleen and Jackie, demanding to go Mary shouted.

'NO. STAY WHERE YOU ARE. THIS IS DAD'S TIME,'

I nodded in approval. Jack walked back to us, carrying his trophy grinning like a Cheshire cat, handing it to Mary, tussled her hair and said.

'You rode a wonderful race. Don't ever do that again. Do you understand? The Colonel was right about skinners horsemen!'...Gone was his embarrassment...'Done well as a family Eh Sarah?' Jackie enquired.

'What's a skinners horse Dad?'

'Oh those. Many years ago there was a British army officer named Colonel James Skinner, he formed an Indian cavalry regiment and dressed them in yellow uniforms. Known as "Skinners Horse" and nick-named the "Yellow Boy's" They were brilliant riders. Maybe Sarah we will have to sign her up in that Regiment.' Even at the thought he roared with laughter He left us to return to the Battery lines for the forthcoming Alarm Stakes.

Over the megaphone The M/C announced the finale was about to start. That brought utter silence among the spectators. As the tension mounted, all eyes focussed on the far side of the racecourse where the two tents were. Charging across the mydam came a lone horseman, blowing his bugle announced the alarm. Immediately the gunners emerged from the tents still buttoning up tunics, as they ran to the horses. A lot of shouting could be heard as the gunners coupled up the gun and limber. The spectators enjoying the spectacle began shouting words of encouragement, as both teams raced away abreast of each other. The most dangerous part of the race. Mary shrieked.

'Mum something is wrong. A rider is climbing onto the back of another horse'....she loudly shouted... 'BE CAREFUL'...I sensed the concern of other spectators as Mary screamed...'MUM HE'S FALLEN' I watched as the second and the third horse reared up followed by the limber and gun. I closed my eyes and yelled...'OH MY GOD PLEASE HELP HIM.'...Both teams pulled up, some gunners had already jumped off running back to a crumpled figure lying on the ground. I recognised Jack galloping across the course to the scene of disaster, then spectators began running to the scene. This was no place for them or us. In the background echoing across the mydam came the wails and screams of spectators. I ordered.

'Mary don't move. Bearer. Michael's ghora jahldi. You three come on we are going.'

I led the way, followed in crocodile file by my tribe. I decided to walk home it would help to ease the shock. Putting up my parasol I began to recite the Rosary. My tribe responded, even the bearer muttered. 'Ai.' Though they were relentless warrior's needless tragedy affected them badly. We must have looked a strange procession walking like this loudly praying. At the Bungalow the Bearer left us, after a short while the wailing started. Little was said no one wanted to eat. Mary helped me with Kathleen and Jackie, before she herself sat with me on the veranda, full of our own private horror, later I sent her to bed She whispered.

'Good night Mum. God bless that poor man.'

I had to do something or I would go mad. I thought of a solution. *"Black armbands."* I got out my sewing box, a pair of Jack's black dress trousers, cutting off strips of the legs. All I could think about was this poor Soldiers life destroyed. It was very late when I finished the armbands for all the household. Then I went to bed lay unable to sleep. Jack arrived back crept into the bedroom, he whispered.

'Sorry. Sarah I've had many things to arrange.'

I got up helped him get his boots off, undressed he lay on the bed very upset, quietly talking to me.

'That young Gunner was the replacement for the other gunner who had just died of fever. The buckle of the lead horse had come loose, without giving it a thought he clambered over the two horses, then fell, trampled by the horses was cut in two by the wheels of the gun.'

We both quietly sobbed until he managed to say....'Thank you Sarah for taken them away. It was no fit place to see that horror. But some stupid women just stood there, their children screaming and crying, some fainted, had to be attended to by the soldiers, stopping them from doing their rightful job.'...We lay there wrapped in our own thoughts for hours until Jack got up....'Sarah I had better gets moving there's a full Military Funeral this morning.'

It was pointless for me lying there thinking, whilst he did his ablutions I got his Number one's out, when he was ready helped him check everything was right. Medals in the correct place, I slipped the mourning band onto his arm. He looked quizzically at it and said.

'Good thinking Sarah'...he kissed me...'I'll order Tonga's to pick you up later Okay.'

We walked out onto the veranda. The Bearer, with a Chico holding a hurricane lamp stood near the top of the steps, he salaamed murmured a few sad words? Below the Syce stood waiting with Jack's horse. Jack going down the steps mounted his horse cantered off. It was going to be a traumatic day. The Dhobie Wallah came up the steps carrying a bowl and cloth for me to wash. The Ayahs appeared they were sobbing quietly, having had a quick wash, between us we got my tribe bathd dressed in their best, even Mary wore a dress. Then I dressed for the sad occasion handed out armbands. Two Tonga's arrived, it was time to go to the Military cemetery. We stopped outside the gates; it appeared that everyone on earth was lined up there? Possibly nobody knew this young gunner but the Army is one huge family I ushered my tribe to a suitable place near the burial site. Arriving on a gun carriage his coffin draped with the Union Jack. The burial party carried the coffin to the graveside. After a short service his body was lowered into the grave. A volley of rifle fire then four Badgie's blew the last post. The saddest most heart rending sound in the world. The burial party marched slowly away. A fitting gesture by the Padre and Colonel was to meet all the Batteries families. There wasn't that many to file past them along with their Bearers. For obvious reasons I was last to file past. I shook the Padre and the Colonel's hands, spoke of my condolences, then Mary spoke.

'Colonel. May I please speak to you sir.' I was taken aback by her remark.

'Yes Mary. What is it?' She blurted out.

307

'Thank you for giving me the privilege of using one of your ponies to ride along with James and Desiree Jordan. But I cannot ride over where this young Soldier has just died.'

The Colonel stepped forward placed his hands on her shoulders, bent down and kissed her cheek.

'Mary Plant. That is a very kind and considerate thought. You are right I thank you on behalf of all the Battery. Now would you please introduce me to the rest of the family?' Mary walked beside him with the Padre and me behind.....

'My Sister Kathleen...The Colonel shook her hand...A very beautiful child the pride of the Regiment.' Kathleen gave him her best blue eyes look and beamed as she took his hand...'My brother Jackie'... He knelt down and shook his hand...'Ah Jackie another brave soldier of mine just like your Father. I hear you swab your own throat now. Wonderfully. Brave young man. Keep it up.' She took Michael from the Bearer... 'And this is Michael the baby colonel.' ...'Well we will have to enrol him as a Badgie won't we?' Mary laughed...'The Bearer Colonel.' The Bearer saluted bowed salaamed, then she introduced the Ayah's, the Khansama, the servants all saluting and salaaming to the Colonel, proud to be introduced to the Burrah Sahib, the Colonel turned to me saluted.

'Thank you Mrs Plant. For being the most loyal family, but a request. May I invite you Mary and all the children, to take chai with my family next Sunday after service. I shall arrange Tonga's for you all.' Thanking him I accepted his invitation, however I thought: *This was a most pleasant thought but it was not due to me but Mary she alone had won the Colonels favour, this girl of ours who we could not control her wild ways.*

As we walked away, out of the corner of my eye. I spotted Ole' Ma Jordan standing there with Desiree and Patricia her other daughter. She had been watching all that went on. In my triumph unfurled my parasol, deftly thrust it open in her direction. As good as a slap in the face for her, a very hollow victory, but I was still smarting from the contagious stigma placed upon the family all because of Jackie. She above all forbade Desiree, to have anything to do with Mary nevertheless, Desiree was just as stubborn. I ordered.

'C'mon Mary quick march.'

We smartly left the churchyard got onto our Tonga's and rode away. I thanked Mary for refusing the Colonels present. This girl of mine never ceased to surprise me.

A pall had settled over the Regiment. All further festivities were cancelled. Nevertheless the following Sunday after service. Tonga's arrived for us to be taken to the Colonels Bungalow. When we arrived the Colonel, together with his wife and son James came out to greet us. We were ushered to a table on the veranda to take chai and later spent a very enjoyable hour. Out on the lawn the Bearer's and Ayahs of both households sat talking, The episode, of my household being invited to the Colonel's, changed our standing amongst other families. When the Colonels servants paid us a visit it was like a Royal Occasion, they were greeted in the roadway with great salaams, the two Bearers, led all the Ayahs onto the veranda. I questioned Mary.

'Mary. What is going on? '

'Mum great occasion the colonels servants are visiting, quickly into the bedroom.'

'But this is our bungalow?' Mary took my hand and I was guided with the rest of my tribe into the bedroom to sit on the bed.

'Mary.' she shushed me saying.

'Mum they are all having a wonderful time, don't spoil it.'

So we had to sit and listen to the goings on and revelry outside. As was their right only the Bearers and Ayahs were allowed into the Bungalow. So that's why the place had been so assiduously waxed and polished by the Chico's.

They sat down formed circle trays of delicacies and chai were served by the Chico's. Then they started to entertain each other. As we watched the entertainers I thought: *How strange I had created work for myself and entertainment for them and here we were being their audience. What a strange place we lived in?* The Ayahs relating the amazing "Story of the black armbands." worn by everybody in respect for the poor dead soldier number One Ayer indicating to her arm and eyes waving of arms, it was all their entertainment about The Burrah Memsahib Plant, working by candlelight had stitched and sewed all night long. They had begged and pleaded with her stop before she went blind? But not this Burrah Memsahib no one could stop her. Great gasps and sighs were uttered. (Mary understanding their conversation, whispered to me all that was going on) I had to stifle a laugh at the story related. One thing I was sure of I could not imagine, Ole' Ma Jordan going blind sewing, even for her own brats? Their visit over, the Ayahs went out into the roadway salaamed waved their goodbyes. Indeed a great honour was bestowed upon the household; this visit of respect was to be repeated by other households. On those occasions to leave them in peace, we visited the Burn's who had by that time out of quarantine. Kitty and I had much to gup about.

The recent death had the strangest effect for some families to visit the Plants. Those that did always would advise their intention to visit. Each time dressed in a different coloured turban and cummerbund the Bearer presented them to me, which must have set their teeth on edge. I rose to receive them, but was cold, deliberately sat Jackie in front of me. Small talk was made, chai was served, I gave no ground hard eyes for everyone. My Ayahs, dressed in beautiful flowing Saris, no old Dung coloured ones for mine, with Kathleen flitting about in her sari raised eyebrows that did not go down well. I could sense that all visitors would have much to relate to each other, once they got back home. Needless to say no one visited twice, however, I had made my point, and my household were the greatest in the land! Kitty who had been there on a couple of occasions noticed my coldness but politeness to the visitor. She made comments after that had m laughing,

'Sarah Plant you're the cats whiskers whenever these women visit. You put on a show of politeness, but underneath your cold as an block of ice. How do you get away with it? If I was in your shoes I would not give them the time of the day. Oh By the way don't forget the Battery will soon be returning to Blighty.'

'Yes. Kitty you keep on saying that but when?

'I don't know? It was banded about. I do know it will happen sooner than later. '

That left me with wondering if it was soon that would mean returning to the cold winter of Blighty. Warm clothing we did not process, there was nothing here in Lucknow for the cold only things to keep you cool. I decided to ask Jack if there was any chance of getting some warm clothing sent out by Mother.

'Well Sarah it's not official but it would be far too late, we would never receive them in time. The best place you can buy that type of warm clothing is up in Mussoorie. Why don't you and the children take some of the servants on a trip up there for a week or so? I can arrange for the same Bungalow. I'll sleep in camp, the Dhobi Wallah and others can remain behind. It would be nice for you to return once more before leaving India.'

Without hesitation I agreed. Within that week Jack got permission for me to leave in two days time. I told Kitty and the reason why.

'Christ Sarah Plant. You think of everything. It never entered my head. While you're there, my tribe are the same size as yours. You must buy two of everything, much cheaper.'

'Kitty. How on earth will I get some things for your tribe?'

'Look here Sarah Plant. I have just told you you'll see. Stand my tribe up against yours. She shouted an order.

'YOU LOT C'MON UP HERE, ALL OF YOU. JACK AND MARY, STAND BACK TO BACK'...Mary shouted.

'GIRLS ARE ALWAYS THE FIRST.' Jack retorted.

'No their not.' A swipe by Kitty missed as she shouted.

'SHUT UP. I'LL THRASH THE PAIR OF YOU. JUST DO AS I SAY.'

Back to back they matched each other in height.

'There you are Sarah Plant. See what I mean?' Mary demanded.

'What's this all about Kitty Burn's?'

'Nothing to do with you, it's between me and your Mother. There you are Sarah Plant, Mary's always dressed in Jodhpurs. Try her with boy's clothes and Kathleen for Andy.' Kathleen retorted.,

'I'm a girl' I'm not putting boy's clothes on.' Pushing Andy, the next thing they are all shoving and pushing, falling into a heap onto the veranda floor. Quickly we separated them.

'Right Sarah Plant. Now we have that all settled. I'll remove my brats from your hair and bid you a nice journey in the morning, I'll see you when you get back from your gallivanting up in the Hills then pay my dues.'.

22nd. (The Residency) Field Artillery Battery Football Team Lucknow 1931

Dvr. Moore- Grn. Lockett – Sig. Skelding.
L/Bdr. Winstanley- Farr. Slade.- Sig. Cowgill
Grn. Southern – Bdr. Lambert –Sgt. Leask – B.Q.M.S Plant B.S.M. Jordan. Grn. Sutcliffe – Sig. Williams.

CHAPTER NINE
FAREWELL INDIA.

With the trip arrange after two days we left. Strange as it seems, I was prepared to travel alone on the train to Dehra Dun, an uneventful journey. However, the Bearer was the guardian and smoothed all paths. At Dehra Dun we stayed overnight in the rest house. Low and behold a new flushing toilet a chain to be pulled until there was no water left in the Hostel. It was time for bed. At the crack of dawn all were up ready for the first stage up to Rajpur. The QM in Charge settled us in Tonga's along with other families from different places, which were far fewer than the last time. Just after sunrise we set off. The black clouds covering the hills above showed signs of rain. The journey to Rajpur ended near midday, lunch was served We transferred to the Jhampanies. It was great fun. I loved it as much as my tribe. Their shrieks as monkeys, swung about in the overhead trees or shouts of delight if a beautifully coloured bird flew across our path, even a snake that Jackie had seen. But this time it was considerably colder, drifting overhead the dark clouds bore rain, out came the black umbrellas. Higher up we encountered the clouds and a heavy chilling mist causing everyone to shiver. Finally out onto the Mall the cavalcade entered Mussoorie. Through the swirling mist, a rickshaw trundled past its passenger's two Indian ladies in white saris, they unaware of the mist, obviously acclimatised to such occasions. We came to a halt and out of the mist a voice boomed out.

'Attention everybody there will be one hours rest, with chai available on the veranda. I will be around to see all families. Thank you.'

We were at the Savoy so knew the drill. First toilets then refreshments before we left for Landour. With those necessaries taken care of on to the veranda for chai, a rare treat cups, saucers and biscuits. We were paid a visit from the "Voice" It was QM Quiggle.

'Aah. Mrs Plant. Returned for another stay. How's Jack. Still playing football?'

'Hello Mr Quiggle nice to see you again. Yes he's still playing football.' But the last match was a bit of a disaster.'

'Oh why was that? Not injured or anything?'

'No far from it. Just Mary's antics.' I related the story he roared with laughter.

'Well done Mary. That stopped your father playing.' ...Mary grinned...'Mrs Plant you're in the same bungalow in Landour. They are leaving soon, so I'll say cheerio, I will see you up there sometime. This weather has been like it for a couple of days but it will soon blow over.' He left on his rounds.

Our final part of our trek along the Mall up to Landour, was through mist. I decided to make a stop at the Kulri Bazaar for the Khansama to get in some provisions. After that we had only gone half way further up, when a shower of hailstones thundered down, umbrellas were quickly opened up as the large hailstones bounced off of the cart road. The noise on the umbrellas was like one continuous dull thud reverberating down the handle. Within minutes it stopped, the cart road was covered in white hailstones; the poor coolies just struggled on up to the bungalow. In the mist the shape of the Church appeared ghostly, beyond you couldn't see the bungalow but the barking of Sue had my tribe shouting. 'Sue.' She appeared running through the mist barking her head off her tail wagging in greeting to the children, as she tried to get into the Jhampanies with them they made a fuss of her. The coolies finally made it placed the Jhampanies down. The Chowkidar appeared, his blanket draped around his shoulders, with a smile on his face recognised us salaamed. We clambered out and followed him into the bungalow.

'Mum holiday home.' They all yelled as they ran from room to room followed by Sue who obviously was delighted with the company. I spoke with the Bearer to arrange transport for tomorrow morning for a trip down to Mussoorie. The Bearer talked with the Chowkidar whilst the Ayahs busied themselves sorting out the room, The Bearer advised.

'Memsahib. Coolie Wallah Michel baba Kal (tomorrow) Jhampanies Du Gora's all Okay, Sue. Holy Sahib's.' Apparently Father O'Hare had taken over looking after Sue.

Lamps were lit, with the night temperatures dropping; fires had to be lit to warm the bungalow up. The Khansama saw to that, going out with the Chico's to collect more wood; having done that prepared a meal for all of us. I had brought little clothing with us hoping to purchase all new warm garments here in Mussoorie. During the night to keep us all warm, I made the children put their pyjamas on over the clothes they had come up in. Tomorrow was a new day and change of clothing. We settled down to sleep, the sleep of exhaustion.

Next morning although there were plenty of clouds about, the sun was trying to break through. After breakfast, with the children playing outside with Sue, I was busy with the Ayahs sorting out the luggage. Then our transport arrived, two horses, one each for Mary and me, two Donkeys for Kathleen and Jackie, the Coolie Wallah for Michael and two Jhampanies for the Ayahs. I decided to leave the rest of the unpacking until we got back from our trip down to the Bazaar. We set off riding quietly down the bridle paths into the Kulri Bazaar for purchases, requesting warm clothing. The Babu shook his head.

'Noa.' In broken English directed me to the Library Bazaar in Mussoorie, where his bhai (brother) was a very fine tailor, he make warm clothing for Mussoorie school children. But I had noticed hanging up on the wall behind him, two full-length black curtains, each with one large Ibis waxed onto the cloth; their outline was embroidered and stitched with heavy golden and beautiful coloured threads, as were the reeds adorning the rest of the curtain. I felt them they were heavy. I had to buy them. I asked.

'Ki kya kitmat hai?' (How much cost).

'Memsahib. Panchchis rupees.'...I thought. *Panchchis! 25. I will do a Kitty Burns on him.* 'Ji nai bahut zydda hai. Das Rupees' (No. Cost too much ten rupees) A lot of bartering ensued before a price was agreed. At 8 rupees. I was rather pleased with myself. The Bearer did his duty paid, made arrangements for the delivery. We left for the Library Bazaar back down to the Mall to the bandstand area, as our party came to a halt the Bearer indicated to a store.

'Memsahib. Iwahd (there) Kapon ki dukan (clothes shop) Wallah. He went into this store, we dismounted and I turned to my tribe.

'Right when we go into the store. I don't want any nonsense from anyone.'

We entered, greeted by the owner. A dapper grey haired Indian in smart attire, tape measure around his neck in perfect English asked.

'Yes Memsahib. What can I do for you?'

'Some warm clothes for the children.'

'Certainly Memsahib. Please sit down'... clapped his hands...'Chai Jahldi Jahldi'. A small boy appeared with glasses of chai. 'Memsahib. What would you like? I mostly have grey cloth'...he indicated the array of cloth and clothes neatly stacked around his store...'Which one of your children is it for?'...fanning his arm in an arc, his English took me aback, this was going to be easy I answered.

'All of them?'

'Yes Memsahib. Shall we start with this one?' He assumed Mary was the first one to be fitted. No messing about here she went forward speaking.

'Babu. Jodhpurs monta hai.'

'Mary stop that this moment. I shall deal with you first, then you can go with the Syce to ride up and down the Mall for half an hour. Now to business Babu. I want some warm clothes for England with a coat to match. Chha (six) pairs of warm knickers, pants, vests and socks, also chha (six) pairs of heavy shoes and coats.'

312

The Babu having finished scrawling this down, turned to Mary with outstretched hand murmured....'This young lady first Memsahib?'...

'Ji han achha' He busied himself sorting out suitable dresses to show her she liked none (I chose one) let her try it on, followed by a heavy coat and shoes. Then I said.

'Short trousers, a blazer.' His eyebrows rose at this request.

'Trousers and blazer Memsahib?'

'Ji han Babu.' He fitted her out -they were put to one side.

'Now off you go Mary. We will meet you at the Band Stand when all this is over. Kathleen now you.' The Babu enquired.

'Memsahib just the dress.' Kathleen answered.

'Ji han only sari.' I intervened.

'No Babu everything same.' I indicated to the pile of Mary's clothes a similar dress was produced certainly not Kathleen's style. We tried a few until she was pleased, coat then shoes.

'Babu trousers and blazers also.' He again looked quizzically at me carried on all matching.

'Babu in that size. I require do (two) sets for girls and ek (one) set for a boy.' Jackie was easily dealt with. The Babu was now agitated at my choice and shaking his head.

'Memsahib which school will the children be attending in Mussoorie?'

'Babu they are not attending any school at the moment.' The Babu stood there arms outstretched waggling his hands.

'Memsahib I do not understand?'

'We are going home to England. The other clothing is for children in Lucknow.'

'Achha . Now I understand'...A big beam creased his face all settled...'Memsahib material for coats I require more, will be ready to collect in two weeks time, is Okay?'

'Ji han. Achha do hafta. Babu 'Ki kya kitmat hai?' He shrugged his shoulders scratched his head. I said.

'Babu work out a price. I shall be back to check tin haji. (3'o'clock) and agree.' We left to meet Mary at the Bandstand.

The sun was then out so, I moved them all across to the bandstand where the Coolie Wallah was sat on his haunches, in his wicker basket Michael was fast asleep, the Ayah's still remained seated in the Jhampanies. My horse and two Donkeys were there but neither Mary nor the Syce. Jackie and Kathleen started to run onto the Bandstand I sat down. Above the sky was blue with woolly white clouds dotted about, in the distance the black clouds were rolling away across the mountain range, the storm of yesterday had passed. There were many more people moving about. I was concerned about Mary, she wasn't there as ordered. Seeking her out amongst the increasing number of horse riders could not see her, a couple of rickshaws trundled past. I waited awhile wondering what I should do? Then in the distance she came cantering up with the grinning delighted Syce astride the back of the horse. Jumping down came to sit next to me.

'I've been up to Gun Hill and back wonderful view. Mum you must go up there before we go back to the Bungalow. It's wonderful!' The Bearer enquired gestured to the Chai house opposite.

'Memsahib. Chai ut Baba's pani?'

'Achha Bearer. C'mon let's all have a drink.'

After our refreshment it was nearly three as we headed back to the Babu's who greeted us with a big beaming smile clapping his hands.

'Chai Memsahib?'

'No Babu we must be off. The price please?'

'For all. Twenty rupees memsahib.'

'No. Too much eight rupees

'Memsahib too little twelve rupees

'Still too much eight rupees. No More.'

'Memsahib. Eight rupees no more?' The Babu looked downcast nodded his head.

'Achha Memsahib.

'Bearer pay Babu.' Now the purpose for our coming to Mussoorie had been dealt with. We could enjoy the stay. Mary persistent as ever.

'Mum can we go up to Gun Hill now?'

We left a defeated Babu. I was pleased about the price and sure Kitty could not have done better. Outside the sun was warm; we had nothing else to do.

'Right we shall go.' Shouts of glee from all of them. Mary already astride her horse was raring to go. I mounted my horse and ordered.

'Bearer. Gun hill jalhdi.'

Our small party set off, making our way up the Mall, up Gun Hill. Mary was right it was a wonderful sight the hills, changing colour in the sunlight, green, browns, blues and purples, eventually dull white, where snow covered peaks lay in the shadow from the black clouds. How I wished Jack were up here now, filled with nostalgia I thought. *"C'mon it's time to go."*

Back at the bungalow, I sat with Sue laid at my feet. I was pleased with the outcome of the day's venture and purchase. Outside my tribe were riding around on their mounts, the vigilant Bearer stood watching them. In the background the quiet chatter of the Ayah's and the lilting voice of the Khansama as he sang whilst preparing lunch, everyone was happy. I reflected upon my previous stays in Khanspur, after the tribe had been put to bed, I used to sit in front of a roaring fire with the Bearer outside sat on the veranda steps, a blanket wrapped around him with a machete on his lap, he quietly dozing, alert at the slightest sound. Now the outside noises never gave me palpitations and understood why the English chose to have settlements in the hills. They were a reminder of home, a more relaxed atmosphere with fires to sit in front of at night and contemplate one's life. India is a hard relentless pitiless country, but it had much more to offer than that. Its vastness, a superior greatness that grabs at your soul that can strangle you, except me. Unfortunately too late, then I had not recognised I was the loser. As I sat there for the first time I realised I was at peace with myself. How could I have missed all this before? No one to put the fear of God up me with wild tales, moreover with the unknown they were just as frightened themselves as for me I fell for it, hook line and sinker. I must have been a trial to Jack.

On Sunday the Priest arrived to his waiting congregation. Father O' Hare was delighted to see us back. Afterwards we took chai in the Char Dukan to gup pass the time of day, so began our last trip up to Landour, exactly as we had done before a peaceful way of life, a fitting one before we left for Blighty. One good thing Mary and I were at peace, probably because she was on a horse, not a cross word from morning to night. With no school to attend, we spent most days out riding sedately along chatting; sometimes she would race ahead, particularly if the abyss below was at its most precipitous, wheel around and race back. Exhilarated shouting.

'OH MUM WASN'T THAT LOVELY?'

In the Bazaar's alongside the Bearer he with glaring eyes, she shouted everybody down as she bargained with the Wallahs. All gave in, she would roar with laughter after each purchase.

'Pukka Bearer. Pukka

'Achchha Teek hai Missy Mary.' Was all he ever said but I noticed he watched over her like a hawk, her wild escapades especially when on a horse. Saying nothing, even during my previous thrashings, yelling and shouting, he stood impassive, probably to him children had to be corrected this way. But if she did attempt something that was dangerous, he would say loudly to her.

'Bahut Kharab Missy Mary. Bahut Kharab. ' (Very bad)

314

That and only that would make her stop. However on the trip down to Babu's to collect the clothing. I took the advantage to ride a Rickshaw with my tribe, it was not far. Leaving the horses and Jhampanies at the Bandstand we climbed up into the Rickshaw with Michael sat on my lap and my tribe around me. The Rickshaw Wallahs took up as far as the Himalaya hotel and back. A strange sensation as its big wheels trundled along the Mall but we had done it and it was good. We mounted our own mode of transport horses, donkeys, wicker baskets and Jhampanies to head back to our bungalow.

Sadly this was the end of my Indian summer, before we left I arranged a party on the veranda for the children and the servants. I left Mary in charge to boss them all. I wanted to be away for a few hours on my own. I needed no distractions from Mary, just to ride over the hills, I wanted to embrace and fix in my mind every tree leaf and flower, all the scents and smells of the Hills of India. This was the India for me; no one was to share it. I had to imprint on my being and never forget. Years later I would sit in front of a fire and recall every moment of this ride. It was to be the greatest solace I could gather strength from. Even from the worst happenings in the family, just to sit and be back in India. With a heavy heart I went out riding, the Bearer forever at my side as we made our way downward through the leafy tracks splattered with the rays of sunshine I had to go to Gun Hill. All of a sudden the Bearer said,

'Memsahib.' Pointed. Stopping just in time. I caught a glimpse of a bird falling in a shallow dive, its split tail fanned as it alighted in a tree below us in the Khuds, a flock of crows mobbing it as they landed in the branches above it, cawing madly down at the bird. Without opening its wings it fell in a diagonal steep swoop downwards, from tree to tree followed by the crows all the way down through the Khuds. The strangest and most thrilling sight. So here at last was "Jackie's mystic Bird" the one with two tails, which doesn't fly. His tale that was treated with roars of laughter from all of us. I don't know whether he was more alert or aware than the others, but he always saw everything first and brought the others attention to it. I am glad and pleased I was witness to this sighting, the Bearer beamed murmured. 'Jackie Baba's piridah.' For the last time I rode on up to Gun Hill just to savour the expanse of the Himalayas, a wonderful sight, moving in my saddle saw below me Mussoorie, farther down in the valley a speck in the  distance was Dehra Dun, unfortunately almost obscured by mist. I sat there my mind pictured Jack on his white charger coming up the path. This man of mine who I loved so dearly, who had brought me out to this place with its entire mystique that only India can provide, which now I had to leave. I sat there tight-lipped listening to the sounds of the birds the chattering of distant monkeys. I could not contain my emotions any longer, with tears streaming down my cheeks uncontrolled I sobbed. The Bearer, forever our guardian understood murmured. 'Achha Memsahib Achha.'Slowly we returned back to the bungalow, as we approached the Church. The sound of the Sue barking mixed with the lilting singing their methodical clapping to a rhythmic of the Ayah's beat, drifted down towards us. Reigning in found no trouble from anyone, everyone had enjoyed this last treat all were happy. I was about to witness without Jack the setting sun in the Mussoorie Hills. The following day we would be packing up for the return journey back to Lucknow, a very sad time for all of us, as we knew this would be the very last time we would be here. Two days later we departed Landour, all were surprisingly quiet on the trip down to Dehra Dun, including the train journey to Lucknow. Probably they in their own way were also feeling venerable. Jack and Kitty were at the station to meet us with transport to take us back home. It was back to the usual routine except, all very much aware of the forthcoming return to Blighty, I had to inform Jack that I was expecting again, he was pleased but said.

'Sarah that's wonderful news, but no time to dilly dally, be ready to leave to-morrow.' I had unpacked essential things repacked them so often; I did not know what was in a box or a case.

315

Some had already been sent ahead nevertheless, we did not leave the next day. However you planned, this was the Army if and when the day actually arrived, I had to be fit and at the head of my family. That day did arrive, when Jack informed me we were leaving the following week. The same week I received an air letter from Mother, Eilish my younger sister had been ill and died. I was distraught with anguish I would never see her again, Eilish a wonderful companion as a sister had been a real brick to me in the Curragh Camp. When I told Jack he just stared ahead and shook his head in disbelief. Jackie was taken ill with his throat again they had to hospitalise him, even though he was still swabbing his own throat. The worry of this along with the packing, the worst part of leaving my household behind, possibly a count of about forty, mostly Chico's, that I had amassed on my travels, who had become a part of my family, which I had with a bit of imagination learnt how to manage them with a different tongue. Whereas I completely lost having nothing to do they saying. 'Ji nai Memsahib Ji nai.' To witness Ayahs or servants mess around for hours, which I could have completed in a couple of minutes, that left me frustrated ready to roar and shout, it was certainly was not easy for me. Now this was the hardest part I had absolutely no idea what to do with them. Jack had arranged and paid the return fares, for the Bearer, two Ayahs and two Chico's to accompany us on the train to Bombay. The rest would be taken over by the new Army family. Jack paid the wages and presents also provided, references for all, giving anything in the house not required as a keepsake. As a parting gift I gave the Bearer my Bike to remember the Memsahibs outings. The Khansama cooked a fine meal for us came in. Handed me a carving set, a knife and fork in an ornate carved wooden handle and sheath. Held my hands in between the palms of his salammed tears welled in his eyes said.

'Memsahib Bahut bahut shukriya shukria.' India was not going to let us go easy.

It was not just a wrench, but heart-breaking. I, who could not wait to get home to Blighty, was crying like a lunatic. From the time I became pregnant, as before I had not felt very well suffered on my own, the worry of Jackie sick, the packing and heartbreak of Eilish. Four days before we were due to leave, I became terribly ill miscarried my baby of two months. Jack had a Private Doctor attend me. If I had seen the MO, I would have been taken off the return home list. As Jack would say, "On your feet soldier." I had to soldier on.

All the families we had become acquainted with came around for private goodbyes; this included the Colonel's family, our Major Doctor who had taught Jackie to care for his throat? He gave him a final inspection. A1 fit to travel. A welcome relief I hoped to God that I was as fit as him. Unfortunately Jack would be staying behind to hand over to the new incoming Battery Quarter Master. Then he and Bobby would follow us down to Bombay.

The entire household had bought, a Kukri Knife for Jack, a Sari for us, and a Pathans suit for Jackie, all had to be tried on the night before we left. They inspected us and cried at the sight, which set me off thinking: *I could cry no more, but still had to face the final farewell.*

The next morning saw a stream of one-way Tonga's en-route to the station. At the station a sea of people had gathered, soldiers at one end, families friends and households gathered at the other. We weren't the only ones shedding tears, the late arrival of the train with the replacement Regiment did not help... Jack bade us farewell he would see us in Bombay. It was pandemonium as we boarded the train. I felt awful and as the train started to pulled out of the station, those of my household on the train and stood waving us off began to wail and shriek. The Ayahs wrung tears out of their saturated Saris; the little Chico's hanging onto the windows. I was terrified they would all be killed. I had to lay down only to have the children lay crying all over me. Kitty was a brick. got her tribe and mine sorted out.

'Christ Plant. What's the matter with you? We are going home to Blighty.' She herself wiping tears away from her red-rimmed eyes I thought to myself. *"Kitty Burns your just as bad. You are on your own again. Come on soldier on your feet there's work to be done."* I got up washed myself and organised my tribe for a four-day train journey to Bombay. Kitty interrupted my enthusiasm.

'Sarah get your Ayahs to do their chores for you. That's what Jack paid their fare for. '

'Yes that's true but they are at the back end of the train. We will have to sort something out.'

The train travelled across central India, the terrain was quiet flat and lush with green landscape and areas of jungle. India is so extensive and seemingly endless. The train only stopped at stations to pick up coal and water. On the second day our first stop for an hour was Jabalpur. I was still feeling ill and was only taking chai with some fruit. Jackie's throat was fine but as a precaution with the smuts and smoke I had him grip a handkerchief in his mouth. Mary pulled it out giving him a raging toothache; his teeth were blackened from drinking Quinine as were the other two. Poor little devil he just sat there at the open carriage door, his feet dangling over the side grizzling and crying watching the life of India speed by. I had nothing to administer for it. On the third day we pulled into a station called Jalan and stayed for about two hours, the heat was intense. We sat there perspiring fanning ourselves trying to keep cool, next stop Bombay and possibly some sleep. Arriving in Bombay station the usual shouting and barking of orders greeted us. We were to stay at The Taj Hotel, for three days until Jack arrived and then to embark on board the troopship, so as they say "we had time to spare".

Kitty and I with our two tribes, booked into the Taj Mahal Hotel, so they could be on hand, the Bearer, Ayahs and Chico's were afforded accommodation somewhere around the back of the Hotel. I went straight to bed. Kitty took charge of everything. The following day I was feeling fit enough to get about. With nothing else to do after breakfast, the Bearer organised Tonga's to take us all to Collabra the local beach and the same the following day, the children playing with the Chico's on the beach, in and out of the sea, our two Ayahs sat in one Tonga they just waved and called to the children. I walked up and down with Kitty, or sat in the other Tonga whiling the time away, the Bearer did not like Bombay. 'Bahut Kharab Memsahib Bahut Kharab.' Spent his time going from horse to horse, talking to them or brushing their flanks, ignoring the drivers or shouting abuse at them. They appeared terrified of him, eventually he would say. 'Hotal Memsahib?'

''Ji han Achchha Achha.' He would salaam organise everything away we would go. So those were my very last days in India. I had very briefly tasted the honey with a breakfast in the Taj on my journey into India, upon my departure was again blessed with a welcome but brief stay of luxury in the Taj. Now I was ready for home.

CHAPTER TEN
BLIGHTY BOUND

On the second day, when we arrived back from the beach Jack and Bobby were waiting in the Hotel reception. The following morning we left the hotel early to embark on the Troopship 'Somersetshire.' It was Christmas Eve 1931. Michael's birthday. We arrived at the quayside, to become just another family to swell the multitude of soldiers and families embarking up the gangways.

I thought. *"Here we go again four weeks of fear."* We found our cabin, the Ayahs helped me and Kitty to unpack make ready the two cabins, Kitty and her tribe were in a cabin on the other side of the ship. Jack and Bobby were bedded down with the rest of the troops. Our two tribes took the Bearer and Chico's to walk around the ship, although they had never been on a ship before they appeared quite at home, they would have much to tell when they arrived back in Lucknow. It was getting on for lunchtime when the ding-dong of the Tannoy system requested all visitors to leave the ship Jack said.

'This is the time Sarah.'

We all went up to the gangway followed by the Bearer, Ayah's, and Chico's, to say our last 'Khuda hafiz' again floods of tears. This time the Bearer Abdullah actually knelt down in front of me, salaamed tears streaming down his face, this was too much for me, I was sobbing as they departed down the gangway, they formed a line in front of us, waved before the Bearer threw up a salute turned to his small line of troops shouted.

'Quick march.' Smartly marched them away, much to Jack's admiration that turned to me.

'Sarah do you remember our little processions on the way to Sunday Mass, this time it's without you Sarah.'

Tears were streaming down my face I did remember thought: *No about the processions but about when I arrived to a mass of servants I did not want and now I was witnessing the departure of them. The family I had grown to love.* As they marched away we all clapped at this splendid show, others lining the rails joined in with the cheering and waving to them, until they got into the Tonga's and were gone out of sight, out of our lives. Up on deck all were distraught. Kitty Burns remarked.

'Sarah Plant you won't get the likes of them back in Blighty. Part of your tribe has flown the nest.' How right she was, I could have trusted all of them with our lives.

We went had lunch. About five o'clock in the afternoon the ship left the quayside of Ballard Pier set sail homeward bound. As the ship headed into the setting sun in the West, we were all up on deck looking back at the slowly receding shores of India. What memories they had now formed in my mind. Jackie broke the train of my thoughts.

'Mum no flies.'

So early to bed. This was the end of my Indian summer The saddest day of all, but tomorrow Christmas Day, much had to be done before then. Late that evening Jack arrived back in the cabin with a case he had kept separate, presents for the children. We quietly made up their stockings. Then to bed India sadly behind us

Sometime during the night I woke up with a start, the unfamiliar movement of the ship had disturbed me; I lay there with sweat pouring out of me, aware that the bed linen was damp. It was Christmas day; it was quiet except the gentle sounds of children deep in sleep, through the open porthole the sound of the sea swishing past far below. I lay there listening, gathering my wits, thinking: *About where I was going, that was home to Blighty,* slowly my lids closed.

The noisy chatter and excitement of my tribe opening their presents woke me up. The rising sun threw a beam of light through the porthole. I glanced at my kneeling tribe, amidst torn wrapping paper, raising myself up moved down towards the other end of the bunk, knelt up looked through the porthole at the blue sea with long white caps rippling across the tops of waves, Mary called out.

'Happy christmas mum.'

I returned her compliment, the rest joined in, before concentrating on presents, getting up went into the little toilet busied myself with my ablutions getting ready for the forthcoming days event. The familiar sound of the gong announced, 'Breakfast servings were about to commence.' We left the cabin and made our way to the Dining room to meet Kitty and her tribe, Jack and Bobby arrived to join us. Christmas Day turned out to be quiet delightful. At midday the ship's Captain had laid on a big party for the children with English fare. Yes we had them out in India nevertheless; there were many things that we did not have, which appeared on the menu with a speciality, Turkey with all the trimmings, Christmas pudding. In the afternoon games were played on the upper deck, everyone joined in regardless of the rolling of the ship. It was a case of learning to get one's sea legs all over again. A dance in the evening had been scheduled at which a couple of familiar faces from the outward trip showed up. There would be much to talk about, during the rest of the voyage. The ships daily routine was unchanged so it was going to be quite easy to adapt to its procedure.

The second day saw the sea quiet calm and a welcome blessing to me, still not quite fit but getting better every day possibly with the sea air and pleasant breeze. On New Year's Day on our starboard side, we passed the port of Aden steaming into the Red Sea onwards towards the Canal. It was first light when we anchored at Suez to join the convoy of ship, into the Suez Canal before reaching Port Said. This part of the trip both out and in had been most frustrating being in sight of land but not able to go ashore. On both sides lay the bleak desert, the only interesting period going through the Bitter Lakes. If ships are on the outward trip they appear to be sailing through sand. Talk about Camels being ships of the desert.

On the third of January 1932 we arrived in Port Said. We were up on deck to see the activities of the Vendors in their bum boats far below, selling their wares shouting out to the passenger's way above them, Jack pointed out another ship and told me it was the troopship "Dorsetshire" the sister ship to ours, she being outward bound to India. I felt pangs of sadness as to what I had left behind me. Realising that I had at least accomplished one of my ambitions as a young girl to visit India to see its brassware then at that time was just a daydream, now a reality I had purchased my own. I turned to Jack said.

'Thank you.' Quizzically he asked.

'What for?'

'Oh something that I remember from years ago.'

'Aren't you going to let me in on your little secret then?'

'I'll tell you later.' He enquired.

'Bobby, Kitty are you going ashore?' That was met with a resounding.

'Yes.' With a big grin he suggested.

'Okay Sarah assembles our tribe, we'll go ashore, get those sea legs of yours working. Jahldi.'

'No thank you Jack. I'll stay on Board.' I was not getting on any bobbing boats. Kitty was all for it.

'Oh come on Sarah, let's get into those Bazaar's and beat the Buggers down.' I gave up.

The same procedure as before. I very wary of the sea did not enjoy the ferryboat trip, although only a few hundred yards. They sat me up the front so I could not see where we were going. All I saw was the boat Wallah standing at the rear swaying with the motion of the boat as

319

he moved one large oar rowing like a coracle with me clinging to the side of the boat for dear life, Jackie couldn't contain his mirth started the others off laughing. Kitty sat beside me said.

'Sarah Plant don't be so daft we won't sink?' I still clung on. Once on shore it was not very inspiring except the arid smell that was entirely different to India. After an uneventful trip around the Bazaar, Kitty was amazed at Mary's bargaining powers and let her carry on. Mary in her element talking Urdu that they could not understand had them shouting back in Egyptian language. Little or no purchase was made which was a blessing, turning to her father said.

'Dad I wish I had the Bearer here with me. He would stop their shenanigans.'

She stomped off in frustration. Jack and Bobby just stood there roaring with laughter at this charade. We made our way back to the landing stage to be ferried back to the ship. She sailed later that afternoon into the Mediterranean, the evening sky was overcast and windy, which didn't look to good to me. Next morning we awoke to a blue sky as the ship steamed for our next port of call. 'Gibraltar.' The atmosphere on board was that of "Blighty Bound". Conversation between wives were of their experiences, many had been posted to Central India, which seemed in comparison with mine, trivial and quite tame. Those without families did not have any wild one's around their legs all day. Dances were held on 'A' Deck very lively affairs and at one of the dances somewhere south of Malta, Kitty and I were relaxing with a shandy, when Jack and Bobby brought over this tall elegant looking Artillery Sergeant.

'Sarah. Kitty. This is Sergeant Dickie Fox. He insisted on being introduced to you two ladies?'

'Ladies. My name is Sergeant. Reginald, Claude De Veer Fox. Royal Artillery, known to my friends as Dickie Fox. I am extremely pleased to make your acquaintances. I've been speaking with Jack and Bobby I must congratulate you both for your bravery.'

Taken aback by his compliment but unsure of what he was on about Kitty jested.

'Oh what bravery? We haven't done anything that was brave, except marry our husbands.' However this sergeant carried on.

'Forgive me. But you are the two ladies, who got mixed up in a riot in a Bazaar near Lucknow?' Kitty realising his comment replied.

'Oh that incident. That was nothing to write home about.'....Kitty was in her element, passing off something at the time that was serious, now just an adventure...'Nothing to it. We just got on our bikes and rode our bikes through the mob. Scattering them to the four corners of the earth.' I said with embarrassment.

'Kitty that's not true and you know it.'

At my remark the three of them broke into laughter. He was very polite bought us another shandy. We chatted about India, He knew Jack from the Sergeants Mess in Lucknow. He even had witnessed Mary's antics at the Gymkhana he was in the same horse race alongside Jack. But was a competitor from another Battery so we had never met him. Nevertheless, he was quite a gentleman and danced with both of us. Much later the M.C. interrupted everyone's conversation to announce. After the dance we shall be passing the "Empress of Japan" on maiden voyage, she will be quite a sight lit up. Much later the ships rail became crowded with the onlookers. She slowly came into view, her upper decks lit up and pinhole lights indicated rows of portholes, which shimmered on the sea surface between the two ships as we sailed past each other into the darkness of the night. It was quite a sight.

Next day south of Malta, we passed a flotilla of the Royal Navy Squadron on manoeuvres however; there was a nip in the air. That day ships orders of the day instructed all to change into winter clothing. The following day with Tobies discarded, anyone on deck reeked of mothballs. Kitty and I sat gupping watching the tribes play deck quoits, not without arguments; however the blowing winds aired the scent of mothballs away, causing rather wavy and choppy seas. The Captain announced rough weather ahead. Advised all to stow away any breakables in cabins, all entertainment would be cancelled until the storm had abated. I quailed at the thought. The winds struck with terrific force, from then on we seemed to be in a constant storm as the ship battled against the elements, everyone clung to their hats or locked themselves in their cabins. I feared the ship would sink at any moment. As the storm abated cold weather set in, apart from seasickness, passengers became ill with the flu. When the ship docked at Gibraltar. Three hundred people were confined to their cabins; the worst cases were taken ashore to a hospital. The ship sailed without them into the Atlantic up through the Bay of Biscay where it was a whirlpool, I was so seasick I thought: *I was about to die.* Kitty had succumbed to seasickness and remained in her cabin. So did everyone else including the Captain. Jack and Bobby informed us that their new postings had been announced. We had been posted to Greenland's, Bobby and Kitty to Newcastle. I could not have cared less. The storm did not abate until the day before we were due to dock at Southampton, then Jackie caught the flu with a roaring temperature. Then news quickly spread around that the ship had lost its Port anchor and chain. My immediate reaction was that of fear. We'll never land, please God let us get into port safely and bring an end to this voyage. Then Michael caught the flu.

Finally the ship docked on the 15th. of February 1932. It was snowing and freezing cold. There were no bands playing. What a welcome home, definitely the end of my Indian summer. Then the Tannoy announced all were to disembark. Jack again fully occupied, had no time to spare for me. I couldn't wait to get out of this cabin it reeked of sick. Kitty and I wrapped all of them up as best we could. Jackie appeared a little better having got over the initial stages of the flu, his nose constantly running, I got one of his father's handkerchiefs and pinned it to his coat. Leaving the cabin without the aid of coolies struggled with the suitcases into the corridor, to be met with an ever-increasing number of people. Their once tanned healthy faces now ashen and tinged with green, red noses dark rings under their eyes all suffering from the flu. Slowly we made progress, tempers frayed as the pushing and shoving continued. It was pandemonium trying to get off this ship. With Michael held in one arm the suitcase in the other, our chattels carried amongst my tribe, we struggled up to the dispersal point passing some unfortunate lady, noisily retching in a corner oblivious to the frantic mayhem passing her by. Gained a quip from Kitty.

'Hasn't she had enough of that already?'

That could not bring a smile to my face, reaching the open deck the rush of cold air had me shivering, but glad to be going down the gangplank for the last time. On the quayside, Kitty blurted out.

'Sarah Plant. Thank Christ that's over.'

As we made our way to a sheltered point. I sat down on some soldier's kit –bag and sighed with relief.

'Kitty. I never want to go to sea, ever again.'

However both our tribes had found their feet having found an icy patch began sliding around much to the consternation of Kitty.

'Where's my crop? I'll thrash the lot of them.'

Nevertheless unable to do anything, least of all me with a sick Michael in my arms, unable to stop any of them. Great fun for them, hopeless telling them to come and stand by me. Kitty exclaimed.

'Christ Sarah. Why can't we be back in India?' A young Gunner approached and asked.

'Ere Missus would you like a drink of tea out of my mug?'

'I'll drink it out of your tin helmet if you like'. He laughed and kept us company until Jack arrived.

'C'mon Jahldi, let's get some breakfast. Kitty Bobby's queuing up.' The Gunner suggested.

'You go Missus. I'll stay and look after your luggage if you like.'

'Thank you that's very kind of you.'

Once inside, out of the freezing cold another cup of hot tea, warmed us up, but I just could not face a meal of any description. I had expected my sisters to meet me but they were not there Jack remarked.

'They would probably be waiting at Waterloo I've sent a wire to your Mother just a few words.

ARRIVED SAFELY STOP WILL SEE YOU IN LONDON STOP

'Now then Sarah, what do you want to do? Shall I put you on the boat train to London with the children along with the Burn's or, will you come with me to Greenland's. It's on the Salisbury Plains?'

I thought; *"God. No not London, with Jackie not fully fit, Baba Michael one very sick baby in my arms, and two reasonably healthy girls."* I decided.

'No. I'll go to Greenlands.'

'Right that's settled. I'll organise the luggage.'

This was going to be a personal wrench for me leaving Bobby and Kitty. I had met some fine women friends in my time but Kitty Burns was someone special. Right from the start in Peshawar we had hit it off. There had never been a cross word spoken between us, although our tribes had been at one another's necks she had been a very good friend, always ready with a quip or a joke, that had me roaring with laughter. She had indeed helped me through some very bad times. Farewell's, had to be faced we had to say our tearful goodbyes on the platform at Southampton; she bound for Newcastle via London. The pair of us clinging together weeping buckets, Kitty's parting words.

'At least Sarah Plant. I'll have some peace for myself, away from your tribe.'

As the two tribes parted, it began to snow again. But my thought was: *Will I ever meet my true friend Kitty again?*

"THE ADVENTURES OF A SOLDIERS WIFE"
BOOK III.

CLIMATIC CHANGES

BLIGHTY 1932 - 1974.

QMS. J. J. PLANT.

ROYAL ARTILLERY

DOVER CASTLE 1940

CHAPTER ONE
GREENLANDS BLIGHTY-1932

Blue with the cold, all shivering like idiots, we stood in a small group on the station platform, furthermore, to add to our misery we were informed that the train's departure had been delayed for some time. Before we boarded the train Jack sorted out our luggage and had some of his gunners load them into the luggage van. Whilst on board the ship I had ensured we all had double of every item of clothing on. Nevertheless, when we got into our allocated compartment it was freezing cold, the only conciliation was, that we were out of the biting wind. Eventually with a deafening whistle a lot of chuffing and a couple of jolts the train did leave Southampton Docks, soon puffing its way out into the countryside covered in snow. Upon reflection, it was exactly the same as when we left for India those many years before. Jack, sittng opposite, had his greatcoat done up tight, with his arms wrapped around Jackie and Kathleen, drawn in close to him, trying to keep them warm, whilst I had Michael laid down beside me with Mary looking after him. After a while she quietly said.

'Mum Michael baba is very hot.'

Feeling his brow she was correct, his temperature was up, he was getting worse. I suggested to Jack to give Michael a little drop of Brandy, he being generous gave him too much and made him sick. Many hours later we arrived at Salisbury. I was very concerned about Michael's condition, urged.

'Jack quick get out and find a Medic. I'll sort the tribe out.' Returning back Jack informed me of what we had to do.

'Sarah, I've spoken to a Major who suggested we should take Michael to the Military Hospital at Tidworth, that's about sixteen miles away. He is organising transport for us, so we have to wait outside the station. I will go and sort out our luggage and get it outside.'

Outside the station we stood shivering in a biting wind, until finally a GS wagon arrived. The driver helped load the luggage, then we clambered up into the back, used the luggage as seats. After an uncomfortable ride, it was late afternoon when we finally arrived at the Greenland camp guardhouse. I knew that Michael was not well enough to travel any further, and explained the situation to Jack, who ordered the driver to stay where he was, he strode into the guardhouse. After a short while he came back out accompanied by a Gunner to inform me.

'Sarah, they have contacted a doctor at the hospital. He is on his way, this Gunner is to direct us to our quarters and let us in.'

We set off, after a short ride we stopped. The Gunner appeared at the back to say.

'Ear Ma. These are your quarters. You're the last family to arrive.'

His passing remark did not please me one little bit. Instead of us charging around a snowbound countryside, we should have stayed on the train. Jangling a set of keys he went to the front door opened it, Jack helped us down, prompted.

'Come on Jahldi, all get inside out of the cold.'

Stumbling through the snow, we entered to be met by the warmth of the quarters and the smell of burning coal, fortunately someone had already lit a fire. Jack guided me into a room where a pot boiler was throwing out the welcome heat, grabbing a chair he positioned it in front of it opened the stove door, then ordered.

'Sarah you sit there, the Doctor should be here soon. C'mon you three sit down around the stove whilst I sort out the luggage.'

Holding Michael in my arms I sat there staring into the fire, contemplating my fate, my heart went back out to Landour, thinking *"Oh how I wished I were back there now?"* Meanwhile the driver and Gunner had left. It was late in the afternoon, the room was in semi-darkness, when Jack tried to light the gas mantle, found the gas was not turned on, typical of the Army. With no servants available to help, I rallied around. Getting up I sat Mary down on the chair and laid Michael in her arms to look after him, whilst I sorted out what the sleeping arrangements were? However the beds in the rooms had already been made up, by whom, mystified me. But I, ready to drop onto one myself, nevertheless still very worried about Michael. Returning back to the room, feeling Michael's brow, I did not like its heat, he had a raging temperature, taking him out of Mary's arms, I pulled the coat tight around him, as Mary vacated the chair I sat down with him. Suddenly there was a knock on the door. Jack went and opened it. I heard a woman's voice say.

'Can I help?'...Jack spoke.... 'Please c'mon inside, we have just arrived.' ...Entering the room this woman immediately seeing my plight said to Jack.... 'Come with me.' It was not too long before they both arrived back carrying a cot, placing it by the fire she said.

'There you are put him in that for the night. Hold on'...again she left, only this time returned with an armful of blankets...'There wrap him up in those.'

As she left I thanked her for her kindness. Settling Michael down into the cot covered him with blankets. Jack manoeuvring boxes around stopped, picked up one of the blankets and wrapped it around my shoulders.

'Sarah, we have not eaten since this morning. I'll take these three down to the cookhouse for something hot to eat. I'll bring something back for you. if that's okay?'

'Go on take them they must be famished. I'll wait for the MO.'

Reluctantly they followed their father out. I did not think the three of them wanted to leave the warmth of the fire, then Michael began yelling his head off, it was all I could do to pacify him. A knock on the door had me jumping, I went and opened it to find the MO along with an Orderly stood there, he enquired.

'Mrs Plant.'

'Yes Sir. Please do come inside. I've been waiting for you, my husband QMS Plant has taken the children down to the cookhouse to feed them some food. Michael my baby is in that room there. The MO headed for the room then shrouded in darkness, he ordered.

'Jenkins. Light up the gas.' I spoke up.

'Sorry doctor no gas.'

'No gas why not?'

'Don't know? We've only just arrived.'

'Uhm. Jenkins light one of those sticks in the fire and give me some light.'

Bending over Michael the doctor, stuck a thermometer into his mouth, feeling his pulse waited, began asking the relevant questions about his ailment. Michael now wide awake was about to cry, shushed him to be quiet. Slipping out the thermometer. the Doctor said.

'Jenkins hold that stick closer, so I can read this thermometer'...peering at it muttered...'Um one hundred four, that is high'...Sounding his chest a couple of times muttered...'He's definitely got a bad dose of flu. I can't admit him to- night. I'll make arrangements to take your son into hospital tomorrow morning, for tonight wrapped up in the cot, he should be all right.have, heres some asprin, crush it up in warm water and give it to him.' ...One thing I did not want, was Michael admitted to a hospital, I quickly answered...'Doctor. I will have his temperature down by the morning.'...'If you can do that, it would certainly help his condition. I'll be back early in the morning. Get your husband to get the gas put on.'

They left, not long after Jack arrived back, by then the room was only lit by the flickering flames of the bright fire I told him of the MOs decision and, he had to get the gas turned on. He had brought back some form of meat pie, that I couldn't face, but he had got some tea, milk sugar and mugs to make up a brew of tea. 'The reviver.' He left to sort out the gas, whilst I rustling about in the kitchen, found a pot to make tea on the fire and do what the docter said with

325

the asprins. While that was brewing, I sorted out the other three for bed, put them into the beds in the first room, spreading plenty of coats on top of them, plus a couple of spare blankets. As there were no lights to turn out, with hot food inside them it wasn't long before they settled down for the night, as it had been a very tiring day for all of us. Returning back to the cot, fed Michael with the warm asprin water, then poured out a cup of tea, sat there in the darkness by the warm glow and flickering light of the fire, to enjoy my first drink since Southampton. Returning back, Jack entered with a few hurricane lamps he set alight, informing me that the gas would be turned on the next day. Nevertheless, whoever had the sense to light the fire earlier, had left sufficient coal for the night... Having stoked up the fire with more coal we sat in front of it until Jack decided to turn in. I could not sleep, having not eaten anything since the previous day, pangs of hunger gnawed at my stomach, but was far too worried to get the cold meat pie to eat. With Michael well covered up, I kept the fire stoked up, until eventually he broke out into a sweat, which soaked him throughout. We stayed all night in front of the fire, until early in the morning Jack entered to stoke up the fire, make another welcome brew up, before my tribe came in to crowd around the heat of the fire. True to his word the MO. arrived early with the ambulance, taking Michaels temperature said.

'Wonderful Mrs Plant. Almost normal. Now I'm here I'll examine all of you.'

All were passed fit except Jackie. His throat was inflamed however, this time it was his tonsils. Therefore instead of Michael, Jackie was put into the ambulance, rushed into Tidworth Military Hospital to be operated on. A further unwanted worry but it happened. Inspecting our allotted quarters in the light of day, discovered it was a converted Barrack hut, with a long corridor leading to five rooms. The end one where we had stayed all night was a large L shaped dining room with the pot boiler in the middle. The Bombadiers wife Mrs Sugden next door came to see how I was coping I thanked her for her assistance before she left. I wrote a brief letter to Mother, told her about the voyage home, the flu and Jackie's operation. It took us a week to sort out the quarters and stow away our luggage, during which time we visited Jackie in hospital, day by day he was getting over it. A letter from mother arrived, according to her, after reading about the 'Somersetshire's ill-fated voyage in the newspaper. She was convinced we were all dead? Jack laughed aloud when he read her comment.

Whilst on our visits by a GS wagon to Jackie in hospital. I found out from Jack where Greenlands Camp was located. All that I knew about it was as Jack had informed me. 'It was on the Salisbury Plains.' Anyway, driving over the plains passing a sign post I noticed Durrington, which had me thinking back to me staying with Mrs. Brampton in Durrington, so I said to Jack.

'I didn't know we were close to Durrington, it's where we stayed at Mrs. Brampton's all those years ago, when you were at Larkhill, seeing that it's not far from Greenland's Camp, maybe we should pay her a visit, what do you say?'

'Sarah. With Dickie at Larkhill along with Jackie Leash, then there is a RAF balloon observation school not far from here, that seems a good idea. But at this moment we are just finding our feet moving in to our new quarters, with Jackie's problem, sorting out the tribe for school we have our hands full. Maybe sometime in the future it might be possible.'

'Well if you say so. But if you remember she did invite us back if we were ever in this locality.'

After three weeks. Jackie was released from hospital. Only then, after being away for so long, it was a good time to travel to London to see the family again. Arriving at Waterloo station, we caught the tube to Stockwell, which was to be our very first journey on the underground railway. It was so quick and it only seemed to be a matter of minutes before we arrived there. Then up to street level by a long moving staircase, out into the streets of London, that to me had not changed much apart from more vehicles. Holding Michael in his arms Jack ran out into the roadway, towards a stationary tram in the middle of the road he shouted.

'COME ON WE CAN CATCH THIS THIRTY- FOUR TRAM.'

With us scampering behind we climbed aboard the tram before it started off. At Loughborough Junction we alighted, to me I was back in familiar territory. Crossing the road, and with Jack at his normal walking pace, we practically ran along beside him, as we turned into Conderton Road. As we approached our old flat my heart fluttered with anticipation. Jack bounded up the steps, gave the knocker two hefty bangs. The door was opened by young Julia, surprised to see us she gasped.

'Oh my God is it really you? Wait until I tell Mother.' Lunging forward she hugged me, I whispered....'No wait I want to surprise her.' Pushing past her entered the hallway, only to find Mother already on her way down the stairs, she shouted.

'ALLAHNAH. AT LAST, MY GOD IS IT REALLY YOU? AND YOU JACK COME ON IN.'

Halfway up the hallway we met, she grabbed hold of me then the tears flowed. Her flat was full of her furniture and spotless. She made a fuss of my tribe, exclaining how big they had grown and so brown, but especially Michael who she sat on her lap. He bewildered by all the fuss just stared at mother.

'Allahnah, you make the tea, while I get acquainted with my new grandson Michael. Tis a fine name that he has got. No wait. Julie you make the tea for these poor unfortunates, who have travelled thousands of miles from India!'

A pot of tea was brewed, out came the soda cake. A knock on the kitchen door heralded the entrance of dear old Dolly, accompanied by young Bertie who had grown into a tall fair-haired lad. 'Coooee just in time for tea I see.'

'Now then, who in God's name invited you up here Dolly?'

'Come on Mrs. Cunningham I heard all the commotion, and you shout out. Allahnah. That could only mean one person. Sarah had arrived.'

'Be japer's you never miss a trick do you? Now your part of the family and you're up here, you might as well have a cup of tea with the rest of them. Now then Dolly what do you think of my new Grandson?'

'Ah isn't he the likeness of you?'

'Get away with you he's more like Jack.'

I laughed, they had not changed however, we were soon informed of the changes that we had missed whilst we were away. Lena had married Bert's brother Wally in Westminster Cathedral and a month after Michael was born, Lena had given birth to a boy named Patrick. After father's death in Ireland and the unfortunate demise of Eilish, my sisters Agnes, Nan and brother Jack had left Ireland, came over to start jobs in England. So all the family had taken root and were living in flats close to their place of work in South Lambeth. Arriving home from work, a very surprised Fan entered the room, so it was Fan and Julia who were staying with Mother, later we would meet the rest of them. Jack suggested to me.

'Sarah while were here, we should go and visit Dick and Edith a few doors down. What do you say is that okay?' Before I could say anything Mother interrupted.

'Jack you won't find them there. Dick and Edith moved lodgings a year or so ago, to somewhere in West Norwood, but I don't know where. Now then Dolly, during their stay, we will have to put up these travellers to sleep with us. Down you go, sort somewhere out there's a good girl.'

Reluctantly Dolly left the chit-chat to do what mother had ordered. I had to grin as when I was there, it was the devil's own job to get her to move out of the kitchen. However, it did not take her long before she was back having arranged some sleeping accommodation for us. Bert arrived on the scene, more salutations, and a good time for the pair of them to visit the Mess for a couple of drinks. Meanwhile I related our adventures in India before they arrived back, rather late but I could not have cared less. The next day we visited Jacks parents in Putney. A big surprise not only to them but to us, as his other brother Alf, whom we had not seen for almost seven years, along with Lillian, Jack's sister, her husband Alf, and their little boy Jack, yet another birth whilst we were away. It seemed as if the whole family were there, so much so we were overwhelmed with the reception we received. Miria was more than overjoyed at the sight of all my tribe to see how tanned and well they looked, she made a great fuss over us whilst the men went out for their customary drink. It was late in the afternoon when we eventually left to return to mothers. Jack had found out where Dick and Edith had moved to. However, it would not be this trip we would meet up with them. After the short but wonderful stay in London, we returned back to Greenland's accompanied by Julia, who turned out to be a blessing in disguise, as the next day I developed a nasty hacking cough. I got Julia to go to the Orderly Office, to get the doctor to give me some cough mixture. Someone there got the message wrong. At nine 'o' clock, that night a army ambulance arrived to take me into hospital. Although I refused, I was bundled into the waiting ambulance and carted off to Tidworth Military Hospital. All I had was a very bad cold and nasty cough. The next day I implored them to let me go home, it fell on deaf ears. For four long wasted days they kept me in, Jack did visit, I complained to him but it was all down to the Doctors. Totally fed up with their treatment, I got dressed and released myself, but with no way of communicating with Jack. I stood outside the hospital entrance with absolutely no transport available and possibly unheard of in Greenland's. Standing there very despondent wondering what or how I was going to get back to camp, when a lady came out of the hospital and stood waiting beside me, she enquired.

'Good morning. Are you waiting for a Taxi?' Whether or not she wanted to hear my problem. I explained....'Well Good morning to yourself. No. I'm not. But I would like to hire one if there are any available? I've just released myself from the hospital, after four unnecessary days inside. I must get back home to my children in Greenland's camp. Hopefully my young sister Julia is looking after them. I am very concerned as we have not long returned from India and I'm not very familiar with the locality.'

'Oh how unfortunate. Look I'm waiting for the taxi I ordered, to take me to Larkhill and if you like you can ride with me. I'll get the driver to drop you off at the camp, its not that far away.'

'Well that is very kind of you. Yes, thank you but I will pay part of the fare.'

'No I would not hear of it. Just say it's my treat.'

We chatted on until the taxi arrived, then we spent the journey talking about my Indian experience. Stopping at the camp gates, I again offered to pay part fare but the lady refused and told the driver she would pay the full fare at Larkhill. I thanked her and bade her farewell, then gave the driver a good tip. Entering the camp, whilst walking on the way to our quarters, I wondered if everything was alright. But my concern vanished when I entered the quarters. I had no cause for worry. Julia had looked after them very well. Cooking all their meals, had even done all the washing, kept the quarters clean and tidy. Albeit with several unpacked trunks lying around. Ready for another move, all due to my previous experiences of the many postings, before we left for India. I was always apprehensive of unpacking any of my things. When Jack arrived home after duty he was very surprised to see me home.

'What are you doing here? Did they release you? How are you now? Three questions and I explained all three then said to him. 'I don't want to unpack any of the Indian stuff.'

'Sarah don't be silly unpack it. I'm not being posted anywhere. I'll be here until I get demobbed out of the army and that is some time away. Unpack the lot then we will have a party to celebrate our homecoming. What do you say to that?'

'Well if you are sure, that's all I want to hear.'

The next day, with my tribe playing outside. Julia and I tackled the unpacking of the luggage. Most of the Indian brass and souvenirs were packed in wooden ammunition boxes, so it was a job to unscrew the screws holding the tops, but we managed. Julia was aghast at the number of brass pieces emerging from within the boxes, when all the brass was unpacked and laid around on the floor, she expressed her opinion in more ways than one.

'Sarah how on earth did you collect all these different animals, I adore that brass table please can I have that?'

Immediately her last remark, caused me to cast my mind back to years gone by. When I too had admired the array of brass souvenirs in some of the Kildare quarters. Now was the time that I wanted to show them off.

'Whoa back Julia that table I got made in Lucknow and I intend to keep it, like the rest of the others as a visual memory of my time in India. The problem is where to put it all on show. But now Jack has said we will not be moving from this posting I'm sure I will find suitable places for all of them.'

It took best part of two days to complete the unpacking and place them in various rooms within the quarters. I made a feature at the main window. Hanging the long black curtains, became a major job, placing the brass table in position between them. When it was done to my satisfaction it had changed the rooms décor, obviousy to Jack'sapproval, as he stood there hands on hips admiring the brass display.

'Sarah it's just like India, what do you say ducks?' A nice compliment, retorted.

'Well Jack they could not stay in trunks until you were demobbed, that is for sure.'

'Sarah. Seeing that you now have the quarters the way you want, and with the money we have saved, how about you order some furniture for the sitting room. Next Saturday, we have to make a trip into Salisbury to see Julia safely on the train. So afterwards we can go shopping in Salisbury. Is that okay?'

'Uhm. New furniture. That is a good idea. But are you positive there is not going to be any more postings coming your way?'

'Look Sarah. The way I see it is when I am demobbed we will not have any furniture to call our own, all I'm doing is just looking ahead that's all.'

'Well it is a good idea. We shall see what they have that suits us both.'

The matter was settled. Julia's stay with us had been short , she had been a God send and good company during her stay. We saw her off on the following Saturday in Salisbury before venturing on our spending spree I was looking forward to. In one of the several big shops we visited, we chose a dining room suite and a new double bed. They were delivered the following week, They were soon put in there place, it did not take me long to place a few pairs of brass animals on the top of the new sideboard with the three monkeys. as a centre piece "Hear no evil, see no evil and speak no evil."" A definite reminder of the monkey's attacking the bungalow.

It was time for the children to go back to school. Mary, Kathleen together with Jackie and the other children in camp, went to the school in Shrewton. They were taken there and back by army transport. As they would be away all day I gave them lunches to take with them, therefore during the day I only had Michael to look after, with time on my hands, I began writing letters to Mother and to my dear friend Kitty Burns. The problem was when we separated at Southampton neither of us knew where to contact each other, so got Jack to find out where to address her letter to in Fenham Barracks. A week later I received her reply, giving me all their news and highlighting the fact. "Its bloody cold in Newcastle, I want to return to India."

A regular visitor to our quarters was Dickie Fox, on his weekly visits, Dickie used to buy several comics for my tribe, nevertheless he and Jack would deliberately tease them. When he arrived he would give some to Jack keeping some for himself, then the pair of them would sit on the rest and carry on reading the comics they were holding, both roaring with laughter at the comic strips, then they would swop them. Much to my tribe's annoyance who sat around with glum looks on their faces, until Mary would get up, toss her head, walk away followed by Kathleen, whereas Jackie would moan.

'Let me have a comic please.' Dickie's answer.

'Not much in this week's comic Jackie. You really don't want to read them. C'mon, we are all going out now. You can read them later.' This used to send Jackie into a right paddy, if I intervened, telling the pair of them off they would reply.

'C'mon Sarah, it's only a bit of fun. We're off now. He will read them when we come back.'

As Jack had promised, he organised a party for the forthcoming Easter holiday, it was going to be a full house with my sisters, Margaret and Francis. Jacks comrades, Jackie Leash, Dickie Fox, a new friend Tom Wilbraham a RAF Sergeant at the local Balloon School, On the Saturday of the party, Jack and Dickie took a horse drawn G.S. wagon, down to Salisbury station to collect my sisters. When they arrived back, Margaret took me out of earshot to say to me.

'Sarah. Your Jack is just as mad as ever. Do you know what the pair of them did?'

'No. How could I? But I'll bet you will tell me. Go on.'

'The ride started off well until we got out to the plains, then Jack clicked the horse into a gallop, driving the horse at full tilt across the plains. The wagon was tipping and heaving about, we were hanging on for dear life. Then much to our astonishment while driving at full tilt, the mad pair changed places. Yes it was fun at the time, but we could all have been killed. What's the other fella's name?'... I sensed her sudden interest in Dickie.... 'Oh Dickie Fox or Ferdie as he is known. He's all right, but you watch your step with that young man or, you'll have Mother after you.' She blushed.... 'I was only enquiring Sarah, nothing wrong in that.'

My warning went on deaf ears, but I did notice during the evening they were getting on quite nicely as Fan was with Tom Wilberham. That Saturday evening party was a roaring success, it was the first of many we held while in Greenland's, weekend parties were always occurring for one reason or another. Margaret and Francis, became regular visitors pairing up with Dickie and Tom, who to get around had bought motorbikes, a new fad for Sergeants they being much cheaper than the car Wally and Lena had purchased. The four of them would roar off for picnics over the plains. I wasn't worried about their relationship, but knew what Mother

would say if they were ever involved in an accident. Nevertheless, the inevitable did happen, but not to them. Inevitably Lena and Wally would also be invited to the parties. One Saturday, with the party well underway, when a knock on the door, heralded the arrival of Wally and Lena. Jack answered the door, however he was there for some time talking, it soon became apparent it was the Police. Everyone was subdued until they left, wanting to know what was going on. When Jack re-entered the expression on his face revealed something serious had happened.

Dickie Fox, Peg & Ray Batten

'Please can all of you listen to what I have to say. The Police have told me Wally and Lena have been involved in a serious car accident. They are in hospital and according to the Constable, it was Wally who informed them of their journey to here, the Constable also told me there were four people in the car. Wally, Lena, Frogie and his girlfriend she was killed. Wally has a broken leg. Lena as well as Frogie had severe head injuries. Another thing he said was the driver was Frogie, Wally was sat in the passenger seat beside him. Lena and Frogie's girlfriend were in the rear seat. Dickie you and I will go to the hospital on your motorbike.'

Jack and Dickie left to see if they could help in any way, but there was nothing they could do. That was the end of the party, it was more of consoling each other. Much later the news they brought back was not good. Wally was basically alright apart from a broken leg. Lena and Frogie were both unconscious and they lay comatosed for days. That incident put an end to parties for some time to follow.

Christmas time. Our first back in England, Jack saw to it that the tribe would enjoy, a totally different time to that of the heat of India. Decorations were strung up with a Christmas tree, that year there was no turkey from Mother, but we did purchase one from a local farmer to feed another full house with Dickie, Margaret a couple of Jack's pals from the Mess. All in all everyone had a good time. It was early in the New Year when Jack and I were at the Mess celebrating someone's birthday, for me, I did my normal thing, put in an appearance and left early to return to our quarters to find the front door open, from the reflection of the the indoor lamp, stood in the doorway I recognised Bombardier Sugden and his wife from next door along with Mary. I noted that the Bombardier was only dressed in his khaki trousers and braces, his khaki shirt sleeves were rolled up, his boot laces were undone, his wife was wearing slippers with a pinafore over her dress. Alarm bells rang in my brain. What has Mary been up too again? Jack hailed the Bombadier who spoke quietly to Jack, after listening he replied.

'Well Done. Good job you were both on hand or, it could have been more serious. Thank you please don't worry. We will sort out the mess. C'mon Mary in you go and tell us what happened.' Following her in, immediately I smelt smoke as she spoke.

'It wasn't me Dad. It was Jackie and Michael they were putting the paper decorations in the stove to burn them up. Kathleen and I were in the kitchen washing up when Jackie yelled out fire. We both ran into the room to see the lino was alight. Jackie was stamping on it, but it was spreading along the floor. So I went next door for help, that's when the Sugden's rushed in and threw lots of water over it.'

Listening to her story and surveying the mess on the floor, the remains of charred and wet decorations, the lino was burnt practically to the doorway, the room awash with water, the ceiling and walls were blackened by the smoke, it did not look a pretty sight. But realised that if Mary had not gone for help. God alone knows what would have happened? I had to say to Mary.

'Well done Mary you did the right thing.'

Both Jackie and Michael were threatened never to play with fire again. As a punishment were not going to read any comics and packed off to bed. I stood there looking at the state of the place Mary and Kathleen watched as Jack and I cleaned up the mess before we all retired. Next morning Jack reported the fire, complained about the state of the quarters. Within days we were allotted new quarters further up the hill, yet another move but this time it was of our own doing. However, I became friendly with our new neighbour Connie another Bombardiers wife who on the then very rare occasions, kindly looked after my tribe, whenever I went to a Sergeants Mess dance. But after the incident of the fire, definitely never stayed too long, nevertheless really enjoyed the small break.

Our tribe's school reports were definitely not good apparently they were well behind in schoolwork, what with all the travelling and upheaval from one school to another, either in England or India, their education had really suffered. Jack and I had good reason enough to discuss their prowess of education. I remembered my convent school days, of the standard of teaching in the Convent schools also talking with Father O'Hare out in India, It crossed my mind of the possibility of sending our three into a convent school in Salisbury. Jack agreeing to my suggestion. sorted out a Convent, wrote them a letter asking about boarders? Their return letter advised of the conditions, fees, new boarders would be able to start in the September. Accepted the conditions agreed.

Kathleen, Ray, Patty, Aunt Fan, Mary, Jackie, Michael.

331

I loved Greenland's, it was so quiet and safe, so unlike India with less to worry about no wild animals. I could send the children out to play without worry but soon it was time for school holidays. When their cousins Ray and Patty Batten along with the McDermott's would arrive they would all stay for weeks. It was bedlam with my sister's tribes along with mine, nevertheless with all the freedom they used to have the time of their lives. However Margaret, who was almost a permanent visitor was known as Aunt Peg she became the escort to the tribes visiting us. Margaret was a very domineering person who always got her way. Upon their arrival all the children were stripped of their clothing, only to wear swimming togs every day, almost nothing else was worn until they returned on their homeward journey. I did complain to her.

'Peg. there's absolutely no need for that.'

'Now Sarah. With three tribes running amok around your feet you would be continually washing and ironing their clothes. So, off they come, and if it rains it will wash them as well.' Nevertheless, when she wasn't there, clothes were permitted. On another occasion, during the school term. I was away for some reason or another, Peg was looking after my household. Upon my return I was confronted by an irate Mary who blurted out.

'Mum she's a viper. Just like Kitty Burns.' Immediately I thought: *It was one of her school teachers....* 'Mary. Tell me who are you calling a viper? What's happened?'

'Aunt Peg. After you left we left for school. We missed the GS Wagon, so we came back and told her we had missed it. She wouldn't let us in, closed the door and told us to walk to school. When we arrived at lunchtime the head teacher told us off. It wasn't our fault and she's still like Kitty Burns. A viper.'

I saw that look in her eye that told a tale. There was nothing I could do but confront Margaret and ask why?

Jackie, Peg, Michael, Patty. 'Well what do you expect? If they dawdle on the way to catch the school wagon, it will teach them a lesson.' Her excuse got my paddy up I retorted.

'Yes. But you making them walk six miles along the roads is not the answer.'

'Well you would have let them stay at home and miss their lessons?'

'Margaret, you know damn well your way was not the right way.' She huffed and puffed at my reason and seeing our argument was going no place she said no more. Towards the end of the summer holidays, the other tribes departed back to their homes in London, leaving me far from being happy. It was time for me to start worrying about my tribe living in at the Convent boarding school. One morning after breakfast Kathleen announced.

'I'm sick of being called Kathleen. From now on my name is Kaye.'

Jackie promptly called her 'Kathleen.' That she ignored, which prompted Mary.

'If that is the case, I shall be called Caroline as it is my first name.'

Jack and I listened to all of this chat going on, thinking it was just another nine-day's wonder. For Mary it was, but Kathleen, unless she was addressed as Kaye, she refused to respond to all, so Kaye remained for the rest of her life.

The day arrived when they had to begin their boarding school days. Leaving Michael in the care of Connie, Sgt. Jackie Leash kindly offered to drive us to the Convent, we set off. As far as I was concerned, doom for my tribe. At the convent I coersed them out of the car with their small cases containing their clothing etc. Jackie Leask stated he would go have a cup of tea then come back to pick me up. I urged them forward, as I knocked on the big black door, they stood silent with their chattels. After a little while the door was opened by a Nun, not a word was spoken, as she bade us enter into a small anteroom embalmed with a cold atmosphere. The walls were draped in holy pictures. Christ being crucified, the Stations of the Cross, barely getting a look in, was a picture of Our Blessed Lady. It's atmosphere was enough to put the fear of God into the worst of sinners, certainly enough to keep my tribe quiet. We stood in silence waiting in the cold room for what seemed ages, until eventually a Nun entered, her head bowed deep in prayer, beckoned us to follow her out into the hallway, she walked down a corridor we followed her towards the Mother Superior, stood at a doorway further down, she too beckoned us to follow her into her room. I had to shove the three of them forward in through the doorway of the room. I it too was very forbidden, empty, with no seat., We came to a halt to stand in front of a very formidable and commanding figureof the Mother Superior. Dressed in her nuns habit with wide wings, her black gown, was pulled in at the waist, encircled by a row of the heaviest rosary beads I had ever seen, hanging close to her feet was a very large black and silver cross. I waited for her to say something. Instead she just glared down at my tribe. Clearing my throat I informed her who we were.

I'm Mrs. Plant and these are my three children.'

With piercing eyes she glared at me, as if I had committed a mortal sin by speaking first. I carried on introducing...'This is my eldest Mary, she is...She looked straight through her...'this is Kaye, (If she was going to ignore people no point in making trouble.)... 'this is Jackie.' She turned, glaring at me questioned.

'Is Kaye. The name of a foreign saint? I know nothing about.' I spluttered.

'Err. No she's English.'

'Which one? Is this Kaye?'

Kaye stepped forward, politely offered her hand. The Mother Superior grabbed hold of her hand, promptly dragged and pushed her through the doorway stood to one side as Mary and Jackie run after her, they were not going to be parted they disappeared into the corridor. I just stood there too shocked to speak, stopping briefly at the doorway she turned addressed me.

'In good time you will be advised of their progress. Mrs. What did you say your name was?' With a rustle of skirts the Mother Superior left banging the door shut behind her.

I stood there bewildered whispered to myself. '*Oh my God, what have I let them in for and not even a chance to say goodbye.*' The door opened, the other nun entered still bent double deep in prayer. I thought: *She is doing penance for interrupting the Mother Superior.* However she tugged the sleeve of my coat, led me out into the hallway, onwards back down the corridor towards the door she opened it, letting go of my sleeve urged me out. I was outside as the door was closed solidly behind me. I stumbled away towards the gateway before turning around looked back at this soundless place. After that very short sharp meeting with the Mother Superior, it struck terror into my heart. What an introduction. I felt like going back in there and taking them home with me. Waiting I blessed myself, started to pray for them. Just at that moment Jackie Leash arrived in the car getting out he asked.

'You alright Sarah? Not been waiting long have you?' I replied.

'A little while.' Not forgetting the silent wait for the Mother Superior and the whole incident of the introduction. I could not bring myself to speak to Jackie so, we drove back in silence.

Back home, I collected Michael from Connie, and for the rest of the day sat pondering in a silent house, until Jack arrived home, then I related all of these frightening events.

'Sarah ducks. Don't start worrying about them. Anyway all schools are just like that. Let's wait for their reports.'

In the confines of a very silent house, not able to understand its ramification's, for a full month all I did was pray for them. The only respite was the Battery swimming championships that Jack had entered for. I took Michael along to watch his father compete. Jack won all his events including the diving competition. At the Medal presentation the winners name was always Jack's, his Major asked.

'Plant. Where on earth had he learnt to swim and dive so well?'

'Off the dustbins into the river Thames Sir.'

Yet another day to be proud of his achievements. Possibly two months later a letter arrived from the convent, expecting it to be a report on their progress quickly opened it. The scribe was to say the least very brief, just two lines, informing us that Kaye had been admitted into their infirmary. Nothing else. After reading this I was at my wits end, went to the admin office to get word to Jack. As it was a Saturday, he would be available to go with me to the Convent. When he arrived home, reading its contents he was more than concerned.

'Sarah wait here. I'll speak with Jackie to see if he can take us there.'

I was already dressed to go to the convent, taking Michael next door to Connie's for her to look after him, briefly explained the situation then waited outside. I did not have to wait long Jackie's car drew up, Jack appeared very agitated he called out.

'C'mon Jahldi Jahldi Sarah let's get a move on.'

I got into the back of the car, even before I had closed the door we were racing off. Jackie drove like a demented soul all the way there braking hard to stop. Jack and I jumped out of the car, ran to the Convent door. Jack gave a few hefty knocks on the door. Soon it was opened by the same nun who still deep in her prayers looked at us, her lips moving silently, Jack questioned.

'Kaye Plant. Where is she?'

Frowning deeply, with no words forthcoming her lips stopped moving, she stepped back beckoned us into the cold atmosphere of the anteroom. Closing the door behind us, she bade us to follow her, as she walked through corridors to stop outside double doors, through its glass panes, revealed two rows of beds on either side, it was their infirmary room. The beds all covered in crisp white sheets and pillows, there was no one in them. The Nun pushing open one door ushered us inside, down at the far end alongside a bed I saw the black draped rear figure of the Mother Superior, standing with another Nun dressed all in white. Hurriedly we walked towards the end, the Mother Superior hearing our advance turned, a look of astonishment appeared on her face, quickly she advanced towards us, looking past her towards the bed I saw the tiny prone form of Kaye lying in bed, the white sheets tightly drawn up to her tiny face, breaking into a run I ignored the Mother Superior, at the bedside Jack came alongside me. We took a long look, staring down at Kaye's white face, her bedraggled fair hair unkept on the pillow, she was shaking like a leaf on a cold winters day. I turned shrieked at the Mother Superior.

'OH MY GOD WHAT IS WRONG WITH HER?' Who in an aloof manner stated.

'Seeing that she has not long returned from India. We think it's some kind of foreign disease. You will have to take them all away from here. They are a bad influence.'

Jack turned to me, with thunder in his face, gritting his teeth he spat raised words at the Mother Superior.

'BAD INFLUENCE INDEED. SARAH YOU SORT THESE PEOPLE OUT. GET OUR TRIBE. I'LL ARRANGE FOR AN AMBULANCE.'

He stomped out of the room in a towering rage. I had never seen Jack so enraged before. I stood at Kaye's bedside, watching the bedraggled state of Kaye's hair, her head moving involuntary, she not uttering a word. The sight of my little girl sent my blood pounding in my head, my heart was beating nineteen to the dozen. I too was in a right paddy, snapped, shouted.

'YOU. WHAT EVERY YOUR DAMN NAME IS. GET MY OTHER TWO. NOW.'

The Mother Superior muttered to the other nursing Nun, who with a rustle of starched clothing ran out of the room. I stood beside the bed, gently swept the strands of hair from Kaye's shaking brow, her eyes held a vacant stare not seeing anything. I took hold of her shaking hand and murmured.

'Kaye it's Mummy, c'mon my love, say something to me.' There was no response. With tears welling up in my eyes I turned to the Mother Superior and blasted her again.

'WHAT IN GOD'S NAME HAVE YOU DONE TO MY LITTLE GIRL?'

'Well there is no need for that language, we assumed it was a tropical disease.' With tears rolling down my face I shouted.

'TROPICAL DISEASE? YOU HAVE NEVER BEEN OUT OF THE COUNTRY. WHAT ON GOD'S EARTH GAVE YOU THAT IDEA? WHERE ARE MY OTHER TWO? HURRY UP I'M TAKING THEM AWAY FROM THIS BAD ENVIRONMENT.'

Not responded blessed herself. I stood there holding Kaye's hand, impatiently waiting with my foot involuntary stamping the floor in the silence of the room. After a little while that to me appeared to be ages. I heard the sound of the rustle of clothing from the doorway, The pair of them appeared in front of the nun in the white habit. She ushered them forward to stand beside me by the bed, they both appeared cowed, together uttered a meek.

'Hello.'

These were not the exuberant children I knew. I was smitten, embraced the pair of them, silently their arms slid around me. At that moment Jack still in a rage stomped in. They did not run to him, I thought: *My God what have they done to my children?* Jack came up to me placed his arm around my shoulders, I looked up to him, saw the anger in his face his jaws set firm, as through his gritted teeth he muttered to me.

'Jackie has gone back for an ambulance'...then he turned to the Mother Superior and in the same tone ordered.

'QUICKLY. GET ALL MY CHILDREN'S BELONGINGS. THEY ARE LEAVING NOW.'

I could see she was more than perplexed. Her previous tone of superiority was lost as she told the nun to make arrangements. She together with the other nun left without any apologies to us. Their clothes and chattels were brought in, we stayed in that room until the nursing nun returned along with the still praying nun, without saying a word. indicating that the ambulance was outside. The nursing nun moved to the bedside to fuss over Kaye. Jack was having none of that, with anger ordered.

'JUST LEAVE KAYE ALONE.'

Hesitating, then she stood back. Whilst Jack drew back the bedcovers, picked Kaye up in his arms, purposely strode out of the room, I took hold of Kaye's parcel, got Mary and Jackie to pick up their parcels, quickly escorting them followed Jack out, into silent corridors, carrying on towards the anti room and main door opened by the praying nun, as I passed by her, there was no movement of her lips but she did bow. Rapidly the door was closed firmly behind us. Jack had got Kaye into the back of the waiting amubukance, we all climbed in to be driven away back to the camp MRS, away from all this mess we had mistakenly got ourselves into. Jackie Leash followed behind in his car. Arriving back at the MRS. Jackie Leash looked after Mary and Jackie, whilst we got the MO to examine Kaye. Unfortunately his diagnose was a case of. 'St. Vitas Dance.' I exclaimed.

'Oh my God Doctor. What on earth is that?'

'That Mrs. Plant is a nervous complaint. I'm afraid she will have to go into hospital.' That suggestion to me was like showing a red rag to a bull.

'She is going nowhere. Doctor. Tell me. What I have to do and I shall get her better.'

'Mrs Plant it will take months of constant supervision with medication. Unfortunately you are not qualified to undertake that course of action. She would be far better off in hospital.'

I was torn between doing what he advised or, carrying out what was necessary to get her better myself. My heart won the day.

335

'Doctor I'll take her home.'...I saw concern appear on Jack's face...'Jack pick Kaye up and let's get back to the quarters. Where we can discuss the matter further.' The MO intervened.

'Mrs Plant. I do see and do appreciate your concern but, if that's the way you want to proceed. I'll give you some medication to administer to your daughter. I'll get the ambulance to take you all back to your quarters.'

We put Kaye into bed. I was beside myself with worry but determined to get my little girl Kaye back amongst our tribe. The other two just sat quietly at the table in the dining room, this was so unlike them. Jack and I were beside ourselves, we both knew we had done the wrong thing. We questioned them on their treatment at the Convent? It appeared that it was not, that they had been badly treated. Only no one was allowed to speak. As they related their story it somewhat became more exaggerated.

Mary: 'Mum as soon as you left. We were separated and only saw each other in Church. The boys were down one side and us girls on the other.'

Jackie: 'Mum. It was no talking all day long, if we twisted our heads they would be twisted right off and back again. When I laughed at the boy in front blowing his nose on the nuns habits. They dragged me by my ears, out of church and beat me. I howled with pain.'

Mary: 'Kaye and I ran out to him and fought with the nuns. Instead we got a thrashing as well. It was after that that Kaye began kicking the pew. They dragged her out and beat her, but it didn't stop her kicking.'

Connie having seen the ambulance draw up arrived with Michael. That put an end to any further of their explanations. Hoping with the presence of Michael, the other two would respond. That did the trick, the pair of them played with Michael, our house soon returned to normality. We arrange for them to return to their army schooling. After a few days Mary and Jackie returned to their old school then Connie, a tower of strength took it upon herself to look after Michael, whilst I tended to Kaye. With the proper medication after a few weeks her constant shaking subsided into spasmodic shakes as she quietened down. Nobody had ever heard of the ailment, not even mother. I would sit on Kaye's bed cuddle and talk to her about India, which seemed to pacify her easing the spasmodic bouts of shaking, which had me tightening my arms around her. I would put Michael in bed with her, so I could carry on with my household duties. Each day when they came back from school, they would all pile on top of Kaye's bed, run through their different lessons, then start entertaining her to make her laugh. However, I not feeling well find I am pregnant again. Although pleased, dreaded the thought of this additional worry with Kaye being so ill. Somehow after months of patience, medication and constant attention to Kaye I managed. Her shaking spasms became less, before they ceased. At her last examination the MO declared she was fit enough to return to school, he gave her the all clear and congratulated me.

'Mrs.Plant. With your patience and determination, you have worked wonders in getting Kaye back to normality. When I first examined her I thought it was definitely a hospital case, but I admire you for your determination in treating your child. Well done. But what about you?'

'Oh. I'm alright sir. I'm just pregnant.'

'Well, if you need too, please do come and see me.'

Christmas dinner was celebrated with Dickie standing up and proposing to Peg, who accepted. Prompting more celebrations. The new year of 1934 arrived, the early months were very cold, with bitter winds that brought heavy snow, causing high drifts over the plains, making it very difficult for the children to get to school. Sunday dinner times in our quarters became a regular social gathering. After the men had returned from the Mess, we sat down to the meal with invited guests Dickie Fox, Jackie Leash and Tom Wilberham. Any current topic was discussed with disagreements, as they tried to put the world to rights. However, the on-going political developments in Germany brought consternation to all the men. They did not like the idea one little bit. Their discussions became more intense. Jack was the only one who had fought in the First World War and expressed his feelings by saying.

'Hitler the so called Chancellor of Germany was only some jumped up Corporal of the German army, and for all who got in his way, big trouble was in store.'

As the situation in Germany intensified their weekly discussions continued. Jack and Dickie spent many hours after the Sunday meal discussing what was really going on in Germany. The new Nazi party had burnt any non-German books, had begun to terrorise the Jews. With me becoming larger every day and not feeling very good, it certainly was not the news I wanted to listen to. I spoke up.

'The pair of you. Go to the Mess and discuss it down there.'

Dickie full of apologies took the hint. Both disappeared with my tribe in tow. However Dickie had applied for promotion, so he was away quite a lot, so the Sunday after dinner discussion waned, unless Jack and Tom were on hand.

Bridie & Peter

In July, I went into labour, gave birth to another son Peter, he was not very strong. A month later, we christened him Peter Joseph, my cousin Bridie Dalton was Godmother. By the beginning of the summer holidays, I had plenty of help around, as an excuse to see the new baby, the Battens and McDermott's turned up, stayed for six weeks, until it was back to school. Only then would I have some peace to myself in our quarters, but to mine and Jack's shock. I find myself expecting again. Peg and Dickie had set the date for their wedding to be held at Clapton East London near Mary's & Bert's home. It was to be somewhat of a military wedding with the men in their Blues. Mary and Kaye were her bridesmaids, Michael a pageboy. On their wedding day Patty Batten became an additional bridesmaid. We all stayed at Mary's and Bert's. Everyone made a great fuss of our new-born son Peter. Mother was at her best ordering everyone around, she took over looking after Peter, ordered me to go and enjoy myself like the rest of them. The wedding went off well, lasted well into the night. On the Sunday we returned back. Not long after that event a letter from Mother informs us that Francis and Tom Wilbraham had set a date to get married, again at the same venue Clapton. However, the last time travelling up there had not done Peter or me any favours. I discussed it with Jack, who unfortunately could not make the date as he would be on duty that specific weekend. He left it to me to reply, politely refused their kind invitation. A week later much to my horror. Jack informs me.

'Sarah. I have been posted to Fenham Barracks Newcastle.'

'Oh no Jack. I thought you said we would stay at Greenland's until you were demobbed.'

'Well Sarah you know what the army are. Oh by the way Dickie has been posted to Bulford.' All said in a matter-of-fact way.

I resigned myself to this latest move, the only one thing good about the posting was. I would meet up with my dear friend Kitty Burns. I wrote informing her the latest news, then set about with packing of all my brass. Early in November on a bleak and raw day, Jack went on parade together with two bombardiers who had served with him in the Battery in India, to be presented with Campaign Medals for service in the Northwest Frontier, another celebration together with a farewell one. Our large luggage was collected and sent ahead of us. A week later we left Greenland's camp. I said my tearful farewells to Connie a true friend.

CHAPTER TWO
NEWCASTLE - 1933

On a cold and miserable day we left Greenland's. I was none too happy, but my tribe could not have cared less, overjoyed with the prospects of once again meeting the Burns tribe. Holding baby Peter well wrapped up in my arms, we caught the train to Waterloo where we had arranged to meet mother and Julia under the square clock, before catching a tube to Kings Cross then the Newcastle train. Struggling through the barriers Jack said something to me, but due to the noise I did not hear, as we headed for the square clock, where mother and Julia stood waiting, however, another pleasant surprise awaited us, stood close by them was Jack's mother and his sister Rose. Both parties unaware of each other's company, at the same time they both moved to greet us. Jack made the introductions, seeing the funny side of the chance meeting, all got on well together. No doubt after we had left they had a long chat together, but with Jack urging us to make a move, for us it was a brief. 'Hello and Goodbye, see you soon.'

At King's Cross we boarded the train found a compartment to ourselves. After it had left Kings Cross careering out of the smoky atmosphere of London, the flat drab countryside passed us by, in the twilight it stopped at a place called Peterborough then off again into the darkness of the night. I had fed Peter and got him settled down on the seat,with a small case placed alongside him, so as he would not roll off but he was too young to move about that much. With the continuous and monotonous clank and rattle of the wheels it soon had everyone asleep. I must have slept a long time, as Jack shook me awake.

'Sarah not long now. Were nearly there, let them sleep on.'

We arrived in Newcastle in the early hours of the morning. The train clanked to a stop, then we woke them. Dazed, shivering with cold they gathered their parcels before we left the train. It was extremely cold with a bitter wind blowing. We shuffled our way down the platform towards the exit and into the station entrance. A soldier approached Jack.

'Sir is your party for Fenham Barracks?'

'Yes that's correct.'

'Right Sir. If you'll follow me. I have transport waiting to take you. There are a couple of other families, already waiting out there.'

We trooped out behind him to where others were waiting by a G.S. wagon, another family joined us. The Driver checked to see that everyone was on his list, asked us to get into the back. Jack helped us all up then climbed up beside us. The journey to Fenham Barracks was short ride through wet deserted streets, turning off into the Barracks stopping briefly at the Guardhouse then carried on, it stopped, with the engine still running the Driver came around the back and called out a short list of names to get off, leaving others still sat or stood in the darkness. The driver assisted in lifting cases and boxes down and away from the rear of the wagon the driver spoke with Jack. I don't know what he said and I could not have cared less, then revving up the engine he left us. Along with several other families we stood in a biting wind shivering with the cold. I had Peter tightly wrapped in a blanket that covered him totally from the wind. All I wanted to do like everyone else was to get to our quarters and sleep. The only audible sound amongst us was the whistling wind, the chattering of teeth and stamping of feet. After a short while, signs of a couple of flash lamps became visible, as they advanced towards our party, then above the whistle of the wind a voice with the lilt of an all too familiar Irish brogue called out.

'Laura is that you?' (Laura was a nickname Bobby named Jack back in Peshawar. After the famous variety actress Laura le Plant, God knows why?) Jack replied.

'Bobby. Yes it is. What's going on?' These families have been left here.'

The flash lamps illuminated us, as out of the darkness strode the rotund figure of Bobby accompanied by some other soldiers.

'Laura. Sarah. I've been waiting for you to arrive. By God, it's so good to see you both once again.' Handshakes/hugs, after the brief greetings were over, He ordered the soldiers to take the remainder of the families to their quarters. As they dispersed Bobby picked up a suitcase pointing the flash lamp ahead said .

'C'mon this way. Sarah we only have to walk into that block of flats in front of you.'

Jack had Michael in his arms, I carried Peter, both of them fast asleep. Mary, Kaye and Jackie all yawning, just about awake struggled along with their little cases, as we followed Bobby and Jack chatting away like long lost friends. We struggled up eight flights of stairs before Bobby stopped on the top landing, pointing the flash lamp at two doors opposite each other he said.

'These two flats are both yours.' (A flat on each side of the top landing). He continued…'First thing is to get your tribe to bed. The sleeping quarters are on your right side of the landing. Stay there while I go in and light the mantle.' Unlocking the door he entered, within seconds a flicker of light turned into a warm glow, he appeared in the doorway….'In here Sarah. Kitty has already aired the two rooms and made up the beds, just put the tribe to bed so they should be okay.'

There was no time for any inspections at this ungodly hour of the morning. As we guided them into the first one, they all flopped onto the beds, fell asleep with all their clothes on. Jack laid Michael in between them removing their shoes, pulled the blankets over them. In the daylight we would sort out other clothing. Bobby took us across into the other apartment opened the door, entered and lit the mantle. He showed us where everything was. I couldn't have cared less, I too was ready to drop, still held Peter cradled in my arms. Now I understood what Kitty meant when she wrote, saying she had two flats. Bobby interrupted my thoughts quietly said.

'Sarah it's so good to see you all again. Kitty will be along in the morning. You all get some sleep of what is remaining of the night. I'll say goodnight and catch up with you in the morning.' I enquired.

'Is she far away from us?'

'Oh no we have two small comfortable flats on the ground floor at the other end of this block.' Bobby left leaving the door ajar.Jack urged.

'Come on Sarah let's get some shut eye. It's no point in going to bed it's gone three a.m. I'll make up a makeshift bed in here for the night. I have to be up again at six.'

Jack as ever never to miss a muster call, went out across to the other flat to check on them, he came back carrying a mattress with a couple of blankets, he murmured.

'They are flat out asleep all tucked up.'…He sorted out the mattress gave me a blanket…'Here wrap this blanket around you and Peter.'

He turned the gas mantle down low. I settled down with Peter in my arms and arranged the blanket around us.

'Jack will they be all right in there?'

'Yes get to sleep.'

'How are we going to manage two flats Jack?'

'We don't start worrying about these things now shush awhile?' His voice trailed off, he was asleep. A constant banging on the door woke me up, someone was trying to get in. In the dim light of the gas mantle, I realised where I was.

'Jack wake up there's someone at the door.'

No answer Jack wasn't there. I moved the blanket off of me, Peter was still fast asleep so I tucked the blanket gently around him, got up, turned up the gas to provide its stark light as the banging on the door continued, then with a rattle of the letterbox a voice shouted.'

'Sarah Plant are you in there or are you all dead? C'mon Jahldi Jahldi.'

It was Kitty Burns. Oh my God what a wonderful way to be woken up. I went to the door opened it, there was Kitty as brazen as ever.

'God Sarah Plant I thought you were all dead, it's not like you to be having a lie in.' We fell into each other's arms hugging each other.

'By God Kitty it's so lovely to see you again, come on in. I don't know where anything is in this place yet. For heaven's sake what time is it?'

'About quarter to seven. C'mon Jahldi, I've brought some tea and milk to make us a cup of tea. No sign of Jack. I take it he's already on parade?' Kitty walked ahead.

'Must be he's not here and I didn't hear him go.' She was at a sink filled the kettle placed it on the gas ring.

'That's for chai, where's the matches?'

'On the table there, I'll get them.'... She continued chatting... 'Bobby said he would call for him to show him where he had to report too. Let those two buggers sort themselves out. Sarah Plant Now are you and Jack trying for a football team?'...Handing over the box she lit the gas...'Anyway what's your other news?' Kitty had not changed and doubted if she ever would.

'No we are not, but c'mon Kitty, have a look at Peter.' I took Peter out of the mould of blankets, Kitty took hold of him.

'What a lovely wee chap you have here Sarah.'

'Yes he is but he is not a very strong baby.'

'Sarah over there in that cupboard are some cups, you finish making chai while I look after this wee fella.' I busied myself made and poured out two cups of chai, placed them on the table where she had sat down with Peter cradled in her arms, sat down opposite her. We talked catching up on our news, in between she fed Peter then I fished out some nappies and towels to bath and change him. It was near nine o'clock when I asked.

'Kitty what about your tribe and school?'

'Oh they are okay. They will sort themselves out. How's that Mary of yours? Lost any of her devilment yet? Let's wake them up.' Obviously Kitty was eager to see my tribe again

'No leave them for a little while longer. It was a tiring journey. '

'Okay Sarah. I'll go now and fetch something back for them to eat. I won't be long.'

Away she went. I got myself tidied up, surveyed the cooking facilities, a tiny kitchen you could hardly swing a cat in, two other rooms plus a toilet, rather a let-down after the wonderful home we had in Greenland's. First impression I was not going to like living here that was for sure. Kitty returned with Andy and Babbs, carrying some bags loaded with cereals and other bits for my tribe's breakfast.

'C'mon you two buggers say hello to Aunt Sarah, take those things through to the kitchen.' They stopped big beams across their faces.

'Hello Aunt Sarah nice to see you again.'

'Hello to yourselves. Haven't you both got bigger.'

'C'mon brats move yourselves put that food on the kitchen table. Now Sarah there's enough there to feed your tribe for a week.'

Half of the table was covered in provisions. At that moment Mary and Kaye appeared on the scene, still dressed in their coats half asleep, no doubt woken by the noise, both slumped down onto two unpacked cases. Mary chirped up.

'Hello Kitty Burns nice to see you again.'

'Hello Mary. Hello Kathleen. 'No response from Kaye just a glower, I thought: I'd better tell Kitty of the name change.

'Kitty you had better get used to the idea. Kaye is her name not Kathleen.'

'Umm. Oh. A right little madam. Hello Kaye.'

This time a response with that sweet smile of hers, she answered.

'Hello Mrs. Burns. Nice to see you again.'

340

The return of Andy and Babb's caused a big response. The meeting of the tribes once again. Mary asked.

'Where's Jack and Marty?'

'At school.' Mary yelled.

'I'll beat him when I see him.'

I looked at Kitty and she at me. I noticed a smile appear on Kitty's face and a twinkle in her eyes. Their meeting had yet to come. I had to intervene.

'Mary. Wake Jackie and Michael up, while I get something for you to eat.'

The four of them rushed out. Kitty followed me into the tiny kitchen began cutting and buttering bread. 'I'll put some jam on this lot Sarah Plant, that will fill them up until you get sorted out.' More tea was made, whilst in the other flat there was pandemonium, with all the yells and shrieks of excitement, Kitty just ignored it and said.

'Leave them Sarah, it won't last, when the fighting starts we will sort them out.'

They all trooped in from the other flat. Jackie was enthralled at Kitty's presence, Michael wary and shy. They sat down and ate their fill, then the chasing began. Kitty fed Peter and changed him, I sorted out a change of clothing, it was way after ten when Jack and Bobby arrived back. It was their NAAFI Break.

'Hello Kitty Burns. Still drinking chai I see.' A warm few words as they hugged and kissed.

'Laura. You haven't changed a bit nice to see you.' There was more chatting between the four of us until Jack asked.

'Sarah have you sorted out what's required?' Having already discovered there was not much needed replied.

'Not much, only foodstuff that Kitty has brought in, and if Bobby had anything to do with the inventory. Do not need anything else.'

'Okay well sort out what we need in foodstuff or anything else and I'm sure Kitty will show you the ropes. Eh Kitty?'

'Yes. I'll take her down the Bazaar's. That's for sure.'

Which brought peals of laughter at her suggestion. After a cup of chai the pair of them returned back to duty.

'C'mon Sarah Plant, Jahldi Jahldi let's get these flats sorted out, then after dinner you can get your bearings and buy the provisions, but be warned, wrap up your tribe well against the blasted wind up here, it cuts you in two.'

I looked out of the kitchen window into a cloud-laden sky, a miserable November day, below was the parade ground. Kitty coming alongside me, began pointing out places.

'Sarah, this is the headquarters of the Northumbrian Infantry. Look, over there is the sergeants mess, across that main road is the soldiers barracks. Behind us is another block similar to this one, but before we venture over to the Naafi, I'll show you our quarters.'

We spent the rest of the morning, sorting out cases, most important clothing. It seemed silly to me that we had two separate flats, so decided we would utilise both, using the opposite one for the four children to bed down, in ours Jack and I would sleep in one of the rooms along with Peter and use it for general purposes. Although small it had more than adequate rooms. However the two flats could not accommodate any of our furniture, so it would have to go into storage, we were back to Army issue. We had some lunch then it was time to visit Kitty's flats, and she didn't waste any time in sorting them out.

'C'mon Jahldi you lot of brats. Get your coats on. Let's get going.'

Noisily we left the flat, down the stairway to the ground floor. It was a bleak outlook there were no gardens only a roadway, then the square. Kitty led us to the end of the block into her two flats, they were very comfortable, then back around the square to the NAAFI shop for provisions. The wind whipped across the deserted open parade ground, by the time we got back

341

into our quarters with the provisions, we had time for a cup of chai to warm us up. There was a noise on the stairway, a banging on the door. Mary opened the door, then a lot of shrieking heralded the arrival of Jack, Marty and Kathleen back from school. The meeting up of the two tribes the joyous moments didn't last too long. Mary and Jack Burns were soon fighting.

The cold of the winter months had turned worse, the winds off the North Sea were biting. Peter became ill, his condition deteriorated, had to be hospitalised. Within a week he died on the 11th December. We had not been in Newcastle a month. Jack and I were devastated, I felt so depressed after all the pain and anguish we had endured with Kaye, then the joyous blessing with the birth of Peter, a lovely baby that I nursed and held in my arms, now that was gone I thought: *I would lose the baby I was carrying,* Cried myself to sleep. The funeral arrangements were made, we buried our tiny Peter Joseph in a tiny white coffin. Instead of December being a happy joyous run up to Christmas with the Burns, it became a very disturbing, sombre time for both families, even the two tribes seemed to be in an armistice together. Whilst I cried, Kitty did all the cooking. She was a tower of strength and helped me to get through that particularly very bad time, throughout Christmas and the New Year, which the Newcastle Geordies like the traditional Scots celebrated. "Hog Mahoney" to the fullest, but not so for us. Newcastle was to become a place I never liked. We struggled through those dark days, got the four children into school at Fenham Convent along with the Burns tribe. Michael was of age to start his education. After their experience at the other Convent there were ructions from the eldest three, nevertheless, we made certain it would never happen again. We both went and explained the situation to the Mother Superior. A totally different character with an outlook on the children's welfare under her care. The Convent was just a tram ride away, the fare cost one halfpenny from the Barracks. The winter months slowly crept by, but the weather was still as windy as hell and it did not seem to change. Unfortunately, my tribe did not like their stay in the Convent, apparently according to them at the least mistake, the Nun's strapped them on their hands with a leather strap, maybe if it was right what they were saying my tribe deserved it, but I think it was all to do with them not liking the convent. Mary was still a devil and with ferocity fought with everybody who even dared to touch her sister and brothers. In a roundabout way her report indicated the antics she got up to, her authoritive way however, their reports stated that they were improving with the lessons so all appeared to be going well. One day Jackie innocently blurted out, that Mary and Kaye used to dare him and Michael to run to school to beat the tram to save money to buy a penny worth of sweets for them all. I turned a blind eye to these shenanigans. At least they were not boarders and would be under my care at home. Kitty was a true friend, did all she could to support my tribe and me, she spent all of her time with me. Nothing was too much for her and Bobby. Jack had an ally in Bobby, another old contemptible of the British Expeditionary Force. Both did not like what they had heard or read about the political situation in Germany and Austria, with Hitler and his party, they voiced their opinions verbally. As Kitty put it.

'You two can't do a damn thing about that fella Hitler, so why don't the pair of you bugger off down the mess and leave us two in peace.'

Kitty never had any malice in her comments or suggestion. I doubt if I could ever have her knack of instant conversation that was riddled with her wit. Both didn't need a second offer with big grins over their faces they were soon out of the flat. In my state of pregnancy. I was getting progressively larger, it was well into May, before the cold winds abated and the so called summer months began. Then I received a letter from Peg informing us that Dickie, who by then had been promoted to the rank of a Sergeant Major, had been posted to Fenham Barracks, they would soon be on their way. This news helped me greatly, delighted Kitty, spontaneously she yelled.

'Lucknow. Sarah Plant. Do you member the riot in that Bazaar?'

'Don't remind me Kitty that was a long time ago.'

This set us both gupping about India. I sent a reply letter to Peg to see if they could get up here before the date of my confinement. Her reply informed me that their date of posting was early in May, she informed of her new address that just happened to be the flat on the second floor below us. When I showed Kitty her letter she exclaimed.

'You know what that means Sarah. There will be three buggers in the mess, we will have to contend with.'

'Well that won't be too bad, at least Dickie is a gentleman he will ensure they don't stay all night?'

Peg and Dickie did arrive, moved in below us, much to the consternation of my tribe, as they knew what was in store for them with their Aunt Peg around. However, on the sixteenth of June, I went into labour was rushed into hospital to give birth to a baby girl, again it wasn't an easy birth, at the time was unaware she was to be the last of my girls. Everyone was delighted with the new addition to our family. I could not fault their gracious intentions. This time Jack did send a wire to Mother before he Bobby and Dickie celebrated the birth in the Mess, whilst Kitty and Peg looked after me and the two tribes, not that Peg had ever seen them together or, what they got up to. Anyway Dickie and Peg were godparents to Margaret Rose. Margaret after Peg and Rose after Jack's younger sister. Dickie called her. "His little Princess." Our choice of them being the Godparents had been arranged long before we were posted to Newcastle, it was great to have them with us. Although I was delighted with my little saviour, my instincts told me she was a strong baby, but I could not totally erase the thoughts of Peter from my mind. Nevertheless, much to Peg's annoyance, their own accommodation was not to her liking she being well aware of the devilment that my tribe could get up to, tried to rule the roost on both of the tribes. However at her first encounter with Jack and Mary's rivalry and fighting, she intervened. Kitty just told her

'Peg. Just don't you bother yourself. Let them fight and get it out of their system. They will be great pal's afterwards. Take no notice of the pair of them.'

Peg rather taken aback, let them fight on but was ever watchful and aware of all their tricks. Somehow she soon discovered their, "Beat the tram" trick and stopped their fare money made them walk there and back. Much to their annoyance another failed lark. I taking no notice, prayed that she would soon have children of her own. Dickie. 'Ferdie Fox,' as nicknamed by the children, was from a military family. His father a senior ranking army officer, served seventeen years in China and India. Dickie was born in Tianksin China. The eldest of five children he spent all his youth out in the Far East. His father died in Karachi in 1914. that's when his Mother decided to enrol Dickie at the Duke of York's Royal Military School in Dover. In 1920 at the age of fifteen, having completed his studies, he joined the Royal Horse Artillery as a Badgie, was posted back to India. He finished up a Sergeant in Lucknow where he met Jack and Bobby, he did understand and spoke Urdu and Chinese. So with the three of them together again, their discussions took on a new slant. Grim faces appeared when Hindenburg died and Adolf Hitler announced he would be called. 'The Fuehrer and Reich Chancellor and Supreme Commander of the German Armed forces.' In other words Lord and master over Germany. All three were cynical about what the future held for all. One day Kitty and I were making sandwiches. Peg was busy feeding Margaret. The three men sat in the kitchen, discussing the latest developments in Germany, the name Hitler kept on cropping up. Kitty wielding a knife laden with butter pointed at them and enquired.

'Who's this Hitler fella anyway?' Dickie replied.

'Surely you have heard us talk about him in the past.'

'Not really, but you're always on about him, who is he?'

'He my dear Kitty, is the new Dictator of Germany and were afraid, not the best of news.' Jack commented.

'He's only a jumped up Corporal from the First World War. Bobby stormed.

'What the hell can he achieve?' Jack quipped.

'You wait and see he's got powerful backing with the people behind him. It won't take him long to start something or other.'

Even Kitty with an open mind and devil may care attitude, adopted an instant dislike to him referring to him as. 'That Blasted Fella Hitler.' Nevertheless It did not take him long to increase his Army to three times the amount allowed by the treaty of Versailles. That to the three of them was a warning very quickly condemned his actions. 'Things will get worse not better.' This soon became evident when Churchill spoke about. "Our defences were weak and that efforts should be made to increase our forces against a future war with Germany."

Towards the autumn the bitter cold winds returned carried on into the winter months. It was to be our second Christmas in Newcastle, not without it's sad memories for me but it was to become quite a large gathering. Early on Christmas Eve morning Dickie arrived at the doorway, his peak cap tucked in under his arm, whilst under his other arm was a very large turkey wrapped in greaseproof paper, its lifeless neck dangling as it swung gently to and fro. Being a gentleman he exclaimed.

'Sarah will this be big enough to fit into your stove? Or should I ask is your stove big enough to take this rather beautiful bird I have acquired for the dinner table.'

At the sight of Dickie, looking totally unconcerned about his appearance. I had to sit down and roar with laughter.

'Dickie you are a fool, but thank you'. He stifling a laugh replied.

'Thank you Sarah, this bird is presented with my compliments.'....Unceremoniously he dumped it on the table and remarked...'After carrying that around. I could do with a cup of tea please Sarah. Then we shall decide what is what.'

My tribe came to a standstill when they saw the size of the turkey on the table with mouths agog they looked. Mary ran out. After a while arrived back with the Burn's tribe, followed by an out of breath Kitty. When she saw its size she gasped.

'Jesus Christ. Sarah Plant that's an Ostrich. I'll bet you're behind this Dickie Fox.' Dickie sat grinning like a Cheshire cat quietly responded.

'Kitty, never say the army can't provide.'

'How the blazes are you going to cook that thing Sarah?' I offered.

'Cup of tea Kitty?'

'Christ, that I do need after running up those bloody stairs! Mary came rushing in and told me you had just killed a vulture. I just dropped everything and ran.'

Her latest remark had Mary in howls of laughter, she had caught out Kitty Burns. I went to the stove, opened its door. Dickie offered.

'Here let me give you a hand.' Kitty moved in and the pair of them lifting up the carcase carried it to the stove, which was far too small. Decided the only way to cook this bird was in the cookhouse, back on the table it went. Dickie left to organise the cooking arrangements. Early next morning everyone was up ready for Mass before preparations for the mid-day feast began. Kitty, Peg and I did all the preparations for the Christmas Dinner, things were moved out, tables and chairs brought in, planks of wood rested between two chairs increasing the number of seats for the two tribes Near to one o'clock the three men turned up, all having had a few drinks in the Mess and between them they carried a rather large silver platter covered by a silver top. That was placed ceremoniously in the center of the table. With a flourish Dickie removed the lid to reveal a very large cooked and dressed Turkey. This act alone brought roars of approval and shouts from the children. Then the three of them stood to attention and chorused. 'Happy Christmas to one and all.' More applause and shouts as each one in turn took a hand in carving the bird. While this was going on Kitty, Peg and myself made ourselves busy fetching and carrying all the vegetables to be laid out on the table for all to feast upon. We had turkey for a week until we were sick of the sight of it. New Year's eve, we were preparing for another party to celebrate the New Year, when I received a wire.

FRANCES GAVE BIRTH TO BABY BOY STOP
THOMAS STOP MOTHER STOP

1935. Jack had only eight months to complete his twenty-two year's service. Also not long after, Bobby was due to leave the Army. Jack and I had previously discussed what he would do. With all the discussions that the three of them had previously had, I was not wholly convinced if events took a turn for the worst Jack would leave the army. I was sure he would extend his time, nevertheless, I kept my fears to myself. We had already made up our minds to return to London and settle down somewhere. But Kitty's idea was.

'Sarah let those two buggers do what they like, we only have eight months left to enjoy ourselves. You and I will go to a few of the mess do's, before we finally leave.'

She was quite happy to enjoy herself when the occasion arose. We did take advantage and spent the odd hour at some of the do's. Mary was quite capable of looking after the rest of them and Margaret, who was then six months old, nevertheless we took it in turns to return from the Mess just to see everything was all right. To me the irregular events gave me some respite from the anguish I had from losing Peter. But dark political clouds in Germany were gathering momentum and by the beginning of March.That 'Fella Hitler' had taken over the Saarland. In response, our Government declared new plans for expansion of the three forces. That 'Fella Hitler' responded with the introduction of Conscription in Germany. I was truly fearful Jack would soon sign on for a further term. Easter passed us by and in anticipation of a return to London life. I wished the months would slip by however, before then King George the fifth and Queen Mary celebrated their Silver Jubilee. So began rehearsals for a grand parade on a Saturday morning in honour of their Majesties King George and Queen Mary's Silver Jubilee. The children enjoyed watching the soldiers rehearsing for hours on the parade ground below. The RSM and Sgt.'s shouting out the orders until they were satisfied all was correct. The parade would be dismissed and the solders marched away, followed by the clatter of horse hooves the grinding noise of the carriage wheels on the hard surface. A full dress rehearsal with all the bands was scheduled to take place a week before the big parade, as they marched onto the square, the sky's opened up. The rain came pouring down; this sent all the children on the parade ground scampering out of the rain up to our flat. Mary had invited them all back to see the parade in comfort, crammed into the two flats. Little faces were flattened against the windowpanes, as they watched from this great vantage point as below the dress rehearsal continued. By the time the rain had ceased all on parade were thoroughly soaked. The day of the parade was a sunny day, we had a grandstand view of the pomp and ceremony going on below. In addition to this the Officer Commanding presented Jack with a Silver Jubilee Medal. A great honour, having completed his time of service with distinction. When he marched up for his presentation all the children cheered. A party for all the children had been organised along with one in the Mess. Nevertheless, Jack invited all back to our tiny flat, to continue his celebration, it continued well into the next day, but it wasn't to be the last. Shortly after that celebration I received a letter from Mother advising me that my sister Kitty had given birth to a baby boy their third boy named Kevin. It was the beginning of June when Kitty came running into the flat she blurted out.

'Sarah Plant have you heard the latest?' With apprehension I sighed.

'No what's happened outside? Has Mary done something to your Jack?'

'No don't be so daft. They can beat the hell out of each other for all I care. Listen, I've just been told by one of the wives, that one of the hill stations in India was hit by an earthquake and a lot of British servicemen have been killed.'

'It cannot be Mussoorie they had one early in the 1910's.'

345

'No Quetta, nowhere near to there, apparently it's totally cut off. Reports say that the Army have taken control of the situation.' I retorted.

'Kitty do you remember the snow leopard fur you bought in Nowshera.'

'Sarah Plant don't you say another word. That was the worst bargain I ever did make in India.' She replied with a twinkle in her eye, the rest of the morning we spent talking about our past escapades. We held a party for the children to celebrate Margaret's first birthday.

We had been in Newcastle for nearly two years, a place I personally for my own reasons was very glad to leave. Jack was allowed to take leave and go down to London to apply for a position in the Post Office also try and find somewhere for a family of seven to live. He stayed with Miria and Pops while he searched for suitable accommodation. He came back having being offered a job as a Postman, but had no luck with accommodation. He also had discussed our pending return with Mother, who by then had moved to Vauxhall, so she was also on the lookout as well. It appeared that times had not changed, but in his usual way said.

'Don't worry Sarah we'll manage somehow something will turn up.'

Kitty and I discussed our prospects in great depths. As she too was much in the same boat, three months after Jack's demob, Bobby's time was also up, both decided Bobby would leave the army, however, did not want to return to Armagh in Northern Ireland, instead to move down South, Bobby like Jack try for a Post Office job in London. Furthermore, much to their pride young Jack had decided, he wanted to join the Army as a Badgie. With Jack's release date confirmed, and when Jack Burns left for the army another small farewell party was held.. As usual Mary and Jack finished up scrapping in the other flat and had to be separated by Kitty.

'Jack Burns. Mary Plant. I'll come in there and macro the pair of you.'

The voice of Kitty boomed out, as she went into the other flat. She gave them both a cuff around the ears...'Now then you two this is the last fight both of you will have for a very long time.'

The fighting ceased, they parted grinning like Cheshire cats. This was how they had cemented their friendship. None the worst for any of their scraps they parted the best of pals. When Mary came back in, she was shaking her head. I noticed tears forming in her eyes, but her jaws were firmly set. It was the end of an era. After that, we did not see young Jack for many a year he following in his father's footsteps, served in India and turned out to become a fine smart young soldier. As for us, once again we began packing our worldly possessions, with our furniture still in storage. It had to be transported down to another store in London to await our collection. We were now ready for the final day. But not without a farewell party to say our last goodbyes to a life which I had now grown accustomed to and loved.

On the eight of August 1935 Jack finally left the army. Whatever will happen next?

I had not realised we had made so many friends in Newcastle. There were dozens of people on the platform who came to see us off. Some I didn't know, obviously friends of Jack's Bobby's or Kitty's. After the handshakes the hugs kisses and the crying session was over, as Kitty and I clung together through our sobs she murmured.

'Sarah Plant we will meet again in London, that's a promise.'

I could not respond to her parting words, but just knew it would happen. We boarded the London bound train, as the train slowly pulled out of the station I sat down to regain my composure. With the children all-peering out of the windows, Jack with a final wave withdrew his head from the open window, pulled the leather strap up to close it, as he sat down next to me said.

'Well. I'm pleased that send-off is over.'

At that moment I understood what a personal wrench this was for him. Knowing his life was only of discipline and regimented procedures. Now this was all behind him, and as the head of our family, had to face the new challenge of civilian life. I turned to Jack thanked him for the life he had provided for us as a family. He turned to me and said.

'Thank you Sarah on many occasions your contribution was very badly needed. It will never be forgotten.' Jack pulled out his handkerchief from his pocket, dusted his nose. We sat their quietly reflecting our memories, as the rhythm of the train wheels gradually increased and took us away from army life.

After an uneventful long train ride, we arrived at Kings Cross late in the afternoon. We made our way over to mothers in Vauxhall, like a lot of waifs and strays we arrived unannounced. She was on her own and delighted to see us. On his previous trip to London Jack had visited and discussed with mother about our accommodation problem. She had put the wheels in motion, discussed it with my sisters, had arranged that Mary and Kaye would go to stay at Bridget's in Vauxhall, Jackie and Michael would stay with Fan living in number 4 a few doors along the lane Jack I and baby Margaret would stay at Lena's in the city. That night we slept on the floor.

The next day witnessed the temporary disintegration of our family. We went first to Fan's then onto Bridget's in Vauxhall. Took a tram ride to the City, with me carrying Margaret in my arms we arrived at Lena's. For us as a family being split up, it was going to be an awkward period to face with the tribe's further education. Although at the time it was the school holiday period. However, Bridget came up with a possible solution. Peter was the caretaker at St Anne's school and if appropriate he could arrange for my four to start school there. Jack began his job in the Brixton Hill sorting office, travelling by the early morning 33 tram to Brixton he spent most of his spare time looking anywhere for new accommodation. One afternoon Lena and I were sat in her kitchen talking idly about nothing of importance, when Jack arrived rather later than usual. He entered in a hurry and ordered.

'Sarah quick grab your coat, one of the lads at the Post Office has told me about a flat. I've already been around to see the Landlady, I told her about our family split up and about Margaret and she didn't say no. I've arranged with her for you to see it this evening. C'mon Jahldi it's a good opportunity.' Getting up I asked.

'Where is it?'

In Brixton c'mon. Jahldi Jahldi. Lena look after Margaret for us there's a ducks.' Lena sat holding Margaret, just nodded.

Leaving her flat we ran all the way to the Kingsway to catch the 33 tram that would take us all the way to Brixton Town Hall, we got off just as the Town Hall clock began striking six.

Grabbing hold of my hand Jack had me running across the road around the side of the Town Hall along Acre Lane, with me still running passing one side road puffing, out of breath I questioned.

'Jack how far do I have to run? I'm puffed out.'

As we turned into the next one, Baytree Road until further along he stopped.

'You can stop puffing now this is it.'

He approached a doorway, gave a couple of bangs with the knocker. I stood there breathing heavy out of breath, then the door was opened by a rather stout lady.

'Yes. Ah Mr and Mrs Plant'...she puffed and wheezed...'I've been waiting for you.'...We eased past her portly frame she closed the door behind us...'Please come this way. It will be ten shillings per week, paid every Saturday morning on the dot, and one week's rent in advance if you don't mind.'

We followed on behind her puffing and wheezing frame, with me puffing in harmony. The flat consisted of two rooms, a bedroom with a double bed, another sitting room overlooking the street, and a tiny kitchen.

'Its let fully furnished but sharing the toilet on the landing.' She wheezed, as Jack waving a ten-shilling note in front of her enquired.

'When can we move in Mrs. Palmer?' She wheezed.

'Well it's vacant. Right away if you want. '

'We'll take it, and move in tomorrow.' All agreed and settled we left this "little gem" of a place. Outside Jack asked.

'What do you say Sarah?' I realised I hadn't said anything during the tour of inspection just puffed until I got my breath back, observed.

'Well it's not Buckingham Palace, I've lived in worse places than that. It's certainly not big enough for all of us. But all right for the time being.'

'Well now we've committed ourselves to taking it, and it's closer to my sorting office and seeing that we have already lived down the road away, you know the area very well so, it's a very good base to carry on searching from, don't you agree?'

He was very philosophical about the set up, it had more going for it than against. I knew the area and it certainly would be a base to work from. We caught the tram back to Kingsway, this time we walked back to the Law Court's where Wally worked and lived. We arrived back and told them about our find. Jack and Wally went out to celebrate.

Next day with grateful thanks we left their accommodation. Jack took some of the things with him to work, I followed at a more reasonable time so that I would meet up with him outside the Town Hall after he had finished his post round, all went according to plan. We moved in and to make it reasonably comfortable for the three of us, we purchased other necessary bits and pieces in the Brixton market. Jack never liked the family being split up. Every Sunday the tribe would arrive for dinner. It was so cramped we ate in relays, before they returned back to their respective aunt's abode. Mrs. Palmer bless her heart did not mind, as I had told her our woeful tale to which she was aghast at the thought, and wheezed even more. Once a week I visited Mother, then I discover I'm pregnant again. So began our search for suitable accommodation for our growing family, which took on a new urgency. We had all the families searching, until by chance Jack's brother Bill (His real name was Harris) arrived in the afternoon at the flat.

'Sarah where's Jack?'

'Out searching he should be back soon why?'

'Well. I think I found a small house for you. I've spoken to the landlord and explained your circumstances. He wants to meet Jack.'

'Where is it then?'

'Upper Norwood number 65 Durning Road down the hill from us. I'll hang on for him.'

Whilst we waited I made him a cup of tea. When Jack arrived back he was surprised at seeing Bill there, soon found out the reason why. Wasting no time, we went into Brixton . caught the No. 2 bus en-route to Upper Norwood. Bill got the landlord to let us in and show us around. A two up two down reasonable new house, a little on the small size but ideal to accommodate us as a family. it also had a small garden also found out it was within walking distance of St. Joseph's Catholic School for my tribe's further education. So there was no problem there furthermore, the Catholic Church was even closer. But the only problem was, it was a long way from Jacks Sorting Office, with only two bus routes available the 2 and 137, meant he had a long way to walk, he suggested. 'No problem. 'I'll get a bike.'

We decided there and then we would take it, agreed the conditions and took procession of the keys. It took three weeks to get the furniture and other possessions out of storage to deliver, also to purchase more beds suitable for our tribe. When Jack was working and there was a delivery to the house, Bill was on hand and available to receive it. Once the last bed was delivered, he helped Jack to get the furniture and beds all sorted out in the rooms. Six weeks to the day, we left the flat we had moved into, thanking Mrs Palmer for her hospitality. We were on the move again. Now the tribe could leave the shelter of the respective Aunts abode and once again become a united family. We enrolled Mary, Kaye, Jackie and Michael at St Joseph's school. Durning Road was a turning half way down the side of Salter's Hill, number 65 was situated on the far corner of a semi-circle row of houses overlooking West Norwood. On a fine day, one could see the Dome of St Paul's the Houses of Parliament and other city landmarks. The area was quite pleasant with plenty of open space and parks around. Norwood Park was at the top of the road, down its lower slopes was a Bandstand, a children's paddling pool. At the top on the opposite side of Central Hill was the Church of the Virgo Fidelis and Convent, our venue for Mass on Sundays. Our shopping areas were Gypsy Hill, further up Central Hill was Crystal Palace Parade. Overlooking the big park, where within its grounds the original Crystal Palace had been relocated, together with all prehistoric stone monsters dotted about in its shrubbery. This is where our tribe would spend their Sunday afternoons or they would walk all the way in the other direction to Forest Hill and the Horniman's Museum, with its extensive collection of the Hornimans Tea family. Although out in the countryside, it was a long bus ride down to visit my mother sisters in Vauxhall nevertheless, they came to visit us on the weekends. Dick and Edith had also moved to a little house just further up the hill in Gibbs Avenue, close enough for them to pop in for a chat. So I was never left as they say. 'Out in the cold.'

After the regimental routine of army life, civilian life certainly was strange. Jack had a job and we had a roof over our heads. I had kept in touch with Kitty as I had given her mother's address to send her letters to, until we found our feet. Nevertheless, by that time Bobby had left the army and like Jack had become a postman, thet had moved with their tribe to a place called Bexley Heath in Kent, as Jack said, not too far from ourselves, therefore we kept in touch through letters. She informed me of young Jack who had joined the Royal Artillery and had been posted to the same camp in Lucknow. He had written home telling how strange it was being on familiar territory, but without his parents and the Plant Tribe. However, while walking through one of the Bazaars, there on display in a Bazaar shop he spotted a photograph of Bobby and Jack mounted on horses. He found. "Nanu" their old bearer, was still employed in the camp, with another family. He wished to be remembered to the Sahibs and Memsahib's with Baba's back in England. So we were not forgotten. Mary warmed to this news of her old adversary and suggested we all return back to live in India. For many a year it was to be our first Christmas in London. Jack provided the family with good food and presents for all. We were happy and content and generally at peace with the world and I was still feeling ill whilst pregnant. At the beginning of 1936, on the twentieth of January. the nation mourned the death of King George the V. His eldest son became King Edward VIII. however, we had to celebrate Jackie's birthday. Mother arrived at the birthday party, her first visit to our new abode. Jackie and Michael went up to Central Hill to meet her and she arrived huffing and puffing about her journey by tram then bus. She was the 'Guest of Honour' after she had regained her composure, she was lorded around the house. All had a good time but she had a little bit of advice to give me.

'Sarah Allahnah, as you have travelled around so much, all your babies have been born in different places. That alone you can write a story about, and I'm sure Allahnah, you with your travels with Jack could write a better story than any of the rubbish I have been reading. Not only that Allahnah, the baby you're expecting will be the second one to be born in London. '

I had not realised. How strange, that I would finish up with only two babies born in London like their father. After her first visit Mother ignored the so called tiresome journey and became a regular visitor to our abode. More to see if I was keeping in good health. It was about this time Jack purchased a wet cell battery operated wireless, which brought a new dimension into our lives, enabling me to listen to dance music to my heart's content. Michael was given the duty each week of exchanging the batteries for re-charging down at a shop in Gypsy Hill. But much to the concern of Jack, broadcast on the wireless was the signs of political unrest that became more evident of Hitler's intentions. His remilitarisation of the Rhineland brought further concern to all. It was the beginning of a very worrying time, and was the topic of conversation that the possibility of another war was the mood of the time. Jack and I discussed the future and what it would mean to us as a family. His comments were.

'Sarah you mark my words this 'Fella Hitler' will stop at nothing. He's up to no good.' I hung on his words trying to grasp their implications.

'He won't do anything silly will he?'

'Well I don't know, but he's got something up his sleeve that's for sure.'

In our own way we both had first-hand knowledge of the effects of a war. I had more important matters to concern myself about the forthcoming birth, which occurred on the twenty-second of June. Joseph was to become the last baby of the family. We were very happy living in the environment of Upper Norwood, although living on the side of a hill, it was very pleasant and suited all of us as a family. Yet with our situation and with our latest arrival it was obvious that the house was far too small for a growing family so, we were back on the hunt for larger premises. Mary and Kaye had become great friends of Maisie and Erma Candler who went to school with them, they happened to live in a house just further up the hill in Bloomhall Road. We had met their mother and father Mr. and Mrs. Candler when we all attended mass on a Sunday. It was Jack who when talking to Mr. Candler mentioned our need for another house, fortunately Mr. Candler knew of one down the road from them that was being let, gave Jack the details of the Landlord. Jack did the necessary and we got to view number 70. It was a four-bedroom house and ideal for us. We acquired it. During a weekend we completed the changeover, everyone was involved including Dick and Edith, gave us a hand to move in. Jack hired a handcart from a local builder to move all our chattels and furniture, with a lot of heaving and shoving up the hill to our new abode. Many trips were made until the very last stick of furniture was safely installed and the handcart returned to the Builder.

Not long after our move we acquired an upright piano from a Mr. Charlie Farnsbarnse a gentleman who lived around the corner in Gibbs Avenue. He had two pianos and was giving one away. Jack along with Jackie, Michael and his brother Dick, gave him a hand to bring home the piano. They arrived at the front of the house with the upright piano held on by a piece of knotted string, half of it overhung the back of the inadequate sized handcart. It was a good job that their journey, albeit short, had been downhill not up. Their main problem was how to get it off the handcart and up the three sets of steps to the front door. Margaret was banned from getting involved. So with Margaret stood in front of me, the pair of us watched from behind the curtain, whilst down below Jack in charge of the operation, was gesticulating at what he wanted everyone to do. The handcart was turned around so that its wheels were jammed against the curb, with the handle resting on the surface of the road. With Jackie and Michael on either side he waving his arms about to instruct them to raise the handle, Jack waved his arm at Dick to take position nearer to one side at the front of the piano. He quickly moved to the other side, so that they both could steady the weight. Slowly the boys lifted the handle the piano tipped backwards as Dick and Jack strained to hold it, by which time the unbalanced weight was far too much for the boys holding the handle. Jackie was on his tiptoes and Michael's feet were dangling in the air, he had to let go dropped to the ground, up went the handle. With a crash a crescendo of tuneless notes, it landed on its end, even I heard the piano's notes as it still tied to the handcart, its wheels slowly revolving, with Jackie still hanging onto the handle his feet dangling freely, sat on the road was Michael laughing. Jack and Dick just stood there howling with laughter. Margaret quietly enquired.

'Mum. what are they trying to do?'

I could not answer, tears were rolling down my cheeks. I had to run to the toilet before I had an accident. When I returned they had managed to move the piano half way through the gateway. The two boys pulling from one end with Jack and Dick pushing from the other towards the first steps. Then the pair of them stopped, discussed new tactics with much waving of arms. Then lifted one end of the piano up with the boys pushing from the rear, finally they managed all three steps and let it stay there. Jackie and Michael were instructed to go to the front to guide it whilst they pushed if from behind. I could not resist it I opened up the window and shouted out.

'JAHLDI JAHLDI. CHAI SAHIB.'

In a fit of laughter Jackie fell over into the flowerbed. Dick did not have a clue to what I was saying, Michael just stood by the piano grinning. Jack let out a roar of disapproval.

'SARAH WILL YOU WHISHED AWHILE. CAN'T YOU SEE WE HAVE A PROBLEM HERE?'

'I CAN SEE THAT SAHIB JACK. JAHLDI. CHAI SAHIB.'

He took no notice, continued pushing as a jangle of un-musical notes floated out of it. Amid fits of laughter they eventually got it through the front door and somehow manouvered it into the front room. What a saga, it had taken them all afternoon. With a broad grin from ear to ear Jack nonchalantly said.

'We will have that chai now Sarah. Jahldi.'

I went out and made chai to the strains of an un- melodious noise from the piano. Within a few months of Joseph's birth, more bad news was broadcast over the wireless. Spain had erupted into a Civil War. These were warning signs that Europe appeared to be on the march once again. This concerned Jack very much and he gave me instructions.

'Sarah you know what these are, the warning signs we should take heed of. Start getting the children rigged out in new clothes. different sizes to grow into.'

This was great forethought on Jack's part. but that was his thoughtful way. The greatest shortages of the First World War were food and clothing, and in the event of another war, they would be the main items that an Island like ours would succumb to. Once the children were back at school, I began my quest gradually buying and storing various articles of clothing. The tinned food would come later. Even I had a problem having such tiny feet a size one in shoes, which were even difficult to buy at the best of times. I wrote to my friend Helen Watson living in New York, her response stated she would buy some shoes at the forthcoming New York World Fair and send me some. I regularly walked to West Norwood, pushing the pram with Joseph and Margaret it was a better shopping centre, to buy clothing. In the early evening of November the 30th. we were disturbed by the constant clanging of fire bells. We had heard the occasional one, but these seemed endless, so it must have been a big fire. It was Jackie who came rushing in shouted.

'CRYSTAL PALACE IS ON FIRE.'

Then ran out again. This was too good to miss, except for the two youngest we all went into the garden, to see the orange glow that lit up the black sky. Now and again mountains of flames would shoot up into the sky, still the constant clanging of the fire bells continued. Seeing that it was basically made from glass, we were quite amazed at the intensity of the fire. After about an hour. three huge explosions rent the air, throwing showers of sparks into the sky, for hours the Palace burnt out of control until all that remained was a mangled heap of twisted metal and two gutted towers. Next day news on the wireless reported five hundred firemen had tried to fight the fire without success. Same day Jack arrived home, stood there hands on his hips and said.

'Sarah. have you heard the latest? Hitler has sent his troops and planes to Spain to help Franco's troops.' Cautiously I asked.

'No. is that bad?'

'Well. this latest move of his shows he's up to no good.'

'Will we have to go out there and help out?'

'No. it's a so called internal affair a civil war. The Spanish fighting amongst themselves. It's nothing to do with us. And we should keep our noses out, but with Hitler getting involved is something else.'

'Well I'd hate for us to get involved with something that has nothing to do with us.'

I was concerned about the news and hoped that nothing would come from it. But England was to hear some bad news. Early in December the King announced that he was going to abdicate, which took everyone by surprise. It had never happened before and the future of the monarchy was in doubt. Nevertheless, his younger brother George the Duke of York was to be our new King. Then it was to be our Christmas time in our new home, we had a quiet Christmas as a family.

In 1937 apart from the anxiety of the troubles that was hanging over everyone, we had our own moments of amusement and laughter. Every Sunday we attended Mass, taking over one of the pews, with Jack at one end and me at the other, the tribe in between with Mary and Kaye looking after Joe. (By then his name had been shortened.) I was deep in prayer, intent on the mass when all I could hear was my tribe giggling, followed by a sudden outburst of suppressed laughter. I shushed them and it stopped, then it began again. I told them to be quite, it stopped but began again. Then I noticed what was so amusing. Joe at the crawling stage had crawled under the pews into the next row, along the kneelers and when he found the men's hats he would sit down and try them on, if he didn't like one he would try on another. Flat hats, trilby's, bowlers which fell over his eyes, I reached out grabbed hold of Mary, shook her quietly mouthing to her.

'Get Joe back here.'

Shaking my clenched fist at the rest of them, Jack with a huge grin spread from ear to ear turned his head away, he was amused, just laughed along with others in the surrounding congregation, nobody seemed to mind, by which time he had managed to crawl three pews further down. Finally I got up moved down the aisle, excusing myself pushed my way past others seated, grabbed hold of Joe, with a very red face returned to our pews and sat down. Joe eager to get down struggled, but I held on tight. Outside they all got a lashing of my tongue. They hung their heads with sheepish grins upon their faces. Michael unable to contain himself, still laughed he received a quick cuff around the ears for his troubles. However, it did not do any good, the following Sunday the same thing happened. I'm sure the tribe used to encourage him but it made me laugh to see Joe's head covered by a big bowler hat. It was nearing Easter time. Mary having finished her schooling was at the age to start work. Jack and I discussed with her what she wanted to do, wrongly we decided to put her into service as a maid. With his contacts in the postal service, Jack had found such an opening locally in a house up Beaulah Hill called "Little

Menlo's". A very nice family occupied it. She went to meet them and was accepted as a maid. She appeared happy with her new found job. She had for all intents and purposes changed and appeared to us much calmer, gone were her wild ways but we did not realise, that the restrictions put upon her by her employers had broken her spirit, until she came home begging, pleaded with us to be taken away from her place of work. Jack and I agreed that something was not right. We discussed it with her, but she just said she didn't like the work. Sensibly we gave in and she found another job as a trainee silk-worker in a silk firm in Great Portland Street up in London. Fan became a regular visitor with young Tommy, whilst we chatted I baked cakes and soda bread, Margaret and Tommy played together. Margaret, being just that much older, was like her Godmother Peg, bossing Tommy around. Why Tommy adored her, I shall never know.

A sombre news broadcaster informed all that Hitler's air force planes had bombed the Basque town of Guernica totally destroying it. Jack, understanding what that meant, was even more perplexed. He stood there with hands on hips and shook his head at Hitler's latest move.However in England a brief spell of national joy. The Coronation of the Duke and Duchess of York in May. It was a new experience for the children. They all had been given a day off from school and were to enjoy the street party. However our brief spell of joy ended and we were brought back to reality when the Royal Navy were mobilised. Jack was very concerned about the whole series of events since Hitler's re-militarisation. Even to me the political horizon looked very bleak. I was worried that if it came to it, Jack would re-enlist, and with Mary at full time work, my tribe were lost without their leader. Nevertheless, their own individual spells of devilment took over. Michael hated being late for school, was the first to leave. On one occasion he refused to eat his bowl of porridge, stubborn as a mule sat at the table, getting more and more agitated about being late for school. Jack who was on late shift, laying down the law said.

'Okay my son, you won't be late for school.'

Promptly got hold of a brown paper bag. Scooping up the cold solid porridge from the bowl, filled up the paper bag, then sent him on his way saying...'I will speak to your teacher about that bag of porridge, so don't throw it away.'

At lunchtime. Michael brought back the soggy brown paper bag home with him. He had learnt his lesson. Jack had gone to work so I got rid of it. He was also responsible for taking Margaret to and from school, after breakfast he was always urging Margaret to hurry herself up. Another day because she didn't want to go, Margaret, was dithering about, Michael was getting more annoyed at being late eventually they did leave. As far as I was concerned that was the end of it. Later I was out shopping down the area called the Pan, when Mrs. Skinner the mother of friends of my tribe spoke to me.

'Morning Sarah I don't wish tittle- tattle, but I saw Michael trying to drag Margaret along the pavement and across the road. He was shouting at her to get a move on. She was screaming blue murder, she sat down right in the middle of Central Hill. He left her wailing like a banshee. I went straight out to get her up and take her across, just as Jackie turned up, the pair of us coaxed her to get up and go to school.'

I was fuming at this revelation. Thanked her for her attention. Unaware of my knowledge, when Michael arrived home with Margaret, he got a thrashing, his responsibility was taken over by Jackie. Not to forget the piano, it was a never-ending saga, a new toy for Margaret and Joe, neither they nor anyone else could play. They just thumped and banged making an endless racket all the time. Jackie was the only one who managed to get a tune out of it. Upon arriving home from school. Jackie would go straight to the piano began putting some notes together, until he had created a tune. It appeared he had a natural ear for music, possibly inherited from his great Grandfather, so we agreed to let him have lessons from Mr. Farnsbarnse, under his tuition, within a short space of time, Jackie was playing the scales and classical pieces of music quite well. Far more pleasing to my ears than the purgatory I had to endure from listening to the

353

youngest two, trying to copy Jackie, just thumping and banging out a crescendo of notes. The only key missing from the piano was the key to lock it.

A letter arrived from Peg somewhere up North, informing us that Dickie had been posted to a Territorial unit at Sidcup, the other side of Crystal Palace. He was in charge of the unit that came with accommodation. A small two roomed flat. It was not too long before they paid us a visit arriving in the road outside in Dickie's motorcar. It was a delight to see them again, much discussion went on between Jack and Dickie about the political situation. Anyway Dickie suggested he would come and pick us up and drive us down to his new unit. Before that happened Mary and Kaye took the opportunity to travel by train to stay with them for the weekend. As Jack was still doing shift work at the Post Office at a convenient time Dickie arrived in his car to pick Jack and I up to take us there for a brief visit to his Unit, which later became a holiday home for the various tribes, whenever Dickie was away on manoeuvres. All were introduced to Dick and Pegs dog a Chow Chow called 'Brutus' with a lovely furry light brown coat with a purple tongue I had never seen such a breed of dog before, but the tribes fell in love with it fussing over it. On one occasion when they were there, they caused a big rumpus. Dickie having arrived back from their Summer Camp, had the men's tents laid out flat on the Drillhall floor, unfortunately the tribe's found a small heavy four-wheeled trolley used to move the furniture and tables around. They proceeded to give each other rides around the hall, those sitting on it were pushed by the others behind rolling all over the tent's, and could not stop it from crashing into stack of chairs at the far end, smashing many of the chairs, those were discreetly hidden behind the others. What made matters worse was the new Drill Hall was about to be opened that night, by none other than Mr. Leslie Hore Belisha a noted Parliamentarian and to be followed by a Ball. It was only when some of the guest sat down the broken chairs gave way, that were discovered. Dick was furious and blew his top, all tribes received a good telling off and Peg handed out many clouts. That holiday period came to an abrupt end, but they still had Aunt Sarah's to fall back on.

When Fan arrived with Tommy one weekend, Jackie used to take them all down Norwood Park, pushing Joe in the Tan Sad pushchair with Margaret and Tommy walking alongside, Michael would be off to play football with his pals, leaving Jackie to contend with the youngsters. When they arrived back home, Joe was still in his pram with Tommy and Jackie stood soaking wet in puddles of water, Margaret just stood there grinning like a Cheshire cat no sign of Michael. At t he sight of Tommy, Fan was far from pleased. Before asking questions I gave them all a clout.

*The family summer 193*8   'Jackie what happened?'

'It wasn't my fault Mum. It was Margaret's. She pushed Tommy in. I was pushing Joe and heard the splash I had to jump in to get Tommy out.' I thought: *A likely story.*

'Go and get changed.' When he came back he received another clout as he was in charge. I warned.

'Don't you lot ever do that again.' Shaking my fist at Margaret, she still grinning likes a Cheshire cat replied.

'I promise Mum. '

I might just as well have talked to a brick wall for all the good it ever did. From then on every time Fan came up with Tommy, out they would go and would arrive back soaking wet. On the last occasion Margaret as well. she seemed to be fascinated by water. More clouts. More promises! They were banned from going near Norwood Park Pond, instead were sent up to Crystal Palace Park. Meanwhile during this period of our own malarkies The Prime Minister Neville Chamberlain had been in talks with that 'Fella Hitler' in Munich all about the future of

Czechoslovakia and arrived back at Croydon Airport waving a piece of paper at arm's length above his head. Declaring it was peace in our time. Strange as it may seem, the picture in the newspaper of his simple action of holding the sheet of paper above his head, reminded me of our "Women's Legion' cap badge". The figure of peace holding a laurel wreath above her head. A week later news declared that Hitler's army had marched into Czechoslovakia. Jack was appalled at this new venture by that 'Fella Hitler' shaking his head muttered. 'He's already marched into Austria what next?'

Soon after that a brown envelope was delivered, addressed to Jack. Picking it up, he opened it and scanned it. A big grin spread across his face. I asked.

'What is it Jack?'

'Sarah. It doesn't look good. I have been recalled for duty again. To join the 'E 'Reserve and report back to a receiving station in Ascot for kitting out on Monday the 17th. When I get there I will be able to find out more about what is going on. Until then let's just carry on as normal okay duck's?'

I could not do anything else, when the Army calls Jack jumps. The situation had now developed into a necessity to start preparing for a War. The 'E" Reservists, long-term professional service personnel were required. On his very first weekend leave, he came home dressed in his uniform with a huge grin over his face and said.

'Sarah I met Bobby at the same camp I'm at. Kitty and the family send their love to you all.' He did not tell me where or what he was training for. On other weekends he arrives home and says.

'Guess who arrived at camp this week Sarah?' None the wiser I would say.

'Tell me Jack. I'm no good at guessing.' Christmas was almost upon us when Jack arrived home stating.

'Sarah. I've a week's leave, then I have to report to Dover Castle'…nonchalantly adding… 'Now Sarah is the time, when we as a family had better make the most of this Christmas. Do you agree?'

I did not like the way he said that. Later on he went down to Vauxhall to meet up with Dickie Fox and Tom Wilbraham to have a few drinks and of course discuss the then present crisis. We did celebrate and our Christmas was to be a joyous one, totally unaware it was to be our last before war broke out.

CHAPTER FOUR
LONDON 1939-1941.

The beginning of 1939 brought with it a year of total uncertainty, as to what the future had in store for us. The only certain item on the horizon was after the Prime Minister, Mr. Chamberlain had returned the previous September from a meeting with that 'Fella Hitler.' Peace was little more than a sheet of white paper, that was all to his so called triumph of success. Meanwhile to add to the deepening crisis of doom and gloom. late in January the newspapers reported that the IRA had set off some homemade bombs in London, Manchester and Birmingham. Yet again in February another bomb exploded in Tottenham Court Road. The police arrested most of them, and to my mind I thought: *We had left that entirely behind in 1922.* On his odd weekend leave. Jack would arrive home, predicting the situation was getting worse not better. A real Jobe's comforter, but how right he was. Then over the radio we were informed, "As a precaution against any future enemy air raid attacks, everyone living in houses were to be supplied with an Anderson Shelter." All too quickly the Easter period was upon us, at least brought good news. The war in Spain was at an end.

Late in April, due to the looming crisis, the necessity to conscript men was to be debated in Parliament before it became law. Now the reasons for Jacks, Bobby's plus other old pal's re-enlistments became very clear. They had been recalled in preparation to train conscripts, if the Bill was passed in Parliament, the Government also announced that the Territorial Army was to be increased to double its strength. About the same time I received a letter from Kitty Burns, informing me that Bobby had been posted to a place called Harrogate, they were on the move. I re-read her letter again and realised the current situation was looking very bleak. Jack's weekend leaves become fewer. with urgency in his tone of voice said.

'Sarah it does not look good. Get stocked up with tinned food for at least three years. I'll get Bill to fetch some tea chests up to store the stuff in okay?'

It was Kaye's turn to leave school and start work. She had an interview at Maison George's Salon in Victoria. She was taken on as a trainee hairdresser. Therefore, as the number 2 Bus stopped outside the Fidelis Church, Mary, Kaye with their friends Maisie and Irma could travel to work there and back together on the same bus route. One morning lorries arrived in the road outside the houses, a gang of men began unloading several pieces of corrugated steel sheeting, leaving them in the front gardens. The last item to be dropped off was a small sack. One of the workmen knocked on the door, when I opened it he doffed his cap and said.

Irma- Aun , Kaye, Maisie Mary & Juby their dog.

'Here you are Missus, one anderson shelter for number 70. All you have to do is dig a big hole, erect it with the nuts and bolts in the little sack down on top of the steel sheets. Use these instruction sheets and if you don't mind, just sign here and I be off out of yer way.'

I looked beyond him to the pile of funny shaped steel sheets lying below inside the gate, wondering how we were going to move them asked.

'Can you carry them around to the back garden then?'

'Sorry Missus not our job, just delivers em that's all. I'll be on me way then, we got many more to drop off up the road.'

With a shaky hand I signed for one Anderson Shelter. They stayed where they had been left, until a weekend when Jack was at home on leave. He got Jackie and Michael to help him dig a big hole, carry all the sheets into the back garden put the sides up and left it where it stood until he was home again. After four weeks the shelter was ready he left instructions for Jackie and Michael to cover it with all the earth they had dug out, when that was finished it stood there as a play house for Margaret and Joe. But ready for anything? In May the Conscription Bill was passed in Parliament.

356

This left little doubt in our minds that the situation was becoming grim and even further bad news was that that 'Fella Hitler' and the Italian Dictator Mussolini had joined forces. The tide of war was becoming inevitable. Dickie Fox left Sidcup, was posted to an Ack -Ack unit stationed at Biggin Hill Airfield. It along with Croydon and Kenley Airfield, were to become fighter aircraft stations. The latter two were less than four miles away from us, with Biggin Hill about eight. So for all intents and purposes, we would be well protected? A knock on the front door had be hurrying to open it . Two men stood there held in the hands were about twenty strings attached to brown boxes dangling around their knees. Declaring they were men from the Ministry of Supply required to know how many lived in the house and their ages? I advised them of all of my tribe and ages. In return they handed over seven of these boxes, as I took hold of the strings, they informed me.

'In the boxes were gas masks one for each member of the family, advising in the event of a war, as a prevention against any aerial gas bombs being dropped, when the air raid warning went, the gas mask was to be put on, instruction inside the box please sign here.'

With these boxes hanging from my arm I signed for their receipt. They left walking back down to the front gate with the remainder iof the boxes bumping about their knees. Shutting the door, took them inside placed them on the table in the front room.seven boxes their strings dangling over the edge of the table. I stood reflecting on their statement of arial gas bombs? I had to look at them, opened one box to reveal a rather ungainly looking rubber object, with a wide glass eye piece, I read the instruction imprinted on the lid of the box then removed the gas mask a face mask with straps to attached the mask over the head a round canister-looking thing was at the bottom, the long piece of string was for carrying it around. One box had "child" printed on it, opening the box found a funny red gasmask, with a flat flapping nose, two blue rimmed eye pieces, a round canisterat the bottom with straps to fit over the back of his head it must have been for Joe. I did not relish putting that thing on him. Rather disturbed at the thought and hoping we would never have to use them lef them where they were, went out and got on doing the washing.

When my tribe arrived home from school. MIchael came in to the kitchen, taking a slice of bread sat down to read a comic, Jackie as usual went into the front room to practice on the piano. As I buttered some bread for them to eat. I heard a few notes of the scale being played then it stopped,silence, a few moments later I heard Jackies footsteps approaching, looking up saw he had one of the gas masks on, tufts of his hair poked out through it's head straps, muffled sounds came from inside his gas mask as he said something. I stopped buttering the bread, stood there laughing, To scare him Jackie lunged at Michael sat reading a comic, surprised he jumped up dropping his comic, a huge grin appeared on his face, he ran around the table out through the door, quickly to return wearing a gas mask. With the pair of them trying to frighten each other, they exhaled their breath the tight rubber over their cheeks began to make funny noises, they ran out. I heard Margaret and Joe screeching outside, they came running in, Joe clutching hold of my apron was certainly frightened. I had to stop their shenanigans, got them to take them off put them away. Hopefully never to be used again. Jackie came home and handed me a letter from Mr Brennan the headmaster, informing all mothers and fathers to attend a meeting on the following Friday night in the school hall. Bring your children with their Gas Masks. All must attend. We attended. Mr. Brennan gave out all the details for the use of the Gas Masks, He also instructed all to practice putting them on. Pandemonium broke out as they put them on and began trying to talk through masks. Muffled sounds came from within. A pair of staring eyes looked out beneath tousled hair, after the initial shock; they became the focus of great amusement amongst the boys, running around the hall trying to frighten everyone. Whilst all these shenanigans were going on, younger girls were crying refusing to put them on. Being pacified by rather vexed mothers cursing. 'That 'Fella Hitler' what's he doing to us all?' A sentiment that was voiced by all. With a sharp order Mr. Brennan brought the mayhem to a halt.

The next couple of months seemed to fly by with nothing but bad news from all quarters. A report in the newspaper stated that the IRA had let off a bomb in London and killed one person and seriously injured many others, it appears that they don't want to give up. In Ireland the Eire Government had declared the IRA as outlaws possible due to the various bombings that had occurred in England over the past months.

I received a large parcel from my friend Helen Watson in the States, containing not one but six pairs of high heeled shoes, with a note saying she had purchased them at the World Trade Fair and hoped they would fit me. They looked fine to me. I sat down tried each pair on, walking up and down the hallway. They fitted me perfectly, so I stored them away along with all the other items I had been collecting months before.

On a weekly basis. I had gradually been collecting tinned food. Nevertheless, during the school holidays decided to collect sufficient ingredients to make eight Christmas puddings and a cake. Tea was another priority that I thought: *Would be in short supply.* I knew that the Home and Colonial provisions shop sold tea in silver foil packets making them waterproof, those would be very good to store away without getting damp. With Jackie and Michael off school. I had them helping me search for tinned food in the shops further afield. Michael went shopping up to the Parade and Jackie down to West Norwood. Gradually our stockpile grew. Tins of corned beef, ham, and butter were horded away in drawer's cupboards and the tea chests Bill had supplied. I was sure the horde would supplement any rationing if ever it came into force, looking on the bright side. If it didn't the tinned food would not go to waste. In July, the King announced that a Women's Auxiliary Air Forces Unit was to be formed. This news made Mary's school chums Maisie and Irma Candler volunteer for the WAAF's. Mary can't make up her mind whether to stay at work or volunteer, finally decides to wait a little while longer. It was later on two separate occasions, Maisie and Irma arrived home on leave came to see Mary. Maisie had been posted to Whitehall, within easy reach of her mother, Irma had been posted to an airfield down in Hampshire.

During the school holidays, we received a letter from the Education Department. Cautiously I opened it, removing the pages began to read them. It began by advising us, that in the event of war it had been decided to include the Borough of Croydon as an evacuation area. This started my heart pounding. I read on through a list of four classified groups of the children to be evacuated. Quickly scanning through the groups, turned over the pages to reveal a list of items each child was to take away. With a final notice advising that in the event of War, an announcement on the evacuation of children would be broadcast over the wireless. With horror I stopped, clenching the letter in my hands, screwing it up exclaimed aloud. *'Oh my God. Holy Mary mother of God. Blessed Joseph and all their saints surely this is not going to happen?'* I hesitated to compose myself. With my heart pounding, unscrewed the sheets, re-read the list on the crumpled paper trying to understand which of the four categories would affect us as a family, only the first two did. School children accompanied by their Teachers. -The second, - Mother with children under five. I felt weak at the knees; I had to sit down at the table as I again read through the forms.

Outside, Margaret and Joe were in the garden playing in and out of the air raid shelter with little Trevor Castle from next door. Reflections of the First World War come flooding back to me, but this was totally different. The reality came within the letter. If, there was a war London the capital was going to be the heart of it. I sat there twisting my wedding ring round and around my finger. What should I do? Mary and Kaye were working. Jackie, Michael and Margaret were to be sent somewhere. That left me with Joe to go somewhere else. I did not want any of them to go. My emotions overcame me, I cried out aloud. *'Jack why aren't you here with me when I need your help.'* In anguish, leant my elbows on the table raised my hands to my forehead, and sobbed at the mere thought of my family breaking up again. It was some time before I had calmed myself down to take stock of what it really meant to us as a family. With Mary and Kaye at home would not effect them, I certainly was not prepared to go myself, therefore Joe and I would stay at home with them.

Under the terms of the letter Jackie, Michael and Margaret were the most eligible. I sat there with my eyes sore from crying. Then I heard Margaret crying outside, getting up went outside to see what was going on, that distraction temporally brought me back to my senses. It was nothing she had just fallen off the top of the shelter, next door Brenda, Trevor's Mother was hanging out her washing, so to share my despondent news, I called out.

'Good morning Brenda, have you had one of those letters about evacuating the children?'

'Morning Sarah, yes but it's only one of those things that would affect us, and I do not want to go anyway, I'm staying put with young Trevor.' ...Knowing that Trevor was the same age as Joe, he did not go to school and was her only child, replied…..'Well. I am of that opinion also, but it does leave me with a problem with my two boys and Margaret. They will be separated, and like you I do not want to leave the house to be sent somewhere else. I have had enough of that in my lifetime.'

We chatted on for several minutes in the hot sunshine, before we went about our chores, with me still thinking about our lack of choice. In the end, with extreme reluctance. I decided that Jackie and Michael could go away with the school, as Margaret was in the infants, she could be sent somewhere different to the boys. However, mulling it over in my brain I did have a notion. Fan would have the same problem with Tommy down in Vauxhall. I had no answer to what she would do, but maybe there was a chance, somehow if possible Tommy and Margaret could go away together with Fan. Deciding to discuss the matter later with the girls when they arrived home, put the letter on the mantelshelf. When they arrived home I let them read the letter, we discussed and agreed, what I had suggested, was the best thing I could do. Although it was also dependant on Fan. The following day I sat down and wrote a letter to Jack, telling him of the pending evacuation plans. Also to Kitty, knowing that it would not affect them up in Harrogate, at least she would be aware of our problem. Then being prepared for the worst, using the list provided. I began sorting out their necessities. Two pairs of socks, a change of underclothes, a pullover, toothbrush, soap and towel, plimsolls and a coat etc., packing them in small cases, which with our travels had an abundance of them.

When Fan arrived the following weekend, she immediately informed me about the similar letter she too had received. She had decided to go with St. Anne's school along with Tommy. She had already told Mother of her intentions. However, Mother had a different plan. If, it could be arranged, she as their guardian would go with Margaret and Tommy, leaving Fan to stay behind and look after both Mother's house No 1 and theirs No 4 in Wheatsheaf Lane. I listened to the wisdom of Mothers suggestion, that suited me, still grasping with the hope it would never happen. So the subject was left with Fan and mother to arrange. A few days later Fan returned to inform me.

'Sarah. I have spoken to Mr Hands the headmaster. Under the circumstances he has accepted mother's plan. He also said that when the time came St. Anne's School would be one of the first to be evacuated. Leaving early in the morning from Vauxhall Station bound for a place called Reading. You know what that means Sarah, Margaret will have to stay with me to get to the school in time. So be prepared for a quick getaway?'

I listened intently to what Fan had said. I was already prepared with her bits and pieces, but was I prepared for her hurried departure? Something I would face when that time came. I went to the education authorities, registered the boys also informed them of a possible solution to Margaret's future arrangements. They had some misgivings but accepted. We had also been given instructions as to where the boys of St. Joseph's school were to meet, that was at Gypsy Road railway station.

Everything was happening so fast. You could not keep up with the events and goings on around the world, It appeared the whole world had gone mad. The IRA let off a bomb in Coventry killing five people, injuring fifty others, maybe they were siding with that 'Fella Hitler' who was determined to go to war, he took over Denmark. Mobilisation of forces in many countries becomes a priority. By August the whole of Europe was on the brink of war. A letter from Kitty provided some assurance. She informed, that they would not be affected but invited us to stay with her, but just for us to look on the bright side of things. A statement that was far from my peace of mind. The Evacuation plans happened sooner than we expected. An announcements was broadcast on the radio, that on the 31st, the last day of August. Phase one of Operation Pied Piper. the evacuation plan would begin. London's children would be entrained to all parts of the country. The announcement on the radio also stated. A list of areas for evacuation was read out, amongst those named was Croydon. On the Wednesday afternoon Fan arrived with Tommy. She was not in a very good state. obviously she had been crying, blurted out her message of woe.

'Sarah I've come to collect Margaret, St. Anne's are leaving on Friday morning.'

'Oh my God. So soon?'

'Yes all of the teachers from the classes went around informing all about the move. Tommy's teacher arrived this morning, so I went to Mothers, informed her, then came straight up here. '

'How has Mother taken it?'

'Mother, she is very calm about it. She told me to stop bawling my eyes out. You will upset the children. Just say they are going on a holiday with their Grandma.'

I could see she was about to start crying again, so I ushered Tommy outside to play with the others....'Well if that's Mothers attitude, why don't we think the same way as her? It seems a sensible way to look at it.'...But knowing in my heart that was not the case. I would not be happy until they all returned back safe to me. ...'Fan sit yourself down. I'll make a cup of tea, before we send you on your way.' She immediately started crying. I was about to do the same, then sternly I said... 'Fan stop that now. listen to what I have to say. You go home, get yourself prepared. I will wait for the girls to come home to discuss the situation with them. Now, before they all go, I want to see Mother so I will bring Margaret down to Mother's with me tomorrow morning. Do you understand what I am saying?'....She nodded, wiped away the tears from her cheeks. I went and put my arm around her shoulder murmured.... 'Come on Fan. we are all in the same boat now.'

An hour later, she left to go home and prepare for the following day. When the girls came home, we discussed the happenings of the day, and how we would manage the next few days. We were sitting there discussing the disintegration of our family within the following thirty-six hours. Mary took charge of the situation started to get things arranged. The following morning she would go with me down to Mothers, leaving Margaret to stay overnight, then she would go on to work. Kaye would look after the three boys until I returned home. Margaret was told what was happening. she did not seem very bothered as she was going away with Tommy and her Granny. I did not sleep at all that night, constantly praying. Maybe I drifted off, but did say many decades of the rosary, worrying what this all meant. It did not make sense. Half of my family would be taken away from me to God knows where? Yes for their safety but what about ours. Just an air raid shelter dug in the ground. I was up early at the crack of dawn. The three of us left the house with our gas mask cases slung over our shoulders. Mary carried the little suitcase packed with Margaret's things. We caught the 2 bus down to Vauxhall, a bus journey was the worst I had ever taken. Mary made polite conversation but my mind was on other things. When we arrived at mothers she looked at me with deep concern on her face.

'Come on in Allahnah, Fan's in the kitchen along with young Tommy.'

We followed her in through to the kitchen, where Fan was sat at the table. Tommy was playing with his toy cars on the floor. Fan looked at me with red eyes, immediately she burst into tears at the sight of us. Mother told her.

'Shut yer noise up in front of the children. They're just going away on holiday with their Grandmother. Don't be a wailing banshee.'

It was all right for Mother, it wasn't her that was being parted from them. Only after mother's rash statement could we compose ourselves. Mary about to leave for work bade her farewells with a parting shot from her Granny.

'Now then Mary, you're the eldest, it's up to you to look after your Mother. She has been a good Mother to all of you, and looked after you for all the past years. Now be away with you. I'll see you after we come back off our holiday.'

They hugged and kissed, Mary left. Then we settled down to talk things over about what was going to happen. Early in the morning all would meet at St. Anne's school, then walk to Vauxhall station to catch a train to Reading. There the three of them, had been allocated to stay with a Mr. and Mrs. Huggins home at Woodley just outside Reading. This appeared all too simple and straightforward, but there again months of organising had gone into these preparations. When we left I put on a brave face until I got outside the front door. Walking away the tears welled up I burst into tears they streaming down my cheeks, forcing myself not to cry on the journey home as I waited at the bus stop. Yet I still had another ordeal to face on the Monday of letting the boys go. I was so glad to get back indoors with Kaye and the boys, then Kaye left to go to work. I kept the wireless on listening to some music until on that dreadful morning of Friday the 1st. of September a news flash broadcast. "Hitler had invaded Poland. Everyone should remain calm and listen in to the wireless for further news and instructions. The country is being mobilised for war. Compulsory military service for men between the ages of Eighteen to Forty-one." The doom and gloom had finally erupted into war.

Next day the newspapers were filled with heart rendering photographs of the young children boarding trains at stations. As their weeping mothers said goodbyes. It came as a great shock to me, as in the back of my mind, I could visualise within two days, I could be doing the very same thing with my two boys. I decided to go to church light candles and say a few prayers. I took Joe along with me, but those pictures showing the anguish of Mothers did not go away. All day long they were imprinted in my mind. For all intents and purposes it was a normal day albeit we as a nation were at war. That evening, my heart missed a beat, as we sat there listening intently to the broadcast. I was twisting my wedding ring so quickly it might spin right of my finger. All I could think of on Monday morning. Jackie and Michael would be evacuated and gone. Sunday, I got up very early, went down got myself ready, leaving the house on my own to attend early morning mass and Holy Communion. By the time I had arrived back everyone except Mary and Kaye were up ready to go to mass at nine. I fed Joe, sat at the table as I pottered about in the kitchen, pondering over how to get through the next twenty-four hours, when the early morning news announced that. 'The Prime Minister would broadcast a statement over the wireless at 11.15 a.m. Shivers ran down my spine what did it mean? Mary and Kaye came down on their way to meet Maisie, who was home on leave. I told them of the announcement. Kaye said.

'At that time we shall be in mass.'

So they left together with Jackie, Michael and Joe, as I continued with the dinner, being extremely aware of the time, constantly glanced towards the clock. (the stolen one) Its hands did not appear to move but slowly crept around towards Eleven o'clock. At 11.15.a.m, with the chimes of Big Ben booming out from the wireless set. The Prime Minister Neville Chamberlain in a very grave and tired sounding voice stated.

'Early this morning the British Ambassador in Berlin had given an ultimatum to "Adolf Hitler". Unless he withdraws his troops from Poland and issues such a statement that we had to receive by His Majesties Government by elevon a. m. that day. A state of war would exist between us. I regret to say that no statement has arrived therefore, we as a Nation are at war with Germany. God Help us all.' Silence. I stood there shocked, wept. Then from outside I heard Mrs. Castle next door call out. 'Sarah Sarah have you heard the news?' Wiping my eyes smoothing my hands down my pinafore, went outside, noticed Joe and Trevor playing in and out of the shelter, I answered.

361

'Yes. I heard. It's started.' She asked.

'Whatever are we going to do?'

'I honestly don't know. We will just have to wait and see what develops in the next few days. Maybe that 'Fella Hitler' has sent an answer and it hasn't been received yet. If you'll excuse me, I must get on and cook the dinner.'

I was in no mood to stand chatting. I needed to occupy my mind. I got on with the Sunday dinner, the last one we would be together as a family except Margaret. Then I heard it. First a strange slow whirring sound that quickly gathered speed into a wail, rising to a crescendo then lowering and rising again, in a continuously banshee of a noise, to herald the warning sound that an air raid was imminent. It lasted several minutes before its wail slowly died away. The silence that had descended over the neighbourhood was eerie. The sheer sound of that siren sent shivers down my spine. I went over to the doorway to see what was going on. Nothing in the sky above, nothing happened, maybe it was a practice? Nevertheless, it was a sound that in the coming months we were to become very familiar with. Not long after. It started again, this time it was a completely different wail that of a continuous note, which stayed for several minutes, before it too slowly died away into complete silence. Apparently that was the wail of the All Clear, it again was going to be heard many times later. Just before midday Maisie's Mother Mrs. Candler, arrived with tears streaming down her chubby cheeks and in her strange broken English she wailed.

'Oh Mrs Plant we are at war. The air raid sirens did you hear them?'

I grabbed hold of her and brought her into the kitchen, sat her down. She certainly had something to cry about. Being French she had plenty of relatives in France and also the Channel Islands, with both her two girls in the WAAF's. I made some more tea, gave her a cup, as she drank gradually her crying stopped, we talked for a little while. Not that I knew any different, the noise of the sirens had stopped me dead in my tracks. I calmed her down and I said.

'Mrs. Candler, they must have been practice ones. I did not hear any planes overhead. Mr. Chamberlain only spoke on the wireless less than an hour or so ago. Now don't you fret yourself.'

Whether it was whatever I was telling her, the possibility of us being invaded by the German Army was so remote. It was silly of anyone thinking they would be marching up our road. It was about this time that Mary, Kaye and Maisie dressed in her uniform arrived back from Mass. Coming in Kaye shouted.

'WE ARE AT WAR. DID YOU HEAR THE AIR RAID SIREN?' I scolded.

'Stop shouting, how did you hear that when you were in church?'

'Oh we heard it all right. A lot of us ran outside and looked up into the sky. Father Larkin came out and ordered us back inside. When the all clear sounded, he said special prayers. A full novena that's why we are late getting home.' She moaned.... I questioned...' Where's Jackie and Michael?'.... 'Gone to the shops, they went when the first siren sounded.' Maisie interrupted.

'Mum I've already been home. Dad said you were down at Mrs Plant's, so I'll walk you back home before I go back on duty. I'm sure I will be needed.' Mrs. Candler began wailing again.

'My God do you have to Maisie? What about Erma?' I intervened.

'Mrs. Candler, now stop that, we have just had a nice little chat, and you realised that it was only a practice, so you don't have to worry none. Maisie is in the WAAF's and she is duty bound to report back. There's nothing in that, c'mon with you.'

I was stirring the gravy as I delivered my little speech. Anyway she saw I was busy cooking and remembered she was cooking dinner herself, she left with Maisie however, in a far better state than when she arrived. Then Jackie arrived puffing and panting blurted out.

'They've all ran out of nuts and raisins. there's none in any of the shops including Uncle Bill's. Did you hear the air raid siren? Just as it went off Mr. Parker my teacher went past me in his car and shouted at me.... 'There's a war on get yourself home.' ... I ran all the way I didn't stop until I got here. Isn't it great were going away to-morrow. Where's Michael did he get any?'

'I don't know. He hasn't got back yet.'

I was upset at his remark about the war but it was all excitement for the boys. No doubt Michael will be the same when he arrives back. He was, but without any nut's or raisins. They would have to go without them, on their train journey. We sat down to a very quiet Sunday lunch. Not a lot was said, all listened very carefully to the wireless waiting for any further announcements about that 'Fella Hitler's' expected statement. It never came. Kaye had made the evening meal, and when it was ready, we sat down. I did not have the stomach for it. As they ate I quietly went upstairs fell on the bed, cried my eyes out until it was nearly twilight. Rising out of my misery, said to myself. "This won't do. On your feet soldier." Then went down to the kitchen, where the four of them sat listening to some light music on the wireless, Joe was sat on the floor playing with some soldiers, as they had a very early morning start. I began to organise them for bed We all retired early.

As I lay there in the darkness, my mind flitting from one crisis to another, over the past weeks happenigs, my thoughts of . *Jack away in Dover, Margaret was with her Granny and Tommy in Reading, and the boys were to be sent away with the school the next day. When I had read the contents of the note they brought home from school, it stated the place they were going to. They were to be billeted out with a Mr. and Mrs. Richardson in a place called Franklin's Village near Hayward's Heath in Sussex. When I told them that they were to be sent away. All they were interested in was. 'For how long?' That I had no answer to give them I said... 'Just for a short while.'...At the same time asking God to make it a very short while. Nevertheless they were full of it. An extension to their summer holidays. It was just a big lark to them. As I lay there the reality struck home. Would I ever see them again? God alone knew?* I lay there trying to rest it was no good I had to get up. I went down to the kitchen, to compose a letter to Jack and poured my heart out. It did me good. When I had finished it, I rallied around, before dawn broke I made some sandwiches for the boys, to take with them and sorted out some nuts and raisins from my store. Then prepared their breakfast before I went upstairs to wake them.

I had to take Joe along with me, waking him out of his deep sleep, he began screaming and shouting because he had been woken up so early. Being a normal working day Mary and Kaye got up, got ready to leave for work. After breakfast, the boys with their labels securely attached to coats, said their goodbyes to Mary and Kaye . We left, wearing our gas masks over our shoulders, they carrying small suitcases, Michael pushed Joe in the Tam Sad pushchair down to the station, not a a great distance to walk , down Alexandra Drive, across the main street to the station. There we were met by a mass of children of all ages, from different schools in the area. All dressed in the correct attire with their gas masks slung over their shoulders. carrying their paper parcel or small suitcase, labels tied to Jackets or pinned to dresses. Some of the elder boys were running around with coats trailing on the floor in abandoned care, gas mask cases being swung around like a mace. The various teachers were trying to organise their own charges into classroom order. Mr. Brennan, their headmaster with some of his other teachers was calling out the children's names as they arrived. Teachers from other schools doing the same thing. It was a state of orderly pandemonium. Afraid to say anything to the contrary, some Mothers were trying to reassure their off-springs of the holiday they were embarking on. Most of the children had never been on a train before, at least mine had "travelled well." When it appeared that everyone had arrived, the classes from the various schools were formed up in columns, to be led through the station barriers onto the waiting train. The last to go through onto the platform were the Mothers. Amidst shouts of cheering, whoops from the children hanging out of the partly open windows, the train of evacuees slowly steamed out of the station. The anguish amongst the Mothers was plainly evident. Many handkerchiefs were bravely waved aloft, before wiping away the tears, some mother's still physically wailing into handkerchiefs trying to suppress their personal anguish.

Very tearfully I made my way slowly back home to an empty house, pushing the pram around to the back door, let Joe out. It was a fine sunny day with a tinge of coldness in the air indicating that autumn was not far off. Although it was still before eight 'o'clock, little Trevor was already outside playing, Joe went up the garden, started talking to him through the garden fence. Obviously seeing Joe Mrs. Castle knew I was backing home, came out politely asked.

'Sarah, how did your boys get away?'

I desperately needed to talk to someone, invited her in for a cup of tea. We talked for a very long while, her presence eased the pain I was suffering inside. After she left, I decided there was nothing I could do but accept the fact that at least they were safe, out of the way of any danger. It was only then that I realised that however long this war was to last. I would be on my own alone with Joe throughout the day. It was Monday washing day. I tore into it, stripping all the beds of sheets and pillowcase. Everything went into that days washing, by mid-day it was all out drying on the washing line. Now I was able to come to terms with the situation, looked on the bright side of things. I still had Joe to look after. I kept the wireless on, it being the central point of all information as I prepared something to eat for us. I gave Joe his dinner whilst not in the mood for much just cut myself a slice of buttered bread and a cup of tea, With all the sandwiches I had made for the boys, we had run out of bread butter and a few other things. Sitting there thinking: *It dawned on me a most important thing had then become mine, exchanging the wirelesss batteries, that was a trip up to the Gypsy Hill electrical shop, that normally was Michaels job, the other shopping was the boy's task, I already did all the mundane household chores, Therefore needed to arrange what my new schedule would be. I decided that afternoon, to go down the Pan to get some shopping from the little store.*

About half past two, we left the house. It was easier and quicker for me to push Joe in the pushchair. In the store I met Mrs. Skinner; she too had seen some of her brood off that morning. We commiserating our losses, walked back together, until she went one way I the other. I was half way up the hill when the air raid siren began its wail. I grabbed Joe out of the pram, dived into the shrubbery of a big garden, crouching there Joe squirming about in my arms I shushed him to be still. Nothing happened all was quiet, it seemed hours before the all clear wailed, even before it had finished got Joe and myself disentangled out of the shrubbery, fortunately the pram was caught in the same shrubbery, which had stopped it rolling back down the hill. Shoving Joe in the pram gathered up the shopping that lay on the ground, then with haste started running in front of me. Mrs. Candler running across the road called out.

'No time to stop. Mrs Plant.'

She was puffing and I was panting, with the effort of pushing Joe up this hill. At the time a most frightening experience, which proved me wrong. It was another practice, but it taught me a lesson it was a warning, to take cover wherever one was shopping either in West Norwood or up the Parade, from any future air raids, even our recent trip down to the little store, had been very arduous and frightening. I was so pleased to get back home and out of whatever danger lay in store for us. I had no sooner calmed down than I had another fright. A banging on the front door had me jumping and running to see who it was. When I opened it, there stood was Fan, she was a bag of nerves, pushing past me, her gas mask case caught me on my arm she urged.

'Quick shut the door Sarah. There's an air raid on.' I enquired.

'Whatever are you doing here?'

'Sarah, I can't stay down in our house on my own. So I've come up to stay with you for a few days. There's an air raid going on. Don't you know?'

'That's all over with. It only lasted for half an hour. I was on my way home when the siren went off. I dived in some bushes for cover. Where were you then?'

'On the bus. The driver stopped the bus alongside the park. Nobody knew what to do. We just sat there until the driver got fed up of waiting, started moving again. When I got off, I ran all the way here.' I ordered.

364

'Sit yourself down and relax. I'll make you a cup of tea. You're more than welcome to stay. I was feeling very lonely myself. And I might add, very frightened about the two air raid two warnings. This afternoons warning was the second one we have experienced up here.'

'Two? Well it's my first one, I don't like the sound of them sirens at all.'

She was still agitated, when Mary and Kaye arrived home from work. They too were surprised to see Fan at home. We sat down shared the meal I had prepared to discuss whatever news they had to talk about. Inevitably about what monument had either been boarded up or removed from its dais or had sand bags piled up around them. On the Tuesday I got Fan occupied doing the ironing for me. Somehow I managed to accept and understand the situation, to take it as it was. It was difficult for her as Tommy was her first and only child. On Wednesday morning Mary and Kaye had already left to go to work. It was nearly eight o'clock, when the wail of the air raid siren disturbed the early morning stillness. I could not believe what I was hearing. Fan came running down from upstairs in her nightgown. Screaming like a mad woman.

'IT'S AN AIR RAID. IT'S AN AIR RAID.' I got hold of her shouted.

'CALM DOWN. WE WILL GO OUT TO THE ANDERSON, AND TAKE COVER IN THERE.' Grabbing Joes hand, he still in his pyjamas, led them both outside to the shelter pushed them inside ordered.

'Now just sit down, be quiet. Listen for the sound of aeroplanes.'

We sat on the two side bunks Jack had put in the shelter. Staring through the door opening, a shaft of sunlight lit up Fan, sitting opposite with her arm around Joe. The sirens mournful tone died down to silence. Then realised. I cried out.

'Jesus Mary and Joseph, the gas masks, I'll have to go and get them.'

I flew out of the shelter, hared across the sparse piece of grass into the house. Grabbing hold of the strings on the boxes hanging on the doorknob, hared back into the entrance throwing one at Fan I shouted.

'HERE FAN PUT THIS ON IMMEDIATELY. JOE YOU HAVE TO HAVE THIS ON.' I took out Joe's Mickey Mouse one, quickly placed it over his face, pulled the blue holding straps over the top of his head, he squirmed a little pulling away but I carried on, seeing he was all right, I struggled with my own gas mask pulling the straps over my head, sat there panting away, gradually with my recent exertion of exercise, the glass eye piece steamed up with condensation. Peering through the mist could see nothing. I had to take it off again to wipe the glass, then again struggled to pull the straps over my head. Looking across at Fan alongside the small figure of Joe, these gas masks covering their faces, sat like two idiots both looking through the doorway gazing skywards. Fan with her nightgown half open, beneath the straps of the mask, her hair a complete mess sticking out from all angles. Joe who did not know what the hell was going on. His tiny face encased in red rubber with the two huge circles of steel rimmed glass eye piece, it's red flap of a nose wobbling as he breathed in and out through the blue canister. At the ridiculous sight they made, I burst out laughing, they unaware that I was laughing at them made it even worse, the stifled sound within my mask of laughter had tears rolling down my cheeks, again the glass began steaming up, reaching across touched Fan's arm, indicated about the mess her hair was in. From within the confines of the mask my muffled voice said.... 'Your hair.'... She shook her head. I think she thought I was trying to tell her to take it off. I shook my head waved my hands about my hair saying. 'Hair Hair.' She moved her hands up towards her hair feeling it, she nodded, made some strange noises, one thing for certain, conversation was going to be very difficult with these masks on. We must have sat there for best part of half an hour, tthere wasn't any sign or sound of aeroplanes. Joe was fed up and now very agitated at having this gas mask over his face, he had tried to take it off a couple of times but Fan had stopped him. I too was fed up, Outside it was deathly quiet. Was this false alarm like the previous ones? I decided to accept the fact that it was a practice and we should at least take off our gas mask, to breathe fresh air again instead of air tainted with the smell of rubber. I made the move and took it off, the air in the shelter was certainly not fresh, I could smell the musty earthy smell of the inside, It was not very pleasant. Fan waved her hands backwards and forwards at me saying I shouldn't, but I spoke freely and told her to take them off. I took hold of Joe's eased the strapped over his hair it made a squeaking sound as the rubber came away from his cheeks, he had been crying his mask was wet inside, he had a runny nose, quickly wiped his nose and eyes telling him it was all right. Fan by this time had taken hers off, was looking flustered, her hair was even worse, I began to laugh again.

'What are you laughing at Sarah?'

'You Fan, your hair. That's why I was laughing about it earlier. If I had a mirror you could see for yourself.'

'You're daft Sarah. Don't you know there's an air raid on?'

She still could not see what I was on about. Sitting opposite each other, I laughing at Fan until she started to laugh herself. At what I don't know? Moving outside took in great gulps of fresh air, ran into the house, where the wireless was blaring out some music. I poured water into the kettle, a shriek from Fan made me jump, she was looking at herself in the mirror smoothing down strands of hair, she began to laugh, that started me me laughing. I made the tea, Joe was already outside playing, when the All-Clear sounded. It was well after nine' o'clock, it had lasted about an hour, we had heard nothing, but it was the turning point for Fan, she decided to go back the following day, it would be much safer where she lived than up with us. Next morning Fan in reasonable spirits left with Mary and Kaye. The rest of the week went by without any further air raids. I was in a constant state of worry. I started biting and chewing my fingernails that quickly became a habit. I would retire early to bed, with Joe fast asleep in our bed, I would kneel down by the bedside and say the rosary.

Next day I worked out a schedule for shopping working around the situation of the change of bstteries,. We had not been at war three weeks, when over the wireless came the sound of a new voice, that of. "Lord Haw Haw" (as he was later nicknamed) telling all that the war was lost. I did not know who this person was and dreaded the worst. Later he was proved to be a traitor by the name of William Joyce, a member of the Oswald Mosley British Fascist Party, who had gone to Germany to join the Nazi Party only to become their mouth piece, spreading alarm and despondency with his propaganda. That whole month of September was filled with rumours, uncertainties, restrictions. Almost immediately blackouts came into force. Every household had to hang black curtains to cover up windows. Fortunately I had already got my black Indian curtains hung, so it was only the other windows I had to cover. A heap of restrictions came into force. Street lighting was cut off. It was pitch black during the night-times. Schools had already been closed and some cinemas closed too, much to Kaye's annoyance. I received a few letters from Jack, not much to say. Just to keep our heads down to be very vigilant as that 'Fella Hitler.' was trying to talk about peace with Britain and France. Only time would tell. In the long run that never happened.

With Fan's regular visits, she became the messenger for the family, so I was never going to out of touch. On one of her weekend visits Fan informed me that Dickie Fox, Wally Thomas and Jimmy Curtis, Nan's husband had been sent to France with the B. E. F. Letters from the two boys and Mother, assured me that everything was okay with them. News of the sinking of the armed Merchant ship the Rawlpindi had me thinking back to the escapades of my tribe at Rawlpindi. Oh if only I could be back there again out of this worrying time. By the end of the month, everyone had to register their families at their local provisions shop. The little store down by the Frying Pan as it was called (I never did find out why it was called that). Fortunately there were no more air raid sirens during that month. I suggested to Mary and Kaye that I wanted to go down to Hayward's Heath to see how the boys were getting on. Peg could possibly stay with Joe while I was away anyway. I wrote to Peg suggesting my plan also to Mr. and Mrs. Richardson, asking if it would be possible for me to go down and see the boys. Their reply, I was more than welcome. Peg wired me back informing she would come and stay. Kaye sorted out the times of the trains down to Haywards Heath, which were early in the morning, but subject to change without notice. Nevertheless, I decided to go. I sent a quick note to the Richardsons informing them of the date I planned to see the boys. After peg arrived I was ready to leave the next day. Starting early in the morning, I made my way down to Gypsy Hill station, bought my ticket, fortunately there were no delays, boarding the train I did not have to change. It took about three-quarters of an hour to get to Hayward's Heath,there to be met by Jackie and Michael running up the platform to meet me yelling at the top of their lungs.

'MUM.' They looked very well and happy, with me brushing tears from my face. They took me to meet Mr and Mrs. Richardson waiting outside the station with their car. A very thoughtful gesture, during the ride I was too busy talking with the boy's to notice how we got there. After they parked the car a short walk took us to their house. The Richardson's were a charming couple. He was a bank manager; without children of their own, were quite delighted to be looking after the boys, who had settled down they were quite happy enjoying their stay. They took me on a guided tour around the house, which had ample rooms, a big kitchen, a rear garden that sloped down to a stream at the bottom providing a most pleasant setting. Unlike some other unfortunate evacuees, the boys had the freedom of the house. Mr Brennan and the other schoolteachers still taught them at the local school. However, the local children held their classes in the morning, and their classes were held in the afternoon. It was obvious to me, the pair of them were quite happy staying at the Richardson's, after an enquiring day out, I returned with my mind at rest, very pleased that I had made the trip. Other post arrived. Mother's letter revealed there was no need for Fan or me to worry about Tommy and Margaret, they were quite happy attending school classes. The Huggins had three boys of their own but no girls.

Although very early in the war, everyone was fully aware of the possibilities of rationing that lay ahead. As the months progressed, the shelves were showing signs of shortages. Supplies were not as plentiful and just as hard to come by. It became somewhat of an excuse. "Sorry Madam. Maybe in a week or so stocks would be in." Nevertheless, items were always snapped up quickly. Whilst out shopping the local mothers, void of their own children would really fuss over Joe. Conversation would become the main subject of how individual children were coping away from home. In the home waters of the Scarpa Flow the Royal Oak had been sunk. A tragedy which shocked everyone it was the beginning of the long war against Germany. The postman delivered a package with our Identity Cards together with three different coloured sets of Ration Books one (Green) for Joe, three (Blue) for Jackie, Michael and Margaret and three (Buff) for Me, Mary and Kaye. Inside were many pages with different coupons on and a warning polite but firm. "Do not to lose them or give them away." Further information would follow, all would all be informed of their use later. I decided for the time being the best place to put them was in the small suitcase with all our policies, important documents and place them in the wardrobe. The wireless became the only important line of communication for the nation and of course the voice of Lord Haw Haw. On one occasion I did listen intently to what he was saying. "Croydon beware we shall bomb it to the ground. All within the area should evacuate immediately." That threw me into a panic. After the three previous air raids was this end for us? I waited for the now dreaded sound of the siren. Nothing happened, in the following weeks and many times throughout the war, many listened to his warnings and there were many like me who turned him off, he was nothing but a blackguard. After the war he was captured he got what he deserved. Hanged. Then news someone had tried to blow up that 'Fella Hitler.' at meetings in Munich. Unfortunately it had failed it became a talking point of great interest. If Only! The subject of evacuees temporarily dropped. Yet in later correspondence from mother she informed me that the Huggins kept begging mother to let me adopt Margaret. Yet in another letter from Mother she informed me. Margaret was driving her mad with her antics. She upset Tommy so badly, he was near to madness with fright. So much so she had had told Mr. and

Mrs. Huggins....'Take her keep her so long as it leaves me with my sanity.' But worse was to come. One day Margaret arrived at the back door looking like a Bisto Kid out of the advert. I was shocked to see her standing there a label on her coat. All she said was.

'Hello Mum. Granny's sent me back to you.' I screeched.

'What on your own?'

'Yes. I was quite all right. Mum.'

'Oh my God why on earth did your granny do that?'

'Granny said she had had enough of me. So I should go back home with you.'

I went mad. Taking hold of her I took her in, read the label pinned to her coat, with a lot of writing, saw it was a list of instructions of how she should get to Crystal Palace. Quite unperturbed about her journey, she took a letter from her pocket handed it to me.

'Granny gave me this letter for you. You known mum nice servicemen and women looked after me on the train. I told them about Granny and what a viper she was, they seemed very cross, but I told them, it's quite all right we are all used to it. At Vauxhall station two ladies in blue uniforms took me to the right bus stop, put me on the 2 bus. They paid my fare, told the conductor to put her off at Central Hill opposite the convent. She can find her own way to her mother's from there.'

She related this to me, as if butter wouldn't melt in her mouth, yet here was something fishy about this tale. I wanted an explanation, so tore open the letter, read its revealing passage of mother's version of events.

Quote:

"Sarah Allahnah. I'm sending this child of yours back to where she came from. I am fed up with Tommy waking up at night-times screaming and crying. I had to take him into bed with me, not one night but many times. I could not work out what ails the child? Eventually I demanded to know what was upsetting him? Between his sobs, Margaret had told him. King Herod was coming to kill all little boys. Little girls were all right, he would not touch them. Only the little boys, who would be killed stone dead in their beds, even Tommy who was sleeping beside her. They would not touch her or any little girls, only little boys just like Tommy. So you had better pray." When I found this out from the little madam. I gave her the thrashing of her life, dressed her packed her bags and threw her on the train. So Allahnah, you can control the little devil yourself.'

Unquote

Obviously Margaret had remembered some of the stories from the Bible, unfortunately had turned Tommy into a nervous wreck. I just did not believe what mother had done. Margaret was only six years old nevertheless, I knew from first-hand experience. Mother would stand for no nonsense from anyone. After I got Margaret sorted out , she was happily playing with Joe, I wrote a letter to Mother telling her. It could have been dangerous for Margaret travelling alone with the possibility of air raids. Also another letter to Jack. Mother's later reply to me was. *"Keep the brat. She's worse than any falling bombs, clouts meant nothing to her. She just tossed her head and gave her Grandmother lip. I never tolerated that from my own brood, and I was certainly not going to take it from any of yours. Maybe you can control this uncontrollable madam. As I have no intention of doing so."* The irony of it was, Tommy loved Margaret or as he called her. "Lor Mayee Yose" (lovely Margaret Rose) clung to her every word. It wasn't long after that that Mother returned with Tommy to London. She too was fed up with being away from the family, had decided to return home.

Since the departure of the B. E. F all the action appeared to be happening on the lower countries and on the Eastern front in Poland. However on the home front it appeared to be a situation of a. "Phoney War". There had been no further air raids. On a couple of weekends Mary had been to visit the boys who were enjoying themselves, however I was not. With Margaret's unscheduled return home, and Mother's return with Tommy, I decided to bring the two boys back home. If things developed for the worse and we were going to be killed, it would be all of us together. I composed a letter to the Richardson's, explained my concern, I would be down to collect them myself. Their return letter with words of reluctance,but accepted my reasoning . I arranged for Fan to bring Tommy up to us and stay to look after Margaret and Joe. Then I left.

The train was packed full of service personnel. Army, Air Force and a few Sailors. A soldier gave up his seat I refused but he insisted. I spotted he was an Artillery Gunner enquired.

'Where you off to Gunner?'

'Down the coast Missus. Can't tell you where though.'

'My Jack's a QMS. serving at Dover.'

'Christ Missus. When the Balloon goes up. Those poor sods will be in the thick of it day and night.' Someone yelled out.

'Hoi! You watch your language. There's ladies present.' An ATS girl chirped in.

'Yes, we might be in the services and are used to it, but there are civilians amongst us.'

'Sorry Lady, no offence intended. Don't you worry what I said? Your old man will be all right inside the Castle.'

'Thank you, but I've heard worse language than that in my time. I served in the first world war, and have spent over fifteen years in the army with my husband.'

'Get away. Hey. You lot. Di'yer hear that? We've an old soldier among us, that's done more bleeding time than all you lot put together.'

That broke the ice. I was showered with offers of cigarettes and chocolate. Politely I refused the cigarettes, but gratefully accepted the chocolate, to give the children. Concerned about his remark, I asked him.

'Do you know what the situation is in Dover then?'

'Nah Ma. It was just summat I said wiv'ot thinking. There'll be all right them Gunners you mark my words. They nose 'owes to look after themselves. You should know that. Yersel being a Gunners wife?'

I warmed to this cockney Gunner. Along with the rest of them, they all seemed quite jovial without any concerns. When the train arrived at Hayward's Heath, I got off with cheerio's ringing in my ears the Cockney Gunner called out.

'Ear Ma. You take care of your youngsters, someday they might become soldiers just like us.' He waved. I smiled and waved back as they departed into the distance. Shouts from Jackie and Michael diverted my attention.

'MUM.' The pair of them came racing up to me, followed in the rear by Mr Richardson walking offering their greetings.

'Hello Mrs Plant, we have just found out there are no trains running back to London until very late today. How would you like to stay overnight and catch the train in the morning?'

I did not have any choice, I thanked him for his offer. We soon arrived at the Richardson's house. After tea and cakes, Mrs. Richardson suggested that the boys should show me around the vicinity. I was taken out for a walk, it was plainly obvious from their chattering, both of them did not want to leave. Accordingly it was quite good fun living down there with their school friends. But I was adamant, they should return home with me. Enough said. In the afternoon they had to go to school I went with them to see Mr Brennan, to explain my reasons for taking them back to London with me. He was very good about it, could offer no challenge to my demands. As he put it, some other mother's had already done the same with their children. At the Richardson's they provided a lovely meal. The boy's did their packing and went to bed, leaving us to talk about life in London with all its problems. It was evident that both of them did not want my boys to return with me. We retired to bed in the comfortable bed provided I was asleep in no time. I slept for about an hour, woke up and lay there thinking about the rest of my tribe back at home. It did not make any difference where I was, if my tribe were split up. Would they be all right? I was up early and ready for the return journey back home with my two boys. Mrs Richardson said a sad welfare to them and   Mr. Richardson drove us to the Station, before he drove off.   I thanked him for their kindness, Back

369

home it took less than an hour before pandemonium set in. Thank God family life was back to normal. I was temporarily at peace with the world. With the return of the boys, with the masses of washing clothes for all of them I resumed my usual household chores, whilst they went about their usual chores shopping, swopping batteries etc. St. Joseph's was closed as were many other schools in London. So the three of them were not getting taught anything, that they enjoyed. Nevertheless the BBC broadcast lessons to compensate schooling or, they had to go to the local library for books. It was a rather haphazard affair. I insisted they listen to the broadcast whilst Jackie in his spare time found himself a little job selling provisions from a horse drawn cart. He had to be up at six o' clock in the morning, to curry the horse before the lady owner arrived, then to restock whatever provisions were available, hitch up the horse. and in the darkness get underway on their selling trip for the day. The lady owner gave him three shillings and sixpence per week. He brought it home and gave it all to me. I gave him sixpence back, he refused but took it.

Since early in September, when the last air raid siren had sounded, most of the war activity appeared to be on the high seas, which was very evident by reports of a sea battle of the River Plate in South America, where three of our warships destroyed the huge German battleship the Graf Spee. So we were not the only ones to suffer, so were the Germans. That news alone boosted our morale no end. Christmas was fast approaching and Peg invites all the tribes down at the Drillhall in Sidcup for Christmas and the New Year. The order of the day was, bring and cook. From my stock I took a Christmas pudding a Christmas cake and some preserves. The Plant's, McDermott's, Thomas's, Wilbraham's and Aunt Agnes, en-masse arrived. Aunt Peg gave them all strict instructions on what to do and not what to do, definitely. 'No. Breakages!' Bridget somehow got a very large turkey, Agnes a leg of ham, Fan brought some tinned fruit. With little or no troops about dinner was cooked in the cookhouse ovens, and served in the Drillhall. Trestle tables were put up and the wooden stacker chairs were used. Everyone was fed, everything cleared away, so that the tribes could be let loose in the Drillhall. Our first wartime Christmas was a very happy time.

January 1940 arrived, so did the snow. It was extremely cold. The coldest winter on record for seventy-three years, with deep snow all about the temperature dropped well below zero. In addition to our misery of the cold, snow and darkness, many shops closed down. Empty of stocks. Then on January 8th., the rationing of food began. Four oz's of butter, bacon, and cooked ham. Twelve oz's. sugar. It was just the beginning of a very long period of deprivation for everyone, which was to outlast the war well into the fifties. Yet people still went about their normal day's routine. Still further restrictions were imposed, even more came into force as the war progressed. Another unexpected visitor to our house was my sister Lena, who arrived with Brutus, Dick and Peg's Ginger Chow dog. It was after Dickie had been sent to France, and upon Peg's insistence, Lena took over the looking after Brutus, why I did not know? Nevertheless, with Brutus being cooped up in Lena's flat all day, attempting to get out tore down her curtains. That is why she brought him to us to look after, so my tribe could take him out for walks in the so-called quietness of the suburb. He was a lovely dog he wasn't any trouble at all, he loved the children and became part of our family. Jackie took charge of him, Brutus followed him everywhere.

Another chore, the Government insisted everybody did. "Dig for Victory" was the call. All householders were encouraged to plant root crops and vegetables. On a rare weekend pass Jack arrived home. His first for four months. He looked well, but red eyes told a tale. He too did not like the idea of us all being split up. It was bad enough for him to be away, never mind his offspring's, but when he did find out Jackie was not having any education, insread was in a job. He was not impressed. Jack started digging the back garden assisted by Michael and Jackie, they flattened out the top part for a chicken run. However, they did not finish it. Leaving he informed me.

'Sarah, I am going to get Jackie down to Dover with me.'

'Why? I have only just brought them back home so we can all be together.'

'Well Sarah, seeing Jackie is not getting any schooling he spends more time doing that job. I will see if I can arrange it and get the Padre to give Jackie lessons.' I thought: *Yes. A great idea. So be it. At least he would be with his father. Agreed.,,,*'That might help I'm sure.'

When he got back from his rounds. Jackie was informed of a change of plans. He was a little reluctant about losing his job, but more than excited to live in a Castle. he asked.

'Can I take Brutus?'

I did not take any more notice of the situation. Alec, Agnes husband arrived on the doorstep, over a cup of tea he suggested he buy some more chickens, build a proper chicken run in the garden to raise them to produce eggs for us. I saw no problem to his suggestion, it certainly would help with the rationing agreed. Alec, Jackie and Michael built a chicken hut, when finished. Alec acquired about ten chicks, He named two of them "Gert and Daisy" As they grew we let them roam the garden so there was plenty of scraps for them to feed on, more to the point they did produce eggs, they became good layers for our supply of eggs. However as the war progressed, a few of them became dinners, with the exception of Gert and Daisy..

During one of the so called Air raids (False alarm) Mary came home with a nasty cough must have caught it whilst in one of the communal shelters in Portland Square, IIt would not clear up and developed into a chesty cough. She visits the Doctors, was given cough mixture told, it will soon go away. On the news all were advised that British Summer Time would start in February. Two months earlier than normal, which meant everyone had to get up well before the dawn breaks. The two girls did not like that particularly Mary who was still suffering from the cold, she decides to volunteer for the A.T.S. She attends the Medical Board, A week later she receives dreadful news, the medical had diagnosed her with Tuberculosis. She was forced to give up her job, took to her bed for about two weeks. The event of Mary's illness had Jack come home on compassionate reasons. Having already written back saying that permission had been granted for Jackie to stay at the Castle, Jackie returned with his father taking Brutus as well. Jackie soon wrote home to tell me he was studying most of the day with Brutus sitting in the room. He was the only civilian in the Castle he loved it. Dover, it being a military zone had been totally evacuated. Nevertheless, he had only been away a week, when rather ironical, with the number of school children returning back to London, made some of the London schools re-open in April. Mary's cough was getting worse, it was contagious, which needed specialist treatment. The Doctor made arrangements for her to be sent to a Sanatorium in Winchmore Hill North West London. Just before Easter she was taken by ambulance and whisked away. Once again our family unit was slowly disintegrating. So began another worrying period of my life.

Hitler attacked Denmark and Norway, so-called neutral countries. The British army was sent to Norway, to help resist the advancing German army. More bad news. Dick, Jack's brother arrived on the doorstep, to inform me that Pop's their Father had died, could I wire Jack to go to the funeral? I received a return reply.

SORRY CANNOT STOP SENT WIRE DIRECT TO MUM STOP

Then meat was rationed, not by weight but by cost. One shilling and ten pence worth per person per week. What could you do with that? We continued with our life style constantly being interrupted by one thing or another. Holland, Belgium then Luxemburg were the next to receive a German Blitzkrieg. The war was steadily advancing towards Britain, then more bad news. The British army retreated out of Norway. Holland, Belgium and Luxemburg, surrendered to the Germans. France was attacked. The B. E.F was in slow retreat. It was about seven weeks since Jackie had left for Dover when late in May, disastrous news for everyone, the B. E. F was cornered at Dunkirk. A massive evacuation had got under way, the events of the month of May were overwhelming, spilling into June. On the news we heard that the B. E. F were being taken off the beaches with heavy losses. Hundreds of small boats were required to cross the channel, to pick up survivors, then return to land in and around the shores at Dover and St. Margarets Bay before being reassembled for further duties and action. I feared for the safety of Jackie down at Dover, but knew Jack was with him. A knock on the front door had me running to open it. It was the Telegram Boy holding a yellow envelope in his hand he said.

'Telegram for Mrs. Plant.' Fearing the worst ripped open the flap with trembling fingers unfolded the note. Read its message

JACKIE STOP OK STOP ON HIS WAY HOME BY TRAIN STOP
ARRIVE TODAY STOP

My face must have shown my relief with the news, as the Telegram Boy asked.

'Any answer Mrs?'

'No that's all right, hold on a minute.'

I went and got a three-penny piece, hurried back to give it to him. He left with a grin on his face. I too had a grin on mine. I could expect Jackie back that day. Late in the afternoon he arrived home without Brutus, but just full of the exiting experience he had witnessed as he related. From the vantage point of Dover Castle, using a pair of his father's binoculars, he saw the Stuka Dive Bombers. The air battles, the massive black palls of smoke, towering into the darkened skies above, the glow of fires that raged on the horizon. When his father told him he had to go he said, he didn't want to, but he was put under the care of the W.V.S. on a train, along with all the wounded soldiers. There were some French soldiers as well. He was kept busy serving tea to the wounded, but he had something he had to tell his Aunt Peg. Jack had heard Dickie was on one of the boats that landed in St. Margaret's Bay. Dickie was all right and was being transported somewhere up north. Not to worry, he was safe and sound. Great news to my ears. I would go to the post office to send a wire to Peg.

DICKIE OKAY STOP LANDED NEAR DOVER STOP SARAH STOP

Within a week, the evacuation from Dunkirk was over with, heavy losses and many prisoners taken. Truly a dent to our pride. It was about this time that Churchill broadcast his famous speech, about us fighting them on the beaches. We were for all intents and purposes. "The front line." God help us. June was beautiful with hot sunny days and blue skies, but with the Germans continuing their build up. Imminent on the horizon loomed an expected Invasion. However two days after Margaret's eighth birthday, the sixteenth of June. The wail of the sirens woke me up. In pitch darkness I lay there listening all was quiet. It was sometime later that I did hear the distant noise of aircraft followed by several thuds, it went quiet again before sometime later the all clear sounded, only then did I drift back to sleep. Next day on the wireless, they announced that during the night German bombers had dropped several bombs near Addington. It also announced that code name. "Steel Ring" Phase Two of evacuees was to begin, the Home Counties Croydon was part of. All were to be entrained bound for Devon and Cornwall. However this time my tribe were staying put with me. Yet more bad news about Mary. I received a letter from the Northern Hospital Sanatorium Winchmore Hill. Under the prevailing circumstances, they were going to transfer Mary with other girls to another Sanatorium in Harrogate Yorkshire. Mary had only been there three months, I along with Michael or Kaye had visited her on every other weekend. Catching many buses across London, that almost took a full day to get there and back. My only consolation of her move was, with Kitty Burns living somewhere close, just knew I could rely on Kitty to visit Mary. Soon I received a letter from Mary at the new sanatorium, with the address, also informing me, that she had found out that the girls already interned there had been badly treated. That little piece of information added a further weight to my existing burden of worry. I wrote to Kitty asking for her assistance to visit Mary at the addressed Sanatorium . I received a wire.

SARAH DON'T WORRY STOP I WILL LOOK AFTER MARY STOP
WILL VISIT HER OFTEN STOP KITTY STOP

Over the past six weeks. the war had turned against us. We were now on the defensive and had to defend our Island sanctuary. News reports of daily bombing raids had been on- going around the coastal areas. However, on the first day of July a news bulletin announced that the Germans had invaded the Channels Islands. I was shocked to hear this latest news. It appeared that 'Fella Hitler'' would stop at nothing. where next? The closest was possibly the Isle of Wight, then the mainland itself. With the pending occupation of England by the Germans threatening, everything appeared against us. What did he have in store for us? Was this to be the beginning of the end of the war for us all? God help us all, blessing myself carried on cooking our breakfast, having finished breakfast, my tribe was either leaving for work Kaye, Jackie now without his job along with Michael and Margaret off to a somewhat de-pleated school, almost void of children, leaving Joe, who was next door fighting with young Trevor. Up to that point we had not used the shelter, which had been made comfortable, with the aid of Alecs assistance, duckboards covered the floor plus two cots and a small table, nevertheless it always smelt damp and earthy. Anyway after my last experience with Fan I preferred to be inside in the relative comfort and safety of the house. Then Mrs. Candler arrived at the back door very distressed out of breath she wheezed.

'Mrs Plant can I come in.'

'Yes please do. Cup of tea?'

'Yes Mrs Plant. I need one badly'...I could see she had been crying, my immediate thoughts went out to her: *Maybe news of one of her French cousins had been killed in an air raid...* 'Have you heard the news?'...she broke down again.... 'Whatever is it Mrs. Candler?'...I put my arm around her shoulders to console her...'C'mon tell me who is it. What's upset you?'

Between her sobs, words mentioned the invasion of the Channel Islands. Relieved that it was not one of her French relatives or her girls.

'Oh that yes. I heard it this morning.That is very bad news

'What am I to do?' She sobbed.

Then I realised her concern. she had some relatives or friends over there in the Channel Islands. Placing a cup of tea in front of her I assured her.

'Oh don't you worry too much. They won't get anywhere near us. They won't even land in Britain. You won't see any Jack boots marching up our roads. You wait and see.'

There was I trying to console this woman, who had a far better reason to be afraid of what the Germans might do to her family, yet half an hour before I was the one who needed to be consoled and reassured myself. I felt like crying with her. I offered

'More tea. Mrs. Candler?'

'Yes please, you're so kind.'

We sat there chatting before she regained her composure she left me with my own thoughts: *About our future, whatever it may be?* Next day the news bulletin reported, bombs had been dropped on the Ports of the Southeast and Southwest of England. To add to our immediate misery, more rationing was imposed. This time sugar was reduced down to eight oz's, margarine at six oz's, cooking fat and tea at two oz's, per person. Tea, something that I feared most at losing. I would have to find ways of preserving our stock. All around the coastal areas the bombing continued throughout July into August, there was still no let up. It was brilliantly hot with clear skies, good for the Luftwaffe but not good for us. Although it was the school holidays. I think everyone prayed for rain. It didn't come. The news, air raids on shipping in the Channell, the ports along the south coast, every time. Dover was mentioned Jackie reassured me.

'Don't you worry Mum, Dover Castle is too big it has great thick walls. No bombs would blow that up.'

But day by day the air raids were intensifying, by then we had got used to the warning wail of the air raid siren. Nobody really took too much notice, until the evening of August fifteenth. everyone was out, when the warning wail of the sirens went off, maybe just another false alarm? Nevertheless, in the far distance I heard a faint droning sound which became closer and closer, increasing in its droning volume, until in the far distance the bang and crack of many guns filled the air, as the Ack Ack began firing. Very much aware this was no practice, this was the real thing. I stopped what I was doing, listened intently to the noises, which did not seem far away, I ventured outside looked into the sky to see if there were any planes above. Nothing that was evident, yet progressively the droning noise was getting louder, mixed with the scream of diving planes but still could see nothing in the skies. I heard some thuds, whoomps, booms and bangs, before the drone of the aircraft began fading into the distance. Half an hour later the all clear sounded. I thought: *It must have been our Boys up there.* I realised I had not taken any evasive action having left Margaret and Joe playing outside they unaware of any danger, I let them play on until later called then in to wash and get then in bed. Listening to the news reported: *Many enemy aircraft had bombed the RAF airfields at Kenley and Croydon.* The latter barely three miles away from us. The front line was now my back door. Now were for it! I lay awake that night restless at the thought of the possibility of being bombed. I was sick with fear and had a dreadful nights of so called sleep.

The next day various rumours were abundant about the dozens of enemy bombers, bombing Croydon airport, destroying the factories of Bourgeois Scents, Mallards, and Phillips all had been wrecked. Houses had been demolished; hundreds of people had been killed. Later we learnt a slightly different story. It was twenty-one bombers that had carried out the air raid. A number of people had been killed and hundreds injured. Though it was true about the factories and houses. This was to be our experience of the first air raid on London, with the bombing of RAF airfields marked the beginning of the Battle of Britain. To us, any civilians living in close proximity to the RAF aerodromes at Kenley, Biggin Hill and Croydon as it was with other RAF aerodromes dotted around London. We all had first-hand experience of the forceful attempts of the Luftwaffe to defeat and destroy the RAF. Later that day the air raid warning sirens sounded. No time to ponder on a false alarm, we grabbed hold of our gas masks and ran for the shelter. Sitting on the bunks struggling to fit our gas masks over our heads. I with Jackie Michael and Margaret with our grown up gas masks on, Margaret had to remove her glasses to fit hers on. Jackie helped Joe with his Mickey Mouse one, as he breathed in and out, its nose was flapping. We sat there waiting. Margaret with her glasses held in her hand, stared out of the open doorway at nothing. Waiting and watching for the unexpected to happen. Margaret was the first to speak, well a mumbled tone of something or other, which had Jackie turn towards me. He grabbed hold of Michaels arm to draw his attention to Margaret. The pair of them began laughing, the muffled sound of snorting and banging through these ungainly gas masks was something else. Unlike Fan, Margaret's hair was prim and proper, I was unsure at what they were laughing at. I touched her arm to attract her attention, as she turned to face me, I spotted it. Her left eye was turned in towards her nose, the reason she had to wear glasses, was a slight cast in her right eye, called a lazy eye, I too, seeing the funny side of it, gave a muffled laugh, before turning to the two boys, shook my fist at them. Instead they laughed all the more. I gave up. Fortunately the wail of the all clear sounded, gratefully I removed this terrible mask. I think that was the last time I ever wore one.

As the house was located half way up the side of a hill, the view from the front provided a panoramic view of the city of London, with basically almost a flat terrain in the foreground. Not that I spent much time in the front. My place was in the kitchen at the rear, where I could watch Joe playing in the garden with young Trevor, in and out of the shelter, with the chicken coup located further up towards the dividing fence with one of the houses in Gibbs Avenue. Nevertheless, the danger of living with the threat of being bombed hung like a shroud over one's head. If you were out shopping when the siren wailed into action, you were unsure of what action to take. Go in the nearest shelter, run home or, just stand and look skyways for sight of the enemy. Even if you were at home, it was a case of listening for the increasing drone of aeroplanes, followed by the rapid crack and boom of the Ack-ack guns. At those times we did not know what to expect.

At least the bombing was directed away from our locality, but that was soon to change. On the eighteenth of August, during the daytime the sirens wailed. By this time we had realised, we did have time to get to the shelter, instead stood in a group outside looking skywards towards South of Crystal Palace, in the distance the approaching sounds of the droning of many engines could be heard increasing in volume, to be joined by the crack of the Ack-Ack guns. In the distance high above in the sky we saw plenty of black puffs of smoke of the bursting shell and could just make out the faint rattle of the Spitfires and Hurricanes machine guns, as they too attacked the enemy planes. We following the little black dots with vapour trailing behind as they weaved and dived. Soon black clouds of smoke drifted high into the sky evidence that bombs had been dropped causeing fires in one or all three of the local airfields. Thankfully the bombers, having unloaded their deadly cargo, flew away. The raid did not last too long before the sirens sounded the all clear. It was then I realised we were all standing outside the shelter, not a word had been spoken. The next day they announced on the news, the bombing of not only our local airfield, but other aitfields surrounding London that were being attacked by a massive force of German Bombers in an effort to destroy the RAF.

Shortly after that. I received a letter from Kitty. Her letter full of concern to see if we were alright, she knowing how close we were to the RAF airfields. Also she had been visiting Mary regularly. She was alright. not to worry. Her words cheered me up. However I had not heard from Jack, Peg had informed me that Dickie Fox had been posted to Malta, I made it a point to write to Kitty and Peg. All throughout that week, the daily attacks on the airfields continued, until one day there were no air raid sirens. I wondered if our boys had shot them all down? But shrugged the thought off as silly. That 'Fella Hitler' had something up his sleeve that was for sure, but on the other hand, our RAF Bombers flew over to Germany, bombing them. So it was a tit- for-tat game, until a wave of German Bombers, diverted their attention away from airfields, started to bomb oil storage tanks, the munition factories, then turned on London itself.

Even I was caught up in the excitement of it all. During the daytime out shopping, if you looked towards the city, you could spot many silver Barrage Balloons floating serenely high in the sky with the sun illuminating their outline like big floating pigs. Once the Air Raid siren sounded reckless to say the least, everyone was eager to be the first to spot the incoming aeroplanes. 'There they are.' A finger indicated where all should train their eyes, as tiny black dots appeared far in the distance above. Slowly they became larger as they flew towards us. Wave upon wave of bombers, on occasions the sky was peppered black with them, and it was not long before each type was identified. 'Dormers, Heinkle's, Junkers, nicknamed the" flying pencils." Messerschmitt's and of course the Stuka bombers with bent up wings. When they dive-bombed, their noise could be heard everywhere as the gradual scream of their so called "Trumpets of Jericho" increased as they descended, to release their bombs under the wings. Then almost silence as they climbed high into the sky for another attack. Eager to enter the battle, the Spits and Hurricanes engaged in dogfights with their escort fighters, as they dived in for a kill, the distant sound of their rattling machine gun fire could be heard. Something we had never seen before, the sky criss-crossed with woolly vapour trails, twisting turning interweaving in and out of a blue sky, with the roar and fading of aircraft engines, as they dived to shoot down a plane, first a trail of white smoke then black from behind a bombers or fighters engine, indicated a hit, before it slowly turned sideways and fell into a steep fall twisting like a corkscrew, its engines turning into a howl, as it plunged downwards to earth to crash somewhere out of sight. Joe sitting outside watching the dogfights above shouts out.

'DON'T WORRY MUM. I'LL LOOK AFTER YOU! I WON'T LET JERRY KILL YOU.'

Such words coming from such a small boy. The dogfights overhead were thrilling to watch and enthralled the boy's. I used to shout at them to come indoors. Pointless, they took no notice. However, over the following days and months, the day and night air raids became constant, the wail of a siren interrupted our normal daily way of life, particularly during the dark, disturbing our night-time sleeping.   We were to become very familiar with the sound of falling shrapnel, it's whirring-- zizz sound clearly audible as it fell from above to land close on the ground or bury themselve in the earth. On many occasion they hit roof tiles smashing them in two, the remnants of a tile sliding down the roof to crash on the ground below. All these sounds happened during the ongoing raids, before the sound of the All- Clear.   The next day comments: *"Portsmouth caught it last night"* or *"Southampton" Whichever name of a city or town seemed to be different every day or, "Portsmouth copped it again last night."* All shared rumours and speculations about how much longer the war was going to continue. Germanys very own heart was targeted. The RAF retaliated and began bombing Berlin. By now everybody knew it was going to be a long war. I received no letters from Jack, adding to my worries of Mary. With the night time raids going on, we would sit in the confines of the shelter in total darkness. It was frightening and eerie, as the continual throb and drone of the German bombers droned on overhead for hours. As did the flashes followed by the sound of the Ask- Ack guns, firing into the pitch black sky above, laced with white beams as many searchlights weaved about trying to locate the bombers high up. Eventually visible to the naked eye, the tiny shape of a bomber would be illuminated. whilst others searchlights locked their beams on it. Then the Ack-Ack guns fired at it, scoring a hit, the plane leaving a trail of flames behind it as it plunged towards the earth, ensured that another bomber would not bomb again. Nevertheless, other bombers carried on, as we listened to the muffled crump as bombs crashed onto houses. To add to the cacophony of noise, the distant clanging of fire engines, the ringing of the ambulance bell never seemed to end.

On Sunday the twenty-fifth, that day we had already had three air raid warnings, without any incidents, yet again in the evening the sound of the siren wailed, there was a raid South of Crystal Palace. It could only mean the airfields were the bombers target again. It did not last long before the all-clear sounded.   However the next day, news announced that London had been attacked by many German airplanes. Bombs hitting the London Docks causing mayhem. This was the first time East London had been attacked. I was beside myself with worry. After the recent air raids we had witnessed locally, we were totally defenceless against any of the bombs dropped. I blessed myself, said a prayer, got out the Holy water bottle and threw some around the room, before I got on with the breakfast. Early in September, there had been somewhat of a lull in the number of air-raids locally. I was alone in the house, Joe was outside playing with Trevor, Kaye was at work and the other three had returned to school, in the distance the sound of the sirens wailed, so for a change it was not going to be us, at lunchtime the three of them came home for lunch, the first thing Michael said was.

'Mum. Have you seen London? It's been bombed.'

'No, the air raid siren did go off but not around here.' Grabbing hold of my hand he said.

'Come and see out of the front door.'

When I did open it and gazed out towards East London, there were many great plumes of black smoke rising into the sky. It must have been the docks they had hit. I shuddered to think of where would it be next? I returned back to the kitchen to give them their lunch before they went back to school. Jackie and Michael were full of the sight they had seen, but not I. It was the start of the London Blitz. Two days later, mid-afternoon the sirens wailed, this time I went out the front to see wave after wave of incoming bombers, heading towards London to drop their bombs. I stood there rooted to the spot to watch the horror of an air raid, for a few minutes I stayed there very disturbed blessed myself, went back inside to blur out the sight, sometime later the siren wailed the all- clear. But during the night they wailed again, it woke up the whole household. I got everyone up and downstairs into the front room. The constant drone of hundreds of aeroplanes overhead went on throughout the night as did the distant crashing and exploding of bombs, the noise of mayhem was awful, very frightening. We just sat there listening to the noise of a frightful air-raid, there was no way we would use the Anderson, nobody wanted to venture outside.   Through a crack in the

376

curtains the boys watched, their faces lit up orange by the fires in the distance. About three o'clock in the morning the all-clear siren sounded, only then did we return to our beds. Laying the bed with Margaret on one side and Joe the other, fearful of a reoccurrence. I vowed that I would not use the shelter at night. After that nights raid we did not use the shelter, we stayed indoors. Next morning massive black clouds of smoke hung over London, as the oil tanks burnt and carried on burning for days, an illuminated target for the night bombers, until they werefinally extinguished. Outside the air was tinged with the smell of burning oil. Mrs. Candler came along to see me, carrying Juby her Jack Russell dog, she puffed and wheezed her way into the kitchen.

'Mrs Plant, can I stay with you during the night? After last night's raid I do not want to be on my own again.'

I fully understood how she must have felt on her own, her husband was one of the local area night-time Wardens, and had been out all night during the raid. After our own previous night's experience. I readily agreed. During the following months she became a constant night-time companion in our house, we would all stay in the front room. After the evening meal, we would take the wireless set into the front room to listen to, as we settled down around the table to play cards. Mrs. Candler would arrive with Juby, carrying a big bag filled with balls of wools and knitting needle slung over her shoulders. Before the war, I knew she had never ever cast a knitting stitch in her life, then at the beginng of the war she took it up, as she said. "To calm her nerves." She would greet all, then sit down at the corner of the table, dropping the big bag on the floor by her feet, she would take out some balls of wool of various colours, then start knitting a scarf. Every night to the sound of clickety-click clickety- click of her needles we played cards. Mrs Candler was knitting a scarf that was never going to be finished. Once she got to the end of this big ball of wool, she would stop; unravel the scarf, rolling up the wool into a big ball, then start all over again. There again we were exactly the same with the never ending card game of Newmarket, listening with one ear to the clicking of needles accompanied by the music from the wireless, Joe and Margaret thumping hell out of our piano with Juby howling beside them, on occasions, it must have been a mad house, nevertheless, as soon as Juby stopped howling she would crawl under the sofa, then we knew the bombers were coming. When the bombs were raining down amid the sounds of the constant crump, crump, crump , the bursting shells of the Ack-Ack , clicking of knitting needles Mrs Candler would call out. 'Mrs Plant, more Holy Water.' My bottle of holy water was always within reaching distance. I would stand up scatter it over everybody and bless all. Then back to the cards and her knitting. I do not think she ever finished the scarf. Long before the all-clear sounded, Juby would crawl out from under the sofa wagging her tail. It was so strange how she knew exactly when to crawl under and come out from under the sofa. The bombing raids got progressively worse. During the daytime you could tolerate it and get on with household tasks. I'm sure the German Pilots used the two old burnt out towers of Crystal Palace as landmarks. But later, one was pulled down the other blown up. it made no difference they still flew over us in their waves. In the far distance the slight audible sound of Ack-Ack gunfire was a pre-warning, bombers were again on their way.

Everyday It took Kaye a few hours travelling to work on the bus to Victoria. It amazed me how anyone would want her hair permed at a time like this, it was beyond me. Yet she would arrive home late and tell us about the bus on her way to work in the morning. After a night raid it rolling over fire hoses that snaked across roads to where groups of terraced houses once stood, the air was filled with dust, smelling of burning wood soot and mortar, God knows what the City looked like at night. She said they spent most of the day in and out of air raid shelters, full of cigarette smoke from people endlessly smoking cigarette after cigarette, just waiting for the all- clear, then they would emerge outside, coughing and spluttering. It appeared that this had become the normal way of working life. Jackie left school, got a proper job employed at a local firm TMC down in West Norwood. One day Michael was out somewhere and I needed flour to bake cakes, instead I sent Margaret down to the "'Pan" to buy some. Whilst she was out the air raid siren went. The sound of

377

the incoming planes grew much louder and closer, putting me into a mad panic. I put my coat on got Joe inside to take him with me, to go out and fetch Margaret, just then much to my relief, she arrived at the back door, looking like a snowman, her glasses partly covered in flour, I screeched.

'Whatever happened?' In an indignant manner she replied.

'Nothing. On my way back the sirens went. so I just covered my head with the shopping basket and began to run home. Then the flour bag burst. It was horrible, It went into my mouth and I couldn't see. I do not want to go shopping ever again.' Needless to say there was no flour for cakes. I wiped her face, cleaned her glasses, made her change and washed her hair. Her mishap was related to all when they came back home and much acclaimed to everyone's enjoyment.

Sunday the fifteenth of September became known as Battle of Britain day. On Monday Kaye arriving home informed all, that one of the German planes shot down on Sunday had crashed into Victoria Station. The pilot and crew had parachuted out, one of them had landed near the Oval Cricket ground, where the local women beat him up with brooms. I thought: *If I had been there I would have done the same.* Regardless of air raids Michael and his pals spent most of their time out searching for shrapnel. They collected shrapnel in buckets, somehow knew which bomb or shell these fragments of metal came from. To me they were just jagged pieces of metal. Michael came home one day struggling with a huge chunk of a bomb, left it beside the back door. Margaret went out to play, fell over it ripping her leg wide open. She shrieked blue murder, and I'm sure all the German Pilots could hear the sound of this wailing banshee, they must have turned about to head back home. With blood pouring out of a gaping wound, we put her in Joe's old pushchair, pushed her all the way to the local Cottage Hospital, to get the wound, stitched up. Michael got a thrashing and a warning... 'Do not bring anymore home.'

It fell on deaf ears. Even Jackie went out during the early part of the night, to listen for the whirr of a piece of shrapnel. When he told me this I forbade him to go out ever again during an air raid. Another day I sent Michael up the Palace parade for shopping. I was in the garden hanging out washing, when the sirens sounded. I knew he would take cover somewhere. I had nearly hung everything on the line, when I distinctly heard the distant chatter of machine gunfire. Then the droning of engines appeared to be closing fast in our direction, had me looking up in the direction of the Palace Parade. Almost immediately, flying very low a twin engine Dornier suddenly appeared. Through the glass cockpit in the front, I saw an airman in a beige coloured suit and helmet. In a split second it was overhead. The noise of its roaring engines was deafening and really frightened me. I stood rooted to the ground dropping the peg in my hand covered my ears, it began banking in a wide circle, its black cross plainly visible on its wings and belly, but it was gone before I could shout out anything. How on earth did it get through undetected? Not long after that the all- clear sounded. When Michael arrived home, he was panting, excitedly he blurted out.

'Mum a Dornier machined gunned all the streets up there. It was so low I saw the gunner's face. A man dragged me out of the way and flung me into an air raid shelter. He shouted at me to stay there. After it had gone, I ran all the way home.' ...After my own sighting, I was pleased to see him in one piece, retorted...'Oh, I'm pleased you did not get shot yourself. Good on that man whoever he was. It must have been the same plane I saw, it flew very low right over here.'

But that experience really frightened me. What if he had machined gunned me? Not only were they bombing civilians, they were machine-gunning them as well? What with the children and the worry of Mary and Jack away. I was at my wit's end. I had no fingernails left. I had bitten them off to the quick. It was late in the evening on a Saturday, we heard the Church bells clanging. A pre warning that the invasion was imminent, something Father Larkin our parish priest had warned us about. The fear I felt in my stomach made me physically sick. I could not bring myself to believe that it was going to happen. But the so-called invasion never happened, and I do not know why the bells had been rung? Our postal letters seemed to take a long time gtting to us, even the Post Office was struggling like every other service. By this time we had totally abandoned the shelter. Instead

378

Jackie and Michael had moved the chickens inside it for protection. With the approaching autumn with double summertime, the twilight was much later and the night bombing was at its worst. We had moved a couple of mattresses downstairs together with a bunk bed, to take turns in getting some sleep if we could or, play a game of two pence halfpenny cards. The stake being halfpenny a game. From time to time I stopped the game; one of us would say a decade of the Rosary, with Mrs Candler intoning with us, yet all the time the steady clickety-click of her needles could be heard. Then it was back to the cards.

As I have already mentioned, before the war, taking Jack's advice, purchased as much tins of food as I could, along with dried fruit, for Christmas puddings, fresh fruit, sugar bottles and jars for making jam preserves and lemonade. Amongst our supplies were bottles and bottles of homemade lemonade I had made from a recipe the Khansama in India had given me. It was quick to brew, it finished up like thick syrup, which had to be diluted with water to drink. However gradually those supplies soon diminished, removed from various cupboards and the larder provided empty space under the stairs. Inside the larder was a very thick slab of slate, used as a cold point to store perishable goods, with its easy access from the hallway, during a very heavy night raid, it was the strongest place to be in for added protection. We began to use the larder, all cramming in, Joe, Margaret, Michael and Jackie with Juby sqeezed in under the slab, Kaye, Mrs Candler and myself, standing then shut the door. A couple of candles would be lit and set on top of the cold slab to provide some light. I really don't know how we all crammed in there. On one such occasion I, doing my usual thing, showered Holy Water over everyone. They blessed themselves then silence…'More please Mum more'…I gave them another dowsing…silence. I was aware of a lot of licking going on…when they again asked for more, I became suspicious. In the dimness of the flickering candlelight. I could make out grinning faces licking lips and hands. In my haste, I had picked up a bottle of undiluted lemonade not Holy water. With the guns blazing away at the night bombers. I just roared with laughter, yet they still wanted more. So I showered them again much to their pleasure. Under the circumstances, a delightful moment

There was no let up with the bombing, Mrs. Candler called in and told us a bomb had hit West Croydon station, killing sixty people outright. Two days later Fan arrived informing us a bomb had gone straight down the stairs at Balham Underground station killing everyone. Not even in the undergrounds were you safe. The night-time bombings were even worse. If you ventured outside some hidden person would shout.

'PUT THAT BLOODY LIGHT OUT. JERRY CAN SEES A PINPOINT OF LIGHT FOR MILES. THE NEXT BOMB WILL BE YOURS.' On another occasion Kaye came home later than usual, which had me worried, however when she did arrive she informed me.

'Sorry Mum, but I got off the bus to visit granny, to see how she was coping. I spent some time banging on the door before she opened it. To me she didn't look too good. She was ill and wanted you to visit her. Can you go down to see her?' I was concerned about her wanting me. If Kaye would stay at home to look after everything, I would go next day.

Outside the convent I caught the 2 bus, it was going to be my first visit to Vauxhall since we took Margaret to stay with Fan months before. All appeared to be all right until we arrived at West Norwood bus garage, from there onwards houses lay in ruins, at Brixton the bus stopped outside Quinn and Axtons, a big store on a corner. It was just a gutted shell. I shuddered at the sight as the bus continued onwards, in the middle of an air raid it arrived at Stockwell. All passengers were ordered off the bus into an air raid shelter. Jostled by others we walked into the gloom either stood or sat down on some forms. It was my first experience in a communal air raid shelter, inside the air stank of stale tobacco smoke, a match flickered into life, then after that, it was like a Christmas tree, everyone lighting up to smoke, I began to cough, soon I'd had enough of it. I thought: *No wonder Mary caught that damn cough. How many more had the same problem?* I decided to get out and into fresh air. Coughing my way to the doorway. I was stopped by an ARW.

379

'Hoi, you missus, where do you think you're going Ma?' I quietly responded....'I have to get out of this smoke.'... 'You ain't going no place, until the all clear sounds, and mark my words. I say's when you can go. Anyway it will soon be over then you can go.'....I waited in the fresh air of the doorway until the all clear went....'Okay Ma. Off you go.'

I couldn't get out of there quick enough, as it was not that far to mothers, I decided to walk the rest of the way. Hurrying sort of half running until, at the Tate Library I began to run the rest of the way. I was puffed out when I knocked on her door. No answer, I banged harder until it was a continual thud. Eventually it was opened by Mother in her nightdress. Distressed at the sight I exclaimed. 'Mother, whatever is the matter with you?'

'Allahnah. Wooo-come on in-Wooo.- Nothing. It's those damn blasted bombs. – Wooo. - Night, after blasted night. - Wooo. - Those blithering idiots of German. - Wooo- hit the docks. Two nights later. Wooo-. They went for- Wooo.- us.' I knew her feelings agreed.

'Well Mother, like it or not, we all have to contend with those bombings.'

'No I didn't feel well. Wooo- so I went to bed. Wooo- on Tuesday. I can't Wooo- stop the - Wooo- wind. Allahnah can you-Wooo- do something Wooo- for it?'

I had to laugh in between this. Wooo- and that Wooo- she would try and say a sentence.

'Mother, all you've got is wind.'

'Yes. Allahnah, but -Wooo- it goes -Wooo-on all night' Wooo-.'

I ushered her inside closing the door, helped her into the kitchen, sat her down then made a made us a pot of tea. She just sat there quietly now and again Wooo- ing. Searching through the cupboards, it was most odd she had no medicine she could take. I enquired.

'What about peppermints, have you got any?'

'Wooo- No'

'Well, I'll see if I can get you some when I've finished this tea. Why did you call for me? Couldn't Fan or Agnes, sort you out and get a Doctor?'

'Fan. Wooo-or, Agnes Whoo . No, -Whoo. - Nether of them pair of blithering idiots have Wooo- your experience. Wooo-. And those blithering idiots of Doctor's Wooo- will only Wooo- come out Wooo- and treat you Wooo- if you're dead.'

She sounded like a foghorn. It was quite comical, yet disturbing. I had to get out and find some peppermints for her...'Can I get your shopping while I'm out?'... 'Wooo- Buy anything - Wooo- Yes.' I made up a list, gave her another cup of tea, sat at the table, she nodded her thanks whilst. Wooo-ing - at every other couple of breaths. I left her Wooo--ing to herself.

I tried the little shop in Wheatsheaf Lane just a few doors away from her house. No joy there, then the stores in Wilcox Road, I tried a chemist opposite the Tate Library. The Chemist gave me a bottle of peppermint essence suggested I try. "Bill's" the sweet shop along the road. Entering Bills, the smell of toffee mixtures, treacle and sugar filled my nostrils, but that was the only choice Black Treacle slabs, Barley Sticks and Peppermints. I bought some peppermints, a treat for my tribe. Treacle Toffee. Back at Mothers I gave her the essence and the lozenges.

'Thank you. - Wooo- Allahnah. I knew you could- Wooo- help... I had to laugh...Allahnah Wooo- It's not a Wooo- laughing matter Wooo-.

I gave her the essence in warm water. It made it worse. Woooooo- she went...Be Jabbers. Wooo- I Wooo- can't take Wooo- that Wooo- stuff....I gave her some lozenge's...'Here Mother. Try these lozenges'....Sucking at the lozenge she coughed at their strength, but the wind seemed to subside... 'Where did you get these from Allahnah?'

'Bill's in the south lambeth road, he makes his own sweets.'

'Be Japers, they seemed to have stopped the wind'

'Now Mother, you can get Fan to get some more. Don't forget it's Bills.'

'Ah well. God Bless you and your tribe. I knew I could rely on you. - Wooo.'

With that finale I left. At home I explained Mothers ailment, imitating the sound of wind she made, that was the worst thing I could have done, that had them all Wooo-ing. So much so, much to everyone's amusement Mothers ailment did continue throughout the rest of the war.

Out of our bedroom window, Kaye and Jackie constantly watched the raids over London, they asked me to watch as well. I declined. I constantly worried that if we were to be killed what would happen to Jack? Who possible would survive but Mary? When if ever would all this bombing end? Fortunately the ferocity of daytime bombings subsided. That 'Fella Hitler' had changed his mind about invading England. Instead invaded the Russians. Good for us not for them. That pleased Mrs. Candler, but she still continued with the endless knitting of her scarf. Jack arrived home with Brutus for a weekend leave. his first leave in nine months he looked tired. Sweeping me in his arms kissing me, all he said was.

'Sarah ducks, it's wonderful to be with you again. It was exciting but now the tide has turned. Now then Sarah. All will be well.'

But what concerned him was the way we appeared, red eyed with bags upon bags under our eyes. However it was not just ours but the way of everyone's life. He brought home a suitcase full of chocolate, goodies including two -dozen eggs and bacon. What a sumptuous three days of breakfast we all enjoyed. He left home to continue his journey north to another posting at a Training Depot in Lancashire. But duty is duty, he was a soldier. Unexpected Kaye arrived home before lunch I enquired.

'What's up Kaye no work?

'No Mum. I was on the bus on my way to ,work, just passing where Mother and Fan lived. Was horrified to see the area bombed. Smoke and fires were raging with fire engines and ambulances everywhere. I jumped off the bus, ran to Granny's, but was stopped by the Air Raid Warden. He said... You can't go down there Miss. We are still putting out fires. The wood yard got hit last night and all the streets behind are ablaze.... Fearing the worst I shouted at him my Granny and Aunt live down Wheatsheaf Lane. What's happened to them? He asked me if she was an old white haired woman. I told him it was. When I said that. He said. She brought out cup of tea to them all. She was a tough old girl she stayed with them. They thought she was mad. They took her to the school next door. So I dashed to the school, asked for Mrs. Cunningham. Someone said she had already left sometime before. So I went to Aunt Ages, banged on her door but there was no answer. Went to Aunt Bridges, knocked on door. Aunt Bridget opened it, moaning about Granny, saying she had had enough ear bashing. I went inside, Granny was sat on a chair moaning about Hitler and what she would do with him, if she could get her hands on him still Whooing.. Fan and young Tommy were also there all comfortable in old easy chairs. Granny's face was rather grimy and smutty, her white hair almost black. She was waving her arms about, ranting and raving and wooing... It was so funny I had to laugh. When I asked if she wanted to come home with me? she bit my head off, looked at me and said. 'Get Away with yus. Wooo- A little bombing won't move me. Wooo.' Anyway they are all okay.'

Not good nrews but at least they were safe and sound. There had already been an announcement that over Christmas a truce would happen, the bombing would cease, when two days before Christmas Fan arrived on the doorstep, with good news. Mad Agie had won a huge Turkey bird in a Pub raffle, all were invited to her flat for Christmas dinner. A turkey dinner! This we were not going to miss. I decided to go. Bugger that 'Fella Hitler.' Christmas day after attending early mass we caught the 2 bus outside the church. At West Norwood the conductors changed over, it just happened that the new conductor was Jacks brother Dick, he cheerfully greets us.

'Hello Sarah. I can see you lot are all right. How's Jack?'

'He was home a couple of weeks ago, then left for Lancashire. I'm worried I have not heard from him.'

'Nah. Don't yer worry yersel, Jack all be all right Sarah, you mark my words.'

381

All Jack's family were alive and kicking, like us surviving the onslaught of the daily routine. The bus stopped at the Tate Library, we got off as the bus sped away Dick shouted.

'ALL THE BEST FOR THE NEW YEAR SARAH. SEND MY REGARDS TO JACK.'

Arriving at Agnes, I banged the knocker twice, when the door opened. Agnes flung herself at me, dislodging my hat, at the top of her voiced shouted.

'SARAH EVERYONE IS WAITING FOR YOU. THEY'RE IN THE FRONT ROOM UPSTAIRS.' Then whispered... 'Keep quiet, Alec is asleep.' She always was a little mad. Adjusting my hat my tribe chorused. 'Hello's Auntie. Happy Christmas.'

Pulling us inside, she ushered us upstairs. First into her tiny Kitchen to see, Big Alec fast asleep slumped like a sack of potatoes on a chair, his blue dungarees caked in mud and dust. In a loud voice she said. 'Poor love. He needs his sleep.'

Alec was one of the Heavy Rescue workers, who worked amid the rubble of the bombed houses. He was the complete opposite to Agnes. Quiet stable a very amicable fellow. However she got him to marry her was beyond my belief. Up in the front room, Mother, Peg, Fan with young Tommy were sat down at a large Christmas table, with Brutus asleep under it, he had been returned to Peg months before. Under the circumstances that prevailed, it was quite something. I questioned.

'Agnes, where's Bridget and her family?' She retorted.

'Oh I didn't have any large tins to fit the bird. So I borrowed Bridget's. We had a row, so I didn't invite the McDermott's.' The wrath of Mother intervened.

'Wooo-.You're a blithering Idiot Agnes. At a time like this. Here we are surrounded by bombing, and you squabbling over Wooo- nothing.' The subject was dropped like a bomb. I helped Agnes with the cooking. The Turkey was a monster far too big for their tiny oven, although Alec had cut off its legs. I provided the Christmas pudding,that was put on into a steamer to heat up also bottles of lemonade. Cooking over, time for dinner. Alec was woken up and he carried in the turkey, placing it on the table about to carve, questioned.

'Who wants the Parson's nose?'...No response...'Who wants a leg?' All chorused.

'Yes please.' Quick as a flash Alec retorted.

'But I've only got two.' Roars of laughter erupted as he quickly cut the bird, dished out the carvings. As everyone helped themselves to the veg, that soon were ravished, filling their stomachs fit to burst. As the table was cleared away Agnes was congratulated on her winning the big bird. chistmas pudding was eaten, after which we played games before Alec left for his night watch. Blankets were brought out for sleeping in chairs or, on the floor. It was very quiet except for a lot of Wooo--ing by mother. Then the tittering started, so began the imitating of their Granny by my tribe, until she got fed up and ordered everyone to.

'Cease or, I'll waylay into the lot of yus '

The next day, all were severely ill, except the Plant's. Mother's comment.

'Wooo- Stomachs like oxen with all those curries. Wooo.'

The turkey was to blame, it must have been as high as a kite? Before the draw it had been laying on the pub counter for over a week. With everyone else too ill to do anything, we left leaving Brutus with Peg to take back with her to Sidcup. We arrived back home, none the worse for the sumptuous meal having taken advantage of the truce, enjoyed the remainder of Boxing Day. Then bed to sleep. Our first night un-interrupted since September. What would Hitler do next? A question that could only be thought of day by day.

Mrs Candler arrived with Juby to spend the night with us. That night the twenty-seventh of December we were all in bed, The distant sound of the bang and crack of guns woke me as the bomber's headed towards London. A very cold chill ran down my spine. I got them all up and downstairs into the larder, Mrs Candler using the bunk bed was already awake. We did not sleep that night. early next morning when the bombing had ceased we staggered outside, looking in the direction of the city to see London ablaze from left to right, clouds of black smoke curling and billowing high into the sky. Then the siren wailded again, the guns started banging away, the incessant droning of the Bombers could be heard. Another big one was on its way. I quickly got them back inside into the larder. I shouted.

'LIGHT THE CANDLES'. Matches were struck, the flames flared up to reveal no candles. Jackie shouts out. 'MUM, I KNOW WHERE SOME ARE.' I shouted back.

'QUICK GO AND GET THEM.' He left and soon returned with a handful, in the darkness he gave them to me, I wondered over these candles, where had they come from? but no matches, we had struck them all.

'Jackie, where did these come from?'

'Outside Mum.' I thought: *That's odd. I'll question him later.*

'The on-going noise outside was at a crescendo. We didn't talk and sat in the darkness until Jackie blurted out.

'Let's go outside, the bombers are all heading for London.' As he got up I detected his movement, immediately shouted.

'STAY WHERE YOU ARE.' Kaye retorted.

'Mum, there's no point. We can't spend the day in here. Jackie said they are all heading for London; there can't be much of it left now. Let's go out and see what's happening?'

I could see her point of view. No bombs had dropped around the area. I reluctantly gave in. Got up and left the larder, quickly followed by them, even the orange glow through the curtains over the front door reflected some light. I opened the front door. In the morning daylight revealed London under siege. Whilst overhead the continuous droning of engines went on and on, with the noise of banging guns, the crack of bursting shells in the distance, the continuous crash of exploding bombs raining down on the city, produced a cacophony of noise. In the distance the red glow of burning, shone on the dome of St Paul's surrounded and engulfed by smoke. In the cold of the day, we stood very quietly watching this siege. Pent up fear and worry finally got the better of me. I sobbed at the sight, tears rolled down my face. I thought: *My God is this the end of us all?* I'd had enough. 'C'mon you lot inside this is not for you to be seeing.'

Mrs Candler, Michael, Margaret and Joe came with me, Kaye and Jackie remained outside, and until later they sat with us. It was a very bleak end to 1940.

The only heartening news, was early in January the Eighth Army had captured Tobruk and was advancing along the North African coast. However due to the very uncertain weather. the sporadic raids continued, London still copped it, as did other major cities. Targets were varied and wide. Mrs. Candler had decided to stay at her own home and do as we did. Take cover in her larder. So we got a little bit of respite from the clicking, One late afternoon an air raid began, the usual noise deafened us, the sound of the loud explosions and thumps close by, had us diving for cover. It didn't last long, then the all-clear sounded, we crawled out of the pantry. I made pots of tea, slices of bread with scrapings of margarine, a smear of jam, something we all had after a raid. I was constantly rationing my accumulated reserves, which unfortunately were reducing. Jackie arrived home exclaimed.

'The Vicarage has bought it, another bomb had created a big hole in Norwood Park and the school got one, blew up the toilets and classrooms.' Michael added.

'Must have been the same stick of bombs.'

The sporadic bombing continued. Depending on the crash, thump or, if you could hear the whistle, they were very close. However, we had become use to them. Some nights there were no raids. Then followed by three or four sleepless nights in a row. We were not the only ones, other cities had been unmercifully bombed causing deaths and mayhem to all civilians. Early March, a raid had just finished, we had heard the whistling, but no crash or boom, Kaye arrives home from work with Mrs. Candler and her dog Juby. She quickly said

'Mrs. Plant, the ARP's have told us to leave everything and get out. There's an unexploded in the opposite garden, they have moved us away towards the park. Can I stay with you?' ...'Sure you can, come in.'

Making room at the table, as normal we chatted about the recent raid. Hours later Kaye answered a frantic knocking on the door. In walks Maisie.

'Mum you all right?'

Mrs Candler sat at the table, with a cup of tea in front of her still knitting.

'Of course I am. Mrs Plant has told me to stay with them until their have sorted out that unexploded bomb.'

Maisie explained her predicament, working in the Ops room. She had heard about the stick of unexploded bombs landing in the area of Salters Hill, had got permission to go home. Found the area cordoned off, her Mother gone. She came to us to ask if we knew her whereabouts obviously very relieved to see her in amongst us. For about a week or so there had been no raids of any magnitude. Mrs Candler had decided to stay in her own house again. A sense of security made me decide, tonight we sleep in our own beds upstairs. I made sure that everything was secure, the black outs drawn. With Margaret and Joe sleeping bedside me in my bed, Kaye and the two boys in their room. I showered all with Holy Water before getting into the comfort of a warm bed, in between two inert bodies, hopefully faced with an uninterrupted night's sleep. The wail of the siren woke all, I lay praying waiting in anticipation for the familiar drone of aircraft. Nothing happened. In the distance only the muffled sound of the Ack - Ack guns. I sighed a relief, it was not going to be over us. In a state of drowsiness, the sound of a plane grew louder and louder, until in the distance I heard an enormous crash, the bomb hit the ground followed by another one, then another one, all too close for comfort. I heard Kaye shout out.

THAT'S ANNERLY. THE PALACE. GYPSY HILL.' Then the noise of a low flying the plane passed overhead, as the noise of its engines rapidly receding Kaye screamed.

'MUM. CHRIST ALMIGHTY. THIS ONE IS FOR US. '

In that very instance. Fear overtook my stomach. My mouth was dry of saliva, why I do not know? It happened in a flash. I quickly put my arms around Margaret and Joe pulling them tight into me for protection. With a terrific whistle, howl and earth shattering crash, the windows were blown in, I felt the bed lifted into the air, then overturning we were flung out landing with a thud on the floor, with the bed coming down on top of us. In a heap we lay under the bed totally winded. I was sprawled across Joe, with Margaret lying on top of me screaming in my ears. The sheets and blankets that covered us saved us from being cut to ribbons by glass. We lay there in the tangle of blankets total darkness, with Margaret still screaming in my ear, Joe squirming underneath me was crying. Dazed from the blast in a state of shock, I was trying to catch my breath, focus on what I should do or could do? Margaret screaming in my ear had her arms wrapped arrond my neck, Joe still crying struggling to push me off him. I don't know how long we lay there? I heard a voice shouting

'MUM. MUM ARE YOU ALRIGHT? QUICK GET OUT.'

Through my daze I recognised Kaye 's voice filtering through the tangle of blankets, frantic hands grasped at blankets, dragging them from over us. Someone was trying to lift the bed up it was Jackie and Michael both shouting.

'GET OUT. GET OUT.'

The blankets were pulled away, Margaret was being dragged off of me then a pair of hands grasped my arm pulling me out from under the bed half kneeling I eased myself off of Joe to crawl out into a blaze of light, someone grabbed Joe. I felt Kaye's hands under my arms as she dragged me out, as we scrambled up, with a whoosh another huge blast of hot air enveloped us, more sounds of breaking glass, tearing the clawing hands away from us, the five of us were physically flung against the wall, knocking the wind out of me I crumpled to the floor. It seemed everyone was shouting screaming or howling. At that exact moment in time, it was indescribable what was happening, yet in the bright light I saw Jackie and Michael grab Joe and Margaret rushed them out of the room. The room was a blaze of orange light, the gas main outside had exploded shooting flames high into the night sky lighting up the room. I felt Kaye's arms around me levered me up, above the roaring noise outside. She was screaming in my ear.

'GET OUT. GET OUT.' In a daze I mumbled.

'I'm all right, go and see to the children.'

'NO. MUM. C'MON OUT QUICK.' Her voice seemed far away but very urgent, still pulling at my arm trying to get me up, my hand feeling around in the glass, somehow found both my slippers put them on. In the glare and heat I glanced towards the shattered windows, all I could see was a fountain of flame. I raised my arm against the heat. Kaye was shouting.

'MUM. C'MON OUT.' I felt Kaye's hand grab my arm again she started to pull me, automatically Totally disorientated I resisted I had to get the documents. I shouted.

'GET THE SMALL SUITCASE AND MY FUR COAT FROM THE WARDROBE QUICKLY.'

The suitcase we always kept packed with any valuables and documents, which were more important to all than anything else. Except life itself. Kaye shouted.

'YOU'RE CRAZY MUM. NO TIME FOR THEM. LET'S GET OUT OF HERE.'

But she joined in the hunt. We stumbled or fell about amongst the glass. We did not need any candles, the bright orange light fully illuminated the room, the double bed was upside down against the wall, the wardrobe was lying on its side fortunately its door was hanging off, but we found what we were after. I found the suitcase. Kaye shouted.

'MUM. ENOUGH IS ENOUGH. C'MON MUM. LET'S GET THE HELL OUT OF HERE.'

A voice from below shouted.

'IS THERE ANYBODY UPSTAIRS?' Through my haze I heard Kaye shout.

'YES TWO OF US.'

'ANYONE INJURED?'

'NO.'

'ANYONE ELSE IN THE HOUSE?'

' YES. FOUR OTHERS.'

'WHERE ARE THEY?'

'DOWNSTAIRS.'

'YOU TWO. GET YOUR BLOODY SELVES DOWN HERE NOW. QUICK AS YOU CAN. WE'LL FIND THE OTHERS.'

The yelling and shouting that was going on, was something I could not grasp, I had hold of the suitcase, the heat on my back was so intense, but coming to my senses, in the fierce glare of the ignited gas, I could see Kaye had hold of my fur coat, realised I did have to get out. Kaye grabbing hold of my arm, forcibly dragged me out through broken glass, crunching under our feet, she guided me through the open doorway, the bedroom door lay at an awkward angle against the broken banister, the orangey glare behind us lit up part of the stairways showing the moving shadows of our bodies. Clambering over the door made our way downstairs, the whole house was aglow, glass was everywhere, stumbling down the stairs found the front door laying on the stairway, as I carefully walked over it, a hand from a rescue worker grasped my arm, spoke encouraging words.

'Okay Ma gently does it, go that way through there into the kitchen.' He helped me down off of the door, we made our way to the kitchen, where the rescue workers, armed with pickaxes, shovels, came in from the back. One of them shouted.

'YOU'RE SURE THERE'S FOUR OTHERS?'

Kaye shouting above the roar of the gas flame outside.

'YES. THEY WERE IN BED UPSTAIRS.'

'WELL THERE'RE NOT DOWN HERE. YOU SURE THEY CAME DOWN.'

'I DON'T KNOW. THEY JUST DISAPPEARED.'

'RIGHT. YOU TWO STAY HERE. I'LL GO UPSTAIRS. DON'T FOLLOW ME.' He hurried past us. I was still in a state of shock. I certainly was not with it. Another warden came in.

'ITS ALL RIGHT MISSUS WE FOUND EM. THEY'RE IN THE ANDERSON.' He carried on through, shouted to the other Warden.

'HARRY. WE' VE FOUND EM. THERE'RE IN THE ANDERSON.' Then shouted at us.

'YOU LOT WERE LUCKY. THE HOUSE OPPOSITE COPPED A DIRECT HIT. DON'T KNOW ABOUT ANY CASUALTIES YET. THE OTHER CREW ARE OVER THERE'.

We were soon informed they were safe in their shelter. Thank God no one was killed. A fire engine and ambulance turned up, both clanging, ringing their bells. A Warden came in with Joe crying in his arms, followed by the other three. Margaret minus her glasses was sobbing. They looked dazed but appeared unhurt. To add to the mayhem and confusion from outside the shouts of the NFS Firemen leaping into action running out hosepipes, were almost drowned out by the constant hissing and roar of the gas flame. A nurse came running through the front entrance shouting.

'DOES ANYONE NEED ATTENTION?' Kaye shouted.

'NO WERE ALL OKAY.'

Miraculously, no one had received a scratch even me feeling for my slippers. With nobody to attend too, the Nurse quickly disappeared. Gradually the house on fire opposite was brought under control, but nothing could be done about the roaring gas main, so it burned merrily on. Although forbidden to go outside, my tribe sat at the table somewhat in a state of shock appeared to enjoy all this mayhem. As the gas had not been turned off, there was gas on the stove rings to brew up tea. With Kayes help brewed up gallons of it. The Wardens took it in turns to have a quick cup? I said a prayer in thanks. Sometime later Kaye and I surveyed the damage in the orange light. Downstairs the house was in a terrible state, glass everywhere, window frames smashed or hanging at awkward angles, pictures hanging drunkenly, their glass shattered. Cupboard doors hanging on by a hinge or lying on the floor. Even worse the men trailing mud all over the floors, we didn't venture upstairs, The house was in a state of controlled pandemonium. The senior Warden arrived, surveyed the damage. Shouted.

'CAN'T STAY HERE TONIGHT MISSUS. CAN YOU STAY SOMEWHERE ELSE'? IF NOT WE'LL TAKE YOU TO THE RESCUE CENTRE. WHILE WE CLEAN THIS MESS UP? Kaye was the one that answered him shouted.

'NO WE CAN STAY UP THE ROAD.'

'OKAY. YOU KNOW MISSUS. THE HOUSE NEXT DOOR IS JUST AS BAD?' ...The Castles. I had forgotten all about them....'DON'T WORRY NOBODY HAS BEEN INJURED. THEY WERE IN THEIR SHELTER LIKE YOU LOT.'...(Little did he know?)... 'YOU GET MOVING WE WILL LOOK AFTER THE HOUSE. UNTIL YOU GET BACK IN THE MORNING. IT WILL LOOK BETTER IN THE LIGHT OF DAY. YOU MARK MY WORDS.'

I was now back in control of my senses, still in my nightdress, as we all were. I rallied them around to sort out coats and shoes from amongst the debris. Then left the scene behind us on our way to Mrs Candler's. Outside, Kaye had Margaret and Jackie had Joe on their backs. as we made our way up the road, the heat and noise from the flames intensified, to add to the confusion and activity, the gasmen arrived. We scurried past them carried on as gradually it became colder. A few people were stood watching the activity behind us. Nods and shouts of concern were uttered.

'You were lucky.'-- 'You all right love?'

Suddenly the glare from behind went out, so we carried on in the darkness, going through Mrs. Candler's gate up the steep pathway to the front door Kaye knocked, that started Juby yapping, after a little while a voice from inside asked.

'Who is it?'

'It's me Kaye with Mum.' Mrs. Candler opened the door. Kaye blurted out.

'We've just been bombed out.' Mrs. Candler issued a stream of French words. Good job we did not understand what she was saying.

'Come in. Come in.'… in the darkness, she ushered us through into her kitchen. She fussed about saying.…'Let me light up the mantle.' Michael blurted out.

'The gas is off, the mains were blown up.'

'Wait, candles, candles, wait a minute.' I heard this noise of a draw being opened. Then a match was struck it flickered into flame close to the wick, which spluttered into a flame, its feeble light illuminated our faces. Mrs Candler let out a cry. …'Oh my God, you poor people look at the state of you all? Here, come and sit down.' She pulled out a chair…. 'Mrs Plant, come sit here the rest of you sit down at the table.'

I sat down on the chair. We must have all looked a sight all stood there, Joe was still on Jackie's back, in delayed shock my tears flowed, Mrs Candler put her arms around me. Kaye began to laugh saying..

'Look at the state of you Mum.' Mrs. Candler muttered in her accent.

'Kaye, this is no laughing matter!'

I looked at my tribe then seated around her table, their grinning faces covered in dust cheeks smeared through their crying, hair dishevelled. All were giggling Michael blurted out.

'Mum, you should see your face.' I muttered.

'Well. What's the matter with it?' Laughing he replied.

'You look like the Golliwog on Robinson's jam jars.' I asked.

'Mrs. Candler have you got a small mirror?' Mrs. Candler, busy lighting other candles said.

'Yes, I do have one, I'll go and get it.'

With more light from the candles, I could see my tribe more clearly, sat smiling with grimy faces tear streaked faces. At least we had all survived, wiping the tears away from my cheeks enquired.

'Is everybody okay? 'A chorus of.

'Yes, Mum.' Returning, Mrs. Candler thrust a mirror into my hand.

'Here you are Mrs Plant.' Taking the small mirror I looked into it to see the reflection my face, blackened by smoke and dust, where I had wiped away tears, my cheeks were smudged with dirt, my straggly hair was all over the place, but I wasn't the only one. Mrs Candler urged.

'Let me get you something to wash yourselves with'

Mrs. Candler busied herself brought in soap, a bowl of water a towel. I washed my face, in the cold water, with wet hands tried to smooth down my straggly wisps of hair. In turn they washed their faces. As I watched them, washing I realised how lucky we had been. The tension now gone, I too began to laugh at the sight of them. Mrs Candler said she did hear the bang but thought it was further down by the Pan. We all laughed at that thought, we were the evidence. At first light, still in night attire, we walked back down the hill. The distinct smell of gas, burnt wood hung in the air. The fire engines and ambulance had gone. The house opposite had been demolished was just a smouldering shell. Rescue workers and gasmen were still in amongst its smouldering embers and debris. The scene provided a grim reminder of the devastation a bomb could and did cause. We saw what had happened. The bomb hit the house and fractured the gas main, the house caught fire, ignited the escaping gas, we and Mrs Castle' next door.caught the full blast, the roadway between the house was covered in rubble with mud everywhere, a gaping hole was where the gas men had dug to repair the main. Our garden gate was lying up near to the front door against the fence where it had landed there were bricks and broken slates laying on the grass. We did not have a front door or any windows, there was no sign of my black curtains. Next door the Castles house

387

had copped it as well, smashed windows, curtains flapping in the breeze, their front door hanging on by one hinge. We had been extremely lucky. Someone shouted out.

'HOI. YOU LOT. GET OUT OF THERE.' Turned around I saw a rescue worker striding up behind us. I answered.

'It's all right we live here.'

'Oh. I thought you were some other people just having a look. Mind how you go in there. We've cleaned up the glass, but still be careful. As soon as we've finished down there. We will board up your windows and doors as well as next-doors.' I enquired.

'What's happened to the Castles next door?'

'Oh, they went to someone local like you lot. The couple, below went to the Rescue Center.'

Entering the house, little remained of any glass, muddy marks of sweeping and many footprints were everywhere. No time for tears. Get stuck in, all would help to clean up the mess. The next few days would be very busy. I sorted out clean clothes for all to change our filthy night attire. Jackie came in from the back garden.

'Mum, look four eggs.' Even the chickens were alive. Marvellous four eggs and no gas to cook on. Dick arrived as did Nan, both lived further up the hill in Gibbs Avenue they were unaware of our strife, until word got around. They just asked how everyone was, then left us to carry on cleaning. The rescue workers arrived back later, they boarded up windows, put the doors back on their hinges. It was all makeshift for the time being, with the windows boarded up the house was in darkness and full of draughts. Hours later when they left, a heap of assorted digging implements were left propped up against the front fence. It appeared the front garden became a storage area, for later bomb clearance of houses in the vicinity. With the house in darkness, presented a problem. Candles were hard to get, so the front and back doors were left wide open, making the house freezing cold. Overcoats and scarves were the order of the day. With the exception of houses further up the hill, our houses in close proximity to the bomb were without gas for a few days. Mrs. Candler cooked our meals. We only ate and slept there, with the two boys sleeping at Nan's just around the corner. With our immediate crisis solved. I went to the Post office to send Jack a wire.

BOMBED OUT STOP ALL OK STOP NOT TO WORRY STOP
LETTER IN POST STOP

That afternoon the Telegram boy came, shouting through the open doorway.

'TELEGRAM FOR MRS PLANT. HELLO . ANYBODY THERE?' I was sat at the table in the kitchen writing the letter. 'Yes, okay. I'm coming.' I ran to the doorway and he handed me the Yellow Telegram envelope saying. ...'Blimey Missus, you lot copped one then?' I tore open the envelope and quickly read the message.

HANG ON STOP LETTER TO FOLLOW JACK STOP

'Yes, You can say that again. But it's all over now bar the shouting.'.... 'Well at least you're not dead. Any reply'... 'No'...Okay Cheerio.' Off he went down the path whistling.

I caught the flu but carried on getting the house in order I received a letter from Kitty informing me, that Mary was okay, young Jack had been posted to North Africa. How were we all coping in the bombing? Coping! We had just been bombed out, she unaware of our recent escape. Jack's letter arrived a week later. He was shocked to receive the wire and now very concerned about our safety. He informed me. "He had managed to find two rooms to lodge in. With an elderly lady and gentleman. He had paid two weeks rent in advance, and if we did not hurry. It would go. He had applied for compassionate leave and would be down as soon as it was granted. Start packing."

Once again on the move, to a place called Bamber Bridge. Lancashire.

CHAPTER FIVE
BAMBER BRIDGE - 1941 –1945.

It took us a week or so to clean up the house the best we could. With all the windows boarded up the rooms were shrouded in darkness. The winds whistling through tiny cracks, turning each room into a cold room. The house had basically become uninhabitable. At least the gas main had been repaired and gas was available for basic cooking and some lighting. Nevertheless, we just could not stay there until everything was repaired properly, which could take months before any work began. I was grateful that we had at least somewhere else to sleep and eat at Mrs. Candler's. The Castle's next door had just upped and left. I think they had had enough and it was only a matter of time before we left.

After our recent traumatic experience. I suppose I was still in some form of shock and the bout of flu had left me very low, having partially got rid of the flu, but still felt like death warmed up, there was only a week before we moved. I was standing in the open back doorway muffled up against the cold watching Michael outside counting his bits of shrapnel. After rereading Jacks letter for the umpteen times, at least this was encouraging to me, he advising. "Only bring essential items and arrange for the furniture to be put into storage, until he had found suitable accommodation?" Had me thinking: *The easy part was collecting the essential items to take with us. The worst, trying to find storage for the furniture. Where in war torn London was a safe place to store anything? If anyone knew it would be Jack's brother Dick. Apart from being separated, we were back in the Army together.* With tears in my eyes, I wished: If only I could wave a magic wand. Then shouted out 'ON YOUR FEET SOLDIER. GET ORGANISING. Had Michael jumping. 'What's up mum?'

'Michael go to Uncle Dick's. Tell him I want to see him, be quick about it.' I got on sorting out other bits and pieces until later Michael arrived back to say.

'Aunt Edith said Uncle Dick's on his route, he will come up later.'

Later that day Dick arrived in his busman's uniform coming in, him quickly surveying the darkened interior said.

'Strewth Sarah you have done well, when I came a couple of days ago. It was in an awful state, I can see you have cleaned up the place. How can I help?'

Like many others, our situation was a common everyday occurrence,. I let him read Jacks letter, so he knew what it was about, after a brief explanation of what we needed he stood there shaking his head said.

'Well you know Sarah, that's asking a lot at such a short notice. But let me see what I can do.' After a cup of tea he left.

With that problem under way. I set about packing the essential items to be taken with us, which I thought would see us through a short period of time. Seeing that we had no army issue boxes to pack stuff in, our precious stocks of food stuff would have to be packed in tea chests. I sent Michael out to see if he could locate any more from any of the shops including his Uncle Bills down in West Norwood. He left taking Joe's pushchair. I organised the others sorting out various things, willing hands helped with everything, soon the pile became bigger. Our clothes I packed in suitcases. Michael spent the whole day searching, making many trips in locating six tea chest all with lids, that was a Gods send, however this created another problem. how do we get all this luggage across London to Euston? I started on an inventory on all our possessions. I was in the middle of doing this when Dick returned. However not with good news, he had contacted about five or six firms without success.

'Look Sarah you leave that matter with me. It will give me more time to sort out the problem in between shifts.'

'You sure you don't mind Dick?'

'Sarah that's all right. Keeps me mind occupied. Good job Jerry has left us alone for a while. Plymouth copped it again last night. Jerry's going for the Navy shipyards down there. Poor buggers got a pasting.' Wearily I questioned.

'When is this all going to stop?'

'Don't you worry, soon you will be out of it with your Jack. Cheer up your going for a holiday away from it all.'

'Well yes your right Dick but let me show you in the rooms what has to go in storage.'

We did a tour of the house, showed him all the furniture, beds, bedding, tea chests packed with food, and the brass pieces. He noticed the pile of boxes and suitcases, I had assembled in the front room to go with us, he exclaimed.

'Blimey Sarah. Is that what you're taking with you? That lot is going to be a problem!'

'Yes I know. Do you know anyone with a van that could help us take it over to Euston?'

'Well it just happens that one of our bus drivers has a van that maybe could take the lot. I'll ask him. When do you plan on leaving?'

'I'm not sure. Jack is supposed to be coming down to take us back up there. Maybe another week or so. I can't say for definite until he arrives anytime from now on.'

'Gor Blimey, it will be good to see young Jack again. I'll tell you what, when I get back to the depot, I'll find out from my mate if he will do it. Where's this place yer heading for?'

'Bamber Bridge. Don't ask me where it is. I haven't got a clue? Dick I will leave the keys with my sister Nan, who lives in number 10 Gibbs Avenue, just up behind us, so that when the time comes. If you're on one of your shifts. Nan can let the removal men in. Is that all right.'

'That's all right, so long as either of us can get in when the time comes. I'm not worried. Now I'll find out when or how the trains are running. Then when Jack gets here, he can decide when the best time to move this lot is. Is that okay? '

Dick was an angel. I fell in with this plan, which gave me more time to finish my inventory. The front room was the largest with all the brass artefacts in there. I lit the gas mantle and stared around the room at the gleam of rather dusty brass. A lump came into my throat as I started taking notes, was dismayed to find, the force of the blast, had thrown them all over the place, and some had suffered casualties. The peacock had its tail smashed off, the fish was broken in two, a few of the deer's antlers had been snapped off, two other deer had their horns bent and the three brass monkeys had been broken. My brass table had a few large dents in its rim, but most of all my two precious elephant's tusks made of ivory had been broken off. Jackie, home from work came into the room.

'What's going in here Mum that we can pack up?'

'Uhm. All of it has to go into storage.'

Two days later Jack arrives. I was so relieved to see him, looking a darn sight fitter than any of us all put together. Happy to see everyone was now none the worse for his or her experience, but was shocked to see the state of the house. After a long chat he went around to survey the house.

'Well everything seems organised as usual Sarah. Right to-morrow I'll sort out the Landlord about this place. I've paid another two weeks rent for the rooms up in Bamber Bridge, when I got off the train at Euston, I booked the tickets back on the eleven o' clock train the day after tomorrow.' He was interrupted by the wail of the siren.

'What do you do now Sarah?'

'Not much one can do. I just stay in say my prayers and wait for the all clear.'

The arrival of Dick stooped further chatting, and as the planes droned overhead, unconcered the pair of them chinwaged over a cup of tea then Jack said.

'Sarah. Dick's pal can take us to Euston, in between his shifts, but we must be ready to leave latest eight 'o'clock, two days time. I know its short but under the circumstances ecessary.'

390

With the arrangements settled, after a few more cups of tea, the all clear sounded Dick left us. We had our meals up at Mrs. Candler's. Kaye had to make arrangements to leave work the next day. However, Jack decided that we should rough it and sleep in the house that night. Rough it? We had been doing that for the past six months or more. Early the next day we visited Nan and told her to be at our house next morning before eight 'o'clock. There was absolutely nothing we could do in the house, everything was packed ready to go. The siren went, why I jumped at its sound I don't know? Suddenly realised. I was physically and mentally exhausted from the constant anxiety that everyone lived under. I now wanted and needed to get out of London for a break. Jack went out to see if he could see anything, returning in was disgruntled unable to see anything overhead due to low clouds. We went to Mrs. Candler's to bid her farewell, she became very emotional when we were leaving. Nevertheless, during the war, those things happened on a daily basis. No sooner had we settled down at home than the sirens went, another disturbed night. It was no use we all went downstairs and played cards, around the tble in a rather packed front room, until the raid was over. That 'Fella Hitler' wasn't going to let us go without his goodbye.

Well before seven. Jack had them all up ready. A loud banging on the front door brought Dick's pal Fred. Before he starts, a quick cup of hot tea was downed. By a quarter to eight the van had been loaded. It was time for us to go. Why I made a quick tour of the upstairs rooms shrouded in darkness I don't know. Force of habit? From the top of the stairs I called out.

'Jack has Nan arrived yet? '

'No don't worry she will be along very soon.'

I did my last minute checks downstairs all gasses off back door shut, I went through the front door to find they were gathered around the back of which looked like an old bread van. I walked down the pathway a round to the back of the van and peered inside, the luggage was piled up on both side. There was plenty of room Jack said.

'Sarah Ducks, you're up in the cab with Fred and I. The others can sit or stand in the back?' Then Nan arrives.

'Good morning everyone, all ready for the off?' I sharply retorted.

'Come with me Nan, you're late.'

I walked her back up the pathway, showed her the right key for the front door and slammed it shut. A home that we had all enjoyed living in and now sad to leave. However, not a fit place to live in. Handing her the keys gave her my last instructions.

'Dick with be in touch, when he arranges the removal men okay. Tell mother I will write when we get there. Nan there are two chickens still in the shelter you might as well take them home with you, they are good layers look after them.'

With hugs and kisses all round, we were ready to leave. Jack got me sat next to Fred and he climbed in after me. With the tribe behind, looking through a half doorway into the cab. Fred started the engine.then advised.

'Look mate, just in case I can't get through the city route. I'll take you the long way around alright?'...Jack looked at him and agreed...'Okay so long as we get there in time..'

We moved off I did not look back. Passing Mrs. Candler's, tears were welling up inside me but I suppressed them thinking: *I have had enough. I want to get away from all this.*

Fred drove through Streatham Common and on through places I had never been to. It wasn't till we got to Putney Bridge road, that I recognised some old familiar places. As we went past I was able to point out a few of the places I was familiar with. Over Putney Bridge, past Bishops Park and that was the extent of my knowledge of the area. Evidence of the bombing was everywhere. I shuddered as I recalled the near miss we had just encountered. I said a silent prayer of thanks.

When we eventually arrived at Euston, Fred was more than helpful he said.

'Hang on mate, while you unload. I'll go and check out the platform number and try and get a barrow or summat to take your luggage. Where is it you're going?' Jack answered.

'It's the Preston train.' Jack got out opening the doors at the back of the van, which was slowly unloaded. Fred returned pulling a trolley behind him.

'It's number five platform, you've got plenty of time.'

The luggage was loaded onto the trolley. Jack sat Margaret and Joe on the top of the luggage, Thanked Fred, gave him something for himself to pay for the petrol.

'Thanks mate, you lot have safe journey. Cheerio to you all.'

The platforms inside appeared choc-o-block full with military personnel and civilians alike, and like us, all travelling north. Jack and Jackie pulled the trolley through crowds to number five platform and stopped outside the guards van, Stood alongside the open doorway the guard enquired.

'Is this lot all yours mate? '

'Yes is there a problem?'

'Cor blimey, where yer heading for China?'

'No Bamber Bridge near Preston.'

'Oh, I'd better mark em then.' He went around the luggage marking everything with a piece of chalk casually he asks.

'What yer got in this lot then mate?'

'Clothing and provisions. The family have just been bombed out.'

'Blimey! You lot have been lucky. Bleeding Hitler. He ruins everyone's lives, he oughta be shot. All right mate, leave this lot to me. I'm going as far as Carlisle. I'll sort it out don't you worry. Hoi Charlie gives us a hand wif this lot mate.'

I was not aware where Bamber Bridge was, never mind Carlisle. We left them to it and moved along the packed train. Jack stopped at an open carriage door and ushered us onto the train. There were no seats available, so we stood in the corridor. After a long wait, with a long drawn out blast from the guards whistle, the train finally left London. On an uneventful tiring journey. we eventually got seats at Crewe, all slumped down and slept. Jack roused everybody, as the train clanked into a station and stopped.

'C'mon, wake up we're here. This is Bamber Bridge.'

We stumbled out of the carriage onto the platform. It was dark, the rain was pouring down. Jack began ushering us towards the rear of the train. The guard shouted out.

'That's yer lot mate. All off nah.'

The luggage was haphazardly stacked on a trolley. He blew his whistle and with a hiss of steam and a clanking of engine wheels. The train slowly started to move away. Stood in the open doorway of his van the guard uttered a cheery shout of farewell.

'Good luck Missus. No bombs up here!' I'd forgotten all about him. Jack was speaking to another porter.

'Can we leave this lot here for a while? I'll arrange transport from the camp and pick it up. ' He replied in a strange accent.

'Ta'll be alreight intwait'ng ruum til t'morrar.'(It will be alright in waiting room till tomorrow.)

With the noise of the chuffing train receding into the distance darkness, he left us standing in the pouring rain, jumping down onto the track he disappeared into the darkness. After a few moments, the sound of a creaking noise came out of the darkness, I noticed two red lights gradually appear, then stop with a rattle quickly followed by engines being started up and lorries noisily began crossing over the railway lines. Then I realised the porter had gone to open the level crossing gates. I thought: *I wonder if he is the Station Master as well. Talk about old Mr. Porter what shall I do.* Jack and the two boys had wheeled this trolley away towards the waiting

392

room; we followed behind them, into a tiny room lit only by a solitary dim oil lamp. We stood there until it was all stacked inside.

'Good, now that's all in, I'll sort that lot out tomorrow. C'mon all stick together follow me.'

Taking hold of my arm, he led us towards the dim red flickering lights on the gates, guided us all through a small gate onto the roadway, walked over the level crossing, turning immediately left into a cobbled street. In the pouring rain stumbling over wet cobbles. he informed me.

'This is Carr Street. It's the last house at the end.' At the far end he knocked on a door and after a short while it was opened. Silhouetted against the dim interior light was the tall figure of a man. Jack spoke.

'Mr. Dewhurst, we've arrived this is my family.'

'Hello. Thur Jack. Cum reight in an t' family too. Welcum t'Brig?'

(Hello. There Jack. Come right in and the family too. Welcome to the Bridge)

Drenched through we scurried into a small dimly lit passageway. The smell of coal, soot and pipe tobacco hit me. Not unpleasant and just like the peat fires back in Ireland. Going through some very heavy curtains entered the warmth of a parlour. A big grey haired woman with a black shawl wrapped around her shoulders was sat next to a blazing fire, she got up. Mr. Dewhurst uttered behind me.

'Tis ess Mrs Dewhurst.' She offered her hand.

'Eee. Ess reight pleesed t' mets te' al tha naws.'

(Ee. I's right pleased to meet thee all you know)

I shook her hand and nodded a hello, not understanding a word she had said with introductions completed.

'Sit Te' sel dow t'might b' cold wit t' rain aside. Teck te weat cooites o' un I'll put Ket'le on t' make tea.' (Sit yourselves down. might be cold with the rain outside. Take the wet coats off and I'll put the kettle on to make tea.)

She busied herself by the fire, where a big black kettle stood on the griddle. We sat or stood around like lost sheep, removing our wet coats. Mr Dewhurst took them into the passageway. The tea was offered in giant size cups and gratefully received. As she busied herself sticking chunks of bread on a long fork and toasted it by the fire. Much to my relief Jack held the conversation. I knew what he was on about, but not their lingo. When we had finished tea and toast. Mrs. Dewhurst got a candleholder with half a candle, lit it with a taper from the fire, beckoned us to follow her upstairs, at the top she indicated two rooms.

'Te privy tis ooitsid, Te potty tis underneath te bed, fre neatteem uos.'

(The lavatory is outside. The potty is under the bed for night-time use)

My first impression and my thought:. *My God. The rooms were small, Kaye, Margaret and Joe, with me in one room. Jackie and Michael, in an even smaller room.* She lit candles in each room. Jack who had come up with us murmured in my ear.

'Sarah I'm sorry, but under the extreme circumstances this is the best I could find. I have to return to camp, I will be back in the morning. Goodnight and sleep as you are. Cover yourselves over with the blankets.' He clumped downstairs and after a short while I heard the door close. We settled down for the night. I whispered to Kaye.

'I hope this is only temporary and we can get something better.'

She just grunted and was asleep. I was exhausted but could not get to sleep. Even without any air raids or bombs. I must have laid there for an hour or so, Kaye woke up. I whispered to her.

'What's the matter?' she whispered.

'I can't sleep. No bombs Mum.' The pair of us cat-napped for the rest of the night.

Early the next morning we were awakened by the noisy clanking of a train. It seemed to be in the room with us. Slowly it came to a grinding halt with a hiss of steam. Then the sound of many carriage doors being opened, strange clumping and scraping, with many foreign voices filled the air. Pulling aside a heavy draped curtain, in the dull light of early morning. I saw a short garden, a small shed against a wooden fence that was all that separated the house from the railway platform. The platform was crowded with female workers wearing funny footwear. The wail of a hooter began, certainly different from air raid sirens. Kaye murmured.

'What's that ? Another air raid?'

'Can't be, nobody is running. Anyway last night that guard on the train said there were no bombs up here. C'mon we had better start moving your father will be here soon. Then we can find out more about this God forsaken place.'

I drew the drapes fully back. Outside it was still raining, with a loud whistle the train clanked away. The only thing I recognised was the waiting room on the opposite platform. In the dim daylight, I noticed the bed was a big iron one, very comfortable, underneath the coats Margaret and Joe were still asleep. An old wardrobe and small chest of drawers was the only other furniture in the room. On the floor was a rag scatter rug. The rest of the floor was bare boards. A guzunder was beneath the bed. No lights, just a candle on the chest of draws. I left well alone and ventured into the boy's room. The compliment of furniture was the same. I shook them and told them to get up. Soon we were all moving about in the cramped rooms. Downstairs a couple of bangs sounded on the front door. I heard Mrs. Dewhurst utter good morning greetings. Then clumping up the stairs, Jack entered the room.

'Sarah. You lot awake yet?'

'No were still asleep.' From my expression, he could see I was not in a very good mood.

'Mrs. Dewhurst, said she had tea and toast for us downstairs. C'mon rally them around. We have a lot to do.'

He clumped back down, with us following in crocodile fashion behind, into a warm parlour. Mrs. Dewhurst was talking to Jack as she toasted a chunk of bread the size of a doorstep stuck on the end of a toasting fork close to the fire. Jack enquired.

'Sarah. How did you sleep?'

'Not too good. I'm afraid it's too quiet. We're not used to this peace. Jack what was that siren all about.'

'Oh that Sarah. I forgot to tell you. That is the mill hooter. You'll hear it several times a day. Nothing to worry about.' Mrs. Dewhurst interrupted.

'Til te Missus aboot yon shed tha no's' (Tell your Mrs. about the shed you know)

'Oh. Err. yes. Sarah. Mrs. Dewhurst has just mentioned about the toilet facilities out the back. It' the shed at the bottom of the garden. Okay?'

His last remark came as a bombshell to my ears. We were going back to basics. I didn't say anything. The silence you could cut with a knife.

Sit te sell's dow.' (Sit yourselves down)

Mrs Dewhurst placed a plate of doorsteps on the table and poured out tea in those ponds of cups. After all had had their fill Mrs. Dewhurst spoke.

'Jack, teck ter sel and missus inte tother room te talks like.'

Jack mentioned this to me and we all dutifully followed him into their front room. In the centre a small round table covered by an open woven dark blue tablecloth. With two chairs, another two were against the wall. A fireplace, two drawn long drape curtains allowed the dim daylight to lighten up the room. We sat down ready to listen to Jack. He having been there for nearly several months was able to brief us on Bamber Bridge. A small cotton village, with six or seven Mills dotted throughout the village. Located in-between Chorley and Preston, and very typical of the cotton industry that flourished in Lancashire. It had Churches, Schools, Working

394

Men's Clubs, a Picture house and Public Houses. Besides the train service to Preston there was a Bus Service. Its streets were cobbled with terraced houses everywhere, and the rain. We soon found out poured down every day. Jacks Barrack was one of the smaller cotton mills converted into a training camp. It was not the back of beyond, as I had imagined. However we were going back to the old days of living out of suitcases. I had to interrupt him and ask.

'Jack. We can't stay here. There's not enough room for two people never mind six. You can't swing a cat around in our bedroom, never mind the boy's, that's even smaller, and on top of that, only candles or, oil lamps for lighting. I'd rather be back in London.'

I think all echoed my comment. Jack said.

'Look Sarah, I'm looking around for another place to re-house us and hopefully, it won't be too long before we can move out of the Dewhurst's. What we need to do now with all our luggage and belongings, is just take our clothes for everyday wear, and I will arrange to take the rest of the stuff, back to the Barracks stores where I can keep an eye on it.' I thought: *Hear we go again, I've heard those stories before.* How right I was, worse was yet to follow.

'Right. We all might as well go around to the station, collect the suitcases and bring them back here.' Jack told Mrs. Dewhurst what was happening. Outside the rain was then pouring down. "Welcome to Bamber Bridge." Retracing our steps to the level crossing, where on the opposite side was the signal box, a level crossing fence, on the right was a small paper-shop. What attracted me most, were the four old style gas lamps perched on top of each gatepost. Going through the pedestrian swing gate, crossed the railway lines to the other side, onto the platform towards the waiting room. There was no sign of the Porter. Our luggage was as we had left it. Jack sorted out the suitcases. Just as we were about to leave the Porter arrived with a railway barrow. He speaks.

'Morn'g. Reight morn'g t'day witrain. Wet t' borrow barra t' move cases?' (Morning. Right morning today with the rain. Want to borrow the barrow to move the cases.)

'That would be handy. We only have to go back down to the Dewhurst place in Carr Street.'

'Theet's al reight not ter far eah?'...Pointing to the boxes... 'T'al leaf te boox's fur te wheele?' (That's all right not too far Eh? .....Your'll leave the boxes for a while?

'Yes. I'll have those picked up around ten is that all right?'

'Reight . Ta'll stil be ere.' (Right they will still be here)

The Porter started to lift the case onto the barrow, when he finished loading them on, he took hold of the handles and started off pushing it down the platform, he went down the ramp out into the road across the railway lines. Following behind, we went through the pedestrian way. By the time we got into Carr Street, he was half way towards the house. He had already unloaded the cases by the time we got to the front door. Jack knocked.

'Thanks Porter. That was a great help.' Gave him a tip. Mrs.' Dewhurst opened the door. The Porter hailed her.

'A'reight Missus Dewhurst. Tease Londoners ye war spate abeet?' Tis nay a geed day for theme's t' arreev ta knows.' Nither Te meend. Sels sin get used tweeter.' (All right Mrs. Dewhurst. These the Londoners you were speaking about? It's not a good day for them to arrive you know. Never you mind. They will soon get used to the weather.) With that he began his journey back to the station.

Mrs. Dewhurst went back inside. We began carrying the cases into the house and up the stairs to the two bedrooms. Each case was unpacked and the clothing placed into the drawers and wardrobes. We had the clothing sorted out by lunchtime. That's when the first hooter went. Half an hour later it went again. Lunch break over. Jack said.

'Sarah I'll take you up to the camp. We can get a bite to eat there and on the way I'll show you what's what.'

Outside the rain had eased to a drizzle. As we walked along Jack provided a running commentary. The main road was called Station Road. I noticed that the pavements were certainly wider than the London ones, along both sides were small terraced type houses, here and there were small shops. On the opposite side behind the houses. Tall chimney stacks were billowing out smoke from one of the Mills. Halfway down, the Blue Lamp of the Police Station hung outside for all to see the mark of authority. There were hardly any cars or lorries, just a couple of horse drawn carts. One with vegetables for sale, its horse motionless stood between the shafts its long mane matted by the rain, a long sack was draped over its back. We crossed the road at a place called the Pear Tree Inn and walked up School Lane. Half way up this lane an army vehicle towing a howitzer, passed us and turned off further up the lane into what I soon found out was the entrance to the barracks.

Jack showed his pass to the armed sentry as we went through the gateway. Its forecourt floor was cobbled everywhere, each building had signs attached to the wall, indicating where different Offices were, outside one building another army truck was parked with its Howitzer. Jack took us into the building it was their canteen. He sat us all down at a trestle table, the only other occupants there were six gunners seated at another table having their dinner, they had only just started, so I assumed it was the crew of the Howitzer outside. Jack came back with a tray of plated food and eating utensils, placed it front of us it was a pie of some sorts, at last it was hot and possibly the remnants of the lunchtime meal and very welcome to all, we had not had a square meal since leaving London. With something warm inside us, it gave me heart to think I was out of the bombing of London. Jack continued telling us of what was in the village. It all seemed miles away as he told us of this and that. But my mind was on other things. Living in cramped bedrooms. How we would cope in the next few weeks, I interrupted.

'How can we cope in Mrs Dewhurst's with washing, eating etc. etc?' Jack's reply.

'Let me and you talk with her, and see what she has in mind about all those things.' Immediately I thought.. *No. Jack You talk with her I can't understand a word she is saying?* We returned to the Dewhurst's.

My tribe were parked in the front room, whilst Jack and I sat down in the parlour with Mrs. Dewhurst. Jack interpreted what was said. Basically their routine was the same as our normal weekly chores. Daily spring-cleaning, shopping. Saturday ablutions night. Sunday a day of rest and Church. The cooking and eating we arranged. Mr. and Mrs.' Dewhurst, would still do what they always did. He was a Mill worker on shift duty. I was very mystified as to how we would cope under the cramped conditions. Jack assured me that he would find other accommodation as soon as possible. Just grin and bear it for the time being, something would turn up. It did?

The first few days were a bit hectic, Jackie went to the labour exchange and was given a job at Dick Kerr's an aircraft factory in Preston building Wellington bombers. Kaye did not know what to do so stayed with me. We got Michael Margaret and Joe started in the local Catholic school and it rained. We had not been there more than two weeks when Jack informs me, he had a temporary posting for a month to six weeks at Brentford London, attached to the East Surrey Regt. He had spoken with one of his friends called George Parkinson at the workingmen's club, who would try and sort out some other accommodation for us, whilst he was away. This was the ultimate as far as I was concerned. *Thoughts of Aldershot whizzed around my head.* Immediately suggested.

'Jack, let's all go back to London.'

'Sarah Ducks, there is no place to go and stay there. You know that. So it's here or nothing. Just be patient.'

I resigned myself to what I had and would try to make the best out of it. Shortly after Jack left. I was forced to take to my bed again. The flu, which I thought I had got rid of returned with a vengeance. I was physically and mentally exhausted. Mrs. Dewhurst was concerned and got a

Doctor Ryan to visit me. Who gave me a tonic told me to stay in bed, keep warm and take aspirins. Kaye stayed with me. Slowly I get better, it was Easter before I was able to venture out. Mrs. Dewhurst, had been more than obliging and really looked after us all. Kaye tried to get a job doing hairdressing without success. There was no call for it in Bamber Bridge. She was given a job working on the Looms in a mill, just off of Station Road. Up at the crack of dawn and out with the rest of the mill workers, clopping along in their clogs. After her first day she arrived back, her wavy blonde hair tightly covered by a knotted turban, she was holding her ears.

'What's the matter?' She didn't answer… I repeated. 'Kaye what's the matter?' … She could see I was talking to her. She began shouting at me.

'I CAN'T HEAR PROPERLY MUM. I'VE BEEN STANDING IN THE MILL ALL DAY LONG. THE NOISE OF SCREAMING, SPINNING LOOMS, AND INCESSANT THUMPING ALL DAY HAS AFFECTED MY HEARING. I'LL BE ALRIGHT SOON.' I shouted back at her, as if she were deaf.

'HOW DID YOU GET ON?' She shouted.

'NOT TOO WELL. ALTHOUGH SOMEONE WAS PUT IN CHARGE OF ME, TO SHOW ME THE ROPES. I DID NOT HEAR A WORD THEY SAID. WOMEN TALKED TO ME WITH HAND MOVEMENTS AND MOUTHING WORDS. BUT I COULD NOT UNDERSTAND ANY OF IT. WITH HUNDREDS OF BOBBINS IN LINES. SPINNING AWAY. THE NOISE OF THE MACHINERY WAS WORSE THAN THE BOMBING. AT LEAST THAT STOPPED FOR LONG PERIODS BETWEEN RAIDS.'

'Stop shouting, I can hear you perfectly well. Let you're hearing get back to normal, then we will talk.' She nodded and sat down. I made her a cup of tea. As she drank from the cup, she kept on banging her ears, as if to knock out the noise. It must have got better as she began to talk normal

'You know Mum, above all the continuous scream of the looms, they hold normal conversations with each other, even with all that deafening noise. They all lip-read, it's fascinating to watch, if you know what they are on about. The woman showing me the ropes, as she handled the cotton, her hands were as quick as a flash. It was hard work trying to keep up with them. Maybe two or three bobbins, all at the same time, become full, and you have to keep an eye open. To catch them and exchange them for empty ones. It takes about three minutes for a bobbin to fill up. Then you have to whip it off the spinning rod quickly replace it with the empty bobbing. Then catch the thread and set it around the empty spinning bobbins, the full bobbins go into a big wicker basket and when that's full, a man comes around with an empty one and takes the full one away. It's never ending. I'm not going to like it there. I can tell you that for nothing, and I'm not wearing those clogs. I'm still going to wear my heeled shoes. At least that will give me some dignity.' I sensed resentment creeping into her voice. It certainly was not Kaye's kind of work.

'Well it's the only work that's available up here. You'll have to put up with it. I added. Suit yourself about the clogs. But it sounds to me, that they are the most sensible things to wear on your feet.'

Even Michael, Margaret and Joe, began wearing clogs. Made out of a wooden soles, the uppers black leather nailed to the sole and steel iron nailed on the bottom, they were solid, warm, comfortable and very cheap to buy and repair. When the irons wore out it was like taking a horse to the furriers to get it re-shod. The first pair of Joe's clogs I took to the menders shop. When I entered, it was warm with the smell of leather, rows of clogs all shape and sizes lay around the floor and hung on the wall. The Mender dressed in a leather apron with a foot last clenched between his legs, was busy nailing an iron onto a huge clog he looked up.

'Re-ironing Eh! Til tha wit for em eh?' (Re-Ironing Eh! Will you wait for them Eh?) I nodded. …'If it's Okay.'

397

Getting up took the clogs and picked out irons for the sole and another two for the heel. Sat down stripped the old irons off and within seconds had the irons nailed to the clog then to the heel. It took less than five minutes.

'Therr Ter ar' as gud as new Missis. Tet be tow bob.' (There There're as good as new Mrs. That will be two shillings)

I paid him and left. During this period of some very disruptive cramped way of life, it was extremely difficult cooking in relays and becoming unbearable to stay at the Dewhurst's, but they were really good people. I had registered at a Butchers ,a Grocery store. then more rationing: Meat came down to one shilling per person, followed by cheese at one oz per person. Preserves were also placed on ration and I could not get to my own horde of supplies, that was at the barracks. I came in from shopping one day and found Mrs Dewhurst had a visitor. I excused myself and was about to retreat upstairs, when she called me.

'Ee Missus Plant, yon fella air, tis George Parkinson ess cum Te see thee.' (Er. Mrs. Plant, this fellow here. Is George Parkinson. He has come to see you.)

I thought: *That's the name Jack spoke about*. I went back into her parlour, where a little man, a bit on the rotund size, with ruddy cheeks, and a twinkle in his eyes he said.

'Wilt ta til Jack tha I stilt trying fo lodging tint Brig?' (Will you tell Jack, that I am still looking for lodgings in the Bridge) I seemed to understand this crazy way of talking. It was more by picking up the lilt of what subject someone was talking about. I answered

'Oh thank you I will tell him.' He left and I was disappointed. *I thought he had brought good news?* The war had spilled out into North Africa as well as various other countries in Europe. News about the Eighth Army was on everyone's lips. The ceaseless bombing of England continued but the RAF retaliated. The Germans bombed Moscow and 'That 'Fella Hitler.' had ordered his army into an Eastern offensive. With the change in offensives the British as well as the Americans were supplying arms and other supplies to the Russians. It seemed senseless to me. but it did not make any difference I also prayed like mad that we would soon find better accommodation. After three months, Kaye had learnt the job and how to lip-read. However, suffered from cramps in the stomach. The Doctor informed her, that it was due to not wearing clogs in the mill. She gave it up. Back at the Labour exchange she was given a job in Dick Kerr's, so she went to work on the bus with Jackie.

Spring had turned to summer, and Jack's six weeks away had long gone since. In his letters he was unsure when he would be posted back. I was very depressed with our situation. Somehow in amongst the cramped living accommodation we had to endure, our schedule seemed to work. Nevertheless, my longing to get back to London never waned. Only on Sundays was I happy to walk to mass at St Mary's Brownedge. Its high alter was the most impressive one I had ever seen. Made out of carved green and white Connemara marble slabs, through ornate metal gates, four wide steps led up to it, behind it ten granite pillars supported the sanctuary. Much later I found out that Augustus Pugin, a famous architect of the nineteenth century had designed it. The tribe's entertainment in T'Brig was a Saturday morning excursion to the Empire, The local cinema commonly called the "Flea Pit" Where the Saturday morning matinees were known as. "The two-penny rush." Their goodies, the stable diet of a penneth of parched peas. A tasty Lancashire speciality, peas, black in colour and covered with salt.The Lancashire people must be the kindest in the world. The neighbours and shopkeepers, having not seen or experienced what it was like in London, understood our predicament and went out of their way to help or, assist. A letter from Mother informed me that the bombs were still raining down in London. Everyone was sound but not safe in his or her beds. Peg had invited her down to stay with her in Sidcup but she had refused. There was no news from any of the other brothers in law. Only news from my sister Mary, about our nephew Ray, who had joined the Fleet Air Arm, as a flying navigator and had been posted out to the West Indies to do his training. The nearest the

German bombers got to us was Liverpool. Concentrating their bombing raids on the docks and they were not that many miles from where we were.

Our situation at Mrs. Dewhurst was unfair to them but to us even more so. Six people living in two bedrooms and sharing their meagre facilities, fed up with living in two rooms I was a a loose end having run out of options seeking accomodations decided to tackle the local Council they were kind and listened to my plea for resettlement somewhere, however there answer was they would try to find a suitable accomadation they took down all details, where I could be contacted? With this information giving I left with the hope sooner rather than later something would turn up. A letter from Jack suggested I should visit Mary in Halifax as it was not too far away. It had been a long time since I had seen Mary. I decided to find out about trains to get there. I wrote to Kitty and told her of my intended visit and could we meet up. She replied, it would be far better if I were to see Mary on our own, and when we eventually got settled somewhere better, she would make the trip to Bamber Bridge and stay over. I was quite happy with her suggestion. On a fine summers day we made the trip to see Mary. We caught one of the early morning trains, changed at Blackburn then Burnley onto Halifax. At Halifax I enquired where the Sanatorium was. 'Take a bus to someplace, a name I cannot remember, then walk up a steep hill to the Sanatorium at the top.' Following instructions. we alighted at the right place and began the walk up the hill in the scorching sun. We finally arrived exhausted, at this gaunt looking building. Entering through its double doors. I made enquires about Mary from a starchy looking nurse. She looked down at Margaret and Joe and curtly stated.

'They shouldn't be in here. You will have to take them outside. Mary Plant is sitting outside on the balcony. Go around the side of the building, that's where she will be.'

I was none too pleased with her tone. Retraced our steps, walked around the building to a wide esplanade of a balcony and found Mary sitting with some other girls they were wrapped up against a slight breeze. After a very emotional reunion the first thing she said.

'Mum. Those two have to stay away from us. Its forbidden.' She too was disappointed, but that was the rules. While we talked they played about in the surrounding grounds. To me Mary's cough did not appear to be any better. Her beautiful face was drawn and her cheekbones were very prominent, very thin almost skeletal. However she was responding to the treatment. The Sanatorium was in a wonderful setting on top of this hill overlooking the Pennines. The time flew past and it was soon time for us to depart. She mentioned Kitty was a regular visitor, as I then knew where she was, I would pay her more visits, but without Margaret and Joe. The next time and on several other visits, Kaye went with me, meeting up with Kitty at the Sanatorium. My tribe were looked after by Mrs Dewhurst. We had a great time cheering Mary up. Then stayed at Kitty's house before returning back.

The tranquillity of summer was almost over. I had by then began to understand the colloquial lingo of Bamber Bridge. With the children back at school I received notice from the Council, they offered us a place in the village providing the address as 190 Chorley Road please attend the Office to collect the keys. I asked Mrs Dewhurst where it was, she kindly directed me to the other end of the village, all the way down Station road, past the Pear Tree Inn, it was near to Duddle Lane? I immediately went to the Office collected the key paid the rent I did not care what it was but it must be better than two rooms, Continued on my way there. I had only been as far as the Pear Tree Inn, opposite was the Clog menders, from there on the aspects of the village changed after a short walk I came to several Bungalows on both sides of the road a total revalation from the other end of the Village noting the numbers of the bungalows soon found the fourth one was 190. Going through a big double gateway into a front garden towards an empty bungalow, at its front porch put the key into the lock, pushing open the door entered

399

into a hallway, on either side doors led to six rooms. A kitchen, bathroom/toilet. In one of the front rooms two stained glass windows were portraits of the previous owner's two old spinsters. (The lady next door later informed uslater) So we were forever to be reminded of our benefactors. Outside it was surrounded by a lawn in the front, a flower garden down one side and a large allotment with two apple trees at the rear. As a family home it was perfect. One problem furniture and bedding that was down in London. Back at Mrs Dewhursts I told her of our intention to move but needed bedding. Leave it with her she would arrange something? Isent a wire to Jack to get Dick to arrange for our furniture to be transported up. Mrs Dewhurst did find some beds and offered her bedding which we had been using since we arrived. Early in October we moved in. It was six months since we had arrived in Bamber bridge. I could not care less about our sleeping arrangements. Three weeks later our furniture arrived I went back to Mrs. Dewhurst and thanked them both for their hospitality and patience returning their beds and bedding.. I was then prepared to start making a home for my family.

Our luck had certainly changed for the better, in more ways than one. By good fortune the bungalow was next to two farms one on either side of Duddle Lane. Milk, chickens, and eggs were of little problem. Powdered egg had been introduced into the food chain and made excellent scrambled eggs and cake ingredients. In November Jack returned back to the Baracks from Brentford at last we could be together once again. In response to the nation's call of 'Dig for Victory' during the evening time and during Jacks spare time, which was not often, soon the digging began in the back garden, which also had gooseberry and raspberry bushes. It soon became a field of trenches, ready for wintering and planting the next season. Very quickly we settled down and became accepted within and part of the community. As Mess Do's at the Camp were a thing of the past, any drinking and entertaining carried out was by courtesy of the Workingmen's Club in School Lane. Jack insisted that I came along with him to meet some of the local people. As I had little to worry about with the tribe, I agreed only if Kaye could come as well. It was in the Club I was formally introduced to George Parkinson and his wife Mary. Jack said.

'Sarah this is George.'

'Hello. agin Mrs Plant, ter es my Murry.' (Hello again Mrs. Plant. This is my Mary) Mary his wife bade me sit down at the table, whilst the men went to the bar. *(No more interpretation normal spoken words. Hereafter.)*

'Mrs' Plant. I wanted to speak to you before, as I always saw you at mass on Sunday, but you were always up and gone.'

'Yes I don't hang around, when I have the Sunday dinner cooking.'

I was puzzled, how did she know who I was. I'd only spoken to her husband at the Dewhurst house. Nevertheless, we were the only London family that had become resident in T'Brig. As they called it. The Club was certainly not the same atmosphere of an army mess. Everyone knew everyone else; they were hard working down to earth people and made anyone feel welcome. George and Mary became great friends of ours. She told me to shop at Melia's opposite the Pear Tree Inn. She would meet me and introduce me to the owner. With the ration books, I changed shops, registered the family with Miss Wells the shop owner of Melia's stores, who said.

'Mrs Plant. I've seen you at Mass on Sundays. Here meet Mrs Billington. She goes to Mass as well, her husband Donald is the organist at St' Mary's. This meeting appeared to be a Catholic mothers meeting albeit in a shop. When I had purchased my shopping I bade them Good Day, however Mrs Billington said.

'Mrs' Plant. I'm going your way I'll walk with you.'

She told me she lived farther down from us on the opposite side of the road and her son Donald knew Michael at school. Soon after this meeting whilst speaking with Miss Wells she mentioned she was looking for a young lad to deliver her groceries. With the possibility of obtaining more tea, I volunteered the services of Michael. She took up my offer and I coaxed Michael into doing it. However he did get paid and I got extra tea. His mode of transport was, a massive big bike with a huge basket in front, it was miles too big for him. Somehow he managed to ride it. He enjoyed doing it after school. On rare occasions when Jack is back off manoeuvres he would take the two youngest up to the camp, on a Saturday evening, when the Army Kinema was showing a Laurel and Hardy or the Marx Brothers film. On the way home he bought them a bag of chips from the fish and chip shop.

The extra hour of summertime, was turned back and autumn was upon us. According to the Nazi propaganda.The Ark Royal was torpedoed and sunk in the Mediterranean. Malta was getting pounded I feared for the safety of Dickie Fox and prayed that he would come out of it unscathed. That news was confirmed as a ship which had had been sunk so many times before, it was like a cat with nine lives. But more good news on our own home front. The tribe's leader Mary returns home to stay. Having lost a lot of weight, then with a slight cough, she was very thin but much better. Her illness appeared to be disappearing and apparently was able to start work again but what? She decides to wait for a little while, before she tries to find work in the New Year. I make up the tiny room at the rear of the house, opposite the toilet, easy access for her and I was joyously happy, we are a reunited family again.

The winter months set in and brought with them bitter cold winds and the rain turns into snow. Then another big shock the first week in December. The Japanese Bomb Pearl Harbour. With serious consequences to the American Navy. The Americans promptly declare war on Japan. At last the Americans join in with us in a total World War. Yet more bad news followed, Hong Kong had been occupied by the Japanese, also they had attacked Malaya, advancing towards Singapore. The situation in the Far East did not look very good. Jack spends more time out on manoeuvres, convoys of armoured vehicles, towing howitzers would rumble past, be away for two-three days at a time, then rumble back. The only thing that seemed of any sense was the run up to Christmas. Michael arrives home from school and informs me.

'Mum I entered the family in the schools fancy dress party. We all have to go.'

He has an idea, but won't tell anyone his secret. I spotted him come home pushing an old pram with no rubber on its wheels. He leaves it around the side of the house out of the way.

'Mum. have you got any old clothes for Jackie, Margaret and Joe's fancy dress?'

This secret was becoming more intriguing. On the night, Jackie and Michael got dressed up in some women's clothes and pairs of Kaye's high heels and stockings. Both wore scarves over their heads. Kaye and Mary made up their faces with rouge and lipstick. Margaret and Joe were dressed in old rags. Only then the pram entered the scene. Michael placed a big bundle of rags in it. They looked a right shambles as they all set off pushing the pram a couple of miles all the way to the school hall. There was a dance before the fancy dress competition, that Mary and Kaye attended, Jack and I arrived nearing the end of the dance. The fancy dress competition was to be judged by Mr. MacMillan the headmaster and the teachers herded all the competitors dressed in their fancy dress outfits into a crocodile line and there were plenty of them to form up in a big circle. To begin their parade around the hall a teacher began banging out a tune on a piano. My tribe were the easiest to spot, as they were the only ones pushing a pram with Jackie and Michael pushing it, both had notices hanging from their backs. "BOMBED OUT" In the pram sat on top of a bundle of clothing was Joe, Margaret was walking holding onto the pram handle, both were crying. Jackie had pinched both of them to make them cry. At every turn of the wheels they squeaked with Jackie stumbling around in a pair of Kaye's high heels, much to everyone's amusement, his stockings kept on falling down. The four of us stood watching this charade with tears of mirth rolling down our faces. A truly amusing sight. They all paraded around twice with loud clapping and cheering to all the contestants. Our BOMBED OUT kids won first prize. A bottle of "Tizer". Something that they kept for Christmas.

Without the threat of bombs hanging over our heads Christmas 1941 was a very joyous time. The children's stockings were filled up with one chocolate wafer biscuit and one Orange each, that Jack had acquired from somewhere. There was no turkey, only a chicken from the farm next door, but Christmas pudding and the first Christmas cake. The icing was rock hard. It did not last very long, but the main thing was that we were all together.

The New Year of 1942, found Kaye fed up working at Dick Kerr's, she quits the job. Mary feeling capable to work went along with Kaye to the Labour Exchange and both became Clippies on the Buses . Due to the shortage of cloth they were not provided with uniforms. Dress as normal. They leave home at four in the morning and cycle into Preston to start their bus routes. From Preston to Lytham St Anne's. Kaye as ever, still very conscious of her dress, her uniform was a fur coat for protection against the cold and still insisted on high heels. Mary came home from work late one evening, apologised for being late and said.

'Mum. Guess who I met in Preston?'

'No I can't guess. Who did you meet?'

'Cousin Percy Plant. I was walking to the bus garage when by chance I bumped into him coming the other way. He's in the Ordinance Corps hes on a ship docked on the Ribble. They are en route to somewhere up Scotland he wouldn't say where though.'

'Percy! How is he? Did you have time to speak with him?'

'I don't want anything to eat. We went and had some fish and chips. Yes he's fit and well and sends his love to you all. His mum and dad (Dick and Edith) were still weathering the bombs but okay He said that Crystal Palace and the surrounding area of Croydon seemed to get a hell of a lot of bombs. We were lucky to get out alive. Dorothy is in the A.T.S. somewhere down South. He hadn't heard from her for some time. We ate our fish and chips and he had to get going back to the ship. He said he was sorry that he couldn't come and see us. I wished him good luck from us all. Then we parted.'

'Well at least he met up with you. The chances of that happening are very slim. Yes good luck to him and God speed wherever he is bound for. I'm sure your father will be pleased when you tell him about Percy.'

Mary did not like working on the buses . She found it far too strenuous and would come home and go straight to bed to rest and sleep. Someone had told me that a couple of the Clippies had been attacked on the busses in Preston. This convinced me that neither of them should stay in that job. I told them to pack the job in. At the labour exchange Mary got a job as a typist in Horrock's Mill in Preston. It was an office job inside and more suitable for her in her current state of health. On the other hand Kaye with her experience in Dick Kerr's, was given a job as a riveter in an Ammunition Box factory up near the Station. Five weeks later she walked out she had refused to wear a protective hat. Next day she went back to the Labour Exchange in the morning. She came home late that afternoon to inform me of her new job. She was full of it. As she related the day's proceedings.

Mum. You know what the chap at the Labour had the cheek to ask me. If I could use a telephone? I told him, of course I can doesn't everyone know? He shook his head and told me to report to a building at Adam's Hall American Army Air force Camp. I had never heard of it. Do you know anything about it?' Rather intrigued about these goings on I replied.

'No. Why should I?' Did you go then?'

'Of course I did. When I got there an American Officer asked me questions and where I came from When I said London. He gave me the job as a telephonist on their switchboard. I start tomorrow.'

That's good. But where is this Camp?'

'It's up the Top end of town past the station up near the hob Inn. It's a supplies depot or something.' I. immediately thought: *The American's had arrived in Bamber Bridge.*

Then more bad news was broadcast on the radio. In the Far East the Japanese has occupied Malaya and the British army are putting up a hell of a retreating fight. Notification of more rationing, this time. "SOAP." Not that it worried Joe. In North Africa the Eighth army were in retreat, then we surrender to the Japs in Singapore, where there is another massive evacuation of civilians and forces from the Island. Those left behind are interned as prisoners of war. It was very bleak news, as the winter snows melted and spring appeared with the bluebells. Although Mary was the leader of our tribe, for all intents and purpose due to her illness, she had succumbed to a restricted life style, whereas, the rest of my tribe had never given up their antics. Since their arrival at T'brig, they had organised the local lads into a gang who spent most of their spare time down in the woods behind us in dug out caves, where they all congregated after work or school, very much to the annoyance of the local farmers, as they were trespassers, who disturbed their cattle and sheep. It was when when Mr. Metcalfe the farmer next door arrived at my door, that I found out about this.

'Mrs Plant can you stop your two boys going down the woods? I've tried to catch them, but they get away swinging on long ropes tied to branches on the trees. I'm at my wits end. I'm going to the Police.'

I'm sorry. I will speak to them.' The Police got involved, and even they couldn't catch them. It wasn't just Jackie and Michael but the whole gang of about fifteen local lads of Jackie and Michaels ages It fell on deaf ears. I spoke to Jack about the visit from the farmer.

'I'll speak to them and stop their antics.' Even that didn't stop them.

Kaye had met George Sandiford and appeared to be courting? George was a Sergeant in Jack's unit who had a good singing voice, for free beers he would entertain all on Saturday night at the Workingmans club, singing to his heart's content. On one such Saturday night George approached me to ask.

'Mrs' Plant. I had a letter from my father in London he is not well and is having a very bad time from all the ceaseless bombing in London'....'Oh I'm sorry George (I had not forgotten about the constant bombing we had been through) Is he taken any medication?',.. ' I don't know but I am worried about him he lives on his own. I was wondering if you could you do my father and me a great favour? Would you be kind enough to put him up a few weeks?'...This indeed was a challenge I thought: *This bungalow could become a retreat for whoever needed a rest* and didn't hesitate to agree ...'Well George I could make room in the bungalow for your father when would he be comng up?' ...'Thank you. I'll write to him then inforn you of his reply.'

At the appropriate date and time George arrived on the doorstep with his father. Mr. Sandiford. A very tall quiet gentleman, in a pinstriped suit, carrying a small brown suitcase. He looked gaunt with sunken eyes that appeared never to stop moving he was rather agitated and shaking. I thought: *He must have had a nervous breakdown.* I bade them enter and took them into the kitchen. Sat them down busied myself making a pot of tea. George thanked me again.

'Dad you'll be safe here with Mrs Plant. She will look after you.'

The first thing Mr. Sandiford did was to take out his ration book from inside his jacket pocket. With a shaky hand gave it, to me.

'Please use this as you see fit Mrs Plant. And thank you for your hospitality.' ..There was not much I could say except... 'You're welcome.'

After they had drunk their tea. I took them into the front sitting room, where I had made up a bunk bed for him. This was the best place for him to be on his own. I left them to talk alone.

I collared Margaret and Joe, taking them aside. Warned them not to disturb the gentleman in anyway. Let him just rest in the garden or in the sitting room whichever pleased him. During his stay Mr. Sandiford kept to himself to himself, spending most of his time wandering around the garden or going for walks, he even had his meals in his room. He was far less trouble than I had expected. The change of location did him the world of good, after a week or so of resting. His gaunt look almost disappeared, he became more relaxed and as far as I was concerned, certainly on the mend. He came in to me one day and asked.

'Mrs Plant could I have my ration book back? Would it be all right if Margaret and Joe, went to the shops to buy some sweeties?'

It sounded okay to me, dutifully obliged, handed it back to him and took no further notice of the incident. A few hours later he came back to me, returning his ration book quietly said.

'Mrs Plant, all I wanted Margaret to do, was to buy some writing paper and envelopes, and with the change buy some sweeties for herself and Joe. I gave her two shillings and sixpence with my month's supply of sweet ration coupons. When she returned, she handed me some greaseproof paper with three pence change. I didn't want greaseproof paper. I wanted writing pad and envelopes.'

I could see he was agitated and I was afraid he would slip back into the same state he was in, when he first arrived.

'Oh I am sorry Mr. Sandiford, I will sort it out. Don't you worry.'

I left him grumbling to himself as he made his way back to his room. Whilst I headed in the other direction, to sort her out.

'Margaret, why did you buy greaseproof paper?' Looking straight at me said.

'Joe and I went to the Post Office stores. Joe insisted we buy the sweets first. I did, but we didn't have enough money left. Instead I bought the greaseproof paper, it was cheaper. We ate all the sweets on the way home.'

I laid into the pair of them. To save any more ructions, gave them money and sent them to buy a writing pad and envelopes for him. It wasn't long after that incident Mr. Sandiford decided to return back to London, however afer six weeks in far better health than when he had arrived.

Our communication with London was by letters, sent on a regular basis. In one of Fans letters, she informs me, Mother was not good. Could she come up and stay with us for a while? No problem. With all the travelling arrangements concluded, we ordered a taxi from Crooks Garage, Jackie and I went up to meet her at the station where we waited until the train eventually puffed and clanked its way into the station as it clanked ast we saw her sat next to a window we waved to her, Jackie ran up to the carriage, when the train stopped opened the door, took out her little case. Out steps Mother dressed in black with her funny black felt hat stuck on her head, underneath her arm was a large brown paper parcel, that was all. I ran up and hugged her. She did not look well. In fact she looked all in. Maybe we looked like that when we first arrived she mumbled. 'Wooo- Allahnah. Wooo- I've arrived Wooo- at this God forsaken place you calls Bamber Bridge. Wooo-.' More to cheer her up than anything else. I lied.

'You're looking well Mother.' She exploded.

'Wooo- Don't be such a Wooo- blithering idiot Allahnah.'

Jackie holding her case was stood behind her, I could see he was about to burst out laughing. He made a face at me, pursed his lips, as if he was saying. Wooo-. I shook my fist at him. I was about to take the brown paper parcel away from her, she moved her body away. I thought: *What on earth has she got in there? She does not want me to unload her of that?* So I took hold of her arm, guided her towards the level crossing exit, where the taxi was waiting. We got her into the taxi sat her in the corner. The first thing she did was to take out some peppermints. Pop them in her mouth, quietly sucked them. As I tried to talk to her about her journey up. The strong smell of peppermint seeped into the taxi, but all she said was.

'Wooo- Later Allahnah. Wooo- later.'

I gave up. it was a good job it was a short ride home. I got her into the bungalow. sat her down in the kitchen, gave her a cup of tea. Margaret and Joe made a fuss of her. She soon put them straight.

404

'Now. Wooo- You two Wooo- little devils. Wooo- I don't want any Wooo- shenanigans. While I'm here Wooo-. Do you hear Wooo-.'

The pair of them stood there with grins over their faces, amused by the Wooo—ing not in the least bit interested in what she had said. I thought: *This is a good start. Maybe she will be better once she has rested for a while.* I moved Jackie out, and put mother into Jackie's bed to sleep along with Margaret and Joe in the other bed. Jackie could sleep in with Michael. *All was set for a peaceful stay with us!* So I thought. Jack was delighted to see Mother again as she was to see him. He always was the apple of her eye. Whilst I prepared the evening meal, they talked for ages about the problems in London. She constantly was interrupting with all the Wooo--ing in between her words. They were still at it when Kaye and Mary eventually arrived home to fuss over her. The one thing she guarded was the brown paper parcel, she took it everywhere with her and I wondered what she had in It? After the meal she retired to bed. When I went in to see if she was all right, she was undoing the parcel on her bed, opened it to reveal. a supply of strong peppermints and some packets of digestive biscuits. She turned to me with a rare twinkle in her eye and said. 'Now then Allahnah Wooo -I Wooo- I don't' want Wooo- you to be letting Wooo- on to your two Wooo- young Wooo- devils. What I have Wooo- brought Wooo- with me.' I'm sure that her ailment had got worse…. 'That's alright Mother, I won't let on to them. But we can buy them up here you know.'

But in her mind, she knew what Margaret and Joe could get up too. It took about a week before she was in a frame of mind to accept the quietness that prevailed in Bamber Bridge. Margaret and Joe were less than happy. They soon complained about the constant Wooo--ing of their granny during the night-times. As she recited the rosary loudly to herself, they feigning sleep so that they would not have to join in. Not only that, Mother used to complain to me, about the antics of Margaret and Joe. But also Mary complained about them and asked me.

'Mum. Why I can't you control them?' I quickly retorted.

'My God Mary you're a fine one, asking a silly question like that. Those two are angels compared to the devilment you used to get up too, and nobody not even your father could control you. Do remember the time?' Then we would spend a happy hour or so laughing about what she used to get up too, totally forgetting about Margaret and Joe's antics. Oh yes they were not the only ones. Michael along with some of his pals from school decided to join the local A.R.P. unit. Jack and I approved of his voluntary action. He is trained to put out incendiaries. All is going well until the Chief Warden turns up at the door to tell me all about what the boy's had got up to. I patiently listened as he droned on.

'Mrs Plant young Michael and his pals, without anyone's authority took one of the incendiary devises down into the woods for their own use. They had set it off in a field. In doing so it produced tremendous amounts of smoke. They tried unsuccessfully to put it out with cowpats, it got out of hand when a local Police constable arrived on the scene, they all ran away leaving the Policeman to put it out himself. I'm afraid, Michael, along with the other boys are not to report back to the unit. They are more of a hindrance than a help.'

He left me on the doorstep flabbergasted by his outburst. So ended Michael's war effort. He got a good telling off for his troubles.

The war was progressing with increased intensity. News of a thousand-bomber raid on the German city of Cologne. It was reported that the raid was four times the size, of any of the worst raids carried out by the Luftwaffe on London the previous April. This was really great news that 'Fella Hitler' was getting a pasting. Our Boys were given back more than what we had received.

I received a letter from Kitty, informing me she was concerned about Jack who was out in the fighting in North Africa? The news on that front was not good. Rommel was pushing back Montgomery's Eighth Army. Announcements that the Americans had defeated the Japs in the battle of Midway. A very good result. The American's were also doing their bit and definitely into

405

the war. The American Camp in Bamber Bridge was a supply unit of the American Eighth Air Force and as it developed, the number of Americans servicemen increased. The sudden increase of lorries into a sleepy village of very few cars and even less buses. Their presence was to cause quite a stir amongst the locals. Apart from the armoured vehicles and guns, which Jack's unit drove through the village. The Americans would drive around in ten wheel lorries, and what they called Jeeps, roaring around at breakneck speeds. As there was a war on, the police could do nothing about it. Kaye working on the camp was able to buy the American candy and chocolate bars that they sold in what they called the P-X. Their goodies were not under the same rationing restrictions as ours were. This pleased the children no end as they saw this as a ready supply. But I made certain that they only received a small amount each week, and only if they had done their chores. I warned Kaye, it was all very well being able to get sweets, but bring them all home to me. So that I could ration them out accordingly. Kaye thoroughly enjoyed working on the switchboard at the camp. She soon came to meet and become acquainted with quite a few of the GI's. She asked me if she could invite them to our home. I saw no wrong in that and agreed.

On occasions, the bungalow became full of American servicemen with their polite ways, every time they visited they all brought something with them as a gift. candies, chocolate,  chewing gum and cigarettes. They all had rather funny names some that I remember were. George Sokaralis, Bing Crosby (no not the crooner) Joe Novak, Johnnie Crivakrucha and Jonnie Zilmann to name a few, there were many more and some who were never to return home. They were soon accepted into the community. They made their local drinking house at the Old Cob Inn. The last pub out and the first one in. With the friends that Kaye had made, Jack made arrangements to get them invited to the Working Men's Club, for off duty drinking, which they appreciated.

Joe Novak Michael Jonnie Zilman   I have mentioned in the previous chapters about the trouble I had with Mary, but the others were just as bad, and I had to put up with a lot of incidents that they got involved in. Late one afternoon Joe came back home his face covered in blood. His shirt was streaked with blood from the wounds to his face. Kaye who was at home let out a shriek at the sight of him. I grabbed hold of him and rushed him into the kitchen over to the sink, to wash away the blood. He winced as I washed it away to reveal two rather deep long gashes both from just below his left eye running down to his chin.

'How on earth did you do that?' He didn't answer directly, just kept on wincing as I tried to stem the flow of blood.

'Kaye fetch me the iodine. Please.' He quickly reacted at this suggestion.

'NO Mum. Not iodine.' I repeated.

'How did this happen?'

'Freddie and I were in the cart and were coming down the hill. When a car came the other way. I steered the cart off the road and we finished up in the barbed wire fence. It was the barbed wire that done it.' Kaye came back with the Iodine. He yelled.

'NO. I don't want that on it.'

I didn't take any notice I took the bottle and some cotton wool she had given me. Poured out some iodine onto the cotton wool and went to dab it on his face, he squirmed away. Kaye grabbed hold of him and between us we administered the iodine. As it stung the open flesh then he yelled. Seeing the extent of the wounds covered with iodine I said to him.

'Your very lucky it didn't catch your eye. Next time don't go down the hill on that cart. How is Freddie anyway?' He mumbled something about he had gone home. The wounds healed but left two scars.

That year we had a blazing hot summer. The skies were as blue as could be. We sweltered with the heat the local's lads used to go swimming in the River Derwent that coursed through Forty Steps, a local beauty spot. One day the local police Bobby arrived on the doorstep. Suddenly confronted by this figure of authority. I feared the worst. My heart leapt into my mouth as he addressed me.

'Mrs Plant'?

'Er Yes.'

'I would like to speak with Michael Plant. If that's OK.' Relieved at the realisation that nothing was very drastic asked.

'Can you tell me why'?

'Yes Mrs Plant. Apparently yon Michael was one of the lads who helped fish out another young lad, who had drowned in the Derwent. He is requested to give a statement at the inquest. I can assure you that he is in no trouble.'

Michael went to the inquest to give a statement. He was commended for his action in the incident. Another afternoon Margaret and Joe with their friends, wanted to go swimming in the Derwent. After the recent tragedy I certainly did not want them to go, and forbade them and took away their swimming costumes.

Jack arrived back home later after his duties enquired.

'Awful quiet around here. Where are the children? '

'Out playing in the garden. They wanted to go swimming but I told them not to.' He answered.

'Well I did not see them.' Immediate panic took over me.

'Oh my God. I hope that haven't gone swimming.'

'Stay here Sarah. I am quicker than you. I'll take the bike and go and look for them.'

With that he was away out of the door. He knew where to head for Forty Steps. I started to pray. Sometime later he came back with them both looking very sheepish. He'd found them with their friends. All without swimming trunks trying to learn how to swim in the River. For their disobedience they both got a good hiding. much to Mother's approval. Chuckling away to herself in between Woooing.

The bungalow next door which was identical to ours, was owned by a middle-aged couple. Mr. and Mrs. Littlefir. He kept an immaculate garden full of flowers, a grass lawn with a fishpond and goldfish. Dotted about in the garden, were all different types of gnomes. Mrs. Littlefir was a bit of a busy body. Always making comments about the ball Michael kicked over, when he was playing football outside. He would climb over the fence and retrieve it. I knew he was always very careful about not doing any damage to their garden. However she would always try to catch him, without success. One day when they were all at school. She came into me and accused Michael of killing her goldfish. I retorted.

'No. Mrs. Littlefir. Michael wouldn't do anything like that!'

'Well they have all gone. You come in and see.'

I followed her back into her garden and around to where the fishpond was. I peered in the water for several minutes and sure enough. "No Fish." I was puzzled, as they were not floating on the top. They had gone. I promised.

'Mrs. Littlefir, when he gets home from school. I'll question him about them.' I left her standing there looking into a fishless pond.

After school he used to go directly to Melia's to do his deliveries. When the other two arrived home. I asked them.

'Did you two know anything about Mrs. Littlefir's fish?

Both shook their heads something wasn't right? I waited until he came home and questioned him. He answered with an emphatic.

'No. I don't know anything about any missing fish. Maybe some herons had a meal.'

A little unsure. I left the matter and forgot about it. A few days later Mrs. Littlefir returned back and said.

'Mrs Plant. Do you know that young Joe was using the cycle pump filled with water and spraying your clean washing hanging on the line.'

'No. but he'll get a telling off for doing it. Oh by the way. I questioned Michael and the other two. About the disappearance of your goldfish. He said he didn't know anything about it and neither did they.'

'Oh. that. Yes' she commented…I forgot to tell you. The fish are all back in the pond again. Very strange isn't it?'

'Very strange' I added thinking to myself: *The heron that Michael mentioned, could not have liked the fish had returned them.*

She left with a smug smirk across her face. I could not be bothered with such trivial things. If I had to sort them out. It would be me and nobody else interfering. Once I had to give Joe another good hiding, for something he should not have been doing. I was at the kitchen sink, I heard him say.

'Look Mum I'm going to shoot something.'

I turned around, bold as brass he was pointing this pistol at me. It was so heavy he could not hold it up, I knew it was not loaded.

'Don't be silly, go and put it back in your father's drawer and I won't tell your Father.'

He left with the German pistol, dangling at the end of his arm, and put it back where it came from. The large bottom drawer of our wardrobe where Jack kept all his trophies and souvenir's. The pistol, a souvenir from the First World War. When Jack came I told him of the day's incident. Jack said. 'Right that's it. I'll get rid of it.' And so he did.

Like most of Lancashire, the village followed the old tradition of closing down everything for a week. However, due to the war this was confined to one day. An outing to Blackpool, being members of the club we joined in. Mother did not want to leave the house.

'What in God's name. Wooo- Do I want to go Wooo- to see the Wooo- sea for? You lot go and enjoy yourselves? Leave me on Wooo my own. For Wooo. a bit Wooo. of peace and Wooo. quiet. Wooo in this Whoo mad house. '

Mother had spoken. Her Wooo--ing was improving. Being our first encounter with an old tradition, we took the youngest two and went with the Parkinson's. Caught the bus to Preston, then a train to Blackpool. After arriving there, our first stop was the big Woolworth's store canteen under the Blackpool Tower. Fish and Chips were the menu. Then donkey rides on the sand for the children. along with all the other amusements still available at that time. When all red and rosy from too much sun and wind, back on the train to Preston then home.

Another Saturday during the summer holidays it was a very hot summer's day. Joe came running into the bungalow shouting.

'THERE'S A FIRE. THERE'S A FIRE.' He grabbed hold of his toy tin helmet and was gone, before I could stop him. It wasn't until later that evening when they all marched in blackened by smoke and smelling of burnt wood, Margaret's dress was covered in black smudges. I demanded. 'What's been going on then?' Jackie answered.

'Well it wasn't much of a too do. I caught a crayfish in the Derwent. Took it down, to the woods, to cook it on a small fire. The trouble was that everything was so dry, the bushes caught alight. I told Joe to run home and tell you. But it spread too quickly the bushes burnt fiercely. We used a couple of old buckets and formed a chain from the brook to throw water onto the fire. We got it under control, just before the Police arrived. We all ran and used the ropes. So if the Police do come around Mum, you don't know anything about it.' He warned me. That did it.

'Your worse than them all put together. Why don't you pack up these malarkeys at your age? What will Josie think of all this?' I threw this in because I knew he was courting a beautiful young lady called Josephine Livesey. from one of the most highly respected catholic families in Bamber Bridge. Whether it made any difference to him, I don't know. But all of them in the woods. acted like Robin Hood and his Merry Men.

More visitors came to see Mother and ourselves. Peg arrived with Julia and Brutus. The pair of them looked worn out from the sleepless nights they were still having. Peg informs us that Dickie is okay, and has weathered the storm of the German's bombardment of Malta. Dickie had been promoted to the rank of Captain, which was more good news. Somehow we put them up for a week, whilst they looked around for a place to stay. Fortunately they found a flat above a little shop right next to the station. They moved in, leaving Brutus with us much to my tribes delight. There were fights as to whose bedroom he would sleep in. Mother solved the problem by banning him from sleeping in her room. In another letter from Fan, she asked if Jack could find to her somewhere to stay in T'Brig. As Tom her husband was based in Stranraer on Coastal Command Duty, she had decided to move closer to us, rather than Stranraer where she knew nobody. With a bit of luck Jack found a small flat further along the road. Then Fan moved up from London with Tommy, to stay in T' Brig where she stayed until they returned in 1944, After three months Peg and Julia having recovered were fed up with the quietness of a sleepy Town, decided to return back down to London.

Jack eager to get back in the front line, volunteers to go with the East Surreys to North Africa. Although he passed his medical, he was turned down. According to the Army, with his record he had done his bit albeit was far too old for foreign active service. What a relief that was for me. Another visitor arrived to visit us while on leave. Marty Burns he had joined the Merchant Navy. He cycles all the way from Harrogate to stay with us for a weekend. Then Kitty Burns came over to stay again. Bobby was still away somewhere on the north coast but was quite okay. Nevertheless, with all the too-ing and fro-ing of people, for us that turned out to be a very busy summer and I being able to afford them some respite from the anxiety and worry everyone was under thoroughly enjoyed having a full house. I still had mother in with the children. Although she had taken to her bed, on occasions she would shuffle around in and out of the rooms, her hand placed on the small of her back rubbing it up and down. to relieve some pain or other. Constantly Wooo--ing away as she did her rounds, before returning to her room with a brief request. 'Allahnah. Wooo- I could do with a cup of Wooo- tea.''All right Mother. Very soon.'

It was around the time that Monty beat Rommel at the Battle of El Alamien That news in itself, was a great national morale booster. However I received a woeful letter from Kitty informing me that her Jack had been wounded out in North Africa, also Andy's ship H.M.S. Zulu had been sunk . He was missing I immediately sent a wire to her to come and stay with us. She arrives and is in a dreadful state of anxiety over her two boys. She had received notice about the incidents. First of Jack then of Andy and nothing else. I set about consoling her and getting her to look on the bright side. She stayed for a week before returning back to Harrogate, much better for her brief stay with us. It was a few weeks later that I received a letter from her with good news. Both her boys are well and now safe and sound. On their way back from North Africa.

Then winter sets in its bitterly cold. Mary catches a nasty cold again and is taken into Chorley Hospital. where she was to stay for a long period. Margaret and Joe are highly delighted with their clogs walking through the snow, it packs tightly within the steel shods and they compete, trying to get the highest snow stilts, before one drops off and they fall over It was not uncommon to go outside and find four lumps of hard packed snow lying in the porch way. Fuel was a scarcity. There was little or no coal to be had. Jack takes all of them, down the woods to gather wood for the fire, with a two handed saw and long handled axe. Michael and he saw up fallen down trees and the rest of them carried the chopped up logs home, so by the time they had finished their many trips. The outer shed at the back was chocker block full of logs, that supply would keep us going over the Christmas period. The Americans were good to all the village children. Just before Christmas, they gave all the school children a Christmas Party. They drove around to all the schools in their big lorries, collected all the children, and took them back to their camp for a Christmas party. Bearing in mind that there was a war on and rationing was at its highest, with all the food, ice cream, and candies available to the Americans, nearly all of the children were violently sick after gorging themselves silly. They even bought home bags of candies for their Christmas stocking. I do not think they lasted that long. Christmas that year went past very quickly, Fan and Tommy sat down with us to Christmas Dinner. We made the best of it with what we could buy, and that wasn't much.

Early in 1943 I received a letter of woe from Kitty, telling me of one her family's cousins had informed he of the plight of one of their nieces, who was the youngest of their family. who was in a desperate state having been abused. Could I go with her, to see what she could do to help this poor little mite she planned to go asap. She lived in Congleton Cheshire. Obviously, if Kitty had asked me, it must be a bad situation. In my reply I agreed. When Kitty arrived she stayed overnight then early in the morning we made the journey to visit the family. On the way Kitty filled me in some of the details that had been given to her by her contact in Armagh. When we arrived at the address we were shown into a room then the mother brought her in. Only then we saw what a state this little girl was in. She was about Margaret's age. Totally bedraggled, thin, and I could see lice crawling through the wisps of her hair. A gaunt pair of eyes focused on us. She was withdrawn and in bad need of care and attention. Looking down at this sorry state, my heart went out to this poor little mite. Shocked at the sight I exclaimed.

'God in Heavens. Kitty, words fail me. How on earth did she get in that state?' Quietly Kitty responded.... 'Sarah, that is why I brought you with me. We need two brains to work this one out. Don't you agree?'... My eyes were fixed on this little girl. Kitty asked... 'What are you thinking?'... 'I don't know Kitty? We cannot leave her at this house. We must do something.' Kitty whispered.... 'Sarah. What if we take her back with us? I will take her home with me and look after her.'

I stood there looking at this bedraggled little girl thinking: *This poor mite definitely needed help, but in the presence of children of her own age. She would respond to good treatment and care, only which a good family could provide.* I made my mind up. If Kitty was going to look after her I would do my bit and take her home. If only to clean her up give her a change of clothes of Margaret's, and treat her with the care she desperately needed. I suggested.

'Kitty I agree. but all your tribe are grown up. I suggest we take her to our bungalow first. Clean her up before you take her home. I'll leave you to do the necessaries with the Mother.'

I took hold of the little girls hand and asked.

'Tell me, what is your name?' Dropping her head she whispered.

'Evelyn.' That was it. No further response.

Taking Evelyn with us, without any luggage, we left the house on our way back to Bamber Bridge. Our trip there and back had taken all day we arrived back at T'Brig late in the evening. At home Kitty and I started to clean her up we de-loused her, washed her and tried to feed her some nourishment, which could see she as having difficulty consuming it. When all this was done, we packed her off to sleep in with Margaret with Joe at the bottom of the bed. It took us a great deal of care and attention as she gradually responded. After about two weeks she was back in the world of the living. Then Kitty took her back to Harrogate, where she was brought up as one of their own and stayed with the Burns family for the rest of her life.

Bamber Bridge saw the first coloured servicemen, to be billeted in the American Camp with the other white Americans. We were not aware of any racial tensions or problems at that time. It certainly didn't bother me, my past travels had enriched my attitude to other races and creeds. At first T' Brig looked upon them with curiosity. They went about the town with a friendly attitude and they caused no problems. Within a short time they were accepted as part of the war machine. It was in June months after they had first arrived, when the first signs of trouble erupted. Being at the far end of the Village we were unaware of what was going on. Around about eleven 'o'clock, we were all woken up by the sound of gunfire, followed by sporadic gunfire shots. Michael called out. 'Mum, that's machine gun fire!' The firing went on for some time. Then the Police arrived at the front door, warned us and everyone else…. "That a riot between the white and black G. I's had broken out up the other end of town. Nobody was allowed out that night. Fighting and shooting between the white and the coloureds, continued well into the night and early hours of the morning, until it was brought under control by the American M. P's. Next day had the whole village talking about the incident. Quite a large number of coloured G.I's from the camp had gone on the rampage, apart from the gunfire, bottles and stones, had been used in the battle that followed. The far end of town was the scene of many trucks roaring up and down station road. Kaye went to work as usual, and it wasn't till she arrived back late that afternoon that she told us what had really happened. First thing I asked her was.

'What was all that shooting about?'

'Well. I got the facts when I got in. According to our Duty Sergeant., it had all started at the Hob Inn. At closing time some G.I's had asked for more drinks. The barmaid refused to serve them. Then an argument started. Two MP's arrived and tried to arrest one coloured G.I. As he was not in uniform without a pass, a row developed. Being that the two MP's were heavily outnumbered they withdrew. Getting into their jeep they drove off followed by a hail of bottles. One smashed the jeeps windscreen, further along station road other coloured G.I's has heard the rumpus, they too started throwing bottles and stopped the jeep. One of the M. P.'s was knocked out the other drew his pistol and fired at a coloured G.I., then all hell broke loose, word got back to the camp and the other black G.I's. raided the armoury and that's when the shooting started. One black G.I. was killed and a Second Lieutenant was badly wounded along with three others. After the night of terror the ringleaders were arrested. A court martial was to be held on charges of mutiny. We have to wait that verdict before me know anything else. But the camp is very quiet now, it's all under control. So don't worry about me.'

So that was another situation of unknown racial tension. That we or anyone else in T' Brig were not accustomed too.

Brutus a lovely dog, who was in our charge was a great pet for the tribe, used to run free, soon got into trouble. He got into the farmers chicken run and was blamed for the chickens not laying. We tried keeping him in, but he would get out and roam around, he never did any harm. The consequent was the farmer stopped given us any eggs, not that he had that many to give. So much to the children's disgust, Brutus had to go back down to London. Apparently according to them, it wasn't Brutus fault but the farmer's. So much to the annoyance of all. Brutus was packed off back to London with Jackie and Michael. During their brief stay, they stayed with the McDermott's, Upon their return they informed me Peg had arrived there to collect Brutus, and take him back to Sidcup so he was back in his own home, they were full of the stories of the bombing. It was about this time that the R.A.F. raided the Dams in Germany with devastating results. After Brutus had gone the bungalow was not the same without the presence of a dog, and the tribe missed him. One evening, Kaye came home from work asked if she could bring one of the dogs home from the camp, as it was running around free after its owner was lost on a Bombing mission, could we look after it, My tribe jumped at the idea, so Kaye arrived home with a mongrel dog called Heppie, who accordingly was used to the wide open spaces of the camp. Heppie did not take kindly to being restricted, although closing the double gates we tried to keep him in. However, with the heavy traffic of R.A.F. plane transporters, armoured vehicle and lorries, that constantly rumbled backwards and forwards past the bungalow, it wasn't long before Heppie ran out into the roadway and was killed. After that we seemed to be the foster home for any of the pet dogs the American Airmen used to keep. If they didn't return from a mission, the dog would just roam around the camp. Kaye would take pity on one and bring it home. During the summer months of the year, we had about seven dogs that were killed on the main road by one vehicle or another. It was a regular occurrence for the tribe, to take a dog down and bury them in the woods. Joe then seven years old, along with other children at the school, was about to take his confirmation and had to attend church for rehearsals, while he was doing those, I took the opportunity to go with him, and say a few prayers. One evening, I rode my bike down Duddle Lane with Joe running alongside of me, without any warning a car came tearing around the corner. I pulled on my brake unfortunately it was the front brake! I sailed over the top of the handlebars to land in a heap in the ditch just in front of me and very close was the barbed wire fence. All Joe did was standing there laughing

'Mum that was good. Do you remember when I ran into the barbed wire?'

Seeing the funny side of it I scrambled to my feet, looked around no one was in sight. The car had disappeared, whether the driver had seen me or not I don't know. We stood there laughing, embarrassed by the incident I said....'Joe promise me. You won't say anything and I'll buy you some extra sweets?' He promised.

The vegetables, Jack and Michael had sown the previous year, had grown into a good crop. I was busy preparing the vegetables for a meal. Having made Mother a warm Peppermint drink I took it in to her, she retorted.

'Be japers. Allahnah. Wooo.... Can you stop Wooo- ... Those two brats of yours. Wooo- making that infernal noise'

'Yes Mother. '

I took no notice and carried on with my vegetables. When I heard a tremendous crash from our bedroom. I dropped the saucepan I had in my hands. From the depth of her bedroom. Mother shouts out. 'IN HEAVENS NAME. Wooo- WHAT WAS THAT Wooo?'

I ran into the bedroom where I saw Margaret standing there with her hands over her ears. Our big wardrobe was laying at an angle. Its top resting on the floor and its base a large draw was open, glaring up at me was Jack's assortments of silver cups and medals. I yelled at her.

'What's happened? Where's Joe?'

'In the wardrobe. We were playing hide and seek. I locked the door on him. Then it just fell over.' From inside the wardrobe a muffled cry identified Joe's whereabouts. To add to my annoyance mother came shuffling in.

'Wooo-. I told you to stop them. Wooo-.' Turning about rubbing her back, she left me to it. I got down on my knees, looked to see if I could open the door, but could not with the top resting on the floor. The only way to get him out was to lift the whole cupboard upright. I got up and made a lunge to grab Margaret. Fortunately for her, she was on the other side of the wardrobe.

'Right let's try and lift it to let him out. You get hold of that end and lift it at the same time.'

With all the weight of the clothes plus Joe it was very heavy, Margaret wasn't strong enough. So I went and got a small stool, together lifting the top end up managed to push it under, then fetched a chair and did the same with that. Each time we struggled to lift it, muffled roars came from within the depths of the wardrobe, until gradually we managed to get it upright, from inside came the muffled yelling of brokem glass. The key was slightly bent but was able to unlock it, as the door opened, out fell two pieces of the long plate glass mirror fixed to the inside of the door, they fell onto the floor, then out tumbles Joe, avoiding the glass none the worse for his imprisonment he was grinning at Margaret. The pair of them got a whacking. Joe an extra one for getting into the wardrobe in the first place. Their whacking received the approval of mother. So that she could Wooo- to herself, in the peace and quiet, thrust upon the household. It didn't

412

last long? I think the last episode of Margaret and Joe's antics was the straw that broke the camel's back. Much to everyone's relief. Mother decided to go back down to London. She went back much better than when she come up, one day just before she left Fan came to visit and announced to mother and me that she was pregnant. We were both pleased for her. It was good news for her and Tom.

By the end of summer our troops had fought their way across from Africa and into Sicily and Italy. As they advanced on Rome Mussolini signs an armistice, then promptly declares War against Germany. What a mad man he was. But the signs to us were all good. The summer turns once again to winter and it's snowing hard. Rationing is still at its height. Our stocks are almost at an end. I was getting more concerned about Jackie as in January he will be eighteen, due for call-up, Sooner than later Jackie received his call up papers He had a choice to go down the pits or volunteer to go into the forces. His decision not to go down

Blackpool Sands with a couple the pits, instaed volunteers to join the Royal Air Force as a pilot.

of the American Boys Jackie decided to make a trip down to London to say his farewells, Michael went with him for their brief stay they stayed at their Aunt Agie's.

Family photo taken in Preston prior to Jackies mobilisation 1943.

Christmas 1943 was to be Jackie's last Christmas at home. To make it a good one, for him to remember, Jack decides to get a turkey for our Christmas dinner he has an idea, maybe Bobbie can get one from his family in Armagh Northern Ireland, He got me she write a letter to Kitty to get Bobby to go with him across to Bobbies home. They return with two one for Kitty. It was really good to see Bobby who I had not seen since Newcastle. He had not changed and was still the same. He returned the following day with his turkey to Harrogate. All gratefully received our Turkey dinner was a quiet but a memorable one. In January 1944. Jackie was called up not for the RAF but to join the Royal Regiment of Fusiliers at this stage in the war, the German front was cracking under the persistence of the allied forces, therefore the call for young men were now required to serve in the Infantry for service in the Far East fighting the Japs. After his basic training he came home on embarkation leave for three days, it was during that time we had time to chat together. Then he revealed some of the escapades my tribe got up to before the war. As a favour to Kaye, who had got tired of spitting on the red cover of her Catechism book in an effort to stain her lips red, she wanted the real thing Jackie obligingly supplied her needs. He organised the children, into a shop lifting team. On one of their shopping forages to Woolworth's in West Norwood, he would be sit Joe on the counter, whilst the counter assistants made a fuss over him. Jackie would cautiously take from the seperate sections on the counter, a lipstick, nail polish, when lifting Joe down into his pram, he would stuff the goods under his nappy, This petty thieving turned into a grand scale stealing of small items from nearly every shop, selling on to other children and splitting the proceeds between them. He told me they even stole to order. Unaware of all these things they used to get up I froze on his words. He went on to say that Margaret threatened to tell all, blackmailed him into giving her his share as well. Jackie had already had a plan arranged with them, if and when they were caught they had to roar and shout to get out of the predicament. Inevitably they were caught, the Police were called, the fright they did get put an instant stop to those antics. Seeing that it was a family of four with a baby in a pram, they escaped with a good telling off. Jackie being the eldest received a cuff around the ear from the Constable and sent on their way. Having escaped the law, once outside the shop, Jackie raced them all up to the Church and confessed at the side alter of Our Lady making them all kneel down in the front with Joe still in his pushchair he told them to recite out loud after me. Dear God forgive us. for we have sinned. Margaret stood up and shouted...'God. I was never any part of this. So I have committed no sin. It was only them.'... Jackie took them all across into Norwood Park, swore them all to secrecy, upon arrivin back home, as they pulled Joe's pushchair up the steps to get into the garden. Margaret said.

'Jackie looks at Joe.' Down behind him he had stuffed a couple of blessed candles he had taken from the box in front of him at the Altar. Jackie quickly buried them in the garden and swore them again to further secrecy. Agast at all these revelation I thought: *God must have smiled on little children*. Then I remembered: *That night during the Blitz, when a stick of bombs fell close by putting all the lights out, there not a candle in the house only a few matches (they were very difficult to get). Jackie said he knew where there was some. went out into the garden and kept us supplied for some time. At the time I did think the candles looked somewhat like the blessed candles they had in church, but being it was candlelight thought nothing more of it.* I scolded him for all these revelations. All he did was roar with laughter the three days was soon up, that was a sad time for us all he was still courting Josie, who was to write constantly to him throughout his tour of the war. Then Michael now fed up with his delivery job, starts a Saturday job at Crook's the local garage further down the road helping to repair cars. He used to come home covered in grease, muck, and smelling of it. It was a devils own job trying to wash his dirty clothing. He seemed to love all the grease and muck.

The war trundled on and never seemed to get any closer to ending. In Italy the Germans were holding fast at Monte Casino, where the Monastery on the top was constantly being bombed accompanied by reports of fierce the fighting on the top. Jack appeared to be constantly away on training exercises, unbeknown to the population, the secret build up for the 'D' day offensive had begun. A letter from Peg provided very good news, that Dickie was back from Malta, he would

 like to see us all, before he leaves for some other place. They would be up the following week. I in turn wrote to Kitty Burns, who was more than glad to come and stay with us during his leave.They arrived Dickie looking very smart in his captains uniform looked really fit, tanned or should I say weather beaten. Kitty arrives together with little Evelyn, what a change in the child with the care Kitty was providing. We all had a wonderful reunion, before they departed back down to London and Harrogate. Upon Pegs return she sent me a letter informing us thst the wood merchants behind mothers house had been hit by an oil

bomb, for the second time the whole lot went up blazing merrily away, as my brother Jack had long gone in the Army, although Bridget and Agnes being the closest to her, visited her when they could Mother was lonely, according to Peg, the last bomb had really dampened her spirits and she had decided to leave she wanted to stay with us. Peg informed me of the train she was catching. I ordered a taxi and went up to the station to meet her. Again she arrived with her small suitcase and brown paper parcel full of Foxes treble strong peppermints and digestive biscuits. Not only that but her cat as well. I certainly did not like the look of mother, much worse than when she first came up to stay with us. Our ride back in the taxi was quite apart from her Wooo--ing she said little. It reminded me of Jackie the last time, when he imitated her wind, I had not heard from him in months. I had a quite laugh to myself, said a quick prayer for his safety. Mother took over Jackie's bed, much to the annoyance of my two brats as she called them. She nearly drove us all mad with her drilling and bossing. She had only been there about two weeks. When she called me into her bedroom and said to me.

'Allahnah. Wooo- To be sure my Wooo -biscuits keep disappearing. Wooo- Are you taking them?'... 'No mother. Nobody can get at them because they are under your bed, in the biscuit tin I gave you. Anyway you're always watching over them. Margaret and Joe have had strict instructions not to touch them.' ... 'That pair of brats. Wooo-.'

I could tell she wasn't happy with the thought of those two brats getting their fingers into her prize possessions. I retorted... 'Anyway. I've told you before that we can buy them up here. I've just made a cup of tea would you like one?'... 'Wooo- Yes. I Wooo-- could do with one.'

I left her Wooo-ing- to herself and went out and made a pot of tea. I only said that to pacify her. A couple of days later there were roars and screams from her bedroom. I ran in to see what had happened. There was Mother hanging half way out of the bed, with a firm grip on the seat of Joe's pants. All you could see of him was a pair of legs, poking out from under her bed, his muffled screams, as she pinched his bottom triumphantly she yelled.

'There. Wooo. I've got you me young bucko.Wooo.- Here you are. Wooo-- Allahnah. Wooo.- This is the culprit. Wooo.- Who's taking my biscuits. Wooo.- I caught him red handed. Me pretending. Wooo- to be asleep Wooo.-. Now give. Wooo.- Him a good hiding for his troubles. Wooo- If you don't .Wooo-- I will.'

I grabbed hold of Joe's ankles, dragged him out, as she let go of his pants, I hauled him upright. A rather cowering little figure waiting for a slap. He didn't get one, instead a good hard whacking from me in front of his jubilant granny. The biscuits were never touched anymore!

Some of the American lad's with Irish descent, made a great fuss of (Ma) as they called her. She loved all this fuss and the attention they made of her. But when they left on a mission and never returned. She was inconsolable and more determined to go back to London. She stayed with us for about four months, before she left to go back down again. She roared and shouted at us. 'That we were all a load of sheep. Cowering in our trenches. She was going back to London, where hero's Wooo- were made every day. Wooo-.'

One of the American soldiers said he would give ' Ma.' The drive of her life in a Jeep. He informs Ma that he will drive her all the way to Preston to catch the London train. When he arrives she was helped into the back of this little jeep, as we stood by the main road including young Tommy, who spent most of his time playing with Joe, to wave her off. As the American driver revved up the engine, he took off at break neck speed, with Mother hanging onto her hat, I said a silent prayer. Now she had departed, we could settle down and pick up the pieces again. Not so. One evening Jack came back off duty and informed me.

'Sarah I've been given orders to report to a unit just outside London. I have to go within the next few days.'

A shock to me. I knew there was no way he would be taking us with him. We would have to remain where we were, although the bombing was on the wane, we ourselves ached to get

415

back down to London. Then the big offensive. 'D' Day. The sixth of June came and went. I was worried that Jack was part of it. Fortunately he wasn't. I received a letter from him a week after the event had taken place, advising that he was still in England. We warmed to the possibility that after the Normandy Invasion had started, the end of the war would not be far away. How wrong we all were. A week later that 'Fella Hitler's answer came back to us. The second Blitz of London. On the 16th June we read in the newspaper the Germans were using a new arial weapon a pilotless plane, called a VI's soon to ne nicknamed ."Doodlebug." According to the newspaper the first of this type of raid had began early o the Tuesday morning, quickly followed by more over the next two days, that quickly became a daily occorrence on London. Kaye had been given some time off from her job at the camp she decides to go back down to London to visit the rest of the family, with the latest news of rebewed bombing I tried to dissuade her not to go but she said.

'If Gran can stand it so can I. Anyway it's only for a week or so.'

So off she went. I prayed myself silly until she returned. She quite excited about her trip. related the events of her week's stay, with her Aunt Agnes and Uncle Alec. Alec, still doing the rescue work looked worn and tired. Mad Aggie was still the same a bit demented, maybe caused by the constant threat of bombs, she would run out and see the latest bomb crater, to witness the blood and gore. Gran and the rest of the family, were all okay and surviving the latest wave of terror bombing. The atmosphere during a raid was so different, when the siren sounded, people still carried on as normal. However gone was the constant throb of hordes of bombers flying overhead instead, one heard the sound of the guns banging away in the distance, before the sound of a Doodlebug became clearer and louder a stuttering noise of its engne All would look up trying to see it as it came into view, the shape of a small fighter plane with no propeller, mounted above it at the rear was its engine, just like a long tube, out of which belched a great big orange flame. As the engine spluttered to a stop it either glided down or, went into a steep dive towards the ground. Thr big problem was no one knew exactly where it would fall. If it stopped overhead, you just held your breath, watch and say your last prayers, waiting for the blasted thing to hit somewhere with an almighty crash. Causing chaos and destruction followed by a huge plume of dust and smoke. Kaye said she watched three of these damn Doodlebugs within a week. In threes or fours they would fly over at any time during the day Not in waves like the other bombers. She made me laugh at mother's antics who would go out, shake her fist at them in defiance. Wooo--ing in between her insults. Adding... 'So do not go worrying about Gran. She is doing okay.'

At the end of June. I was in attendance when, Fan gave birth to a little girl they were to call Julia. It was strange that with all the death and distraction, that was going on in the world., life was created and still carried on. In France things were going just as well for our troops. The Germans were fighting a war of retreat, back to their own borders. Unlike us at Dunkirk we had somewhere to retreat to. When and if the Germans reached their borders they would have nowhere to run to, on the other side the Russians were attacking their rear defences? In September news of another mass evacuation took place in London. Mothers and children were being sent back into the country to escape the oncoming bombardment by the Doodlebugs. Kaye arrived home one evening and informed me news had filtered through to the camp, an attempt to blow up Hitler had failed. Apparently some of his Generals had plotted against him and tried to assassinate him. Unfortunately he escaped, was still alive. It was good to think that even some of his Generals didn't like what he was doing.

More encouraging news was our armies were rapidly advancing northwards. By mid-August Paris had been recaptured by our boy's. Then in turn the Russians advanced and took Romania, a place I'd never heard of. The Poles start to dig in at Warsaw. Hitler was being pounded from all sides.The tide od war had definitely turned in our favour. The quicker they advanced north, the quicker they would take over the launching sites of the Doodlebugs and stop any more being fired at us back in England. On the battlefields of France that 'Fella Hitler' Was getting some of his own medicine being pounded from all sides.   In return that 'Fella Hitler.' unleashed yet another new secret weapon. VII Rockets. Far more deadly than the Doodlebug, without warning it just landed. No chance for anyone who was unfortunate to be in the wrong place at the wrong time. Mainly aimed at London once again to demoralise the civilian population. But we retaliated with more daylight and night-time bombing hitting Berlin and the major cities of Germany. Then real good news, our troops are seizing all places. Salonika, Flushing, and then another announcement in November, fter many attempts to sink her, the giant battle ship Tirpitz had finally been sunk by Lancaster bombers, dropping big armour piercing bombs on her. Now she lies deep in the icy waters of a Fjord in North Norway. All these announcements were positive indication that we were now winning the war. After four and a half years, the home guard was to be disbanded and to cap it all the lights were to be turned on in Piccadilly. Wonderful stirring news. One evening Kaye came home from the camp and said they had been told, Glen Miller the Bandleader, while flying to Paris to entertain the American troops, his plane had crashed into the sea, he was missing.

It was Christmas Eve 1944, not long after five in the morning, the distant roar of a stuttering engine woke me from my sleep. Then silence before an almighty explosion, happened somewhere further up the village. Margaret and Joe came rushing in and leapt into bed beside me. Squirming their way down underneath the blankets, I said a prayer, as I thought: *It might be one of the American bombers. returning damaged from its raid over Germany. But it could not have been. This was a sound I had not heard of before. It was unlike the sound of any bomber engines, I could remember. If I wasn't mistaken that was the sound of a very big bomb.* I looked over toward the dressing table where the clock stood and saw by its luminous hands That it was nearly twenty-five to six. I lay there blessed myself. Then I heard the distant clanging of the fire brigades bell, as they made their way to whatever had happened. That sound brought painful memories back to me. It had also woken up Michael out of his deep sleep. He wandered in through the doorway and stated.

'I guess it's something to do up at the Hob Inn.' Then wandered out again. The clanging of the fire bells had ceased, so they must have reached the incident. I shook the other two, still fidgeting about under the blankets and told them. 'To get back into their own beds and get some more sleep.' Moaneing and groaning, still stayed where they were. Now that I was fully awake. I decided to get up and start getting ready for the day. I swung my legs out of the bed, when another large explosion went off. This one not as close, but definitely big likes another bomb, this brought Michael and Kaye back into the bedroom all mystified by the explosions, but all with the same opinion, definitely big bombs. I glanced at the clock again it was nearly a quarter to six. Michael decided to go outside and listen for any more bombers. He left us, Kaye went back to bed, leaving the other two still underneath the blankets. I put on my dressing jacket slipped my feet into my slippers and left for the kitchen, vert aware that some type of an air raid was going on. In the darkness found the matches and lit the gas under the kettle for a cup of tea while I waited for the kettle to boil, I fumbled around in the darkness, getting the pot for tea ready, Then I heard another big explosion that was much closer. Just after that Michael came back in from outside stumbling in the darkness. He mumbled.

'Where's the light's Mum? There's not a raid on.'

I realised that there had not been any air raid sirens going off. So I guessed it would be okay to light the gas mantle. I struck a match reached up, turned on the overhead mantle. With the light now on saw Michael still in his pyjamas wearing his overcoat he muttered.

'Did you hear that one mum? That was closer than the other one but still some distance away. Whatever they were, they were big. I heard another one go off just after I went outside.

That seemed even further away but still a big one.' Making the tea poured it out, gave it to him and wished him a. 'Happy Birthday.' he said.

'Thank you Mum, you know what? I didn't hear any bombers, only the sound of a single engine. I reckon they were Doodlebugs. What do you think?'

'I don't really know but the first one woke me up by its noisy engine. You might be right. Why don't you go back to bed? It's only a quarter past six. I'm going to get myself ready for early morning mass. I have a lot to do to- day getting ready for to-morrow.'

'No I'll get up maybe read some book.'

With the unexpected early morning call, it seemed pointless that everyone should laze about in bed. Within half an hour they were all up messing around that made my mind up. As it was Sunday we would all go to the early morning mass. That would leave the rest of the day free. When we were all ready to go. I made them all wrap up against the cold wind that had developed. After mass as they normally did, the congregation would stand chatting about whatever was going on. On this occasion there was an air of curiosity, but the talk was centred on the big explosions that had occurred earlier that morning. Mary Parkinson was flustered to say the least. She informed me

'Bombs had been dropped on T' Brig.'

That alone was not a good thing. As they had not really experienced any of the intensity of bombs, that had rained down during the course of the Blitz. Michael got chatting to one of his pals who informed him. That a giant bomb had landed on some farm up near Brindle.' He said to me. 'Mum. I'm going up to Brindle to see what had happened.'

I warned him to be careful and be back in time for his Sunday lunch. We left the questions and answers to the diminishing congregation, headed back home. I got on with my chores and started preparing the dinner. It was after twelve, when Michael finally arrived home to inform me.

'There's been an air raid on the North by Doodlebugs. Quite a number had landed outside of Manchester. That last big bang was at Brindle. When Rob and I got there the Police stopped us from going too far. It demolished some cottages, and no casualties had been reported. I heard him talking to another man telling him that others had landed at Oswaldtwistle, Turton, and Tottington. With more landing all around the Manchester area. Some had landed in Yorkshire, but he did not know where. There was not that much to see, but on our way back it seemed that all the town's population was heading that way. The Doodlebugs must have been aimed at the American Camp.'

As far as he was concerned he was out looking for more shrapnel pieces but he didn't find any. I was certainly not going to bother walking to see the sight, whereever it was. I'd seen enough of bomb damage in London.

There were no further raids during the following days. Christmas of 1944 we had turkey that Jack had ordered from Metcalf's farm earlier in the year. That gave us a little bit of extra at Christmas. To say the least with the rationing it was rather bleak. Kaye had fortunately got some candy from the PX to fill up their stockings. At least they were happy for five minutes. Snow had fallen on the ground, although we didn't know at the time it was to be the last Christmas we were to spend in T'Brig. As the new year of 1945 approached the war appeared to look likely to finish in the near future? It didn't. Another visitor arrived early in the New Year. Ray Batten now a navigator in the Fleet Air Arm. Who was stationed at Insip Airfield just outside Preston. He along with one of his pals, came to spend a long weekend with us. The pair of them cycled all the way. A warm welcome was given and they had the time of their life while they were there. He said his father and mother Bert and Mary still living in Clapton, had so far survived the bombings. The pair of them returned back to their base, much the worse for wear, as they rode back to camp on their cycles.

In February I had Kitty Burns arrive on the doorstep with Evelyn. A total different being, but still very quiet and shy. However Kitty was very depressed. She had heard that her Jack had been wounded again. This time during the fighting in Holland. He had lost an eye. Another two weeks of consoling before they both return home.

As the time goes by I was getting more concerned about Jackie, I had only received infrequent letters from him. They were not letters as such, more like photographs and highly censored. It was the same with Josie, when she received one she would come around to tell me he was all right. We did not have a clue where he was. More worry for me Mary is sent back to the Convalescent Home in Halifax. She had a re-occurrence of the TB. I got Kitty to visit her. Fan with Tommy and Julia had already made the move and returned to London. She wrote to me she got a little flat a few houses away from Bridget. Yet the war in the Far East was still on-going, we still had not heard from Jackie in month. I continually worried about his safety. The Americans were advancing towards Japan, after very intense fighting they took Okinawa. Our own troops had re-entered Malaya, were moving down to Singapore. I was really worried for Jackie's safety. Jack came home after duty one evening and said.

'Sarah Ducks, I've heard a rumour. Now the War in Europe had ended, it is only a matter of time that before the Japanese would capitulate it seems that I and many of the old Soldiers, including Bobby will be demobbed. If that is the case and I believe it will happen quickly, we need to start thinking about our return to London. That will mean I need a job and I want to be the first in the queue. I have accumulated leave, so I will go back down and see what is available and also start looking for accommodation. What do you say to that?'

'Yes. I can see your wisdom. Where will you stay, at Agies?'

'I suppose so . They have a spare room, Kaye has stayed there before.'

'Okay, where are you going to look for a house? Near Vauxhall?'

'C'mon Sarah, I don't think we can be that choosy. Not after the damage the bombs have caused. You have been away nearly four years.' That made me think.

'Well yes. Mother, Fan, Kitty and Bridget not forgetting Mad Agie, all live in that area, but if it's possible, I would like to be near Mother and the rest.'

Okay, I put in for some leave, get myself down there to see how the land lies.'   I enquired.

'Are you going to try for your old job in the Post Office at Brixton?'

'We shall see after I get down there.'

Jack along with Michael left a couple of weeks later for a spell at Agies. I received a letter from him saying. He had applied for a Post Office job at the Victoria Sorting Office and had received a positive answer. Advising him- when he was demobbed to get in touch with them again. That was indeed a positive move and encouraging to me. He had seen nearly all of our close relatives. All were well. Mother was still Wooo--ing and with the recent announcement about ending the war, she was in a far better frame of mind, Fan had moved into a Flat in Langley Lane opposite Julia and a few doors away from Bridget's house. With his limited time available, he had contacted his brother Bill and Bert Thomas, to seek their help in looking for a suitable place in either of the two areas. But I wondered if he or they had found any housing for us. The following week the Telegram Boy arrived on the doorstep. I immediately feared the worst about Jackie.. With trembling fingers I opened up the flap.

FOUND HOUSE . NOT FAR FROM DOLLY STOP

START PACKING STOP

JACK STOP

I nearly fainted with relief. I gave the boy a sixpence for his troubles. This time I was overjoyed about we are on the move again.

419

My main concern now was to get us back down to London. Knowing of the problems we had previously encountered in past years, Kaye being employed by the American Air Force could not be released just like that. So she was to remain behind. George and Mary Parkinson offered to put her up and stay with them, until she could get her release. This suited Kaye. So that problem was solved. Next thing packing and removal.

Jack returned without Michael, he was staying with his Aunt Bridget. He said.

'I've got the keys and paid for a month's rent up front. Get ready to move. There is a bloke in the club who has a removal company down near Walton Le Dale, I'll speak with him about getting the furniture back down to London.'

Now it was all rush rush. We went to a few parties before he left. Jack plan was to take Michael back with him to stay in the house, get it fixed up for when we arrived. Jack got some crates from the camp stores then we began to pack We spent the week packing then the first lorry arrived and left with a part load to return in three days time for the second load. Then Jack left. I booked our train tickets to leave on the night train after the second lorry had picked up and gone on its return journey. We made a point of going to all our neighbours and friends to pay our thanks, say our farewells. The second lorry turned, all the furniture was moved into the lorry, all completed the removal Van left early in the afternoon, leaving us with plenty of time to spare, as the train for our return journey home to London, would not be leaving from Bamber Bridge station until early evening.

Our stay in Bamber Bridge had been a few years break away from the bombing of London, and certainly not without its many incidents. Now this interlude was over, we just had two small cases and the pack of sandwiches to carry. I decided not to get a taxi, instead walk with Margaret and Joe to the station, thinking: *It would be fitting for our final journey, to walk back through the village to the station, just as we had done when we first walked to the Bungalow.*

I made my last walk around the now empty and silent rooms of the bungalow before. I went out the front door, closed it with a bang. It was back to London and hopefully a much brighter future.

CHAPTER SIX
LONDON DEVASTATION - 1945

Arriving at the station in good time, we found something I had not bargained for. Mary Parkinson, had organised a group of friends that were not working at the mill, to be there to say goodbye. As the train approached it clanked noisily into the station, it was time for a tearful farewell to all the good friends we had made there. Boarding the train found an empty compartment, settled ourselves down for the long journey, which gave me time to contemplate our future, having long since given up the lease of number 70 Bloomhall Road, Jack's statement of a bigger house to live in, gave me a good feeling and was not too concerned about our future accommodation. He would meet us at Agie's then take us there. During the night we slept with some comfort. We arrived at Euston in the early morning, I woke Margaret and Joe. Gathering up our chattels, ushered them off along a near deserted platform towards the Underground station. I bought tickets to Stockwell and made our way down the escalator stairs to the train platform. When the Morden train came in. it was already packed, unceremoniously we were pushed and shoved into a carriage, by the time we had travelled four stations as passengers got off. seats became available for us for the rest of our journey. Arriving at Stockwell we got off and went up the escalator stairs into the vestibule, as a steady stream of people entered the vestibule we made our way out. We stood on the pavement in the morning sunshine, watching the Trams, Buses and cars go by. I noticed the clock tower opposite showed exactly 8.00a.m. I thought: *We are too early, we have plenty of time to walk down to Agies.* I ordered.

'Your Auntie's, is not too far away, so we will walk there.'

As we walked along the South Lambeth Road. the clanking sound of the trams provided me with a sense of well being, a few buses and cars passed us by, but as we passed the remnants of a row of terraced houses, two houses, more gaps, a single house, a huge gap, showing nothing but piles of bricks, rubble with timbers poking out at awkward angles. I was aware and horrified at the awful sight and smell of destruction, yet in amongst those was the smell of fresh bread being baked at the local bakery, which added warmth to the existing smell. To my dismay when we arrived at the Tate Library saw that it too had been hit. At the traffic lights we crossed the road, in silence I guided them into Old South Lambeth Road towards Agies. Outside of Agies in the roadway was a brick built Communal Shelter, a stern reminder of the blitz. I gave two hefty bangs with the knocker on Agies door, looking around saw opposite next to a large bombsites, still standing was the Crown Pub, behind that the Victoria Mansions had been hit and badly damaged thought: *Agnes you have been very lucky.* The door opened, Alec with his very soft-spoken manner greeted me.

'Hello Sarah, it's wonderful to see you all again.' He bent down and kissed me. Alec was a big strapping fellow of a man, well over six feet in height,

'Alec. It is good to see you after all this time. How are you?'

'I'm good. Hello you two. Welcome come on in' He stood to one side to allow us to pass then closed the door he murmured.

'Go on Sarah, lead the way up the stairs.' I lead the way up and into their tiny kitchen. Agnes still in her night attire stood up.

'Sarah.' She literally threw herself at me in welcome. Very pleased to see her but thought: *The events of the war had not curbed her, it had made her worse.*

We sat down, were provided with weak tea and toast to eat as we caught up on all the news. Finally Jack arrive with Michael, we stayed until after lunchtime,then left en-route to this house located between Loughborough Junction and Herne Hill, areas I was already familiar with. We walked back to Stockwell to catch a 34 tram. As we walked along I still could not believe the devastation that was very evident I mentioned my fears to Jack. He replied.

421

'Sarah Ducks this is nothing. London did get it rather badly, and so did other cities. You have not seen the worst yet?'

At Stockwell we caught the tram, but what I was not ready for was the sight of more devastation. There appeared to be nothing left from one end to the other of houses on either side of Stockwell Road. Just large areas of bombsites piled high with rubble. Here and there were the skeletons of houses.Their blackened walls stuck out like sore thumbs. Tree trunks burnt scorched, bare of branches. Openings to side roads leading to nowhere, were clear of debris, along pavements stood old lamp standards, some leaning at drunken angles. The main road on both sides were identical, halfway towards Brixton, still standing was 'Pride and Clarke's.' The tram clanked to a stop outside the Astoria. Opposite I remembered the sight of the shell of Quinn and Axton, hit years before.. Micahel was chatting to the other two, Jack broke our silence. 'See what I mean Sarah?'

The tram clanking into motion crossed the Brixton Road into Gresham Road where it stopped outside the Police Station, briefly changed from below ground pick-up to overhead wires. On the move again. The scene was the same, more devastation. Isolated buildings, proudly left standing out of piles of rubble, almost whispering. "They did not get me." I sat there numbed as we carried on. Jack interrupted my daze.

'C'mon we get off here.'

Getting off the tram with our chattels, took my mind away from my previous encounter. However, having been very familiar with the area many years before, I was aware of where we were, Jack urged us.

'C'mon each of you carry something. The house is not too far away to walk.'

Crossing over at the Green Man Pub, walked towards the Railway Bridge, having passed under that met the same sights, large bombsites and gaps between terraced houses, huge timber frames supported walls to stop the houses falling down. We bought some milk and bread before we arrived at a pub. "The Milkwood Tavern."

'Sarah. This is Heron Road. Our house is at the far end, not far now.'

However, this Road was no different, large bombsites on both sides, at the end of the bombsite we were walking past, there was a row of patched up three-storied Victorian terraced houses, at the far end we stopped outside Number 56.

'Here we are this one's ours.'

Taking the two steps up into a porch archway, he opened the front door. Following behind we entered a dark cheerless, passageway with a musty damp smell. Jack led the way through to a kitchen, on one wall was a dirty window covered in bomb blast tape, through which daylight could hardly penetrate on the other wall was a cooking stove, the only piece of furniture in the kitchen was an old wooden table under the window, either side of the range were low cupoards cupboards, another door led through into a tiny scullery, with a deep sink with one tap, a small gas cooker and in the corner a brick built coal fired boiling pot. A back door provided access to a yard and an outside lavatory. A tour of the house revealed, a cellar and two rooms on the ground floor, the one in the front room contained part of the first load of our furniture, going upstairs revealed, a lavatory, another kitchen, up a small flight of stairs, were two bedrooms beds had already been assembled. Yet another two flights, led up to a very large bedroom, a nother couple of the beds assembled also the room had box windows at either end all the windows. I noticed that all the windows in the house were the same, filthy dirty criss crossed with blast tape.. All rooms had fireplaces, however, the house was extremely damp. The first load of our household goods including the beds had been set up by Jack and Michael,so at least we had something going all we needed was blankets. In the next load.

Unimpressed by what I had seen and foresaw I never would be happy whilst living in this house. Nevertheless, we were there and had to make the best of it. Margaret and Joe were running up and down the bare staircases like Indians until Jack stopped them. When he spoke, everyone took notice. Quietness reigned while we discussed where to sleep everyone, there were plenty of rooms. Late in the afternoon, the second furniture lorry arrived. Then all became too occupied, to worry about the outside world. Most of the stuff was stored in the lower two rooms. I sorted out a tea chest containing all the kitchen utensils, plus a couple of pots to cook the tinned food, which Jack had brought from his camp. It was very late when the removal men eventually finished unloading and left on their journey back to T'Brig, in the fading light Jack lit the gas mantles in the rooms we had sorted out for that nights slepping bedstead were Margaret and Joe were given the task of making up beds, while they were oganisng bedding arrangement, I started cooking a makeshift meal in the tiny kitchen, lighting the gas rings, the gas flame faded, with a pop went out. No gas. Quickly brought screams and shouts from Margaret and Joe upstairs. I heard Jack going upstairs, then quietness, the sound of footsteps coming downstairs as they all entered the kitchen Joe was whispering.

'There's a bogey man upstairs.' That was all we needed. In frustration I yelled at him.

'BE QUIET DO NOT BE SILLY. TRYING TO FRIGHTEN EVERYONE.' Mind you in this strange house and darkness, I could sense he was scared. Jack giving Michael some money said....'Michael here, feed the meter in the cupboard with these pennies.'

He left the room, I heard the faint sound of clicking then coins dropping onto metal, coming back in said.... 'Light the gas mantle.'... that was producing a hissing sound of escaping gas gas from the mantle. Jack struck a match to light it, in its stark light I relit the gas rings to continue with cooking, They returned back upstairs to finish off the bedding. I soon had the meal ready, clearing the table arranged the seats at the old wooden table then called them down to eat, a meal of powdered scrambled egg, tinned beans, slices of bully beef with chunks of the bread we had bought down at the bakery washed down with tea then all retired to bed. The following day would be very busy sorting out the place properly, furthermore discovering what the surrounding area had to offer.

Shouting, banging of doors, the noise of car engines woke me from a sleep of exhaustion after the events of the precious two days. Outside It was dawn I lay there wondering what was going on with all the noise, then the rasping of gears and reving enginss. Jack was snoring his head off I shook him.

'Wake up Jack there's a disturbance going on outside.' Covering myself up I got out of bed and crept across to the window to see loads of van's in front of the houses parked on both sides of the road, with many men moving about. Some of the vans were coming out of a large gateway next to us, on the side of the van's I read. "NEVILL'S BREAD" Joining me at the window Jack said.

'Oh I forgot to tell you Sarah, we live next door to Nevill's the bakery company. C'mon back to bed.'

Back in bed, I heard a tram clank past then stop. I exclaimed.

Jack. I thought I heard a tram go past.' A muffled response informed me.

'That's the 48. It goes past here to West Norwood.'

I thought: *Now he tells me*. Fully awake I decided to get up and make tea. Going down the creaking stairs crept into the scullery, filled up the kettle, very aware of the strong smell of baking bread obviously coming from Neville's next door, which happened to be one of the biggest bakeries in South London, with their van's noisy exits outside, they must have been leaving on their rounds. Later in the afternoon they returned,soon found out it was a daily occurrence I was to endure for the rest of my days at Number 56, with the exception of Sunday, a day of rest.

I had just finished making the pot of tea, when Jack entered the scullery.

'Morning Sarah, my it's warm in here.'...I had not noticed, but the heat from the gas flame warmed the whole scullery up. It was so tiny; even I could touch the sloping ceiling by the backdoor.,,, 'Jack while I make toast, go and get them up?'....'No, first a cup of tea. Sarah Ducks, you're not very pleased with this place are you?' I retorted....'No I'm not. It's far too damp for my liking and I don't think it will improve.'... 'Sarah, at this moment in time we have no options. When we get settled, we can look around for a better place.' Conversation over.

He left leaving me making toast, unfortunately without any marge. One by one, they entered the kitchen dressed, but still sleepy. Joe refused toast unless it had marge. He was sent to find some in a packing case, he returned in triumph, exclaimed.

'I've found it.' He ate his toast.

When they had finished I sent the pair of them out to find what was available from the local shops. Margaret refused but with the threat of. "No sweets." They quickly disappeared, whilst Jack, Michael and I started on the unpacking. About an hour later they arrived back with information of grocery shops and other assorted providers. A paper shop that sold sweets and comics. Noting what they said I ordered.

'Right. You two sort out what provisions are in the packing cases and take them into the kitchen put them on the table.'

So we were all occupied. When they had completed that chore I checked ove it to make a list of our basic needs, then sent them out again armed with Ration books and sufficient money, to buy their weeks ration, two oz's of sweets. Much later they returned with only half of the list. With a woeful tale Margaret retorted.

'It's not on sale, and there are long queues at the shops.' I answered.

'That can't be the case. There must be. I'll go myself. Joe you come with me and show me the shops.'

I got my coat on, grabbed the ration books, out we went down the Road. I soon found out, they were right. there was not much to buy and at every shop there were queues outside. We walked to Loughborough Junction, where Kingston's the Greengrocers was, before the war they always had plenty of fruit and vegetables now very little on view, but they did have long queues. We joined the end of the queue. Slowly we moved up his had me thinking: *We are now back in London not T'Brig and shopping was going to become a big problem also I realised we were close to Doctor Smythe's surgery. I was not going to waste an opportunity like this after shopping we would see if she was still working.* We did not get much veg just enough to bide us over for a couple of days Then across to Doctor Smythe. The brass nameplate indicated she was still there. I ventured in and asked the receptionist.

'Can I register my family please?' She replied.

'Sorry Doctor Smythe has more than enough patients to deal with.'

'Look many years ago.I was registered here. Will you please ask her if I could re-register?' Sharply she asked.

'What's your surname?'

'Plant.' She went into the surgery, I noted there were plenty of customers waiting. after a little while came out followed by a much older looking Doctor Smythe she greeted me.

'Mrs Plant. Is it really you? After all these years? How's that baby of yours?'

'He's no baby Doctor Smyth. He's nearly twenty, hes in the Army in Burma.'

'My Goodness me. Doesn't time fly? I hope he's all right. What's the address you are living at?' I told her she said.

'That's' all right. We can fit you in. How many in your family now?'

'All together, eight including three boys and three girls.'

'My word, hasn't your family grown. The receptionist will take your details down. Next time you're in. I'll catch up on your news.' She returned into her surgery.

Pleased that I had achieved something important, we left. Outside I realised that the little Catholic Church. we used to go was further up the Road, thought: *Did that get bombed?* So,

424

with Joe dragging behind we found it was still standing, and popped in to say a pray of thanksgiving. That we had all survived the war. Outside I asked.

'Joe, do you know where our house is?' He retorted.

'Don't know.'

'Look we walked down to the Junction but back a different way, we will have to retrace our steps.' He paused before saying.

'Don't know, I'm not walking all the way back down there.' He was not very helpful, possibly because he was tired of walking around.

I did remember the church was almost at the foot of a hill that went up to Red Post Hill, but Heron Road was flat and the Road opposite the church went downwards. Taking a chance decided to walk downwards.'Right if you don't want to walk back, let's walk down that way.'

Crossing over we took the road down in the middle was a single set of tramlines, carrying on passed another big bombsite. Then further down I noticed back of a parked NEVILL'S van, we were close. 'There you are son, I was right.' Passing the van, I vaguely remember a Hall was opposite the house, a dirty notice board outside stated. "St John's Mission Hall" A few more steps, revealed the large entrance to the bakery, next to it our house. I was quietly satisfied and pleased with myself. Having registered at the Doctors, found that our Church, was only three minutes' walk away. I gave two hefty bangs on the front door. Jack opened it, his sleeves were rolled up and he was sweating.

'Sarah. Quick come in. I thought you had got lost, you've been gone ages.'

Michael half way up the stairs holding onto our wardrobe, yelled.

'Hurry up Dad I can't hold it much longer.'

'Okay coming. Sarah makes us a cup of tea. I'm parched.'

My news would have to wait. I made some tea, listening to grunts, groans, bumps, and knocks, had the tea made when they came down.

'Now then Sarah, what did you get?'

'Bread and milk, a few vegatables nothing else just as they said long queues at shops with something to sell, other shops empty.. We went all the way down to the Junction. David Greigs the butchers had no meat; Kingston's did have long queues for potatoes and cabbage, which I did join. However, I now know what and where everything is, I also have registered us back at Doctor Smythe's. She is still there, though looking very tired. She remembered me. After that, I decided to find our old church which just happens to be three minutes walk away.'

'Oh, so that's what's taken you so long, I might have guessed. You've being praying in church. '

'Well I could not walk past it could I? It's closer than the walk was from Dolly's. Now I know where we are. After we have settled in, I'll pay her a visit.'

We were indeed back on familiar territory, which helped us to settle down more quickly. We had been back nearly a week, it was early April and the War still trundles on, Jack had returned back to camp, Michael was looking for a job, I had letters to write, but my first priority was schooling for Margaret and Joe. I found out there was a school just around the corner, but not a catholic school. St Anne's at Vauxhall was to far away, with the 48 tram stopping almost opposite the house I decided, it would be easier for them to ge back to St. Josephs, if, it was still standing? And if, Mr. Brennan was still alive?

On the Wednesday morning. we set off on our journey, much to the disgust of both of them, but they had to go to school. At West Norwood we caught the 2 bus, we got off at the bottom of Central Hill and Norwood Park fond memories flooded back of pre-war days however they were in the past we went the opposite way up the hill towards the school. Low and behold it was still there,entering through its side gate went down the slope and entered the top part of the school where   Mr Brennan's office was. Knocking on his door an Irish voice called out.

'Please enter.' Opening the door peeked around the edge and saw the familiar face of Mr. Brennan; immediately he recognised me standing up exclaimed.

'Mrs. Plant! Please come in.' I pushed the other two in first. He came around from behind his desk with an extended hand as we shook.

'It's a delight to see you once again. How are all your children? They must be all grown up by now?' We had a good chat about what happened throughout the war. He was still the headmaster. The school had been hit by a bomb but not severely damaged. He accepted both of them to start the following week. I left with the knowledge that they would get a good education whilst they were there. As we were not far from Dick and Edith's, we visited them on the way back. Edith was surprised to see us, Dick was out at work, over a pot of tea, we caught up on the past few years. Percy was in the D' Day landing's he was somewhere in Germany. Dorothy was still in the ATS, somewhere down south. They had weathered the onslaught of the bombs, doodlebugs, and rockets that had rained down on Croydon and the surrounding area. We must have spent an hour or so talking; before Joe reminded me we had to get home. Good news awaited, Michael was fortunate to get a job as a trainee mechanic in an engineering firm in Victoria. That left me with running the household, not a problem to me. However, at that moment in time I was unaware of what lay ahead, for Londoners, amongst the destruction that lay everywhere, their biggest problem was finding sufficient food, to make edible meals for the family, my problem was to sort out, how and wherever you could buy food.

Monday, I was up early to fill the boiler up with water, light fires, before I made them a meagre breakfast. After they had left, I stripped all the bedding to wash in the boiler, using cut pieces of soap for a cleaning agent, swept right through, remade the beds with another set, then went shopping. Wrong move. I was too late. Yes there were some queues that I joined, but soon was turned away. 'No more available.' I was lucky enough to get some basic provisions, for a meagre meal that evening. I felt very despondent as I walked back home, my attempts to begin a new life for us in war torn London was very disappointing, gone was the life of what I only could reflect back on in Bamber Bridge there it had been a far better way of living, whilst here in London it was sheer purgatory and I was sure it would remain as such. Arriving back at the house, opening the door was greeted with the smell of dampness, seeping from every pore of the building that did nothing to help my flagging spirit. I was so low I could have cried. However, I banged shut the door behind me and carried on through to the kitchen, where the smell of boiling clothes somewhat changed my attitude. There was work to be done. Making myself a cup of tea sat down at the table, in the quietness of the house mulled over how I would meet this crisis. The laundry and cleaning was important, but drying with only a tiny back yard was going to be difficult, that chore could be done throughout the week. On the table lay the shopping bag, tipping out its contents, there was little of it, decided that shopping was the number one priority, picking up our four Ration books, scanned the pages began to work out all our allowances, jotting them down as a weekly shopping list. ½ a pound of tea, 1-pound bacon, 1 ½. pounds of butter, ½ pound of lard, 2 pounds of sugar. 6 eggs. 4 shillings and 8 pence worth of meat. As a treat when available, a pot of jam if you could get it. 8 oz's of sweets. Not a lot to feed a family, however I was determined to get the best meals out of what we were allowed.

Sunday would be a meat dinner. Mondays, bubble and squeak with bread, the rest of the days wait and see what was available, but everything would be with bread. Bread pudding without the currants, bread, milk and onions, the tea leaves, could be re-used until there was hardly any taste. Dried egg powder and bacon (if you could get it?) Pie, with potatoes and greens. Michael hated greens and would not eat them at any price, so the other two could have his share, leaving the six eggs for another meal, egg and chips, Friday's boiled fish if available and potatoes with bread. After completing this exercise, this presented a great challenge for me. It was my job to keep the home fires burning. Milk was delivered so for the daily bare essentials bread, foraging around, trying to see what was available from the local shops, inevitably little or nothing. Apart them. I had to start looking further afield for provisions. It would take time, but I was determined to do it and sort out various areas with shops for individual produce whatever was on offer, the other options was fresh fish, for Fridays meal which we had not had for ages, decided Thursdays and Fridays were to be my searching days, which turned out to be cvery frustrating, every shop had queues of women waiting their turn. The longer the queue meant that there was something on offer. You would just join a queue and ask the lady in front.

'What's it for.' She would reply.

'Biscuits' or, whatever was on offer. You either took a chance waiting your turn, hoping the supply would not run out or, leave to join another queue at a shop further up the road. Often you would get at least as far as the shop window, as soon as you saw the shopkeeper or his assistant, leave the counter come out and count the women in front of you. Hold your breath and hope that he would count you in on his sale or. as he put an arm between two ladies he would say. 'Sorry ladies, nothing after this lady.'

In the early days, the queues would disperse. However as time went by, abuse started to flow out from frustrated women, shouts of... She pushed in front of me.' Or. 'Serving your mates only are you? ' ... These scenes were too common and I wouldn't be a bit surprised if fights didn't break out. I heard of them but never saw any. Rumours that cuts of meat were available the next day, had a queue form a couple of hours before the shop opened? Food was a big problem. I like everyone else, would pound the streets looking for something, which I could make into a decent meal, one day having bought potatoes and carrots at Kingston's, I was about to go over to the horseflesh shop, when someone on the opposite side innthe queue hailed me.

'Yoo-hoo. Sarah?'

It was Dolly waving her arms above her head, a beaming face she hailed.

'C'mon over.' She grabbed hold of me, got me into the queue gave me a big embrace then of course the endless chat, we were in the queues for over half an hour before we got served. I promised I would go down and visit her, which I did a few days later.

Good news that the Italians had turned against Mussolini, captured him, shot and hanged him, .whilst In Germany all forces are trying desperately to reach Berlin and capture that "Fella Hitler." The end of the war appeared to be very close. Then three days after Mussollini's death, news that. 'Hitler Dead.' that 'Fella Hitler' had committed suicide. I couldn't believe it was true. Was this the end of the struggle? Nevertheless it was true, how long would it be before the war was finally over? Yet the war in the Far East had not ended. News that Rangoon the Capital of Burma had been recaptured against great opposition. Now the tide has turned. I had not received any letters from Jackie for nearly seven months. I had spoken to Jack about my fears, who in turn had assured me not to worry. If anything had happened, we would be the first to hear about it. No news was good news. I still worried. On May eighth the war was finally declared over in Europe, it was eight days after that "Fella Hitler" suicide before the German army finally surrendered. Then I said my prayers in thanksgiving. The mood was that of jubilation and rejoicing, the War was finished and that people could get back, to the lives they lead before the start of the war.

I began taking the 48 tram to large shopping areas of Herne Hill, Tulse Hill and West Norwood, however in each locality, it was much the same, queues. In West Norwood I ventured into Woolworth's, to meander around, at the lipsticks counter, memories came flooded back of my tribes pinching sprees. I laughed aloud causing the serving girl to look very quizzically at me as if I was deranged from the bombing, hurriedly I left, but pleased something had touched a funny nerve, somehow it gave me more strength. In each of the three areas, I found which shops would be the most liable source, returning home with a different variety whale meat that did not go down very well. Nevertheless, I had other places to go to. I walked to Brixton Market, but with the crowds, it seemed like half of South London had the same idea. The following week I went to visit mother in Vauxhall to see how she was getting on, did she need any help with her shopping from the open market in Wilcox Road. However Mother was in fine fettle.

'C'mon in Allahnah. I'll make you a cup of tea.'

We talked, laughed over old times. I told Mother of my plans to sort out the best shops and asked her if she wanted any shopping. She let out a roar.

'Be japers, Allahnah, there's nothing in that market except queues. Waste of blithering time.' Then cupping my hand in-between hers she whispered...'Now Sarah Allahnah all my food I get from Fox's. A little gold mine, that it is. Somehow they have nice things'...She, raising one eyebrow....'Mind you it's all on ration.' This little bit of information interested me.

'Where is this shop Mother? Why the secrecy?'

'Aah. Allahnah now we don't want everyone to know about that. Do we?'

'Why you telling me then?'

'Allahnah. Yus ave sparrow mouths to feed, and yus are the one telling me yus cannot get hardly anything. Yus go, see for yourself. Yus cannot miss it Allahnah. Go past the school next door, turn left yus will see it opposite the Builders Arms pub, they are the only things standing amongst piles of the rubble.'... she began pulling me up...'Away with you, and buy me some mints. Here take my ration book.'

I had no choice I walked around to this little shop., true to her word saw standing on one corner was the pub, on the opposit corner, surrounded by heaps of rubble stood a shop, mothers. "Gold Mine." A sole reminder of the destruction caused by one bomb. I walked to the shop, joined the end of the queue, gradually moved along entering into a tiny. 'L' shaped counter, with many shelves behind it. Quickly I surveyed the contents. Jam, soap, biscuits, tea, coffee, tins of this and that, but no sugar, this little place was indeed Aladdin's Cave.

The woman behind the counter was about my age, smartly turned out with a bandana tied around her hair, a pencil was stuck behind her ear, she asked.

'Good afternoon what can we do for you?' I ventured.

'Um. Have you got any sugar. please?'

'Can I have your ration book?'

I handed over one of mine. She looked curiously at the front.

'Sorry you don't live around here. Can't serve you.'

Quickly I sorted out Mothers. Offered it saying.

'Sorry I gave you the wrong ration book.' Glancing at the address.

'Oh! You shopping for Old Ma Cunningham?'

'Yes. I'm her eldest daughter.'

'Oh that's different then. She's all right. Tough 'ole one that one, but a heart of gold. How is she? I can let you have half a pound with your two books.' She offered. I thought: *In for a penny might as well be a pound*. 'Can you spare a pound? I have more, three other books.' Quickly providing the others.

'Well seeing it's your Mother, we can do that for you.'

Bending slightly to her right from under the counter she produced a blue coloured 1lb. bag of sugar. I thought. *So that's where they kept it*. A man entered through the doorway from behind the counter with some more provisions to stack up. He cheerfully called out.

'Afternoon ladies.'

'Afternoon. Mr. Fox. Wotcha got on offer today then?'

'Nothing much. You all right to-day?'

'Yerse. Ear. Mrs Fox. Yer' ole man's a right one ain't he?' The woman behind me quipped as Mr. Fox retreated through the doorway. Presumably, the woman serving was Mrs. Fox. She prompted.

428

'Anything else?' This opportunity I was not going to miss.

'Some biscuits, Jam, soap, two tins of carnation milk, two tins of condensed milk, and some other things I cannot remember, but all were precious to me. She queried'

'Can you pay for all this lot?' I politely answered.

'Yes I have the money.' Removing the pencil from behind her ear.

'Let's have all your ration books then.' Very quickly I handed them over, she marked off the amount of rations I was allowed saying.

'You have two oz's left on this one. Do you want to make it up with sweets for your children?' She offered.

'If that's all right.'

'Yes that's all right. It is Mrs. Cunningham isn't it?' She was prompting me

'Er. That's right.' I was accepted, she called out.'Two ozs of sweets for Ole Ma Cunningham.' She totted the sums up. Mr. Fox entered with a brown paper bag.

'There you are two ozs of Mint Imperial's...That will be five shillings and two pence halfpenny please.' Handing over the money. I thanked her, bade her good day as she called out.

'Your very welcome come again Mrs. Cunningham. Give our regards to your Mother. Next please.'

With my shopping bag near full. I left the shop, overjoyed at my purchases and at mothers insistence. 'To see for yourself.' When I informed her of my priceless gains and the fair deal, I had been afforded at Fox's. all because of Mother's name. I presented her with the Mint Imperials. She asked with a twinkle in her eyes.

'How did you know. Wooo- I liked them?'

'I didn't. Mr. Fox gave them to me. '

'Ah. He knows. He is a nice man. I'm well in there along with a few other shopkeepers. I don't take any buck from them and they enjoy my chattering.' she chuckled.

'Look Mother next time I come down I'll do your shopping and bring Margaret and Joe to see you. Take them along to Fox's. So they will be known as your grandchildren.' She looked at me with a furrowed brow.

'That will be nice to see them two brats of yours I don't want that brat Joe. taking my digestive biscuits.' She added. 'Now you hear, you tell him from me.' Aware of the rapid improvement of her condition I questioned.

'Mother. What has happened to your wind? You don't do it so much now.'

'Aah well now Allahnah, that was brought on by indigestion; I got through the blasted bombs.'

I laughed at the thought of her eating bombs, but I knew what she meant. I left her happy sucking her Mint Imperials. On the way home with my goodies, I was pleased with my recent forage and thought up a plan of shopping sprees. I arrived home before them, presented them with, buttered bread, smeared with jam, along with two biscuits each. A real luxury. Margaret asked.

'Where did you get this Mum?' Her question had me thinking: *On their way home from school they could do some shopping at West Norwood and Tulse Hill.*

'If you want any more of that, I'll take the pair of you shopping, show you where you can get these things. This Friday I will meet you outside your school okay?'

They did not appear to mind that suggestion.

I met them on the Friday afternoon. First thing I took them back to see Mrs. Candler. To see if she had survived the war? Maiking a slight detour, walked past number 70 that had been repaired. Memories of that dreadful night came flooding back, so I hurried them up towards Mrs. Candler's. Margaret and Joe had already knocked on the door when the yelps of a dog stopped. As the door was opened by Mrs Candler. Juby wagged his tail in greeting. Seeing us stood on her doorstep, she burst into tears. As they rolled down her cheeks; we were dragged in, sat down. The tea flowed. Maisie and Irma had married. Maisie to an American and Irma to a Canadian, both had left England. She informed me they too had applied to immigrate to Canada and would soon be on their way. Then it was my turn to bid them farewell. I left her promising to get the rest of my tribe up to see them before they left.

We caught the 2 bus down to West Norwood, where at the United Dairies the first shop of their intended shopping route, I bought half a dozen eggs, then walked to Tulse Hill and bought fish for Friday, then caught the 48 tram home. Early Saturday mornings, for them it was down to the Junction with me, to queue at David Greigs for bacon and any meat available, if not onto Thurtles to buy horsemeat. They did not like the smell. At Kinston's we queued for vegetables. The following week I took them down to visit mother and introduce them to Fox's. I accompanied them on all these shopping trips. They were frustrating and took a long time queuing for specific items. Nevertheless, that way of shopping, you were recognised as a regular and got served. The variety of provisions obtained provided some variety of meals. Joe's only other chore was taking the battery down to the bike shop, to get it recharged. The summer school holidays began. Then it was time for them to take over. Their reward sweets and jam sandwiches.

The rationing was to say the least, a necessary pain, the queues seemed to get longer and longer. Margaret and Joe spent more time out further afield on their shopping expeditions, whilst I shopped locally, so we covered all areas. My early shopping plan had reaped the benefits of choice. However, everyone was doing the same thing. Lena, Wally and Pat had moved not far from us into a house in Rolls Court Avenue off Red Post Hill. On Sunday after Mass, she and Dolly would chat about where you could buy, this, that and anything on offer. Lena told me that one of her friends. June and her husband Reg owned a wet fish shop in Tulse Hill. I should go and buy my fish from them. I told her.

'I have been buying from their shop for ages.'

'Well next time you go, speak to June. Tell her you're my elder sister. She'll see you all right.' Informed with this piece of chat, Joe on his next visit to the fish shop on his way home from school. announced who his Aunt was, he came home with extra fish. If you were a regular customer at most shops, the shopkeepers would pass the word to them.

'Tell your Mum. I'm getting such and such on Wednesday. Does she want any?'
They would come home tell me. It did not matter what it was they always said. 'Yes.' Kennedy's the meat pie shop down at Herne Hill, began making sausages for sale- Only on Saturday's and only half a pound per family. They opened their doors sharp at eight o' clock. Two weeks running the pair of them came home with nothing and a woeful tale.

'Sausages sold out by half past eight.'

So to be first in the queue on a Saturday they had to be down waiting at Kennedy's, an hour before opening time. All to buy half a pound each. Hail rain or shine I got them up at 6. 30 in the morning, to catch the ten -minute to seven tram opposite. As a treat Joe would run down to the paper shop just around the corner and collect the Film Fun and Dandy comics, to read while they were in the queue. I threatened them.

'You're not brother and sister. Never speak to one another in the queue. If you do. I'll thrash you when you get home.' They must have done as they were told. They always arrived home armed with two half-pounds of sausages. Another meal solved.

That was only the start of Joe's Saturday shopping chores. To earn his pocket money, he as well as Margaret, like all the rest of my tribe, carried on with the tradition of shopping for the family. After Kennedy's he would go to Thurtles queue for horsemeat for us and Mrs. Bushnell down the road. She gave him sixpence pocket money. On his way back he would queue up at the bakers for the freshly baked bread. Then off to brixton market to buy whatever cheap vegetable bargains were available. Those items were the only things not rationed. But oranges or any foreign fruits were, or whatever the Costermongers were selling. Even they imposed their own way of rationing, by restricting the number or by weight you could purchase. The food chain appeared to be getting worse not better.

Every night, after Michael came home was the time that he and Joe, disappeared up to their bedroom at the top of the house with its two box windows. They became goal areas. It was an ideal indoor football pitch. Their football, a tied up sock full of paper. This was their haven, where every night The Cup Final was re-enacted. Michael was Arsenal and Joe, Preston N.E. The thumps, bangs and shouts, which echoed from the top room resounding throughout the house, were too much for me.

Then it was election time. The Coalition Government that had served during the war was disbanded. Blue and Red posters soon appeared in the front room windows. Vote for Conservative. Vote for Labour. With what everyone had endured and suffered throughout the war everyone was fed up and disillusioned. The miners, dockworkers, you name them were restless. It was time for a change. By the end of July the Labour party were voted in. After all the good work Churchill had done, he resigned.

Early in August, came the terrible news. An Atom bomb had been dropped on the city of Hiroshima with devastating effect. This was followed three days later by another Atom bomb on the city of Nagasaki, and masses of civilians had been killed. On Wednesday the 15th. I was listening to the wireless, when the news reported that the Japanese had unconditionally surrendered on the 14th and a two-day holiday had been granted. To mark the victory over Japan. What a celebration that was everybody out shouting and waving flags. The pubs overflowed with revellers. I just prayed to God that after all the fighting was over. Jackie would get home safe and sound. Late the same day, Tommy arrived to tell me, his Grandmother had had an accident and had been taken into St. Thomas's Hospital. I dropped everything I was doing. Told Margaret and Joe about their Granny. To stay where they were in doors and tell Michael when he came home, to take over until I got back. Then left with Tommy to get there as quickly as possible. I arrived at the hospital and did get into see her. Mother was unconscious with her head swathed in bandages. Peg, Julia and Fan were sat at her bedside. Soon after me Bridget arrived. We were told that she had slipped on some fat in the Butcher's and hit her head on the Butchers Block. Bridget and I stayed the night at the hospital. In the morning the Doctor examined her and said she. 'Was stable. A tough old girl. Just wait and see.'

However, the situation didn't look too good. When Fan and Julia arrived back. Bridget and I left. On the third day after her fall, Mother had developed a clot and slipped into a coma, then she died. We were all in a state of shock at her sudden demise. She has lived through all the bombing, only to finally end her life, by slipping on a mere piece of fat. Was beyond belief. We all decide, no grandchildren would attend the funeral, and as a compliment to her upbringing. Mother's Hearse would be by a horse drawn hearse. A method long since gone from being used in London.

Jack being available took it upon himself, to make the necessary funeral arrangements. The Hearse carriage was not too much of a problem, it was the horses. Somehow through his contacts in the Terriers. Jack managed to obtain a team of black horses. On the day of the funeral I was shocked to see Lena, turn up in a Pink outfit along with a friend nobody knew, that was not taken lightly by any of us. Then Kitty's son Kevin the only grandchild to turn up, that caused more ruction amongst all of us, sadly we buried Mother, as she would have liked to go, drawn by horse's, the animals she loved and cared for. I believe it was the last one of its kind in London. The only other horse drawn carts in everyday use were. The Milkman's and Dustcarts with their big Dray Horses, which later disappeared off the streets.

On the 20th. August another news report stated, that a Japanese army force have finally surrendered to the Russians in Manchuria China. That meant the war was finally over.

431

Jack returned back to Bamber Bridge to be officially demobbed from the Army on August 30th. A few days later he returned looking entirely different dressed in a demob suit. His leaving present from the army after 28 years' service. I was more than happy for him and the family. He had always been their figurehead and done more than his fair share. I told him so.

'Jack, now you leave it to the youngsters.'

He just grinned, but in his heart he knew his Army days were finally over. Dickie Fox was posted out to Germany, leaving Peg in a small flat down in Coronation Buildings at Vauxhall. Jack started work at Victoria Sorting Office as a Supervisor. Unfortunately Jack's change from service life to civilian life. became a big wrench. He did his job and would be home by mid-afternoon with nothing to do. He would help out with the normal household chores and go out shopping for whatever he could get hold of. He then acquired a second job, cleaning cars in a garage. As far as he was concerned, he had to be fully occupied. On his way home he would call in the Milkwood Tavern for a quick pint. It was in there that he met up with the Towner's, another family that lived in Heron Road. Bill Towner had been demobbed from the Navy, and became a constant companion to Jack. Both would put the world to rights over a pint. Jack invited me to go down on a Saturday night to meet Bill's wife Lil. When I did agree I met her. A charming person, they were typical Londoners. Fed up with their lot, but happy to have a sing and drink down the local. It transpired that Margaret and Joe had become great friends of their daughter Lily and son Maurice, they used to play together in the street. At least the kids seemed happy. On Sundays after mass. Bert and Jack would meet outside, and Dolly, would keep me standing there. Chatting for hours if she could. I would excuse myself.

'Dolly, must fly. Got the dinner in the oven.' Leaving Jack to walk down with Bert and Dolly, to Bert's local the 'Cambridge.'

Life seemed to pass by so quickly in this drab place, with Jackie still in the Far East. I was not aware of his whereabouts and whether he was dead or alive. One thing I clung too was if the worst was to happen. God forbid. I would be informed by telegram. A letter from Mary informed me, she was being released from the Sanatorium in Halifax.

Jack and I were both were delighted at the prospects of having her back home with us. So we made up her room next door to ours, making it as comfortable as possible. Jack met her at King's Cross and brought her home. The last time I had visited her was before we moved to London. Then she looked pale but in reasonable good health and spirits, so I was expecting an improvement. When they did arrive, I was shocked to see the state of her very tired and drawn after the train journey, it was her first time out anywhere. I was worried about her condition, and got her into bed to rest for a few days to feed her up with whatever I could. I got Dr Smyth to come home and check her over. Slowly lying in bed she gained strength and made doily mats out of cotton on a set of wooden frames, which was all she could really do, nevertheless Margaret and Joe were always up to something always arguing, fighting and running up and down the stairs. I would take her in a cup of tea to wet her lips. One day she said to me.

'Mum. can't you stop those two making such a noise. It's bad enough when Michael gets home and he starts playing football with Joe.' My answer to Mary was.

'Mary you're a fine one to talk about all their antics. When you were their age you were the ringleader. They are angels compared to you. Do you remember the time when!'

We both would reminisce for ages about the old times in India, killing ourselves with laughter. The antics of Margaret and Joe totally forgotten. I did enjoy those little breaks as a welcome reward.

However I would get Jack to put a stop to their racket. He would shout up the stairs.

'Come on you two. That's enough now.' Back down would come their reply.

'It's a draw. We have to have a winner. Until the next goal. All right Dad?'

432

Jack would call out something. They played on. Twenty minutes later or even a half hour would pass by. The racket was still ongoing. Not one but many goals were scored during that period. This happened every night, until Jack went up and blew the final whistle, much to their disgust. Their football season never ended until Michael went into the Army a couple of years later. In those early days just after the war, football was a sport that every man and boy, went to watch the professional games being played in London and other cities. On a Saturday afternoon, the grounds would be packed to capacity. Jack and Joe would be out of the house, from eleven o' clock and come home late either frozen stiff or soaked through. Michael another keen footballer together with his cousin Pat Thomas had joined St Anne's Club youth club in the Settlement Vauxhall in the early part of 1945 when Michael was staying down in London. It was a club where all the cousins went to and it became a meeting place for the "gathering of the clans."

Michael and Pat played for the team every Sunday afternoon on pitches such as Clapham Common, Brockwell Park plus others. They were good and had spectators coming from far and wide to watch their matches. They became a very formidable side winning several cups at the end of the season. The winter months finally succumbed to summer times, which turned out to be a glorious one very hot. Michael like his father was keen on athletics, so at the start of the Athletics season, he ran for the Club.

At last I received a Forces letter from Jackie in Palembang the Dutch East Indies. They had joined forces with the Dutch clearing out the Japs. It was such a relief. At least he was alive and well. In the October to add to the existing problem of acquiring food, the Dockers came out on strike. The troops were called in to handle the imports at the docks. This went on for seven weeks until an agreement was reached. During that period, it became harder to get any provisions and the queues became longer. Winter had set in.

Being regulars attending Sunday mass, Father Dodd suggested Joe, should become an Alter boy. As Jackie and Michael had done their stint. I saw no objections for Joe not to do it. He learnt Latin and became one of the servers at the daily 7 o'clock Mass. before he went to school. Christmas 1945 he was chosen to serve at Mid-night Mass and the church was packed. Jack came in late from the pub and in front of me, took a place kneeling down between the front row pews and the Alter. Halfway through the service, at the Offertory, a very silent part of the Mass the bells sounded, but all you could hear was snoring. Jack had dozed off, someone shook him awake. What I wasn't going to do to him, when I got him home was no bodies business. Nevertheless Joe and his mate Ginger could not stop giggling the rest of their responses to the Priest were said through giggles. I was fuming. Christmas or no Christmas, when we all got back home Jack and Joe, got a good telling off. Jack for snoring, Joe for giggling. For our Christmas dinner Jack managed to get a chicken, but no Christmas pudding.

The winter of 1945 extended well into 1946. It was bitterly cold, with heavy falls of snow. However we were to experience further cuts in rationing. Almost taking us back to war-time cuts and of all things. Bread was rationed, yet a further blow to our flagging existence meant additional queuing for Margaret and Joe. They would arrive home, blue with the cold, their legs chapped from the wind, rain, and snow. I did feel sorry for the pair of them, and in an effort to beat the shortage I decided to make Soda Bread without currants. Then Whale meat appeared on the Butchers slab, we tried it but nobody liked it, that was something even I drew the line at. Like thousands of others, just about surviving and to make the meals go further, proportions got smaller. At least, Margaret and Joe had school dinners, but they grumbled about those. In Joe sentiments.

' Yuk! Do we have to have school dinner Mum? They're 'orrible. My mate Stanley, sicked up at the table, the smell was 'orrible, we all ran.'

Regardless of Joe's excuses. They still had school dinners.

My concern over Mary grew. She was very frail and not well at all. Lena's, Christian mothers group, had planned a trip to Lourdes. She suggested that maybe Mary could go with them? I talked it over with Jack and Mary. Would she like to go? In desperation she agreed. During the trip Lena and Mrs. Clinton would be Mary's chaperone. After the weeklong trip. She arrived back from Lourdes. not cured but certainly stronger and appeared better for her experience. Dr. Smyth checked her over and in her opinion. No worse off, but far better in spirit.

Early in June the planned Victory Parade took place. To mark the Victory. The regulars of the Milkwood Tavern had collected monies in preparations for a Children's street parties in Heron Road. Buntings appeared and houses were daubed with painted V.E. V.J. and V. for Victory. All the old servicemen donned their Service Uniforms. Jack wore his Blues, possibly the last time

he was to wear it. The day was a clear sunny day and a great time was had by all. Also to mark the occasion. A special award was given by HM the King to every schoolboy and girl in schools a signed message with a little gold coloured medal to mark their participation during the London Blitz. The following in day we attended a firework display, a big one down at Vauxhall Embankment, where they attached fireworks to a Bailey bridge crossing the river Thames in front of the Tate Gallery.

As the heat of summer grew everyone from far and wide. Made for the open-air swimming pool at Brockwell Park. Even there, you had to queue up to get in, and that was only for a half hour session. When they came out they just re-joined the queue. It was always packed. Kaye would go with her then current boyfriend Cyril. Michael, Margaret and Joe with their friends and Tommy, who stayed with us during the school holidays. In the afternoon's, even I went along with Jack, who used to have a quick dip. Tommy who himself had developed into a fine swimmer. (Most likely after all the ducking's he took from Margaret years before). Was in the St Anne's swimming team. Somehow it got around to him challenging Jack to a race. Who took the bait and the race was on. Joe started the race? After three false starts. Jack won the race but not by much. He came back to me with that big grin all over his face. Puffing like mad and happy as a sand boy, they shook hands and Jack said.

'Thank you Tommy that was a quick race. You're a fine swimmer keep it up.'

It wasn't the last time Jack went for a swim. St Anne's Club organised an outing for all the families. Six to eight Charabangs would make their way down to Bracklesham Bay near Selsey, for a day's fun by the sea. The cost was little, so we joined in with all the other families. Fan, Julia, Bridget. There Jack used to go for a swim in the sea. Life in London seemed to be getting back to normal. The four local bomb sites, three in Heron Road, and the one in Lowden Road, had been cleared to erect prefabricated houses, to re-house families. Much to the annoyance of all the local children, who used the sites as happy hunting grounds, building camps from the remnants of timbers and doors that littered the areas? If a tree was still standing, a tree top camp was erected, how they did it I shall never know?

On the food front. Things began to brighten up. More food was gradually appearing. queues would still form and people were not being turned away, so stopped the squabbling although, more varieties of food started to appear in the shops, at first in small quantities. Bananas went on sale to make them go around. One pound only per family. To share them around. I made Banana Custard. Limited quantities of dried fruit; currants sultana's, figs, and dates began to appear, which provided Sunday with steamed puddings of Spotted Dick, Date puddings, and Soda Bread. With these little infrequent extras, one had to improvise and make it go a long way. It appeared we had got over the worst, but I was not convinced.

But dark clouds were looming once again this time it was with Russia. The allied countries having fought against the Germans could not come to any sensible agreement about the division of Occupied Germany, it all seemed senseless to me. Nevertheless, their disagreement on the 9th.October. Marked the beginning of the Cold War. However at home, we had our own daily war to fight, existing on the meagre ration of available food. We got the house wired up to electricity doing away will the fragile gas mantles? So Jack rented a Radio, our first electric appliance, which pleased Joe, no more batteries to exchange. However like everyone else in the road, Joe became an ardent listener to a new serial "Dick Barton.". Every night at quarter to seven, the road would miraculously become empty until a quarter of an hour later, precisely at seven o'clock the road would be full of boys. reacting the episode they had heard.

Then Mary caught a cold, to keep her warm. I lit the fire in her bedroom, she refused anything to eat even the soup I offered. I sent Joe down to the chemist, for Doctor Smythe's prescribed medicine however, after a fit of coughing she just lay there, drained of any strength. I was so worried. The household became strangely quiet, as the evening progressed her cough got worse turned into pneumonia. I felt helpless inside my own body, knowing my poor child was gradually slipping away from me. I spent the whole night by her bed we prayed soundlessly together, just the murmur of her uneasy and laboured breathing. Early in the morning I heard Jack go to work, leaving the house quietly soon followed by Kaye. I kept my vigil. Almost an hour later a couple of knocks on the door, had me down to open it. Kaye arrived back home, she whispered.

'Mum. I kept crying at work. The Inspector came in and asked what was wrong?'

'My sister is dying.' He sent me home'. We returned to Mary's room. Not long after, Jack arrived back and came up to sit in with us. He just said.

'Kaye. Go and wake up the rest of them. Feed them and get them out of the house.'

She left without saying anything. Michael Margaret and Joe came in to kiss Mary. All said they would see her when they come home. I lit some candles, Mary had brought back from Lourdes, we prayed with Mary. I felt her cold hand on mine, she quietly murmured.

'Don't worry Mum. Everything will be all right."

Then closed her eyes, her lips moving as she quietly prayed to herself. I knew of her concern. In the Sanatorium of other girls at the end had haemorrhaged. I prayed as I have never prayed before. God please let her have her wish to die peacefully. After what seemed an age her breathing trailed off. I looked up to see my poor baby had gone. The three of us broke down

435

and cried helplessly. I told them both to leave me with her. I thought my heart would break as I brushed her hair for the last time. My tears falling freely on her face, wiped them away kissed her cold lips. Bade farewell. Unfortunately, Mary had left me years ago, all that lay before me, was the husk of my wild untameable, Irish spirited girl. She gone forever.

I withdrew the blinds to reveal a wet dismal November morning. Such as only London provides to dampen your spirit and blight your soul. Quietly Jack and Kaye returned, I grabbed hold of Kaye and guided her out as Jack said his personal goodbyes. I heard his suppressed anguish spill out over his eldest daughter. Twenty five years old. Gone forever. He stayed for some time before he came out his face was grey and drawn, he said nothing. Kaye and I returned, washed her, and laid her out, lighting more candles around her bed. Before leaving her in peace. I went into our bedroom where Jack was staring out of the window, for the first time in my life I said to him.

'Come on soldier on your feet, make some tea. I want you to go to the Priest and also inform the Nuns, and when your out go and tell doctor smythe she has to be informed.'

He dusted his nose with his handkerchief he had been given orders. He quietly left the house, then Kaye and I both set to and started work. The best way to grieve quietly, is on your own and while you work keep your hands busy. We both spring-cleaned the house from top to bottom. Father Dodd and two Nun's arrived, we entered her peace to pray as the Priest administered the holy oils. Before they left we arranged the date of the funeral. After they had left Jack arrived back with Doctor Smythe she had to sign Mary's death certificate I got Jack to write a letter to Jackie and one to Kitty and Bobby invite them down for the funeral. When Margaret and Joe came home from school, when I told them that Mary had gone we all cried together I brushed away my tears, waited for Michael to get home from work he could go down to Vauxhall and inform all of Mary's death, he could also take Margaret and Joe down to their aunt Julia's to stay until after the funeral,.arriving home he went straight up to her room. After he came down. I gave the three of them something to eat before they left. I did not sleep that night instead concentrated on baking cakes, making sandwiches for the expected arrival of the families, to offer their condolences. Very late I crawled into bed and called Mary to me, she came and we talked, we even laughed about old times. Later whenever I was worried. I only had to call on Mary and she would be there in spirit to help me to get over whatever was my worry. With this personal contact I had with her, I was able to get through that dreadful week until after the funeral. Kitty and Bobby arrived the day before the funeral. I found solace and comfort with Kitty and Bobby, who stayed on after the funeral. It never dawned on Jack or I, the influence Mary held over our tribe. Gone was their leader, but she had left her mark on all of them. It took a very long time for them to come to terms with their individual loss. In my mind, I placed Mary's death solely on the dampness of the house, told Jack.

'I wished to God. We never stepped a foot in this house. I wish we were out of here.'

He nodded he knew of my concern, but he was always applying to be re-housed. Always receiving the same answer. 'Mr. Plant. You're on the list.' Nevertheless, the Council arrived to fumigate out Mary's room. Sealed it up including the windows and doors with tape. It lasted two weeks until they came back and reopened the room. Every time I went past that room I blessed myself.

Kaye found another job with the Greyhound Racing Association (GRA) as it was called. It provided more money and a nine to five job. Another blessing in disguise, which helped to release the anguish we had all felt since the loss of Mary. Being in that job Kaye was able to get complimentary tickets. To Ice Hockey at Harringey Arena. Although as a mother, this did nothing to replace my loss, but it gave us the outlet, which she would have wanted us to have. By this time Margaret and her friend Lily Towner, attended the Fidelis Convent. They became avid followers of the Harringey Racers Ice Hockey Team. After one night's shouting and cheering for the Racers. She arrived home with a discarded hockey stick of her favourite player with his name "Wynn Cook" printed on it on it. What a trophy that was for her. She treasured it. However much later.it did cause a problem. Just before Christmas Kaye came home with complimentary tickets to see the Tom Arnolds Circus. What a spectacular display that was. But Christmas that year was one we all wanted to forget. To add to our recent distress, the dreadful winter of 1946/47 began with a white Christmas, it stayed until about the mid March. The snow lay thick everywhere and it became unbearably cold, it even froze up Big Ben. Striking miners caused more misery with no coal, there were power cuts therefore no lighting only candles. These strikes seemed to becoming more frequent as the winter progressed. The house was frozen, there was nothing to do except retire early. After school Joe who had acquired an old pram without rubber from a bombsite pushed it to Brixton market to collect any old wooden boxes for firewood he would return home with boxes piled high, tied up with string to keep them from falling off, unloading them he would go out again, to collect tarry block from tram road works. Very good items to burn, however not so good was the smell of tar and the mess. I did not complain at least it was fuel to provide some warmth to a cold and damp house I hated so much? Tommy arrived to imform me that the Vauxhall Gas Works were selling rationed coke, one hundred weight per week per family. Good news but we needed at least double, that amount to keep the house warm. It was a long way to go just for one bag of coke but w did need it . Saturday morning Joe set off in the snow pushing his chariot down to the gas works, he was away for hours, however, with the aid of Tommy's mates, they joined Joe in the queue, became his next door neighbours, to buy an extra bag. He was happy with that arrangement pushing two cwts and only one trip to make. I'll never know how the pram managed it, with all the loads it used to carry, yet the pram, 'his chariot,' lasted out until we finally left number 56.

One Friday night in January, we were in bed fast asleep when a loud banging on the front door woke us up. Jack went down to see who was making the infernal noise. I heard voices and someone come in, then the sound of heavy boots coming up the stairs. I just knew it was Jackie my heart started beating quickly, I was partly out of bed when in burst Jackie.

'Mum. It's me Jackie. I'm home.'I grabbed hold of him to hug him, his great coat was covered in snow that made my arms wet. I was crying with relief with him arriving home in the early hours of the morning, against mine his face was so cold, he must have been frozen to the marrow. Our reunion was in the pitch darkness. I said.

'Thank God your home son. Your freezing look, find your way back down stairs I think your fathers making some tea.'

'He said he would, he told me where you were, so here I am.'

'We have no lights, so find your way down your Dad must have some candles alight. Go on down then I'll wake the others up.' I got my coat off the top of the bed and slipped it over my shoulders, as I guided him out onto the landing pointed the way down stairs, he clumped back down the stairs, I went into Kaye's room, who had taken over Mary's bedroom. Excitedly I said.

'Jackie's home. Go and wake the others up, bring them downstairs.' Startled by the news she exclaimed. 'Jackie where downstairs?'

'Down with your father hurry up.' I retraced my steps out going back into the bedroom removed a blanket off the bed, I heard her going upstairs to wake up the rest of them. With the blanket over my shoulder I groped my way down stairs, into the kitchen, where Jack was busy raking the fire, trying to get some warmth out of the embers. Some candles were already alight on the table. In their meagre glow I saw the tanned grinning face of Jackie. I put the blanket around his shoulders sat him down at the table. The others came charging in to the kitchen and showered him with hugs and kisses. In a vain effort to warm him up, more candles were lit and placed on the table. It was wonderful to see him sitting there shivering with a huge grin spread across his brown face. Everyone was asking questions. Tea was made the gas rings were left alight to give added warmth. Without any heating the house was freezing cold, he had arrived at two a.m. Jack said. 'The best place for you son is in bed. We'll all talk in the morning. When you have thawed out.' We all trooped behind him carrying candles up into the top room. I urged.

'Just get into bed as you are Son.'

Removing his gaiters took of his boots still in his uniform he got into bed. I made Margaret and Joe get into bed with him to keep him warm. A few hours later Jack got up to go to work with all the excitement of a couple hours before I couldn't sleep so got up with him. Jack got the fire going, on the stove top boiled water in the kettle. I made tea, Jack took Jackie up a cup to warm him up, then he left for work. I sat there to say a few prays of thanks thinking: *Of what food we had for his breakfast? As it was Saturday it was sausage day, the only thing we could purchase off ration, a weekly chore for Margaret and Joe. They had to be down in the queue very early.so at the appropriate time.* I got them up made another pot of tea and took Jackie up another tea. In the bedroom all four of them were already awake. By the light of two candles the glow on their faces was something to behold,as they listened to Jackie telling them tales he said..

'Morning Mum.'

'Morning Son. Come on you two you have to go to Kennedy's Sorry Son. But we haven't got much food. Would you go with Margaret and Joe down to Kennedy's? To buy some sausages. Remember. You are not with them and no talking to them either. You ask for a full pound. As you have only just arrived back.' He asked.

'Why?'

'They will tell you on the way down.. Otherwise they won't be able to purchase their ration of half a pound each.' He found this very funny, but agreed to go with my suggestion. He had to see this for himself. At five to seven they are off to catch the tram. Jackie in uniform with his Bush hat on. I waited anxiously for their return with the spoils. Michael left for work as I made up the fire in the top bedroom to keep it warm and made up the one in the front room where the old piano was. Just in case? When they arrived back, they trooped in through the front door. all were cold, it was snowing again. Jackie was laughing his head off I gave him a cup of tea as he related what it was all about.

'Mum. Is it always like that? When we got there two people were already in front. We joined the queue, soon the queue formed very quickly, within minutes it disappeared around the corner. A Cockney behind me, got chatting to me, he wanted to know where I had come from. With my bush hat on and S.E.A.C. Burma flashes. I told him the gory side of it. Eight o'clock the shop opened, we moved up to the counter. Margaret and Joe got their ration and left, I asked for five pounds please.'....The Butcher shouted.....'Here mate. Who do you think you are? Half a pound only each family.' ...The Cockney behind him shouts back... 'You bleeding give it to him. He's just come back home from fighting the Japs out in Burma to keep you bleeding well safe. So you can rob us.'...'Then others joined in, shouting at him. The Butcher saw a riot was about to break out and gave me five pounds. Good Eh?'

He placed his five-pound worth on the table besides Margaret and Joe's, tiny parcels Joe left do his normal Saturday chores. We would eat after he came back. My problem was cooking the sausages the stove was not hot enough I had used the remnants of the coke on the other fires so the coke was all gone, another chore Joe had to do. it was going to be slow cooking with only a low gas Another chore Joe was due to do that morning. Jackie couldn't wait. From out of his kit bag he produced a round tin with a folded up tripod wrapped around the inside of the tin, with some round white tablets. Said it was a Tommy Cooker, they used in the jungle when they were lucky enough to stop for food, setting up this tiny contraption placed a white tablet in the middle lit it with a match, soon the blue heat from the white tablet was intense. On went the frying pan and in went some sausages. Joe arrived back with some fresh bread. We had the most wonderful picnic breakfast of sausages. Jackie's first sausages for years.

438

We sat there agog, as he related tale after tale, made us all laugh. about their homeward journey on the ship. All of them on board had heard about the big freeze up in Britain, even the people in Suez had become shivering wrecks, from their unexpected cold weather. Jackie said he prayed that there might be snow still on the ground. Joe left on his way to get the coke, so I sent Jackie back up to bed to keep warm, he slept for hours.

Although on disembarkation leave, he had to return to Colchester to be demobbed. However Jack advised him about the strikes, the shortage of generally everything. Disillusioned, he took his Fathers advice volunteers for service in Germany. He wrote to me from Germany giving his address etc., Jack looked it up on the map discovered his posting was not far from Dickie Fox who was serving on a War Grave Commission in Dusseldorf, Peg was out there with him, fortunately Jackie got posted to a unit not far from his aunt and uncle. It wasn't until late March the snows finally disappeared, winter turned into spring causing wide spread floods and more cuts in food rationing and a countrywide shortage of potatoes, rationed at three pounds per week. I found a substitute powder called POM. I served it as roast potatoes, made potatoes cakes and mashed it with corned beef as and when available. The Butcher would ask.

'Something extra this week Mrs. P?' As soon as he said that. You knew he had some tinned meat either Corned Beef or Spam on offer. Never ever refuse, take whatever is on offer.

I had joined the Mother's Guild at St Anne's, who had arranged a ten-day trip to Lourdes. Still grieving the loss of Mary, who had told me about it, more out of curiosity and dedication. I wanted to see Lourdes for myself. Jack said.

'You go. We have enough able bodies here.'

We travelled by coach then train, stayed for a week in Lourdes. There I reflected upon the change in Mary after she arrived back. Both having shared the same experience, possibly my feelings were similar to hers. But Joe the youngest, just like Mary used to be was always up to something he should not be doing I was constantly on my guard against what would happen next. It wasn't long after my trip. I received a letter from Mr Brennan. Joe's Headmaster. Advising me. Joe and three of his pals had volunteered to go out to Africa to help with the Missionary work of the Silesian Brothers. Apparently they had all been so enthralled with the talk, by one of the Brothers at the school, they went to St Joseph's College and volunteered their services. They were taken in given some tea and cakes, told to come back later in about six years' time! He being an Altar boy, had also been chosen to hold the Bishops Mitre at a confirmation at our local church I ensured he was scrubbed clean warning him not to get dirty. We all attended the service, from inside the vestry the Altar boys walked out onto the alter. Joe with a white silk stole around his neck with his comrade in arms Ginger, swinging the incense burner. Followed by the entourage of Priests and Bishop. The ceremony proceeded and the Bishops Mitre was removed. Joe moved into position, ready with the silk stole to receive the Mitre. I proudly watch then horror, I saw his hands black with dirt. Instantly I knew he had been playing football in the street. I caught his eyes and shook my fist at him. Then he presented the Mitre to the Bishop, he bowed, returned to his place turned to face all revealing two dirt handprints on the silk stole. Another thrashing awaited Joe when he got home.

The summer was very hot everyone heads for Brockwell Lido to cool down causing long queues to get in.. Kaye is provided with complementary tickets for the Three A's championships, the Horse of the Year Show and Boxing Promotions which Jack along with Dickie Fox when he was home on leave always went to. Joe then eleven leaves St. Joseph's and starts the new term at another St Joseph's Secondary school in Camberwell much closer. This was the period of time that India became Independent. It was of interest to Jack and me. For many years before the end of the Raj finally came. There had been much turmoil and unrest. Unfortunately, fighting intensified between religious beliefs. In Amritsar, over a thousand Indians were killed. How times change attitudes? But more joy for us. At Christmas. Jackie arrived home on leave. And it was

Michael's eighteenth birthday he held a party, for his mates from the football team at St. Anne's. Somehow Jack was able to buy a small turkey for a traditional Christmas Dinner accompanied by with my last Christmas Pudding. There were no trappings, but we relished that dinner. I thought: *I had finished with seeing Khaki around the house. But not so!*

January 1948. Michael receives his brown envelope to do his National Service. And is selected for the R.E.M.E. In March he leaves home to start his "Square Bashing" at Honiton in Devon followed by Trade Training, at Catterick camp. Whilst there, he paid regular week-end visits to Kitty and Bobby's upon finishing his Trade Training he arrived home on embarkation leave, with a posting to Nigeria West Africa. His first night back home. "The Cup Final" starts again. The thumps and bangs from the football pitch in the top room, which had lain silent from the time he joined up, erupted into the roar of Wembley Stadium. I did not take any notice, my mind firmly fixed on Michael's overseas posting thankfully, there were no hostilities there. He had a farewell party invited his football mates most of who were already in the services. Jack was in his element serving drinks from the makeshift bar in the kitchen. Yarning and joking with the new conscripts. He was well respected. Jack said to me one night.

'Sarah do you notice anything?'

'Yes I wondered when you were going to ask. No noise upstairs.'

"The last Cup Final had been played."

No sooner has one son gone away. When another come home Jackie arrives home demobbed. He gets a job working in the Scottish Highlands for the Forestry Commission, planting trees. With them both away the family income, had been drastically reduced. Jack would never allow our standard of living to fall, a thoughtful husband and good father to our tribe, found another week-end job Friday to Sunday, as a night Porter in an Office building off Park Lane. Another chore for Joe after Sunday Mass take sandwiches for Jack's lunch. All this extra money provided the family with some little extras whatever they were? However Jack did miss the Army and obviously the Mess. On occasions, he went down to meet up with. Tom and Alec at their local in Vauxhall or, on a Sunday night. when we both went down to the Milkwood Tavern and share an evening with the Towner's and Bushnell's. Both the Towner's son's had been conscripted into the Army. In June. the Russians, Blockaded Berlin cutting off all supplies in or out of the city and to transport supplies to the occupants. A massive airlift began by the British and Americans, left everyone thinking: *Was it going to become a third world war?* Only the next few months would tell but it carried on.

One Saturday Joe returned from Brixton, with a bag load of peas. It was the pea season and an abundance of Laxton's. Extremely proud of his purchase.... 'Best Buy in the market Mum. One penny a pound.'... However, far too many for us and certainly not what I ordered. I sent him back with them. He protested.... 'Mum. I've eaten half of them.'...'Well .You had better follow your trail of pea pods back. Off you go, protest to the costermonger. Not to me. Get them exchanged for what I told you to buy. Money doesn't grow on trees.'... Reluctantly he eft. Returning much later, with what I had asked for, plus a further hole in his pocket money. Having paid two pence halfpenny for the eaten peas. He didn't do that again. Two well learnt lessons.

I did not go out very much and only visited Vauxhall on the rare occasion, it was more to the point that my sisters would come to visit me. My sister Kitty, on one of her visits invited me to a whist drive, she being a bit of a card player, had found that on a Wednesday evening once a fortnight the Catholic Mother's at St Helen's in Brixton held a Whist Drive she urged... 'C'mon Sarah. It will just be like old times.'...'Kitty it wasn't me or Bridget it was you and Mary that played cards ' Anyway I agreed.

These whist drives were held in a little wooden Church Hut behind Pride and Clarke's and right in the middle of the large bombsite. I got Joe to accompany me there, then come back for me later. It was Okay during the summer evenings, until the nights of autumn and winter took

440

over. He armed with his torch would arrive to collect me we would walk back through the rubble, his torch beam was not directed at the rubble in front. Instead directed skywards, like a searchlight. Exclaimed. 'Looking for Russian planes. Mum. '.. When I tripped over some rubble, he helped me up, I swung a clout that caught him around his ear, stopped him playing searchlights. Very soon it began to get colder a sure sign winter was about to set in and the London fog's returne, so did Jackie. Having got fed up of the cold Scottish Highlands he got a temporary job of selling Vernon's football pools, nevertheless, he did not like the London fogs and the damp weather, so applied to join the Merchant Navy.. Christmas for us was a quiet affair.

In February 1949. Jackie was accepted into the Merchant Navy sailed on the RANCHIE Merchant ship taking immigrants to Australia, he was away for nearly four months at a time, the house was much quieter certainly not the same. But each time he returned, he brought caseloads of tinned food and fruit, there was no rationing in Australia also he brought home all his ex-servicemen or sailors pals. That was the start of his parties and great ones they were. To combat the increasing number of cases of TB. The New National Health Service. Introduced Mass X Rays. X-Ray Vans would be located in various areas for all to be X-Rayed. And glory be at last in May, the Berlin Blockade by the Russians finally ended, supplies could get through by Road transport. It somewhat eased the tension of another War.

Margaret was no trouble and had grown into a charming young women and was nearing the age where she would soon be working. Joe sat for his Technical Entrance Exams for college, and passed to go to an Engineering college in Kennington. The only problem was all had to wear a school uniform, our money was tight. Jack took him to their college outfitters to buy everything they required including football gear and cricket whites, in fact Joe apart from his devilment had become somewhat of a sportsman himself, played football for the Heron Road team, as well as the school. Out in the street the boys played cricket or kicked a tennis ball about then when the Olympic Games at Wembley captured everyone's imagination, the boys and girls of Heron Road. decided to hold their own long distance races? Running around the Mission Hall so many times, milk crates became hurdles and placed in lines along the middle of the road, all these events happened until the arrival of the Police stopped all. Futile protesting by the young athletes, fall upon deaf ears the Law is the Law. Off the Roads.   Undaunted another stadium is created - an unused bombsite opposite the Milkwood Tavern and the Games continued. Once the Olympic Games were over. another sport captured their imagination, motorbike speedway. Their circuit around the Mission hall on their bikes, racing around skidding around the corners. Joe used his father's bike, far too big for him, so he sat on the crossbar and pedalled like fury. He worried the life out of me. Jack would have a go at him particularly about his rear wheel tyre that had somehow become very worn down. Of course nothing to do with Joe? But the events carried on for a few weeks until Mike the butchers son, was nearly killed. When he collided with a Taxi, which brought the end of Speedway. Late one Saturday. I had a blinding headache, it was close to six and called Joe in.

'Joe. Run down the Chemist and buy me some aspirins. Be quick before they shut.' He responds....'I'll take Dad's bike.' I said …'No.' But he was gone bike and all. He retuned sometime later, crying his eyes out, minus the bike. I demanded…. 'Where's your fathers bike? Why are you crying? Where are my aspirins?' Handing me the aspirins he whined….'A car ran over it, when I was in the shop. When I came out it was underneath a car'… Don't hit me Mum. It wasn't my fault.'… I did hit him. But it wasn't for the bike. It was because he did not do. What I had told him to do. I snapped. 'Were is the Bike now?' He wailed… 'In the bike shop. Can Dad go down on Monday to speak with the shop owner?'

His Fathers punishment. Relinquish his football boots for one month. No football games, but plenty of jobs without pocket money. In the September Joe starts at his new College and was old enough to join St Anne's Youth Club. He plays in their football team, and on occasions,

441

played for his school. However more disturbing news. The Russians had exploded an atom bomb although two atomic bombs had already been dropped this new threat was like a burning taper between the Americans and Russians. It was the beginning of the Atomic Age. Nevertheless some good news came in November Princess Elizabeth gave birth to Prince Charles. Yet again, with Michael and Jackie away it was going to be a quiet Christmas for us. However that was not the case. Christmas Eve unexpected Michael arrived home from Nigeria. His Bush Hat cocked at an angle on his head and three stripes on his great coat a Sergeant just like his father. Rapturous welcomes all around and hot water bottles in his bed. The very next day after over a year of silence! The whistle blows to restart the Cup Final in the top bedroom. What a delightful sound to our ears the boy's doing what they enjoyed doing then I did open the goodies. With Christmas and the New Year out of the way. Michael's returns to Aldershot to get demobed.

February 1950. Michael starts back at work in his old job in Victoria. Jackie arrived back from Australia, fed up with moaning immigrants, changes shipping companies and goes to South Africa, hen trouble arrives to my household, Jack and Michael had been to the Mobile X-Ray Unit. Michael received a letter informing to report to St. Thomas's, was diagnosed with a shadow on his lung contacted whilst out in Nigeria. Confined to bed in the old back kitchen upstairs, basically isolated, his friends from St Anne's visit and play cards. Within six weeks Jack was also diagnosed with it. Being gassed in the First World War had not helped, he was isolated in Mary's old bedroom. Kaye was moved up stairs with Margaret and Joe all was reshuffled. A new drug called Streptomycin was to be administered by a visiting nurse. She arrived every day and injected both my men. However, with the history of it in the family, we were all suspect cases and had to attend St Thomas's Hospital once a month to be screened. Jackie arrived home in the June yet again changed his Company, over the following months, changed them a few times more. He enjoyed the life and definitely wanted to see the world.

With summer almost over, Jack was transferred to Benenden in Kent, Michael was sent to Hastings in Sussex. Possibly their delay was due to shortage of beds. I had not forgotten the length of time my Mary had been away herself I feared the worst, with three of my men away and Michaels 21st. due. Jack had left me to pay bills and other matters etc. I had approached the Council many times, complaining bitterly about the illness, which had hit the family, all due to the state and dampness of the house, reminding them, they had fumigated and sealed Mary's room off. My argument was full-filled. I was informed that we would soon be re-housed. The Christmas and New Year passed uneventfully by.

In the New Year good news to us, visiting was allowed. Together with Margaret and Joe, we made an arduous trip by charabanc from Camberwell Green down to Benenden. What a trip it was freezing cold and snow everywhere. Unfortunately at the sanatorium they were too young to see him. So they had to stay out on the veranda and shout to him. Michael was different, a train journey down to Hastings where he met us. He had progressed very quickly, in getting better and walked with us along the sea front, but tired very quickly. Then back to the station and home. The challenge went out to start the Cup Final as soon as he got back home. Joe was very eager nevertheless it was never to happen ever again. March 1950 we received a letter from The Council. Notice to move to a new four bedroom Maisonette. No. 17 Evans House. Fount St. Wandsworth Road...further details would be issued later. I did not exactly know where it was but its district Post Code was, SW8. I decided to pay a visit to Agnes, she would know where this place was. Mad Aggie was more than delighted. 'Sarah. It's right next to the Granada. I'll take you there now.'

Leaving Alec in charge of her two youngsters Kathleen and Michael. I was dragged out, at break neck speed, across the road down the Wilcox Road past Fox's. At the end we crossed over a wide road, still galloping along, we came to the Grenada Cinema. According to the street

442

sign opposite it was Fount Street and EVAN'S HOUSE. on the side of a four storied block of flats. Agnes shouted.

'THERE IT IS SARAH.' At her outburst I retorted.

'Agnes. Not so loud. I'm here standing next to you.'

We crossed over and walked down the side street, there was a roadway between that and another very long block of six storied flats. Agnes grabbing my arm said.

'C'mon Sarah. Let's walk to the end.'

We began walking along the pavement went past two wide entrances to the Flats,at the end of the block a wire fence was stretched across the road cordoned off any further progress. I noticed that it was a building site with another block of flats in progress. I murmured.

'It must be in there.' She shouted.

'C'mon we'll see from the main Road.'

She began running back. I followed in her wake up to the main road further down by the end of the block of flats, spotted this crazy little woman, dancing up and down beckoning to me. I thought: *She is mad, that cannot be my sister?* She was pointing and urging me on that had me running towards her she began shouting.

'SARAH. THAT'S IT, NUMBER SEVENTEEN. THAT'S IT.'

Drawing level with her saw what she was pointing at. Nearing completion was our new abode. A square two storied building attached to the end of the Flats. I could not see how it had four bedrooms. On the other side of the wire fence the adjacent building site, was another block of flats that appeared to be a mirror image of this EVAN'S HOUSE. I walked away slightly baffled. Nevertheless, grateful and very happy with the fact that it was brand new. Even the vicinity was nearer too my sisters, certainly central for all our needs. Satisfied we leisurely walked back to Agnes, she informed me.

'Sarah. Fox's is a new self-service store. Far bigger than that little shop behind Mothers.'

I pondered about this but thought. It being so close. It would please Joe with his shopping chore. Back in Agnes flat, Alec made us a cup of tea and offered.

'Sarah. When the time comes for the move. I'll help you move. Also my mate owns a small van that we can use Okay?'

I returned home with a far greater sense of relief. It was time for packing up, without the assistance of my three men. I wrote to both of them, Jackie was expected home soon, so he could wait for our good news, also to Kitty telling of our good fortune. However, surveying all we had accumulated over the years of our many possessions and furniture. Visualising what I had seen could not see how. It all would fit into a tiny so called four-bedroom maisonette? I thought. *The old piano will have to go, since Mary had died Jackie had never played a note on it. Maybe the Towner's would like it?* I busied myself preparing a meal for when the others arrived home. When we all sat down, I told them the good and bad news. They would have to get rid of their stuff. Gradually items appeared that weren't wanted. Two weeks later.The letter from the Council informed us. 'Moving date May. Please collect keys from Head Office.'

I went and saw Alec, agreed a Saturday move. I gave the piano away to the Towner's. As the boys manhandled it outside they pushed it down the centre of the road, as a jangle of unmelodic notes played goodbye. On the Wednesday, Jackie arrived home, to provide an extra pair of hands to help with the move. On Friday I went into Brixton to the Council Office's collected the keys, signed papers. Informed the Gas, the Electric Boards to turn on the Gas and Electric in Evans House, do whatever they had to do in 56. That I could not care less. I was then ready for Saturday's move.

Alec and his Mate arrived with a small van, just big enough for large items nevertheless, it was to make many trips. On the first trip I went down with the keys to open the door. We left the house, made rapid progress down to Fount Street then turned into the roadway up to the far

443

end where the wire fence had been moved further back. Stopping outside the maisonette Alec got out, helping me out thoughtfully he murmured....'Sarah. You go on ahead and open up. You deserve that privilege.' I walked up a pathway into a tiny entrance. Warily I opened the front door. The smell of fresh paint hit me as I stepped inside into an L shaped hallway, a staircase in front of me. Joe followed in behind me we walked around the rooms downstairs. A lovely kitchen fitted cupboards even a space for a small refrigerator and gas cooker, neither were included. A separate toilet and two larger rooms, the stairs led up to a small landing with five doorways, four bedrooms with fitted cupboards and my God. A bathroom and toilet with hot and cold water. This was sheer luxury beyond my wildest dreams. I was overjoyed at its possibilities. Small but what a lovely house, plenty of windows and light. I looked out of a window down at Alec still stood beside the van, opening the window called to Alec.

'Come on in and see.'

We went around the house again, quickly unloaded the contents of the van into the hall. Leaving Joe behind, to unpack the kitchen items, wait for the Gasman to install the new gas cooker. On the journey back to 56 I was in my element having seen the inside was completely reassured of its size, nevertheless, more things would still have to go. The second van load was quickly packed up and gone. Within the hour they were back

'Sarah the gasman's been and installed your new cooker. Joe promised a pot of tea will be ready when we get back.'

Six van loads later late in the evening, only two items remained in the backyard. The old tin bath still hung on its hook, and Joe's "Chariot". Alone I entered Mary's old room, in the silence of the house. I said my final farewell. Went back downstairs out through the front door of number 56. Banged it firmly shut. All the time I had lived there. It had brought me. Nothing but grief and anguish a chapter well forgotten.

CHAPTER EIGHT
FAMILY TOGETHERNESS - 1950 -1965

With the move to a new house. Yet another chapter in my life was about to begin. That was to become the happiest time I was to spend anywhere. EVAN'S HOUSE. With both hands I grasped the advantages it had to offer us, within a complete new environment. Gone was the boiling up of washing on a Monday. Below ground level at the far end of the block, was a small laundry with two large washing machines and hot air cupboards for drying wet clothing. Unlike the old days, there was strictly. No washing lines to be used. A group of lockup sheds were allocated to each flat for prams and bikes, but only sixteen, not one for us. Grass areas surrounded the Block. The tenants of the other flats came from all walks of life, like us; all were friendly with medium sized families. We were next door to the Grenada Cinema A big Co-op was directly opposite with rows of shops along the Wandsworth Road, Close by was the Wilcox Road, where shopping was more centralised with an open market. A variety of shops and of course Fox's was then a very large a self- service stores, owned by Mr. & Mrs Fox possibly the first one in London, all wonderful facilities within walking distance. Within a couple of days of our arrival. Jackie went back to sea, leaving Kaye, Margaret and Joe, to settle down into our new environment and dispose of anything that we did not need Both Jack and Michael had been away for close on a year their treatment had taking effect and three months after our move Jack was allowed home. Under his own steam he arrived home, grinning, the picture of health and of course, delighted with the house. With the exception of sweets, sugar, tea food rationing had all but finished I did not have to worry about too much, as Jackie kept us supplied with any extras that we needed. At the Butchers,where mother had her unfortunate accident. I was able to get more meat and provide Jack one of his favourite meals. "Steak and Kidney pudding." A month later Michael arrived home. For a few months both were not allowed to work. until our Doctor declared them fit for work. In Jack case he was transferred to Main Post Office in Victoria. Unfortunately, Michael could not return to his previous work was told. " Only a desk job." He takes time in making up his mind about how his future is going to turn out.

In May of 1951 the Festival of Britain site on the South bank opened and lasted for five months before it was closed, although we did not go into the exhibition, Jack and I walked around the site. The buildings were impressive. The Dome of Discovery, the Skylon and Festival Hall. What really caught my eye was the replica of the Crystal Palace. Memories of pre-war and wartime came flooding back. We reminisced and laughed about those times.

In 1952 the King dies and everyone is shocked by his death. But life has to go on and Princess Elizabeth becomes the Queen. However, the Korean War had been ongoing for nearly eighteen months, when Jack receives a brown envelope from the War Office. I was always aware of brown envelopes marked O.H.M.S. Leave it on the windowsill until he arrives home. I held my breath I thought: *Surely, he wasn't going to be recalled and mobilised yet again.* Not so. When he opened it a broad smile creased his face. 'You know what Sarah. They have awarded me the "MERITORIOUS MEDAL" for long service and good conduct in the Army.' He was delighted and so was I, another proud event in his life. Margaret was working as a typist in a office in the city it was also easier for Kaye to get to work, iIn June Joe. In his final year at the Engineering College. Passes his exams. His Father tries to get him into the Post Office as an apprentice. But he did not want that, his prospects were firmly set on becoming a Draughtsman. He went to several interviews before he left College, but they did not suit his needs, he went to the Labour Exchange. fortunate must have been shining over him. He got a job as a Trainee Draughtsman at a local firm in Stockwell within walking distance. He was happy, he had got what he wanted.

When there is trouble in the family. I gird myself together and got stuck in, surmounting whatever has hit me, but when it is all over, iInwardly I collapsed. Unfortunately the previous year's worries and anxieties, had taken their toll. I was unwell and the Doctor sent me to the St. Thomas's, where I was examined, X-rayed, sent home to await results. They diagnosed that I had developed a shadow on my right lung. I refused to go to a Sanatorium. So they agreed for me, to be treated daily at home, with tablets and injections, administered by the Nun's from Cedar Road. The treatment lasted six months. All my tribe took on all manner of household chores. Jack and Michael controlled the running of the house. Jack did the weekly washing, down in the washing room at the end of the block. Kaye, Margaret, cooking and ironing, Joe all the shopping, all cleaned the house. We were all happy to be solving the problem in our own way. Now laid up in bed with nothing to do, other than pray. Is when I took to reading, Kaye vetted all books, so that I should not read anything worrying or upsetting. Father O' Byrne after his Sunday services would visit, say Mass and give Holy Communion to me in my bedroom. He was a great character and made me laugh with his old tales about Ireland. Eventually I overcome the sickness, we had somehow contracted in that other awful place.

Joe and his mates Derek, Kenny, and Brian were into bikes in a big way, the other three, all had well known sports bikes. Joe tries to coerce Jack into buying him a bike, saying he always had to borrow a bike every-time the club go on a cycle outing. However Jack remembering what Joe did to his own bike! Would not have anything to do with it, but Joe kept on until Jack eventually gave in and agreed. Seeing he was earning a wage. Jack paid the deposit, Joe paid him back and all the instalments. It took six weeks for the bike to be made, then Joe was happy.The passage of time changed our life for the better, as things started to come together, Jackie, enjoying travelling around the world, made his career the Merchant Navy. Arriving home on leave with plenty of food, accompanied by his shipmates Ken, Tony, Tom and George with girlfriends, they were welcomed and it was party time, which occurred every time he arrived home, on the New York run. It was every two weeks. His Father asked.

'Jackie. how many at the party tonight?'

'Usual crowd Dad. Here's the money.'

'Right, I'll get the beer and glasses.'

Jack back running the mess bar. Always there to welcome all that came into our house, having only a few drinks, kept the parties on an even keel. The parties lasted well into the early hours of the morning. Very quickly invites to friends of Michael, Kaye, Margaret's and Joe's turned up. Geoff and Betty friends of Kaye's were always there Geoff and Jackie had something in common, both had been in the fighting in Burma, Jackie the foot slogger and Geoff the Pilot they did not talk about their time out there. How we slept them all amazed me, but we did. With the dining table dismantled to make more room for dancing and jiving, it became a crush with nearly everyone dancing. It was at one of these parties, when Michael made up apple pie beds for all. Nobody knew who did it? Nevertheless, it was the beginning of practical jokes. All manner of vegetables appeared in beds. Next morning, I had to go all around the house collecting vegetables from the stairways and various rooms, for Sunday lunch. Jack thought it was harmless good fun and never stopped it. However, on the Sunday morning he would be up early. Wash, wipe glasses, clear away cigarette debris, open all the downstairs windows, make tea for everyone. Then at the stroke of nine 'o 'clock turn the radio on full blast, to the sound of. "Marching with the Bands." Then he would stomp up and down the stairs, blowing an imaginary trombone, hollering.

'Come on you lads and lassies. Time to get up you'll all be late for Mass.'

Groans and moans, echoed from all quarters of the house.

'Please turn the radio down.'

'If you can't stand the pace. You lot shouldn't drink.' He replied as he served tea to the incapacitated. Furthermore, he would open all upstairs windows to let in the FRESH AIR. He loved it and so did everyone else. There was never any malice at any of the parties. One early morning he found Michael's mate. Keith Ager, under the table fast asleep, his face covered in powder, lipstick, and rouge, administered by the girls where he slept. All Jack said was.

'Come on son, Wakey wakey. It's time you went home.'

He sent him on his way, Keith unaware of his lipsticked powdered face. It is strange, not everyone was a Catholic, but all attended mass. Then to the local for a few drinks. Jackie's ship-mates would all come back for Sunday lunch. It was always a full house. Come Monday, back to the ship. Christmas Eve, Michael's Birthday, another all-night party, it became a tradition. After midnight Mass all friends would come back, and never finish until late into the morning. An excuse to lie in and recuperate before Christmas Dinner. Followed by the ensuing party game. "Ludo for Money" Small stakes but endless games. Somewhat reminiscent of our endless games of New Market, during the air raids.

1953 saw the end of the rationing of sweets and later by sugar, which was another reminder of what we had endured throughout the war. The main event of the year was the Queen's Coronation, like a lot of other families we rented out our very first Television Set; it was amazing to watch the pomp and ceremony in our own front lounge and to cap it all, the day before the Coronation. Edmund Hillary and Shirpa Tensing reached the Summit of Mount Everest. My thoughts: *Went back to those glorious sights that I had witnessed when I was up in the Hills of India: Oh how I longed to be back there, even for a short holiday but that was never to be.* Instead a holiday in August. Jack and I returned back to Bamber Bridge staying with George and Mary Parkinson before a week's stay in the Isle of Man. It was a good reunion and a most welcome break for both of us. We left inviting them both down to stay with us in London. It was sooner than we had expected.

Trouble amongst two of my tribe. It all started when we were away and upon our return, got the full story. Margaret and Michael could not see eye to eye were constantly arguing. When Margaret was out Michael as a joke, took. 'The Trophy.' Wynn Cooks Ice hockey stick. Tied a string around it, hung it out of her window facing the main road. Margaret discovered its disappearance enquired about its whereabouts. Michael denied all knowledge saying. It must have been Joe, who sided with Michael. She was furious refused to speak to Michael ever again. Margaret complained to Jack, but the boys stuck by their story. There was nothing he could do. This went on for about three weeks until one Sunday Jack returning from mass saw "The Trophy" hanging from the Margaret's window. He had a quiet word with both Michael and Joe. Michael up to his pranks again. However Margaret refused to speak to Michael, which lasted three months. I witness to this malarkey thought.: *The situation was quite funny. At mealtimes in the kitchen. Margaret sat at one end, Michael at the other with Joe in the middle, as a go between.*

Margaret: 'Can you ask him down there, to pass me the salt and pepper please.' Margaret would tell Joe to pass on the message. Michael: Deliberately keeping the salt down his end would reply, via Joe.

'Yes with pleasure. Tell the madam. down that end of the table.' The message was passed over via Joe siding with Michael. He would pass the salt and pepper.

Margaret: 'Tell him down the other end. Thank you. '

This passing back and forth of messages, via Joe continued throughout every meal, after a while, I asked Jack.

'What can we do to ease the situation between Michael and Margaret? Poor Joe's stuck in the middle.' Jack retorted.

'Poor Joe. Don't worry about Joe. He'll take no notice. Anyway. He's on Michael's side. Just let the situation takes its course. The pair of them will get over it you'll see.'

End of conversation. Not the end of the feud. It continued wherever they were in the house. Neither would give in. If Michael was hogging the bathroom Margaret, would get whoever was upstairs, to convey a message to Michael through the closed door. 'To vacate the bathroom.' Whilst she would stand waiting on the landing, arms folded tapping her foot. It eventually got past a joke and got on my nerves. Three months later, Joe sat between the pair of them. Taking up his dinner moved out remarking. ...'That's it. I'm fed up of being piggy in the middle. Mum from now on. I'll have all my meals. On my own in the dining room. Please.' I spoke to Jack again.

'Okay. I'll sort the pair of them out.'

He stopped it and normal mealtimes resumed once again. This all happened about the same time as the war in Korea was to end. With the signing of the peace treaty. Nothing to do with Jack negotiating a peace deal between my two.

We had a telephone installed. A party line shared with the neighbours of the adjoining flats. Jack only agreed if everyone paid for their own calls and a share of the rent, he would keep the books. It worked very well, all called home telling me. If they were going to be late. Therefore I did not have to worry where they were.

1954. The final end of rationing arrived, the legacy the war had left us with fourteen years of struggling and endurance, to feed our families on the pittance allowed. Only too well did I remember in 1938? When Jack advised me. 'To start storing tins.' The struggle throughout and the worst times immediately after the war. However, from 1948 Jackie upon his return trip from Australia was able to provide goodies for the table. Always giving never wanting anything in return. he was a good-natured son and a blessing to have. In April the tribe's first wedding occurs. Kaye marries Robin Edney a young shop owner from Croydon. We held the reception at home with not much money, not a lavish do. In May the anticipated arrival of Mary and George Parkinson. For a holiday and a trip to Wembley Stadium. Where Preston N.E. we're playing West .Bromwich Albion. In the F.A. Cup. Much to the delight of Joe, a Preston supporter. But it was Jack that went with them. Preston lost to W.B.A. 3-2. But the result did not dampen their spirits. They had a whale of a time when we went out to our local for a drink. Poor old George walking ahead with Jack, his hands clasped behind his back his fingers twitching, as a signal to Mary. He wanted some money and she was the one who controlled the purse strings.

Joe's mate Derrick who was a few month older, received his marching orders for National Service and within a month. Is called up to join the Royal Signals up at Catterick. Derek on his a weekend leave always visited us. He looked very fit and brown from all the outdoor life that they were treated to. However, it was not long before it was Joe's turn, his Brown envelope arrived in the post, to attend a medical. He passes A1. But for some reason, his call to arms is delayed and he waits and waits. Finally he gave up hoping they had forgotten him. So on the spur of the moment, he and Kenny. Decide to have a week's holiday at a holiday camp, and by all accounts, they had a good time and were quite tanned when they came back.

Summer turns to autumn. I have already mentioned the London fogs and the first bad one. I ever experienced was in 1922. But now we were experiencing them more frequently. These fogs were extremely bad and called Pea Super's, so thick you could not see your hand in front of your face, almost yellowy green in colour, with a horrid smell, caused through the smoke laden atmosphere that engulfed London. Jack could not stand them. they got into his throat into his lungs, regularly he comes home with his handkerchief covering his mouth and nose with his scarf wrapped tightly around his face for protection. No sooner is he indoors, than the barking coughing and wheezing would start.

'Sarah. Get the swabs out. There's a good girl.'

Then I would administer swabbing his throat. The same treatment as I used to do to young Jackie. (And did likewise with all the others whenever they have sore throats) As soon as the swabbing was over, he retreats to bed and stays there until the fogs lifts. He was dreading the next one, which inevitably did happen sooner rather than later. Within no time at all Christmas was upon us. Joe understanding it would be his last Christmas as a civilian. Decides to make the most of it and in more ways than one, enjoys the Christmas festivities until mid-January 1955 he receives his calling up papers to join the R.E.M.E. like Michael he goes to Honiton, for square bashing upon his completion, a short weekend's leave before reporting to a camp near Malvern there to do his trade training. He like most of the other National Servicemen if, unless on Guard Duty if, were allowed weekend passes they could get home they did. On a Friday evening he would telephone me.

'Mum. home for the weekend.'

That meant Margaret, Lily, and I would start baking his favourite cakes. Oh no. Not to be ate at home. But to be taken back to camp, to share around. According to him the grub was not fit for pigs to eat. On Saturday he would hitchhike lifts, from any vehicle travelling in the direction of London. Arriving home in the evening, have a good meal a good night out. Sunday evening armed with his cakes, return by train. June 16th was Margaret's 21st. Birthday, we held a party on the weekend. Margaret and Lily like Joe and Derek, all liked this Jazz music in the West End clubs. Margaret had invited some of the Jazz Musicians to her party. With the party in full swing, four of them arrived after midnight, with their instruments. Very nice people and gave an impromptu rendering of Jazz. I think the chap playing the saxophone was Tommy Whittle, a strange name but cannot remember the others. It all went down very well and everybody had a wonderful time. Jack couldn't stand this music as he called it the "Heebie Jeebie's". Joe would play his Jazz records as loud as he could, until Jack had had enough and shout out.

'Joe turn that blasted Heebie Jeebie music down or better still. Off.'

'Okay Dad. I'm going out now.' Off he would go with Derek to the Jazz clubs for more noise. Quietness would descend on the house, until the next time he would be home on a weekend pass. Within four months into his Service having passed his Trade Training course. He was home on a week's embarkation leave with a posting to Singapore. We had a farewell Sunday lunch for him, early Monday Morning he is away, gone to join a troopship sailing to the Far East. Four weeks later I received a postcard from Port Said telling me he is enjoying the trip. Reading his words reminded me of when we landed at Port Said in 1929. He appeared to be, following in his Fathers and brothers footsteps.

I received word from George Parkinson that Mary had died; this sudden shock set me back, yet a month later, further bad news, another letter from George informed me. Miss Wells had died, both of them from Cancer. God rest their souls. With my constant worrying over Joe, that was news I did not like, still no news from Joe until mid-October, he was not in Singapore but on Active Service in Malaya at a place called Ipoh. I had heard of Aden, Cyprus, Kenya to mention a few, only Malaya when Jackie was out there during the war. It seemed at that period of time, there were few places of the dwindling British Empire, where a serviceman got posted to, which was not a hot bed of military action. Then I remembered the Hansen Boy they lived next door to the Towner's in 1953 John got killed in Malaya. I really started worrying again.

Margaret had started courting a handsome young man by the name of Pat, come Christmas our depleted family of four sat down to Christmas Dinner. I am in no mood for any festivities, the previous months harrowing news,with Joe in the Far East I succumb to nervous exhaustion. Jack tells me not to be silly, stop worrying. The Doctor confines me to bed. Again Jack, Michael and Margaret do the household chores, allowing me to get the rest I badly needed. I spent hours thinking about the life we had experienced all we had been through as an Army family, always on the move, that is when I took to writing my memoirs. Very slowly I became fit once again. During that summer Michael's illness had prevented him to "Not much physical activity" He takes up the gentle art of Bowls playing at the Vauxhall Park Bowls Club, and soon wins cups and medals for their which supposedly at that time, had the youngest Bowls team in

England? On one of Jackie's shore leaves he takes Jack and I down to Salisbury to see Wilton House, amongst some of the old places we were posted to, during the twenties and thirties, we visit Shrewton. Jack as usual gets talking to some of the locals, who provide us with some of their home brewed wines. Rhubarb, Elderflower, and Beetroot with recipes to take home. This new activity was to occupy my time, fermenting them in a big Demi John, placed in the warmth of a cupboard in our bedroom. One night we were fast asleep a Demi - John exploded. Jack shot out of bed. Exclaimed.

'What the hell was that Sarah?'... As I slowly came to my senses, realised what it was and laughed.... 'Sorry Jack. I forgot to put an air lock on the bottle.'

We investigated the cupboard and found all of the clothes, covered with rhubarb wine. A very expensive lesson at the dry cleaners.

One October afternoon, I was busy ironing when there was a knock on the door, I went and opened it, I recognised a familiar face?

'Mrs Plant. I'm Alan Keene. I was with Joey out in Ipoh, he asked me to come and see you when I arrived back and tell you how it was out there.'

'Oh. Please do come in and have a cup of tea. I recognised you from a photograph.'

'That's Okay. Thank you I won't stay long.' He answered following me into the kitchen. I heard him say.

'Don't worry about Joey. He's alright.'

'Sit down there Alan. Is it alright if I call you Alan?'

'Yes that's my name. Mrs Plant. Is that right, your sister lives a few doors away from where we live, she lives opposite the Crown?'

'Yes she does.'

'Dad. Sometimes has a drink with her husband Alec. The Crown is not my local. I use the Mawbey, but do drink in the Crown sometimes.'

I provided tea, and we sat at the table. I noticed he was much older looking than Joe. But didn't wish to pry into his age. Asked him what it was like out there. I wasn't surprised when he replied that.

'Oh. It's alright. Very hot, plenty of work to do, our only recreation was playng football..'

He chatted amicably about Malaya, without giving me the benefit of doubt. Mentioned another of Joey's mates Dennis, who lived further along the Wandsworth Road, co-incident or what? Three of them unknown to each other, all living within a mile of each other would meet up in Ipoh thousands of miles away. Making his excuses got up to leave when Jack arrived from work, Jack knew his father through Alec. Alan invited him for a Sunday drink. It was an unexpected but total welcome visit. It gave me more comfort with the knowledge that Joe was safe and sound. Nevertheless anything could happen? Another Christmas came and went with four sitting down for Christmas Dinner.

End of January 1957. a couple of days after Jack's birthday it was late we were sat watching some television programme, before we retired to bed. Michael was out and Margaret, had gone to the pictures with Lily she was staying overnight at Lily's home. When the phone rang. Jack got up went outside to answer it was brief, coming back in already with his coat on, wrapping his scarf around his neck said.

'Sarah. Good news. That was Joe ringing from Charing Cross. He's home. He wants me to get some beer in. Got to dash to the Nott, before they shut. He should be home in about half an hour. Okay. I'll be back before then.'

With that parting shot he was gone with a bang of the front door. It then dawned on me what he had said. Joe's home. Wonderful news another weight off my shoulders. I immediately went to call the Towners. Bill Towner answered. ...'Hello. Who's there?'... 'Bill. Its Sarah. Can I speak with Margaret please.... 'Yes hold on. I'll get her for you.' Then silence.

450

'Hello Mum. What's up?'... 'Joe's home. Are you coming home?'... 'Joe's home? Where?'...'He's on his way from Charing Cross.'... 'Yes. I'm on my way. I'll get a taxi home.'

That done, I headed for the kitchen, one thought in my head:: *The cold. Hot water bottles.* I did that and put them into his bed, returned to the dining room put more coke on the fire lit the gas, when a knock on the door, had me running to open it. There to be confronted by a grinning Joe. Tanned, looking much older, dressed in civvies shivering with no overcoat. An overnight grip in one hand and a small white kitbag in the other.

'Hello Mum. It's me.'

'I can see that Son. Where's your overcoat?'

'Don't have one.'

'C'mon get inside out of the cold.' He came in, shut the door, dropped his kit, then we hugged each other, he was shivering. I was crying with relief he said.

'Stop that Mum. I'm home now. I'm freezing I got a taxi home from Charing Cross, Christ it was so bleeding cold on the tube. I could not bear the thought of another train journey?'

I dragged him into the front room, sat him down in front of the fire. Jack arrived back with clinking bottles. More greetings, exchange of handshakes. I could tell that Jack was relieved to see him. The drinks flowed not tea, then the inquisition begins. Jack stood, feet together and hands on his hips.

'Why didn't you tell us you were coming home? And why civvies? Are you demobed?'

'I did write, just before I left Ipoh. But I must have been on the same plane as the letter. The reason for the civvies. No military personnel are allowed to fly via India in uniform. No. I'm not demobed but will be in next week.'

'When have you got to report back then?'

'Tonight. But they lost my kitbag at London airport.' A big grin appeared over his face... 'I missed the train to Aldershot didn't I? ' Jack wasn't at all pleased with this. Not his style.

'You should have tried to get to the camp any old how.'

'Cor. This is rich. Theirs me been away for nigh on two years and I get told off as soon as I get through the door. Anyway it's great to be home.' His father looked at him quizzically. 'Uhm?' ...Then we let him tell us all about his trip home. Margaret arrives home more hugs and kisses, then Michael arrives home more handshakes, long chats before bed. I slept very well that night. Jack had him up at the crack of dawn. This time out dressed in his uniform. Jack brought me a cup of tea all he said to me was.

'Joe's gone Sarah. Silly young Bugger. He could be put on a charge for that.'

I could not have cared less. I don't think Joe cared either, he was finally back with us safe and sound. About three weeks later he arrived home demobed. Much to his disgust. He had served more than two years. With Joe home the 'Heebie Jeebie' music sounded from the spare room. Jack took no notice. After about a fortnight at home, trying to pull together his old roots, meeting Derek once again, who was courting a young lady, both go back to St Anne's club. Find it's changed so much, with Kenny and Brian still in the Army. He can't get a game of football with their team. finds himself at loose ends having spent his army allowance. Decides he must get back to earning an honest living, seeks his old job at his previous firm. He arrives back rather disillusioned.

'Mum. No Bleedin' Job. Their business is folding up all because of the Suez crisis. John told me to go to the Labour Exchange and tell them.'

I could see from his mannerism. That he was in the doldrums, at a loose end. He came home one Friday night sits down. I wondered what was going on in his mind then he says

'D'yer know what Mum? Derek has asked me, to emigrate to New Zealand with him. He wrote and asked me the same question when, I was out in Malaya. I told him Yes.'... I was startled by this revelation but he went on... 'But not now, maybe later in the year, I've already been away too long.'

I was relieved by his last comment, but concerned about his future? However, he meets up with his mate Alan who gets him playing for the Mawbey Arms football team. He then gests a job as a Draughtsman with a firm in South Kensington, for all intense and purposes he is quite settled after his initial bad luck. He starts courting Annette a beautiful young local girl, who just happened to be Alan's sister, she was a rather shy person. In June, three memorable events took place. On the 22nd. Joe celebrated his 21st birthday. We held a big party for him. On the following Friday, Derek his mate sailed to New Zealand. To me their parting was a relief. Joe would not be leaving us for another foreign land. Then on the Saturday. Joes pal Alan married Pat. we were invited to the reception.

The telephone a useful blessing in disguise for us all, but trouble over it. Michael at loggerheads with Margaret again she was forever on the telephone to Pat, she spent hours on it, every time Michael phoned home. It was engaged. Jack resolved the situation by increasing the rental cost, which Joe did not agree with, in the end Jack put a time limit on Margaret's calls. Later in the year Margaret and Pat announce that they are engaged planned to marry the following September with their wedding reception at home, to stock up, Jackie, keeps on bringing bottles of Champagne back. Christmas saw a full family gathering all at home for the festivities and the start of the endless game of Ludo, gambling of course.

The beginning of 1958. Lily got married to an American, emigrates to America, Margaret wanted Annette to be her bridesmaid. The list of guest included Kitty and Bobby Burns. With all arrangements finalised the bath was filled with ice and bottles of Champagne. Their wedding was

in our local church,afterwards Father O' Byrne's came back for a "Wee Dram."

During the celebrations, Joe and Annette announced to Jack and I. They were engaged and planned the wedding for the following September. We were both delighted. Everyone had a great time and nursed heads the following day. This Photo was taken on Sunday the day after the wediing. Kitty said.

'Come over here Annette you sit next to me I know that young fella from way back. You don't want anything to do him that's for sure.' Annette did, which brought much laughter from all.

By the Monday all back to work. Kitty and I were gupping in the Kitchen. When about ten o'clock. Joe arrives back home with his bike carried on his shoulder, the front wheel totally buckled. He uninjured except for his pride. He shouted.

'SOME STUPID PEDESTRIAN. WALKED STRAIGHT INTO ME. IT HAPPENED IN SLOAN STREET . I'VE JUST WALKED ALL THE WAY HOME, I HAVEN'T EVEN BEEN TO WORK.' Quick as a flash Kitty winking at me retorted.

'You should not have drunk so much at the wedding. Anyway its quicker by shank's pony.' We both roared out with peels of laughter followed by...'Do you remember the time?'... Joe saw the funny side of his encounter, just shrugged his shoulders and walked out. With Joe and Annette's wedding the following year. It was an open invitation to Kitty and Bobby. It was about this time that Dickie Fox. Long since finished with the Army, paid us a visit and informed us. They had decided to immigrate to America with their daughter Caroline. As Bobby and Kitty were still with us. We arranged to have a farewell party for Dickie and Peg, which was the reason they extended their stay to a fortnight. The reminiscing that went on was no bodies business. The party with much drinking and dancing, the men spent most of the time in the bar (kitchen) gupping about India.

452

Margaret and Pat rented a flat in Chelsea, whilst Joe and Annette began planning their wedding, saving up to reduce the cost, they decide to hold their reception at Annette's parent's home. Michael was to be Joe's best man. On the day of their wedding. Kitty and I was driven in style to our local Church in a tiny but gleaming. "Austin Seven". Owned by Michael, driven by his pal Tony Gange. Father O' Byrne performed the Marriage ceremonies the wedding went off without a hitch. Everyone nursed heads the following morning. After their honeymoon in Switzerland. They move into a tiny flat locally, a bit of a hovel but ,that was all they could afford.

Our depleted household was down to four, the others had decided to purchase their own homes. Gradually they move away from our close proximity, but still in London. The house became very quiet without the other two, gone was the chattering and bantering between Margaret and Michael, the sound of Joe's Heebie Jeebie's music. As Annette worked all day Saturday Joe visited us Jack always looked forward to any of his sons, having a drink with him.

'We are just popping out for a quick pint. Is that all right with you Sarah?'

'I know your quick pints Jack. Go on off with you and make it only one.' It never was. 'Just the one.' But Jack still continued with his Marching with the Bands on Sundays, at least once a month they came home for a meal, then house erupted into life.

On Sunday's after dinner, late in the afternoon. Jack would coerce me out to visit a church in Victoria or Westminster to attend evening Benediction. It was the only time I would venture out. Afterwards to have a quiet pint in one of the locals he knew. A letter arrived from Kitty Burns with the sad news Bobby has suddenly passed away, together with Kaye we went to his funeral in Harrogate stayed for two weeks. Another chapter in our lives had closed. By then Annette and Joe had bought a house in Balham. Having learnt to drive in the Army Joe buys a second hand car. During the winter of 62/63 that It lasted well into April. Joe experienced a lot of problems with his car, he decides to purchase a better one. Nevertheless tragedy strikes again. Joe has a car accident and his face is a mess his most vital asset his eyes, are lacerated by glass, fortunately he sustains no other damage. Pat his passenger received a broken bone in his foot badly bruised ribs, otherwise he was Okay. Joe is taken to Moorefield's Eye Hospital and is operated upon to remain immobile with the treatment the doctors provided. Annette was only permitted to visit him. Annette moved in with us, it being more convenient to get to and fro to Moorfields. Annette keeping me well informed of his progress. Annette was a brick to me. I warmed to her genuine concern over her husband Joe. Full of anguish that only mothers and fathers go through Jack and I were deeply concerned about our youngest son. I prayed like mad for God to save his sight. It was almost two weeks before visitors were allowed. Jack and I went to the hospital, what a shock awaited us he lying there inert on his back, the upper part of his head swathed in bandages, unshaven unable to move his head. He murmured.

'Who's there?' All Jack could say was.

'Hello Son.' It was four weeks before they found any glimmer of him seeing light in his left eye. His right eye was too far-gone, was removed the day after his 27th.birthday. Leaving the evening visiting to Annette. Jack and I visited him on several occasions in the afternoons and none was more rewarding than the afternoon we saw him sitting up in a chair beside the bed, still unshaven with only tear pads stuck on his cheeks, a pair of black glasses shielded the normal days glare. We had a wonderful hour-long chat and laughed. When it was time to go Jack took his hand and pressed a bottle of beer into it.

'I understand from Annette. That on top of your Guinness ration, you can have another pint later, that's from Mother and me, there's one waiting in the bar at home. Also. Young un'. You keep your hands off the nurses, I've heard rumours? That's a sure sign you're on the mend.'

We left both elated with his progress. He was released from hospital much later and returned to work four months after it happened. In September Jack receives notice from St James Palace. That the H.M the Queen. Has awarded him THE IMPERIAL SERVICE ORDER. For

453

long service to the crown, yet another addition to his decorations. On the day of his presentation we all trooped up with Jack to receive his medal, except Joe who was still under the Hospitals supervision. Courtesy of Jackie we celebrated the occasion, at the Trader's Vic Polynesian restaurant, in the London Hilton Hotel. We thoroughly enjoyed it, with taxi's back home to finish off the celebrations. Someone turned on the television to reveal a news flash. President Kennedy had been assassinated the date 22nd of November. We were shocked and could not believe what we were seeing on the screen? Then good news Annette announces she is pregnant.

Michael who had been courting Wendy, a lovely young nurse from Kent announced that they were going to get married the following year in September 64. They were going to hold the wedding down near where her parents lived. Joe was to be Michael's best man. A few weeks before the wedding .Annette gave birth to our first granddaughter. 'Laura' A fitting name after her Grandfather. We are both overjoyed at the new addition to our family. We all made our way down to Greenwich for Michael's wedding, it was a grand do and a beautiful day, they were married with a wonderful reception. Annette took less than a month old baby. 'Laura' along. Oh what a delight it was for me to hold my first grandchild in my arms. Looked on by an equally proud Grandfather. His face creased with that old grin. Michael and Wendy like the others purchased a house outside London, in the little village of Ashington, a lovely place that we were to visit many times later. Christmas of that year saw us, as a family all get together with the first of many grandchildren to follow. On the Boxing Day Joe, had to go back into hospital for another operation on his left eye, which was successful. Early in the New Year both Margaret and Annette announce that they are expecting. Annette's second, Margaret's first.

With Jackie away for very long periods at a time Jack and I are now basically on our own. Having lived in that lovely house for fourteen years. I had many happy memories to reflect upon not only were my own sons and daughters gone their separate ways, so had my own sisters and their families, only Bridget who still lived in Vauxhall. Kitty, Fan, Nan, had moved way outside of London. Julia who had married Vincent an American soldier had immigrated to the States, years before, as did Peg Dickie Fox, also Agnes. The rest had since passed away. So our connection with Vauxhall was sadly at an end. The devastation I had witnessed after the war had mushroomed up around us into large multi storied estates. Gone was the London we loved. This was not our scene. Number 17 Evans House had served its purpose.

454

CHAPTER NINE
THE TWILIGHT YEARS - 1965 - 1974

1965 was the year Jack retired. Kaye's husband Eddie sold his shop and bought a large Victorian house in Clapham Park. They asked us. If we would move in with them. It was not a hard decision to make, with Jackie away for up to six months, we agreed. With the help of Joe, Michael and Pat, they turned it into two self-contained flats. The flat on the first floor, had been modernised and decorated throughout by the boy's. It was adequate for our needs, spacious with big rooms and high ceilings, a lounge, kitchen, bathroom, toilet, and two bedrooms, one for Jackie when he came home. Outside it had a lovely front and back garden, with a goldfish pond. Gardens were always something, I longed for in any of my homes. Late in the year once again we are on the move, moving seemed to be part of my life. Nevertheless with a scattered family, I made a welcome home for my family when they all made it back for a weekend reunion that occurred at least once a month.

Early in the New Year, two new Grandsons are born, Julian to Margaret and Pat, followed a fortnight later by Elliot, to Annette and Joe. Again proud grandparents. Joe and Annette, lived within walking distance of us. Every Saturday afternoon, they would push Laura and Elliot around in the big pram to visit us. Jack and Joe doing the necessary discussing the World affairs over a pint down at our local. Eventually Annette and Joe find that their accommodation is too small for their growing family, they sell up buy a new house in Norwood Junction. It was later that Annette informed me that she was pregnant again. As they say new house new baby. Annette within days of Christmas gave birth to another granddaughter Meier. Later Michael and Wendy have a little granddaughter, Claire, and a grandson Mark. As they all grew older and more boisterous. Elliot was nicknamed 'Butch' by his grandfather, which stuck. We still had our gathering of the tribes every six or eight weeks. On one occasion Julian, somehow got pushed into the fishpond, his yells and screams, brought Margaret tearing downstairs, to find out what was going on. Julian standing there soaked to the skin wailing in discomfort. Butch was the culprit. Margaret went berserk saying...'It should never happen. Pat do something about it.'.... Pat a rugby player. Just laughed. ...'It won't do him any harm he's all right.' I called out to her.

'Margaret don't you remember the times you pushed Tommy into the pond in Norwood?'

This was greeted by howls of laughter from everyone, much to Margaret disapproval. Jackie another one when on leave, took all the kids up to the Round pond on Clapham Common, where Laura got pushed in, followed by Meier. Jackie came back with two soaking wet girls, laughing his head off, denying all knowledge of the incident, but I knew better. After all helped with the preparation, then the sit down dinners, washing up then followed by relating of time gone by regaling with laughter. It was happiness to me just like old times, a full house a complete family. Then the Children would play, the noise was horrendous. Nobody took any notice, except Jack. When the football results began at five' o'clock. "A time for peace and quiet, to see if he had won a fortune?" The tribe would be whooping around full of beans, he would look over his glasses and say.

'Whished awhile Sarah. Keep them quiet for five minutes will you? There's a good girl.'

I took no notice. They were more precious to me, than one can think. The happy laughter of the tribes reminded me of mine as they grew up.

Jackie on leave always took Jack and me to visit some of England's beautiful stately homes. Longleat, Wilton, Blenheim Palace, maybe stay a weekend and then visit places where we used to live. Greenland's in Wiltshire was so wonderful, we could walk over the grounds, and think of the happy times we had had there. Margaret and Pat took us across to Ireland to visit Pat's relatives. I had not been back to Ireland since 1927. We spent two weeks travelling around, at times I riding side saddle, on the pillion of Pat's motor scooter. We laughed the whole

455

of the time. It was so good to be back. Then Margaret, Pat, and Julian moved up to Bolton. Where we were to spend some delightful and restful days with them.

For our fiftieth Wedding Anniversary. Jackie took us back over to Ireland. We flew over, my very first trip in an aeroplane. I thoroughly enjoyed the adventure, but the Irish weather poured with rain the whole of the time. In Kildare we visited the Church, where we were married all those years before. Though Jackie got to kiss the Blarney Stone. We did not attempt to do that. The rain never ceased, after three days we flew home, instead Jackie took us along with Kaye, to Paris for a weekend. Another wonderful time, in contrast the weather was beautiful, Jackie was tireless, we never stopped, Versailles, Fontainebleau, Mal Maison, the Louvre, he knew Paris well and his French was not too bad. After we had visited the Notre Dame Cathedral we were crossing the square he called out to me

'Mum look in there. They have some beautiful flowers for sale.'

I quickly tripped in to find not flowers, but a French man going to the toilet. Who roared at me? I flew out, much to the delight of the other three watching. It was a French public convenience. We went up the Eiffel Tower and thrilled to the wonderful views of the whole of Paris. Jackie   pointed out the Sacre Coeur. We enjoyed some delightful meals and came home in high spirits but both Jack and I were very tired after this hurried but most enjoyable trip.

Jackie changed his ships companies so he could work on the children's cruise ship the " Devonia ". He came home with tales of the children's antics at sea. Sea sickness, laid in droves on deck, clutching spew bags, past caring, hoping to die. Next day dancing all around, their previous incapacity forgotten. Jackie had a way with exaggerating his tales and insisted we go on one of these cruises, after listening to his tales I was not willing to go but between him and Jack I was co-ersed into going. We flew to Malta, where Kaye and Eddie were there on holiday, we stayed two nights before going aboard the ship. It was strange when I saw the ship, gone had my fears of water from years before. Jack and I had a comfortable cabin to ourselves far better than the troopships of bye gone days. I began to look forward to this mini cruise, sailing from Valletta bound for Nauplia, Piraeus, Istanbul Izmir, and Malaga, before returning back to Tilbury. The weather was glorious as we sat on the top deck a light breeze the sea was blue and it took two days before we reached the port of Nauplia on the Greek mainland of Peloponnis. Jackie advised us of what we should do he would be our guide. After breakfast we disembark onto a pontoon, then into a motor boat, which rapidly filled up with children, and headed for shore. All the children were chatting excitedly as they sorted out their packed lunches and started swopping their likes and dislikes. We disembarked onto the quay whilst the children piled into bus's, which took them up to a castle above Nauplia. We waited for Jackie, he arrived on the last ferryboats. We boarded the bus with the other children and upon our arrival at the castle. One of the boy's on our bus called out to another boy.

'What's it like in there?' A disinterested reply.

'You've seen one, you've seen them all mate. Just brick walls, and hundreds of steps to climb.'

We laughed at this interchange. Jackie said.

'We will take that lad's advice and stay here.'

What a sensible suggestion. Our party arrived back and we re-joined the bus and drove onto Epidauros to an ancient ampi-theatre. We sat on one of the tiers in amongst the school children, whilst a group of schoolgirls stood in the centre and sang. Nymphs and Shepherds, everyone clapped and cheered. We were driven back to Nauplia. But a strange thing happened. Jack said.

'You know what Sarah? For the first time since I left Benenden. The ringing in my ears has stopped.'

It was a side effect from that Streptomycin for T.B. Jackie interrupted.

456

'You know Dad. Epidauros once was a Hospital and Sanatorium.'

So it was still curing people. We arrived at Argos got off of the bus, to face an ancient road of very warn large cobble stones. and a similar incline. With Jack holding onto me I got so far. Jack gasping for breath shouted.

'Jackie we are going no further this is dangerous.' He questioned.

'Now what's wrong with you two?' Jack retorted.

'This Son. Is no place for high heel shoes.'

Just then, one of the Teachers was knocked flying by an over excited schoolboy, determined to be the first to the top. Jackie came back to assist the Teacher who had damaged her arm. He suggested.

'Right I suggest you get back on the bus Miss.'

We followed them back, the driver gave him the First Aid Box, which he used to clean, plaster and put her arm in a sling. She asked Jackie.

'Seeing as you work on the ship. Would you escort my party to the fortress?' Without hesitation he replied.

'That's Okay. I'll take care of them.'

They both left the bus. Jackie was introduced as their Guide.

After about fifteen minutes, they emerged at the top of this ancient Acropolis. Waving and jeering at the other children arriving at the top. They all returned safe and sound.

Back on board the ship did a short trip to Corinth. Where all went ashore. Jackie took a taxi up to the top where we walked across the bridge over the Corinth Canal. A narrow gorge cut out of the rock with sheer sides wide enough to take a large ship. It made the Suez Canal look puny. At a café, we had lunch of fish with baby artichokes and a bottle of wine, with no use for our packed lunches we gave ours to some of the children, who devoured them. Then back on board where Jackie ordered us.

'Have a shower and get to bed straight away.'

We were packed off to bed, just like the students. Nevertheless a memorable day. Overnight the ship sailed for Piraeus. Next day as a surprise Jackie took us by train to Ammonia Square in the centre of Athens to the Museum it was splendid. A Taxi ride up one of the hills in the City. Where we sat in a cafe and drank some Retsina, whilst we gazed over to the Acropolis, mounted on top of another hill. That was certainly a far nicer way to view it. Instead of clambering over fallen columns. I think Jackie was getting the idea, that we were not all agile monkeys like him. Back at sea we had a full day of rest before the next port of call Istanbul.

Next morning we had an early breakfast as the Captain had invited us and some Teachers onto his bridge, for the passage through the Bosphorus and the Sea of Marmara. As we passed the Anzac beaches in Gallipolis. an old army Captain, who had been at those landings. Gave us a talk on the landings. The carnage and suffering, endured by the British and ANZAC troops. Australian New Zealand and Indian and other members of the Empire Troops with the frightful casualties on both sides was appalling. I was as interested as Jack. We were served drinks. Jack was in his element talking to this ex-army Captain being able to discuss the tactics and movements that took place those many years ago.

The following morning we arrived in Istanbul. It was very hot and the first stop on the bus tour was the. Aya Sophia once a Christian place of worship then a Mosque. It was enormous but very dark and gloomy, Next on the schedule was the Blue Mosque. It compared to the Aya Sophia was all light and airy, a myriad colour of blue tiles and magnificently fretted white marble like icing sugar everywhere. Of the two my preference would have been the Blue Mosque. Outside Jackie pointed over the other side of the water to a large square building. he said.

'That's the Scutari building built for Florence Nightingale as a hospital for the sick and wounded soldiers from the Crimea war. Another one was built in England near Southampton at

457

Netley.' We took a Taxi to the Grand Bazaar. This brought back many memories of our Kitty and mine trips to the Indian Bazaars He took us to so many places. I can't remember them all, but at one place we overlooked the bay and saw our ship berthed. Great surprise. Jackie. produces a bottle of chilled wine and glasses, that he had brought along from the ship. We enjoyed our packed lunch in fine style.

Next day the ship slowly cruised back down the Sea of Marmara on to the next port. Izmir. Once the ancient port of Ephesus. In the morning Jackie took us up into the mountains to a church, built on the site of where our Blessed Lady ascended into heaven. It was a long drive and cold, but the sun was brilliant and warm. It was a lovely little place and we said a pray there. Then they both left me to pray on my own. I was so happy and at peace with myself just praying here on this hallowed spot. I later joined them outside and we quietly ate our packed lunches. No wine this time only water, Jackie collected from a tiny stream running down the side of the mountain. I could have asked for nothing finer. Then back down to Izmir. For Jack and I. this was a far better way to see it all from the mountain. We returned back to the ship for a good rest.

The next day neither of us felt well and asked the steward to fetch Jackie.

'Take it easy and rest. If necessary I'll get the ship's doctor to pay you a visit tomorrow let's see how it goes?'

Next day the Doctor did visit us and said.

'We had caught a chill up in the mountains. Just sit out on deck in the fresh air.'

We took his advice and rested. Next stop the homeward journey first to Malaga in Spain a long sea trip. After docking we waited until everybody had disembarked. Jackie took us by taxi to the Cathedral and local market. All very lovely but neither of us felt up to it, and were very glad to get back to the ship. We sailed in the evening and later Jackie took us back up on deck again to see all the lights along the coast of Spain and Gibraltar truly a wonderful exciting sight. The ship passed close by the loom of the water catchments along the side of the Rock, and above us vanishing into the blackness at the top. It was ghostly and as we sailed round Europa point to see the full splendour of Gib. brilliantly lit from the docks along the front of the town. This was always a magical moment for most Service people leaving for a tour abroad or returning. A Goodbye or a hello. Both Jack and I had tears in our eyes. Jackie took us back to his cabin for a drink where we thanked him for his advice on so many things. He had been invaluable. Each evening after dinner we sat in the Lounge and watched the children dancing. All jigging around and roaring with laughter. Until the Tannoy piped them to bed at nine p.m. The final scuffle as their Teachers, herded them off the deck had us both in fits. We would join Jackie in his cabin for a drink and chat about the day's events before we retired for the night. I was sea sick in the Biscay, but only once. (Am I becoming a hardened sailor at last?). On arrival in Tilbury he told us to wait in the Lounge until everyone had disembarked. Wendy, Michael, Kaye and Eddie arrived in their cars, to take us home we regaled them all with tales of the cruise before we left the ship and went home together. Jackie had to leave early the following morning to re-join the ship for another cruise. All in all we had a splendid holiday never to be forgotten. But this cold hung on with Jack. Not like him to be ill. Though he recovered, he never really was the same. He who always looked so bright and cheerful had almost aged overnight. I made him go to see the Doctor and was packed of to hospital, for the removal of the Prostate after which, he deteriorated and felt every chill wind, his breathing was laboured. I was worrying about him, as I never had to before. He. once the fully fit one all the time. Many a time in the evening he left me on my own to watch television, while he would go to bed early. Tired out after only doing bits of shopping for me. On Sundays the Priest came to the house to say Mass and give him Holy Communion. Whatever was coming over him? But also myself, I never seemed to have the energy to do anything.

One Sunday as Eddy was working. Charlie Howley. Joe's Brother in law came over to take Kaye to Bletchley for a cricket match, After they left Jack went to bed early. I followed him

458

later and was fast asleep, When Kaye arrived back. They came up to see how we were. Jack asked Kaye to telephone for a Doctor, as he felt very bad. I stayed in bed, whilst Jack dressed himself and went into the sitting room, until the Doctor arrived. He promptly telephoned for an Ambulance. When it arrived Kaye came back into the bedroom to tell me her father was being taken into hospital. would I like to go in the Ambulance I said.

'No. I will stay here and pray for your father.' He came in to say he was off and gave me a quick kiss.

'Sorry Sarah. I don't feel too good. I will just go to the hospital for a check-up.'

I awoke in the morning cold and worried. No one was in the house. They must still be at the Hospital. I got up and dressed went into the sitting room, and waited for someone to turn up, to tell me what was happening. When I heard the sound of Charlie's car draw up and stop. I heard footsteps coming up the stairs then Kaye followed by Joe came into the sitting room. I was surprised to see him there. Joe sat down beside me to tell me the awful news that their Father had just passed away peacefully. I could hardly take it in. I dissolved in tears. When Joe put his arm around me. Through my sobs I listened as he told me that the hospital had informed Kaye that Jack's condition was not good, it would not be long before he passed away. Kaye phoned Joe, Charlie picked up Joe. They arrived back in time for Kaye and Joe to hold their fathers hands as he slipped away. All I could say was.

'Not my Gallant Sergeant.' I told Joe. 'Leave me on my own for a while son. You phone around to pass on the sad news.'

Jackie. Who at the time was staying up with Margaret and Pat in Bolton. Came back on the next available train. Margaret followed afterwards for the funeral.

On the day of the funeral. Jackie would not let me go. He told me it was far too cold and nobody wanted me sick. So I stayed at home and helped Eddie to prepare the buffet and drinks in Kaye's sitting room, for when they all trooped back. Jackie brought them one at a time, in to see me so we could all quietly talk and cry together. It was the presence of Dickie Fox that upset me most. He cried like a baby, he thought the world of my Jack. It seemed the end of everything. I was so lost and so low.

After the funeral I missed him at every step and found myself talking to him all day long and at night I prayed. Remembering all his old ways, all the wild things he did to worry the life out of me. Oh how I missed him. At times when he nearly drove me insane playing all that football, like a madman in the heat of India then in the early hours of the morning. Arriving back from a match to inform me. 'Sarah you are moving tomorrow. Get packed and ready. With all the children and servants. C'mon no time to start crying. On your feet Soldier. You are in the Army now.' With which I could have screamed, not realising in his eyes, he was paying me the greatest of compliments.

'Sarah can manage. I could and I did. But oh Jack. My Gallant Sergeant. How am I going to manage without you?' Her shining light had been extinguish.

POSTSCRIPT

I Jack. No longer Jackie. Now my father has gone. Left the sea to stay at home, as I knew that my mother would not last long, now that Dad had died. It gave mother a boost to have me at home. The sad news that her great friend Kitty had also passed away, was a further blow too her waning existence. But for her there was no purpose left in her life. She steadily declined. Would barely eat, and found nothing amusing any more.

Kaye and I were watching television with her one night, and I made her laugh out loud, over something. She said.

'Oh I never thought I would laugh again. But I think I shall go to bed now.'

Kaye went to her bedroom with her and then we stayed talking for a while, before we both retired. During the night mother came to my room and asked If I would come and sit with her, as she felt awful. I roused Kaye to quickly telephone for an ambulance. We sat on her bed each holding a hand, the three of us praying. Kaye and I trying not to break down. We went in the ambulance with her, and were told by the nurses, to come back the following morning. For three days, the whole family were with her at intervals. She complained of the drip and oxygen mask they put on her, her lung had collapsed.

The nurses telephoned us during the early morning to say. Mother had refused all medication and had passed away peacefully – She would suffer their ministration no longer. But lay there her hands folded in prayer, closed her eyes and waited.

Dad her gallant sergeant came for her and said.
'Come on Sarah on your feet soldier.'
She got up, smiled, Jack put his arms around her.
They left together to eternal peace and quiet.
God rest their souls.

460

About the Author

Joe Plant was born in the Crystal Palace area of Lambeth London. During the Blitz of March 1941, his family was bombed out. They travelled North to Bamber Bridge Lancashire to seek refuge, before the end of the war they returned back to a devastated Lambeth. In 1955 he was conscripted as a National Serviceman and served in Malaya during the Emergency (War). Demobbed in 1957, in 1959 he married his wife Annette. From their marriage they have three children and seven grandchildren. In 1963 through a car accident Joe was left partially sighted. Having trained as a Design Draughtsman, he had to change his profession to become a Materials Purchasing Manager, which took him to several overseas assignments, before he was seconded to Devonport Dockyard in 1987. His family moved to Torpoint Cornwall. He retired from Commercial life in 1995 and took to writing as a hobby.

Other Titles from Joe. P. Plant.

Cornwall's First Town In The Front Line: Torpoint's War Diaries 1939- 1946
ISBN: 978-1-90761-103-2

Up To Their Necks - The Story of a National Serviceman.
ISBN: 978-1-78222-054-1

'The Spirit Liveth On' A Trip Down Memory Lane - The History of St. Anne's Vauxhall.
ISBN: 978-1-78222-400-6

KIndle editions:
THE ADVENTURES OF A SOLDIERS WIFE PART I.
IRELAND/ENGLAND 1915-1928

THE ADVENTURES OF A SOLDIERS WIFE PART II.
THE MEMSAHIB'S INDIAN ADVENTURE 1928-1933

THE ADVENTURES OF A SOLDIERS WIFE PART III.
BLIGHTY CLIMATIC CHANGES 1933-1974

Published by Joe Plant

Publishing partner: Paragon Publishing, Rothersthorpe

First published 2016

© Joe Plant 2016

ISBN 978-1-78222-446-4

Book design, layout and production management by Into Print - www.intoprint.net - 01604 832149

Printed in the UK, USA and Australia by Lightning Source

Lightning Source UK Ltd.
Milton Keynes UK
UKOW06f0838270616

277156UK00001B/3/P